17th International Conference on Cognition and Exploratory Learning in Digital Age (CELDA 2020)

AA005072

Lisbon, Portugal
18 – 20 November 2020

ISBN: 978-1-7138-2226-4

Printed from e-media with permission by:

Curran Associates, Inc.
57 Morehouse Lane
Red Hook, NY 12571

CURRAN ASSOCIATES INC. proceedings.com

Some format issues inherent in the e-media version may also appear in this print version.

Copyright© (2020) by International Association for Development of the Information Society (IADIS)
All rights reserved.

Printed with permission by Curran Associates, Inc. (2021)

For permission requests, please contact International Association for Development of the Information Society (IADIS) at the address below.

International Association for Development of the Information Society (IADIS)
Rua Sao Sebastiao Da Pedreira
No. 100, 30, 1050-209
Lisbon, Portugal

Phone: 351 21 3151373
Fax: 351 21 3151244

secretariat@iadis.org

Additional copies of this publication are available from:

Curran Associates, Inc.
57 Morehouse Lane
Red Hook, NY 12571 USA
Phone: 845-758-0400
Fax: 845-758-2633
Email: curran@proceedings.com
Web: www.proceedings.com

TABLE OF CONTENTS

TOO MANY DULL WORDS EXCEED THE LIMITS OF VISUAL PERCEPTION: THE EFFECTS OF CLUTTER AND COLOUR ON LEARNING

Olivia Foulds
The University of Strathclyde, United Kingdom

ABSTRACT

When too much visual stimuli is present, the phenomenon of clutter is known to degrade an individual's perception across a variety of domains, ranging from completing search tasks incorrectly, to decreasing reading speed when letters are too close together. However, research is lacking as to whether the negative effects of clutter impact learning when too many words are visible at any one given time. Furthermore, colour has been implicated in affecting clutter. Thus, the present study created a recognition experiment whereby 42 participants had to learn target words that were presented in black or red font and positioned amongst no clutter, clutter words (distractor words surrounded the target), and clutter non-words (sequence of random letters surrounded the target). Results found that words learned in isolation were identified faster and significantly more accurately than words learned in both forms of clutter. Although red target words did not eliminate the negative effects of clutter, red words did show a trend towards higher accuracy of recognition compared to black words. These results would appear to be explained by existing clutter theories that state the limits of attentional resources and short-term memory cannot process excess visual stimuli. These findings have real-world implications for establishing optimal reading formats to improve learning.

KEYWORDS

Clutter, Crowding, Colour, Memory, Reading

1. INTRODUCTION

During human development, vision is fundamental to facilitate learning, knowledge, and cognition (Chokron & Dutton, 2016). However when too much visual stimuli occurs, human cognitive capacity is overloaded. Specifically, the detrimental effect of excess visual stimuli has been defined by the concept of clutter –otherwise known as crowding- which refers to the negative impact of nearby contours that interfere with and reduce visual discrimination when trying to focus on a target (Rosenholtz et al, 2007). Clutter then overloads cognitive resources such as attention and short-term memory, which leads to a bottleneck that impairs object perception (Levi, 2008). Clutter therefore occurs in a multitude of areas, from everyday errands such as finding something in the refrigerator, to essential visual search tasks like X-ray baggage scanning for dangerous items (Adamo et al., 2015). Consequently, it is vital to ensure that when people learn, the amount of visible clutter is minimal.

1.1 Visual Crowding

Defining clutter simply as the number of items around a target, many experiments have discovered a similar theme– increasing clutter impairs efficiency of individuals performing search tasks by increasing response times and the number of errors made (Moacdieh and Sarter, 2015, Yeh et al., 2012, Adamo et al., 2015). A recent review on the types of stimuli that have been found to exhibit clutter involve studies that have investigated letters, shapes, objects, digits, abstract symbols, and natural scenes (Patro & Huckauf, 2019). As clutter has been implicated in affecting letter identification, some studies have tested whether reading words results in more clutter when letters are closer together. Theoretically, by increasing the interletter spacing, each individual letter in a word should appear less crowded and thus enable a more accurate perception of the letter resulting in faster reading times (Perea et al., 2011). In a lexical decision task, Perea et al. (2011) confirmed that participants did have faster response times to identifying words or nonsense-words when spacing between letters was increased (Compare casino vs. c a s i n o). However in another lexical decision task, Montani et al. (2015) reported different results: increased letter spacing did not result in statistically significant faster response times, but response times were significantly slower when default letter spacing was reduced. These results would appear to suggest that either readers have adapted to the default presentation of words, or that due to increased spacing, fewer letters can physically be viewed in the visual span thus resulting in longer reading times when letters are further spaced apart (Chung, 2002). Although findings on interletter spacing using lexical decision tasks appear inconclusive, studies using different methodologies have replicated the finding that reduced interletter spacing results in poorer reading fluency. For example, reading times were faster when increased interletter spacing was used in a standardised word reading fluency test (Van-Den-Boer and Hakvoort, 2014). With differing research designs finding complementary results, the validity that clutter of individual letters does impair reading of single words is increased.

However, despite many different types of research design exploring the effects of clutter on interletter spacing, to the best of my knowledge, no studies have yet investigated whether the effects of clutter extend onto more everyday reading scenarios, such as reading words that are surrounded by other words. Yet in the current era of technology, apps have been designed to provide alternative ways to read, such as VelocityReading (2018) and Spritz (2016). These apps display text in a rapid-serial-visual-presentation (RSVP): words do not appear in a block of sentences or paragraphs as they would in a normal book, but instead are quickly, sequentially presented one-by-one. It is believed that using RSVP methods results in faster reading times because an individual's eyes do not have to move (Spritz, 2016). Although one study would appear to confirm that reading using RSVP does result in faster reading speeds than for text that is static– 1171 words were read in a minute of RSVP reading, compared to 303 words for normal text (Rubin and Turano, 1992)– little empirical research evidence explains the mechanisms behind this finding. Additionally, it is unknown as to how well the words that are read at such faster speeds are retained. If the phenomenon of clutter increases errors made in search tasks and increases reading time when letters are too crowded together, perhaps the results of reading through RSVP are also indicative of the phenomenon of clutter: words in a paragraph may be muddling the identification of the specific word that the reader wishes to focus on.

1.2 Colour

Generally, the negative perceptual effects of clutter have been shown to increase depending on the similarity of colour, contrast, and visual complexity between the target and clutter that is present (Cheung & Cheung, 2017). Therefore, when participants were asked to identify a target letter surrounded by other irrelevant letters, the effects of clutter were found to reduce when the target and clutter differed in colour (Põder, 2007). Specifically, Põder's (2007) three experiments demonstrated that when distractor letters were black and the target letter was either red, or highlighted in red or yellow, identification times of the target were significantly faster for all 7 adults that participated. Põder (2007) suggested that these results further accentuated clutter theories which state that excess visual stimuli exceeds the limits of attentional resources– by highlighting a target in a particular colour amongst cluttered distractors of a different colour, exogenously controlled attention was automatically attracted to the salient colour, thus reducing the cluttered illusion from the distractors. Although these experiments have not been replicated and the sample was small, the initial findings from Põder (2007) would appear to suggest that colour does have the ability to affect reading of letters. This is in line with other research irrespective of clutter, that has found faster reading speeds when every alternate word in a sentence was displayed in a different colour (Zhou et al., 2020), or when coloured overlays have been used (Wilkins et al., 1996). Similarly, coloured overlays have been used as a clinical intervention for individuals with dyslexia and autism to improve their attention, which demonstrates the power that colour can have on reading (Wilkins, 2003, cited in Dzulkifli and Mustafar, 2013; Ludlow and Wilkins, 2009).

Related to the theory that clutter doesn't just exceed attentional resources but is also implicated in memory (Levi, 2008), colour has also been identified as impacting upon generalised memory recall. For example, patients with Alzheimer's Disease were presented with a picture such as a purple cow, and later asked to identify what they had seen from a choice of answers such as a pink horse or yellow elephant (Cernin et al., 2003). Results found that participants were significantly better at remembering what they had seen when stimuli were presented in colour compared to black and white. A more recent review on the effect of colour on memory reaffirmed these results and concluded that colour can increase memory on certain tasks depending on the choice of colours used (Dzulkifli and Mustafar, 2013). For instance, when recalling letters in an experiment, slides with a white background elicited higher immediate retention rates than slides against a blue and green background (McConnohie, 1999, cited in Dzulkifli and Mustafar, 2013). Furthermore, Greene et al. (1983, cited in Dzulkifli and Mustafar, 2013) explained that colours such as red and orange elicited greater attentional capture compared to colours like brown and grey, and that this was contributing to enhanced memory performance. Despite converging evidence indicating that colour impacts upon memory, little is known as to whether the colour of words affects memory during reading and learning.

1.3 Summary and Hypotheses

To summarise, clutter increases response times and the number of errors made in search tasks (Moacdieh and Sarter, 2015), and clutter of individual letters impairs reading speed (Yeh et al. 2012). However, little is known for whether the detrimental effects of clutter extend onto an individual's perception when reading and learning words that are surrounded by other words. In accordance with the measure of clutter proposed by Yu et al. (2014), the present study quantified clutter by the amount of similar image features that merge into a perceptual scene. Thus, when reading words, 'clutter' was defined by multiple irrelevant words and non-words visible on the same screen. It was firstly hypothesised that words learnt amongst either form of clutter would be associated with worse and slower accuracy in a recognition task than words learnt in isolation. Furthermore, as research has identified the colour red as eliciting greater attention, increased object recognition, and faster reading times (Põder, 2007; Dzulkifli and Mustafar, 2013), words that are learnt in red font should hypothetically elicit greater and faster accuracy than words learnt in black font. Finally, since Põder (2007) established that colour interacts with clutter, such that red letters among black distractors reduced the negative perceptual effects of clutter, it was hypothesised that target words learnt in red font would result in similar accuracy and response times to words that were learned in isolation.

2. METHODOLOGY

A 3x2 repeated-measures factorial design experiment was programmed and run using OpenSesame (Mathôt et al., 2012). 42 participants ranging from 19 to 78 years old (29 female; 13 male; mean age= 42.6 years) were recruited through a university experimental participation website and completed the study. After a practice task to familiarize users with the system, each participant completed 6 blocks in a randomized order to reduce any order effects from occurring. For each block, 10 target words were sequentially positioned in the centre of the screen for 6000ms each, and participants were informed they must try to remember these. Participants were also informed that the word they were to remember would sometimes be presented in isolation whereas sometimes other words would be visible on the same screen, and that they were only to attend to the central word, where a fixation point would direct them to in-between screens. After all 10 target words had appeared, participants underwent a recognition task, where the same target words were randomly interspersed with an additional 20 words, and participants had to individually select whether they had previously seen the word or not. Average reaction times and correct responses for the recognition task in each block were measured as the dependent variables. The system generated answer logs for each participant, which were then transferred into SPSS software for statistical analysis.

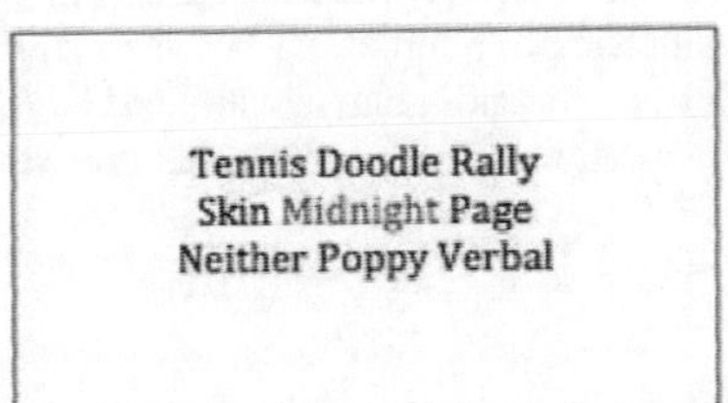

Figure 1. Block 5, where clutter-words are present in the red condition

The 6 blocks represented the different conditions for the study. Firstly, clutter was defined by what surrounded the target word that participants were instructed to remember: 1) isolation- no other words were around the target; 2) clutter-words- 8 irrelevant words symmetrically surrounded each target (See Figure 1 for an example); and 3) clutter non-words- 8 irrelevant words that did not make sense symmetrically surrounded each target, Eg. 'vinsoi'. Non-words were used to reduce the potential confound that any results found were in fact due to clutter, and not just related to the linguistic structure that distractor words would automatically be read by the reader. Secondly, colour was operationalized so that target words were either presented in 1) black or 2) red font. Between each block, participants were informed that they no longer needed to remember the previous words, and that they could initiate the next block when they were ready.

All stimuli were presented in 32-pt font with default interletter spacing against a white background. Words were selected through generating a list of items on the English Lexicon Project database and chosen to ensure each condition had an equivalent word for: Word length (4-8 letters); number of syllables (1-2); beginning letter; Freq_HAL > 1000; and a I_Mean_RT range of 500-900 (Balota et al., 2007). Plural and distressing words were excluded. The additional words for the recognition task, always presented centrally in black font, were as alike to the target words as possible by sharing the same number of letters, syllables, beginning letter, and frequency range. The non-words were created by rearranging letters from each clutter word, ensuring that each 'non-word' had an equivalent normal word with regards to: beginning letter, word length, syllabic structure, and looked linguistically pronounceable. For example, 'tennis' was changed to 'tesnin'. Both clutter words and non-words always appeared in black font.

Finally, all participants: gave online informed consent; were able to read English; had normal or corrected-to-normal vision by self-report; were naïve to the purpose of the experiment; and received no payment for participation. Overall, the experiment lasted about 20 minutes. Afterwards, a virtual debriefing statement was displayed that thanked individuals for participating, explained the purpose of the experiment, and provided the researcher's contact details for any future concerns they may have had.

3. RESULTS

Multiple repeated-measures ANOVAs were conducted to compare the accuracy and response times to identifying target words depending on whether they had been learnt in isolation, amongst clutter-words, amongst clutter-nonwords, or in black or red font.

3.1 Accuracy

The results of a 3x2 repeated measures ANOVA with a Greenhouse-Geisser correction revealed that there was a significant main effect of clutter on participant's accuracy at identifying target words (F(1.67, 68.28)= 9.10, p=.001, np2=.182). Bonferroni Post Hoc tests confirmed that mean accuracy scores were significantly higher when identifying target words that had been presented in no clutter (mean= 8.92) compared to target words that had been presented among clutter words (mean=7.93) and clutter non-words (mean=8.13). The difference between accuracy on clutter words and clutter non-words did not reach significance.

While descriptive statistics revealed that participant's mean accuracy scores were slightly higher when verifying red target words (mean=8.49) compared to black target words (mean=8.16), the ANOVA with sphericity assumed revealed that this difference was not significant (F(1,41)= 3.93, p=.054, np2=.087).

Furthermore, there was no significant interaction between clutter and colour (F(2,82)= 1.07, p=.346, np2=.026). However, for each clutter condition, participants did have slightly higher accuracy when the target word had been initially presented in red as opposed to black font (See Table 1 and Figure 2a).

Table 1. Descriptive statistics (Mean ± Standard Deviation) for: Accuracy as the number of correctly identified target words per condition; and Reaction times to identifying target words

	Accuracy		Reaction time (ms)	
	Target Word Colour		Target Word Colour	
Clutter Type	**Black**	**Red**	**Black**	**Red**
Isolation	8.76 ± 1.66	9.07 ± 1.13	902.96 ± 517.82	871.54 ± 418.92
Clutter words	7.62 ± 2.00	8.24 ± 2.26	947.54 ± 624.94	973.26 ± 745.75
Clutter non-words	8.10 ± 1.82	8.17 ± 1.85	942.98 ± 577.62	938.67 ± 627.65

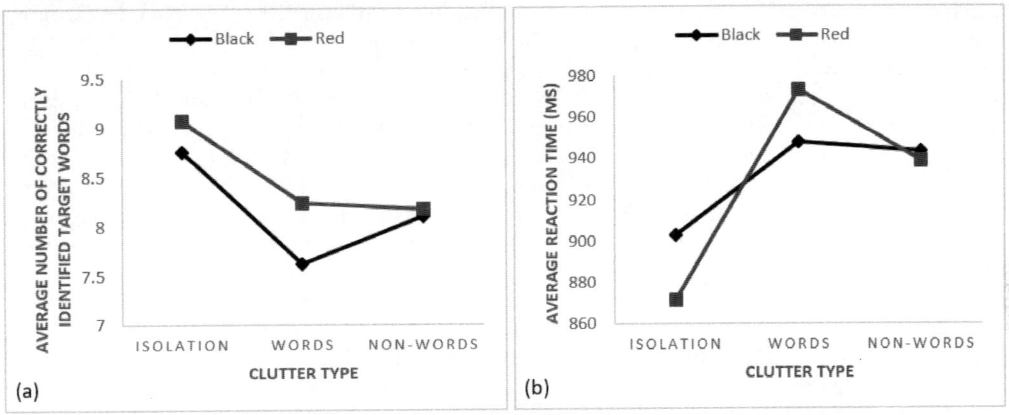

Figure 2. Mean results for each condition, where black and red refer to the target word colour: (a) Accuracy for the number of correctly identified target words; (b) Reaction times for target word responses

3.2 Average Reaction Time

A repeated measures ANOVA with Greenhouse-Geisser correction identified a significant main effect of clutter on reaction time (F(1.94,2384.28)= 11.35, p=.000, np2= .009). Bonferroni Post Hoc tests revealed that reaction times to target words presented in no clutter (mean=887.25ms) were significantly faster than both clutter words (mean= 960.60ms) and clutter non-words (mean=940.82ms).

Although reaction times for the red words were slightly faster (927.82ms) than the black words (931.29ms) this result did not reach significance (F(1,1229)=.07, p=.789, np2=.000).

Furthermore, a visible interaction occurred between colour and clutter (See Table 1 and Figure 2b): When there was no clutter or clutter non-words, participants responded slightly faster to red words than black words. Yet when clutter words were present, participants responded slightly faster to black words than red words. However, this interaction did not reach significance (F(1.99, 2440.43)= 1.82, p=.162, np2=.001).

4. DISCUSSION

As hypothesised, words that were learned in clutter elicited significantly impaired accuracy and longer reaction times when recalling them in a recognition task compared to words that were learnt in isolation. Additionally, despite the hypothesis that red target words would result in greater accuracy and faster reaction times compared to black target words, no significant differences were found. However, a trend did appear that red target words elicited higher recognition accuracy and were recalled slightly faster than black words. Furthermore, whilst it was predicted that red target words presented amongst black clutter might reduce the negative effects of clutter and lead to similar accuracy and reaction times to words that had been learned in isolation, there was no significant interaction found between clutter and colour.

The finding that clutter around a target word, either in the form of irrelevant words or non-words, increased the number of errors made and reaction times in response to a recognition task, would appear consistent with a multitude of previous research that identified clutter as degrading accuracy and response times in search tasks (Moacdieh and Sarter, 2015; Yeh et al., 2012; Adamo et al., 2015). Additionally, the present findings assimilate to faster reading times when the clutter surrounding an individual letter in a word was reduced (Perea et al., 2011; Van-den-Boer & Hakvoort, 2014). As the present study found a significant impairment of target word recognition when the word had been learned in clutter as opposed to isolation, the most reasonable conclusion for these results would appear to relate to other study's explanations of clutter– negative perceptual effects of clutter do extend onto more everyday reading scenarios, such as words surrounding other words: clutter automatically attracts vision away from the target and this excess of visual stimuli exceeds the limits of attentional resources and short-term memory (Levi, 2008). For example, when participants are attempting to memorise a target word, if other words or non-words are surrounding the target, these may be mistakenly processed as the target word and cause a degradation of memory because only a certain number of items can be processed at one time (Chastain, 1991). Furthermore, an interesting finding with the present study is that the participant's attention was not automatically directed towards the excess clutter because they were not expecting it, as participants were explicitly pre-warned that they did not need to look at the words beyond the center of the screen. Therefore, it is unknown whether the effects of clutter are so strong that they overrule overt attention and distract a user's vision regardless of whether they want to process it or not, or whether the effects may be a result of more subconscious and covert behavior that participants are unaware of, perhaps through their peripheral vision subtly processing the excess stimuli. Consequently more research is needed, perhaps using eye-tracking, to explain how exactly visual attention responds to clutter during reading.

In keeping with theories related to attention, colour has previously been thought to capture attention and thus enhance memory performance (Dzulkifli and Mustafar, 2013). Although the present study did not find a significant effect of using the colour red, compared to black, on accuracy of identifying target words in a recognition task, this finding only marginally missed out on reaching significance ($p=.054$). Therefore, it could be tentatively assumed that a larger sample size may have resulted in a significant result that words learned in red font do in fact elicit better recognition than black. This explanation would reiterate the findings by Greene et al. (1983, cited in Dzulkifli and Mustafar, 2013), who stated that red elicited greater attentional capture compared to colours like brown and grey, and that this impacted upon memory performance. However, other research has claimed that long wavelength colours like red illicit worse performance in certain tasks (Shieh and Lin, 2000; Hall and Hanna, 2004). Furthermore, unlike research that identified colour as increasing reading speeds (Wilkins et al., 1996) the present study found minimal differences in response times for either red or black target words. Thus, further research is needed to clarify the contrasting results of whether the colour red enhances or hinders individual's performance in tasks.

It is unsurprising that as the present study found no significant benefit of presenting the target word in red, compared to black, red target words also failed to reduce the negative effects of surrounding clutter. These results are in contrast to Põder's (2007) experiments that found when target and surrounding clutter differed in colour, the process of mentally eliminating distractors was easier (Levi, 2008). However, these findings should not automatically reject the theory that colour can reduce negative effects of clutter because: only two colours were used- red and black; participants were not screened for colour-blindness; and due to variations in computer browser that the experiment was viewed on, the brightness could not be controlled for across participants. Additional examination using different methods would be useful to clarify these methodological problems of how the colour red contrasted to the colour black.

The results of the present experiment are not just theoretical, but could also have vital importance in many aspects of everyday life because the finding that clutter does impair individual's performance across a multitude of tasks has been replicated. More specifically, the present study provided the first evidence (to the best of our awareness) that the negative perceptual effects of clutter extend onto reading words surrounded by other words. As this is how many textbooks and websites present information, the present experimental findings could evolve current learning strategies and alter popular opinion on how best to read and retain words. With vision being a huge facilitator of learning (Chokron & Dutton, 2016), it may be a more positive and beneficial learning experience if clutter is considered for future design of learning materials. Therefore apps that operate rapid-serial-visual-presentation, or handheld devices like typoscopes which ensure only a few words are visible at any one time, could potentially offer a more optimal reading environment in comparison to a standard book.

This alternative way to read should then hypothetically promote greater memory of what has been read, and in a faster time-period. Presenting words in a minimalistic structure may also enable more inclusive education to occur, as other research has identified that children with cerebral visual impairment or dyslexia particularly struggle with clutter (Chokron & Dutton, 2016; Morris et al., 2018).

However, it is worth noting some limitations of the present study. Firstly, in contrast to clutter studies conducted in a controlled laboratory, anyone with OpenSesame could participate in the experiment. Therefore, although all words were presented in a consistent size, due to variation among computers and distance from the screen, some participants would have seen the words in different sizes, resolutions, and colour contrasts. Other studies on clutter have removed this confound and ensured a fixed viewing distance by using a chin rest (Yeh et al., 2012; Adamo et al., 2015). However, this may not be necessary when other research has concluded that clutter perception is invariant to image size, but dependent on the content (Zelinsky and Yu, 2015). Furthermore, as the experiment was conducted virtually, it was unknown whether participants varied in terms of factors that may affect their memory such as: their mood; the time of day the experiment was completed; distractions that were present; and alcohol or drug consumption. Nonetheless, these limitations could in fact be seen as a positive– no data was excluded from analyses, yet results were still significant. Therefore, the overall finding that clutter does significantly impair word recognition may extend onto a population irrelevant of individual situation or distractions present.

In order to fully establish whether the effects of clutter similarly extend onto other populations, further research would firstly be needed. In particular, it would appear worthwhile to examine whether the degradation of word recognition among other distractor words exists among children- after all, it is children who are expected to memorise what they learn through textbooks and websites that contain a plethora of clutter. It may be possible that children are unaffected by clutter, and that it is a concept that develops and worsens with age. Alternatively, it is unknown whether the negative effects of clutter can be alleviated through practice, and therefore reading words surrounded by other words in a normal paragraph do not result in clutter effects if readers are familiar with reading in that way. Correspondingly, as the present experiment only tested recognition of individual words, it would be interesting to expand the ecological validity and see whether clutter affects word recognition at a sentence level. Furthermore, future research should develop the design of the current experiment to explore whether learning words amongst clutter impairs memory recognition beyond the immediate short-term memory, and not just instantly after words have been presented. Consequently, the present research is only the beginning of a topic that could potentially improve learning in many domains. All of these unanswered questions therefore raise many interesting avenues for future research that could have hugely important real-life consequences for how best to learn when clutter is present. If more understanding of clutter is had, then hopefully strategies can be implemented to reduce the negative effects it causes.

5. CONCLUSION

To summarise, the current experiment identified that clutter, either in the form of distractor words or non-words, significantly impaired accuracy and increased response times for recognising target words. This finding would appear to extend other theories that when excess visual stimuli are present, the limits of short-term memory and attention are exceeded. Although no significant findings were found in relation to the colour of a target word or the interaction between clutter and colour, some interesting patterns and trends emerged that require more investigation. Finally, as this experiment provides the first evidence that clutter effects do extend onto words surrounding other words, these findings motivate further research for creating an optimal reading format for learning. For example, if clutter can be reduced during reading, through ways such as apps that operate rapid-serial-visual-presentation, then reading speed should be faster while improving memory for what has been seen.

ACKNOWLEDGEMENT

This paper was revised from work undertaken as part of the author's undergraduate degree with The Open University. The author would like to thank their tutor at the time, M Louise Kelly, for their original feedback. Additionally, appreciation goes to the anonymous reviewers for providing helpful suggestions.

REFERENCES

Adamo, S., Cain, M., & Mitroff, S. (2015) 'Targets Need Their Own Personal Space: Effects of Clutter on Multiple-Target Search Accuracy', *Perception*, vol. 44, no. 10, pp. 1203-1214.

Balota, D.A., Yap, M.J., Cortese, M.J., Hutchison, K.A., Kessler, B., & Loftis, B. (2007) 'The English Lexicon Project', *Behavior Research Methods*, vol. 39, no. 3, pp. 445–59.

Cernin, P., Keller, B., & Stoner, J. (2003) 'Color Vision in Alzheimer's Patients: Can We Improve Object Recognition With Color Cues?', *Aging, Neuropsychology, and Cognition*, vol. 10, no. 4, pp. 255-267.

Chastain, G. (1991) 'Effects of abruptly appearing clutter on a peripherally precede covert attention shift', *The Journal of General Psychology*, vol. 118, no. 1, pp. 31-44.

Cheung, L. & Cheung, S. (2017) 'Chinese-character crowding–Effects of structural similarity', *Journal of Vision*, vol. 17, no. 11, pp. 1-13.

Chokron, S., & Dutton, G. (2016) 'Impact of Cerebral Visual Impairments on Motor Skills: Implications for Developmental Coordination Disorders', *Frontiers In Psychology*, vol. 7, no. 1.

Chung, S. (2002) 'The effect of letter spacing on reading speed in central and peripheral vision', *Investigative Ophthalmology & Visual Science*, vol. 43, no. 4, pp. 1270-1276.

Dzulkifli, M., & Mustafar, M. (2013) 'The Influence of Colour on Memory Performance: A Review', *Malaysian Journal of Medical Sciences*, vol. 20, no. 2, pp. 3-9.

Hall, R., & Hanna, P. (2004) 'The impact of web page text-background colour combinations on readability, retention, aesthetics and behavioural intention', *Behaviour and information technology*, vol. 23, no. 3, pp. 183-195.

Levi, D. (2008) 'Crowding—An essential bottleneck for object recognition: A mini-review', *Vision Research*, vol.48, no. 5, pp. 635-654.

Ludlow, A. & Wilkins, A. (2009) 'Case report: color as a therapeutic intervention', *Journal of Autism and Developmental Disorders*, vol. 39, no. 5, pp. 815-818.

Mathôt, S., Schreij, D., & Theeuwes, J. (2012) 'OpenSesame: An open-source, graphical experiment builder for the social sciences', *Behavior Research Methods*, vol.44, no.2, pp.314-324 [Computer Program]. Available at: https://www.ncbi.nlm.nih.gov/pubmed/22083660

Moacdieh, N., & Sarter, N. (2015) 'Clutter in Electronic Medical Records, Examining its performance and attentional costs using eye tracking', *Human Factors: The Journal of Human Factors and Ergonomics Society*, vol. 57, no. 4, pp. 591-606.

Montani, V., Facoetti, A., & Zorzi, M. (2015) 'The effect of decreased interletter spacing on orthographic processing', *Psychonomic Bulletin & Review,* vol. 22, no. 3, pp. 824-832.

Morris, M.R., Fourney, A., Ali, A. and Vonessen, L. (2018) 'Understanding the needs of searchers with dyslexia', *In Proceedings of the 2018 CHI Conference on Human Factors in Computing Systems* (pp. 1-12).

Patro, K., & Huckauf, A. (2019) 'Asymmetries in flanker-target interference at different levels of number processing', *Acta psychologica*, vol. 201.

Perea, M., Moret-Tatay, C., & Gómez, P. (2011) 'The effects of interletter spacing in visual-word recognition', *Acta Psychologica*, vol. 137, no. 3, pp. 345-351.

Põder, E. (2007) 'Effect of colour pop-out on the recognition of letters in crowding conditions', *Psychological Research*, vol.71, no.6, pp.641-645.

Rosenholtz, R., Li, Y., & Nakano, L. (2007) 'Measuring visual clutter', *Journal of Vision*, vol.7, no.2.

Rubin, G. & Turano, K. (1992) 'Reading without saccadic eye movements', *Vision Research,* vol. 32, no. 5, pp. 895-902.

Shieh, K. & Lin, C. (2000) 'Effects of screen type, ambient illumination, and color combination on VDT visual performance and subjective preference', *International Journal of Industrial Ergonomics*, vol. 26, no. 5, pp. 527-536.

Spritz (2016) '*Spritz*' [Computer application]. Available at: http://spritzinc.com

Van-Den-Boer, M., & Hakvoort, B. (2014) 'Default spacing is the optimal spacing for word reading', *The Quarterly Journal of Experimental Psychology*, vol. 68, no. 4, pp. 697-709.

VelocityReading (2018) '*Velocity Reading'* [Computer application]. Available at: https://velocityreading.com/learn

Wilkins, A., Jeanes, R., Pumfrey, P., & Laskier, M. (1996) 'Rate of Reading Test®: Its reliability, and its validity in the assessment of the effects of coloured overlays', *Ophthalmic and Physiological Optics*, vol. 16, no. 6, pp. 491-497.

Yeh, S., He, S., & Cavanagh, P. (2012) 'Semantic Priming From Crowded Words', *Psychological Science*, vol. 23, no. 6, pp. 608-616.

Yu, C., Samaras, D., & Zelinsky, G. (2014) 'Modeling visual clutter perception using proto-object segmentation', *Journal of Vision*, vol. 14, no. 7.

Zelinsky, G., & Yu, C. (2015) 'Clutter perception is invariant to image size', *Vision Research*, vol. 116, pp. 142-151.

Zhou, W., Ye, W., & Yan, M. (2020) 'Alternating-color words facilitate reading and eye movements among second-language learners of Chinese', *Applied Psycholinguistics*, vol. 41, no. 3, pp. 685-699.

INFORMATION SECURITY EDUCATION SYSTEM IN SECONDARY SCHOOL AND ASSESSMENT OF THE LEVEL OF ANXIETY OF SCHOOLCHILDREN

Mikhail I. Bocharov[1], Irina V. Simonova[2], Tatyana I. Bocharova[3] and Anna Y. Zaika[4]
[1]Moscow City University, Vtoroy Selskohoziajstvenny proezd, 4, Moscow, 129226, Russia
[2]Herzen State Pedagogical University of Russia, Moika River, 48, St. Petersburg, 191186, Russia
[3]Moscow Technical University of Communications and Informatics, Aviamotornaya Street, 8A, Moscow, 111024, Russia
[4]National University of Kyiv-Mohyla Academy, 2 Skovoroda St., Kyiv, 04655, Ukraine

ABSTRACT

The analysis of the results of scientific research has revealed the necessity to track the level of anxiety of a student while studying aspects of information security in a particular subject area. And in accordance with the results, it was necessary to justify the choice of methods for management and content of information security training in order to minimize the negative impact on the psychological state of a child of middle school age. The purpose of the research is to determine the impact of educational elements from a specific subject area related to information security guaranteeing on the level of anxiety of secondary schools students.

The authors identified the need to assess the level of anxiety of students while studying aspects of information security in a particular subject area and proposed tools for tracking the level of anxiety. In the middle school, during the formation of a comprehensive idea of professional activities in the field of information security, especially at the pre-profile stage, an approach that forms the basis for the formation of the content of information security training is substantiated. It combines the knowledge from a wide range of different sciences for teaching secondary school students. The study shows that the level of situational anxiety of secondary school students while studying aspects of information security in a particular subject area can increase due to the natural reaction of the body, adapting to new potential threats for it. It was experimentally established that the level of personal anxiety as a result of assimilation of new knowledge about information security did not change both before studying the educational elements of information security in a particular subject area, and after studying them.

KEYWORDS

Digital Education, Information Security of Students, the Conceptual Apparatus of Information Security, Sources of Information Threats, Information Security Training, the Level of Anxiety of Adolescents

1. INTRODUCTION

During the transition from elementary school to secondary school, the level of independence of the student and, accordingly, his/her autonomy in decision-making process in the situation of information threat, which implies the choice of a particular action, increases. In elementary school, the child is under the supervision of adults to a greater extent, therefore, while teaching information security issues in elementary school (Bocharov M., 2019), one can limit oneself to a description of the information security problem itself and a certain set of typical situations in which a primary school student may be without the immediate proximity of his/her guardians. Such situations require the "inclusion" of protective mechanisms. This approach is justified at the elementary school stage, when the student is under the close supervision of parents and teachers, and the set of situations that a younger student may encounter is limited. However, with an increase in the degree of independence of the child during the transition to secondary school, the number of such "typical situations" tends to increase sharply. More effective in secondary school is an approach based on the use of a conceptual apparatus, which allows to highlight common points in almost any real situation and explore them using well-known concepts.

More and more researchers and practitioners are paying attention to the need for active development of the problems of information and psychological security of the individual, society and the state. This is due to the fact that without the solution of these problems it is impossible to further sustainable social development and ensure the security of the individual, society and the state in the political, economic, social, spiritual, military and other fields.

The place of information security in the system of modern scientific knowledge is determined mainly by the fact that information security is a branch of a computer science. Methods and tools of informatics can be general, fundamental, and applied, taking into account the specifics of pedagogy, medicine or law. Hence, it is proposed to subdivide computer science into theoretical (fundamental) and applied. Applied informatics includes pedagogical informatics, medical informatics, legal informatics, etc. Therefore, information security is present both in theoretical (fundamental) computer science and in applied science, i.e. in legal, medical, pedagogical informatics, etc. (Abissova M., 2006).

2. COMPONENTS OF INFORMATION SECURITY TRAINING IN SECONDARY SCHOOLS

In the middle school, during the formation of a comprehensive idea of professional activity in the field of information security, especially at the pre-specialized preparation stage, it is necessary to take into account the integrative principles that form the basis for the formation of the content of information security training, combining knowledge from a wide range of different sciences. So, the basis for the development of the content of vocational training for information security of education system employees T.L. Partyka and I.I. Popov put the following principles (Partyka T., 2007): universality, integration, the integrity of the scientific picture of the world, fundamental nature, professionalism, variability. (Chou H. et al, 2016).

The middle level of the school is the main link for the formation of key concepts in the field of information security. These concepts are grouped by type of information security. The information security system includes the following types of security: *organizational support*, *psychological support*, *legal support*, *information support*, *linguistic support*, *social and ethical support*, *spiritual and moral support*, *software*, *hardware*, *math support*, *engineering and technical support*.

Let us define the subjects (educational areas), the content of which can highlight the educational elements related to the field of information security in the Russian federal basic curriculum of basic general education and in the system of additional education of schoolchildren. Within each subject, we define a key concept that reflects to a large extent the substantial part of information security elements related to this subject. Let us compare the types of information security with the content for each subject selected for studying the basics of information security. As a result, we obtain the following correspondences between basic subjects, substantive elements, and types of information security guaranteeing, presented in Table 1.

Table 1. Correspondence between basic subjects, substantive elements and types of information security

Basic subjects in basic general education for teaching the basics of information security	Content elements of teaching the basics of information security	Types of information security support
Informatics	Software	Software
Math	Cryptographic	Mathematical
Physics	Physical	Hardware
Social Studies	Social, legal	Psychological, socio-ethical, legal
General History	Historical, factual	Socio-ethical
Life Safety Fundamentals	Organizational	Organizational
Literature	Spiritual, moral, ethical	Linguistic, socio-ethical, spiritual, moral
Foreign language	Communicative, ethical	Organizational, linguistic
Art	Spiritual, moral, ethical	Social and ethical, spiritual, moral
The subject area "Technology"	Hardware and technical	Hardware
The subject area "Fundamentals of spiritual and moral culture"	Spiritual, moral, ethical	Spiritual and moral

Key states on the role of intersubject connections in the formation of concepts in students, formulated by A.V. Usova, can be applied to the formation of basic concepts in the field of information security. Interdisciplinary connection is a reflection of the relationship between the sciences, the foundations of which are studied at school, in the content of the educational material, in its structure and teaching methods (Usova A., 1986).

3. INTEGRATIVE MODEL OF TEACHING INFORMATION SECURITY TO STUDENTS OF MIDDLE SCHOOL AGE

In our opinion, an effective way to improve the quality of understanding concepts in the field of information security by schoolchildren is to solve problems of an interdisciplinary nature. According to A. V. Usova, the solution of such problems requires students to establish links between concepts formed in the study of various academic subjects, which plays an important role in the formation of students' natural science picture of the world (Usova A., 1986). An effective method for solving such problems is the method of (creative) projects.

The consistent formation of independent critical thinking in schoolchildren in the process of all educational subjects can be facilitated by the introduction of a media education course in school curricula (Larsson K., 2017). Media education is a subject area that studies the specific language of various media, primarily television, radio, the press, and the Internet.

M.A. Abissova in the field of information security training distinguishes three levels depending on how much material is provided for training information security according to state educational standards of higher professional education: 1) future specialists in the field of information security and other areas of computer science (several general professional and special disciplines); 2) future specialists not in the field of computer science (one general professional discipline "Information Security" for some specialties); 3) students of humanitarian and socio-economic specialties (section of basic informatics – a general discipline called "Informatics" or "Informatics and mathematics"). All students study a small section in the basic course "Jurisprudence" (Abissova M., 2006).

Based on this, certain priorities can be identified in the content of pre-specialized training of schoolchildren in information security in one or another educational area.

In relation to natural sciences (areas), the content of such training will be determined by the theoretical foundations of the security of information systems. In technical specialties (areas) issues related to protected information technologies will be disclosed. In humanitarian specialties (directions), attention should be paid to studying the issues of combating computer crimes.

The ideas received by students during the study of various school subjects about certain aspects of information security should be generalized and systematized for subsequent career guidance and the implementation of pre-specialized training. This can be done on the basis of the organization of intersubject communications and the involvement of students in project activities in the manner presented in Figure 1 as an integrative model for teaching information security to students of middle school age.

A feature of teaching schoolchildren at this age stage compared to primary school is the increased influence of the Internet and network communities both in educational activities and in the student's personal, social extracurricular life (Chou H. et al, 2017).

The following statements can be identified as sources of threats to the information security of students using the Internet in the educational process:

1. The nature of the incoming information and how to set the computer according to the content of the incoming information from the Internet is known to a small number of parents of secondary school students, which indicates the absence of parental censorship.

2. Minor Internet users are aware of many ways to overcome locks from the reception of unwanted information.

3. Many parents have superficial ideas about the psychological problems of adolescents associated with the uncontrolled use of Internet resources, do not give their children an idea of the problem of maintaining privacy, do not use any means to filter negative information (Lau W. et al, 2016).

4. Juvenile Internet users are not aware of the legal rules regarding their rights and the principle of "democracy" of the Network.

5. Due to the physical and mental characteristics of childhood and the lack of life experience and life support for a child, in comparison with adults, it is much more difficult to defend one's own rights. Excessive enthusiasm for "virtual reality" leads to a decrease in the experience of real interaction.

6. Most students while working on the Web consider the information interaction on the Web anonymous (actions, messages to chats and letters).

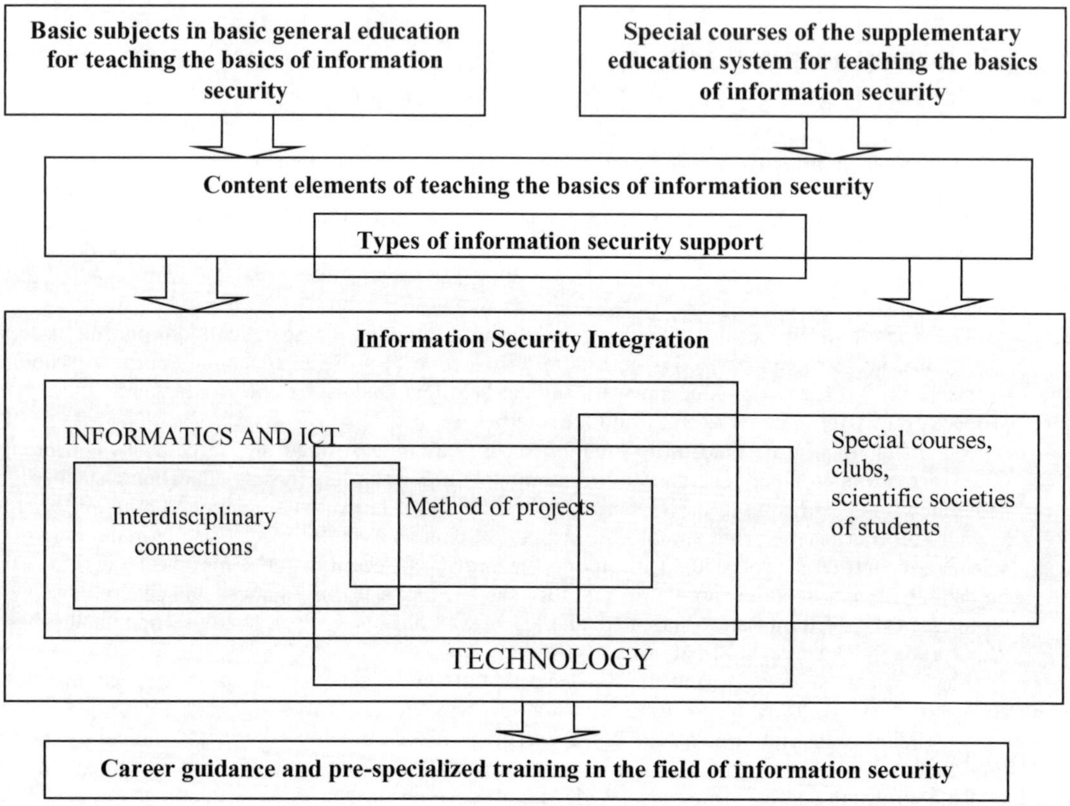

Figure 1. Integrative model of teaching information security to secondary school students

Sources of information security threats on the Internet can be such negative social manifestations as the following (Dzhonson S., 2006.): porn industry, paedophilia, crime and terrorism, cyberbullying, invasion of privacy.

The porn industry is a source of pornography and obscene information on the Internet. There are hundreds of thousands of Web sites containing information that may be considered obscene.

Pedophiles use the Internet to track down children. Pedophile is an adult who has a sexual desire for children. Pedophiles use the Internet to organize the distribution of child porn photographs, as well as to select specific children and establish contacts with them.

Crime and terrorism. Not only children can easily find pornography, but they can also easily get information about committing crimes, such as making bombs, making drugs and stealing money, making fake IDs and etc (Thompson N. et al, 2017).

Cyberbullying – attacks through electronic devices. This can be defamation on Web sites, threats made through mail or mobile phone. Cyberbullying is the equivalent of street bullying in the information society. It is necessary to closely monitor the child for signs of its manifestation (Plaza-de-la-Hoz J. et al, 2018). Signs of cyberbullying can be determined by observing the reaction of children when they receive instant messages on a computer or SMS to their cell phone. Other symptoms may include a refusal to go to school, a sudden drop in self-esteem, depression or a refusal to use a computer or mobile phone (Yhomee S. et al, 2012.

Invasion of privacy. The worldwide disadvantage of the Internet is the possibility of violating the privacy law, which can also endanger the privacy of the child when he uses the Internet.

Through the Internet, an advertiser can obtain information about a child in three main ways: when they subscribe to free services on the Internet; when they participate in competitions and lotteries; when they launch a viral advertisement with a click of the mouse.

The collected information may include the following: personal information such as name, address, and phone number; software applications installed on computer; the websites you visit and the details of the forms you fill out on web pages; advertising that you click on the mouse; a list of all the files that you download; your data for accessing the Internet, including your IP address, user login and Internet password.

All of the above factors with particular acuteness raise the question of the need for a comprehensive study of the entire set of socio-psychological phenomena caused by the emergence of a new information-psychological environment in relation to: teaching students to identify threats to information security and counter them to reduce the consequences of mental, moral and physical influence; determining the place of information security in the future professional activities of schoolchildren.

4. METHODS

To assess the child's training in information security aspects in a particular subject area in the experimental and control classes, a conceptual level in the field of information security was determined before and after the experiment. Studies were conducted in schools of Moscow, the city of St. Petersburg, the city of Novokuznetsk.

So in the framework of the subject "Fundamentals of Spiritual and Moral Culture", an important aspect of information security was considered as "Network etiquette" – netiquette (from the English net "network" + French etiquette "etiquette") - neologism of the rules of behavior, communication on the Web, the traditions and cultures of the online community, which most people adhere to. After studying the topic "Network Etiquette" by students, statistically significant differences in the child's training in knowledge of information security concepts related to network etiquette are established.

During the experimental training, the level of anxiety of schoolchildren was assessed, while studying the aspects of information security in a particular subject area, measurements were performed twice: before training and after training. To determine the level of anxiety, the Spilberger Alert Scale methodology, also known as the State-Trait Anxiety Inventory (STAI) developed by Charles Donald Spielberger, was used. STAI was adapted into Russian by Yu. L. Khanin.

This questionnaire consists of 20 statements related to anxiety as a state (state of anxiety, reactive or situational anxiety) and 20 statements to define anxiety as a disposition, personality traits (anxiety property or personal anxiety). Each statement is evaluated on a four-point scale from 1 to 4, after which, in accordance with the STAI scheme, the total result of the obtained values is calculated, based on which the level of anxiety is determined: 1) up to 30 points – a low degree of anxiety; 2) from 31 to 45 points – an average degree of anxiety; 3) from 46 points or more – a high degree of anxiety.

C.D. Spielberger generally understands anxiety as "Anxiety is characterized by subjective, consciously perceived sensations of threat and tension, accompanied or associated with the activation or arousal of the autonomic nervous system."

Personal anxiety as a personality trait, apparently, means a motive or acquired behavioral disposition, which obliges the individual to perceive a wide range of objectively safe circumstances as containing a threat, prompting him to react to them with states of anxiety, the intensity of which does not correspond to the magnitude of the real danger. The Spielberger Reactive and Personal Anxiety Scale is a complex technique that allows you to differentially measure anxiety both as a personal property and as a state.

Situational (reactive) anxiety is the state of a person at a given moment of time, which is characterized by subjectively experienced emotions: tension, anxiety, concern, nervousness in a given specific situation. This state arises as an emotional reaction to an extreme or stressful situation, it can be different in intensity and dynamic over time.

Using STAI, anxiety levels in interpersonal interaction were identified as indicators of the psychological state of schoolchildren before and after studying the information security aspect associated with network etiquette.

As a result of an experimental study, an analysis of typical mechanisms of psychological defense in children of secondary school age was made and the levels of anxiety were determined.

Since schoolchildren were included in the educational process and other educational influences, in addition to the experiment, could affect their level of anxiety, for the experiment two independent groups of subjects were formed – the experimental and control groups, according to which the corresponding independent samples were obtained.

The homogeneity of the experimental and control groups was established prior to the experiment. Data on situational anxiety obtained before the experiment are presented in table 2. Data on personal anxiety obtained before the experiment are presented in table 3. Data on situational anxiety obtained after the experiment are presented in table 4. Data on personal anxiety after the experiment are presented in table 5.

To determine the change in the level of situational anxiety, let us compare the data obtained in table 2 with the data in table 4. To determine the change and the level of personal anxiety, let us compare the data obtained in table 3 with the data in table 5.

Table 2. Pre-experiment situational anxiety data

	Experimental group		Control group	
Level	Number of people	%	Number of people	%
High	19	30,65	14	21,54
Average	27	43,55	31	47,69
Low	16	25,81	20	30,77
Total	62	100,00	65	100

Table 3. Personal anxiety data obtained before the experiment

	Experimental group		Control group	
Level	Number of people	%	Number of people	%
High	15	24,19	18	27,69
Average	36	58,06	38	58,46
Low	11	17,74	9	13,85
Total	62	100,00	65	100

Table 4. Post-experiment situational anxiety data

	Experimental group		Control group	
Level	Number of people	%	Number of people	%
High	27	43,55	14	21,54
Average	26	41,94	29	44,62
Low	9	14,52	22	33,85
Total	62	100,00	65	100,00

Table 5. Personal anxiety data obtained after the situational anxiety experiment

	Experimental group		Control group	
Level	Number of people	%	Number of people	%
High	22	35,48	16	24,62
Average	32	51,61	34	52,31
Low	8	12,90	15	23,08
Total	62	100,00	65	100

To identify significant differences in the level of anxiety for independent samples, the Pearson $\chi 2$ criterion was used. In this case, it was applied to three gradation levels of the studied feature.

In our case, for three rows and two compared columns, two degrees of freedom are obtained (we determine the number of degrees of freedom by the formula: f = (number of rows – 1) × (number of independent compared columns – 1) = (3-1) × (2-1) = 2), for which we select the tabular critical values $\chi2cr = 9.210$ for 1% significance level and $\chi2cr = 5.991$ for 5% significance level and compare them with the obtained $\chi2emp$ values in table 6 and table 7.

Table 6. Comparison of the level of situational anxiety of students in the experimental and control groups before and after the experiment

	The value of the uniformity criterion $\chi2$
Comparison of the level of anxiety of students before the experiment	1,407801684
Comparison of the level of anxiety of students after the experiment	9,671731181

Table 7. Comparison of the level of personal anxiety of schoolchildren in the experimental and control groups before and after the experiment

	The value of the uniformity criterion $\chi2$
Comparison of the level of anxiety of students before the experiment	0,456169728
Comparison of the level of anxiety of students after the experiment	3,069255771

5. CONCLUSION

In accordance with the developed model of the research, based on the results of the study of the section "Network etiquette" included in the subject area "Fundamentals of Spiritual and Moral Culture" by students, statistically significant differences were established in the training of a secondary school child in information security concepts. At the same time, during the training, the level of anxiety of schoolchildren while studying the aspects of information security in the subject area "Fundamentals of Spiritual and Moral Culture" was assessed, measurements were taken twice: before training and after training in the section "Network etiquette".

The data presented in table 6 indicates that prior to the experiment there are no statistically significant differences in the level of situational anxiety between the experimental and control groups.

At the end of the experiment, statistically significant differences were observed with a 1% significance level between the experimental and control groups. This is confirmed by the fact that $\chi2emp = 9.671731181$, more than $\chi2cr = 9.210$ for 1% significance level. This indicates that the level of situational anxiety among schoolchildren of the experimental group in the middle of information security training is increasing. Our observations show that an increase in anxiety is associated with the study of information threats by secondary school students and an analysis of their possible consequences, which is a natural reaction of the body adapting to new potential threats for it. After some time, the differences decreased and at the time of studying of another educational element related to information security, there were no statistically significant differences in the level of situational anxiety between the experimental and control groups. In any case, the high level of situational anxiety that has arisen requires the organizers of the educational process to take certain operational steps to reduce it, for example, switch to another type of activity or require the creation of previously prepared situations that dilute the stressful psychological situation.

The data presented in table 7 indicates that prior to the experiment there are no statistically significant differences in the level of personal anxiety between the experimental and control groups.

After completing the training, statistically significant differences in the level of personal anxiety of schoolchildren in the experimental and control groups before and after the experiment, as can be seen in Table 7, are not observed for the obtained $\chi2emp = 3.069255771$, since the obtained value is less than critical as $\chi2cr = 9.210$ as at 1% , and at a 5% level, $\chi2cr = 5.991$ for two degrees of freedom. This may indicate that the study of educational elements related to information security issues does not increase the personal anxiety of secondary school students.

The results of the study described in the article show that while studying the aspects of information security in a particular subject area, secondary school students meet the requirements of the modern stage of the development of the information society.

It has been established that the level of situational anxiety in the learning process can increase for a short time due to the natural reaction of the body, adapting to new potential threats for it. It is shown that the level of personal anxiety as the assimilation of new knowledge about information security is not critical.

Thus, the set goal of the research, which was to determine the influence of educational elements from a certain subject area related to information security guaranteeing on the level of anxiety of middle school students was achieved, a method for determining situational anxiety and personal anxiety was proposed for analyzing the psychological state of schoolchildren during the study of aspects of information security within the framework of the developed integrative model of teaching information security for students of secondary school age. The revealed patterns will allow to take into account the peculiarities of teaching information security issues to secondary school students and to organize this process more effectively.

REFERENCES

Abissova M., 2006. Servisy obucheniya informacionnoj bezopasnosti v teorii i metodike obucheniya informatike studentov gumanitarnyh i social'no-ekonomicheskih special'nostejRos. gos. ped. un-t im A.I. Gercena, SPb.

Bocharov M., 2019. Systematic information security training in elementary school, Atlantis Press, Vol. 105, pp 600-605.

Chou H. et al, 2017. The moderating roles of gender and social norms on the relationship between protection motivation and risky online behavior among in-service teachers, Computers & Education, Vol. 112, pp 83-96.

Chou H. et al, 2016. Beyond identifying privacy issues in e-learning settings – Implications for instructional designers. Computers & Education, Vol. 103, pp 253-265.

Dzhonson S., 2006. Kak zashchitit' detej ot opasnostej Interneta: virusov, programm-shpionov, spama, pornosajtov, vsplyvayushchih okon. NT Press, Moscow.

Fallon T. et al, 2018. Investigating social vulnerability in children using computer mediated role-play, Computers & Education, Vol. 125, pp 458-464.

Gratian M. et al, 2018. Correlating human traits and cyber security behavior intentions, Computers & Security, Vol. 73, pp 345-358.

Larsson K., 2017. Understanding and teaching critical thinking — A new approach, International Journal of Educational Research, Vol. 84, pp 32-42.

Lau W. et al, 2016. The relative importance of paternal and maternal parenting as predictors of adolescents' home Internet use and usage, Computers & Education, Vol. 102, pp 224-233.

Partyka T., 2007. Informacionnaya bezopasnost': uchebnoe posobie dlya studentov uchrezhdenij srednego professional'nogo obrazovaniya. FORUM: INFRA-M, Moscow.

Plaza-de-la-Hoz J. et al, 2018. The family, key agent in youth empowerment in ICT society / La familia, agente clave de empoderamiento juvenil en la sociedad TIC, Cultura y Educación, Vol. 30, Issue 2, pp 338-367.

Poos J. et al, 2017. Battling bias: Effects of training and training context, Computers & Education, Vol. 111, pp 101-113.

Rooney P., 2018. A cultural assets model for school effectiveness, Cambridge Journal of Education, Vol. 48, Issue 4, pp 445-459.

Thompson N. et al, 2017. «Security begins at home»: Determinants of home computer and mobile device security behavior, Computers & Security, Vol. 70, pp 376-391.

Usova A., 1986. Formirovanie u shkol'nikov nauchnyh ponyatij v processe obucheniya. Pedagogika, Moscow, pp. 115–120.

Yhomee S. et al, 2012. Computer use and stress, sleep disturbances, and symptoms of depression among young adults – a prospective cohort study, BMC Psychiatry, – Vol. 12, Issue 176, pp 1-14.

LEARNING TO USE A DIGITAL WORKBENCH TO DEVELOP COMPETENCE-BASED TESTS IN VOCATIONAL EDUCATION: GUIDED OR EXPLORATIVE?

Josef Buchner, Anne-Cathrin Vonarx, Peter Pfänder and Michael Kerres
Learning Lab, University of Duisburg-Essen
Universitätstr. 2, 45141 Essen, Germany

ABSTRACT

This study arises from the question of how learners experience different learning arrangements while learning to develop competence-based tasks with a new digital workbench. The study compares a guided arrangement with worked examples to an exploratory learning scenario. Leading questions for the design of the study and analysis are as follows: Does the guided group develop more tasks? Does the explorative group test more functionalities of the digital workbench? Does the guided group report lower cognitive load and a more positive attitude toward the workbench?
The analysis of the elements created within the workbench reveals that the guided group was able to develop more tasks, while there was no difference in quality. The data show that the explorative group was able to test more functionalities; however, the difference was not significant. The results of the questionnaire show that the overall cognitive load also did not differ significantly. There are differences in the scales, which are discussed more deeply in this article. Regarding the further use of the digital workbench[1], both groups report a positive attitude. It can be concluded that learning to use a new digital environment for developing examination tasks should be supported; however, the form of guidance can be subject to further investigation.

KEYWORDS

Worked Examples, Cognitive Load, Role of Attitudes, Exploratory Learning, Scaffolded Learning, Task-Based Learning

1. INTRODUCTION

Which learning arrangement helps learners most? This question has occupied educational and psychological science for a very long time and has led to intensive discussions between researchers around the world. One of the best-known debates is between Kirschner et al. (2006) and Hmelo-Silver et al. (2007). While the former argue against unguided exploration (i.e., pure discovery learning), Hmelo-Silver et al. claim that discovery, exploratory and problem-based learning are effective under certain conditions, such as through scaffolding. More recent studies report that different instructional approaches also pursue different learning goals; therefore, different learning goals need different instructional methods (Koedinger et al., 2012; Renkl, 2015). For example, the promotion of interest, motivation or attitude toward scientific disciplines in explorative learning scenarios can be an important (learning) goal (Newman and DeCaro, 2019). Likewise, different approaches can also moderate the learning process (Hmelo-Silver, 2004), as demonstrated in Likourezos and Kalyuga (2017). Their study provided evidence that participants in an unguided group accepted the learning of new content as a challenge more strongly than a guided group. The authors explain that this compensated for the higher cognitive load that was otherwise associated with this type of learning approach (Likourezos and Kalyuga, 2017, p. 214).

According to cognitive load theory (CLT), excessive cognitive load can unnecessarily strain working memory and hinder learning. This is especially relevant for beginners who have little prior knowledge of a certain domain (Sweller, 1988; Sweller et al., 2019). If they are confronted with low-guidance learning

[1] Project ASPE: https://learninglab.uni-due.de/forschung/projekte/aspe-kompetenzorientierte-pr-fungen

methods, these learners are quickly overwhelmed and must invest more time, e.g., to solve a task or a problem (Sweller et al., 2007, p. 116). One way to counteract this challenge is to reduce extraneous cognitive load. CLT has identified many effects related to this phenomenon, such as the worked example effect (Sweller, 2020). This effect has been demonstrated in many empirical studies and shows that the use of worked examples to learn domain-specific knowledge is more effective than teaching approaches without such guidance. The reduction of extraneous load also leads to better results in understanding and transferring knowledge to other problems (Renkl, 2014; van Gog et al., 2011; Wittwer and Renkl, 2010).

Worked examples are elaborated samples of problems that lead step by step to the solution to the problem. Novices can use them to follow an expert's approach, and as their level of expertise increases, they can detach themselves from the supportive materials. Worked examples mostly use practical, highly structured problems (Atkinson and Renkl, 2007). However, there are also examples of worked examples for less structured problems, e.g., writing, argumentation training or studying teaching methods (van Gog and Rummel, 2010). The learning of digital tools can also be supported with the help of worked examples (Hilbert and Renkl, 2009).

It must be noted that the worked examples effect is sufficient for beginners. Experts or advanced learners may perceive worked examples as not conducive to learning. This effect is called the expertise reversal effect and has been proven in many empirical studies (Kalyuga, 2007).

Furthermore, worked examples limit the exploration of other possible solutions, which is known as learning through failure (Kapur, 2008). Achieved learning goals within a worked example learning scenario are usually based on a very clear and restrictive structure, which can hinder the acquisition of learning objectives beyond the constructed setting (Hmelo-Silver, 2004).

2. PRESENT STUDY

Based on the abovementioned findings on learning with worked examples, this study examines how a fully guided instructional design with worked examples affects different learning goals compared to an explorative approach. The first learning objective involves participants' creation of tasks for vocational training examination with a new digital platform, called the digital workbench. This objective is divided into two parts: the quantity and the quality of the tasks created. The second learning objective is the examination of the functions of the digital workbench. The cognitive load as well as the attitude of the participants toward the workbench will be examined since learner characteristics such as attitude can influence the perception of cognitive load (Scheiter et al., 2009). The following hypotheses will be tested:

H1: The group guided through worked examples scores better than the unguided group on the 1st learning objective (quantity and quality of the prepared examination tasks).
H2: The unguided group explores more functionalities (learning objective 2) of the workbench than the guided group.
H3: The guided group reports a lower cognitive load than the unguided group.
H4: The guided group shows more positive attitudes toward the workbench than the unguided group.
H5: Attitude toward the workbench positively influences the perceived cognitive load.

3. METHOD

3.1 Design and Participants

A total of 31 participants (four women, 22 men, five did not specify) with an average age of 50.6 (SD = 8.9) years participated in the study. The participants worked as teachers and research assistants for schools and a state organization for nationwide examinations in vocational education and training. We used a randomized experimental design. Sixteen participants were randomly assigned to the fully guided worked examples group (FG) and 15 to the unguided exploratory group (UG).

3.2 Materials

3.2.1 Prototype of the Workbench

Within the framework of the ASPE project[2], a digital workbench was developed to support the participants of this study in the future creation of examination tasks. In this study, the first prototype was tested for the first time. An examination in vocational education and training consists of several parts, all of which can be created in the digital workbench and then combined to form an examination. The prototype allows the research team to access all the content created. This created content is evaluated and used to determine how successfully learning objectives 1 and 2 have been achieved.

3.2.2 Learning Tasks and Objectives

The tasks were handed out to the participants in written paper-based form. Each element of an exam had to be worked out at least once by the participants in the same way as for a real exam. The other learning objective was to explore the functionalities of the digital workbench.

3.2.3 Instructional Worked-Out Example

The step-by-step instructions were issued only to the guided group in paper-based form. The manual consisted of text-image combinations with regard to design principles of the cognitive theory of multimedia learning (CTML) (Mayer, 2019).

3.2.4 Measurement of Cognitive Load

Cognitive load was measured with the Nasa Task Load Index (NASA-TLX). The NASA-TLX is a self-reported questionnaire with six subscales on a scale of 0-20 (Hart, 2006; Hart and Staveland, 1988). It is used frequently because it meets the requirement of multidimensional measurement of cognitive load compared to one-dimensional scales (de Jong, 2010). Participants filled out the NASA-TLX after working with the workbench (Cronbach's alpha = 0.7).

3.2.5 Survey of Attitudes

We used an adapted version of the personal digital assistants' attitude survey (Cheng, 2017) to investigate the participants' attitudes toward the use of the workbench. This questionnaire consists of four scales: usability ($\alpha = 0.9$, four items), usefulness ($\alpha = 0.9$, four items), concerns ($\alpha = 0.6$, three items) and intention to use ($\alpha = 0.7$, three items). The Likert scale ranges from 1 (do not agree at all) to 5 (agree completely).

3.2.6 Procedure of Measurement of Cognitive Load and Attitude

The participants were randomly assigned to one of the two conditions, guided with worked examples (FG group) or explorative without guidance (UG group), by means of colored markings on the name tag. Two to three participants met in a small group to test the workbench. Each FG group received the worked example and the paper-based task. The small groups in the UG group received only the printout with the task. After the intervention, the participants completed the questionnaires on cognitive load and attitudes. All elements created in the workbench were saved anonymously.

4. RESULTS

For the evaluation of the learning success regarding the two learning objectives, the data from the workbench were first prepared in tabular form, and then the values were calculated together with the values from the questionnaires on cognitive load and attitude in SPSS 26.

---

[2] https://learninglab.uni-due.de/forschung/projekte/aspe-kompetenzorientierte-pr-fungen

4.1 Descriptive Statistics

In Table 1, we present the descriptive statistics for each variable. Learning success is divided into learning objective 1 with the quantitative and qualitative components. Learning objective 2 involves testing the functions of the workbench.

Table 1. Descriptive statistics with means and standard deviations for all variables

	FG (n = 16)		UG (n = 15)	
Variable	M	SD	M	SD
Learning Obj. 1 – quantitative	3.50	1.38	1.71	0.95
Learning Obj. 1 – qualitative	6.50	5.68	4.00	3.00
Learning Obj. 2 – functions	8.00	5.40	10.00	6.90
Cognitive Load				
Mental Demand	10.06	5.13	10.53	5.84
Physical Demand	5.12	6.12	4.40	3.23
Temporal Demand	4.00	3.76	8.92	4.73
Performance*	8.50	4.65	12.20	4.78
Effort	8.00	5.48	8.33	4.98
Frustration	6.25	5.62	8.80	5.67
Overall CL	6.99	3.31	8.85	3.05
Attitudes				
Usability	3.14	0.46	2.98	0.50
Usefulness	3.09	1.11	3.68	1.16
Concerns	1.46	0.47	1.58	0.56
Intention to Use	3.65	0.93	3.98	0.92
Overall Attitude	2.83	0.44	3.00	0.46

*Note: Scale performance is reverse coded.

4.2 H1: Does the Guided Group Score Better?

To test the first hypothesis, "the group with the support of worked examples scores better than the unguided group on the 1st learning objective (quantity and quality of the prepared examination tasks", we calculated an independent t-test with the values for small groups per condition (Table 2). Levene's test for equality of variance showed no significant values for learning success quantitatively (p = 0.07) or qualitatively (p = 0.46), so we can assume homogeneity of variance.

Table 2. Results of the independent t-test to test hypothesis one

Variable	FG		UG		t(11)	p	Cohen's d
	M	SD	M	SD			
Learning Obj. 1 – quantitative	3.50	1.38	1.71	0.95	-2.75	0.019	1.50
Learning Obj. 1 – qualitative	6.50	5.68	4.00	3.00	-1.02	0.33	-

The results in Table 2 support part of our first hypothesis. The FG group differed significantly from the UG group in quantitative learning success, $t(11)$ = -2.76, p = 0.019. This means that the FG group solved the required task significantly more often than the UG control group. The effect size according to Cohen (1992) was high (d = 1.50). No significant differences were found in the quality of the actual tasks for final vocational examinations that were created by the participants. The FG group created more tasks but did not create them at a higher quality than the lesser tasks created by the UG group ($t(11)$ = -1.02, p = 0.33).

4.3 H2: Does the Explorative (Unguided) Group Test More Functionalities?

To answer hypothesis two, a t-test was again calculated for independent samples (Table 3), this time with the variable functions explored as a dependent variable. Levene's test again showed no significance. We again assume homogeneity of variance ($p = 0.41$).

Table 3. Results of the independent t-test to test hypothesis two

Variable	FG		UG		t(11)	p	Cohen's d
	M	SD	M	SD			
Learning Obj. 2 – functions	8.00	5.40	10.00	6.90	0.57	0.58	-

The mean values in Table 3 show that the UG group explored the functionality of the workbench slightly more. However, this difference is not significant, $t(11) = 0.57$, $p = 0.58$, so we reject this hypothesis.

4.4 H3: Does the Guided Group Report a Lower Cognitive Load?

To determine whether the unguided group (UG) reported a higher cognitive load, we compared the mean values of each scale and the overall cognitive load using a t-test. Except for the physical demand scale (Levene's test, $p = 0.029$), all scales showed variance homogeneity (p-value between 0.45 - 0.90). For the overall cognitive load, there was no significant effect between the groups, $t(29) = 1.63$), $p = 0.12$. Additionally, the scales of mental demand ($p = 0.81$), physical demand ($p = 0.67$), effort ($p = 0.86$) and frustration ($p = 0.22$) did not differ significantly between the FG group and the UG group.

We found significant differences for the temporal demand and performance scales (Table 4).

Table 4. Significant results of the independent t-test to test hypothesis three on cognitive load

Variable	FG		UG		t(29)	p	Cohen's d
	M	SD	M	SD			
Temporal Demand	4.00	3.76	8.92	4.73	3.12	0.004	1.21
Performance*	8.50	4.65	12.20	4.78	2.18	0.037	0.78

*Note: Scale performance is reverse coded.

As Table 4 shows, the participants of the UG group found the processing of the task in the workbench more time-consuming than did the FG group, and the effect size according to Cohen (1992) was large, $d = 1.21$.

We also see a large effect in the results of the participants' own assessment of the performance that can be achieved with regard to the task ($d = 0.78$). This means that the group with the worked examples believed more strongly that they could successfully complete the task set compared to the UG group.

4.5 H4: Does the Guided Group Show More Positive Attitudes Toward the Workbench?

We must reject this assumption. The results from the independent t-test do not show significant differences between the FG and UG groups for any scale or for the summary of all scales (overall attitude). We interpret the results as indicating that both free exploration and a guided instructional approach fostered positive attitudes toward our developed workbench.

4.6 H5: Does the attitude toward the workbench influence the perceived cognitive load?

To test hypothesis 5, we calculated linear regression models with the overall cognitive load as the dependent variable and the individual attitude scales as independent variables. The results are shown in Table 5.

Table 5. Effect of attitude on cognitive load

	Unstandardized		Standardized		Coefficients Std. Error	
Variable	FG	UG	FG	UG	FG	UG
(Constant)	19.19***	6.45				
Usability	-3.92**	-1.23	-0.54**	-0.20	1.32	1.78
Usefulness	-1.43*	1.50	-0.48*	0.57	0.66	1.07
Concerns	0.52	3.00	0.07	0.54	1.38	1.89
Intention to Use	1.03	-1.02	0.29	-0.31	0.72	1.28
R^2	0.67	0.36				
corr. R^2	0.55	0.11				
F-FG(4,11), F-UG(4,10)	5.63**	1.41				
f^2	1.11	-				

*p=0.05, **p<0.05, ***p<0.01

As we can see in Table 5, the model is significant only for the FG group ($F\text{-}FG(4,11) = 5.63$, $p = 0.01$, $N = 16$). The effect size $f^2 = 1.11$ corresponds to a strong effect according to Cohen (1992). The attitude toward the workbench among the participants of the FG group therefore had an influence on the cognitive load. Only the scales usability ($p = 0.01$) and usefulness ($p = 0.05$) were significant. If the positive attitude toward these two variables decreases, cognitive load can increase. This effect is stronger for usability (unstandardized beta = -3.92) than for usefulness (unstandardized beta = -1.43). In the UG group, however, we did not find any significant influences for any of the attitude scale variables that can be reported as predictors of cognitive load ($F\text{-}UG(4,10) = 1.41$, $p = 0.30$, $N = 15$). We also calculated a linear regression with the overall attitude scale as an independent variable for both groups. The model was not significant for the FG group, $F\text{-}FG(1,14) = 1.70$, $p = 0.21$, $N = 16$, or for the UG group, $F\text{-}UG(1,13) = 0.78$, $p = 0.39$, $N = 15$.

Based on the results found in 4.3, we calculated linear regression models with temporal demand and performance as dependent variables.

A scale from the attitudes scale was not a significant predictor for the sense of temporal demand in either group; $F\text{-}FG(4,11) = 1.49$, $p = 0.27$ and $F\text{-}UG(4,8) = 1.72$, $p = 0.24$.

For the variable performance, it was found that usability (p = 0.02) and usefulness (p = 0.012) were significant predictors in the FG group; $F\text{-}FG(4,11) = 5.38$, $p = 0.012$, $f2 = 1.08$. This was not true for the UG group. None of the variables showed significant values in the sense of assumed performance; $F\text{-}UG(4,10) = 2.07$, $p = 0.16$.

5. DISCUSSION

This study examined how different learning arrangements affect learning goals, cognitive load, and attitudes toward a new digital workbench. One learning objective was to create vocational education examination tasks using the workbench, and quantitative and qualitative aspects were investigated. In terms of quantity, it was found that the group led by worked examples (FG) was more successful than the explorative group (UG). No differences were found in regard to the quality of the tasks created by the participants. Both groups showed similar performances. The second learning objective was to explore the new workbench and test its functions. Here, the descriptive statistics data show a small advantage in favor of the UG group; however, the difference is not significant. These results are consistent with other research results on worked examples. Highly structured and clear tasks are much better fulfilled by guided groups (Atkinson and Renkl, 2007). This was not the case for more explorative aspects of the task, where both groups performed similarly.

The overall cognitive load did not differ significantly between the groups, and only the scales of temporal demand and performance differed significantly. The UG group found working on the tasks more time consuming than the FG group. The FG group showed much stronger confidence in their own performance and reported higher values for performance. The time requirement for unguided instructional designs was also reported by Kirschner et al. (2006). Instructional designers should take this into account when designing learning arrangements and, in the case of more explorative approaches, give learners more time to solve tasks. Perceived performance can have a lasting effect on learning success, as Bandura's theory on self-efficacy shows (Bandura, 1977). Instructional designers should also be aware of the extent to which explorative learning environments may hinder learners' confidence in their success. No differences were found regarding attitudes toward the workbench. Both groups reported high values on all scales and were positive about further use.

The scales of usability and usefulness were found to be predictors of cognitive load, but only in the FG Group. For learning arrangements that are digitally supported, it can be concluded that the handling of the respective platform or technology should be perceived as simple by the users. With this in mind, the potential risk of cognitive load can be minimized. In conclusion, the technology used should also help to process certain tasks; otherwise, the risk of cognitive overload increases.

ACKNOWLEDGEMENT

The ASPE project is funded by the Federal Ministry of Education and Research, funding code: 21AP007AA.

REFERENCES

Atkinson, R.K., Renkl, A., 2007. Interactive Example-Based Learning Environments: Using Interactive Elements to Encourage Effective Processing of Worked Examples. Educational Psychology Review 19, 375–386. https://doi.org/10.1007/s10648-007-9055-2

Bandura, A., 1977. Self-efficacy: Toward a Unifying Theory of Behavioral Change. Psychological Review 84, 191–215.

Cheng, K.-H., 2017. Reading an augmented reality book: An exploration of learners' cognitive load, motivation, and attitudes. Australasian Journal of Educational Technology 33, 53–69. https://doi.org/10.14742/ajet.2820

Cohen, J., 1992. A Power Primer. Quantitative Methods in Psychology 112, 155–159.

de Jong, T., 2010. Cognitive load theory, educational research, and instructional design: some food for thought. Instr Sci 38, 105–134. https://doi.org/10.1007/s11251-009-9110-0

Hart, S.G., 2006. NASA-Task Load Index (NASA-TLX); 20 Years Later., in: Proceedings of the Human Factors and Ergonomics Society 50th Annual Meeting. Presented at the Human Factors and Ergonomics Society 50th Annual Meeting, HFES, Santa Monica, pp. 904–908.

Hart, S.G., Staveland, L.E., 1988. Development of NASA-TLX (Task Load Index): Results of Empirical and Theoretical Research. Advances in Psychology 52, 139–183. https://doi.org/10.1016/S0166-4115(08)62386-9.

Hilbert, T.S., Renkl, A., 2009. Learning how to use a computer-based concept-mapping tool: Self-explaining examples helps. Computers in Human Behavior 25, 267–274. https://doi.org/10.1016/j.chb.2008.12.006

Hmelo-Silver, C.E., 2004. Problem-Based Learning: What and How Do Students Learn? Educational Psychology Review 16, 235–266. https://doi.org/10.1023/B:EDPR.0000034022.16470.f3

Hmelo-Silver, C.E., Duncan, R.G., Chinn, C.A., 2007. Scaffolding and Achievement in Problem-Based and Inquiry Learning: A Response to Kirschner, Sweller, and Clark (2006). Educational Psychologist 42, 99–107. https://doi.org/10.1080/00461520701263368

Kalyuga, S., 2007. Expertise Reversal Effect and Its Implications for Learner-Tailored Instruction. Educ Psychol Rev 19, 509–539. https://doi.org/10.1007/s10648-007-9054-3

Kapur, M., 2008. Productive Failure. Cognition and Instruction 26, 307–313. https://doi.org/10.1080/07370000802212669

Kirschner, P.A., Sweller, J., Clark, R.E., 2006. Why Minimal Guidance During Instruction Does Not Work: An Analysis of the Failure of Constructivist, Discovery, Problem-Based, Experiential, and Inquiry-Based Teaching. Educational Psychologist 41, 75–86. https://doi.org/10.1207/s15326985ep4102_1

Koedinger, K.R., Corbett, A.T., Perfetti, C., 2012. The Knowledge-Learning-Instruction Framework: Bridging the Science-Practice Chasm to Enhance Robust Student Learning. Cognitive Science 36, 757–798. https://doi.org/10.1111/j.1551-6709.2012.01245.x

Likourezos, V., Kalyuga, S., 2017. Instruction-first and problem-solving-first approaches: alternative pathways to learning complex tasks. Instructional Science 45, 195–219. https://doi.org/10.1007/s11251-016-9399-4

Mayer, R.E., 2019. Thirty years of research on online learning. Applied Cognitive Psychology 33, 152–159. https://doi.org/10.1002/acp.3482

Newman, P.M., DeCaro, M.S., 2019. Learning by exploring: How much guidance is optimal? Learning and Instruction 62, 49–63. https://doi.org/10.1016/j.learninstruc.2019.05.005

Renkl, A., 2015. Different roads lead to Rome: the case of principle-based cognitive skills. Learning: Research and Practice 1, 79–90. https://doi.org/10.1080/23735082.2015.994255

Renkl, A., 2014. Toward an Instructionally Oriented Theory of Example-Based Learning. Cognitive Science 38, 1–37. https://doi.org/10.1111/cogs.12086

Scheiter, K., Gerjets, P., Vollmann, B., Catrambone, R., 2009. The impact of learner characteristics on information utilization strategies, cognitive load experienced, and performance in hypermedia learning. Learning and Instruction 19, 387–401. https://doi.org/10.1016/j.learninstruc.2009.02.004

Sweller, J., 2020. Cognitive load theory and educational technology. Education Tech Research Dev 68, 1–16. https://doi.org/10.1007/s11423-019-09701-3

Sweller, J., 1988. Cognitive Load During Problem Solving: Effects on Learning. Cognitive Science 12, 257–285.

Sweller, J., Kirschner, P.A., Clark, R.E., 2007. Why Minimally Guided Teaching Techniques Do Not Work: A Reply to Commentaries. Educational Psychologist 42, 115–121. https://doi.org/10.1080/00461520701263426

Sweller, J., van Merriënboer, J., Paas, F.G.W.C., 2019. Cognitive Architecture and Instructional Design: 20 Years Later. Educ Psychol Rev 31, 261–292. https://doi.org/10.1007/s10648-019-09465-5

van Gog, T., Kester, L., Paas, F., 2011. Effects of worked examples, example-problem, and problem-example pairs on novices' learning. Contemporary Educational Psychology 36, 212–218. https://doi.org/10.1016/j.cedpsych.2010.10.004

van Gog, T., Rummel, N., 2010. Example-Based Learning: Integrating Cognitive and Social-Cognitive Research Perspectives. Educational Psychology Review 22, 155–174. https://doi.org/10.1007/s10648-010-9134-7

Wittwer, J., Renkl, A., 2010. How Effective are Instructional Explanations in Example-Based Learning? A Meta-Analytic Review. Educational Psychology Review 22, 393–409. https://doi.org/10.1007/s10648-010-9136-5

A TAGSET FOR UNIVERSITY STUDENTS' EDUCATIONAL GOALS

Felix Weber[1] and Elen Le Foll[2]
[1]*Institute of Cognitive Science*
[2]*Institute of English and American Studies*
Osnabrück University, Germany

ABSTRACT

Self-set educational goals are central to self-regulated learning and an observable manifestation of students' motivation. In this paper, we develop and trial a tagset for the characteristics of university students' self-set goals. The novelty of this approach consists in using data-driven, non-exclusive tags, rather than theory-derived, exclusive categories, on the basis of freely formulated goals in natural language. A 400-goal sample out of the 2,262 educational goals collected from 732 students at three universities was used to develop a tagset of six metatags and 28 tags. Six coders independently assigned tags to the collected goals. Based on these tag assignments (n = 376,458), Krippendorff's α was used to approximate intercoder reliability. Surprising intercoder agreement scores are discussed. Further, relative frequencies for each of the tags were calculated. These point to relevant aspects of students' motivations. The tagged dataset may serve as input for AI-powered study assistant systems, whilst the tagset itself may be used in future studies to gain further insights into university students' study motivations.

KEYWORDS

Goal Setting, Goal Characteristics, Goal Classification, Study Goals, Higher Education

1. INTRODUCTION

Goal-setting theory (Locke and Latham, 1990; Locke and Latham, 2019) postulates that by explicitly formulating personal goals individuals are more likely to attain them. Goal-setting individuals are hypothesized to be more capable of directing their effort and attention towards goal-relevant tasks and of ignoring distractions. Indeed, the setting of goals can, in itself, bolster individuals' self-regulation capacity. Furthermore, goal setting boosts persistence, thus reducing the impact of negative influences such as anxiety, disappointment or frustration. In addition, well-defined goals are thought to encourage individuals to develop more efficient strategies to meet their aims (e.g. Locke and Latham, 2002). Over the past four decades, more than 400 experimental and correlational studies have provided evidence for the validity of goal-setting theory (e.g. Locke and Latham, 2002; Latham and Locke, 2007).

Goal-setting theory is key to social-cognitive learning models of academic achievement. Within such frameworks, goal commitment and self-efficacy positively influence each other in a virtuous cycle of goal attainment (e.g. Pintrich, 2000; Morisano, 2013; Schippers *et al.*, 2015). Crucially, competences such as self-regulated learning, self-initiative, self-management and self-efficacy are all considered fundamental skills for successful studies and careers. In the context of higher education, these "future skills" are also expected to gain in importance as universities shift towards more active learning forms involving more student choices and greater learner autonomy (Ehlers, 2020, p.22). Since self-regulated learning is known to largely depend on intrinsic motivation and, crucially, the ability to set personal study goals, the ability to formulate meaningful goals is seen as a key quality for students to successfully complete their university studies.

Indeed, Locke and Latham's (1990) proposal that high but achievable goals correlate positively with performance outcomes has been shown to generalize to academic learning (cf. Morisano, 2013 for a review; also Schippers *et al.*, 2020 for a recent study). In addition, Alessandri *et al.* (2020) conclude that students' self-set goals are more likely to be attained if the goals formulated are highly specific and of moderate difficulty.

In the German context, the EU-wide Bologna reforms have introduced new challenges, particularly for Bachelor students, for whom the transition to the world of work requires an increasingly high degree of professional goal orientation and self-control (Olos *et al.*, 2014). However, a considerable proportion of students are known to be rather poor at formulating intrinsic study goals. Studies suggest that they can greatly benefit from support to both formulate and maintain commitment to self-set goals (Schippers *et al.*, 2020).

1.1 Objectives

The present paper aims to uncover and quantify the types of intrinsically motivated study goals that university students spontaneously formulate in a brief, online goal-setting exercise. To further analyze these self-set goals, a coding scheme is generated on the basis of the natural language data collected. Intercoder reliability scores and the relative frequencies of the different types of goals are calculated.

The results may inform future attempts to support students in developing and pursuing their individual study goals. Digital study assistants have the potential to support university students in self-monitoring their progress and assist them in their development, application and evaluation of strategies and behaviors for successful goal achievement (Weber, 2019). It is hoped that the successful implementation of such software may substantially improve students' learning outcomes, grades and self-efficacy.

1.2 Existing Study Goal Classifications

Two broad categories of achievement goal constructs have traditionally been contrasted. These have been alternatively termed learning and performance goals (Dweck, 1986), mastery and performance goals (e.g. Ames and Archer, 1987), or task-involvement and ego-involvement goals (Nicholls, 1984). Achievement goal theorists hypothesize that these two types of goal constructs are linked to "a divergent set of competence-relevant affect, cognition, and behavior" (Elliot, 1999, p.169). With performance (or ego-involvement) goals, students focus on their abilities and sense of self-worth, whereby ability is achieved by surpassing normative-based standards and/or the performance of others. By contrast, learning, mastery or task-involvement goals reflect the belief that effort and outcome covary. They thus highlight intrinsic motivational patterns. In contrast to performance goals, mastery goals are evaluated on the basis of self-referenced standards (Ames, 1992).

Adding to the prevailing performance-mastery goal dichotomy, Elliot (1999) added the notion of approach and avoidance and thus introduced the trichotomous framework of mastery, performance-approach, and performance-avoidance goals. In this framework, performance-approach goals focus on attaining normative competence, whilst performance-avoidance goals home in on avoiding normative incompetence. Pintrich (2000) subsequently added the, at first sight, somewhat counterintuitive construct of mastery-avoidance goals. This latter category may be associated with some forms of perfectionism; typical motivations for such goals might include *"make sure I don't make any mistakes"* or *"not get a single question wrong"* (Elliot and Thrash, 2001, p.146). At the functional level of analysis, these distinct, theoretically mutually exclusive, achievement goal categories are assumed to be associated with different outcomes, such as levels of cognitive engagement, self-regulation, affect, interest, persistence, and choice behaviors (Pintrich, 2000).

Although these goal categories have traditionally been theorized as dichotomous and in opposition to one another, empirical correlational studies based on survey data have reported conflicted results with some positive, negative and non-significant correlations between the supposedly opposing types of goals (Pintrich, 2000). A further issue with such goal classification schemes concerns the consciousness or cognitive accessibility of motivational constructs and thus whether students can accurately report on their own motivation (Murphy and Alexander, 2000). Goal-setting theory assumes that goals are cognitive representations of what individuals are trying to accomplish and their purposes or reasons for attempting a task. As such, they are inherently cognitive and assumed to be accessible by the individual. This, however, is not necessarily a given and, in real world contexts, students spontaneously formulate much more varied goals. Indeed, such self-set goals have been reported to "take on a much more personalized, idiographic flavor" (Elliot and Thrash, 2001, p.146) Furthermore, each achievement goal category potentially encompasses very many different sub-levels of goals. By way of illustration, Elliot and Thrash (2001, p.146) differentiate between high-level striving, e.g., "*learn as much as I possibly can at school this year*" and lower-level striving, e.g., "*get at least 45 out of 50 problems correct on my math exam*". Hence the kind of goals that students freely formulate may be simple task-based target goals, overarching goal orientations or goal complexes. In addition, goals are cognitive representations and, as such, are expected to be adapted on the basis of contextual sensibility (Pintrich, 2000).

One known issue in designing and evaluating goal-setting interventions is the difficulty of reliably classifying and coding participants' self-set goals in natural language. As a result, many studies have resorted to using study goal questionnaires designed to capture the different types of goals that students set themselves. For instance, Elliot and Church (1997) devised a questionnaire to assess college students' adoption of mastery, performance-approach, and performance-avoidance achievement goals. Participants responded to six items, such as "*It is important to me to do better than the other students*" and "*I want to learn as much as possible from this class*", on a 7-point Likert scale ranging from "*not at all true of me*" to "*very true of me*".

An early, data-driven attempt to classify students' self-set goals includes Krause (1995), who investigated the individual planning and decision-making processes that students go through before choosing a university course. In her analysis, students' goals were subdivided into two broad categories: subject-related goals (e.g. *pursuit of personal interests and development of personality*) and social goals (e.g. *contact with other students, communicating with lecturers*). Also in the German higher education context, Ahn *et al.* (2012) applied both previously established goals categories and added new categories on the basis of interviews and questionnaires with students and lecturers. These categories reflect goals related to the choice of a particular course of study. The authors classified them into six supra-categories. On the basis of the data collected, Ahn *et al.* (2012) proposed a four-level hierarchical model of study goals. The highest level represents the overarching aim of *living a good life*. The second level makes a temporal differentiation between goals concerning students' university studies and those concerning life after graduation. The model's third level is about the goal's contextual environment: at university vs. outside of university, and private vs. professional lives. The fourth, most fine-grained level, distinguishes between self-focus vs. other-focus, high vs. low involvement in the learning process, professional vs. personal considerations, and fulfilling personal wishes vs. those of others.

As part of a personal growth goal-setting program, Travers *et al.* (2015) explored the types of academic performance-related growth goals that students choose to set themselves. The authors subsumed these goals into three broad categories: (1) personal organization and time management; (2) emotional and psychological control; and (3) interpersonal-skills development, stressing that these need not be discrete categories. Similarly, as part of a large quasi-experimental goal-setting intervention program, Schippers *et al.* (2020) categorized students' self-set goals with a set of seven categories: academic, career, social relationships, material, physical health, mental well-being, and miscellaneous. Two independent raters classified the goals according to these seven categories and Schippers *et al.* (2020) report high interrater agreement scores of $k = 0.85–0.87$.

Prior studies on students' self-set study goals have tended to focus on one or two study disciplines (most frequently economics, management and psychology) and attempts to classify freely formulated study goals have usually been restricted to a handful of very broad goal type categories, with only few studies reporting inter-rater agreement scores. By contrast, the present study seeks to create and validate a tagset that can capture the full breadth of study goals students set themselves and that can be applied to a broad range of both under- and postgraduate studies. Ultimately, it is hoped that such a tagset, together with a large reliably manually tagged training dataset may later be used by a digital study assistant to automatically analyze students' self-set goals in order to design personalized goal-setting interventions.

2. METHODS

The procedure is summarized in Figure 1. First, students from three German universities across all study programs were invited to participate in the study using existing university- and faculty-specific email mailing lists, as well as advertising on the universities' local learning management system (LMS) platforms. As such, the sampling technique used was a combination of self-selection and convenience sampling (Oates, 2006).

The link provided in the emails and the LMS adds redirected students to a web-based interface embedded in the universities' local LMS. The webpage detailed the project's wider aims (creating a digital study assistant) and encouraged students to participate by citing research that has shown that the formulation of personal goals can, in itself, positively contribute to attaining them (Locke and Latham, 2002). Further motivation was provided by informing students that, on submission of their goals, they would be able to see the goals most frequently submitted by other students and that they would see as many as they had submitted themselves.

Thus, by submitting four goals, students would be shown the four most frequently submitted goals thus far in the study. In the first text box of the input interface (Figure 1), participants were informed of the pseudo-anonymization procedure of their personal data and could opt in to have personal information concerning their course and their current semester of study saved alongside their goals. The exact information saved was displayed next to the check box. The data collection procedure was checked by the data protection officials of the universities involved and approved to be in line with GDPR regulations. The second text box required participants to input their goals one by one. They also had the option of deleting previously submitted goals.

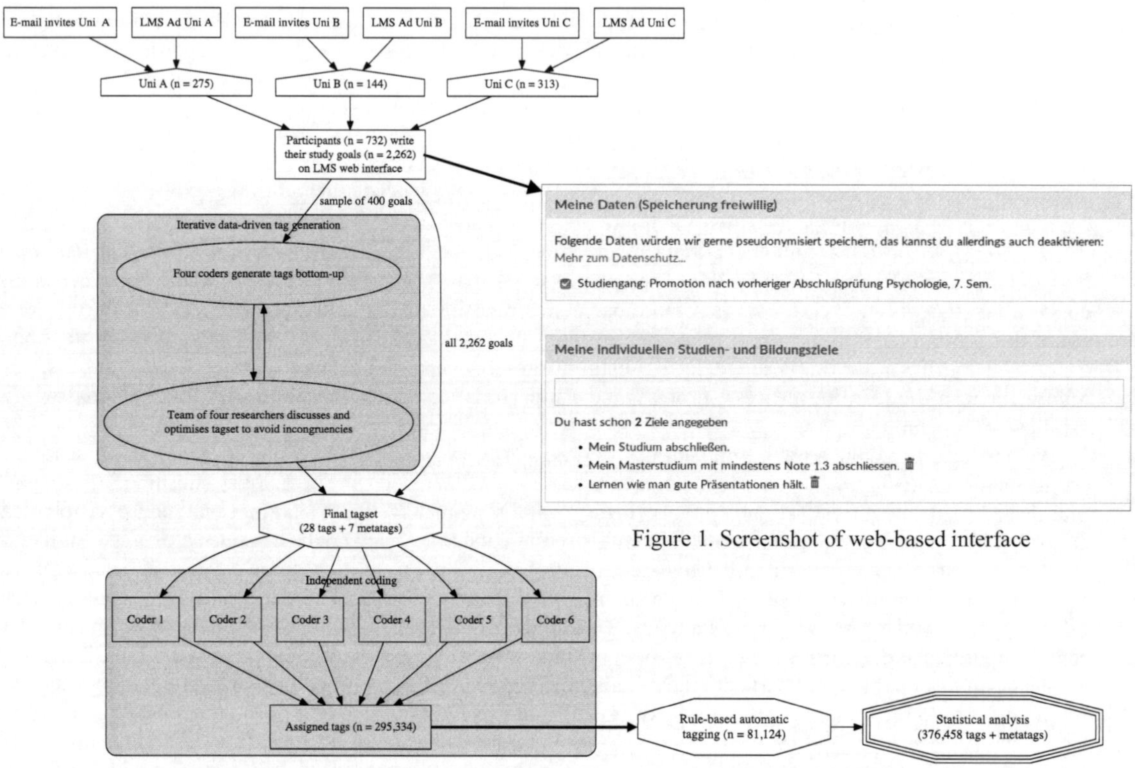

Figure 1. Screenshot of web-based interface

Figure 2. Flowchart outlining the data collection and processing procedure

Post-data collection, a random sample of 400 goals were iteratively tagged by one of the researchers following a cyclical, data-driven process, and four project members discussed and improved the proposed tags. Thus, rather than imposing preconceived categories, commonalities and key themes were identified from the data (Braun and Clarke, 2006). Six independent coders then applied the final tagset to the full set of goals collected. They were instructed to use as many of the tags for any one goal as they felt necessary.

Post-manual coding, rule-based algorithms were run to add the corresponding metatags to the goal ratings made by the six coders. For instance, if a coder assigned the tags ORIENTATION to the goal *Promotionsstelle bekommen* [get a PhD position], the metatag CAREER was automatically added. Additionally, following Bloom's (1956) taxonomy of educational objectives, the tags subsumed under the metatag *Education goals* were hypothesized to be sequentially dependent: PERSONAL GROWTH > COMPETENCES > COMPREHENSION > KNOWLEDGE. Consequently, if a goal was tagged as COMPETENCES, the tags KNOWLEDGE and COMPREHENSION were automatically added to the list of tags assigned to that goal.

Krippendorff's α (Krippendorff, 2004) was used to measure intercoder agreement. This measure was deemed most appropriate to gauge intercoder reliability since it can handle missing data and can be compared to a number of other well-known metrics (Krippendorff, 2004). Relative tag frequencies were calculated for each tag across all ratings by all raters. Data analyses were carried out in Python 3.7 using the Pandas (McKinney, 2010), NumPy (Oliphant, 2006), and Statsmodels (Seabold and Perktold, 2010) libraries.

3. RESULTS

In total, 732 students participated in the study. Among the participants, 74.69% percent agreed to provide data about their subject, degree type and semester. 2,262 goals were generated so that, on average, participants provided around 3 goals each. The length of goals varied from single words (e.g. *Abschluss* [Graduation] or *Praktika* [Work experiences]), to several elaborate sentences, e.g.:

> Ich möchte wissen wie ich realistischer Weise [sic] eine positive Auswirkung auf die Umwelt und Gesellschaft haben kann. Hochgesteckte Ziele klingen unerreichbar und niedrighesteckte [sic] Ziele klingen sinnlos. Ich möchte das Gefühl haben (und das Wissen dazu) etwas verändern zu können. [I want to know how I can realistically have a positive impact on the environment and society. Ambitious goals sound unattainable and modest goals sound pointless. I want to have the feeling (and the knowledge) to be able to change something.]

The full tagset derived from the data is listed below. As shown in Figure 3, the tags were grouped under seven metatags. This means that, for example, when a coder assigned the tag GRADES to a goal, the metatag CAREER was also automatically assigned to it.

Figure 3. Final tagset with 28 tags and seven metatags

In total, 2,262 goals were tagged. Due to time and resource constraints, the six independent coders did not all code the full dataset. A total of 295,334 manual ratings were made. Post-coding, the data cleaning process involved excluding goals identified by the coders as NON-SENSICAL utterances and NON-GENUINE goals ($\alpha = 0.712$), e.g. *Gucci Socken* [Gucci socks], and resulted in a total of 2,204 goals to be further analyzed. The results are summarized in Tables 1 and 2, which list the decreasing relative frequencies of the metatags and tags and provide an indication of intercoder reliability in the form of Krippendorff's α.

The overall very low intercoder agreement rates reveal that, in practice, many of the tags proved rather difficult to distinguish. Thus, it was originally assumed, in line with Ahn *et al.*'s (2012) hierarchical goal model, that every goal would be assigned the metatag PRIVATE OR PROFESSIONAL; in other words, that every goal would be classified as either related to (future) private, or professional life plans. In practice, however, 57.19% of goals were not be assigned this metatag. By contrast, it was not infrequent for both the PRIVATE and the CAREER tags to be assigned to the same goals. Thus, it would appear that educational goals are often tied to both personal and professional interests and that, in many cases, the two are not easily disentangled.

Conceived as a pragmatic operationalization of the concept of distal and proximal goals (Latham & Locke, 1991), the temporal scope of goals was also often hard to determine without additional background information. The α scores for the three temporal tags WITHIN THIS SEMESTER, DURING STUDIES and POST-GRADUATION are among the lowest. Theoretically, these three tags cover all the possible temporal scopes of study goals. Hence, in principle, at least one of the tags should apply to each goal formulated. However, as many as 67.14% of goals were not assigned a temporal tag. This was due, on the one hand, to participants not assigning clear temporal scopes to their goals and, on the other, to implicit temporal scopes not being inferred by the coders.

Similarly, the intercoder agreement rates reported for the EDUCATIONAL GOALS tags are also strikingly low. This is largely due to participants' often very sparse elaboration of goals. Thus, many participants formulated goals that simply read *Lernen [learn/revise]* or *Neue Inhalte erlernen [learn new things]*, for which even the four broad EDUCATIONAL GOALS tags of the present tagset (Figure 3) were already too detailed.

Table 2 shows that the tags STATUS & WEALTH and (job and financial) SECURITY (referring to job and financial security) were also frequently difficult to ascertain. Again, goals that explicitly mention these factors are rare, e.g. *Ein eigenes Haus haben [be a homeowner],* and coders often disagreed as to when they could reasonably be inferred, e.g. *Lehrerin werden [become a teacher]* was assigned the tags STATUS & WEALTH and SECURITY by exactly half the coders.

Raters also reported that the tags NETWORKING (assigned to 46 goals) and SOCIAL CONTACT (assigned to 76 goals) were hard to distinguish from one another. The tagset included this distinction in the hope of tapping into the motives behind the two goal types. On a pragmatic level, however, coders frequently lacked contextual information to disambiguate the two so that 22 goals were assigned both the NETWORKING and SOCIAL CONTACT tags. It is worth noting that, in German culture, admitting to building relationships purely for professional reasons is often not regarded as socially acceptable and may be perceived as selfish.

Table 1. Results for metatags

Metatag Label	Krippendorff's α	Rel. freq.
PRIVATE OR PROFESSIONAL	0.409	42.81 %
CAREER GOALS	0.744	35.65 %
TEMPORAL HORIZON	0.184	32.86 %
EDUCATIONAL GOALS	0.516	32.26 %
CONCRETE GOALS	0.706	19.65 %
SOCIAL GOALS	0.685	6.43 %

α ≥ 0.800 tentative conclusive in grey, α ≥ 0.667 acceptable in light grey (Krippendorff, 2004, p. 429)

Table 2. Results for tags

Tag Label	Krippendorff's α	Rel. freq.
PROFESSIONAL	0.525	37.85 %
KNOWLEDGE	0.516	32.26 %
DURING STUDIES	0.254	24.36 %
COMPREHENSION	0.446	20.20 %
COMPETENCES	0.533	17.39 %
GRADUATION	0.831	17.15 %
SMART (SPECIFIC, MEASURABLE, ACHIEVABLE, REALISTIC, TIME-BOUND)	0.398	12.88 %
PERSONAL GROWTH	0.477	12.74 %
JOB OPPORTUNITIES	0.612	10.73 %
POST-STUDIES	0.245	8.05 %
WORK-(RELATED) EXPERIENCES	0.697	5.24 %
GRADES	0.776	4.80 %
PRIVATE	0.262	4.66 %
GOING ABROAD	0.889	4.13 %
COMMUNICATION & CONTACT	0.716	4.06 %
FOREIGN LANGUAGES	0.903	3.90 %
TOO VAGUE	0.281	3.65 %
ACADEMIC & SCIENTIFIC SKILLS	0.582	3.60 %
FUN, HAPPINESS & SATISFACTION	0.587	3.01 %
PROGRAMMING SKILLS	0.794	2.82 %
ORIENTATION	0.487	2.68 %
STATUS & WEALTH	0.411	2.47 %
VOLUNTEER WORK & IDEALISM	0.622	1.87 %
NON-SENSICAL/NON-GENUINE GOALS	0.712	1.75 %
NETWORKING	0.664	1.48 %
DURATION OF STUDIES	0.869	0.86 %
SECURITY	0.614	0.33 %
WITHIN THIS SEMESTER	0.203	0.05 %

α ≥ 0.800 tentative conclusive in grey, α ≥ 0.667 acceptable in light grey (Krippendorff, 2004, p. 429)

On the other hand, CONCRETE GOALS tags, such as those referring to learning a foreign language, studying abroad, graduating quickly, acquiring programming skills, obtaining good grades and gathering work experience, have a high intercoder reliability. This is probably due to their specificity and the fact that they are very frequent and, consequently, familiar to the coders, who were university students themselves.

Due to the number of students ($n = 732$) and, in particular, the uncontrolled variables in the selection of the participants, the external validity of the relative frequencies presented in Tables 1 and 2 towards a generalization to the goal characteristics of university students is inherently limited. Nevertheless, they reveal that the most frequent tags assigned to participants' self-set goals are CAREER, KNOWLEDGE, DURING STUDIES, COMPETENCES and GRADUATION. CAREER, here, refers to goals clearly related to either studies or work, as opposed to PRIVATE goals, hence this finding was to be expected. The fact that many of the goals were also tagged as DURING STUDIES suggests that the majority of students' goals do refer to their current student status, as opposed to more long-term goals referring to their professional lives beyond their studies.

Indeed, many of the participants' goals revolved around learning objectives and were thus assigned the tag KNOWLEDGE. However, these goals were often highly unspecified: many simply stating *Wissen [knowledge]* or *Lernen [learning],* courses or broad disciplines, e.g. *Biologie [biology], Statistik bestehen [pass statistics].* Other students formulated longer, but even more general goals such as *mehr Wissen sammeln, allgemein und fachspezifisch [gather more general and subject-specific knowledge].* Nevertheless, a relatively high proportion of goals were also assigned the tag COMPETENCES, which refers to the application of comprehended knowledge. Such goals were often more specific, so that the tag COMPETENCES is highly correlated with the tags corresponding to specific skills such as PROGRAMMING and FOREIGN LANGUAGES skills, though it was also frequently assigned to goals referring to critical thinking and soft skills, for which no specific tags are included in the present tagset. Across all degree programs, many students articulated a wish to improve their foreign language skills. It is striking that such goals are also frequently formulated in a very abstract manner, e.g. *eine weitere Sprache erlernen [to a learn another language].*

Given these examples, it will come as no surprise that the relative frequency of SMART goals is low. The intercoder agreement rate for SMART goals is also surprisingly low: this is due to a disagreement between the coders as to whether goals referring to GRADUATION, which were also among the most frequent, e.g. *Master abschließen [complete my Masters]*, should be considered specific, measurable and time-bound.

4. CONCLUSION

This study encouraged students to submit their personal study goals via an online interface embedded in universities' local LMSs. Previous research has shown that the very process of formulating such goals may induce learning and contribute to actually reaching these goals (e.g. Locke and Latham, 2002; Seijts *et al.*, 2004). In particular, Morisano *et al.*'s (2010) study concluded that detailing personal goals and strategies can significantly improve educational performance. Thus, such personal goal-setting interventions can both contribute to making the value of goals more salient, as well as help develop strategies to attain them. However, this study has made clear that, without any support, students tend to formulate very brief, unspecified goals, whereas meta-analyses have shown that specific and challenging, yet attainable goals are most likely to be reached (cf. Locke and Latham, 2002). Alternatively, Schipper *et al.* (2020) hypothesize that developing detailed strategies for goal attainment may compensate for a lack of specificity in the goal formulated. In either cases, the results of our study suggest that university students could benefit from additional support to both formulate their goals and develop specific strategies to attain them.

We suggest that a digital study assistant could provide this kind of support, at large scale, in a personalized manner. Further, such a tool could support the monitoring of goal progress, which is also known to improve effective self-regulation and increase the likelihood of successful goal outcomes (Harkin *et al.*, 2016). The present results suggest that CONCRETE goals may be most easily supported by a digital study assistant on the basis of simple rule-based algorithms. The coded data for these goals could serve as labeled training data for machine learning algorithms that can process user input in natural language. For the tags with lower α levels, more explicit rules agreed between the coders, in particular regarding information inference, may prove beneficial. Given the low intercoder agreement rates for many of these tags, this ought to be considered in future studies.

To conclude, the goal characteristics derived from the present dataset may be understood as dimensions of a multidimensional study goal space. In comparison to established categorical classification systems, which do not allow for the assignment of multiple categories to any one goal, such an approach allows for a better representation of the high complexity of goal representations.

REFERENCES

Ahn, H. *et al.* (2012) 'Entscheidungsanalytische Strukturierung fundamentaler Studienziele: Generische Zielhierarchie und Fallstudie'. *Zeitschrift für Betriebswirtschaft*, 82(11), pp. 1229–1257.

Alessandri, G. *et al.* (2020) 'Self-Set Goals Improve Academic Performance through Nonlinear Effects on Daily Study Performance'. *Learning and Individual Differences*, 77, p. 101784.

Ames, C. (1992) 'Classrooms: Goals, Structures, and Student Motivation'. *Journal of Educational Psychology*, 84(3), pp. 261–271.

Ames, C. and Archer, J. (1987) 'Mothers' Beliefs About the Role of Ability and Effort in School Learning'. *Journal of Educational Psychology*, 79(4), pp. 409–414.

Braun, V. and Clarke, V. (2006) 'Using Thematic Analysis in Psychology'. *Qualitative Research in Psychology*, 3(2), pp. 77–101.

Dweck, C.S. (1986) 'Motivational Processes Affecting Learning'. *American Psychologist*, 41(10), pp. 1040–1048.

Ehlers, U.-D. (2020) *Future Skills: Lernen der Zukunft - Hochschule der Zukunft*. Wiesbaden: Springer Fachmedien Wiesbaden DOI: 10.1007/978-3-658-29297-3.

Elliot, A. and Church, M. (1997) 'A Hierarchical Model of Approach and Avoidance Achievement Motivation'. *Journal of Personality and Social Psychology*, 72(1), pp. 218–232.

Elliot, A.J. (1999) 'Approach and Avoidance Motivation and Achievement Goals'. *Educational Psychologist*, 34(3), pp. 169–189.

Elliot, A.J. and Thrash, T.M. (2001) 'Achievement Goals and the Hierarchical Model of Achievement Motivation'. *Educational Psychology Review*, pp. 139–156.

Harkin, B. *et al.* (2016) 'Does Monitoring Goal Progress Promote Goal Attainment? A Meta-Analysis of the Experimental Evidence.' *Psychological Bulletin*, 142(2), pp. 198–229.

Krause, G. (1995) *Lehrveranstaltungen im Studium: Herleitung und empirische Prüfung eines Modells zur individuellen Planung des Besuches von Lehrveranstaltungen*. Münster: Waxmann.

Krippendorff, K. (2004) 'Reliability in Content Analysis'. *Human Communication Research*, 30(3), pp. 411–433.

Latham, G.P. and Locke, E.A. (2007) 'New Developments in and Directions for Goal-Setting Research'. *European Psychologist*, 12(4), pp. 290–300.

Locke, E.A. and Latham, G.P. (1990) *A Theory of Goal Setting & Task Performance.* Englewood Cliffs: NJ: Prentice-Hall.

Locke, E.A. and Latham, G.P. (2002) 'Building a Practically Useful Theory of Goal Setting and Task Motivation: A 35-Year Odyssey.' *American Psychologist*, 57(9), pp. 705–717.

Locke, E.A. and Latham, G.P. (2019) 'The Development of Goal Setting Theory: A Half Century Retrospective.' *Motivation Science*, 5(2), pp. 93–105.

McKinney, W. (2010) 'Data Structures for Statistical Computing in Python'. In Python in Science Conference. Austin, Texas, pp. 56–61.

Morisano, D. (2013) 'Goal Setting in the Academic Arena'. In Locke, E.A. and Latham, G.P. (eds.) *New Developments in Goal Setting and Task Performance*. Routledge, pp. 495–506.

Morisano, D. *et al.* (2010) 'Setting, Elaborating, and Reflecting on Personal Goals Improves Academic Performance.' *Journal of Applied Psychology*, 95(2), pp. 255–264.

Murphy, P.K. and Alexander, P.A. (2000) 'A Motivated Exploration of Motivation Terminology'. *Contemporary Educational Psychology*, 25(1), pp. 3–53.

Nicholls, J.G. (1984) 'Conceptions of Ability and Achievement Motivation'. *Research on Motivation in Education*, (1), pp. 39–73.

Oates, B.J. (2006) *Researching Information Systems and Computing*. London: Sage.

Oliphant, T.E. (2006) *A Guide to NumPy*. Trelgol Publishing USA.

Olos, L., Hoff, E.-H. and Härtwig, C. (eds.) (2014) *Berufliche Zielklärung und Selbststeuerung*. Wiesbaden: Springer Fachmedien Wiesbaden.

Pintrich, P.R. (2000) 'Multiple Goals, Multiple Pathways: The Role of Goal Orientation in Learning and Achievement'. *Journal of Educational Psychology*, 92(3), pp. 544–555.

Schippers, M.C. *et al.* (2020) 'Writing about Personal Goals and Plans Regardless of Goal Type Boosts Academic Performance'. *Contemporary Educational Psychology*, 60, p. 101823.

Schippers, M.C., Scheepers, A.W.A. and Peterson, J.B. (2015) (1) 'A Scalable Goal-Setting Intervention Closes Both the Gender and Ethnic Minority Achievement Gap'. *Palgrave Communications*, 1(1), pp. 1–12.

Seabold, S. and Perktold, J. (2010) 'Statsmodels: Econometric and Statistical Modeling with Python'. In *Proceedings of the 9th Python in Science Conference*. SCIPY 2010. Austin, TX, pp. 57–61.

Seijts, G.H. *et al.* (2004) 'Goal Setting and Goal Orientation: An Integration of Two Different yet Related Literatures'. *Academy of Management Journal*, 47(2), pp. 227–239.

Travers, C.J., Morisano, D. and Locke, E.A. (2015) 'Self-Reflection, Growth Goals, and Academic Outcomes: A Qualitative Study'. *British Journal of Educational Psychology*, 85(2), pp. 224–241.

Weber, F. (2019) 'Goal Trees as Structuring Element in a Digital Data-Driven Study Assistant'. In Sampson, D.G. et al. (eds.) 16th International Conference on Cognition and Exploratory Learning in Digital Age (CELDA 2019). Cagliari, Italy: IADIS Press, pp. 413–416.

BECAUSE IT IS FUN: INVESTIGATING MOTIVES OF FAKE NEWS SHARING WITH EXPLORATORY GAME QUESTS

Patrick Jost
Department of Computer Science
Norwegian University of Science and Technology, Trondheim, Norway

ABSTRACT

Exploratory learning has become a widely applied, pedagogical concept. One approach to encourage exploratory knowledge creation are situated game experiences. Putting learners in quest-based environments can thereby support engagement through exploration and at the same time, allow for a variety of supportive learning strategies. However, examination of progress and investigation of success or motivational factors remain challenging in exploratory pedagogy. Evaluation in learning quests can interrupt the flow experience that supports engaging and successful learning in exploratory environments.

This paper presents an approach for unobtrusive dialogic investigation in quest-based learning environments. Building on the results of an existing exploratory game quest to raise privacy awareness, the study conducts a dual between-subjects investigation to identify the motives of sharing fake news. The study, therefore, extends a mini-quest with a character to build a dialogic investigation for evaluating the intentions behind sharing of fake headlines. Concurrently, the impact on perception of flow and the robustness of the suggested dialogic inquiry is assessed by comparison to the prior non-dialogic evaluation.

The results of the experiment with participating educators and students ($N = 92$) from two European universities confirm students more likely share fake news than educators and suggests hedonic rather than pragmatic motives as drivers of the sharing decision. The dialogic investigation with the mini-quest shows that students perceive fake news headlines as significantly funnier than educators while also spending less time reflecting if they are real or fake. Flow experience did not improve significantly by changing to dialogic questioning. However, positive tendencies in all flow sub-measures indicate that adding a character and inquiring with dialogue rather supports than breaks the sense fluency in exploratory learning quests. Implications for the design of analytical mini-quests as well as further research directions are outlined conclusively.

KEYWORDS

Exploratory Learning, Evaluative Mini-Quests, Game-based Investigation, Serious Games, Decision Making, Fake News Sharing

1. BACKGROUND AND RESEARCH OBJECTIVES

Deciding if information is trustworthy has become an invaluable skill in our environment that is technically and socially connected in every perspective. Teaching about (digital) information and the value of private information is thus an educational mission to educators. However, the skill to judge if information is honest or if sharing of private data is appropriate or not strongly depends on the context of social interaction. Whereas in one situation it might be appropriate to share (e.g. within a close friend's chat group), this shared information can leave context and become a severe privacy concern in another situation as pointed out by Nissenbaum (2009). Aside from this contextual permeability, the indelible nature of digital data in social networks complicates decisions on what can cause privacy issues. Simply put, once shared, it cannot merely be deleted sometime later when a contextual change is becoming evident.

Sharing and thus multiplying and spreading potentially false and harmful news on networks, for example, is a process that cannot be just stopped by one authority. Even a relatively obvious hoax can therefore spread and circulate in social media without being identified for an extended period. Notably, such hoaxes are not only a nuisance but can develop into serious threats, conflicts and consequences affecting politics and policies

(Zannettou et al., 2019) but as well personal life and security (Muthaqin, 2020). As spreading wrong information is also a fast-rising issue on social media (Sulistyawan & Pinilih, 2019), researchers identified a lack of media literacy (Higdon, 2020) leading to the spread of false news.

Our recent investigation with an exploratory game to raise awareness about data sharing concerns (Jost, 2020) confirmed that students are considerably more susceptible to share fake news headlines than educators. However, for finding adequate pedagogical strategies to raise media literacy and awareness of possible dire consequences in sharing of hoaxes, it is essential to learn more about the motives that drive the younger generation in sharing fake news. In this regard, Leeder et al. (2019) recently found that students' willingness to share news was unrelated to trustworthiness evaluations and accuracy of identification as real/fake. This present study is consequently extending the research objective to learn more about the motives involved in students' fake news sharing decision. In addition to assessing sharing decisions and the pragmatic quality of real/fake the investigation is extended with evaluating the emotional/hedonic quality of fun perceived from the news headline following the model of Hassenzahl (2007).

As several researchers have established the benefits of exploratory pedagogical approaches such as situated learning/cognition (Lave & Wenger, 1991) and problem-based learning (Ertmer & Glazewski, 2018) the problem-solving practice is generally also in line with exploratory game experiences (de Freitas & Oliver, 2006). Quests as inherently problem-solving endeavours can be seen as challenges to overcome by engaging in a situated problem-solving task. They can allow learners to learn from relatable real-world oriented scenarios and learn from experiencing failure and consequences in a safe environment (Dahlin et al., 2018).

Further, the social frame where dialogues happen in a problem situation with a peer or in a group could be designed in quests and influential factors on decisions judged with evaluation. People could meet other players or game entities such as virtual agents to engage in a dialogue. Similarly, advanced chatbot technology could be applied (Bergen et al., 2018) in problem situations to investigate influential factors on decisions about sharing personal data.

1.1 Evaluation in Exploratory Game-Based Learning

Beneficially, exploration can promote engagement in learning environments when combined with the concept of knowledge discovery (Yee & Ducheneaut, 2018). Eventually, the exploratory quest could represent a situated learning environment with discoverable points-of-interests (POI) which present decision challenges to overcome. Such POI, however, may also be configured as investigative mini-quest scenarios that allow assessment of learner progress or research questions. Nevertheless, to allow a reliable assessment of sharing decisions or other measures, an investigative game experience requires balancing of cognitive influences (Jost, 2020; Jost et al., 2020). Story aligned inquiry in dialogical form could thereby help both, controlled evaluation and unobtrusive investigation for maintaining an engaging game flow without interruption of a narrative (Nakamura & Csikszentmihalyi, 2009).

Having a dialogue, of course, requires characters and a context fitting the narrative. In other words, a situation, and thus possible extraneous workload originating from presentation or interaction with it (Sweller et al., 2011). Ifenthaler et al. (2012) provide a good overview of learner-centric game-based assessment (GBA) with a recent update to the state of research (Ifenthaler & Kim, 2019) including data-driven approaches informing event-streams, technical threshold concepts and games as formative assessment tools. Several discussed methods of assessment could thereby extend the investigative approach to a broader social research context. Effectively, extending the learning to an investigation approach contributing to domain research goals. When, for example, evaluating exploratory learning quests that include dialogic situations, knowledge creation in decision-making influences could contribute to the scientific knowledge base of cognition and risk-taking. Taking this perspective essentially evolves GBA to a bidirectional research instrument that transmits as well as emits knowledge. While the natural sciences intensively apply parametric simulations for knowledge creation, the social context possesses a hedonic dimension that is difficult to quantify. When trying to evaluate a decision in a narrative quest, for example, the visual presentation of an artificial character matters not only cognitively but at the same time emotionally. Not dissimilar to a real-world interviewer and relatedly subject to emotional biases or preconceptions (Baylor, 2009; Veletsianos, 2010). Which leads to the question of what hedonic influences a dialogic evaluation entails and how they would affect evaluation results or reliability of complementary metrics such as unobtrusive embedded measurements/analysis. The prior test cycle of the presented exploratory learning quest has demonstrated expectable and accurate assessment of fake news sharing tendencies (Jost, 2020) with decision-making metrics while reaching adequate perceptions of flow. As expected, a higher propensity of sharing fake news was found with students compared to educators.

1.2 Research Objectives

Consequently, to better understand this sharing tendency for pedagogical alignment, this study extends the evaluative mini-quest to assess the pragmatic/hedonic motives of sharing. In other words, following the question, if students inadvertently share more because they also are less able to rationally identify fake news or deliberately because the headlines trigger a more impulsive sense of hedonic pleasure. Moreover, the mini-quest is adapted to a more relatable real-world scenario to encourage contextual knowledge creation and maintain flow by aligning to the overarching narrative.

Therefore, the participant engages in a dialogue on the qualities of fake news headlines and sharing intentions with a character from the overarching exploratory environment. In comparing the non-dialogic assessment with the quest-based evaluation robustness of decision-making measures and influences of the character-based inquiry on fluency and absorption of the quest experience is valued. Consequently, the two research objectives of this present study aim to contribute to:

1. Identifying the motives behind students' tendency to sharing fake news headlines to guide pedagogical approaches for learning about the threats of data sharing.
2. Evaluating the assessment of decision making with situated mini-quests regarding the robustness of measures and influences on flow perception when combining metrics with character visualisation and dialogic inquiry.

2. EMPIRICAL RESEARCH APPROACH

2.1 The Quest Game-Frame: Configuration of a Dialogic Mini-Quest

To address the first research question, the established reflection time metrics of the prior evaluation cycle were again applied. Just as well as the overarching exploratory learning quest implemented with the Quest Game-Frame (QGF) (Jost, 2020). However, in the "City of Data Sharing", the prepared mini-quest for assessing the sharing decision tendencies regarding real/fake news was extended with a character visualisation (Figure 1) and dialogic questioning instead of prior simple text box indicating slider input without a relation to the overarching quest. The character named "John" was a friend of the protagonist met in the mini-quest before and engaged in a dialogue when both noticed a newspaper stand at the sidewalk. The character was designed and integrated into the QGF by using the library of Adobe Fuse CC/mixamo.com.

Figure 1. Exploratory quest environment (left) and dialogic mini-quest to investigate motives in fake news sharing

The mini-quest triggered when the player walked into a POI in the city, or the exploratory 3D environment, respectively. A static image of John was displayed while he was first starting to ask how likely the protagonist would share some of the headlines to replicate the prior user study in a dialogic form. As before, it was made clear that some of the six headlines are real and some are fake news and asked how likely s/he would share the news. However, John then progressed to ask the protagonist to express her/his perception of fun regarding the headlines. After that, he challenged the participant to judge how likely they are real or fake. The same headlines were used as in the prior study (Jost, 2020) to maintain comparability of study results. Equally, the same rating scales (from 1 to 10) were applied on all three dialogical stages – sharing intention, perception of fun and perception of reality). Figure 1 displays the extended dialogic evaluation. For evaluating flow experience, again a digital rating possibility of the 10-item flow short scale (ranging from 1 to 7) (Rheinberg et al., 2002) was presented following the last quest, and it was optional to provide this feedback. The exploratory quest game was built for web browser supporting WebGL 2.0. No personal data was assessed; all players were prompted with information on data collection and only advanced to playing after informed consent.

2.2 Research Design and Hypotheses

To investigate the two outlined objectives, both examinations followed a between-group design. The investigation with extended dialogic mini-quest was planned to match the prior study cycle for comparability of results. Therefore, educators/students from the same two universities in Austria and Norway but different departments/courses were invited to take part in the study. Two members of the departments invited to engage in the quest-based exploration game via e-mail to their colleagues and students.

The experimental design for investigating the motives of sharing decisions (research objective 1) is outlined in Figure 2 and combines the reflection metrics established in the preceding study with character dialogue on sharing intention and pragmatic/hedonic qualities regarding the fake headlines.

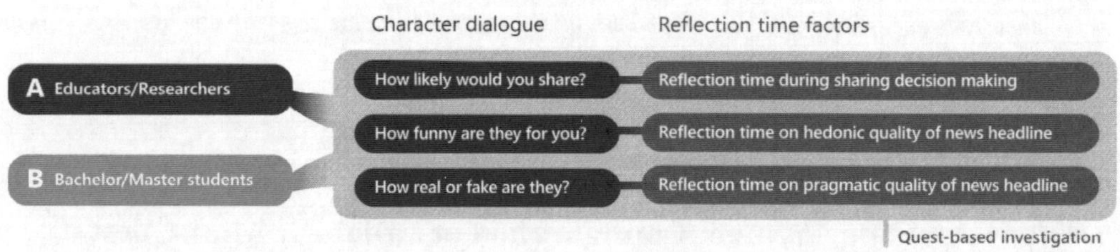

Figure 2. Experimental design for investigating fake news sharing motives with a dialogic mini-quest [RO1]

For monitoring the impact of the dialogue-oriented evaluation with a visualised character on sharing, perception of fluency and absorption by the experience (research objective 2), the results of the group of the earlier study were valued against the present study group (Figure 3).

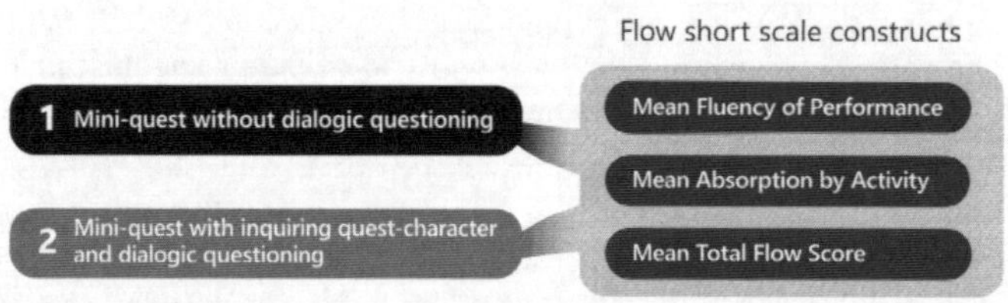

Figure 3. Experimental design to evaluate influences of dialogic investigation on an engaging experience [RO2]

According to the research objectives, the null hypotheses established for the empirical investigation were:

H_{0A}: 'There are no significant differences between educators and students in the propensity of sharing news headlines.'

H_{0B}: 'Educators and students do not differ in their perception of news headlines as fun or real.'

H_{0C}: 'There are no significant differences in experiencing flow when evaluating decision making situations with visualised dialogic questioning compared to the non-dialogic inquiry.'

2.3 Data Collection and Analysis

The invitations were distributed to two research groups and three university courses at an Austrian and a Norwegian university. Ethical approval for the project was granted by the Norwegian Centre for Research Data. Informed consent was obtained before participation with an introductory screen before starting the quest. Data was collected with the mini-quest evaluation modules of the QGF (Jost, 2020) by the provided dialogue scoring and reflection metrics. Using in-game events, each mini-quest result was stored non person-related over a secure connection to the data controller's database. E-mail invitations resulted in 92 participations from two departments and three university courses. All participants (Table 1) played the game using a web browser. Data was subsequently analysed using IBM SPSS Statistics (version 25).

Table 1. Distribution of participation in dialogic mini-quest [between-subjects experiment A/B]

	Participators in dialogic mini-quest			Distribution by age group						
	Educators	Students	Σ	16-19	20-29	30-39	40-49	50-59	60-69	Σ
N	25	67	92	10	57	14	7	3	1	92
Quota %	30.8	69.2	100	9.3	61.7	15.9	8.5	3.7	0.9	100

3. RESULTS

The collected data of participation entries was not consistently normally distributed but showed comparable distribution and homogeneity of variance; thus non-parametric Mann-Whitney *U* analysis ($\alpha = 0.05$) was conducted following Field (2009). Statistical testing revealed significant differences on sharing tendencies between educators and students on both, sharing real and fake news as well as in hedonic perception of fake news as fun and the reflection time when judging veracity (Figures Figure 4/Figure 5; Table 2).

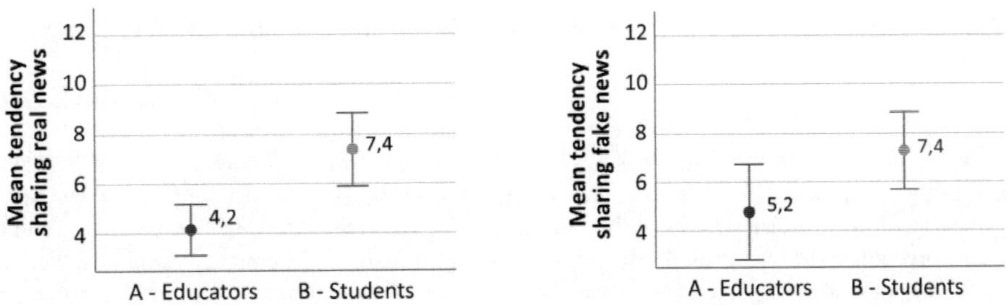

Figure 4. Mean tendency to decide sharing real/fake news [min 3; max 30]

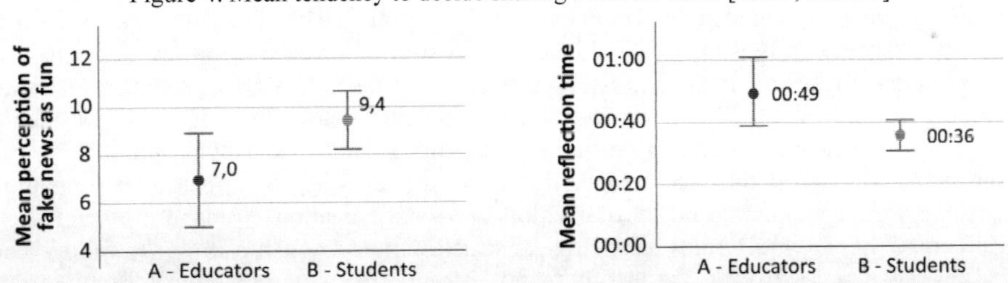

Figure 5. Mean perception of fake news as fun [min 3; max 30] and mean reflection time on real/fake decision in seconds [mm:ss]

Although the median does not differ in tendency of sharing fake news, the mean rank comparison revealed a significant difference for tendency of sharing fake news originating from a smaller range (Table 2) which is better displayed in this case when looking at the mean (Campbell, 2006). Consequently, the results suggest rejecting the null hypotheses H_{0A} as there are differences in sharing tendencies and H_{0B} since students and educators differ in their perception of news headlines as fun or real. Statistical results showed no significant differences when looking on flow perception by comparing study group 1 ($N = 31$) of the preceding study to the 75 participants of the present study 2 that provided the optional feedback. The extension to dialogic evaluation was neither perceived significantly different in perception of fluency of performance between group 1 ($M = 4.64$) and 2 ($M = 4.94$), $U = 1010$, $z = -1.06$, $p = .289$ nor absorption of activity between the first study ($M = 3.44$) and the second ($M = 3.52$), $U = 1075$, $z = -.61$, $p = .543$.

Table 2. Statistically significant differences between educators and students when deciding on sharing real/fake news

		Mean	Median	Range	*U*	*z*	*p*	*r*
Reflection on real/fake decision (pragmatic quality)	A B	0:00:49 0:00:36	0:00:46 0:00:34	0:02:29 0:01:30	597	-2.11	.035	.22
Tendency to share real news [min 3; max 30]	A B	4,16 7,37	3 5	9 27	545.5	-2.82	.005	.29
Tendency to share fake news [min 3; max 30]	A B	5,20 7,43	3 3	17 27	634.5	-1.98	.047	.21
Perception of fake news as fun (hedonic quality) [min 3; max 30]	A B	6,96 9,43	5 9	18 18	582	-2.28	.023	.24

The total sense of flow was as well not differing significantly between the group investigated without dialogical evaluation (M = 4.16) and the group assessed with a dialogue (M = 4.37), U = 1054, z = -.75, p = .451. Thus, the analysis indicates to keep hypothesis H_{0C}.

4. DISCUSSION

4.1 Motives for Sharing Fake News and Reflective Decision Making

When analysing what the results regarding the first research objective, the study disclosed primarily two valuable insights on sharing of fake headlines and the motives behind propensity to share.

First, the results made again clear that students are more inclined to share fake headlines than educators. Thus, confirming the findings of the preceding study on sharing propensity of fake news. However, they are also generally more willing to share headlines than educators regardless of the grade of veracity. The tendency was notable in the preceding study and likely strengthened to significance in the present study by the larger sample.

Secondly, students shared fake news more because they were perceived as fun, not because they were considered real or fake. Compared to educators, students perceived the fake headlines as 34% more amusing, and obviously, they are not determined to reflect too long about the truth of a headline either. When it comes to judging the authenticity of headlines, the empirical evidence of this study showed students are deciding on average 36% faster than educators on the pragmatic decision between fact or fake. This hedonic/pragmatic relation is in line with the findings of Leeder (2019) and suggests that the students' sharing attitude regarding fake news is more related to a faster and instinctive decision making (Evans, 2003) than the educators' approach.

Taking the educators view, this recommends fostering explorative, problem-based learning approaches since they can encourage critical thinking and help contextual knowledge creation (Kumar & Refaei, 2017). Exploratory quest frames could thereby function as balancing construct in three ways, a pathway to follow learner progress (Ruipérez-Valiente et al., 2016) (i.e. the learning goal), a supportive environment for aligning rewarding game achievements and engaging narrative plot situations (i.e. the game goal) and investigating decision-making process and outcome for knowledge creation considering situated contexts (i.e. the domain goal) (Jost, 2020). However, balancing these goals is a continuous requirement for achieving successful outcomes on all points of this intertwined triangle. Comparable to balancing flow of a user experience but with the additional challenge of achieving learner progress.

4.2 Implications for Evaluation in Exploratory Game Quests

Accordingly, this study monitored the influences on flow experience when aligning decision making investigation with a more quest-based dialogic inquiry. When interpreting the data for this second research objective, also two main implications arise for the design of evaluations with mini-quests.

First of all, dialogue-based situated investigation aligned on overarching narrative with a pictorial character does not change the perception of game flow. Although, both flow sub-constructs and total flow perception show positive tendency, the addition of dialogue with pictorial impression of a character alone is not significantly changing flow experience. Since there is a generally positive trend, the data nonetheless suggests following this approach with further investigation for improvements. In particular, as this finding is also the origin of the next subsequent design implication for exploratory environments.

Evaluation with mini-quests displays investigative robustness when applied in situated decision-making research. Adding character visualisation and adapting the inquiry to a dialogue-style inquiry confirmed prior results on sharing decisions. Students' again were found to be more susceptible to spreading fake news than educators. Considered both implications together, dialogic evaluation with pictured non-playing characters is not showing great benefits for flow experience, but on the other hand, is not breaking or distorting it either. This suggests following a point-of-interest structure and aligning investigations in dialogic mini-quests along a narrative can be a way to probe for success factors on decision making. By considering the domain goals arranged in an overarching exploratory scaffolding, situated mini-quests could be applied for probing success factors that influence different outcomes. Specifically, when considering dynamic adaptions of decision situations and potential influences to examine. The configuration of such a game approach should, however, be considered starting with the conceptual phase to balance the experience accordingly.

4.3 Limitations and Further Research Trails

This study revealed valuable insight and conclusive implications on the two research objectives while also confirming results of the preceding examination cycle with the investigative quest environment. Nonetheless, the results must be considered with constraints. One reason is that the binational sampling was limited to universities and thus a specific population. The findings cannot be translated directly to other contexts such as organisational or industrial investigation scenarios. Further research approaches should also apply the quest game frame to other use cases than data sharing to create insight on balancing factors for quest configuration. Another limitation is the visualisation of the character that has been pre-determined by applying a character creation tool defining an abstract appearance. Implications on the design of mini-quest evaluations should be regarded concerning similar visual styles. More investigation is needed to disclose influences from other visual representations with a dialogic inquiry, including photographs, videos, or animated characters. Eventually, the possibilities of generative media should be explored with quest-based scenarios to extend the possibilities of mini-quest probing.

5. CONCLUSION

This study extended a situated mini-quest in an exploratory learning environment with dialogic examination and character visuals to investigate motives of sharing fake news headlines as well as influences from dialogic evaluation on the measures. The results demonstrated robustness of the quest-based investigation approach by confirming results of a prior investigation cycle in the finding that students more likely share fake headlines than educators. More importantly, however, the findings of this examination disclosed the motives of sharing are rather originating from a more hedonic perception of the fake headlines than from judging authenticity. Exploratory, problem-based approaches such as quest-based learning can thus be an appropriate strategy for improving critical reflection on the threats of sharing false information. Additionally, the results suggest that while the dialogic evaluation the designed mini-quest is not improving flow experience, it is not breaking it either. Mini-quests that assemble to learning pathways in an overarching exploratory environment bears the potential to be both, motivating for students and knowledge-creating for researchers. Future research can follow several significant strands: advance unobtrusive in-game evaluation that regards situated context, examine the potentials of generative media for creating social environments (e.g. generated characters), or investigate how game-based quests can become a tool for meaningful social knowledge creation. Ultimately, balancing the interdependent objectives of learning, engagement, and assessment remains a continuous challenge.

ACKNOWLEDGEMENT

This research was supported by the Research Council of Norway (Norges Forskningsråd) by funding the IKTPLUSS project ALerT, #270969.

REFERENCES

Baylor, A. L. (2009). Promoting motivation with virtual agents and avatars: Role of visual presence and appearance. *Philosophical Transactions of the Royal Society B: Biological Sciences*, *364*(1535), 3559–3565.

Bergen, E., Solberg, D. F., Sæthre, T. H., & Divitini, M. (2018). Supporting the Co-design of Games for Privacy Awareness. *International Conference on Interactive Collaborative Learning*, 888–899.

Campbell, M. J. (2006). Teaching non-parametric statistics to students in health sciences. In *ICOTS 7*. IASE, ISI Salvador, Bahia, Brazil.

Dahlin, K. B., Chuang, Y.-T., & Roulet, T. J. (2018). Opportunity, Motivation, and Ability to Learn from Failures and Errors: Review, Synthesis, and Ways to Move Forward. *Academy of Management Annals*, *12*(1), 252–277.

de Freitas, S., & Oliver, M. (2006). How can exploratory learning with games and simulations within the curriculum be most effectively evaluated? *Computers & Education*, *46*(3), 249–264.

Ertmer, P. A., & Glazewski, K. D. (2018). Problem-based learning: Essential design characteristics. *Trends and Issues in Instructional Design & Technology*, 286–295.

Evans, J. S. B. (2003). In two minds: Dual-process accounts of reasoning. *Trends in Cognitive Sciences*, *7*(10), 454–459.

Field, A. P. (2009). *Discovering statistics using SPSS: (And sex, drugs and rock 'n' roll)* (3rd ed). SAGE Publications.

Hassenzahl, M. (2007). The hedonic/pragmatic model of user experience. *Towards a UX Manifesto*. HCI 2007, Lancaster, UK.

Higdon, N. (2020). *The Anatomy of Fake News: A Critical News Literacy Education*. Univ of California Press.

Ifenthaler, D., Eseryel, D., & Ge, X. (Eds.). (2012). *Assessment in Game-Based Learning*. Springer New York.

Ifenthaler, D., & Kim, Y. J. (Eds.). (2019). *Game-Based Assessment Revisited*. Springer International Publishing.

Jost, P. (2020). The Quest Game-Frame: Balancing Serious Games for Investigating Privacy Decisions. In *Proceedings of the 11th Scandinavian Conference on Information Systems (SCIS2020)* (pp. 1–17). Association for Information Systems (AIS). https://aisel.aisnet.org/scis2020/5/

Jost, P., Cobb, S., & Hämmerle, I. (2020). Reality-based interaction affecting mental workload in virtual reality mental arithmetic training. *Behaviour & Information Technology, 39(10),* 1062–1078. https://doi.org/10.1080/0144929X.2019.1641228

Kumar, R., & Refaei, B. (2017). Problem-based learning pedagogy fosters students' critical thinking about writing. *Interdisciplinary Journal of Problem-Based Learning*, *11*(2).

Lave, J., & Wenger, E. (1991). *Situated learning: Legitimate peripheral participation*. Cambridge university press.

Leeder, C. (2019). How college students evaluate and share "fake news" stories. *Library & Information Science Research*, *41*(3), 100967.

Muthaqin, D. I. (2020). Rehabilitation Concept of Legal Protection for Citizen in Hoax Defamation. *2nd Annual Civic Education Conference (ACEC 2019)*, 82–86.

Nakamura, J., & Csikszentmihalyi, M. (2009). Flow theory and research. In C. R. Snyder & S. J. Lopez (Eds.), *Handbook of positive psychology* (pp. 195–206). Oxford University Press.

Nissenbaum, H. (2009). *Privacy in context: Technology, policy, and the integrity of social life*. Stanford University Press.

Rheinberg, F., Engeser, S., & Vollmeyer, R. (2002). Measuring components of flow: The Flow-Short-Scale. *Proceedings of the 1st International Positive Psychology Summit*.

Ruipérez-Valiente, J. A., Muñoz-Merino, P. J., & Kloos, C. D. (2016). An analysis of the use of badges in an educational experiment. *2016 IEEE Frontiers in Education Conference (FIE)*, 1–8.

Sulistyawan, A. Y., & Pinilih, S. A. G. (2019). The Reality of Spreading Hoaxes on Social Media: A Sociolegal Approach. *2nd International Conference on Indonesian Legal Studies (ICILS 2019)*, 436–441.

Sweller, J., Ayres, P., & Kalyuga, S. (2011). Cognitive Load Theory in Perspective. In J. Sweller, P. Ayres, & S. Kalyuga, *Cognitive Load Theory* (pp. 237–242). Springer New York.

Veletsianos, G. (2010). Contextually relevant pedagogical agents: Visual appearance, stereotypes, and first impressions and their impact on learning. *Computers & Education*, *55*(2), 576–585.

Yee, N., & Ducheneaut, N. (2018). Gamer motivation profiling: Uses and applications. In *Games User Research* (First edition, pp. 485–490). Oxford University Press.

Zannettou, S., Sirivianos, M., Blackburn, J., & Kourtellis, N. (2019). The web of false information: Rumors, fake news, hoaxes, clickbait, and various other shenanigans. *Journal of Data and Information Quality (JDIQ)*, *11*(3), 1–37.

EXPLORE FOREIGN LANGUAGE LEARNERS' EXPERIENCES UNDER A METACOGNITIVE LISTENING WEBSITE

Tao Pei[1] and Jitpanat Suwanthep[2]
[1]*Tongling University, Tongling, Anhui, China*
[2]*Suranaree University of Technology, Nakhon Ratchasima, Thailand*

ABSTRACT

This study aimed to explore Chinese English as Foreign Language (EFL) learners' experiences in a metacognitive listening website based on a metacognitive approach. 40 Chinese low-intermediate EFL learners participated in the study and conducted the web-based metacognitive listening practice for 14 weeks. The UEQ and post-interview were used to detect their experiences and perceptions of the practice. The results indicated that these learners had good experiences with the metacognitive listening practice, especially in terms of dependability, novelty, and stimulation. The good experiences may be due to their perceived development of listening comprehension, listening strategies, and the involvement of video listening materials. However, learners' favouring test-based listening practice may affect their perceived efficiency of metacognitive listening practice. This study could provide a sample for further investigation of metacognitive intervention with CALL.

KEYWORDS

Listening Comprehension, Metacognitive Listening, User Experience, Web-Based Learning

1. INTRODUCTION

Recent years have seen increased attention on metacognitive instruction in second/foreign language listening research. Metacognitive instruction was vaguely defined in second language (L2) listening research and entangled with the strategy instruction (Cross, 2015). Cross (2015) unravelled the differences by pinpointing that metacognitive instruction aimed to develop the metacognitive knowledge and listening strategies, as opposed to the strategy instruction that mainly emphasized developing strategy use. Thus, designing metacognitive instruction should involve reflective activities that could elicit learners' thinking on their metacognitive knowledge (Goh, 2008). Vandergrift (2004, 2007) ever proposed a pedagogical cycle —as a typical metacognitive listening model (Cross, 2015) — involved learners through metacognitive processes of listening and peer discussion and reflection. In this way, the cycle could increase listeners' metacognitive knowledge and orchestration of the deployment of listening strategies. Many studies (e.g., Bozorgian & Alamdari, 2018; Vandergrift & Tafaghodtari, 2010; Wang, 2016) have verified the effectiveness of this pedagogical cycle on L2 listeners' listening comprehension and metacognitive awareness in different contexts. On the other hand, e-learning has become a trend since the 1990s and offers learners more chance of monitoring and regulating their learning process (Prastiyo et al., 2018; Rodríguez-Ardura & Meseguer-Artola, 2015). However, although substantial studies investigated the metacognitive listening training inside the classroom, rare research tackled how to implement the metacognitive approach in an online learning environment.

In terms of ISO 9241-11, user experience or usability means the "extent to which a system, product or service can be used by specified users to achieve specified goals with effectiveness, efficiency and satisfaction in a specified context of use" (International Organization for Standardization, 2018). Hassenzahll et al. (2000) indicated that the evaluation of user experience should capture two quality dimensions of a product: ergonomic quality and hedonic quality. Ergonomic quality (EQ) means "the usability of the product, which addresses the underlying human need for security and control" (Hassenzahl, 2001, p. 483) and is related to the task-oriented aspects of the product. A good EQ could make task implementation in a product effective and efficient. Hedonic quality (HQ) "refers to quality dimensions with no obvious—or at least a second-order—relation to task-related goals such as originality, innovativeness, and so forth" (p. 483). HQ deals with users' needs for "novelty or change and social power (status) induced, for example, by visual design, sound design, novel interaction techniques, or novel functionality" (p. 483). By combining the two qualities, users could shape an overall judgment of the product attractiveness.

Hassenzahl *et al.* (2000) further indicated that the appraisal of the user experience induced two consequences. One is the behavioural consequences, such as the increased or decreased usage frequency and time, and the quality of work results. The second is the emotional consequences of the increased or decreased enjoyment, interest, and satisfaction. From this, the user experience appraisal may impact learners' engagement, performance, and motivation in web-based listening. Given the importance of user experience, this study explored second language learners' experiences in web-based metacognitive listening practice.

2. METHODOLOGY

2.1 Settings and Participants

The study recruited 40 EFL learners from first-year students from a Chinese university with 33 females and 7 males, ranging from 18 - 22 years old. The TOEFL scores before treatment indicated that they were low proficient listeners. Most of them had formal English of 12 years, and none had learning experiences in English as native language countries. All of them admitted they were regular internet users with mobile phones or computers.

2.2 Design of Metacognitive Listening Website

There are 28 sets of listening practice on the metacognitive listening website. Each set of listening practice is constructed based on metacognitive instruction cycle (Vandergrift, 2004, 2007) and aims to lead learners through the metacognitive processes of listening comprehension. Also, since previous researchers (Cross, 2011; Goh, 2008; Graham & Santos, 2015; Vandergrift & Tafaghodtari, 2010) have called for the inclusion of bottom-up listening training into the latter stages of Vandergrift's cycle to enhance its effectiveness, we added the sentential dictation tasks (as the bottom-up practice) in the third listening stage of the listening practice. The steps of each listening practice are shown in Table 1.

Table 1. Stages of the online metacognitive listening practice

Stages	Metacognitive processes
1.Pre-listening—Planning/predicting stage	
Learners were informed of the topic, related words, and text type of the listening material. Then they answered some questions to plan their listening goals, strategy use, and potential listening problems, and make predictions of information and possible words.	Planning strategy; person, task, and strategy knowledge.
2. First Listening—First Verification Stage	
Learners verified their initial hypotheses, made corrections as required, and noted the additional information as they understood. They evaluated the effectiveness of strategies and planned new strategies for the second listening.	monitoring and evaluation strategies; task and strategy knowledge.
3. Second Listening—Second Verification Stage	
Learners verified listening again, supplemented the missing information in the first listening, and then evaluated the effectiveness of listening strategies for the second listening and the degrees of comprehension. They could choose to listen again if they had perceived the low degrees of comprehension of the video clip. Then they answered two or three listening comprehension questions and summarized the main contents of the listening text. After completion, they checked the answers.	Monitoring, evaluation, and problem-solving strategies; person and strategy knowledge

4. Third Listening—Final Verification Stage	
Learners completed the sentential dictation tasks and checked the transcripts. Then, they wrote the difficult words during listening and evaluated the difficulty level of the listening materials and their general performance.	evaluation and problem-solving strategies task and person knowledge.
5. Reflection Stage	
Learners summarized listening problems and useful strategies in the listening process and plan strategies for next listening.	Evaluation and problem-solving strategies; person, task, and strategy knowledge.

2.3 Research Design and Instruments

The study adopted a mixed method design. The mixed method design used a quasi-experimental one-group posttest and the qualitative methods of interviews. The learners' experience was examined with UEQ (User Experience Questionnaire) and the post-semi-interview. Both instruments were administered after learners practised listening on the website for 14 weeks. UEQ was constructed and validated by Laugwitz et al. (2008). UEQ was built based on Hassenzahl's (2001) model of user experience. Under the model, users' perceived ergonomic and hedonic quality could reflect the assessment of the appealingness towards the target product. The target product in the study was the listening website. UEQ was composed of six scales under three dimensions. The six scales were attractiveness, perspicuity, efficiency, dependability, stimulation, and novelty: attractiveness means users' overall impression of the product; perspicuity means the extent to which the product was easy to use; efficiency means the extent to which the tasks could be solved without unnecessary efforts; dependability means the extent to which the product is dependable and predictable, and could achieve the expected goal; stimulation means the extent to which the product is motivating and exciting; novelty means the extent to which the product is innovative and engage the users. Among these, attractiveness represented the overall impression of the product; perspicuity, efficiency, and dependability represent the ergonomic quality dimension; and stimulation and novelty were under the hedonic quality dimension. Laugwitz *et al.* (2008) validated the UEQ in several studies with participants in Germany and the USA, which showed that the reliability of UEQ was above the acceptable level on each scale, with the coefficient α >.60. The researcher translated UEQ into Chinese and piloted it with four listeners to reduce their misinterpretation of each item. The reliability for the translated UEQ in the study was above the acceptable level, with the coefficient α = .88. Also, the first researcher conducted a semi-interview to elicit learners' responses on their perceptions of listening practice under the website. 19 learners were randomly selected to join in the post-interview with their consent. This number reached that of gaining saturation (N = 12) in interviews by Guest et al. (2006). The interviews lasted about 10 minutes for each participant.

2.4 Procedures

The whole experiment lasted 15 weeks. Before engaging in the practice, they received a 90-minute training by the researcher to know how to conduct the web-based listening practice. For 14 weeks, learners completed two sets of listening practice on the website each week with computers or mobile phones. The first researcher checked learners' responses in the listening practice and reminded those learners who failed to complete the listening practice each week. Learners were informed to contact the researcher through the QQ at any time if they had problems or difficulties in the listening process. They could also choose to browse over other content on the website. In the 15th week, learners took UEQ and 19 learners were randomly selected to receive semi-interviews by the first researcher.

2.5 Data Analysis

The data from UEQ were analysed with the data analysis tool on the UEQ website (https://www.ueq-online.org/). The data analysis tool also made possible the comparison with the benchmark that contains data from 18483 persons of 401 studies concerning different internet-related products (business software, web pages, web-shops, social networks), to assess the "goodness" of user experience. Interview data were transcribed verbatim and firstly coded by the first researcher to observe the emergent themes. Another researcher helped recode the interview data again with the original themes. After negotiation, we reached the final themes by controlling the percentage of agreement at 90%, a good indicator for the inter-rater reliability.

3. RESULTS

3.1 Results from the UEQ

To detect learners' experiences of the website, the researcher conducted the descriptive statistics to observe the mean scores and standard deviations of each dimension in UEQ, as shown in Table 2.

Table 2. Descriptive statistics of means and standard deviations

Scales	Mean	SD	N
Attractiveness	1.88	0.86	40
Perspicuity	1.57	0.90	40
Efficiency	1.64	0.82	40
Dependability	1.81	0.83	40
Stimulation	1.84	0.87	40
Novelty	1.96	0.88	40

Table 2 shows that the learners performed a positive evaluation on all scales in UEQ, indicating good experiences to work with the metacognitive listening website. Meanwhile, learners had a general better evaluation of the hedonic quality than the ergonomic quality of the website.

In order to generate a more reliable evaluation and detect whether the web-based metacognitive listening practice could fulfill users' general expectations (Schrepp, Hinderks, & Thomaschewski, 2017), the data analysis tool of the UEQ authors also provided the analysis of comparing the mean scores with a benchmark containing the evaluation of a large sample of data, shown in Table 3.

Table 3. Comparison of the means of user experience to the benchmark

Scale	Mean	Rank	Interpretation
Attractiveness	1.88	Excellent	In the range of the 10% best results
Perspicuity	1.57	Good	Less than 25%, better than 50% of results
Efficiency	1.64	Good	Worse than 10%, better than 75% of results
Dependability	1.81	Excellent	In the range of the 10% best results
Stimulation	1.84	Excellent	In the range of the 10% best results
Novelty	1.96	Excellent	In the range of the 10% best results

Learners' responses in 4 dimensions from UEQ were excellent (among the 10% best results) and 2 were good (better than 50% results) compared with benchmark data, indicating that learners had positive feelings towards the metacognitive listening website. Specifically, learners' experience of the listening website was excellent regarding attractiveness and the hedonic quality, suggesting that these listeners felt attracted by the web-based listening, especially impressed by the innovative design and much motivated by this kind of listening practice. Meanwhile, the high score in dependability, one of the ergonomic quality, also revealed the learners' tenacious belief that they could rely on the online listening practice to improve their listening comprehension ability. Also, scores on the other two dimensions of ergonomic quality — perspicuity, and efficiency —represented that the learners were still satisfied with the conciseness and efficiency of the online listening practice.

3.2 Results from the Interview Results

To ensure confidentiality, the researchers used the name codes (S plus the number, e.g., S1, S2) for interviewees in the following data presentation.

3.2.1 Improvement of Listening Comprehension Ability

Most learners reported notable improvement of listening comprehension ability, as illustrated in Excerpt 1.

Excerpt 1:

While listening, I could get a more logical understanding than before. (S3)

I got improved in filling the blank, listening to numbers, and answer the listening

comprehension questions. (S10)
I became more patient since I could endure two-hour listening practice one time. (S11)
I got improved in listening ability…I have been in a better state during listening than before. (S12)

Excerpt 1 indicates that these learners gained more understanding, better listening state, more patience, and more success in completing listening tasks. Their perceived improvement in listening could be due to the effectiveness of the metacognitive listening approach in the website and also could be reflected by the high dependability in UEQ, denoting that these learners felt the listening practice was dependable to achieve their listening goals.

3.2.2 Good Experiences

Most learners used "quite good" to evaluate the metacognitive listening practice, suggesting their affirmation of attractiveness in UEQ — a general evaluation of the website. Some learners pointed out the innovativeness of the listening website, as shown in Excerpt 2.

Excerpt 2:
The listening website is quite good and innovative. Before, we just listened to the audio. (S9)
It [the listening website] is quite good, and the form of practice is quite innovative…the website has the predictions before listening and videos, not merely the multiple-choice as the test. (S18)

3.2.3 Preferences

Preference for the metacognitive listening practice
Some learners reported the preference for metacognitive listening practice to the test-based listening practice. Some of them indicated more fun and closeness to life of the listening practice, possibly owing to the appearance of videos, as seen from the Excerpt 4.

Excerpt 4
This kind of listening practice asked us to extract some information through prediction and verification after listening. In this case, we could grasp the whole meaning of the listening materials. (S5)
I preferred this kind of listening… I think this kind of listening was not formal…when in the test, I was very anxious. (S12)
um…I like this kind of listening; because I could watch videos and engage the ears and eyes into understanding. In traditional listening practice, only ears are involved. (S7)

From Excerpt 4, S12 perceived less anxiety in the web-based metacognitive listening practice; S7 indicated her enjoyment of the video contents; S5 suggested the benefits of undergoing the metacognitive listening process of planning (prediction), verification, and reflection on their listening comprehension.

Choice phobia
Some learners demonstrated their like or positive evaluation of the metacognitive listening practice but admitted that they had to practice the test-based listening, seen in the Excerpt 7.

Excerpt 7
I like this kind of listening practice because it provides intensive training for us. However, I must practice the test-based listening for getting scores from the test and practice the multiple-choice listening items. (S17)
I am personally interested in this kind of listening practice. But if you want to gain high scores in tests, you must choose the traditional test-based listening. (S2)

From the above, these learners' positive evaluation could again confirm the high attractiveness and dependability in the UEQ. However, they still perceived the importance of listening tests and that the development of listening comprehension ability should be reflected in test scores. On account of the long-established test-oriented culture in China (Guo, Diaz, & Liyanage, 2016; Hu & West, 2015), language teachers and learners were highlighting the outcomes of tests as their main instructional or learning goals. Learners' emphasis on listening tests could also explain the relatively low efficiency in UEQ as they may deem that the website may not be as efficient in improving listening scores as the listening tests.

Besides the role of tests in their English learning, some learners indicated the test-based listening was more formal and rendered them more focused in Excerpt 8.

Excerpt 8:

Both kinds of practice are ok for me… I think the test-based listening should be more formal. (S6)

I also like traditional test-based listening because I am easily distracted when practising listening after class. If I practised the listening tests, I would be more focused. (S13)

Preference for the test-based listening practice

Still some learners supported the test-based listening practice and indicated the importance of listening tests in gaining scores and concentration, as seen in Excerpt 9.

Excerpt 9:

I think the test-based listening is more systemic and has some questions I must answer. It is complete. It could help improve my listening scores. (S12)

The test-based listening could make a little nervous, and I could become more focused. From childhood, listening is always in the form of testing. In my spare time, I sometimes listen to news or music. (S19)

From the above, S12 indicated the systemic of tests and its role in improving listening scores, reflecting her idea that listening should produce some products like answering some questions; S14 and S19 indicated that the test-based listening could contribute to concentration, due to the formal atmosphere and some nervousness it produced. This is consistent with the view that mild anxiety could alert people to be more concentrated and improve performance in specific situations (Goleman, Boyatzis, & McKee, 2013; Miller & Stoeckel, 2019; Wiseman & Hunt, 2013). S19 further indicated that for her, English listening mainly meant testing since the routine listening tasks came from the tests.

3.2.4 Modification

When asked about how to modify the website, many learners mentioned the overloaded questions in metacognitive listening practice to increase their metacognitive awareness, as seen in Excerpt 10.

Excerpt 10:

I think there should be fewer questions [about the planning, strategies, and problems] before listening. (S9)

Some repetitive questions, such as the prediction questions, appear three times for me to make prediction and verification. Maybe you could reduce some questions about these. (S10)

Every time the questions are the same. These questions [about listening problems] should appear after four or five weeks because listening problems of today and tomorrow are usually the same, and they don't change so quickly. (S12)

These appeals for less questions could reflect the redundancy in the listening practice, which resulted in relatively low scores in the perspicuity and efficiency of UEQ.

Still, some learners suggested the addition of dictation exercises and categorization of listening topics, shown in Excerpt 12.

Excerpt 12:

Maybe you could classify the listening tasks according to the topics of listening materials. (S15)

I think maybe you could categorise listening practice tasks and put together the listening materials with more connected speech (S12).

It is better to add some practice for the number of dictations or other dictation exercises. (S13)

You could add some dictation exercises. (S19)

S12 and S15 indicated the categorisation of listening tasks based on different criteria. S15 hoped for the grouping by the topics, possibly to increase listening motivation. S12 suggested the grouping by different types of "connected speech" and expected some improvement in this skill. S13 and S19 suggested the addition of dictation tasks, perhaps partly because the dictation tasks (e.g., the dictation of large numbers) were included in their textbooks and in the high-stake TEM-4 tests that these learners were required to pass for graduation. These learners' emphasis of dictation and connected speech could indicate that they longed for more practice of bottom-up listening skills in the online listening practice and the relations between the development of listening ability and bottom-up listening skills.

4. DISCUSSION

The study indicated that the current low proficient L2 listeners had good experiences with the web-based metacognitive listening practice.

Regarding UEQ, four scales were at an excellent level, and two at a good level, suggesting this website arrived at the general user experience expectation (Schrepp *et al.*, 2017). The positive evaluation of the listening website from the interview supported the high attractiveness revealed in the UEQ. Learners' high scores in dependability— suggesting that they have achieved predictable goals—could be reflected by their improvement in listening comprehension ability and the development of metacognitive knowledge and strategies. Learners' high scores in stimulation was confirmed by learners' "feeling interested and fun" in the listening practice. The involvement of videos and authentic listening materials could contribute to this feeling. Also, the "relaxing" environment with less anxiety could bring more motivation to engage in the listening website. The high novelty in the UEQ was predictable since the website contained many metacognitive listening activities, rendering it different from traditional comprehension-based listening websites. Learners also confirmed this in the interview, as some indicated that this listening practice could help develop listening strategies, different from the traditional test-based listening. The high scores in stimulation and novelty represents the high hedonic quality of the website, revealing learners' high satisfaction in using the website (Laugwitz *et al.*, 2008). The other two ergonomic quality falls into the "good" level, suggesting some room for improvement. In the interview, some indicated they were overloaded with metacognitive questions, weakening their perceptions of the perspicuity and efficiency of the website. Meanwhile, perceived slowness of the website and concerns about the listening test results also reduced their perceived efficiency.

In the interviews, the current learners felt they could not abandon the test-based practice, and some test items such as dictation should be added. It also implied their emphasis on listening tests and bottom-up skill development. The focus on the test-based practice could be due to the influence of high-stake English tests in the Chinese context. These high-stake tests were of great importance not just for students to select the access to prestigious or commonplace higher institutions (Fang & Warschauer, 2004), but for schools and individual teachers to earn praises and bonuses (Cortazzi & Jin, 1996). Hence, "[language] teachers … find it impossible to resist pressures that too frequently lead them to focus on test preparation" (Guo *et al.*, 2016, p. 5). Emphasis on test results would transform the listening classes into a 'testing' rather than teaching" (Siegel, 2015, p. 40). It is of no doubt that learners in this context hope to practise listening tests, which for them, was a more efficient way to improve their listening comprehension.

5. CONCLUSION

This study attempted to examine the Chinese EFL low-intermediate learners' experiences of the website. In general, they had good experiences with the listening website, especially in terms of dependability, novelty, and stimulation. The follow-up interview indicated that their good experiences on these aspects could be due to their perceived development of listening comprehension ability, the novelty of the listening practice in developing listening strategies, and the involvement of authentic video listening materials. Still, some learners favoured the bottom-up listening training and the test-based listening practice, probably due to the test-based education environment in China and the ideology of language teachers.

Meanwhile, good experiences could yield positive emotions of learners and engage them more in the self-directed listening website, thus promoting the emergence of the desired outcomes of the metacognitive listening website. Also, the blended learning or flipped classroom could operate with the availability of the metacognitive listening website. There was evidence on the advantage of the web-based metacognitive listening practice over traditional comprehension-based online listening practice in developing listening comprehension ability. However, more evidence was still needed. No evidence was about whether the web-based metacognitive listening practice could exert better results in listening development than the metacognitive instruction inside the classroom. Besides, although many studies (e.g., Cross, 2011) pinpointed the benefits of metacognitive were confined to the less-skilled listeners, some researchers indicated that adding bottom-up listening training could allow the metacognitive listening approach to benefit even the skilled listeners. However, according to Yeldham (2016, 2018), intermediate listeners could gain more benefits from the top-down way of listening (e.g., strategy or metacognitive instruction) than the "bottom-up" way of listening (e.g., training of bottom-up skills). Thus, this is still open to question whether the training focus should switch to the bottom-up skills for the skilled listeners who already had a rich repertoire of metacognitive awareness.

REFERENCES

Bozorgian, H., & Alamdari, E. F. (2018). Multimedia listening comprehension: Metacognitive instruction or metacognitive instruction through dialogic interaction. *ReCALL*, Vol. 30, No. 1, pp 131-152.

Cortazzi, M., & Jin, L. (1996). Cultures of learning: Language classrooms in China. in H. Coleman (ed.) *Society and the Language Classroom* (pp159-206). Cambridge: CUP

Cross, J. (2011). Metacognitive instruction for helping less-skilled listeners. *ELT Journal*, Vol. 65, No. 4, pp. 408-416.

Cross, J. (2015). Metacognition in L2 listening: Clarifying instructional theory and practice. *TESOL Quarterly*, Vol. 49, No. 4, pp 883-892. https://doi.org/10.1002/tesq.258

Fang, X., & Warschauer, M. (2004). Technology and curricular reform in China: A case study. *TESOL Quarterly,* Vol. 38, No. 2, pp 301-323.

Goh, C. C. (2008). Metacognitive instruction for second language listening development: Theory, practice, and research implications. RELC Journal, Vol. 39, No. 2, pp 188-213.

Guest, G., Bunce, A., & Johnson, L. (2006). How many interviews are enough? An experiment with data saturation and variability. *Field Methods,* Vol. 18, No. 1, pp 59-82.

Guo, X., Diaz, A., & Liyanage, I. (2016). Exploring the professional agency chasm in exam-driven English language education contexts. In H. V. Rensburg & S. O'Neill (Eds.), *Deep languages education policy and practices: Stimulating languages learning - global perspectives and local practice* (pp 215-232). Blue Mounds: Deep University Press.

Hassenzahl, M. (2001). The effect of perceived hedonic quality on product appealingness. *International Journal of Human-Computer Interaction*, Vol. 13, No. 4, pp 481-499.

Hassenzahl, M., Platz, A., Burmester, M., & Lehner, K. (2000, April). Hedonic and ergonomic quality aspects determine a software's appeal. In Proceedings of the SIGCHI conference on Human Factors in Computing Systems (CHI '00). Association for Computing Machinery, New York, NY (pp 201–208).

International Organization for Standardization. (2018). Ergonomics of human-system interaction — Part 11: Usability: Definitions and concepts (ISO Standard No. 9241-11:2018).

Laugwitz, B., Held, T., & Schrepp, M. (2008). Construction and Evaluation of a User Experience Questionnaire. In A. Holzinger (Ed.), *HCI and Usability for Education and Work* (pp 63–76). Berlin: Springer Berlin Heidelberg.

Prastiyo, W., Djohar, A., & Purnawan, P. (2018). Development of YouTube integrated google classroom based e-learning media for the light-weight vehicle engineering vocational high school. J*urnal Pendidikan Vokasi*, Vol. 8, No. 1, 53-66.

Rodríguez-Ardura, I., & Meseguer-Artola, A. (2016). E-learning continuance: The impact of interactivity and the mediating role of imagery, presence and flow. *Information & Management,* Vol. 53, No. 4, pp 504-516.

Schrepp, M., Hinderks, A., & Thomaschewski, J. (2017). Construction of a Benchmark for the User Experience Questionnaire (UEQ). *International Journal of Interactive Multimedia and Artificial Intelligence*, Vol. 4, No. 4, pp 40-44.

Siegel, J. (2015). *Exploring listening strategy instruction through action research*. New York: Palgrave Macmillan.

Vandergrift, L. (2004). Listening to learn or learning to listen?. *Annual Review of Applied Linguistics*, Vol. 24, pp 3-25. http://doi.org/10.1017/S0267190504000017

Vandergrift, L. (2007). Recent development in second and foreign language listening comprehension research. *Language Teaching,* Vol. 40, No. 3, pp 191-210.

Vandergrift, L., & Tafaghodtari, M. H. (2010). Teaching L2 learners how to listen does make a difference: An empirical study. *Language Learning*, Vol. 60, No. 2, pp 470-497.

Wang, W. (2016). Learning to listen: The impact of a metacognitive approach to listening instruction. *The Asia-Pacific Education Researcher*, Vol. 25, No. 1, pp 79-88.

Yeldham, M. (2016). Second language listening instruction: Comparing a strategies-based approach with an interactive, strategies/bottom-up skills approach. *TESOL Quarterly*, Vol. 50, No. 3, pp 394-420.

Yeldham, M. (2018). L2 listening instruction: More bottom-up or more top-down? *Journal of Asia TEFL*, Vol. 15, No. 3, pp 805–810.

THE MEDIATING ROLE OF OPTIMISM IN RELATION BETWEEN WISDOM & KNOWLEDGE VIRTUES AND SCHOOL WELL-BEING IN ADOLESCENCE

Bagus Hary Prakoso[1], Zulmi Ramdani[2], Asrijanty Asrijanty[1], Rahmawati Rahmawati[1], Safari Safari[1], Heni Waluyo Siswanto[3] and Nina Purnamasari[3]
[1]*Center for Assessment and Learning, Ministry of Education and Culture*
Jl. Gunung Sahari Raya No. 4, Jakarta, 10710, Indonesia
[2]*Faculty of Psychology, UIN Sunan Gunung Djati Bandung*
Jl. A.H. Nasution No. 105, Cibiru-Bandung, Indonesia
[3]*Center for Curriculum and Book, Ministry of Education and Culture*
Jl. Gunung Sahari Raya No. 4, Jakarta, 10710, Indonesia

ABSTRACT

School well-being for adolescents is a condition that is expected to be one form of educational success. Many personal factors certainly play a role in producing the well-being include positive character of the student. This study aims to look at the role of optimism in mediating the influence of wisdom & knowledge virtues consisting of the character of creativity, curiosity, open-mindedness, love of learning, and perspective on school well-being. The quantitative research design was used involving 339 respondents selected by non-probability sampling techniques. The results showed that optimism plays a significant role as a mediator of creativity, curiosity, open-minded, and love of learning for school well-being adolescents. While the strength of character curiosity, creativity, open-mindedness, and perspective become significant predictors that influence optimism itself. This study explains that the importance of developing these positive characters in daily activities at school.

KEYWORDS

Adolescence, Character, Optimism, Positive Psychology, School Well-being, Wisdom and Knowledge Virtues

1. INTRODUCTION

Adolescence is a stage of development which certainly involves a variety of psychological challenges and demands that must be resolved properly. For adolescents, school is one of the places they spend at that time to develop the positive potential they have, so it becomes important when school becomes a place other than at home, for them to get happiness in their life development (Ramdani, Amrullah and Tae, 2019). The concept of school well-being is often the best indicator that can determine whether schools provide fun things so that youth become individuals who are said to be prosperous (Heller-sahlgren, 2017; Dillon *et al.*, 2020; McCalman *et al.*, 2020).

School well-being certainly occurs because of various internal and external factors. External factors refer to the theoretical dimensions of school well-being such as the availability of complete and supportive facilities in schools, programs that upgrade the interests and talents of adolescents, as well as positive relationships and communication between teachers and young people themselves (Konu and Rimpelä, 2002; Ramdani and Prakoso, 2019). Meanwhile, internal factors involving positive characters possessed by adolescents also determine the formation of school well-being in adolescents. Theoretically, many internal factors that determine the success of adolescents in getting a school well-being are wisdom and knowledge virtues (Toner *et al.*, 2012; Banicki, 2014). In the context of positive psychology, wisdom and knowledge virtues are the personal parts of individuals whose function is to direct them into individuals who have a wise mindset, full of consideration when facing problems, serious in the learning process and try as much as possible to get good knowledge. Then the personal part is manifested into 5 characters, namely creativity, curiosity, open-mindedness, love of learning, and perspective (Peterson and Seligman, 2004).

The strengths of character which are part of the wisdom and knowledge virtues are considered unable to directly influence the formation of adolescent school well-being (Gillham *et al.*, 2011). In this case there are other variables that become mediators between wisdom and knowledge virtues towards school well-being. The author assumes that optimism is an effective mediating variable in mediating the relationship between wisdom and knowledge virtues and school well-being. Theoretically, these variables are included in the construction of positive psychology which will produce a significant correlation in the relationship (Martínez-Martí and Ruch, 2017). In addition, previous studies also confirmed that optimism is a condition when individuals already know well that the strengths of character needed in the learning process are felt deeply by the individual, so that the strength of these characters will produce an optical condition for what individuals have which will ultimately create their well-being in the context of education (Smokowski *et al.*, 2014; Chen *et al.*, 2016). Theoretically, optimism plays a significant role in directing a person's individual potential towards achieving happiness and well-being. This reasoning refers to the statement that these good potentials must be channeled first into a positive container and are able to pass them on to the intended goals. This study itself aims to see the role of optimism as a mediator of the relationship between wisdom and knowledge virtues towards school well-being. Specifically, these wisdom and knowledge virtues are manifested in the 5 characters described earlier. Thus based on theoretical exposure and interconnection between variables in the study, the authors propose the hypothesis that optimism can be an effective mediator that mediates the relationship between the strength of character in wisdom and knowledge virtues towards adolescent school well-being. More clearly, the relationship between the three variables can be seen in Figure 1.

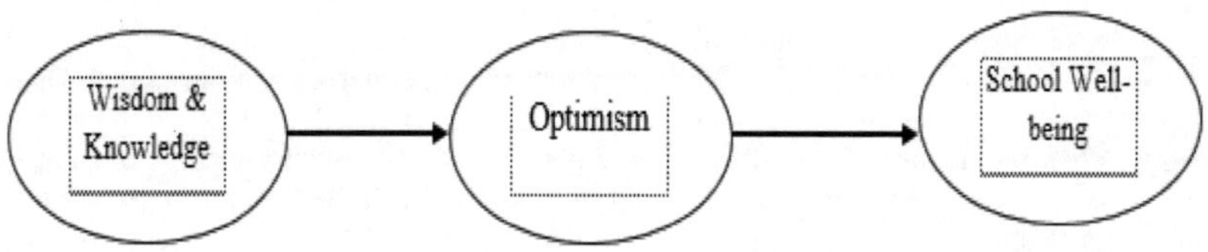

Figure 1. Theoretical Model Optimism as Mediator between Wisdom & Knowledge toward School Well-being

2. CONCEPTUAL FRAMEWORK

2.1 Wisdom and Knowledge Virtues

Wisdom can be defined as "the power of judging correctly and following the healthiest actions, based on knowledge, experience, understanding, etc"(Ahamed, 2017). There are several reasons why it is important to develop wisdom in school settings. First, the purpose of schools should not only be to provide knowledge, but to help students develop the wise use of that knowledge. Knowledge can be used for better or worse purposes, and schools must help students use their knowledge for good. Second, the teaching of wise thinking is always implicit in the school curriculum in any case. Third, if adults do not make wise decisions, schools may deserve a share of mistakes if they never prepare adults today to make such decisions (Park, Peterson and Al, 2004; Peterson and Seligman, 2004).

Wisdom and knowledge virtues are divided into 5 strengths of character, namely creativity, curiosity, open-mindedness, love of learning, and perspective (Peterson and Seligman, 2004). Creativity refers to the nature of individuals to discover new things, create other opportunities, and solve problems with alternative ideas. Curiosity is a character associated with a great tendency to find out all the information that is important in accordance with the purpose of individual life. Then, open-mindedness focuses on the openness of one's attitude, thoughts, and desire to get new information and important new things. The love of learning character leads someone to be serious about learning and gaining knowledge. And finally the perspective character directs individuals to have an ideal and firm attitude towards the circumstances that should occur in life. These five characters will be important for individuals to succeed in the field of education (Park, Peterson and Al, 2004; Sternberg, 2010).

2.2 School-wellbeing

The school well-being model is based on Allardt's sociological well-being theory and values well-being as an entity in school settings (Konu and Rimpelä, 2002; Konu *et al.*, 2002). Well-being is a state in which it is possible for humans to fulfill their basic needs. Well-being is connected with teaching and education, and with learning and achievement. School well-being indicators are divided into four categories: school conditions (having) which refer to material conditions and impersonal needs in a broad perspective; social relations (loving) means the need to relate to other people and to form social identities; the means for self-fulfillment (being) indicate the need for personal growth, that is, integration into society and living in harmony with nature; and health status (health).

2.3 Optimism

Optimists are people who expect good things to happen to them. Whereas pessimists, on the other hand, expect bad things to happen to them. People who are optimistic and pessimistic have a different perspective on the world, including how they face problems, overcome difficulties, and differ in their resources, both social and socio-economic. The nature of optimism can provide cognitive, coping, and contextual resources that improve mental health.

The scientific definition of optimism and pessimism focuses on expectations for the future. Theory that is close to the concept of optimism is the motivation theory known as expectancy-value (Carver, Scheier and Segerstrom, 2010). Expectancy-value theory assumes that individuals are set by goals which are desirable actions and expectation are self-confidence or doubt in the achievement of something. The more important the goals given to the person, the greater the value (Carver, Scheier and Segerstrom, 2010). If people doubt that they can achieve a goal, then they might withdraw efforts in that direction. They may stop prematurely, or even they will never take an action. While those who believe that they can achieve results they will survive even when faced with great difficulties.

3. METHOD

3.1 Design & Participant

The author uses a quantitative approach to answer the research hypotheses proposed in this study. A set of questionnaires was distributed to a selected number of respondents involved in the study using a non-probability sampling technique with a purposive sampling technique selection specification (Warsihna, Ramdani and Prakoso, 2019). Characteristics of respondents involved in this study are those who are currently studying junior high school and senior high school in the city of Bandung with an age range of 12 to 18 years. All respondents involved agreed with informed consent that proves that they participated in the research voluntarily and without coercion.

3.2 Instruments

This study uses 3 measuring devices that represent 3 variables in the study. The first measuring instrument is Value in Action Inventory Scales (VIA-IS) which is used to measure wisdom and knowledge virtues instruments as an independent variable in research. Furthermore, the second measuring tool, the School Well-being Instrument, is used to measure the welfare conditions of respondents at school as the dependent variable. Meanwhile, the third measuring instrument is the Optimism Scale which is used to measure the mediator variables in this study.

3.2.1 Wisdom and Knowledge Virtues

o measure wisdom and knowledge virtues, the writer uses the Value in Action Inventory Scales (VIA-IS) measuring instrument which was originally used by Peterson and Seligman (2004) to describe the strengths of individuals. Wisdom and knowledge virtues consist of 50 items that measure 5 character strengths namely creativity, curiosity, open mindedness, love of learning, and perspective, where each character is represented by 10 items in it. The author uses the instrument in the Indonesian version which has been modified by Fahmi and Ramdani (2014) dan Ramdani, Amrullah, and Tae, (2019), while still referring to the same number of items as the original gauge. The reliability coefficient values for each character strengths in this study are creativity (α = .787), curiosity (α = .749), open-mindedness (α = .802), love of learning (α = .739), and perspective (α = .787). As for the 50 different item power values are .249 - .636.

3.2.2 School Well-Being

To measure school well-being, the writer uses a measurement made by Ramdani and Prakoso (2019), by constructing the main theory put forward by Konu, Alanen, Lintonen, & Rimpelä, (2002); Konu, Lintonen, and Rimpelä (2002); Konu and Rimpelä (2002). The instrument measures 4 dimensions in school well-being, having, being, loving, and health. The number of items in the gauge is 26 items representing the four dimensions of the school well-being. The psychometric property for measuring school well-being that has a reliability coefficient of (α). 862, with a range of different power values of .281 - .559.

3.2.3 Optimism

To measure the condition of optimism in respondents, the authors refer to the theories conveyed by Scheier, Carver, and Bridges (1994 in Augustiya, Nurislamiaty, Al-fatoni, & Rachma (2019). Optimism in individuals can be measured by looking at behavioral indicators that appear including positive aspects and negative aspects. This study uses a measurement tool in the Indonesian version which has been modified into 14 items that measure positive aspects and negative aspects on the optimism scale (Augustiya *et al.*, 2019). The instrument used has a reliability coefficient (α) of .715 with discriminatory power reaching .300 to .478.

3.3 Data Collection and Analysis

The author collects data offline by distributing all instruments directly to selected respondents. Then proceed with tabulating data for analysis. Data analysis uses SPSS software to get descriptive statistical results from existing data and Lisrel software to test hypotheses by looking at the function of each variable in a research model.

3.4 Preliminary Analysis

For school well-being data that is used refers to descriptive data with an average value of 92.4 and a standard deviation of 10.1. Then obtained low, medium, and high categories of respondents. The low category is those who have a score below 82.3, those who are medium are with a score from 82.3 to 102.5, and those in the high category are those who have a score above 102.5. Researchers conducted a Chi Square test to see whether age and sex differences in subjects played a role in increasing or decreasing school well-being in respondents. Chi Square test results for the respondent's age data showed .083 ($p > 0.05$), and for gender data the results obtained were .924 ($p > .05$). Both of these data, both age differences and gender differences did not play a role in increasing and decreasing school well-being in respondents.

4. RESULTS & DISCUSSION

The data collection process is carried out for one week while maintaining the code of ethics in psychological research. The number of respondents involved in the study was 339 respondents (see table 1).

Table 1. Demographic Features of Respondents

No.	Category	N	Percentage
1	SEX		
	Male	168	49.6
	Female	171	50.4
2	AGE		
	12 years	20	5.9
	13 years	59	17.4
	14 years	103	30.4
	15 years	70	20.6
	16 years	67	19.8
	17 years	18	5.3
	18 years	2	0.6

No.	Category	N	Percentage
3	ETHNIC		
	Sunda	266	78.5
	Jawa	44	13
	Batak	9	2.7
	Minang	7	2.1
	Betawi	5	1.5
	Melayu	3	0.9
	Aceh/Bugis/Gorontalo/Kendari	1	1.2
4	RELIGION		
	Islam	334	98.5
	Kristen	4	1.2
	Catholic	1	0.3

Note: S.E. (Standard. Error). Est./S.E. (Estimate for Standard Error). (* Significant).

As explained in table 1, the difference in the number of respondents by sex is very small, only 3 people differ where the female teenage respondents are slightly more than the male. The age of respondents is dominated by the age of 14 years which reaches 30.4% of the total respondents. Meanwhile, the largest ethnic group in this study came from Sundanese, which reached almost 78.5% of the total respondents. This is a natural thing because the locus of this research was conducted in the city of Bandung, which is historically and culturally the origin of the Sundanese. Furthermore, the authors conducted a correlation analysis to see how the relationships between the variables in this study can be seen in table 2.

Table 2. Correlation between variables

No.	Variable	1	2	3	4	5	6	7	8
1	Creativity	1	.476	.508	.348	.504	.743	.502	.292
2	Curiosity	.476	1	.460	.482	.461	.766	.515	.399
3	Open-Mindedness	.508	.460	1	.452	.551	.780	.540	.426
4	Love of learning	.348	.482	.452	1	.423	.719	.455	.384
5	Perspective	.504	.461	.551	.423	1	.777	.481	.370
6	Wisdom & Knowledge Virtues	.743	.766	.780	.719	.777	1	,658	.495
7	School well-being	.502	.515	.540	.455	.481	.658	1	.620
8	Optimism	.292	.399	.426	.384	.370	.495	.620	1

Note. All correlation are significant.

Table 2 presents information related to the correlation coefficient obtained by each variable in this study. Referring to the correlation results in table 2, almost all correlation values have a score above .3. This shows that theoretically, all variables involved in this study are variables that have a linear research construct. Next to see the test results on the role of the mediator variable in mediating the independent variables on the dependent can be seen in tables 3 and 4. Table 3 explains the role of the variable directly meaning without the mediator, while table 4 explains the role of the variable indirectly or the role of the mediator in research.

Table 3. Direct Effect of Variable

Variable	Estimate	S.E.	Est./S.E.	P-Value
School Well-being ON				
Optimism	.455	.058	7.910	.000*
Creativity	-.074	.057	-1.299	.194
Curiosity	.101	.056	1.796	.072
Open-Mindedness	.045	.060	.750	.454
Love of Learning	.113	.052	2.182	.029*
Perspective	.016	.056	.280	.780
Optimism ON				
Creativity	.250	.049	5.146	.000*
Curiosity	.180	.049	3.677	.000*
Open-Mindedness	.304	.050	6.129	.000*
Love of Learning	.131	.046	2.882	.004*
Perspective	.030	.049	.610	.542

Note: S.E. (Standard. Error). Est./S.E. (Estimate for Standard Error). (* Significant).

Table 4. Indirect Effect of Variable (Mediator Effect)

Variable	Estimate	S.E.	Est./S.E.	P-Value
Wisdom & Knowledge to SWB				
Creativity	.114	.027	4.256	.000*
Curiosity	.082	.025	3.335	.001*
Open-Mindedness	.138	.029	4.800	.000*
Love of Learning	.060	.022	2.714	.007*
Perspective	.014	.023	.608	.543

Note: S.E. (Standard. Error). Est./S.E. (Estimate for Standard Error). (* Significant). SWB (School Well-being).

The information obtained in table 3 explains that optimism significantly influences school well-being ($p < .05$). While the variables of creativity, curiosity, open-mindedness, and perspective do not have a significant effect on school well-being if done on the direct path ($p > .05$). Only the love of learning variable has a direct effect on school well-being. Whereas the indirect pathway (table 4) shows that the optimism variable acts as a mediator of the influence of the variables of creativity, curiosity, open-mindedness, and love of learning on school well-being ($p < .05$). The role of the mediator does not function in mediating the effect of perspective variables on school well-being.

The results of the study in general showed that the mediator in this study had a significant role in mediating the influence of various character strengths that exist in wisdom and knowledge virtues on school well-being. These results support several previous studies that also convey the same information that effective optimism mediates the strength of personal character possessed by individuals towards increasing their happiness and well-being (Malinowski and Lim, 2015). Optimism itself is certainly a positive psychological variable has a linear relationship with other positive characters such as school well-being. Theoretically, the two variables are part of a positive character that if the correlation between the two will produce significant results and is directly proportional. This means that when individuals have high optimism it can improve their welfare in any context (Ho, Cheung and Cheung, 2010; Kimberly, Laura and Elizabeth, 2010).

If referring to table 2, each variable has a high and significant relationship. This can be seen by the magnitude of the correlation coefficient values obtained more than .3 (Ramdani, 2018). Correlations for each strength of character and optimism include creativity-optimism (r = .502), curiosity-optimism (r = .515), open-mindedness-optimism (r = .540), love of learning-optimism (r = .455), and perspective-optimism (r = .482). The correlation between the 5 characters with optimism shows positive and linear results, meaning that the greater the strength of character in adolescents, the greater the likelihood of them to be optimistic about what they have. Likewise the relationship with optimism and school-wellbeing is shown by a correlation value of r = .680, which also shows that the higher optimism that exists in adolescents will produce high school well-being as well. Thus, the results of table 2 support the existing research model that the role of a mediator relationship between independent and dependent can be optimal if the correlation between the variables involved is also significant (Fairchild and McQuillin, 2010; Jaenudin *et al.*, 2020; Ramdani, Marliani and Rahman, 2019).

Meanwhile, tables 3 and 4 explain how the mediator's role functions in research. Table 3 shows the direct influence of the strength of wisdom and knowledge virtues character on school-well-being. Of the 5 existing character strengths, only the love of learning character is significant for school well-being ($p < .05$), while the other 4 characters namely creativity, curiosity, open-mindedness, and perspective do not directly influence school well-being. This means that the four characters need mediator variables so that their influence can be significant on school well-being. Meanwhile for perspective character (table 3), it is the only character that has no effect on optimism ($p > .05$), if tested on the direct path so that these results indicate that the existence of perspective is not able to present the optimism situation for adolescents in this study. Thus, if it is continued on indirect analysis or through mediators, optimism plays an effective role as a mediator of the character of creativity, curiosity, open-mindedness, and love of learning towards school well-being. This can be seen in table 4 which shows the 4 strengths of characters that have an appropriate P-Value ($p < .05$), with details of creativity (p = .000), curiosity (p = .001), open-mindedness (p = .000), and love of learning (p = .007).

This study certainly supports the results of previous studies which assume that optimism acts as an effective mediator in the relationship between character strength and well-being. Even well-being in a school context is also largely determined by the optimal psychological situation when adolescents truly believe that the good things they will get during the learning process. In this study, only the love of learning character can significantly influence school well-being either directly or indirectly. This fact is also supported by theoretical assumptions which state that a person's tendency to succeed in school is largely determined by his desire and seriousness in learning, which is operationally manifested in the achievement of learning achievement so that his influence can be directly or indirectly on school well-being. Likewise, with perspective being the only variable that does not affect school well-being through optimism. That is because since direct influence, perspective has no significant effect on optimism so it also has no effect on school well-being through optimism.

This study explains the significant correlation between the variables tested. Optimism as a mediating variable certainly plays an important role in explaining the relationship between character identities possessed by individuals and the happiness or well-being felt by students at school. By adding more respondents, it is hoped that in the future they can provide more definite recommendations regarding internal and external factors that must be directly controlled by any party to create optimal conditions for school well-being. The use of the measured experimental method is also expected to be applied in future research, so that it can also strengthen the existence of dependent variables. In the future, it is also necessary to develop measuring instruments that are more in line with the developmental conditions of the respondents if it is to be carried out at the age of children, because it will be faster to anticipate the factors that need to be considered in their development.

5. CONCLUSION

The results of this study indicate that optimism acts as a significant mediator in the relationship between wisdom and knowledge virtues towards school well-being. Specifically optimism mediates the strength of character in wisdom and knowledge which includes creativity, curiosity, open-mindedness, and love of learning towards school well-being. Thus, these results indicate that the optimization of the strength of character will be the main source for adolescents to create effective optimism that will ultimately make them well-being.

ACKNOWLEDGEMENT

This study is the result of routine collaboration conducted by the Center for Assessment and Learning, Ministry of Education and Culture of the Republic of Indonesia with the Faculty of Psychology of UIN Sunan Gunung Djati Bandung. We would like to thank all the respondents involved in the research, especially for SMPN 44 Bandung, SMP Tunas Unggul Bandung, and SMAN 8 Bandung for helping to facilitate the authors to retrieve data during the process.

REFERENCES

Ahamed, S. V. (2017) ‘Knowledge and Wisdom Across Cultures’, *Evolution of Knowledge Science*, pp. 5–21. doi: 10.1016/b978-0-12-805478-9.00001-7.

Augustiya, T. *et al.* (2019) ‘Hubungan orientasi karier dengan optimisme pada mahasiswa jurusan keagamaan UIN Sunan Gunung Djati Bandung’, *Jurnal Psikologi Islam dan Budaya*, 2(1), pp. 31–42. doi: 10.15575/jpib.v2i1.4014.

Banicki, K. (2014) ‘Positive psychology on character strengths and virtues. A disquieting suggestion’, *New Ideas in Psychology*. Elsevier Ltd, 33(1), pp. 21–34. doi: 10.1016/j.newideapsych.2013.12.001.

Carver, C. S., Scheier, M. F. and Segerstrom, S. C. (2010) ‘Optimism’, *Clinical Psychology Review*, 30(7), pp. 879–889. doi: 10.1016/j.cpr.2010.01.006.

Chen, W. *et al.* (2016) ‘Socioeconomic status and life satisfaction in Chinese adolescents: Analysis of self-esteem as a mediator and optimism as a moderator’, *Personality and Individual Differences*. Elsevier Ltd, 95, pp. 105–109. doi: 10.1016/j.paid.2016.01.036.

Dillon, A. *et al.* (2020) ‘Support for Aboriginal and non-Aboriginal Australian students’ wellbeing at school’, *International Journal of Educational Research*. Elsevier, 99(November 2019), p. 101520. doi: 10.1016/j.ijer.2019.101520.

Fahmi, I. and Ramdani, Z. (2014) ‘Profil kekuatan karakter dan kebajikan pada mahasiswa berprestasi’, *Psympathic : Jurnal Ilmiah Psikologi*, 1(1), pp. 98–108. doi: https://doi.org/10.15575/psy.v1i1.471.

Fairchild, A. J. and McQuillin, S. D. (2010) 'Evaluating mediation and moderation effects in school psychology: A presentation of methods and review of current practice', *Journal of School Psychology*. Society for the Study of School Psychology, 48(1), pp. 53–84. doi: 10.1016/j.jsp.2009.09.001.

Gillham, J. *et al.* (2011) 'Character strengths predict subjective well-being during adolescence', *Journal of Positive Psychology*, 6(1), pp. 31–44. doi: 10.1080/17439760.2010.536773.

Heller-sahlgren, G. (2017) 'Smart but Unhappy: Independent-school Competition and the Wellbeing-efficiency Trade-off in Education', *Economics of Education Review*. Elsevier Ltd. doi: 10.1016/j.econedurev.2017.10.005.

Ho, M. Y., Cheung, F. M. and Cheung, S. F. (2010) 'The role of meaning in life and optimism in promoting well-being', *Personality and Individual Differences*. Elsevier Ltd, 48(5), pp. 658–663. doi: 10.1016/j.paid.2010.01.008.

Jaenudin, U. *et al.* (2020) 'Work-family conflict toward marital satisfaction with self-efficacy as a moderator variable', *Humanities & Social Sciences Reviews*, 8(2), pp. 373–380. doi: 10.18510/hssr.2020.8242.

Kimberly, R., Laura, D. and Elizabeth, M. (2010) 'Stress, Self-Esteem, Hope, Optimism, and Well-Being in Urban, Ethnic Minority Adolescents', *Journal of Multicultural Counseling and Development*, 38(April), pp. 99–111.

Konu, A. *et al.* (2002) 'Factor structure of the School Well-being Model', *Health Education Research*, 17(6), pp. 732–742. doi: 10.1093/her/17.6.732.

Konu, A. I., Lintonen, T. P. and Rimpelä, M. (2002) 'Factors associated with schoolchildren's general subjective well-being', *Health Education Research*, 17(2), pp. 155–165. doi: 10.1093/her/17.2.155.

Konu, A. and Rimpelä, M. (2002) 'Well-being in schools: a conceptual model', *Health Promotion International*, 17(1), pp. 79–87. doi: 10.1093/heapro/17.1.79.

Malinowski, P. and Lim, H. J. (2015) 'Mindfulness at Work: Positive Affect, Hope, and Optimism Mediate the Relationship Between Dispositional Mindfulness, Work Engagement, and Well-Being', *Mindfulness*, 6(6), pp. 1250–1262. doi: 10.1007/s12671-015-0388-5.

Martínez-Martí, M. L. and Ruch, W. (2017) 'Character strengths predict resilience over and above positive affect, self-efficacy, optimism, social support, self-esteem, and life satisfaction', *Journal of Positive Psychology*, 12(2), pp. 110–119. doi: 10.1080/17439760.2016.1163403.

McCalman, J. *et al.* (2020) '"It's all about relationships": The place of boarding schools in promoting and managing health and wellbeing of Aboriginal and Torres Strait Islander secondary school students', *Children and Youth Services Review*. Elsevier, 113(April), p. 104954. doi: 10.1016/j.childyouth.2020.104954.

Park, N., Peterson, C. and Al, P. E. T. (2004) 'Strenghts of character and well-being', *Journal of Social and Clinical Psychology*, 23(5), pp. 603–619.

Peterson, C. and Seligman, M. E. P. (2004) *Character strengths and virtues: A handbook and classification*. United States of America: American Psychological Association.

Ramdani, Z. (2018) 'Construction of academic integrity scale Implementation School Inclusion View project Psychometric Properties of Psychological Constructs View project Construction of academic integrity scale Construction of academic integrity scale', *International Journal of Research Studies in Psychology*, 7(1), pp. 87–97. doi: 10.5861/ijrsp.2018.3003.

Ramdani, Z., Amrullah, S. and Tae, L. F. (2019) 'Pentingnya kolaborasi dalam menciptakan sistem pendidikan yang berkualitas', *MEDIAPSI*, 5(1), pp. 40–48.

Ramdani, Z. and Prakoso, B. H. (2019) 'Integritas akademik: Prediktor kesejahteraan siswa di sekolah', *Indonesian Journal of Educational Assesment*, 2(1), p. 29. doi: 10.26499/ijea.v2i1.14.

Ramdani, Z., Marliani, R., & Rahman, A. A. (2019) 'The individual work perfomance scale: A psychometric study and its aplication for emloyee performance', *Humanities & Social Sciences Reviews,* 7(5), pp. 405–414. doi: 10.18510/hssr.2019.7545

Smokowski, P. R. *et al.* (2014) 'Ethnic Identity and Mental Health in American Indian Youth: Examining Mediation Pathways Through Self-esteem, and Future Optimism', *Journal of Youth and Adolescence*, 43(3), pp. 343–355. doi: 10.1007/s10964-013-9992-7.

Sternberg, R. J. (2010) 'Why Schools Should Teach for Wisdom: The Balance Theory of Wisdom in Educat...: University of Warwick eResources', *Educational Psychologist*, 36(4), pp. 227–245. Available at: http://0-eds.b.ebscohost.com.pugwash.lib.warwick.ac.uk/eds/pdfviewer/pdfviewer?vid=2&sid=6db070f4-59d9-40af-b54f-5f949e42d2f4%40sessionmgr103.

Toner, E. *et al.* (2012) 'Character strengths and wellbeing in adolescence: Structure and correlates of the Values in Action Inventory of Strengths for Children', *Personality and Individual Differences*. Elsevier Ltd, 52(5), pp. 637–642. doi: 10.1016/j.paid.2011.12.014.

Warsihna, J., Ramdani, Z., & Prakoso, B. H. (2019) 'Using Kahoot to improve students' achievement and critical thinking in undergraduate of psychology students', *IADIS International Conference Cognition and Exploratory Learning in Digital Age 2019*, pp. 144–150.

THE DEVELOPMENT AND VALIDATION OF A CONCEPT MAPPING EMOTIONS SCALE (CM-ES) FOR UNIVERSITY STUDENTS

Xinyuan Li, Yanyan Duan, Tong Lu and Guoqing Zhao
School of Educational Technology, Faculty of Education, Beijing Normal University, Beijing, China

ABSTRACT

Concept mapping is a practical approach to meaningful learning, and emotion is one of the most important factors that affect students' learning. However, few studies have focused on learners' emotions of concept mapping. This research aims to develop and verify a CM-ES and to investigate university students' emotions of concept mapping with the aid of this scale. A total of 88 freshmen participated in the study by attending a two-week thinking skills course provided by the researchers. The CM-ES translated and modified from the Academic Emotion Scale of Govaerts and Grégoire (2008) was used to collect the students' emotions of concept mapping. A five-dimensional scale, including *frustration*, *anxiety*, *shame*, *enjoyment*, and *hope,* was obtained through exploratory factor analysis, and Cronbach's reliability coefficient indicates good reliability and validity of CM-ES. The result shows that the emotion of the students' concept mapping is relatively positive. The development of the CM-ES provides the researchers and educators with an effective tool to measure the emotion of concept mapping and helps researchers understand students' emotions when using concept maps.

KEYWORDS

Concept Map, Emotion, CM-ES

1. INTRODUCTION

As a thinking visualization tool, concept maps (Novak, 1984) have similar functions to cognitive tools (Jonassen, 1992). They can help students focus on thinking tasks with a high cognitive load by reducing their low-level cognitive load (Jonassen, 1992; Lajoie and Derry, 1993). Many studies have shown that concept maps can promote students' critical thinking and other higher-order thinking skills (Hwang *et al.*, 2020). Research also shows that concept maps have an impact on students' learning motivation and academic performance (Chiou, Tien and Tang, 2020). However, the concept map itself is an external tool for learners, and it may also bring the cognitive load to learners, thereby affecting students' emotions and willingness to use concept maps (Machado and Carvalho, 2020).

Emotion is one of the important factors that affect students' learning (Chiang and Liu, 2014); it can affect the important factors of students' self-system opening and closing. When the self-system is closed, the cognitive system and the metacognitive system are also difficult to function (Marzano and Kendall, 2006). Studies have shown that students' learning is deeply affected by emotions, which are related to specific learning situations and learning behaviors (Govaerts and Grégoire, 2008). Therefore, more and more researchers have begun to pay attention to the emotional experience of students in different learning situations.

However, research related to concept maps seldom pays attention to the emotions of students using concept maps to learn. Therefore, it is very necessary to understand students' emotions when they use concept maps to learn. This study intends to develop a Concept Mapping-Emotion Scale by revising the Student Academic Emotion Scale and tailoring it to the context of the concept mapping and test the reliability and validity of the scale. Compiling a scale to measure the application emotion of concept maps can not only help researchers understand the emotions of students in constructing concept mapping, but also provide a theoretical basis for the application of concept maps in teaching.

2. LITERATURE REVIEW

2.1 The Role of Concept Mapping in Instruction

Concept maps are usually used as cognitive tools or evaluation tools in teaching. Research on concept maps as a cognitive tool mainly focuses on the impact of concept maps on student learning. For example, Hwang et al. (2020)found that the problem-producing method based on concept maps can improve students' academic performance, critical thinking tendency, and the quality of problem-producing. When the concept map is used as an evaluation tool, it usually includes the evaluation of the concept map and the evaluation of the students' knowledge construction through the concept map. For example, Cañas, Novak and Reiska (2015) elaborated the criteria and scoring method of a good concept map. In the study of Gracia-Moreno et al. (2017), the concept map was used as a tool to evaluate student learning in order to explore the use of private digital workspaces and public workspaces by French high school students.

However, concept maps are not useful in all situations, nor are they useful for all students. Immelman's (2018) research results show that concept mapping does not promote the conceptual understanding of South African accounting students. This is in contradiction with the research results that concept maps can promote the understanding of physics concepts in 10th-grade students (Farrokhnia *et al.*, 2019). Conflicting research results suggest other factors that influence the application of concept maps, such as students' cognitive factors, emotions, and teaching methods. A study found that concept mapping has less effect on students with higher prior knowledge level, so the mastery of prior knowledge of students may be a factor that affects the use of concept maps. At the same time, the study also pointed out that the length of time that students use concept maps and their mastery of concept maps before experiments may have an impact on the promotion of concept maps to learning(Brandt *et al.*, 2001).

The teaching method is also an important factor affecting concept mapping. Roessger, Daley and Hafez (2018) explore whether exercises, feedback, and relational frameworks help to improve students' concept mapping skills in the long term. The results of the research show that repeated practice and feedback improved the structural quality of students' concept maps, and also increased the number of autobiographical explanations in these concept maps. Furtado, Hirashima and Hayashi (2019) describe the Airmap interface, using automatic layout management and space separation to reduce the cognitive load in the concept mapping process, thereby improving the effectiveness of the concept map application.

Emotions and cognition in the learning process of students influence each other, and concept maps can be used as cognitive tools to assist students in learning, and emotion may be a factor that affects the application effect of concept mapping. The researcher pointed out that some students show a certain resistance to the concept map (Brandt *et al.*, 2001). Because concept maps can promote meaningful learning for learners, and it is a difficult task to inspire students to change from rote learning practice to meaningful learning mode.

Many studies have studied the reasons that influence the application of concept maps from the perspective of cognition and teaching methods, but few studies have elaborated from the perspective of emotions, which may be due to the lack of tools for measuring the emotions of concept maps.

2.2 The Influence of Emotion on Student Learning

Emotions are people's psychological and behavioral responses to objective things (James, 1884; Cannon, 1987; Damasio, 2005). A large number of studies have shown that there is a close relationship between students' emotions and learning. For example, some scholars have found that positive emotions can improve the efficiency and effect of learning. In contrast, negative emotions can reduce the efficiency and effect of learning (Tauber *et al.*, 2017). In this regard, the *Dopamine Handbook* explains that positive emotion will gradually increase the dopamine transmitter in the peripheral cortex. Transmitters can strengthen people's thinking flexibility to a large extent and enable people to have stronger response capabilities (Iversen *et al.*, 2009).

It should be noted that due to different measurement methods, research methods, learning tasks, and other factors, the conclusions drawn from different studies may differ. Some research results show that positive emotions may not necessarily improve the effect of learning. For example, the experiment of Oaksford *et al.* (1996) found that neither positive nor negative emotions can interfere with certain reasoning. Other studies have found that happiness can promote simple reasoning, interfere with moderately difficult reasoning, and sadness can influence any reasoning. Interfering with difficult tasks, neutral emotions have a better effect on moderately difficult reasoning (Forgas, 1995). In addition, the specific context of emotions will also change the impact of emotions on learning (Götz *et al.*, 2003).

2.3 Measurement of Emotions

One of the research fields on emotion is the measurement of emotion. Emotion is a multi-dimensional structure and multi-component compound process, including internal experience, external expression, and physiological activation. Its manifestations are divided into explicit emotions and implicit emotions (Strongman, 2003). Commonly used self-reported measurement scales include ISO Project Mind Mirror Adjective List (MACL), Multiple Affective Adjective Checklist (MAACL), etc. But these scales do not reflect the emotional state of specific situations. The Academic Emotion Scale (AES) compiled by Govaerts and Grégoire (2008) contains six kinds of emotions related to academic work. Each emotion is represented by multiple items. The scale comprehensively measures multiple dimensions of emotion; the compilation process is standardized and has good reliability and validity. In this study, the academic emotion scale developed by Govaerts and Grégoire (2008) was Chineseized and adapted to form the CM-ES.

2.4 The Present Study

In the existing studies, the research on concept maps has focused on testing the validity of concept maps in different teaching situations, and concept maps are used to evaluate students' academic performance. Few studies have focused on students' emotions when using concept maps. Machado and Carvalho (2020) found that students' frustration with concept maps can be reduced by teachers' counseling or peer discussions. However, there is still a lack of scales that can comprehensively measure various emotional states of students when using concept maps.

Measuring students' emotions towards concept map tools can help teachers understand students' emotional experience in teaching practice, to make targeted interventions, thereby improving the effectiveness of teaching and students' learning experience. The purpose of this research is to develop a scale to measure the emotional state of concept mapping and to improve the research on the application of concept maps.

3. METHOD

3.1 Research Context

The purpose of this study was to develop the CM-ES and to investigate the emotional experiences of Chinese undergraduate students with concept maps when using them to solve problems.

The study was conducted at a Chinese university that offers a long-standing thinking course. That is a public elective course, so students of the course have different majors. In this course, students learn to use many thinking tools, such as Thinking Maps (Hyerle, 2011), Mind Map (Buzan and Buzan, 2010), and Concept Map (Novak, 1984). The course is delivered online by Dingding, which is an online education platform. In that platform, the teachers can arrange online meetings, and students can turn on the microphone to interact with the instructor at any time during class. In learning concept maps, the teacher first introduces the origin and usage of concept maps. Then the teacher demonstrates how to construct concept maps by CmapTools software.

3.2 Participants

A total of 88 college students from a college in China participated in this study. These students came from different majors, including physics, chemistry, history, and English, etc. Of all the participants, 86 completed the concept mapping task. For the CM-ES questionnaire, a total of 52 data were collected in this study, two of which were repeatedly completed by the same person, and the responses of which took less than one minute were deleted. Matching the concept mapping task and the CM-ES questionnaire, a total of 48 students completed the whole process, and the data were valid, with a valid response rate of 54.44%. 14.58% (n=7) of them are males and 85.42% (n=41) are females. All students were freshmen.

3.3 Data Collection and Analysis

3.3.1 Concept Map Task

After students have a basic understanding of concept maps, students are required to create a concept map of the topic of their choice, such as figure 1, use the concept map to assist in analyzing the question and responding to the question (Novak and Cañas, 2006). Finally, they are required to submit their concept maps.

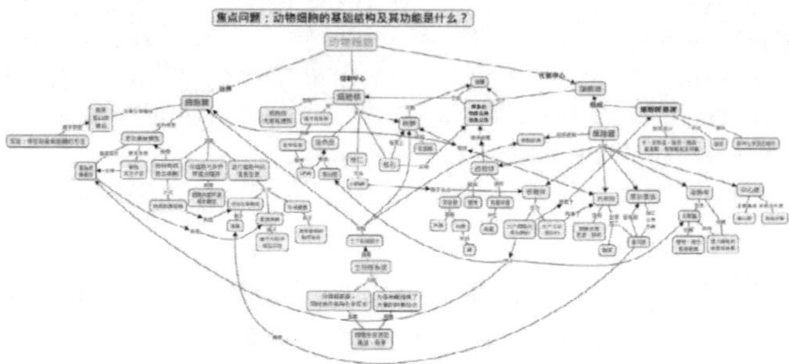

Figure 1. A concept map prepared by a student

3.3.2 CM-ES

Immediately after students completed the concept mapping task, they were given a digital version of the CM-ES questionnaire, also created by the Questionnaire Star tool, to investigate students' emotions about using the concept maps.

The questionnaire consisted of two parts. The first part of the questionnaire included questions asking for the participants' background information, including major and gender. In the second part of the questionnaire, a total of 26 items adapted from an English emotion scales proposed by Govaerts & Grégoire (2008) were used to examine students' emotion.

The context we conducted the CM-ES is different from the initial scales we adapted investigated in the situation of a math exam preparation. Hence, all "math" words in the items were replaced with the "concept map". To distinguish from the original ones, we add the suffix "CM" to the name of every construct, which means the scales are constructed in the context of drawing concept maps. So, the final names of the six constructs are Frustration-CM, Anxiety-CM, Shame-CM, Enjoyment-CM, Hope-CM, and Pride-CM, respectively.

The initial CM-ES was designed to measure six components of emotions concerning the construction of concept maps, with six items for Frustration-CM, five items for Anxiety-CM, four items for Shame-CM, four items for Enjoyment-CM, four items for Hope-CM, and three items for Pride-CM. All items were designed on a seven-point Likert scale from 1 "I do not agree at all" to 7 " I totally agree". An educational technology specialist and three graduate students majoring in educational technology reviewed the items to improve the readability and content validity of the instrument.

3.4 Data Analysis

SPSS 25.0 was used to analyze the data. Firstly, exploratory factor analysis (EFA) was conducted with all original items to clarify the structure of the CM-ES, and Cronbach's alphas (α) were calculated to determine the internal consistency of each component of the CM-ES.

Secondly, a t-test was performed to examine the differences between students of different genders. Lastly, correlation analysis and stepwise regression were implemented to explore the prediction of Frustration-CM, Anxiety-CM, Shame-CM, Enjoyment-CM, Hope-CM, and Pride-CM, respectively on their CM-ES.

4. FINDINGS

4.1 Validation of the CM-ES

Exploratory factor analysis with a varimax rotation was used to clarify the structure of the CM-ES survey. Through the first factor analysis (see Table 1), the initial items from Anxiety-CM construct, Hope-CM construct, Shame-CM construct, Enjoyment-CM construct, and Frustration-CM construct were all classified into the corresponding components as expected. However, one initial item from the Pride-CM construct was classified into the Hope-CM component, and the other two initial items from the Pride-CM construct were classified into the Enjoyment-CM component. Also, the items Frustration-CM4 and Enjoyment-CM1 were removed as these items did not fit the expected component. After removing these two items, factor analysis was conducted again with these 24 items.

The validated CM-ES questionnaire contains 24 items in the five new components: Anxiety-CM (five items); Hope-CM(five items); Shame-CM(four items); Enjoyment-CM(five items), and Frustration-CM (five items). α was computed to assess the questionnaire's reliability. Results showed that α of the total scale was .765, and α of each dimension(Anxiety-CM, Hope-CM, Shame-CM, Enjoyment-CM, and Frustration-CM) were .900, .884, .908, .830, and .859, which suggested high reliability.

Table 1. The first exploratory factor analysis

Item	Factor component				
	1	2	3	4	5
Frustration5	.760				
Frustration2	.711				
Frustration1	.702				
Frustration3	.699				
Frustration6	.673				
Frustration4	.637	.546			
Anxiety5		.810			
Anxiety2		.798			
Anxiety1		.671			
Anxiety3		.665			
Anxiety4		.603			
Hope4			.867		
Hope2			.789		
Pride1			.749		
Hope1			.747		
Hope3			.661		
Enjoyment3				.867	
Enjoyment2				.789	
Enjoyment4				.749	
Pride2				.747	
Pride3				.661	
Enjoyment1		-.517		.523	
Shame1					.893
Shame2					.887
Shame3					.886
Shame4					.796

4.2 Students' Scores on the CM-ES

The means and standard deviations of the participants' scores on Anxiety-CM, Hope-CM, Shame-CM, Enjoyment-CM, and Frustration-CM were provided in Table 2. It`s easy to find that students had positive emotions about using concept maps to solve problems. The mean scores for all the dimensions of positive emotions were above three, the mean scores for the frustration and anxiety dimensions of negative emotions were below three, and the mean score for the shame dimension was 3.16, which was slightly above three.

Table 2. Descriptive statistics of CM-ES

Item	N	Mean	S.D.
Frustration-CM	48	2.52	0.24
Anxiety-CM	48	2.43	0.30
Shame-CM	48	3.16	0.21
Enjoyment-CM	48	3.48	0.19
Hope-CM	48	3.22	0.27

4.3 Gender Differences in the CM-ES

As presented in Table 3, five emotions showed gender differences. No significant mean differences were detected. However, male students reported more frustration and hope, but less shame than female students.

Table 3. Gender differences of CM-ES

Emotions	Male		Female		t	Sig.
	Mean	S.D.	Mean	S.D.		
Frustration	2.71	0.55	2.48	0.73	0.80	0.43
Anxiety	2.43	0.57	2.43	0.76	-0.02	0.99
Shame	2.79	0.59	3.22	0.97	-1.14	0.26
Enjoyment	3.43	0.68	3.48	0.57	-0.23	0.82
Hope	3.37	0.52	3.19	0.62	0.73	0.47

5. DISCUSSION

This study developed and validated a five-dimensional CM-ES to measure students' emotions about concept maps when using concept maps to analyze problems. The results of the study showed that students had positive emotions on concept mapping, and there were no significant differences between students of different genders on each dimension of the CM-ES.

5.1 Instrument Validation of the CM-ES

In this study, the original PRIDE dimension of the CM-ES was eliminated, ultimately presenting five dimensions of the CM-ES. Two of the items in the Pride dimension were classified as enjoyment, and one was classified as hope. This is inconsistent with the findings of Govaerts and Grégoire (2008) for two possible reasons, firstly, the Pride dimension itself has a smaller number of items of only three compared to the other dimensions, and secondly, Pride, Enjoyment, and Hope are all positive emotions, and different people may interpret and feel emotions differently, and this perception of emotions is influenced by the sample (Terracciano *et al.*, 2003). Thus, it is not uncommon for emotions containing intrinsic associations to be clustered under the same factor in studies related to academic emotions.

5.2 The Emotional State of Freshmen while Concept Mapping

From the results of the study, students had positive emotions about using concept maps to solve problems. This shows that students do not reject the use of concept maps to solve problems and have a positive attitude towards the results of using concept maps. The frustration and anxiety levels of students using concept maps are relatively low. This may be because the teacher instructs students to learn enough knowledge and skills to draw concept maps before completing tasks (Brandt *et al.*, 2001). This also indicates that although concept maps can aid cognition, there is still a need to train users in basic knowledge before using them to reduce their negative emotions when using them.

The present study also found no significant difference between male and female students' emotions towards the use of concept maps to solve problems. Whereas, Chiang and Liu (2014) found that male students in the college student sample experienced stronger emotions during science learning than female students, which is inconsistent with the results of the present study. The reason for this phenomenon is that the sample size of this study was small, with only seven male students, and the sample may have been underrepresented.

5.3 Implications for Practice

The results of this research show that college students' emotions when using concept maps are positive. Therefore, university teachers can use concept maps to teach complex concepts. At the same time, this research suggests that students should first learn about concept maps before using them. This can effectively reduce students' negative emotions towards concept maps. When teachers use concept maps for teaching, they can use the scale developed in this research to measure students' emotions, and then adjust the subsequent teaching strategies using concept maps according to students' emotions, and provide students with necessary scaffolding so that students can make better use of concept maps for learning.

6. CONCLUSION

This research has developed and verified a five-construct CM-ES. The five dimensions are *confusion*, *anxiety*, *shame*, *enjoyment*, and *hope*, which are used to measure students' emotions of concept mapping. The results of the study show that students have an overall positive attitude toward concept mapping. Therefore, it is recommended that teachers use concept maps in the teaching process of complex concepts. However, students need to be trained in concept mapping before using them, and teachers need to pay attention to students' emotions during concept mapping. Teachers can use the scale developed in this research to investigate the emotions of students after concept mapping to provide a basis for the next use of the concept map.

However, this study has some limitations as followed. The first limitation of this study is the small sample and the low proportion of male students, so the perception of emotions may be biased by the sample. In future studies, a larger sample size can be used to improve the validity of the questionnaire developed in this study, and further research can be conducted on the effect of emotions on applying concept maps in instructional activities. Also, the emotions measured in this study were static, whereas emotions change dynamically during the students' learning process, and future research could also be conducted with AI to dynamically identify the students' emotions when using concept maps to improve further the research related to the effect of emotions on the use of concept maps.

REFERENCES

Brandt, L. *et al*, 2001. 'The Impact of Concept-Mapping and Visualization on the Learning of Secondary School Chemistry Students', *International Journal of Science Education*, 23(12), pp. 1303–13.

Buzan, T. and Buzan, B., 2010. *The Mind Map Book: Unlock Your Creativity, Boost Your Memory, Change Your Life*. 1st edn. Edited by J. Harrison. New York, NY: Pearson Education Ltd.

Cañas, A. J., Novak, J. D. and Reiska, P., 2015. 'How good is my concept map? Am I a good Cmapper?', *Knowledge Management & E Learning: An International Journal*, 7(1), pp. 6–19.

Cannon, W. B., 1987 'The James-Lange theory of emotions: a critical examination and an alternative theory. By Walter B. Cannon, 1927', *The American Journal of Psychology*, 100(3–4), pp. 567–586.

Chiang, W.-W. and Liu, C.-J., 2014. 'Scale of Academic Emotion in Science Education: Development and Validation', *International Journal of Science Education*, 36(6), pp. 908–928. doi: 10.1080/09500693.2013.830233.

Chiou, C.-C., Tien, L.-C. and Tang, Y.-C., 2020. 'Applying structured computer-assisted collaborative concept mapping to flipped classroom for hospitality accounting', *Journal of Hospitality, Leisure, Sport & Tourism Education*, 26, p. 100243. doi: 10.1016/j.jhlste.2020.100243.

Damasio, A., 2005. *Descartes' Error: Emotion, Reason, and the Human Brain*. Reprint. London: Penguin Books.

Farrokhnia, M. *et al.*, 2019. 'Computer-supported collaborative concept mapping: The effects of different instructional designs on conceptual understanding and knowledge co-construction', *Computers & Education*, 142, p. 103640. doi: 10.1016/j.compedu.2019.103640.

Forgas, J. P., 1995. 'Mood and judgment: The affect infusion model (AIM)', *Psychological Bulletin*, 117(1), pp. 39–66. doi: 10.1037/0033-2909.117.1.39.

Furtado, P. G. F., Hirashima, T. and Hayashi, Y., 2019. 'Reducing Cognitive Load During Closed Concept Map Construction and Consequences on Reading Comprehension and Retention', *IEEE Transactions on Learning Technologies*, 12(3), pp. 402–412. doi: 10.1109/TLT.2018.2861744.

Götz, T. *et al.*, 2003. *Emotions, learning and achievement from an educational-psychological perspective*, pp. 9–28. Available at: https://kops.uni-konstanz.de/handle/123456789/13904 (Accessed: 21 August 2020).

Govaerts, S. and Grégoire, J., 2008. 'Development and Construct Validation of an Academic Emotions Scale', *International Journal of Testing*, 8(1), pp. 34–54. doi: 10.1080/15305050701808649.

Gracia-Moreno, C. *et al.*, 2017. 'Collaborative Knowledge Building Through Simultaneous Private and Public Workspaces', in Lavoué, É. et al. (eds) *Data Driven Approaches in Digital Education*. Cham: Springer International Publishing (Lecture Notes in Computer Science), pp. 553–556. doi: 10.1007/978-3-319-66610-5_61.

Hwang, G.-J. *et al.*, 2020. 'Effects of a concept mapping-based problem-posing approach on students' learning achievements and critical thinking tendency: An application in Classical Chinese learning contexts', *British Journal of Educational Technology*, n/a(n/a). doi: 10.1111/bjet.13007.

Hyerle, D. N., 2011. *Student Successes With Thinking Maps®: School-Based Research, Results, and Models for Achievement Using Visual Tools*. Second. Thousand Oaks, Calif: Corwin.

Immelman, S., 2018. *Concept mapping as a technique for scaffolding concept literacy in accounting: The case of an extended programme*. Dissertation. University of Pretoria. Available at: https://repository.up.ac.za/handle/2263/68033 (Accessed: 20 August 2020).

Iversen, L. *et al.*, 2009. *Dopamine Handbook*. 1e edn. Oxford ; New York: Oxford University Press.

James, W., 1884. 'WHAT IS AN EMOTION ?', *Mind*, os-IX(34), pp. 188–205. doi: 10.1093/mind/os-IX.34.188.

Jonassen, D. H., 1992. 'What are Cognitive Tools?', in Kommers, P. A. M. et al. (eds) *Cognitive Tools for Learning*. Berlin, Heidelberg: Springer (NATO ASI Series), pp. 1–6. doi: 10.1007/978-3-642-77222-1_1.

Lajoie, S. P. and Derry, S. J., 1993. *Computers as Cognitive Tools*. Lawrence Erlbaum Associates, 365 Broadway, Hillsdale, NJ 07642 (paperback: ISBN-0-8058-1082-X, $32.

Machado, C. T. and Carvalho, A. A., 2020. 'Concept Mapping: Benefits and Challenges in Higher Education', *The Journal of Continuing Higher Education*, 68(1), pp. 38–53. doi: 10.1080/07377363.2020.1712579.

Marzano, R. J. and Kendall, J. S., 2006. *The New Taxonomy of Educational Objectives*, *Corwin Press*. Corwin Press, A SAGE Publications Company.

Novak, J., 1984. *Learning How to Learn*. 1st edn. Cambridge Cambridgeshire ; New York: Cambridge University Press.

Novak, J. D. and Cañas, A. J., 2006. 'The Theory Underlying Concept Maps and How to Construct and Use Them', *Florida Institute for Human and Machine Cognition*, 1(1), pp. 1–31.

Oaksford, M. *et al.*, 1996. 'Mood, reasoning, and central executive processes', *Journal of Experimental Psychology: Learning, Memory, and Cognition*, 22(2), pp. 476–492. doi: 10.1037/0278-7393.22.2.476.

Roessger, K. M., Daley, B. J. and Hafez, D. A., 2018. 'Effects of teaching concept mapping using practice, feedback, and relational framing', *Learning and Instruction*, 54, pp. 11–21. doi: 10.1016/j.learninstruc.2018.01.011.

Strongman, K. T., 2003. *The Psychology of Emotion: From Everyday Life to Theory*. 5th edn. Chichester, West Sussex, England: Wiley.

Tauber, S. K. *et al.*, 2017. 'The effects of emotion on younger and older adults' monitoring of learning', *Neuropsychology, development, and cognition. Section B, Aging, neuropsychology and cognition*, 24(5), pp. 555–574. doi: 10.1080/13825585.2016.1227423.

Terracciano, A. *et al.*, 2003. 'Individual Difference Variables, Affective Differentiation, and the Structures of Affect', *Journal of personality*, 71(5), pp. 669–703.

DESIGN OF THE TIME MANAGEMENT SKILLS ACQUISITION SYSTEM USING LEARNING ANALYTICS

Hiroyuki Watanabe[1], Li Chen[2], Xuewang Geng[2], Yoshiko Goda[3] and Atsushi Shimada[4]
[1]*Faculty of Arts and Science, Kyushu University*
744, Motooka, Nishi-ku, Fukuoka 819-0395, Japan
[2]*Graduate School of Human-Environment Studies, Kyushu University*
744, Motooka, Nishi-ku, Fukuoka 819-0395, Japan
[3]*Research Center for Instructional Systems, Kumamoto University*
2-39-1, Kurokami, Chuo-ku, Kumamoto, 860-0862, Japan
[4]*Faculty of Information Science and Electrical Engineering, Kyushu University*
744, Motooka, Nishi-ku, Fukuoka 819-0395, Japan

ABSTRACT

Learning skills include abilities, habits, understanding, and attitudes which are utilized to achieve learning. Students will not achieve good grades unless they properly manage their limited study time. However, it is not easy for them to organize their own study time and learn how to use it efficiently. Notably, learning analytics has not been used in previous research for time management. Learning analytics provides students with accurate data that they can use to manage their study time. Therefore, in this study, we designed a system based on a learning analytics approach with functions that allow students to make their own learning schedules and reflect on their learning behaviors. The system has visualization, calendars, and reflection functions, which are used by both students and their instructors.

KEYWORDS

Learning Analytics, Learning Skills, Learning Analytics Dashboard, Time Management Skills

1. INTRODUCTION

Self-regulated learning (SRL) is an important factor in students' learning processes and environment. Zimmerman et al. (1996) refer to self-regulation as the active involvement of learners in their own learning process in metacognition, motivation, and behaviors; accordingly, these are effective perspectives to achieve learning performance and academic goals. Recently, with the advances in information and communications technology, the data of learners' actual learning behaviors can be captured by the learning analytics approach. Yamada et al (2016) and Yamada et al (2018) indicated that SRL awareness have relationships with learning behaviors. Thus, learning analytics is promising approach to investigate the factors of SRL in behavioral level.

In particular, learning data extracted and collected by the learning analytics approach present students' learning behaviors, which can be related to their learning skills. Therefore, it is necessary to identify what basic learning skills can be measured by learning log data that is based on previous research. Learning skills can be divided into three types based on the previous referenced review.

The first is "Information-processing," which includes the competencies associated with acquiring, recording, organizing, synthesizing, remembering, and using information (Hoover and Patton 1995).

The second is "Skills of learning attitudes and habits of learning," which refers to the abilities, habits, understanding, and attitudes that are necessary to achieve the goal of learning (Cottrell 2019). Tanigawa et al. (2014, p.57) described learning skills as "the comprehensive skills needed to learn effectively in higher education institutions, some related to learning skills and others to learning attitudes and habits." Specifically, this refers to time management, taking classes (how to learn to prepare, review, and prepare for exams, how to take lecture notes); reading (how to find literature and the skill of effectively reading it); and writing (summarizing ideas, writing in a clear manner).

The third type is "Study Strategy," which includes the use of time management and time planning, test anticipation and preparation, and reading and writing strategies as the characteristics of successful students. (Zimmerman et al. 1996).

Gettinger and Seibert (2002) used an information-processing framework to divide learning skills strategies into four categories: (1) repetition- or rehearsal-based skills, (2) procedural study skills, (3) cognitive-based study skills, and (4) metacognitive skills.

Finally, regarding the assessment of basic learning skills, learning skills inventories were mainly used as tools to assess the achievement of learning skills. The Study Skills Inventory was created by Dennis H. Congos of the University of Central Florida; accordingly, it is used by universities, mainly in the United States. It consists of six scales: reading, note-taking, memory, test preparation, concentration, and time management; moreover, there are 51 subscales (Congos 2011).

Although learning skills are classified into different categories, time management is a common element in all categories. The efficient management of learning time is an essential skill for students to implement their learning plans; it is also essential to achieve excellent learning outcomes (Zimmerman 1996).

Thus, time management is regarded as an essential part of learning skills. For example, even if students have prepared and adequately made plans for their work, they will still have difficulties in completing the work as planned without proper time management, since it inhibits their self-efficacy.

Therefore, this study aims to design a learning analytics-based system that helps acquire learning time management skills.

2. LITERATURE REVIEW

2.1 Time Management and Learning Outcomes

Time management is an essential learning skill for the enhancement of learning performance. Goda et al. (2009) showed that students gradually developed study habits and subsequently felt that having a learning plan is beneficial for their learning. Britton and Tesser (1991) examined their hypothesis that college students' performance was predicted by time management practices. The results showed that time management practices could positively affect college performance (academic performance).

How is time management skill enhanced? Talib and Sansgiry (2012) demonstrated that factors such as time management and test anxiety were significantly related to students' academic performance. Furthermore, Misra and McKean (2000) reported that time management behaviors have a greater buffering effect on academic stress than leisure satisfaction activities. The enhancement of time management is related to the awareness of time. Yamada et al. (2015) indicated that learners who have high timely-awareness, reflected by both negative and positive self-concept about learning, tended to have less procrastination awareness and had high learning performance—but these studies depend on self-report data.

From the insights of the above studies, it is indicated that time management behaviors and practices show positive relationships with students' learning outcomes and positive effects on academic stress. Therefore, it is important to take time management into consideration when teaching and learning.

2.2 The Relationships between Time Management and Learning Analytics

The following section presents previous studies that investigated learning time management skills using a learning analytics approach. Many of these studies on time management skills were mainly conducted in educational psychology research—in particular, as a part of self-regulated learning. However, learning analytics, is in fact research that contributes to improving learning and educational environments using various data in not only psychological data but also learning logs. For example, Okubo et al. (2016) investigated effective learning behaviors to predict learning performance using neural networks. Yin et al. (2019) indicated that reading previous pages many times on learning materials promotes learning performance. Shimada et al. (2015) indicated that learning outside of class enhance highly-learning performance, as the perspectives of learning analytics.

Tabuenca et al. (2014) used mobile devices as tools to facilitate self-regulated learning in online courses and stated and measured the actual time spent in learning over a four-month period. The results show that tracing time can improve time management skills.

Uzir et al. (2020) conducted an exploratory study using data collected in a graduate computer course. It detects time management strategies from actual students' learning activities. The results showed that time management strategies were significantly associated with academic performance. Thus, to measure time management in terms of student behavior, a learning analytics approach could be very useful. Nevertheless, these studies did not specify the processes of acquisition of time management skills.

Schumacher and Ifenthaler (2018) investigated students' expectations of the features of learning analysis systems and their willingness to use these features for learning. The five most commonly accepted learning analysis features by students were: (1) the deadline reminder function; (2) the function of revising learning based on the previous semester outcomes; (3) the function of receiving prompts with self-assessment questions with just-in-time feedback; (4) the function of receiving feedback on assignments created in an online learning environment; and (5) a learning recommendation function for the successful completion of the course.

One of the features of this study is to take the students' perspective (e.g., students' expectations) into consideration. By using the learning analysis functions listed above, the students are expected to monitor their learning during the entire learning process. In particular, it is found that the deadline reminder function is an important function for the students to organize their self-regulated learning and time management activities. These previous studies have shown that the learning analytics approach is effective in measuring time management skills. It was also found that the students themselves wanted to manage their learning activities. Based on the results of the above studies, we designed a system that enables users to manage time to monitor their own learning activities (hereinafter, referred to as the "TM system").

3. DESIGN

3.1 The Design and Function of Visualizing Time Management

First, this application focuses on visualization and descriptive information such as time spent, access to resources, progress, and comparison to other students in the same class. Therefore, through the implementation of this application, students can understand their own learning, especially in the areas of poor schedule management. In addition, it is expected that knowledge retention will be improved by facilitating the metacognition of time management. The application designed in this study links the data with the BookRoll e-book viewer, the Metaboard dashboard of the learning analytics system, and the displays of the corresponding learning progress of these systems. Figure 1 shows the screen transition of the entire TM system.

3.2 Application Functions

The functions of this application are presented in this section and correspond with Table 1. The top screen layout includes graphs, calendars, and schedule lists for quick access. Graphs are visualized with the information of users and classes.

Thus, users can compare their own information with the class information. A schedule list is used to list the contents. Reflection deepens learning content. The calendar also has a reminder function. In addition, instructor-only functions include registration of class information and download of access logs.

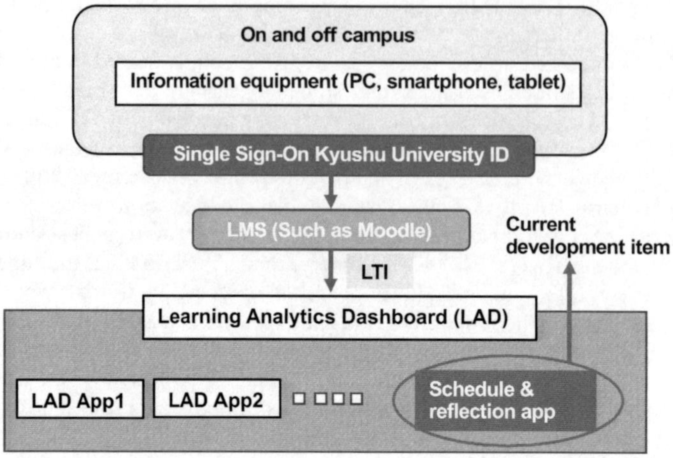

Figure 1. The screen transition of the entire TM system

Table 1. The functions of the TM system

Function	Description
①Top Screen Layout	The top screen layout includes graphs (daily, weekly, and monthly); calendars (daily, weekly, and monthly); and schedule lists.
②Visualization in graphs	Users can select a graph (daily, weekly, or monthly) to visualize their learning behaviors.
③Comparison	Users can compare their behavior with that of the class.
④Schedule List	The list displays users' plans in date and time order.
⑤Reflection	Reflection function allows users to reflect their learning and make plans for the next time. They can also refer to their previous reflection contents.
⑥Link with learning analytics dashboard, E-viewer system	Users can check their assignments by linking to the Metaboard learning analytics dashboard and the BookRoll e-book viewer system.
⑦Reminder	E-mails are delivered to help users to learn according to the schedule. Instructors must register class information (classes, tests, assignment submissions, etc.) on the calendar. Color the calendar to alert students.
⑧Class Information Registration (Instructors only)	Instructors must register class information (classes, tests, assignment submissions, etc.) on the calendar. Color the calendar to alert students.
⑨Download (Instructors only)	The access log can be obtained from the class information registration page.

Concerning the interface of this application, in Figure 2, the graphs on the upper part of the top screen show the learning history (daily, weekly, and monthly). The learning history refers to BookRoll and the Metaboard. The BookRoll system is an e-book viewer, which is used to save digital lecture materials such as slides and notes (Ogata et al. 2015; Ogata et al. 2017). Metaboard is a learning analytics dashboard that aims to provide students with visualized processes and actions based on learning log data from the BookRoll system (Chen et al. 2019; Min et al. 2020).

The bottom left is the monthly graph screen, and the bottom right is the reflection input screen.

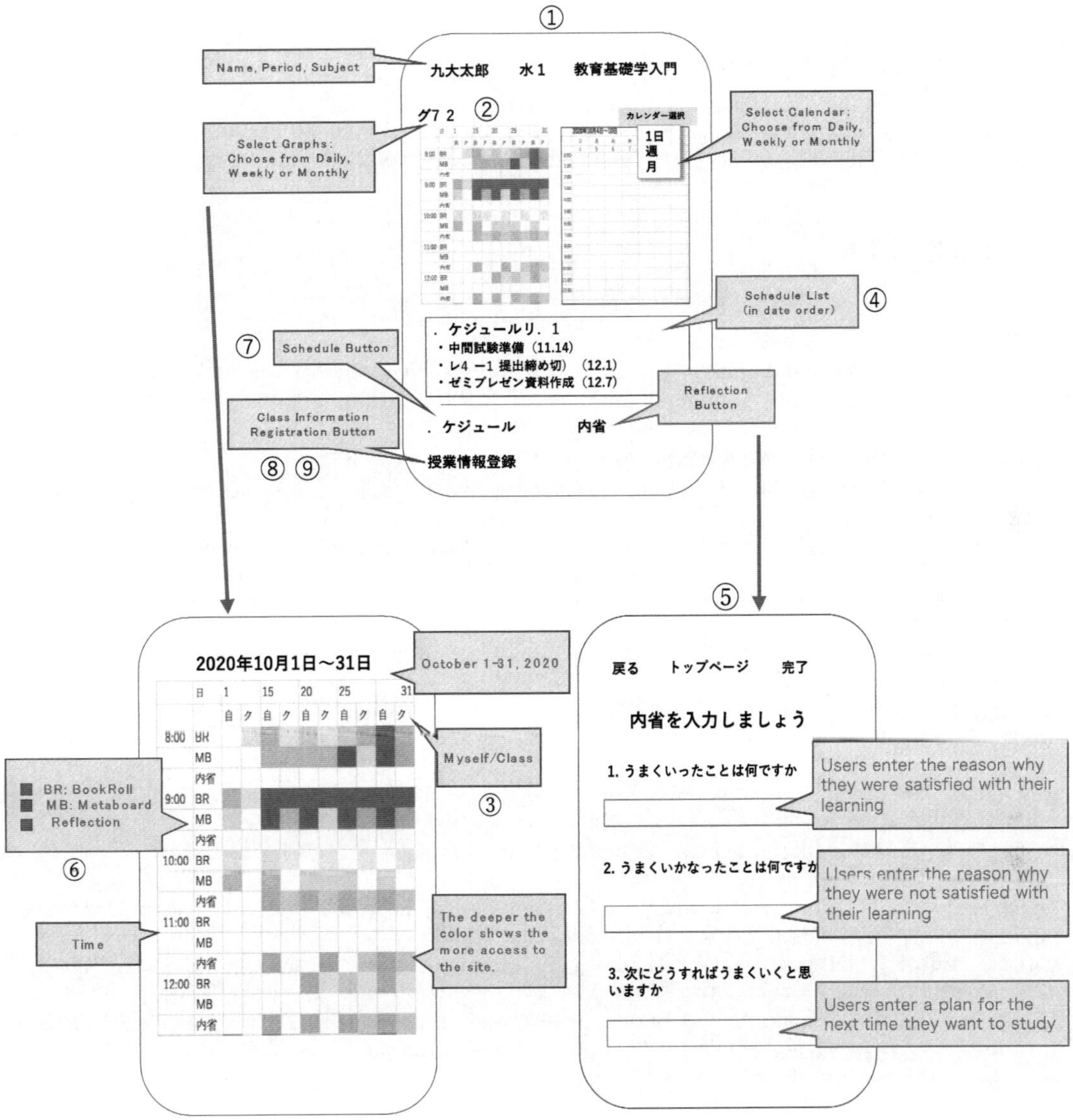

Figure 2. The screen transition of the entire TM system (the numbers in this figure refers to the numbers in Table 1)

4. CONCLUSIONS AND FUTURE WORK

In this study, we examined previous research on learning skills, and designed a new application to help students manage their learning time. It is offered to students and teachers. In the design of this application, the functions of graphs, calendars, schedules, and reflections were necessary for time management to aid the monitoring and management of learning plans. We designed a heat map to allow for learning progress comparisons of individual students and classes. In addition, the minimized screen transition is designed to adapt to the use of smartphones. We will develop and evaluate the application. In next phase, we will evaluate the effects of the application designed in this study, including the analysis of students' access logs, effectiveness and usability (Motiwalla 2007) through a practical experiment.

ACKNOWLEDGEMENT

This study was supported by Japan Society for the Promotion of Science(JSPS) [grant number JP19H01716,JP20H01727], and JST AIP [grant number JPMJCR19U1].

REFERENCES

Britton, B. K. and Tesser, A., 1991. Effects of Time-management Practices on College Grades. *Journal of Educational Psychology*, 83(3), pp. 405-410.

Chen, L et al, 2019. Design of Learning Analytics Dashboard Supporting Metacognition. *16th International Conference on Cognition and Exploratory Learning in Digital Age (CELDA 2019)*, Cagliari, Italy, pp. 175-182.

Congos, D. H., 2011. *Starting Out in Community College*, McGraw-Hill, Chicago.

Cottrell, S., 2019. *The Study Skills Handbook 5th ed.* Red Globe Press, London.

Gettinger, M. and Seibert, K., 2002. Contributions of Study Skills to Academic Competence. *School Psychology Review,* Vol. 31, No. 3, pp. 350-365.

Goda, Y. et al, 2009. Ingenious Attempts to Develop Self-Regulated Learning Strategies with e-Learning: Focusing on Time-Management Skill and Learning Habit. In T. Bastiaens et al (Eds.), *Proceedings of World Conference on E-Learning in Corporate, Government, Healthcare, and Higher Education 2009,* Chesapeake, VA, USA, pp. 1265-1274.

Hoover, J. J. and Patton, P. R., 1995. *Teaching Students with Learning Problems to Use Study Skills: A Teacher's Guide.* Austin, TX: Pro-Ed.

Lu, M. et al, 2020. Development of a Learning Dashboard Prototype Supporting Meta-cognition for Students, *Companion Proceedings 10th International Conference on Learning Analytics & Knowledge (LAK20)*, Frankfurt (online), Germany, pp. 104-106.

Misra, R. and McKean, M., 2000. College Students' Academic Stress and Its Relation to Their Anxiety, Time Management, and Leisure Satisfaction. *American Journal of Health Studies*, Vol. 16, No. 1, pp. 41-51.

Motiwalla, L. F., 2007. Mobile learning. A framework and evaluation. *Computers & Education*, Vol. 49, No. 3, pp. 581-596.

Ogata, H. et al, 2015. E-book-based Learning Analytics in University Education. *Proceedings of the 23rd International Conference on Computers in Education (ICCE 2015),* pp. 401-406.

Ogata, H. et al, 2017. M2B System: A Digital Learning Platform for Traditional Classrooms in University. *7th International Learning Analytics & Knowledge Conference (LAK17): Practitioner Track,* Vancouver, Canada, pp. 155-162.

Okubo, F., et al, 2016. Learning Activity Features of High Performance Students. *Proceedings of the 1st International Workshop on Learning Analytics Across Physical and Digital Spaces* (Cross-LAK 2016), pp. 28-33.

Schumacher, C., and Ifenthaler, D., 2018. Features Students Really Expect from Learning Analytics. *Computers in Human Behavior*, Vol. 78, pp. 397-407.

Shimada, A. et al, 2015. Informal Learning Behavior Analysis Using Action Logs and Slide Features in E-textbooks. *Proceedings of IEEE ICALT 2015*, pp. 116-117.

Tabuenca et al, 2015. Time Will Tell: The Role of Mobile Learning Analytics in Self-regulated Learning. *Computers & Education,* Vol. 89, pp. 53-74.

Talib, N. and Sansgiry, S. S., 2012. Determinants of Academic Performance of University Students. *Pakistan Journal of Psychological Research,* pp. 265-278.

Tanigawa, H. et al, 2014. *Peer Tutor Training.* Nakanishiya ed., Kyoto.

Uzir, N.A. et al, 2020. Analytics of Time Management Strategies in a Flipped Classroom, *Journal of Computer Assisted Learning*, Vol. 36, No. 1, pp. 70-88.

Yamada, M. et al, 2015. The Relationship Among Self-Regulated Learning, Procrastination, And Learning Behaviors In Blended Learning Environment. *12th International Conference on Cognition and Exploratory Learning in Digital Age 2015* (CELDA 2015), pp. 67-74

Yamada, M. et al, 2016. Learning Analytics in Ubiquitous Learning Environments: Self-Regulated Learning Perspective, The *Proceedings of the 24th International Conference on Computers in Education* (ICCE 2016), pp. 306-314.

Yamada, M. et al, 2017. Are Learning Logs Related to Procrastination? From the Viewpoint of Self-Regulated Learning. *International Conference on Cognition and Exploratory Learning in Digital Age* (CELDA 2017), pp. 3-10.

Yamada, M. et al, 2018. BR-Map: Concept map system using e-book logs, *International Conference on Cognition and Exploratory Learning in Digital Age 2018* (CELDA 2018), pp. 248-254

Yin, C., et al. , 2019. Exploring the Relationships between Reading Behavior Patterns and Learning Outcomes Based on Log Data from E-books: A Human Factor Approach. *International Journal of Human-Computer Interaction*, 35(4-5), pp. 313-322.

Zimmerman, B. J. et al, 1996. *Developing Self-Regulated Learner: Beyond Achievement to Self-Efficacy*. American Psychological Association, Washington DC, USA.

PROBLEM-BASED PROJECTS: A CATALYST FOR ENHANCING STUDENTS' SELF-DIRECTED LEARNING IN AN INFORMATION SECURITY COURSE

Marietjie Havenga[1] and Lynette Drevin[2]
[1]*Unit for Self-Directed Learning, North-West University, Potchefstroom, South Africa*
[2]*School of Computer Science and Information Systems, North-West University, Potchefstroom, South Africa*

ABSTRACT

Although postgraduate students are required to be self-directed, this is not always the case. The aims of this study were twofold. Firstly, we investigated whether the use of problem-based projects supported students in implementing different cryptography algorithms as part of a group assignment. Secondly, we determined to which extent the use of problem-based projects enhanced students' self-directed learning. A qualitative methodology was followed. A cohort of 21 honours students enrolled for this elective course in Information Security. Students worked mainly in small groups of two on a project. Data collection involved completion of open-ended questions regarding information security and students' previous experiences in problem-based environments, completion of project sheets and narrative reflections regarding their project work. The data were manually coded to identify certain patterns of meaning. Results showed that problem-based projects provided opportunities for learning 'useful things in life' and strengthened team members' knowledge and skills. Problem-based projects served as a catalyst for enhancing students' self-directed learning in this Information Security course, which is beneficial for addressing real-life scenarios in the Information Technology profession. Additionally, an integrated model for self-directed learning skill development in a problem-based context was proposed.

KEYWORDS

Information Security Course, Problem-Based Project, Programming, Self-Directed Learning, Students

1. INTRODUCTION

Self-directed learning (SDL) comprises an educational space for the incremental development of lifelong and responsible learning where students need to take ownership of and manage their own learning processes (Knowles, 1975; UNESCO, 2015). This notion is emphasised as part of the mission statement of the university to "provide meaningful teaching and learning experiences and responsive and enabling environments … so that its students can progressively become self-directed and lifelong learners who make distinctive contributions to society and the world of work" (North-West University Teaching and Learning Strategy, 2016:10). To instigate the development of SDL, several pedagogical approaches can be applied to prepare students for the development of employability skills. Problem-based learning (PBL) is acknowledged as a powerful student-centred strategy that provides the opportunity for authentic learning and enables students to develop professional skills (Mohd-Yusof, 2017). Ulseth and Guerra (2017) are of the opinion that various PBL approaches can be used for example, "problem-based, project organized learning" (Ulseth & Guerra, 2017:vii). In this research, honours students developed problem-based projects in an Information Security course relating to cryptography algorithms. Honours students are selected for post-graduate studies according to their achievement in undergraduate courses. These students are expected to be driven by the desire to learn. Although it is expected from post-graduates to be able to manage their own learning processes, this is not always the case. In a study by Taylor and Goede (2012) regarding honours students' SDL readiness in a Data Warehousing course, they emphasise that lecturers need to assist students in developing a higher level of SDL to prepare them for careers in the IT environment. Consequently, the aims of this research were the following: we investigated whether the use of problem-based projects supported students in implementing different cryptography algorithms, and determined to which extent the use of problem-based projects enhanced students' self-directed learning. This paper is structured as follows: a literature overview is given and this is followed by the empirical research, the results and discussion, and the conclusion.

2. LITERATURE OVERVIEW

This section gives an overview regarding the aspects concerning this study.

2.1 Work-Related Qualities in IT

Obtaining a degree does not necessarily guarantee success in real life. Friedman (2014, no page) reports on an interview with Bock (senior vice-president of people operations for Google). According to Bock, "Too many colleges ... don't deliver on what they promise. You generate a ton of debt, you don't learn the most useful things for your life." Bock shared five criteria that Google uses when evaluating job candidates, namely integrative cognitive ability (pull together unrelated bits of information, "it's not I.Q."); emergent leadership (lead and sometimes let someone else lead); intellectual humility ("step back and embrace the better ideas of others"); ownership (responsibility and ownership, solving problems collaboratively); and expertise (e.g. coding ability). Bock reveals that the first four are the main qualities required for Google employees. According to the Association for Computing Machinery and IEEE Computer Society (ACM/IEEE) (Sahami, Danyluk, Fincher, Fisher, Grossman, Hawthorne & Cuadros-Vargas, 2013) essential characteristics of IT graduates include that they need to be able to: analyse a problem; design, implement and evaluate a program; function effectively in teams; understand professional and social issues and responsibilities; apply skills, tools and practices; integrate IT-based solutions effectively into the user environment; understand and apply best practices; and assist in the creation of an effective project plan. Such characteristics are also associated with computational thinking and participation.

2.2 Computational Thinking and Participation

Computational thinking relates to problem solving, system development and an understanding of the human way of life with regard to fundamental concepts in Computer Science (Kafai, 2016; Wing, 2006). Wing (2006:33–35) is of the opinion that "Computer Science inherently draws on engineering thinking, given that we build systems that interact with the real world ... solve problems, manage our daily lives, and communicate and interact with other people." Computational participation involves creating a tangible artefact that can be shared with others as Kafai (2016:27) asserts, "Coding was once a solitary, tool-based activity. Now it is becoming a shared social practice." Thus, to learn how to code, students need to learn computer science fundamentals as well as to participate in sharing their work with one another. Computational thinking and participation may be addressed by using various teaching–learning strategies.

2.3 Problem-Based Projects

Problem-based learning (PBL) is a pedagogy that is based on authentic learning, it is student-centred, collaborative and requires reflective learning (Da Silva, Kruta de Araújo Bispo, Rodriguez & Vasquez, 2018). Students are challenged with the problem of inquiry whereas the lecturer serves as the facilitator. According to Bagheri, Ali, Abdullah, and Daud (2013), PBL has the ability to enhance students' SDL and real-life experiences in a specific field. Essential features of PBL involve the following (Savery, 2015): it is an approach where students are actively involved, team members work together to solve fuzzy problems, students take responsibility and ownership of their learning processes, problem scenarios require integrated knowledge and skills, and team cooperation is essential. Distinctive team cooperation, critical thinking, innovative construction of an artefact, as well as self- and peer group assessment are of particular importance in PBL (Havenga, 2015). Chorfi, Hedjazib, Aouaga and Boubicheb (2020) highlight that the combination of PBL and teamwork enhance responsible learning as well as the development of essential problem solving and programming skills for a changing society. Moreover, Sarkar, Overton, Thompson and Rayner (2020) concur that the development of such qualities are highly valued by employers. In this research, PBL was *structured* around the development of a project.

2.4 Real-Life Skills and Self-Directed Learning

It is essential that students develop real-life skills to cope with future demands since continuous changes are inherently characteristic of career trajectories (Beagon & Niall, 2015; Borgen & Hiebert, 2014). As a result, higher education needs to prepare students for employability, skill development and future careers. Learning capabilities should accordingly be occupied with real-life experiences to contribute towards the needs of society. The NWU's Teaching and Learning Strategy defines desired graduate attributes in relation to six domains. One of the domains is "Innovative, critical thinkers" which entails "The ability to solve complex and unfamiliar problems through the discovery and creation of new knowledge and understanding". Another domain is listed as "self-directed and lifelong learners, who are able to work independently, utilise resources effectively, and exercise initiative" (NWU, 2016:12,13). SDL is a process towards independent and responsible learning where goals are explicitly formulated, appropriate strategies are implemented, and reflective activities are used to direct an individual's learning (Knowles, 1975). Students need to engage in their learning, transfer their knowledge to new situations and take ownership of their learning processes. Personal attributes of self-direction involve responsible and strategic abilities, perseverance, autonomous learning and the ability to challenge real-world problems (Merriam, Caffarella & Baumgartner, 2007).

2.5 Information Security Course

'Information security' refers to strategies involved to protect confidential, private and sensitive data, information and systems from unauthorised access, (mis)use, destruction, modification or disruption (Pfleeger, Pfleeger & Margulies, 2015). The Information Security course aims to provide students with insight into the weaknesses of computerised environments and encryption and decryption techniques among others. As part of this course, students need to investigate the following three encryption algorithms.

The Vigenere algorithm is a poly-alphabetic substitution cipher (Whitman & Mattord, 2016). A table with the 26 x 26 alphabet letters is used for encrypting and decrypting messages by permuting all letters with all the others (e.g. A could become an a, b, c … z). A keyword is chosen, which is combined with the plain text and repeated over the length of the plain text (Pfleeger & Pfleeger, 2007).

In the Vernam cipher, a long sequence of numbers is used in combination with the plain text to provide a strong cipher. A plain text is combined with the long non-repeating key (random numbers). The cryptogram is the sum mod 26 (alphabet of 26 letters) of each coded letter ('mod' is the remainder after division).

The aim of using the Columnar transposition algorithm is to get diffusion of the plain text characters by spreading them over the whole length of the message to be encrypted. The message is written row by row in a fixed column size. This is followed by reading the message back column by column, getting the resultant cryptogram (Pfleeger & Pfleeger, 2007). For example, the words ENCRYPT is presented as follows: EY NP CT R* (by reading the text column by column). Variations can be carried out to get improved diffusion, or the columns can be rearranged in order to enhance the complexity of the cipher.

1	2	3	4
E	N	C	R
Y	P	T	*

Figure 1. Message displayed using the columnar transposition algorithm

The research questions were the following:

1) How can problem-based projects support students to implement different cryptography algorithms?

2) How can problem-based projects enhance students' self-directed learning in the Information Security course?

3. EMPIRICAL RESEARCH

3.1 Research Approach and Methodology

Research was done from the social-constructivist point of view where reality is constructed by students working in collaboration and challenging each other's perspectives. A qualitative methodology was followed.

3.2 Study Context

The cohort of honours students in the Information Security course involved 21 students (68% of all the honours students selected this course). The study was approved by the ethical committee of the university. In the Information Security course, students are required to participate in seminars, submit assignments, search for appropriate information, present their project to the class, and write tests as well as an examination. It is also expected of the students to work in groups, explore solutions and take control of their own learning processes. Honours students need to solve security-related problems and recommend measures to address and counteract these. Two students worked in a group and selected the peers themselves. Members were required to develop a program to manage the encryption and decryption of messages and files (Table 1). Each team had to develop one program involving four different algorithms (Vigenere, Vernam, Columnar transposition) as well as an own choice cipher. A graphical interface was developed to demonstrate the algorithms. Students worked after class time and were allowed to use any programming platform (Drevin, 2016). They compiled a concise report comprising a table of contents, introduction, aims, topic selected, summary and conclusion as well as a complete reference list. All programs had to install from a CD during demonstration. Formative assessment included individual as well as group assignments that covered creativity, application of knowledge, scientific communication and reporting. Summative assessment comprised the project, the scientific report as well as the final examination. Prior to project submission, students received a rubric regarding: the time schedule, weekly project sheets, group reflection, software project and report, team presentation as well as group assessment. A final score out of 100 was assigned to each project.

Table 1. The research design in this study

Activities prior to the intervention (individual)	Intervention (10 weeks) (team completion)
Completion of questions: 1) information security knowledge; and 2) PBL (understanding of and previous experiences with PBL)	Plan the project and complete a time schedule Submit weekly project sheets (responsibilities and progress). Develop a project that implements different cryptographic algorithms and a project report as deliverables. Obtain students' reflections regarding their responsibilities and experiences with problem-based projects

3.3 Data Collection and Analysis

Qualitative data collection prior to the intervention involved completion of open-ended questions regarding students' knowledge about information security as well as their initial experiences about PBL (Table 1). This was followed by gathering the teams' weekly project sheets and narrative reflections regarding their project work. Students feedback were analysed according to abilities such as responsibility in learning, ownership, perseverance, active and autonomous learning, cooperation and the ability to solve challenging problems. In the weekly project sheets students had to respond to the following:

Give feedback regarding the assistance and support among your team members
Give feedback regarding your team's personal interaction and communication
Give feedback on the extent to which you as a group have achieved your goals
Which problems or challenges did your team experience in not achieving your goals?
Explain how your team has solved or managed the problems or challenges mentioned above
Reflect on the pace of your team's progress in project development.
Specify which information you searched for regarding the development of your project. List all resources

Give yourself and your teammates a mark allocation in relation to your contribution to the project, with motivation.

The data were manually coded. Both concept coding (broader meaning) and descriptive coding (labelling a word or phrase) were used to identify certain patterns of meaning as the outcome of the coding and categorisation of data. Differences among the groups and re-occurring themes and concepts were identified and agreed upon by the researchers.

4. RESULTS AND DISCUSSION

4.1 Results

The following themes were identified: Theme 1: Experiences concerning PBL (prior to the intervention), Theme 2: Team obligations, Theme 3: Participants' challenges and reflections, and Theme 4: Knowledge and skills obtained regarding information security. All quotations are reflected verbatim and unedited.

4.1.1 Experiences Concerning PBL

Students mentioned that working on a project was an impetus for learning, which enabled a deeper understanding and programming of distinct ciphers. Some examples were the following: "Learning while applying knowledge in a practical manner, asking a project as a catalyst for learning" (Participant 11 (P11)). "Study through practical and visible experience instead of sitting in class and given limited knowledge" (P13, P18). "Applying various or new techniques as part of a project to fully understand a specific subject domain. I like this" (P19). "Consequently to obtain a deeper and better understanding of the topic" (P20). "Being given a project that requires self-learning and self-motivation in order to learn and overcome a problem that has not been physically taught to us" (P21). "Though the project took a lot of effort hour, it was fascinating and has enlightened us about the complications of working on a real-life/deployable project and made us to understand why it takes software companies lot of time to deliver a stable version of software products" (P14). One student was not sure what PBL entailed and mentioned, "Not 100% sure. Learn by doing. Not passive" (P17).

4.1.2 Team Obligations

Examples of teamwork, interaction and management of collaborative activities involved meetings, essential group discussions as well as assistance and support to one another. "Each team member was allocated an algorithm to research on … The team had a progress status meeting … Ensure that everyone on the team is on the same page with the project expectations" (P13). "The support is great and they are always eager to give assistance when certain requirements … are not clear" (P13). Students discussed ways to enhance their understanding: "Team members again discussed the programming of the Vernam and Vigenere to enable that both understand and do the programming" (P2). However, members experienced challenges with the columnar transposition algorithm: "Research was again reviewed and different aspects was explained by different members to support the … programming of the algorithm for Columnar Transposition … All the previous work was debugged and tested" (P19).

4.1.3 Participants' Challenges and Reflections

Some challenges entailed problems with the format of documentation, decisions regarding an appropriate programming language and time concerns: "As the format of documentation differs between the team members, the integration of algorithms also differs since members make use of different user interfaces. After hard work we achieved our aims" (P1). "It was challenging to decide on the programming language … which language will execute the work accurately [as] expected … the coding process took longer than expected. However, the team managed to get all work completed on time" (P13). Programming of the fourth algorithm challenged students: "We experienced problems to decide on how to efficiently program the fourth algorithm … found new ways to solve the programming problems" (P2). Moreover, time concerns involved: "There was an enormous time shortage issue … it takes software companies a lot of time to deliver a stable version of software products … we devised a time schedule to guide the project, rethink our approach, adjusted our personal schedules" (P19). "The first three phases went as planned but … development and testing was rigorous … to ensure that the program works" (P14).

4.1.4 Knowledge and Skills Obtained Regarding Information Security

Students obtained knowledge and programming skills regarding the different algorithms: "Check which languages support the Vigenere algorithm … The team was able to be on schedule and deliver [the] expected outcome" (P13). "Obtain the appropriate background knowledge … involving different encryption algorithms and to decide which of them to include or combine with others to use as the extra one for the project" (P19). Participating students persisted in solving the four encryption algorithms: "The accumulated knowledge about the different encryption algorithms cannot be taken away … therefore we can say that it is bug free to some degree, and fully functional to do what it is intended to do" (P19). "We as a team have achieved our goal of completing all four algorithms at this stage and combining all into one program, as well as starting off with the final documentation" (P20).

4.2 Discussion

This section answers both the research questions. The first research question was: How can problem-based projects support students to implement different cryptography algorithms?

Problem-based projects (PBP) enable students to apply new techniques to enhance a deeper and better understanding of Information Security. Theme 1 outlined some views and experiences regarding the learning in problem-based contexts: "A project as a catalyst for learning" (P11). "Practical and visible experience" (P13, P18). "Learn by doing" (P17). Project development requires self-learning and self-motivation: "In order to learn and overcome a problem that has not been physically taught to us" (P21). "It … has enlightened us about the complications of working on a real-life project and … why it takes software companies lot of time to deliver a stable version of software products" (P14). Applying PBP provided opportunities for the development of skills and enabled students to elaborate on their knowledge (Theme 4). Students obtained background knowledge, different approaches to the algorithms and the programming thereof (P19), and they checked which languages were better suited to implement the Vigenere algorithm (P13). Initially, students experienced some problems with the decryption of the columnar transposition algorithm (P1, P19). Nevertheless, Participant 1 (P1) decided to program the fourth algorithm efficiently and found new ways to solve the problems, whereas another team searched for a programming language which could execute the program "accurately as expected" (P13) (Theme 3).

Some members ensured that the program worked by applying rigorous testing of their programs (P14). The knowledge obtained about the encryption algorithms is clearly outlined by P19 as he stipulated, "the accumulated knowledge about the different encryption algorithms cannot be taken away … applying various or new techniques as part of a project to fully understand a specific subject domain. I like this." Emerging from these examples is the use of PBP as a catalyst for learning by doing. Students were required to figure out what the problem entailed and explored possible solutions, e.g. the columnar transposition algorithm had not been taught to them previously – only the mechanism was explained. Consequently, the emphasis was on the process of solving the problem rather than on merely finding a solution. The importance of knowledge and skill development in real-life contexts was also revealed by Friedman (2014), Kafai (2016) and Wing (2006). Results underscore the view that PBP are problem-focused and student-centred and integrate IT-based solutions into the user environment (Sahami et al., 2013). Similar studies also found that PBL enabled students to practice and develop skills, such as ownership and management of the project, as well as to generate solutions that could not be done as part of general coursework (McManus & Costello, 2019). They also noted that individual responsibility and accountability enforced time management skills.

The second research question was: how can problem-based projects enhance students' self-directed learning in the Information Security course? Participants mentioned their responsibility as individuals and as a group (Theme 2). Each team member was allocated an algorithm on which to do research, and participants had meetings to indicate their progress, they gave assistance and supported one another (P13), and reviewed and explained some aspects (P19). Since the teams where small (comprising mostly two members), members were required to establish goals, share responsibilities and be accountable for group tasks. Assisting each other (P13, P19) and balancing challenges enhanced opportunities for developing interdependence and SDL.

Debugging and testing of programs were also part of group responsibilities as mentioned by P19. Participants strengthened one another's understanding of encryption algorithms (P2). Group members therefore owned a project and they were responsible for all aspects of the encryption project. Ownership is also outlined by Friedman (2014) as one of the important criteria that Google uses when evaluating job candidates. Sahami et al. (2013) further elaborate that students need to understand social issues and responsibilities.

Participating students mentioned some challenges as outlined in Theme 3. They experienced technical problems, such as the format of the document, and the integration of algorithms, which was problematic as a result of using different user interfaces (P1). A main concern was time constraints, as the coding process took longer than expected. P19 also noted, "There was an enormous time shortage issue." Time constrains are of importance to ensure successful delivery. Some students managed their time challenges by rethinking their approach, and they adjusted their personal schedules accordingly (P19, P13). Management of own time, persistence in learning and viewing problems as challenges, are characteristics of highly self-directed learners as emphasised by Merriam et al. (2007). As a result, problem-based projects served as an appropriate method to enhance students' SDL and real-life experiences in an Information Security course. Figure 2 displays a proposed integrated model for SDL skill development in a PBL context.

The model in Figure 2 is based on the integrated findings in this study. PBP provided opportunities for knowledge, skill development and collaboration to foster students' SDL where they needed to solve real-life problems in new ways. The model comprises three main entities, namely collective responsibility and ownership, collaborative knowledge construction and real-life experiences, on the outside of the triangle. These entities were also mentioned in the literature overview for example, collective responsibility and ownership (intellectual humility and ownership – Friedman, 2014), collaborative knowledge construction (integrative cognitive ability – Friedman, 2014), and real-life experiences (develop real-life skills to cope with future demands – Beagon & Niall (2015); Borgen & Hiebert (2014)). Associations, presented as verbs, indicate the dynamicity between two entities. For example, the collective responsibility and ownership entity contributes toward collaborative knowledge construction (especially in a cooperative team). Likewise, collaborative knowledge construction may contribute towards collective responsibility and ownership (thus indicated in Figure 2 with bi-directional arrows). Similarly, collective responsibility and ownership and real-life experiences enhance one another whereas collaborative knowledge construction develops real-life experiences. In the same way, real-life experiences may provide for the development of collaborative knowledge construction where team members solve a complex problem. Selected exemplars are presented within the triangle. For example, achieve team goals ("After hard work we achieved our aims" [P1]), solve real-life problems in new ways ("found new ways to solve the programming problems" [P2]), and apply new techniques ("Learning while applying knowledge in a practical manner, asking a project as a catalyst for learning" [P11]). The attributes mentioned here are part of SDL as Knowles (1975) emphasises independent, responsible learning, the use of strategies and reflective activities to direct the learning process.

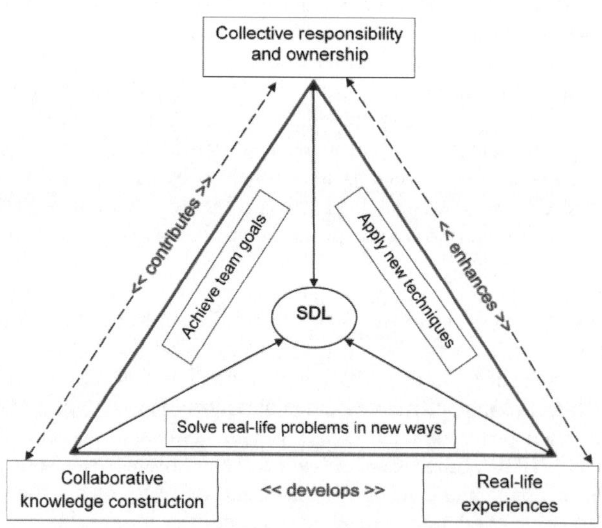

Figure 2. A proposed integrated model for SDL skill development in a problem-based context

5. CONCLUSION

This research explored the application of problem-based projects to enhance honours students' SDL in an Information Security course where cryptography algorithms had to be planned and implemented. PBP supported participants to apply new techniques, increase their knowledge and develop real-life skills. Although it emerged that students initially experienced some challenges, the use of the cryptography project resulted in the improvement of students' SDL. Participants enhanced their knowledge and technical experience, and developed employability skills. Therefore, synergy between theoretical knowledge and practical programming experiences should be emphasised in problem-based projects as a reflection of real-world IT settings. Moreover, a model for SDL skill development has been proposed in a PBL context as a way to integrate responsible learning and ownership, collaborative knowledge construction and the experience of real-world settings, as these are beneficial for the IT profession.

For future work, teaching practices, such as problem-based projects, could be applied in various Computer Science courses to enable students addressing real-world problems while working in small group settings. Some limitations of this research were that the class size was small and generalisations cannot be made, although good insight into the project experiences of these students was obtained. In addition, the emerged model needs to be evaluated in computer science contexts.

REFERENCES

Bagheri, M., Ali, W.Z.W., Abdullah, M.C.B. & Daud, S.M. 2013. Effects of project-based learning strategy on self-directed learning skills of educational technology students. *Contemporary Educational Technology*, 4(1):15–29.

Beagon, U. & Niall, D. 2015. *Using problem based learning to develop graduate attributes in first year engineering students*. [Online]. Available: https://arrow.dit.ie/engschcivcon/92/ [Viewed 04 January 2019].

Borgen, W. & Hiebert, B. 2014. Orienting educators to contemporary ideas for career counselling: An illustrative example. In *Handbook of career development, international and cultural psychology.* Edited by G. Arulmani, A.J. Bakshi, F.T.L. Leong & T. Watts. NY:Springer-Verlag, pp. 1–771.

Chorfi, A., Hedjazi, D., Aouag, S. & Boubiche, D. 2020. Problem-based collaborative learning groupware to improve computer programming skills. *Behaviour & Information Technology*. [Online]. Available: https://scholar.google.com/scholar?hl=en&as_sdt=0%2C5&q=Problem-based+collaborative+learning+groupware+to+improve+computer+programming+skills+Atef+Chorfi&btnG= [Viewed 26 October 2020]

Da Silva, A.B., Kiula de Araújo Dispo, A.C., Rodriguez, D.G. & Vasquez, F.L.F. 2018. Problem-based learning: A proposal for structuring PBL and its implications for learning among students in an undergraduate management degree program. *Revista de Gestão*, 25(2):160–177.

Drevin, L. 2016. ITRI 615 PEC Computer Security 1. Study guide, Potchefstroom campus, Northwest-University. Ivyline Technologies.

Friedman, T.L. 2014. How to get a job at Google. The New York Times. [Online]. Available: https://www.nytimes.com/2014/02/23/opinion/sunday/friedman-how-to-get-a-job-at-google.html?_r=0 [Viewed 10 March 2017].

Havenga, H.M. 2015. Project-based learning in higher education: exploring programming students' development towards self-directedness. *South African Journal of Higher Education,* 29(4):135–157.

Kafai, Y.B. 2016. From computational thinking to computational participation in K-12 education. *Communications of the ACM,* 59(8):26–27.

Knowles, M.S. 1975. Self-directed learning: A guide for learners and teachers. New York, NY: Association Press.

McManus, J.W. & Costello, P.J. 2019. Project based learning in computer science: a student and research advisor's perspective. *Journal of Computing Sciences in Colleges,* 34(3):38–46.

Merriam, S., Caffarella, R. & Baumgartner, L. 2007. Learning in adulthood. 3rd ed. San Francisco, CA: Jossey-Bass.

Mohd-Yusof, K. 2017. Sustaining change for PBL at the course level. In *PBL in engineering education. International perspectives on curriculum change*. Edited by A. Guerra, R. Ulseth & A. Kolmos. Rotterdam: Sense, pp. 13–32.

NWU (North-West University). 2016. *North-West University. Teaching and learning strategy: 2016–2020.* Potchefstroom. [Online]. Available: http://www.nwu.ac.za/sites/www.nwu.ac.za/files/files/i-governance-management/documents/2017.NWU.TeachingLearningStrategy.pdf [Viewed 04 January 2019].

Pfleeger, C.P. & Pfleeger, S.L. 2007. Security in computing. Upper Saddle River, NJ: Prentice Hall.

Pfleeger, C.P., Pfleeger, S.L. & Margulies, J. 2015. Security in computing. 5th ed. Upper Saddle River, NJ: Prentice Hall.

Sahami, M., Danyluk, A., Fincher, S., Fisher, K., Grossman, D., Hawthorne, E., & Cuadros-Vargas, E. 2013. *Computer Science Curricula 2013: Curriculum guidelines for undergraduate degree programs in Computer Science*. Association for Computing Machinery & The Institute of Electrical and Electronics Engineers Computer Society. doi:10.1145/2534860.

Sarkar, M., Overton, T., Thompson, C.D. & Rayner, G. 2020. Academics' perspectives of the teaching and development of generic employability skills in science curricula. *Higher Education Research & Development,* 39(2):346–361.

Savery, J.R. 2015. Overview of Problem-Based Learning: Definitions and Distinctions. In: Walker, A., Leary, H., Hmelo-Silver, C.E. and Ertmer, P.A. (Eds), *Essential Readings in Problem-based Learning. Exploring and Extending the Legacy of Howard S. Barrows*. Indiana: Purdue University Press.

Taylor, E. & Goede, R. 2012. Computer science students, learning styles and readiness for self-directed learning. In *Proceedings of the ISTE International Conference on Mathematics, Science and Technology Education.* Pretoria: UNISA Press, pp. 291-300.

Ulseth, R. & Guerra, A. 2017. Introduction. PBL in Engineering Education. International Perspectives on Curriculum Change. In *PBL in engineering education. International perspectives on curriculum change.* Edited by A. Guerra, R. Ulseth & A. Kolmos. Rotterdam: Sense. pp. vii-x.

United Nations Educational, Scientific and Cultural Organization. 2015. *The role of higher education in promoting lifelong learning.* Hamburg: UNESCO Institute for Lifelong Learning.

Whitman, M.E. & Mattord, H.J. 2016. *Principles of information security*. Boston, MA: Cengage Learning.

Wing, J.M. 2006. Computational thinking. *Communications of the ACM,* 46(3):33–35.

RELATIONSHIP BETWEEN LEARNING BEHAVIORS AND SOCIAL PRESENCE IN ONLINE COLLABORATIVE LEARNING

Yufan Xu[1], Yuta Taniguchi[2], Yoshiko Goda[3], Atsushi Shimada[2] and Masanori Yamada[1]
[1]Graduate School of Human-Environment Studies, Kyushu University
744, Motooka, Nishi-ku, Fukuoka 819-0395, Japan
[2]Faculty of Information Science and Electrical Engineering, Kyushu University
744, Motooka, Nishi-ku, Fukuoka 819-0395, Japan
[3]Research Center for Instructional Systems, Kumamoto University
2-39-1, Kurokami, Chuo-ku, Kumamoto, 8600862 Japan

ABSTRACT

This study examined the factors of learning behaviors in digital-learning-material reader that predict university students' productive participation identified by social presence indicators in online collaborative learning. Data were collected from 76 Frist-year university students, including learning behaviors in digital learning-material readers, and frequency of each social presence indicator classified by coding discussion scripts with automated text classification. The results of the stepwise multiple regression analysis revealed that the learning behavior of drawing red markers, highlighting important content predicts social presence. Furthermore, the study's findings showed that different learning behaviors predict different social presence indicators, which are related to metacognition and critical thinking.

KEYWORDS

Online Learning Participation, Computer-Supported Collaborative Learning, Learning Analytics, Learning Behaviors, Social Presence, Community of Inquiry

1. INTRODUCTION

Online learning has become a popular learning experience based on a pedagogical approach—Computer-Supported Collaborative Learning (CSCL) (e.g., Barria et al., 2012). Online learning participation is related to learning satisfaction and learning performance (Cobb, 2009; Hrastinski, 2009). However, there are variations in online learning participation due to an apparent lack of information on learning behaviors and monitoring from other learners (Swan and Hiltz, 2006). According to previous studies, sharing learners' information by the developing visualization system enhances online learning participation (Barria et al., 2014; Jin, 2017). However, according to a study, identifying productive participation by discussion using quantitative variables, such as frequency of logging in and length of discussion scripts, is not sufficient (Richards, 2011). In addition, individual learning behaviors with respect to preparation of learning materials affect participation (Vonderwell and Zachariah, 2005), and are considered for designing a visualization system. However, factors of learning behaviors that have an influence on participation have not been clarified. Moreover, an effective online learning environment underlying appropriate CSCL design must be established (Stahl and Koschamann, 2006). In line with this, the Learning Analytics (LA) approach is applied to collect and analyze learning log data from Learning Management Systems (LMS). In this study, we investigate the relationship between learning behaviors and productive participation using LA.

2. LITERATURE REVIEW

2.1 Online Learning with Computer-Supported Collaborative Learning

Online learning is a widespread learning method uses advanced Information and Communication Technology and CSCL— a field of research and activities wherein people learn together by utilizing computers (Stahl and Koschamann, 2006; Xing et al., 2015; Yamada et al., 2015). With the benefits of CSCL, online discussion aims at hosting knowledge building exercises based on social interaction, including information exchange and information integration. Such discussions can be conducted at the time and place of the learners' choosing (Razmerita and Brun, 2010). In addition, learning logs data from LMSs can be collected and analyzed to facilitate CSCL. For example, Yin et al. (2017) examined the sequence of learning behaviors in "BookRoll" (Ogata et al, 2015; Ogata et al, 2017) —a digital-learning-material reader— and they found one sequence showing that deleting markers follows adding markers. Accordingly, Yin et al's (2017) study concluded that a teacher's affordance, including pointing out important content, should be provided by using "BookRoll." Teacher's affordance helps learners prepare their discussions in CSCL. Furthermore, CSCL with Community of Inquiry (CoI) provides an online learning environment where learners build knowledge socially and become critical thinkers (e.g., Garrison, 2011).

2.2 Online Learning Participation with Community of Inquiry

As mentioned above, online learning participation affects learning satisfaction and learning performance (Cobb, 2009; Hrastinski, 2009). However, online learning participation is inherently lower than that in classrooms or face-to-face (Swan et al., 2006). Online learning environment helps learners who fail to monitor themselves or other learners' progress hide themselves from others easily. There are several studies to enhance collaborative learning and participation in active discussions. Visualization of concept mapping in CSCL affected active collaborative learning from the view of social presence and learning (Yamada, 2010; Yamada et al, 2016). Barria et al. (2014) argued that providing learning information can enhance participation by visualization systems, and they provided learners with a Social Network Analysis (SNA) result to improve participation in online learning. In addition, Jin (2017) developed a visualization system by encouraging participation identified by the frequency of logging in, and the frequency or length of discussion scripts and proved that the system can enhance participation in online learning.

However, these studies focused on group level information, such as discussion scripts, neglecting individual level information related to preparing for online learning, such as learning behaviors including reading learning materials, highlighting important contents, etc. In addition, Richards (2011) indicated the necessity for qualitative variables to identify productive participation, such as opening threads, advising, agreement with others' ideas, etc. According to this, quantitative variables that emphasize these visualization systems (Barria et al., 2014; Jin, 2017) are insufficient. In the current study, we need to identify productive participation by qualitative variables.

The CoI framework is a powerful model for creating social consciousness and knowledge building exercises in online education in the absence of face-to-face interaction (Garrison et al., 1999; Yamada and Kitamura, 2011), and it has three components or presences: social presence, cognitive presence, and teaching presence.

Social presence is the ability of participants to project their personal characteristics into the community in order to present themselves to other participants as "real people" (Garrison et al., 1999). Cognitive presence indicates constructing and confirming the meaning-thought discourse (Garrison et al., 2001). Teacher presence is identified as "design and organization, facilitating discourse, and direct instruction" to support social and cognitive presence. In previous studies, social presence was identified as productive participation in online learning (Cobb, 2009; Garrision, 2011; Zou, 2020), and it was divided into individual, inter-individual, and granular social presence to show the senders' and receivers' cycle in CSCL design (Yamada and Kitamura, 2011). Through this analysis, learners' social presence, based on CSCL design, can be enhanced, and it can help them focus more on discussions (Gada and Yamada, 2013).

In this study, we identify productive participation based on social presence indicators, which is re-examined by Shea et al. (2010). Thus, we analyze the relationship between learning behaviors and participation by LA, in terms of the CSCL design.

2.3 Learning Analytics and Learning Behaviors

LA is a promising method for collecting and analyzing learners' learning behaviors and processes. Yin et al. (2015) suggested that data from a learning log can be useful in predicting a learner's learning style and performance. For example, learning behaviors, such as "NEXT," "PREV," "MEMO," and "MARKER" in a "BookRoll" can be recorded to prove which of these behaviors can predict learning performance and test scores using a machine learning algorithm. The result showed that "MARKER" can predict learning performance (Nian et al., 2019). In addition, some learning behaviors related to attendance or absence, submission of reports, and quiz scores can predict the learning score (Okubo et al., 2016). Learners who participated in out-of-class learning activities on "BookRoll" tended to gain higher scores than ones who did not (Shimada et al., 2015). Moreover, by analyzing the frequency and area marked in the "BookRoll," Xu et al. (2020) found that the area marked was more strongly correlated with learning performance than the frequency of using markers. The result indicates that a teacher should give hints to highlight important content in an appropriate area when using digital-learning-material readers like "BookRoll." These studies suggested that LA can examine the relationship between learning log data to design and facilitate a learning environment.

As mentioned above, learning behaviors affected productive participation identified by social presence in CSCL. By using learning analytics, we can identify factors of learning behaviors which affect participation and are associated with social presence. Regarding CSCL and visualization design, it is also significant to find out the indicators of social presence that can be predicted by learning behaviors. In this study, we set two research questions (RQs).

RQ1: Which factors of learning behaviors affect social presence?

RQ2: Which indicator of social presence can be predicted by learning behaviors?

3. METHODOLOGY

3.1 Participants and Class

In this study, an instructor teaching a seven-week online educational technology course in K university's 2020 spring semester was recruited to participate. The participants were 76 Frist-year university students from different faculties.

The time of each lecture was 90 minutes per week. The participants possessed fundamental skills, such as computer use, conversation, and self-learning. In the first lecture, the instructor introduced the purpose of the course and how to use "BookRoll" to prepare and review learning materials, which the instructor uploaded. For each lecture, the participants were asked to access the "TEAMS" conference software to take the online class. In each of the 2nd–7th lectures, the discussion about practical educational questions was conducted in groups using a chat system called "CQCHAT" (Yamada et al., 2016). Participants were randomly assigned into groups of four or five. After each lecture, participants were asked to submit a mini-paper about what they had learned and were unfamiliar with. One week after the last lecture, the participants prepared the final reports.

3.2 Data Collection

Data were collected from two aspects—learning behavior logs and discussion scripts. The first data collection was based on learning behavior logs, recorded from "BookRoll" where the participants read digital learning materials using some reading functions. In this study, 10 types of 32,626 learning behavior logs were collected as follows: Turning to the next page (NEXT); Turing to the previous page (PREV); adding red (ADD_MK_RED) or yellow markers (ADD_MK_YEL); deleting red (DEL_MR_RED) or yellow markers

(DEL_MR_YEL); adding (ADD_BK) or deleting a bookmark (DEL_BK); adding (ADD_MO) or deleting (DEL_MO) a memo.

The second data collection was based on discussion scripts. We collected 4,198 discussion scripts from the "CQCHAT" chat system during the 2nd–7th lectures. In the current study, such scripts were encoded into 3 categories of social presence including 18 indicators by using an automated text classification system (Yamada et al., 2015; Taniguchi et al., 2019) as follows: "affective" includes expressions of emotions (EMOTIONS), use of humor (HUMOR), self-disclosure (SELF-DISCLOSURE), use of unconventional expressions (PARALANGUAGE) and expressing value (VALUE); "open communication" includes continuing a thread (THREAD), quoting from other's messages (QUOTING), referring explicitly to other's messages (REFERRING), asking questions (QUESTION), complimenting or expressing appreciation (APPRECIATION), expressing agreement (AGREEMENT), expressing disagreement (DISAGREEMENT), and personal advice (ADVICE); "group cohesion" includes addressing or referring to participants by name (VOCATIVE), addressing the group as group (INCLUSIVE), serving a purely social function (PHATIC), social sharing (SOCIAL-SHARING), and course reflection (REFLECTION).

4. RESULT AND DISCUSSION

4.1 Descriptive Data of Learning Behaviors and Social Presence Indicators

The dataset was collected from two aspects—learning behavior logs and discussion scripts coded by social presence indicators. Table 1 shows the descriptive data (Average, Standard Deviations, Minimum and Maximum) of 10 types of learning behaviors, 6 social presence indicators (excluding 12 social indicators because of their empty values) and a sum of social presence scores called SOCIAL PRESENCE.

Table 1. Descriptive data of learning behaviors and social presence indicators during the course

Variable	Average	SD	Minimum	Maximum
NEXT	298.87	272.10	21	1696
PREV	88.33	87.46	3	462
ADD_MO	0.64	1.47	0	8
DEL_MO	0.05	0.22	0	1
ADD_BK	0.07	0.30	0	2
DEL_BK	0.05	0.28	0	2
ADD_MR_RED	27.74	33.56	0	147
ADD_MR_YEL	9.49	26.96	0	156
DEL_MR_RED	3.00	8.45	0	55
DEL_MR_YEL	1.05	4.59	0	28
PARALANGUAGE	2.74	3.78	0	16
VALUE	7.34	5.87	0	26
REFERENCE	0.29	0.78	0	4
QUESTION	1.32	2.28	0	8
AGREEMENT	1.05	1.83	0	10
PHATICS	2.71	1.92	0	8
SOCIAL PRESENCE	15.45	12.24	0	44

4.2 Effects of Learning Behaviors on Productive Participation

To answer RQ1, a stepwise multiple regression analysis was conducted to clarify which of the learning behaviors predict the productive participation identified by the 6 social presence indicators. First, we set the sum of social presence scores as the dependent variable; the independent variables ADD_MR_RED ($\beta = .304$, $p = .007$) accounted for 8.0% of the variance of social presence: $F(1, 74) = 7.560$, $p = .007$. The results are shown in Table 2. The regression results indicate that ADD_MR_RED can predict social presence identified by coding discussion scripts. As a learning strategy, the learning behavior of ADD_MR_RED means highlighting important content, which is related to one basic aspect of metacognition — knowledge monitoring ability (Van Horne et al., 2016). If learners cannot differentiate between what they know and do not know, they can hardly participate in metacognitive activities like discussions (Tobias and Everson, 2002). Additionally, in Wyre's (2007) study, metacognition influences critical thinking, which is associated with the discussion. For example, learners who are aware of important contents can focus on topics and assess others' speech during discussion.

Table 2. Results of the regression analysis predicting social presence with learning behaviors during the course

Variable	B	SE B	β	t
ADD_MR_RED	.111	.040	.304	2.750**

$R2 = .093$, Adjusted $R2 = .080$, $**p<0.01$, $*p < .05$

To answer RQ2, we set 6 social presence indicators as dependent variables and conducted stepwise multiple regression analysis, respectively. Regarding dependent variables PARALANGUAGE, VALUE, and QUESTION, independent variables DEL_MR_RED ($\beta = .259$, $p = .024$; $\beta = .236$, $p = .040$; $\beta = .304$, $p = .008$) accounted for 5.4% of the variance of PARALANGUAGE: $F(1, 74) = 5.312$, $p = .024$; 4.3% of the variance of VALUE: $F(1, 74) = 4.377$, $p = .040$; 8.0% of the variance of QUESTION: $F(1, 74) = 7.511$, $p = .008$, respectively (tables 3, 4, and 5). DEL_MR_RED, which means deleting important contents highlighted by learners, is also related to knowledge monitoring ability, as mentioned previously (Van Horne et al., 2016). According to the coding scheme for social presence, PARALANGUAGE indicates unconventional expression of emotions, such as repetitious punctuation and emoticons (Shea et al., 2010). In Hoy's (2018) study, metacognition is associated with emotions. For example, during a discussion, when a learner is empathetic in their speech, he tends to use some unconventional expressions of emotion due to the lack of facial expressions in a text-based environment. VALUE is defined by expressing personal values, beliefs, and attitudes (Shea et al., 2010); it is associated with DEL_MR_RED, one of the metacognitive strategies. Tyshchuk et al. (2018) demonstrated that VALUE which is one of elements of human behaviors was represented by perceived behavioral control. The findings suggested learners' beliefs are largely congruent with their behaviors; however, the mechanism between learners' beliefs and behaviors is not apparent (Kamiya, 2018). In addition, learners' attitudes and beliefs are important concepts in understanding an action while teaching others (Richardson, 1996). That is, the attitudes and beliefs affect the way of teaching other group members, such as preparation for the focus area. The results show that QUESTION, which means asking a question, is associated with DEL_MR_RED. Learners who highlighted the important contents generally deleted these before discussion. However, during a discussion, others' speech about these contents induce questions on reasons that these contents are important. In addition, asking a question—not consistent with one's thought—is associated with critical thinking (Sharan, 2010).

Table 3. Results of the regression analysis predicting the social presence indicator PARALANGUAGE with learning behaviors during the course

Variable	B	SE B	β	t
DEL_MR_RED	.116	.050	.259	2.305*

$R2 = .067$, Adjusted $R2 = .054$, $**p< .01$, $*p < .05$

Regarding the dependent variable REFERENCE, the independent variables DEL_MR_YEL ($\beta = .364$, $p = .001$) and DEL_MO ($\beta = .222$, $p = .040$) accounted for 15.7% of the variance of REFERENCE: $F(2, 73) = 7.965$, $p = .001$. DEL_MR_YEL and DEL_MO imply that they had comprehended what they did not previously know and REFERENCE indicates direct references to contents of others' post (Shea et al., 2010). Moreover, markers can help learners decide what they should focus on (Yue et al, 2015). During the discussion, other learners discuss topics which have been comprehended by one learner; this can make the learner interested in the topic and propose his ideas.

With respect to the dependent variable AGREEMENT, the independent variable DEL_MR_YEL ($\beta = .355$, $p = .002$) accounted for 12.6% of the variance of AGREEMENT: $F(1, 74) = 10.644$, $p = .002$. In a previous study, markers helped learners retrieve their knowledge (Yue et al, 2015). For example, learners can think of approaches or means through which the unfamiliar content can be comprehended. During the discussion, this content was proposed by learners because those who know about it had agreed to discussing it.

Table 4. Results of the regression analysis predicting the social presence indicator VALUE with learning behaviors during the course

Variable	B	SE B	β	t
DEL_MR_RED	.164	.078	.236	2.092*

$R2 = .056$, Adjusted $R2 = .043$, $^{**}p < .01$, $^{*}p < .05$

Table 5. Results of the regression analysis predicting the social presence indicator QUESTION with learning behaviors during the course

Variable	B	SE B	β	t
DEL_MR_RED	.082	.030	.304	2.741**

$R2 = .092$, Adjusted $R2 = .080$, $^{**}p < .01$, $^{*}p < .05$

Table 6. Results of the regression analysis predicting the social presence indicator REFERENCE with learning behaviors during the course

Variable	B	SE B	B	t
DEL_MR_YEL	.062	.002	.364	3.432**
DEL_MO	.770	.368	.222	2.092*

$R2 = .179$, Adjusted $R2 = .157$, $^{**}p < .01$, $^{*}p < .05$

Table 7. Results of the regression analysis predicting the social presence indicator AGREEMENT with learning behaviors during the course

Variable	B	SE B	β	t
DEL_MR_YEL	.141	.043	.355	3.262**

$R2 = .126$, Adjusted $R2 = .114$, $^{**}p < .01$, $^{*}p < .05$

In terms of PHATIC as a dependent variable, the independent variable NEXT ($\beta = .397$, $p = .000$) accounted for 15.8% of the variance of PHATIC: $F(1, 74) = 13.844$, $p = .000$. According to Shea et al.'s (2010) study, PHATIC is identified by greeting. NEXT means turning to the next page while preparing for discussion, which can motivate the learners to participate in the discussion and greet other learners. Conversely, according to Yin et al. (2015), NEXT may possibly mean that learners have just read their learning materials. However, in this study, we cannot prove whether the learners just learned their materials. Hence, in the future, we will analyze the correlation between learning behavior patterns and social presence.

Table 8. Results of the regression analysis predicting the social presence indicator PHATIC with learning behaviors during the course

Variable	B	SE B	β	t
NEXT	.003	.001	.397	3.721**

$R2 = .158$, Adjusted $R2 = .146$, $^{**}p < .01$, $^{*}p < .05$

5. CONCLUSION AND FUTURE WORK

In this paper, we analyzed the factors of learning behaviors in "BookRoll," predicting productive participation in discussion which are identified by social presence indicators in an online learning environment. The results show that highlighting important content, which help learners decide on the focus area, can promote participation in a discussion. In addition, deleting important or unfamiliar content related to a basic aspect of metacognitive learning — knowledge monitoring (Tobias and Everson, 2002) — promotes discussion scripts expressing emotion by using paralanguage; such discussion scripts are based on learners' beliefs. The learner behavior of deleting markers can also affect discussion scripts based on agreement to others' ideas, questions, and references to the content of other learners' posts. However, whether learning behaviors of turning to the next page is positive and why such behaviors are related to PHATIC needs further analysis.

In our future work, we will use these findings to improve our visualization system which aims to promote productive participation in online discussions. The visualization system's contents related to learning behaviors, like frequency of markers, memos, and bookmarks in "BookRoll," should be reconsidered. In line with Yamada et al. (2015) 's research, we will investigate which functions of system affect perceived and expressive social presence. Moreover, according to the advantages of highlighting learning contents (Yue et al, 2015), we can visualize some detailed information regarding markers, such as highlighting those contents which were deleted by learners.

ACKNOWLEDGEMENT

This study was supported by Japan Society for the Promotion of Science (JSPS) [grant number JP18K18657, JP19H01716, JP20H01727] and JST AIP [grant number JPMJCR19U1].

REFERENCES

Barría, J., Scheihing, E., & Parra, D. (2014). Visualizing student participation in a collaborative learning environment. In F. Cena, A. S. da Silva, & C. Trattner (Eds.), Hypertext HT (Doctoral Consortium/Late-breaking Results/Workshops), CEUR Workshop Proceedings (Vol. 1210). Santiago, Chile: CEUR-WS.org.

Cobb, S. C. (2009). Social presence and online learning: A Current view from a research perspective. Journal of Interactive Online Learning, 8(3), 241-254.

Garrison, D. R., Anderson, T., & Archer, W. (1999). Critical inquiry in a text-based environment: Computer conferencing in higher education. The Internet and Higher Education, 2(2-3), 87-105.

Garrison, D. R., Anderson, T., & Archer, W. (2001). Critical thinking, cognitive presence, and computer conferencing in distance education. American Journal of Distance Education, 15(1), 7-23.

Garrison, D. R. (2011). E-learning in the 21st century: A framework for research and practice. In Taylor & Francis, Routledge.

Goda, Y., & Yamada, M. (2013). Application of CoI to design CSCL for EFL online asynchronous discussion. In Akyol, Z. & Garrison D. R. (eds.), Educational communities of inquiry: Theoretical framework, research and practice (pp. 295-316). IGI Global, Hershey.

Hoy, R. C. (2018). Emotion and metacognitive monitoring: The role of Emotion in the development of learning beliefs. Individual, Family, and Community Education ETDs, New Mexico.

Hrastinski, S. (2009). A theory of online learning as online participation. Computers and Education, 52(1), 0-82.

Jin, S. H. (2017). Using visualization to motivate student participation in collaborative online learning environments. Educational Technology & Society, 20(2), 51-62.

Kamiya, N. (2018). Teacher and Student Beliefs. The TESOL Encyclopedia of English Language Teaching, 1-6.

Nian, M. W., Lee, Y. H., & Wu, J. Y. (2019). Using machine learning to explore the associations among e-reader operations and their predictive validity of learning performance. International Conference on Learning Analytics & Knowledge (LAK19) (pp. 1-6).

Ogata, H., Yin, C., Oi, M., Okubo, F., Shimada, A., Kojima, K., & Yamada, M. (2015, January). E-Book-based learning analytics in university education. International Conference on Computer in Education (ICCE 2015) (pp. 401-406).

Ogata, H., Taniguchi, Y., Suehiro, D., Shimada, A., Oi, M., Okubo, F., ... & Kojima, K. (2017). M2B system: A digital learning platform for traditional classrooms in university. Practitioner Track Proceedings, 155-162.

Okubo, F., Hirokawa, S., Terai, M., Shimada, A., Kentaro, K., Yamada, M., & Ogata, H. (2016, January). Learning activity features of high performance students. In CEUR Workshop Proceedings (Vol. 1601, pp. 28-33). CEUR-WS.

Razmerita, L., & Brun, A. (2010, December). Assigning Students in Groups: Self-formed Groups versus Automatically-formed Groups. In 7ème Colloque Technologies de l'Information et de la Communication pour l'Enseignement-TICE.

Richards, G. (2011). Measuring engagement: Learning analytics in online learning. electronic Kazan, 2011.

Richardson, V. (1996). The role of attitudes and beliefs in learning to teach. Handbook of research on teacher education, 2(102-119).

Saltz, J. S., Hiltz, S. R., & Turoff, M. (2004, November). Student social graphs: visualizing a student's online social network. In Proceedings of the 2004 ACM conference on Computer supported cooperative work (pp. 596-599).

Sharan, Y. (2010) Cooperative learning for academic and social gains: Valued pedagogy, problematic practice. European Journal of Education, 45(2), 300–13.

Shea, P., Hayes, S., Vickers, J., Gozza-Cohen, M., Uzuner, S., Mehta, R., ... & Rangan, P. (2010). A re-examination of the community of inquiry framework: Social network and content analysis. The Internet and Higher Education, 13 (1-2), 10-21.

Shimada, A., Okubo, F., Yin, C., Kojima, K., Yamada, M., & Ogata, H. (2015, July). Informal learning behavior analysis using action logs and slide features in e-textbooks. In 2015 IEEE 15th International Conference on Advanced Learning Technologies (pp. 116-117). IEEE.

Stahl, G., & Koschmann, T. S. (2006). Computer-supported collaborative learning: An historical perspective. In R. K. Sawyer (ed.), Cambridge Handbook of the Learning Sciences, p. 409Á426. Cambridge University Press, Cambridge.

Swan, K., Shen, J., & Hiltz, S. R. (2006). Assessment and collaboration in online learning. Journal of Asynchronous Learning Networks, 10(1), 45-62.

Taniguchi, Y., Konomi, S., & Goda, Y. (2019, January). Examining language-agnostic methods of automatic coding in the community of inquiry framework. In 16th International Conference on Cognition and Exploratory Learning in Digital Age, CELDA 2019 (pp. 19-26). IADIS Press.

Tobias, S., & Everson, H. T. (2002). Knowing What You Know and What You Don't: Further Research on Metacognitive Knowledge Monitoring. Research Report No. 2002-3. College Entrance Examination Board.

Tyshchuk, Y., & Wallace, W. A. (2018). Modeling human behavior on social media in response to significant events. IEEE Transactions on Computational Social Systems, 5(2), 444-457.

Van Horne, S., Russell, J. E., & Schuh, K. L. (2016). The adoption of mark-up tools in an interactive e-textbook reader. Educational Technology Research and Development, 64(3), 407-433.

Vonderwell, S., & Zachariah, S. (2005). Factors that influence participation in online learning. Journal of Research on Technology in Education, 38(2), 213-230.

Wyre, S. H. (2007). Critical thinking, metacognition, and epistemological beliefs (Doctoral dissertation, University of Phoenix).

Xing, W., Wadholm, R., Petakovic, E., & Goggins, S. (2015). Group learning assessment: Developing a theory-informed analytics. Journal of Educational Technology & Society, 18(2), 110-128

Xu,Y., Geng, X., Chen, L., Hamada, S., Taniguchi, Y., Ogata, H., Shimada, A., and Yamada, M. (2020). Can the Area marked in eBook Readers Specify Learning Performance? Companion Proceedings 10th International Conference on Learning Analytics & Knowledge (LAK20), pp.638-648.

Yamada, M. (2010). Development and Evaluation of CSCL Based on Social Presence. In E-Learn: World Conference on E-Learning in Corporate, Government, Healthcare, and Higher Education (pp. 2304-2309). Association for the Advancement of Computing in Education (AACE).

Yamada, M., & Kitamura, S. (2011). The role of social presence in interactive learning with social software. In Social media tools and platforms in learning environments (pp. 325-335). Springer, Berlin, Heidelberg.

Yamada, M., Goda, Y., Matsukawa, H., Hata, K., & Yasunami, S. (2015). A computer-supported collaborative learning design for quality interaction. IEEE MultiMedia, 23(1), 48-59.

Yamada, M., Kaneko, K. and Goda, Y. (2016). Social Presence Visualizer: Development of the Collaboration Facilitation Module on CSCL. In T. Yoshino, G-D. Chen, G. Zurita, T. Yuizono, T. Inoue, & N. Baloian (Eds.) Collaboration Technologies and Social Computing – Lecture Note of Communications in Computer and Information Science, 647, 174-189.

Yin, C., Okubo, F., Shimada, A., Oi, M., Hirokawa, S., Yamada, M., Kojima, K., & Ogata, H. (2015). Analyzing the features of learning behaviors of students using e-books. In Proceedings of the International Conference on Computers in Education (pp. 617-626).

Yin, C., Uosaki, N., Chu, H. C., Hwang, G. J., Liu, G. Z., Hwang, J. J., Hatono, I., Kumamoto, E., & Tabata, Y. (2017, January). Learning behavioral pattern analysis based on students' logs in reading digital books. Proceedings of the 25th International Conference on Computers in Education (pp. 549-557).

Yue, C. L., Storm, B. C., Kornell, N., & Bjork, E. L. (2015). Highlighting and its relation to distributed study and students' metacognitive beliefs. Educational Psychology Review, 27(1), 69-78.

Zou, W., Hu, X., Pan, Z., Li, C., Cai, Y., & Liu, M. (2020). Exploring the relationship between social presence and learners' prestige in MOOC discussion forums using automated content analysis and social network analysis. Computers in Human Behavior, 106582.

STUDENTS ENGAGING IN MATHEMATICAL PROBLEM-SOLVING THROUGH COMPUTATIONAL THINKING AND-PROGRAMMING ACTIVITIES: A SYNTHESIS OF TWO OPPOSITE EXPERIENCES

Said Hadjerrouit and Nils Kristian Hansen
University of Agder, Institute of Mathematical Sciences, Kristiansand, Norway

ABSTRACT

This paper aims at exploring students' experiences when engaging in mathematical problem-solving through computational thinking and programming by a combination of theoretically derived insights and task-based activities. The main method used is a semi-structured interview with two undergraduate students who were presented with a mathematical task to solve while responding to questions about the mathematical solving process. The results reveal two students' opposite experiences. While one struggled to get acquainted with the task and the associated programming activity, the other was able to handle and solve the task using computational thinking (CT) and programming skills very easily. Conclusions are drawn from the students' experiences to promote mathematical problem-solving through computational thinking and programming in mathematics education at the undergraduate level.

KEYWORDS

Algorithm, Computational Thinking (CT), Matlab, Mathematical Problem-Solving, Programming, Usability

1. INTRODUCTION

In parallel to emerging programming languages (Wing, 2014), students in mathematics study programmes are expected to acquire basic algorithmic and computational thinking skills. These are considered important competencies for future work in society and should be acquired by all university mathematics students who could improve their mathematical problem-solving skills by benefitting from computational thinking and the power of programming languages (Shute, Sun, & Asbell-Clarke, 2017). It is assumed that with easier access to digital technology in universities, the integration of programming activities and computational thinking into teaching could be easier than in school mathematics.

This study explores students' experiences when engaging in mathematical problem-solving through CT and the programming language MatLab. The article is structured as follows. Firstly, the theoretical framing is outlined. Secondly, the context of the study, research question, methods, and the mathematical task given to the students are described. Then, the results are reported and analysed. This is followed by a discussion of the results. Finally, some remarks and future work conclude the article.

2. THEORETICAL FRAMING

Programming has had a relatively long history in mathematics education. Today, CT by means programming languages is becoming an important learning goal of mathematics education from primary to university level. It is therefore important to reflect on the conditions of integrating CT and programming skills into mathematics education and the importance of these skills in the work of today's mathematician (Broley, Caron, & Saint-Aubin, 2018). Given this introductory statement, the theoretical framing is outlined in three sections as follows.

2.1 Computational Thinking (CT): Literature Review

Several definitions of the term "CT" exist in the research literature. Wing (2014) describes CT as "the thought processes involved in formulating a problem and expressing its solution(s) in such a way that a computer—human or machine—can effectively carry out". Ejsing-Duun (2015) describes CT in similar words. It is the ability to work with algorithms understood as systematic and structured descriptions of problem-solving and construction strategies. Filho and Mercat (2018) define algorithmic thinking as the process of solving a problem step-by-step in an effective, non-ambiguous and organised way that can be translated into instructions to solve problems of the same type by an individual or a computer.

Wing (2008, 2014) points out that the main commonality between CT and mathematical thinking is problem-solving and structured construction process step-by-step. CT is also quite similar with engineering thinking in terms of design and evaluation of processes (Pérez-Marína et al., 2018). Moreover, CT and programming constructs such as variables and flow statements (if-then-else, for, and repeat) are closely connected to arithmetical and mathematical thinking (Lie, Hauge, & Meaney, 2017). This close connection between mathematics and CT might provide opportunities for mathematical problem-solving. In contrast, programming skills alone without the mediation of CT are important but may not be sufficient to improve mathematical problem solving. Thus, CT skills are critical for building efficient algorithms for mathematical problem-solving rather than trial-and-error and getting the program to run (Topallia & Cagiltay, 2018). In other words, CT requires students to be engaged in a continuously changing problem-solving process by designing effective algorithms that can be translated into efficient computer programs.

2.2 Mathematical Problem-Solving through CT and Programming

Drawing on the research literature (Kotsopoulos, et al., 2019; Lee, & Malyn-Smith, 2019; Romero, Lepage, & Lille, 2017; Santos et al., 2020; Weintrop, et al. 2016), the paper proposes a three-step approach to connect mathematical problem-solving to CT by means of programming languages. *Firstly*, students should have a good mathematical background to benefit from CT and programming languages. More specifically, they should be able to benefit from their knowledge to make sense of the task and have a mathematical understanding of it before formulating an algorithm and starting programming. *Secondly*, CT, in turn, should enable students to analyse and decompose the mathematical task and design an algorithm and how to perform it step-by-step before programming it. Engaging students in mathematical problem-solving through CT may enable a better understanding of mathematics beyond textbook mathematics and paper-pencil techniques. *Thirdly*, students should be able to translate the mathematical solution with the associated algorithm to the constructs of the programming language. This presupposes that the language is usable. Performing programming activities in mathematics education should provide opportunities to help students do mathematics and gain new knowledge that is otherwise difficult to acquire without experimenting with the program and thinking algorithmically. However, this might be difficult to achieve unless the mathematical tasks are well-designed, mathematically sound, correct, and faithful to the underlying mathematical properties.

2.3 Programming and Usability Issues

When referring to the notions of usability or usable technologies in mathematics education, the research literature focuses on educational software such as GeoGebra, CAS, and SimReal (Artigue et al., 2009; Bokhove & Drijvers, 2010; Hadjerrouit, 2019). However, programming languages differ from educational software and how they are used to implement mathematical problems where one can graph a function or compute an integral simply by entering the function and pressing a button in GeoGebra, for example. Hence, evaluating the usability of programming languages might not be as straightforward as it may seem. Still, three usability criteria can be applied to programming languages with slight modifications. Firstly, the extent to which the user interface of the programming language is easy to use and understand. Secondly, a usable programming language should allow a quick familiarisation with it in terms of learning the language constructs, such as variables, if-then-else, for and while loop, or repeat. The third criterion is the quality of feedback provided by the program in terms of semantic and syntax error messages, and whether these are useful to foster a successful implementation of the algorithmic solution through testing, correcting and improving the program.

A purely technical approach to programming will however not succeed unless students' engagement with mathematical problem-solving through CT is placed in a pedagogical context. A pedagogy-based approach to programming should enable a good degree of autonomy so that the students can work on their own and have a sense of control over their mathematical learning. Clearly, students should be able to acquire knowledge without being completely dependent on the teacher. Moreover, CT and programming languages should be a motivational factor for learning mathematics. In other words, CT should support students' engagement with problem-solving by means of intrinsically motivating tasks that are tied to the students' mathematical activities. Finally, interacting with a programming language when engaging in mathematical problem-solving should be supported by computational thinking skills through a structured construction of effective algorithms.

3. THE STUDY

3.1 Context of the Study and Research Question

This work is a single case study conducted in the context of a first-year undergraduate course on programming with applications in mathematics. The participants were two students from one class of eight students enrolled in the course in 2019. The students had varied knowledge background in mathematics, but no experience with the programming language being used in this course, that is MatLab. The course introduced the basic constructs of MatLab, that is variables, flow statements (loops, if-then-else, for, and repeat). These were then used to solve mathematical problems. The research question addressed in this paper is: *How do students engage in mathematical problem-solving through computational thinking and programming activities?*

3.2 Mathematical Task

The mathematical task presented to the students in this research is: The length of a curve may be approximated using Pythagoras' theorem by positioning a triangle adjacent to the curve (Figure 1, left, below). The length of the green line between A and B may then be approximated as $\sqrt{x^2 + y^2}$. The task is to write a MatLab function approximating the curve length of $f(x) = 2^x$ between two given x-values (Figure 1, right, below).

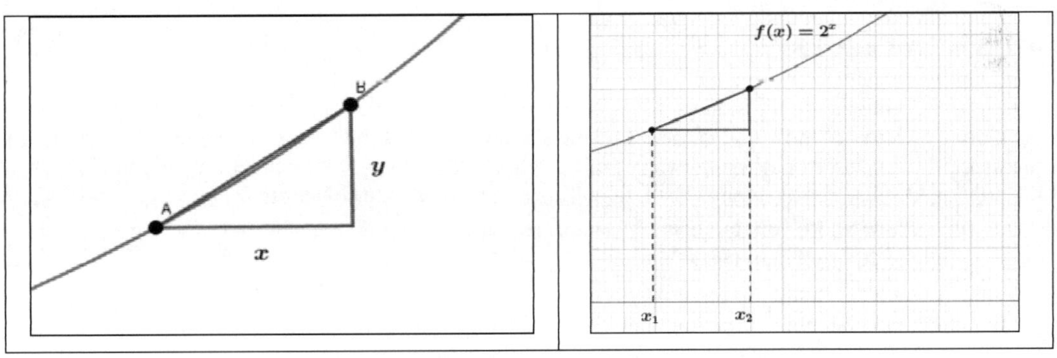

Figure 1. The mathematical task

The students were presented with the following skeleton of a MatLab function: function length=length estimate (x1, x2), length=? The students were then asked to enter the formula, based on x1 and x2, and replace the question mark. The MatLab function sqrt(x) can be used to calculate the square root √x.

3.3 Data Collection and Analysis Method

The main data collection method used is a task-based semi-structured interview of two students with different knowledge background in mathematics. The students were presented with a mathematical task to solve, while responding to questions in a dialogue with the teacher on the mathematical solving process, mathematical understanding, the role of CT and algorithms, possibilities and limitations of MatLab, feedback and interactions with MatLab, teacher help, and pedagogical considerations. Open-ended questions were also used to gain a deeper understanding of some important issues.

In terms of data analysis of the results, the three-step approach presented in the theoretical framing (section 2.2) served as a reference for analysing the students' problem-solving process, that is:

a) Understand the mathematical problem
b) Analyse and decompose the mathematical task, and then design an algorithm and how to perform it step-by-step before programming it
c) Finally, translate the algorithmic solution to the programming language code.

More specifically, the students were expected to solve the mathematical task presented to them in section 3.2. in three steps as follows:

a) Understand the task, that is, using Pythagoras' theorem to calculate the hypotenuse.
b) Formulate an algorithm, that is find the lengths of the triangle hypothenuse using the function $f(x) = 2^x$ and relate it to x_1 and x_2
c) Translate the algorithm into MatLab code, corresponding to: function length = lengthEstimate (x1, x2); length = sqrt((x2-x1)^2 + (2^x2 - 2^x1)^2)

The analysis of the results seeks indications of students' problem-solving through CT and MatLab according to this three-step approach. This is not the same as analysing and coding in the sense of grounded theory without theoretical background. Rather, it is an analytical tool that tries to address the research question about how students engage in mathematical problem-solving through computational thinking and programming activities drawing on students' interviews when solving the mathematical task. The interviews were transcribed and analysed according to an inductive strategy based on the interplay between the three-step approach to problem-solving and the empirical data collected using semi-structured interviews (Patton, 2002).

4. RESULTS

The results describe how the participating students engage in mathematical problem-solving through CT and MatLab. The students were given the task described in section 3.2, and paper and a pen to use. The abbreviations S1 and S2 are used for the students, and T for the teacher.

4.1 Student 1 (S1)

It took some time before the student made sense of the mathematical task. The teacher asked the student to develop a skeleton of the solution. The student did, and started thinking about the length, but suggested an incorrect solution, based only on the values of x1 and x2. After some calculation trials, the student noticed that the attempted solution was wrong. Then, the teacher encouraged the student to think computationally.

T: But before you start using MatLab, are you going to make an algorithm (…), for problem-solving before you start using MatLab?

S1: I just have to sit and think about it.

But still, the student continued guessing and calculating without thinking computationally. After an attempt to make sense of the task and calculate the length of the curve connecting it to the hypotenuse with a trial and error approach, the teacher provided a hint.

T: Now you say you know the hypotenuse and calculate y. But the hypotenuse is the unknown parameter here, the one you are supposed to calculate.

S1: Yes.

T: So now you have turned the problem around (…). It is just that that thought was a little backwards, maybe.

S1: Yes, it is quite possible.

Following this short dialogue, the student started using MatLab without developing an algorithmic solution or a clear strategy for solving the problem. The teacher then engaged in a discussion to guide the student step by step towards an algorithmic solution. Then, the teacher tested the function *"on zero and one and then I got 1.4"*. Likewise, the student tested the formula and found 1.4142. The dialogue continued as follows:

T: (…). Do you have anything to say about (…) like that afterwards?

S1: No, I am, I was a little bit in doubt about how to (…) First, it was the task you asked about (…) and then it was (…) and then I thought (…) f(x) is the function in x2 would be that point minus the function of that point (…) that it would be the length. But that is where I was wrong, I felt (…) Because you meant it to be here (…) and I understand that now.

T: Yes, that is the point, (…). That is why you have to use Pythagoras to find (…). Did you think (…) There was a hint here, wasn't there? Square root?

S1: Yes, yes, yes, the square root (…). I knew it was probably wrong, but I just didn't quite understand what it was.

T: Well, because there was a clue there that you couldn't use, wasn't there. Then you realise that there is something (…)

This excerpt shows there is little indication that the student was following a clear problem solving strategy, which confirms that making sense of the problem and having a mathematical understanding of the task is of crucial importance before formulating an algorithm and starting programming, which is not the case in this excerpt. A few minutes later, the teacher asked the student if there is a tendency to favour pen and paper to solve the task algorithmically before starting using MatLab since developing an algorithm does not automatically require using the computer.

S1: If I have it in my head, sometimes I start with MatLab, and then I write some sort of sketch before going through it carefully. If I am not sure, I will start with paper.

T: Maybe the task was not quite clear?

S1: Yes, so far, but I had probably forgotten some of the principles there.

T: Principles related to MatLab or to the mathematical assignment?

S1: To the mathematical problem.

Again, the interview shows that the problem-solving process requires a good understanding of the mathematical task and computational thinking skills before programming it. Here again, the teacher reminded the student about the importance of algorithmic thinking before translating the task into MatLab code.

T: Now, the point of the assignment is that you should be able to translate the mathematical task into code in MatLab. That is really the point here.

S1: Yes, I felt that when I understood the mathematical thing, I had no trouble putting it into MatLab. It was simply that I had (…) forgotten a bit the length thing there. That f of that minus f of that is delta y, then.

4.2 Student 2 (S2)

After a short dialogue with the student on the menu structure of MatLab, which does not seem to be much appealing, the student started studying the assignment. The following excerpt shows making sense of the task to be solved is of crucial importance before formulating a solution by means of computational thinking. The teacher highlighted that these are the kind of tasks that have started to appear on the exams. So, it is very useful. After this short introduction, the student read the mathematical task described in section 3.2. Then, the teacher asked how to handle it.

T: Just, I have to ask you … How will you proceed to attack such a task? Will you go straight for the keyboard, and then …? You see, you have got a small skeleton here; will you go straight for the keyboard and start programming it, or will you …

S2: No, first I really try to think it through carefully, what the task is really about, here. And then I tend to make a draft as a first thing. (…) That I write down what the assignment actually asks for, and then that I make myself, in a way, a kind of design, then.

T: A design, yes.

S2: And what is it that the program is supposed to be able to calculate here, then? And then, when it is plainly clear to me, I would have gone into more depth on … on … what is somehow … how I am supposed to describe the code here. And here, in this case, there is a function, which is an estimate of length. And then I had to go in and have a look at the length. And then put it in a formula … Oh, I do not know if you want me to do the task itself, kind of.

T: (…) you do not have to spend so much (…) what we are a looking for? that is the thought process. You say you create a draft, do you write code then, or draw boxes, or?

S2: Sometimes I have drawn one of these … in a way a line, then. And then I have drawn a box. Or, if it involves if-statements, then I have drawn something a bit like this. (Shows sketch like figure 2, left, below.) If you look here. And then I have sort of a condition inside here, and then I have, if there is an *if* at the conditions, then I put this there (Shows sketch like figure 2, right, below, pointing to the new line.)

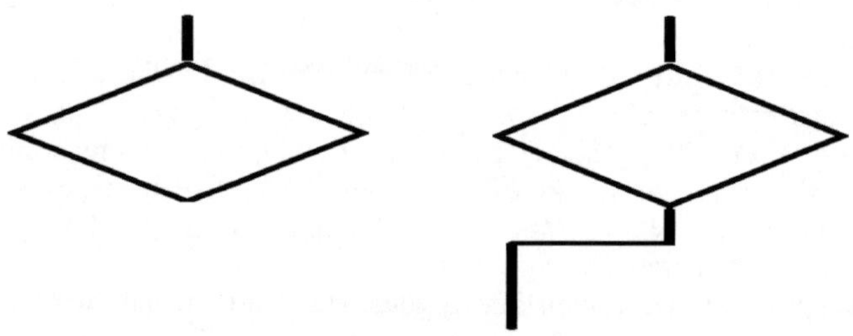

Figure 2. Student's sketches

T: That is what we call a flow chart.

S2: Flow chart, simply.

T: Yes, that is probably something you have learned once, maybe.

S2: Yes, I learned it in this study.

This excerpt shows that the student was aware of the importance of designing an algorithmic solution with a flow chart before starting programming the task, in stark contrast to student 1 who struggled to understand the mathematical task and formulating an algorithm. There are indications that the student understood how to proceed. Words like "design", "draft", "box", and "assignment" point to algorithmic and computational thinking; and "if-conditions" and the associated sketch to programming code.

T: Yes, okay, yes. Very good, for it has turned out that people are very slow to adopt … They often go straight on to the programming. And that works fine when the task is easy, but when it gets a little more complex, then you need to split things up a bit.

S2: Yes, I had not thought about it until I, in a way, read it in this study, but after that I've started to … then I spend a bit of time in the process before I start typing the formula. If I have already started typing the formula, and then want to change it afterwards, then I have discovered that I do a lot of mistakes, then. So now I have tried to spend plenty of time on the preparatory work, so that I am one hundred per cent sure of what it is my function or program is supposed to do. And now I know it is a function I am supposed to write, and what is it … what is it I am actually supposed to calculate here?

Clearly, the second participant was not only able to spend time on some preparatory work, but the student was also reflecting on the function that is supposed to solve the task. Moreover, the student was aware of possible programming mistakes that could be made, and the time needed to correct them iteratively, and how the program will handle the errors and provide feedback to the student.

T: Yes, but that is really good. That is something we would love for more to be better at, so we should probably have stressed it more when teaching. You mention it yourself a bit, the algorithmic thinking. And that is a bit what we are looking for then, considering that algorithmic thinking is to become part of the subject of mathematics in school. So that is what we are trying to fish for, how are these students thinking?

S2: It is the kind of like you analyse this pretty carefully, and then you divide it, and then … in a way … I do not know, I work kind of structured, then, with one piece at a time.

T: Yes, but that is really good. It is a concept one has in programming, you make a design, then you divide it into pieces, where you can look at one piece at a time.

This way of computational thinking was confirmed by the teacher who pointed out to algorithmic thinking and structured design step-by-step, and decomposition of the task in small pieces, (…). Then, the student continued explaining the way of thinking algorithmically and computationally, including the programming process and the testing of the program.

S2: And then after I have made … made one, then … if it … now this task was a little bit different, then … but … but if I have made a program … after I have written the entire program code … If it typically is with for-loops and everything, then I always run through the program in my head. And write down that okay, now, *n* is equal to 1, What happens to that and that value. In that way I always get to put it to the test, and then I detect possible errors, then.

This last excerpt shows that the student is knowledgeable in some constructs of the programming language being used, the way the program code can be run and tested, and what happens if the program contains errors.

5. DISCUSSION AND CONCLUSIONS

The research question addressed in the paper is: *How do students engage in mathematical problem-solving through computational thinking and programming activities?* As one can see from the results, the participating students had two opposite experiences. They engaged differently in the mathematical problem-solving process. While the first student felt challenged by the mathematical task and the way to handle it, the second student made good use of CT, algorithms, and MatLab to solve the task.

Concerning student 1 (S1), the first challenge is the lack of mathematical knowledge, which hindered the student in making sense of the task, having a mathematical understanding of it, and then developing a problem-solving strategy that can be translated into an algorithm. According to the approach presented section 2.2, it seems that students should have a good mathematical understanding of the task as a basis for further development and use of computational and algorithmic thinking skills. The second challenge is related to the implementation of the algorithm using the constructs of the programming language. As the results show, student 1 struggled to use MatLab because of lack of background knowledge in the programming language. The student was therefore unable to relate it to the mathematical task using an algorithm. Clearly, the problem-solving process in three steps as described in the theoretical framing was challenging for the student.

Student 2 (S2) was more prepared to make use of CT than Student 1. Student 2 had sufficient mathematical knowledge and a good understanding of the task to make sense of it, and then design a structured problem-solving solution that can be translated into an algorithm. The excerpts show that the student had a good understanding of the task as a basis for further algorithmic development. Moreover, in contrast to student 1, student 2 had good background knowledge in the programming language MatLab and was able to relate it to the mathematical task using an algorithm. As a result, this student demonstrates that a combination of background knowledge in mathematics, algorithmic thinking, familiarity with the programming language are a pre-requisite to apply CT skills for mathematical problem solving.

These opposite students' experiences show that the minimum requirement for applying CT is a good combination of background knowledge in mathematics, algorithmic thinking skills, and familiarity with the programming language in question. These requirements should become integral parts of university mathematics education. To ensure success in integrating these elements, the pedagogical setting around mathematics courses should be well designed in terms of varied and intrinsically motivating tasks, student autonomy and differentiation. Moreover, as this study shows, the role of the teacher is still important to assist students in formulating solutions. Clearly, student autonomy cannot be fully expected for novices without good knowledge background in mathematics and familiarities with CT and programming. Hence, mathematical problem-solving should consider pedagogical modalities when using CT and programming practices.

Summarising, the study is limited to be generalised to all participating students. Hence, more elaborated and in-depth analysis with mixed methods and more participants is required to ensure more reliability and validity. Although the participating students are not representative for the average student enrolled in the course, two preliminary conclusions can be drawn from the study. Firstly, the connections between mathematics, CT, and programming languages are quite complex, and need to be clearly articulated and related in pedagogical settings. Secondly, engaging in mathematical problem-solving through CT and programming requires good background in mathematics, algorithmic thinking, and familiarity with the programming language constructs.

Future work will include all course participants and a mix of quantitative and qualitative methods to ensure more validity and reliability and assess the role and impact of CT in mathematics education in more depth.

REFERENCES

Artigue, M. et al. (2009). Connecting and integrating theoretical frames: The TELMA contribution. *International Journal of Computers for Mathematical Learning 14*, pp. 217-240.

Broley, L., Caron, F., & Saint-Aubin, Y. (2018). Levels of programming in mathematical research and university mathematics education. *Int. J. Res. Undergrad. Math. Ed. 4*, pp. 38–55.

Bokhove, K., & Drijvers, P. (2010). Digital tools for algebra education: Criteria and evaluation. *International Journal of Mathematics Learning 15*, pp. 45-62.

Filho, P., & Mercat, C. (2018). Teaching computational thinking in classroom environments: A case for unplugged scenario. *Conference: Re(s)sources 2018 - Understanding Teachers' Work Through Their Interactions with Resources for Teaching*. Lyon, France.

Hadjerrouit, S., & Gautestad, H.H. (2019). Evaluating the usefulness of the visualization tool SimReal+ for learning mathematics: A case study at the undergraduate level. In: D. Sampson et al. (Eds.), *Learning Technologies for Transforming Large-Scale Teaching, Learning, and Assessment*, (pp. 71-89). Springer Nature Switzerland AG.

Kotsopoulos, D., Floyd, L., Nelson, V., Makosz, S., & Senger, N. (2019). Mathematical or computational thinking? An early years perspective. In K. M. Robinson, H. P. Osana, and D. Kotsopoulos (Eds.). *Mathematical learning and cognition in infancy and early childhood: Integrating interdisciplinary research into practice*. New York: Springer.

Misfeldt, M., & Ejsing-Duun, S. (2015). Learning mathematics through programming: An instrumental approach to potentials and pitfalls. In K. Krainer, & N. Vondrová (Eds.). *Proceedings of CERME9* (pp. 2524-2530). Prague, Czech Republic.

Lee, I., & Malyn-Smith, J. (2019). Computational thinking integration patterns along the framework defining computational thinking from a disciplinary perspective. *Journal of Science Education and Technology.* https://doi.org/10.1007/s10956-019-09802-x

Lie, J., Hauge, I. O., & Meaney, T. J. (2017). Computer programming in the lower secondary classroom: Mathematics learning. *Italian Journal of Educational Technology*, *25*(2), pp. 27-35.

Pérez-Marín, D., Hijón-Neira, R., Bacelo, A., & Pizarro, C. (2018). Can computational thinking be improved by using a methodology based on metaphors and scratch to teach computer programming to children? *Computers in Human Behavior,* pp. 1-10.

Patton, M. Q. (2002). *Qualitative research & evaluation methods*. London: Sage Publications

Romero, M., Lepage, A., & Lille, B. (2017). Computational thinking development through creative programming in higher Education. *International Journal of Educational Technology in Higher Education 14*, pp. 1-15.

Topalli, D., & Cagiltay, N. E. (2018). Improving programming skills in engineering education through problem-based game projects with Scratch. *Computers & Education*, *120*, pp. 64-74.

Santos, S. C, Tedesco, P. A., Borba, M., & Brito, M. (2020). Innovative approaches in teaching programming: A systematic literature review. *Proceedings of the 12th International Conference on Computer Supported Education* (CSEDU 2020), Volume 1, pp. 205-2014. Prague, Czech Republic.

Shute, V.J., Sun, C., & Asbell-Clarke, J. (2017). Demystifying computational thinking. *Educational Research Review*, pp. 1-10.

Weintrop, D. et al. (2016). Defining computational thinking for mathematics and science classrooms. *J Sci Educ Technol 25*, pp. 127–147.

Wing, J. M. (2008). Computational thinking and thinking about computing. *Philosophical Transactions of the Royal Society A*, *366*(1881), pp. 3717-3725.

Wing, J. M. (2014). Computational thinking benefits society. *Social Issues in Computing,* 40th Anniversary Blog, University of Toronto. Retrieved from http://socialissues.cs.toronto.edu/index.html%3Fp=279.html

JIGSAW IN THE TIME OF PANDEMIC

Maria-Cristina Marinescu[1] and Jose L. Marzo[2]
[1]CASE, Barcelona Supercomputing Center, Jordi Girona, 29, 08034, Barcelona, Spain
[2]Institute of Informatics and Applications, University of Girona, Plaça Sant Domenec 3, 17004, Girona, Spain

ABSTRACT

Based on our positive, but limited experience with Jigsaw at the university level, half a year ago we initiated a more extensive experiment with a larger sample of students, and incorporating changes that relate back to some negative comments we have received during the previous course. Jigsaw is a collaborative inquiry-based learning technique that works by dividing the learning material into different tasks and the class into different groups. What set out to be a controlled experiment in increasing motivation and participation through collaboration, turned into a much more complex scenario due to the arrival of the Covid-19 pandemic, which gave us some interesting results to report. We have seen more positive results this year than the last: the number of students that felt that Jigsaw requires more effort than traditional methods has fallen, they consistently thought that Jigsaw improved teamwork, and they felt they have learned more from their expert peers as the experiment advanced. Some of the results may be due to the confinement forcing people stay indoors, with no social outings and fewer distractions – so more time to study. Another factor that may be relevant are the implicit expectations that were set by the confinement about distance learning and the need to cooperate.

KEYWORDS

Autonomous Learning, Collaborative Learning, Active Learning, Jigsaw, Blended Learning

1. INTRODUCTION

During the 2018-2019 academic year we adapted the Jigsaw methodology to the structure of the *Cloud computing and distributed systems for videogames* course, offered during the 3rd year of the design and development of videogames degree at the University of Girona, Spain. This was motivated by a desire to increase the students' interest and participation in class and complement the purely technical skills with skills that relate to decision making, analysis, and teamwork. To assess the results not only quantitatively, we asked the students to take a series of surveys during the course of the Jigsaw experiment. The results were encouraging, and there were several comments that deserved closer attention. Given that this class only consisted in 12 students, we decided to repeat the experiment with a larger class, while applying only a few, rather small, modifications. Then the one-in-a-decade change came unexpectedly – Covid-19 – and what was supposed to be a controlled case study became an unprecedented one, with interesting, but hard to prove correlations.

The *Cloud computing and distributed systems for videogames* course is a rather technical course, of the type that usually relies on incremental building of knowledge, but it does lend itself to learning various topics independently. One of the concerns we had in the previous year with the Jigsaw method was that, after a certain age, students are already settled into their roles as leaders or followers which, in turn, could make it harder for them to work in collaborative environments that lack hierarchy. Nevertheless, some of the comments did show that sometimes students prefer to work with colleagues of their own choosing – and we assume that this is because of a known group dynamics where people easily assume their roles.

Just like last year, we decided to apply the Jigsaw method to only part of the course contents to limit the possibility of negative outcomes for those students that don't adapt to this approach. We applied the same approach to the same course and contents, but with several new aspects: the number of students increased from 12 to more than 30, and we gave the students some initial guidance before starting the Jigsaw activity, in the form of a 10 minutes introduction to the Optical Networking topic. Lastly and drastically different from last year, due to the COVID-19 pandemic, an initial activity in the classroom during the first week was followed by activities at distance using videoconference tools, in a blended fashion. The impact of these aspects provided new knowledge, interesting enough to be shared.

2. BACKGROUND

The purpose of learning is to acquire knowledge and problem-solving skills and peak the students´ curiosity to continue this process. Every student has a different personality, strengths and weaknesses, interests, and background. They therefore learn at different rates and with different incentives but being engaged is fundamental to learn and retain. More often than not, comparing notes and ideas with colleagues is positive, and cementing positive behavioral changes – such as teamwork – is important.

2.1 Collaborative Learning

Collaborative learning techniques are based on student cooperation to achieve a common goal and come with the challenge of explaining concepts to fellow groupmates. Due to this, students develop their communication, argumentation, and debating skills, rather than not only being guided by their teachers. The focus is shifted to working in groups, where instructors are facilitators rather than dispatchers of knowledge (Zarei, 2016). Cooperative learning also considers that the students can learn better by doing and by working in groups, than by receiving the information from the presentations of the instructor (Slavin, 1995) (McConnel, 1996) (Jones, 2007) and (Pow Sang, 2016).

The social aspect of learning was highlighted by Bruner, who introduced the concept of reciprocity in learning as an incentive (Bruner, 1966). Theoretical studies and practical applications have shown that the students' performances in school can become better if the course combines traditional teaching with modern techniques, which implies that traditional methods will be partially or fully modernized. (Johnson 2014) cites as a learning challenge the development of interpersonal relationships that affect personal identity. Additional elements of cooperative learning are a) face-to-face verbal interaction, b) individual accountability, c) group processing and d) appropriate grouping. All of them are particularly relevant to enhancing social skills in higher education (Kaufman 1997). In (Terenzini 1994) it is shown that individualized and collaborative approaches are more effective than traditional (lecture) approaches because they respond better to differences in students' levels of preparation, learning styles, and rates; the authors support to the use of cooperative learning at the university level – not necessarily an initial target. As in our approach, collaborative learning was used in Science and Technology courses at university level by (Altun 2015).

2.2 Active and Inquiry-Based Learning

Active learning hypothesizes that when students are more involved in active, rather than passive, activities, such as reading, writing, discussing, problem solving, or interacting via questions, they pay more attention. Some studies of specialists in pedagogy and educational psychology have shown that the students are only aware of the lecture about 40% of the time, retain around 70% of the contents presented in the first 10 minutes, and only 20% of those shown in the last 10 minutes (USCTA) (Stuart, 1978). (Guido, 2017) discusses that, when the student is investigating a problem or a question using evidence-based reasoning and creativity, active learning is enriched and becomes inquiry-based learning.

2.3 Jigsaw

In 1978, Elliot Aronson proposed Jigsaw as a collaborative inquiry-based learning technique that works by dividing the learning material into different tasks and the class into different groups (or teams) (Aronson, 1978). In a Jigsaw group, each student has to perform one of the tasks, which will eventually be integrated by the group to conclude the training process. Jigsaw iterates between tasks (expert groups) and team-based work (working groups). The experts work is carried out in groups of increasing size, starting with individual work and ending with all the students that were assigned to a specific task. During the process, students contrast and complement their understanding to reach a common understanding. The jigsaw method is also known as the "mosaic" (Maftei-2011).

A number of investigations support the favorable impact of Jigsaw during the teaching/learning process. (Sharan, 1980) studies the effect of the Jigsaw method on learners' attitudes and achievements, concluding that it helped create interdependence among learners as a result of the learning task being divided up among them. (Zakaria 2016) reports a positive change in the attitudes of the students towards their fellow classmates, an increase in the students' sense of responsibility. (Sahin, 2010) (Durmus, 2008) (Walker 1998) and (Maftei 2011) report an increase in participation and improvements in communication skills.

(Felder, 1998) defines the sequential and global dichotomy learning styles. Most formal education involves presenting material in a logically ordered progression (sequential). Some students are comfortable with this system; they learn sequentially, mastering the material (more or less) as it is presented. Others, however, learn globally, so they may be lost for weeks, until suddenly they "get it". Jigsaw helps to combine the two types of learning and ripping off the benefits: as an expert a student learns sequentially, and as a working team member, globally. Blended learning offers an approach for increasing the impact of both face-to-face learning and online learning as supportive and motivating method for students (Sulisworo 2016).

3. OUR APPROACH

3.1 Case Study

We developed the present study with the thirty 3rd year undergraduates registered in the *Cloud computing and distributed systems* course of the "Design and development of videogames" specialization during the 2020 Spring quarter. The activity was structured around three subtopics that could be independently studied – the same as in the previous year. We selected Optical Technologies because it can be more easily split into independent subtopics: A) Optical fiber properties, B) Optical components and C) Optical networking (Marinescu 2019). Optical Networking stands for an eighth of the course content and grade. The chosen subtopics can be studied in any order, then assembled as Jigsaw pieces. This was a challenge given that in engineering fields, learning is mostly sequential and based on concepts that are already fully understood. The learning process starts with online content search based on a set of keywords that the teacher provides for each subtopic.

3.2 Organization of the Experiment

(Felder, 2003) states fundamental skills such as motivation, positive interaction, cooperation, leadership, decision-making capabilities, tolerance and trust, and the ability to think critically. Following these criteria, we have organized the experiment as follows. The thirty students were organized in two (super)groups, I and II. For each of them, three expert groups were defined for the three subtopics. At the same time, students were organized into four working groups - each consisting of one expert per subtopic, following the suggestions of previous work (Dumus, 2008), (Nooritawati, 2010) (Khine, 2019). The expert groups were randomly formed as a way for students to learn how to collaborate, discuss, and debate with any of the colleagues. Each student was also randomly assigned to a working group. As a notation, student "C2" was assigned to the expert group C, i.e. dealing with subtopic C), and to the working group 2.

3.3 Jigsaw Phases

To carry out the Jigsaw activity, the following phases were planned over the course of three weeks:

Table 1. Phases of the Jigsaw activity

Phase	Activity	Group	In classroom /at distance	Evaluation
1	Every student works individually on the assigned subtopic (A, B, or C), and delivers a short report to the instructor.	Individual	Distance	Report
2	During class, students present their findings (on their assigned subtopics) to their working group members, who worked on different subtopics. Each student is required to take notes of questions, missing points, misunderstandings, etc., to be able to address them in the future phases.	Working	Classroom	None
3	Expert groups meet in small groups building a common understanding of the subtopic and refining their corresponding material. Expert groups can be A1+A2, B1+B2, C0+C1+C2, etc.	Expert	Distance	Report of small expert group
4	During class, each small expert group presents the improved material to the larger working groups consisting of all the members of their teams (e.g. A1+A2, B1+B2, and C0+C1+C2).	Working	Classroom, carried out at distance	None
5	The entire expert group meets and puts together their material for the final version.	Expert	Distance	Final report of the entire group
6	In a "plenary" meeting, the three expert groups present each subtopic. This is the only time when the instructor is present for all the activities, as all previous phases occur in simultaneous presentations.	Plenary	Classroom, carried out at distance	Students presentation, based on their oral skills.

Table 1 shows that during these phases a student alternates between expert and working groups and acts as peer with the expert mates and as instructor to the working group members. The students were informed about the overall structure and activities of Jigsaw, but the new work partners after each phase were announced at the end of that phase. This was meant to get ready to collaborate with any partner without any prejudice based on previous collaboration.

Phases 2, 4, and 6 were initially planned to be carried out in classroom during 15 to 20 min. Due to the COVID-19 pandemic, phases 4 and 6 were carried out using videoconferencing tools.

3.4 Learning Objectives and Evaluation

Among the competences of the course (as defined in the course syllabus), the Jigsaw activity addresses the following learning objectives: a) analyze complex situations and design strategies to address them, b) compile and select information efficiently, c) teamwork and d) decision-making. The goal of this work is to report on a case study rather than setting up to answer an experimental question, which implies delicate ethical issues. The surveys taken by the students are an evaluation tool for the *opinion* of the students with regard to learning with Jigsaw – a first experience for all, versus the traditional method – which they have implicitly used throughout, rather than a tool for the evaluation of the learning outcome.

As in previous work (Marinescu 2019), we could not risk treating individuals as experimental subjects; as a result, to avoid any significant negative impact on the grades of those students who may not find Jigsaw productive for them, we weighted this activity to only count for 10% of the final course grade. For ethical reasons, *all* students were involved in the same activity at the same time, which means we can´t compare the actual learning results with and without Jigsaw, or with other methods. The items to be evaluated and the corresponding phases are detailed in last column of Table 1. The two final plenary meetings (supergroups I and II), were organized in two videoconferencing meetings at a different time, hence the instructor could attend both assessing the students' activity as initially planned. Even if the students are graded individually, students need others for a good mark and therefore this technique requires cooperative working (Altun 2015).

4. RESULTS

We use reports and presentations during the course to quantitatively asses the level to which students acquired the technical target skills and knowledge. At the same time, this evaluation cannot assess aspects such as the level of engagement, the attitude towards their colleagues, the probability that they would use these techniques in the future, etc. These are factors that are easier recorded by surveys, as they refer to opinions and intentions when comparing jigsaw with traditional teaching. Similar to last year´s Jigsaw activity, we surveyed all of the students three times during the course: after phase 3 (1st expert meeting), after phase 5 (2nd expert meeting), and at the end of the activity. Replies were voluntary.

4.1 First Jigsaw Survey

The first survey is a mix of two multiple choice and one free text questions. The multiple choices evaluate the students´ quantitative opinions about the work that was presented by themselves and their team members. The open-ended questions referred to the students´ attitude towards collaborative learning. This survey was taken just after the onset of the Covid-19 pandemics and referred to activities that took place in person. At this point the expert groups had delivered the first report. The questions in the first survey are the following:

1) Rate from 0 (very poor) to 10 (excellent):
   a) In your opinion, which is the level of knowledge of the subtopic that you prepared?
   b) In your opinion, which is the level of knowledge of the subtopic, that other students prepared?
2) The preparation of your topic compared to other students (is: "better", ·equal", "worse").
3) Reply with free text: What aspect of the Jigsaw activity do you a) most like, b) not like.

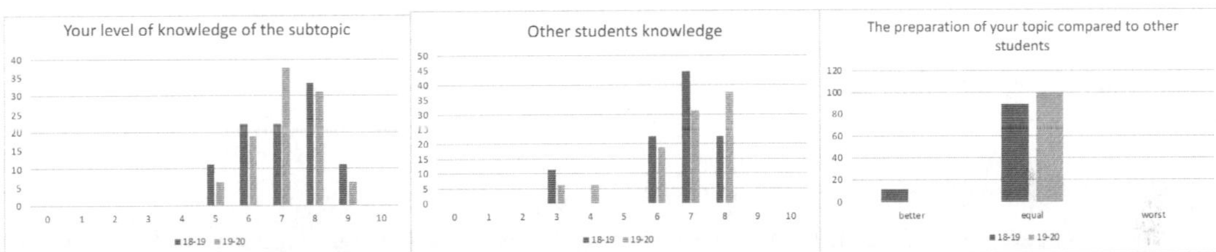

Figure 1. Jigsaw survey 1. The y axis represents the percentage of students

Students considered that, in general, their level of knowledge is good, with a mean of 7.1 (both years) and a standard deviation of 1.27 and 1.02. The distribution is more of a Gauss bell than the results from the previous year given the larger number of surveyed students (last year 9 students, this year 12 students.

For question 1.b students had a similar response as last year, most of them rating the others very closely to their own rating. With more respondents this year, all students perceived that the preparation of their respective topic was "equally good" compared to the others. Last year outlier also disappeared. Looking at the results combined, there is a slight tendency to consider that most of the others have about the same, if not more knowledge after the first expert meeting.

From the replies to question 3.a, it seems that what students liked the most was the fact that they had to look for the information by themselves, understand *small, contained* pieces well by doing research on the topic, then contrast it with their colleagues. The second most cited fact was the teamwork of putting together the content that each has studied separately. Somewhat differently, last year´s comments focused mostly on the social setup of the groups, but putting information together makes one realize details one may have missed.

The negative comments in 3.b are very similar to last year´s, and they refer mostly to the activity being too long and the insecurity of not knowing that you looked up everything relevant, or how to solve a conflict when two students have extracted contradicting information. There were also a few students that wanted to be able to choose their groups – not clear whether because of the particular group dynamics or reluctance to work as a team, when usually you don´t get to choose the members – and one that hadn´t understood the purpose of the activity altogether.

4.2 Second Jigsaw Survey

After the 2nd session of expert meetings (phase 5), students were requested to answer the following questions with the responses limited to "a lot", "some", a little" or "did not increase":

1. The knowledge on the subtopic that you prepared has increased.
2. The knowledge on the subtopic, that your colleagues prepared has increased.
3. The preparation of your subtopic in relation to the other´s subtopics.

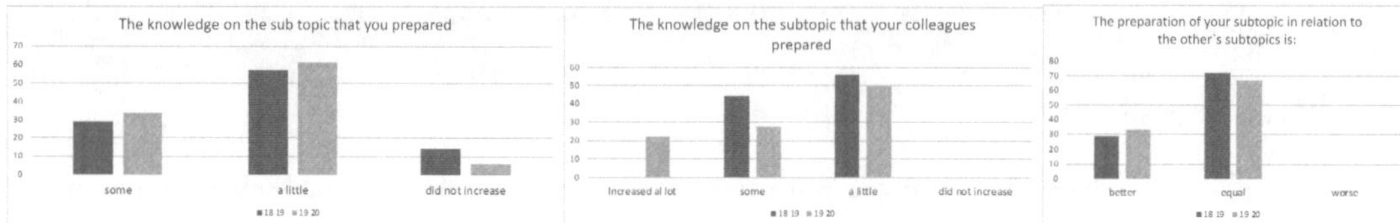

Figure 2. Jigsaw survey 2

The results are rather contradicting those from the previous year, although the differences are minimal. Students report to learn more on the subject they have prepared, after the second expert meeting, relative to the previous year. They also report to have learned considerably more during the second expert group meeting, with about 20% of them having learned "a lot" compared to none last year. Nevertheless, two of the students still reported (in free text) that they don´t feel that the other experts have come up with anything very different after their working group meetings.

These are results for meetings that occurred after Easter week, and thus there may be an effect of paying more attention to work as a result of the confinement, the on-line setting, or both. It is likely that the variation is more connected to the fact that students could not spend time on live social activities and instead studied.

4.3 Third Jigsaw Survey

At the end of the Jigsaw activity, students were asked to fill in a 3rd survey that contains a general question about the technique and two open-ended questions.

1. Compared to traditional classes, how was the Jigsaw experience (more, equal, or less) regarding: a) Effort in the preparation, b) Level of knowledge of one's own subject, c) Improvement in teamwork, d) Satisfaction with others' presentation level and e) Level of knowledge of others´ subject
2. What is your opinion about the Jigsaw technique?: a) Positive comments, b) Negative comments

From the first question we can see that a much lower percentage of students then last year thought that Jigsaw requires more effort than the traditional method. The difference could come partially from a 10 minutes introduction to Optical Communications right before starting Jigsaw. We were happy to see that a lot more students thought that their level of knowledge about the subject they prepared is higher with Jigsaw. This is not surprising given that learning actively is usually more effective than listening to a teacher, if the subject is not prohibitively difficult, but may also be an indirect effect of the confinement, which minimized the distractions.

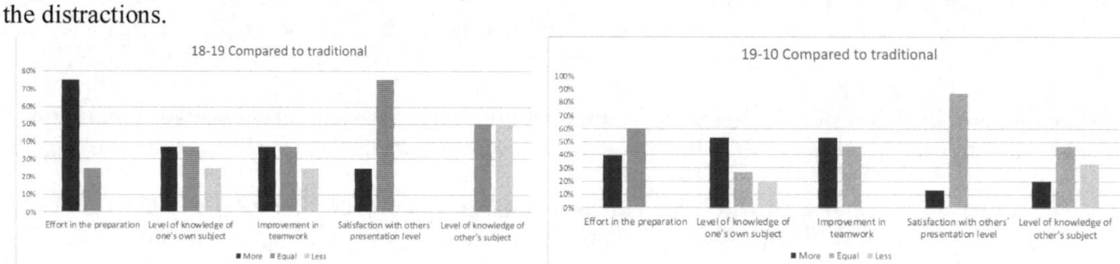

Figure 3. Jigsaw survey 3: the y axis shows the percentage of students that completed the survey

In terms of teamwork, no student considered that this was worse with Jigsaw, while this wasn´t the case last year. It is possible that the expectation of exclusive online collaboration makes people be more effective, and possibly lower their expectations – which would result in higher rating of the same activity. Somewhat surprisingly, some students considered that they have more knowledge of others´ subject with Jigsaw, up from none last year - although even more think the opposite. This survey was taken *after* the final presentations. We hypothesize that this may be the effect of only seeing the material (i.e. slides) and hearing the talks, rather than being present in person and getting distracted by other factors, including faces and body language. We could be observing the opposite result of not seeing a person speaking, when having to process technical information rather than understanding the emotional message.

The *positive comments* are mostly about the fact that students felt that this was a good way to learn a subject, that they have learned a lot about their subtopic, and that this is an interesting type of exercise. One difference from last year is that nobody referred to explaining the material to the others; we don´t know whether their online collaboration was less interactive than it would have been live. Several of the *negative comments* refer back to the first question of the survey: "I don´t think it substitutes the professor´s explanation perfectly", "I feel that I could have learned much more with a (traditional) class", "We don´t understand very well the other subtopics, I would do three different subtopics myself. A last comment was about the group size, which they felt shouldn´t be too large (about 5 or 6 people). This was precisely the case so we understand this is a positive comment

In general, we saw more positive results this year than the last. This could be partially true due to the indirect effects of the confinement, or it may be a better approximation to reality due to pure statistics. In any case, other authors have also commented on the mixed results of the Jigsaw technique. We want to reiterate that surveys relate the *impressions* of students and must be taken as an indication rather than a recipe for success.

5. CONCLUSION

This work presents a study that implements the Jigsaw method with the thirty 3rd year undergraduates registered in the *Cloud computing and distributed systems* course at the University of Girona, Spain. This is a more extensive experiment for the same course as last year, with very minor modifications. The expansion of the Covid-19 pandemic forcefully changed the conditions under which we conducted more than half of the Jigsaw process. This resulted in some interesting outcomes, which are nevertheless not easy to correlate with the effects of confinement, the change to distance learning, or a combination thereof.

Students have generally valued important aspects of learning more positively than last year. Some students still felt that they were not sure whether the information they discovered by themselves was complete and they would have liked to have had more guidance or go through the Jigsaw expert team process for all of the subtopics – a call for an incremental, more traditional learning method, applied in a collaborative team - rather than instructor - context. Some students also proposed to skip the initial individual phase, starting in groups of two or three. This would allow reducing the number of phases from six to four, by skipping the two initial ones. This proposal seems quite realistic at the university level and we consider applying it for next Jigsaw experiences.

ACKNOWLEDGEMENT

This work has been partially supported by the *Generalitat de Catalunya* research support program SGR-1551 1469].

REFERENCES

Altun, S. 2015. *The Effect of Cooperative Learning on Students' Achievement and Views on the Science and Technology Course.* International Electronic Journal of Elementary Education, IEJEE. 2015, 7(3), 451-468

Aronson, E. 1978. *The Jigsaw Classroom,* Sage, Beverly Hills, CA, USA.

Bruner, J. (1966), Toward a Theory of Instruction, Harvard University Press, pp. 125-126

Dumus, Kilic. 2008. The Effect of the Jigsaw Technique on Learning the Concepts of the Principles and Methods of Teaching. World Applied Sciences Journal, Vol. Supple 1. pp. 108-114.

Felder, R.M., Silverman, L.K.1988. *Learning and teaching styles in engineering education.* Eng. Education, 674–681.

Felder, R.M. and Brent, R. 2003. *Designing and teaching courses to satisfy ABET Engineering criteria.* Journal on Engineering Education. Vol. 92 (1) pp. 7-25.

Guido, M. 2017. *All About Inquiry-Based Learning: Definition, Benefits and Strategies.* https://www.prodigygame.com/blog/inquiry-based-learning-definition-benefits-strategies/

Jones, L. 2007. *The student-centered classroom.* Cambridge University Press. Cambridge, UK.

Johnson, D. W., & Johnson, R. T. (2014). Cooperative Learning in 21st Century. Annals of Psychology, 30(3), 841-851.

Khine, S. M., Nyunt, T. T. S., Maw, A. A., & Min, S. S. 2019. *Effective Learning for Higher Education Using Jigsaw Approach.* Myanmar Universities' Research Conference (MURC).

Kousa, Maan. 2015. *Jigsaw Cooperative Learning in Engineering Classrooms.* IEEE Global Eng. Education Conference

McConnell, Jeffrey J. 1996. *Active learning and its use in computer science.* In Proceedings of the 1st conference on Integrating technology into computer science education (ITiCSE '96). ACM, New York, USA, 52-54.

Maftei G., Maftei, M. *The strengthen knowledge of atomic physics using the "mosaic" method (The Jigsaw method).* WCES, Procedia Social and Behavioral Sciences 15 (2011) 1605–1610. 2011.

Marinescu, M. C., Marzo, J. L. 2019. *Using cooperative teaching techniques in engineering courses. The Jigsaw Case.* International Conference on Cognition and Exploratory Learning in Digital Age, CELDA.

Moreillon, J. 2007. Collaborative strategies for teaching reading comprehension: Maximizing your impact. American Library Association, Chicago, USA.

Nooritawati Md Tahir, Kama Azura Othman. 2010. *The Jigsaw Cooperative Method amongst Electrical Engineering Students.* 2nd International Congress on Engineering Education. Kuala Lumpur, Malaysia.

Pow-Sang, José Antonio. 2016. *The Jigsaw technique to teach object-oriented design: A replication study with graduate students.* IEEE Global Engineering Education Conference (EDUCON) pp. 1212-1217.

Sahin, A. 2010. Effects of jigsaw II technique on academic achievement and attitudes to written expression course. Educational Research and Reviews, Vol. 5, pp. 777-787.

Sharan, S. 1980. Cooperative learning in small groups: Recent methods and effects on achievement, attitudes, and ethnic relations. Review of educational research, Vol. 50 (2). pp. 241-271.

Slavin, R. E. 1995. Cooperative learning: Theory, research, and practice. Allyn and Bacon, Boston, USA.

Stuart, J. and Rutherford, R. 1978. Medical Student Concentration During Lectures. The Lancet, Vol. 2, pp. 514-516

Sulisworo, D., Agustin, S.P. and Sudarmiyati, E. 2016 *Cooperative-blended learning using Moodle as an open source learning platform.* Int. J. Technology Enhanced Learning, Vol. 8, No. 2, pp.187–198.

Terenzini, P.T., Pascarella, E.T. 1994. *Living with myths - undergraduate education in America.* Change, pp. 28-32.

USCTAWiki, *Active Learning Strategies.* <http://uscta.wikidot.com/ize-active-learning-strategies>visitedat 2020.06.10

Walker, I., Crogan. M. 1998. *Academic Performance, Prejudice, and the Jigsaw Classroom: New pieces to the Puzzle,* Journal of Community,and Applied Social Psychology Australia, no.8, pp.381-393 .

Zakaria, E., Solfitri, T., Daud, Y. and Abidin, Z.Z. 2013. *Effect of cooperative learning on secondary school students mathematics achievement, Creative Education, Vol. 4, No. 2, pp.98–100.*

Zarei, Abbas Ali and Adbi, Venus. 2016, Blended Learning, Computer-based, and Conventional Reading Instruction Affecting EFL Learners' Self-regulation and Critical Thinking. Intl. Journal of Humanities and Cultural Studies.

ASPECTS ON E-LEARNING DURING THE COVID19 PANDEMIC AT THE UNIVERSITY

Vlad Drăgoi[1] and Dorin Herlo[1]
"Aurel Vlaicu" University of Arad, Romania
[1]PhD

ABSTRACT

The rapid developments in educational technologies and the conditions of pandemic period provoked the academic staff and students for assessing the value of different technologies, new or existing, and for deciding how or when these technologies make sense for them to use. Due to crisis, face-to-face learning process was change with Emergency Remote Teaching. In this article we approached the case study for university education, on the use of learning platforms, to increase reflective learning, critical reflection and concrete action of students in real life which are clear elements of transformative learning and related to the new educational paradigm – paragogy (peer-learning). In order to have a significant outcome of our proposed solutions, we proceed in two-steps. Firstly, we detail and test some of the existing e-learning tools (platforms), and secondly, based on a focus-group experience with groups of students enrolled in computer-science Bachelor degree, we propose adapted solutions for online learning and teaching for the next academic year.

KEYWORDS

E-Learning, Transformative Learning, Paragogy, Case Study, Focus Group

1. INTRODUCTION

Being involved, like everyone else in this world in the pandemic days, in the need to take online university courses, we proceeded, with students from exact sciences, to shift to the Emergency Remote Teaching (ERT) that involves the use of fully remote teaching instead of courses delivered face-to-face or as blended. Under the given conditions we set out to offer students the same curriculum but exploring various tools like platforms.

However, we kept the idea of producing transformative and not transmissive learning that appeals very well to e-learning. Transformative learning (Mezirow, 1991) involved *critical reflection, reflective discourse* and *action.* In our case, *critical reflection* is converted in thinking about what tools, offered by virtual learning environment, could be used easier and more effective for accomplishing the objectives of learning. *Reflective discourse* and *action*, consist in using the e-learning tools, chosen in critical reflection phase, for a good and efficient learning.

In our study we addressed these three essential parts of transformative learning related to e-learning, especially, in this particular case, with ERT studying with the students the behavior of three platforms - Skype, Zoom and Discord.

At the same time, we think that our case study also highlighted few elements of new educational paradigm - *paragogy.* The concept of *paragogy* (literally, "para-" alongside, "-gogy" leading) it's used to characterize the critical study and practice of *peer learning.*

In the idea of supporting our approach, we conducted practical case study with students enrolled at a public University in Romania, having a rather scientific background and orientation. As we were aiming for qualitative responses to new and challenging questions, we used focus-groups interviews on which an online course proposal oriented to individual with low resources was developed.

2. METHODS

2.1 E-learning

E-learning - learning system helped by electronic resources - is known as a network enabled transfer of knowledge and skills, to a large number of recipients (educables) at the same or different times, using different kind of IT tools, aiming for "delivering" education.

As an educational paradigm "E-learning is defined as information and communication technologies used to support students to improve their learning" (Ellis et al., 2009).

A Delphi survey was used to determine experts' perceptions and knowledge, that might converge to a final consensus of an inclusive definition for e-learning. This method (Delphi) makes possible to deal with complex problems (Linstone & Turoff, 1975). Recently, 33 experts from over the world were asked to evaluate e-learning definition, in the final Delphi round. Their conclusion was: "E-learning is an approach to teaching and learning, representing all or part of the educational model applied, that is based on the use of electronic media and devices as tools for improving access to training, communication and interaction and that facilitates the adoption of new ways of understanding and developing learning."

We can say that in their definition the experts mainly characterized e-learning as a "way of teaching and learning" moving towards a "new educational paradigm" and, from our perspective, the new educational paradigm is the paragogy.

The term *paragogy,* as per its founders Corneli and Danoff (2011), it is employed to characterize the critical study and practice of *peer learning* (here adapting the classical concept of *pedagogy* and the notion of *andragogy* to a peer learning context). In essence, Corneli and Danoff's paragogy thesis is premised on the argument that online environments are now sufficiently developed to support *peer production of content* which can be shared freely and widely, and can promote learning for all within any given community. So, paragogy deals with a very important challenge, i.e., of analyzing and co-creating the educational environment as a whole by the peers, which share their learning situations and experiences, benefiting of information technology, used for connecting people. This means creating "wisdom" starting from "data", "information" and "knowledge".

In special conditions of pandemic period a sort of e-learning that we used was Emergency Remote Teaching. "ERT is a temporary shift of instructional delivery to an alternate delivery mode due to crisis circumstances. It involves the use of fully remote teaching solutions for instruction or education that would otherwise be delivered face-to-face or as blended or hybrid courses and that will return to that format once the crisis or emergency has abated." (Hodges & all, 2020).

2.2 Case Study

A case study is a research method involving an up-close, in-depth, and detailed examination of a particular case and can involve both qualitative and quantitative research methods. A case study implies the observance of the following steps: *case identification; objective documentation on cases and identification of intervention modalities; applying the modalities of intervention on the case, of solving it; monitoring the evolution of the case.* Our case study is qualitative and exploratory, mainly because its basic function is to help identify questions and select types of measurement prior to the main investigation.

2.3 Focus Groups

The technique of regrouping a set of individuals in order to discuss on a specific topic, aiming to analyze and built constructive qualitative decisions based on the personal experiences, perceptions and attitudes of the participants, is known as focus group discussions (Cornwall & Jewkes 1995, Hayward et al., 2004, Morgan 1996). The method was already applied in education (Flores & Alonso, 1995). The four major steps in a focus group are:

- **Research design.** Here we define the objectives by fixing the main purpose of the focus group, develop a set of possible questions, recruit the participants (ensure homogeneity, max 15 participants per group, number of groups), identify the possible locations.

- **Data collection.** This step is mainly focused on the preparations, recording, tapping the content, and implementing the sessions by following four major principles, namely Introduction, Discussions, Questions, and Conclusions.
- **Analysis.** Here we analyze the content of the meetings by various methods, e.g., Coding, Discourse analysis, Ranking, Conversation analysis.
- **Results.** Depending on the target audience different reporting methods are used. In our case we address our study to the academic audience and hence conclude our report in a constructive manner, by proposing an e-learning method combined with classical tools, part of which we tested at our university.

3. RESULTS

We started the case study at the beginning of March 2020.

In the first step we identified the case – how the academic curriculum can be delivered as efficiently as possible through e-learning platforms for producing transformative and not transmissive learning for the students.

In the second step – objective documentation and identification of intervention modalities – we requested the students to search the information concerning the Skype, Zoom and Discord platforms. For this action they had to install the application in order to test it and compare it with other similar applications. In this step we used, for communication, the classical tools such as the email, social networks and phones. For academic staff it was a very short period of adapting the course or seminar to the needs of the student for accessed them online (either synchronously or asynchronously) to produce critical reflection, then a reflective speech (after understanding) and, finally, application in practice of notions understood by action. In other words, to produce transformative learning. In the first two weeks we tested three different platforms for video conference (see Table 1).

Table 1. Video conference platforms (free version)

	Skype	Zoom	Discord
Popularity (students)	Very popular, 100% of the students already knew the platform before we started.	Popular, 80% of the students heard/knew the platform before our study.	Almost unknown, 5 % of the students used this platform in the past.
Participants	Max 50. At 35 users we experienced video and voice problems during the sessions.	Max. 100. More reliable than Skype regarding the voice and video quality at high number of participants.	Max 99. We only tested a group of 8, and the voice and video quality were exceptional.
Video recordings	Available for 30 days	Until 1GB on the cloud	Unlimited (as mentioned by the developers)
Quality	Video and voice quality were acceptable for small groups. When two or more participants speak/turn on their camera the quality drops down.	The quality is very good for small groups and acceptable for large ones. Even when several cameras are turned on the image remains clear.	Excellent for small groups, both the image and sound quality are very good even when several users are activating these options.
Security	Skype – Skype chats, both video and audio are encrypted.	Zoom 5.0 introduced an option for secure communications.	There are some doubts regarding its security.
Screen sharing	Yes	Yes	Yes
CPU	Extremely high use of CPU.	High	Low
Time limits	In the platforms specifications there is no time limit.	40 minutes for basic members.	No time limits mentioned.
User-friendly	Easy to use but ambiguous in identifying users or Skype ids.	Easy to use and the connection is very easy once the conference rooms is set up.	Easy to use once we were invited on a server.

We rapidly realized that we could propose a solid way based on completely free, online available platforms. Setting up such an environment, with no technical discrimination between the students, was necessary to release the pressure students started to experience at the beginning of the isolation. In this manner we created similar, non-discriminate, and uniform infrastructure for all the participants.

Finally, we have decided to continue with Zoom. One of the leading arguments for this choice was the possibility of having, in the free version, simultaneous webcams switched on. As simple as it might look, this option kept our connection and relations closer to the face-to-face scenario. This is a real advantage when we are dealing with long periods of isolation.

In the third step – applying the modalities of intervention on the case, of solving it – the academic staff provided the official curriculum for the student's specialization via Zoom, using ERT. For this action it was necessary a schedule/timetable. By the way, planning projects and group meetings is a basic feature one needs to take into consideration when working online. The application chosen by us for such activities was Doodle (www.doodle.com). The application does not require any installation or sign-in process by the participants. The administrator/creator or the pool designs the online voting procedure by creating multiple choices possibilities. After each participant has voted a majority voting gives the output, which can be exported in several different formats, among which the most common one is pdf files.

When the delivery of the online course started, from the faculty point of view, student learning outcomes were of primary interest. For this reason they proposed various learning activities supported by interactive methods such as brainstorming, online editing, problem solving, inquiring, algorithmization, collaborative learning, projects etc. supported by well-known platforms such as Overleaf (www.overleaf.com). Overleaf allows users to edit, modify, save LaTeX documents on the Cloud. The main advantage of using such a platform is that one can use all the resources, namely the editor, the compiler, the templates, without having to locally store any software/documents/libraries. The platform proposes a chat and comments frame alongside the text and pdf document, fact that allow users to discuss directly on the platform regarding the modifications to be made on the document. Also, the large list of templates proposed by IEEE, Springer, ACM and others, are available directly on the platform. Among the most popular tags proposed by Overleaf we recall here, presentations, project/lab report, thesis, formal letters, CV, posters, etc.

For students, issues such as interest, motivation, and engagement are directly connected to learning satisfaction and success of applying all the concepts/ notions in the real life (environment).

In the fourth step - monitoring the evolution of the case – we proceeded to do a **focus group.**

Let us detail the main steps of our focus group.

Research Design. The purpose of our focus group was to determine "good"/ "bad" practice on e-learning implementations, due to the Covid 19 global pandemic. We have implemented our research on homogeneous mixed gender groups of students. They are all enrolled in Bachelor degree scientific studies, in mathematics and computer science, at different levels. We organized three groups, i.e., a first group of 15 first year students in computer science, a second group of 7 second year students in mathematics, and a third group of 2 third year students in computer science. All three groups present the following characteristics. They are uniformly distributed between rural and urban provenience, the students do not have any part time jobs except for 2 out of the 15 students of the first group. Also, they all share a modest financial situation, and finally, their scholar performance being close to the average (here we considered the discrete probability distribution of the grades for each year separately). Our choice is based on some well-known principles, such as group dynamics (Green & Dowler 2003, Thomas et al., 1995), homogenous principles (Krueger, 1994), and mixed gender groups (Freitas et al., 1998). The number of participants follow typical focus groups guidelines, suggested in (Krueger & Casey, 2000, Fern, 1982, Mendes de Almeida, 1980). We organized two focus groups with the first group of students, and one focus group with the two others. These were organized on an online platform, in our case the Zoom platform, and are known as online focus groups in the literature (Kamberelis & Dimitriadis, 2005).

Let us present a selection of the questions asked during the focus groups.

- Did you talked with your classmates or teachers about the technology used for teaching?
- Did you had any discussion with your friends about how you felt during the look down?
- How the selection of the technologies was made? Were you consulted in this process?
- On a scale of 1 to 7 at what level was the online teaching, in average? Which are the extreme cases?
- Let us suppose that next academic year does not start in the classic manner. What do you propose as viable solution?

- What exactly do you think the online teaching/learning revealed about yourself? In what way did it help you?

Data collection. We have decided to collect our data by recording the sessions, fact that was mainly imposed by the context of that time. In order to keep the meetings as active and dynamic as possible we have maintained a 2-hour limit. Surprisingly or not, the smallest group was the most dynamic one, and the discussions inside this group were extremely interesting pointing out several roads of future developments and applications of the e-learning methods. One of the key advantages of using a web-based platform is that younger generations manipulate and feel natural in using such tool. Also known as the connected generation, our students felt extremely relaxed and comfortable during the sessions, and as stressed out by several participants this is due to the online wall between them. The main drawbacks of our collecting the data is that it was almost impossible for us to collect non-verbal data, such as body language, displacement or posture and their use of the physical space to communicate. However, some informal data such as speech markers (volume variations, pitch, gaps) were included in our analysis.

Analysis. We have analyzed our recordings and proceed to an encoding of the data transcripts from the meetings. We have classified the data into three major folders, i.e., "Illustrative quotations", "Positive points", "Less positive points", fact that allowed us to discover several patterns.

Results.

Illustrative quotations. During our study we have noticed key elements of the psychological impact, such as weakening attention during learning activities, long moments of fatigue, and feelings of loneliness. Some of the students felt sad and alone, mainly due to the lack of human contact. The students confessed that they felt the need to socialize, to physically interact with each other, and also with their teachers, fact illustrated by the following quotation made by one student: *After several weeks of lock down and online teaching, we finally understood what "students live" really means. I miss the long coffee breaks, the time our colleagues are late for the computer graphics course and being punished by our teacher, the long nights spent with our project colleagues while trying to finish the report and the final implementation, and the time we all look at each other when the algebra teacher was asking questions. We lost all those simple and beautiful things during the pandemics.*

Since the isolation naturally induces such feelings, the online teaching and learning should clearly not enforce such pessimistic moods.

Positive points: The e-learning process could potentially come into help by steering the students mind to new fields, and also by providing satisfaction, pleasure and curiosity regarding the learning process. Interactive methods and using the adequate tools induce a desire/curiosity for how the application works, how groups of students can use it in order to build a project, organize their ideas and finally to learn. The fact that many of the modules tend to closely imitate the physical objects, like boards, stamps, pens, etc., gives us the impression of handling real physical objects through our computer. However, the overall idea pointed out by the students was that e-learning might provide an effective and healthy environment but for short term activities and it should not completely replace the face-to-face teaching. As long as the both the students and the teachers are equipped with adequate technology the learning/teaching process does not induce any particular initial differences. Another point revealed during the sessions was that all the effort done by the teachers to make students learn, use, combine, and adapt technology for learning and teaching was highly appreciated by the students. Students' confession: *A math teacher has had preoccupation to demonstrate us, on a digital tablet equipped with white-board emulator, how could be explain and prove theorems for algebra, in an interactive and pleasant way. We felt like we were in the classroom and our teacher was in front of us.* The students confessed that they realized that interactive learning means effective participation on both side: teacher-student and academic staff used teaching learning assessment methods very well, suited to the online environment.

The focus-groups revealed positive qualities and abilities developed by the students, that are strangely related to the effect of the online teaching/learning. Several students confessed that they became much more organized, fact that they believe it was induced by the online process. They had to keep a complex updated agenda with their courses, project, meetings etc. Also, they are willing to help their colleagues in a more accentuated and frequent manner, which was not always the case before the lock down.

Less positive points: A first idea detached is that more than three months of physical isolation could potentially induced irreversible psychological damage to the individuals. Even though psychological impacts or measures for dealing with this new type of human relations were previously identified and published (Taylor, 2019), these methods were not sufficiently explained or taught in high-schools or universities. Another point deduced from focus groups was that many students, for various reasons, were not able to provide themselves with the necessary materials, e.g., cameras for the laptops, software for editing, programming etc. This fact induces a polarization among the students, which would clearly affect their performance and utterly change the dynamics of the groups. Eventually, the lack of a technological infrastructure could induce psychological disorder. That is why, we chosen to eliminate as much as possible discriminatory variables, and proposed to students as few software/applications as possible in order to complete the course. Respondents from focus groups pointed out another critical fact - the physical location that students used for their online courses. 32% of the students mentioned physical infrastructure problems cause by different factors, such as, neighbors, roommates, family, outdoor activities, etc. For half of them the main reasons were the living conditions, namely, they were living with their parents, grand-parents, in small flats. Another relevant aspect, provided by the few quantitative data collected (e.g., level of online teaching per course) revealed a phenomenon of polarization. More exactly, we computed the distribution of levels (on a scale of 1 to 7) of online teaching for each course. We noticed an average grade equal to 3,8. However, the distribution of the grades was not at all Gaussian (as expected). The majority of the courses were either "good" (6) and "very good" (7) or "bad" (2) and "very bad" (1).

4. DISCUSSIONS

When the Universities were closed and the teaching went from face-to-face to online, both students and professors had to adapt their behavior for teaching and learning. For academic staff was a great challenge to shift their courses from face-to-face into online, appealing for a way that in the literature is called Emergency Remote Teaching. As we were confronted with a new paradigm in terms of behavior, education, health the communication process was not always convincing and stable, e.g., the content of the program was updated during the teaching process, and the evaluation methods were changed during the semester from work tasks, from one meeting to another, up to short project presentations and the creation of e-portfolios, evaluable at the end of the semester.

Students seem to easily adapt to digital technologies, Internet based platforms for communication, or any other computer-based technology (Dede, 2005, Howe & Strauss, 2000, Oblinger & Oblinger, 2005, Prensky, 2001, Tapscott, 2008), what we found, as well. They appreciated and felt involved in the whole process when planning and collaboration where decided together with the teacher. For that, they stressed out the importance of platforms such as Doodle and Zoom. Their contribution was valued, e.g., they proposed the Zoom platform for video conference, application that we tested together. They were also pro-active in the teaching/learning process and substantially contributed to the design of online lecture architecture.

We can give, here, a detailed example of an online learning activity, combined with discussions and project proposal that was implemented at our university. We worked with a group of seven students in their third year of Bachelor degree in computer science. The subject we proposed was to study the security of a post-quantum cryptosystem. All combined, we had three presentations on this subject, and after the students prepared a project. Technologies such as YouTube video, Zoom, Doodle, Miro and WhatsApp were used in order to achieve our goal. Also, we had a Windows 10 Pro for Desktop Stations equipped with the Microsoft Whiteboard application.

The first course was a presentation of the fundamental notions that we were about to study. We used the Zoom platform and the Microsoft Whiteboard in order to detail, and comment on these initial requirements. While this first course looked very likely to classic lectures, the two following sessions were completely different from a classical computer science lecture. More exactly, during this first course we set up the strategy for learning and getting really into the subject of cryptography. The main goal was to make the students discover by their own the subject (discovery learning), and force them to take some deep thinking (critical reflection) on the issues raised by the topic. Based on the idea that the information gets saved and remembered more efficiently if several physical senses are used, we propose them audio descriptions/definitions, video recordings on the topic, as well as written notes to be taken. In this way the students used their sight, touch, and hearing in order to record the information. The videos are free online MOOC tutorials.

In this way, we challenged the students to build their own reflective discourse based on their previous reflections to then, implement it.

The second and the third courses were interactive, using the questionnaire with open-end answers, e.g., how does a public key encryption scheme work, what is the security of a cryptosystem, what issues are to deal with when implementing such a solution, etc. We were discussing on Zoom and adding content to a spreadsheet on Miro. The technique was extremely appreciated by the students, for several reasons.

- First of all, the classical learning methods using transmissive techniques and repetitions was changed into a process of discovery, research, reflecting and using in a positive way the knowledge. This procedure revealed students that they are able to find the information, select, understand, analyze, synthetize, evaluate and create their own knowledge (following somewhat modified Bloom's taxonomy), guided by the academic staff.
- Discussing all together, students and professor, in a collaborative style, tends to strengthen the relation between the two sides. The learning process becomes in this way a vector for a more human and social relation involving the respect and responsibility of the parties for a job well done.
- Another constructive aspect was that it shapes student's characters with rigor, respect, a high sense of responsibility and collaboration. They had to sustain their ideas in from of the others and by doing so they were confronted with questions and doubts. In order to successfully achieve their goals, they developed their skills, abilities and attitudes with elements of transformative learning and even of peer learning (paragogy).

The last step was a project proposal were the students came with the idea of implementing one solution the general cryptographic problem. We organized private groups on WhatsApp, planned meeting with Doodle, and used overleaf to collaborate on the project development.

5. CONCLUSION

Starting from a reality - the pandemic - in this article we tried to capture, through a case study, aspects of online learning carried out in the university, with students from exact sciences specialization.

Academic staff was forced to adapt their courses very quickly to deliver them online using the so-called Emergency Remote Teaching, which involves the use of fully remote teaching solutions for instruction or education that would otherwise be delivered face-to-face or as blended courses.

The whole process started with the study of several free IT solutions for online collaboration, video conferencing, online editing, scheduling or even project management, such as, Zoom, Overleaf, Miro, Doodle.

The way to move from transmissive to *transformative learning* was also pursued by the teaching staff, in condition to use effectively IT tools. By means of different devices the students were connected peer-to-peer and with academic staff for emphasized the idea of *visible learning* (Hattie, 2011). More precisely, the teaching and learning methods used (interactive) provide a well-being experience, induced by curiosity and the online collaboration. At the same time, through *critical reflection, reflective discourse, action* caused by professors and produced by students the foundations were laid for transformative learning. This way leads us to a learning model between uniform and equal individuals, under an academic supervision.

This particular state-of-mind helped students to overcome feelings induced by the isolation, such as loneliness, sadness.

In our examples of good practices, we highlighted that the teaching/learning/evaluation methods we proposed, helped by IT solutions, enabled the student to self-discover the nature of the objects, their relation with the real life, and the true relation with its colleagues, and finally, itself.

One might find some disadvantages in our case study, e.g., the size of the groups is limited to 15 students or the fact that teachers are not all trained/ prepared for the exclusively online teaching/learning. Another important issue induced by our approach is how to solve the schedule of the lectures given the students number constraint, which is a non-trivial optimization problem.

In the near future we plan to develop this strategy to a broader set of students. We plan to cooperate with fellow researcher from different fields, such as psychology, educational sciences and sociology in order to extend our knowledge about this phenomenon.

We also plan to improve this method for the next academic year and implement it to students from other faculties.

REFERENCES

Corneli, J. and Danoff, C. J., 2011. Paragogy, In: *Proceedings of the 6th Open Knowledge Conference,* Berlin, Germany.

Corneli, J. and Danoff, C. J., 2011. Paragogy: Synergizing individual and organizational learning, published on *Wikiversity.*

Cornwall, A., and Jewkes, R., 1995. What is participatory research? *Social Science and Medicine*, 14, 1667–1676.

Dede, C., 2005. Planning for neomillennial learning styles *EDUCAUSE Quarterly*, 28(1), 7–12.

Ellis, R. A., et al, 2009. E-learning in higher education: Some key aspects and their relationship to approaches to study. *Higher Education Research & Development, 28*(3), 303

Fern, E. F., 1982. The use of focus groups for idea generation: The effects of group size, acquaintanceship and moderation on response quantity and quality. *Journal of Marketing Research*, 19, 1–13.

Flores, J. G., and Alonso, C. G., 1995. Using focus groups in educational research: Exploring teachers' perspectives on educational change. *Evaluation Review*, 19, 84–101.

Freitas, H., et al, 1998. *The focus group, a qualitative research method: reviewing the theory, and providing guidelines to its planning.* 1–22.

Green, J. M., et al, 2003. Shortcuts to safety: Risk and 'rules of thumb' in accounts of food choice. *Health, Risk and Society*, 5, 33–52.

Hattie, J., 2011. *Visible Learning for Teachers: Maximizing Impact on Learning,* Trade Paperback

Hayward, C., et al, 2004. Still left out in the cold: Problematising participatory research and development. *Sociologia Ruralis*, 44, 95–108.

Herlo, D., 2016. IT tools in initial teacher training, in *Proceedings of the International Conference e-Learning 2016*, Madeira, Portugal, July 1-4, 2016, Edited by Miguel Baptista Nunes, Maggie McPherson, ISBN: 978-989-8533-51-7, pp. 85-92

Herlo, D., 2016. Paragogy. New concept of learning in the information society, pp. 159-174, in Volume: *Crașovan, M., (coord), Educație-evaluare-integrare*, Editura Universității de Vest din Timișoara, ISBN978-973-125-489-0

Hodges, C., Moore, St., Lockee, B., Trust, T., Bond, A., 2020. The Difference Between Emergency Remote Teaching and Online Learning – Retrived from https://er.educause.edu/articles/2020/3/the-difference-between-emergency-remote-teaching-and-online-learning

Howe, N., and Strauss, W., 2000. *Millennials rising: The next great generation* New York: Vintage.

Kamberelis, G., and Dimitriadis, G., 2005. Focus groups: Strategic articulations of pedagogy, politics, and inquiry. In N. K. Denzin, and Y. S. Lincoln (Eds.), *The Sage Handbook of Qualitative Research*, 3rd ed. (pp. 887–907). Thousand Oaks, CA: Sage Publications Inc.

Krueger, R. A., and Casey, M. A., 2000. *Focus groups: A practical guide for applied research*, 4th ed. Thousand Oaks, CA: Sage Publications Inc.

Mendes de Almeida, P. F., 1980. A review of group discussion methodology. *European Research*, 8, 114–120.

Mezirow, J., 1991. *Transformative Dimensions of Adult Learning*. San Francisco, CA: Jossey-Bass

Morgan, D. L., 1996. Focus Groups. *Annual Review of Sociology*, 22, 129–152.

Oblinger, D. G., and Oblinger, J. L., 2005. *Educating the net generation* Boulder, CO: EDUCAUSE.

Prensky, M., 2001. Digital natives, digital immigrant *On the Horizon*, 9(5), 15–24.

Sangrà, A., et al, 2012. *Building an Inclusive Definition of E-Learning: An Approach to the Conceptual Framework*, Retrived from http://www.irrodl.org/index.php/irrodl/article/view/1161/2146

Tapscott, D., 2008. *Grown up digital: How the net generation is changing your world* New York: McGraw-Hill.

Taylor, S., 2019. *The psychology of pandemics: Preparing for the next global outbreak of infectious disease*. Cambridge Scholars Publishing.

Thomas, L., et al, 1995. Comparison of focus group and individual interview methodology in examining patient satisfaction with nursing care. *Social Sciences in Health*, 1, 206–219.

Yousuf, M.I., 2007. The Delphi technique. *Essays in Education, 20*, 80-89.

LONGITUDINAL CO-TEACHING PROJECTS – SCOPING REVIEW

Jaroslav Veteska[1], Martin Kursch[2], Zuzana Svobodova[3], Michaela Tureckiova[4] and Lucie Paulovcakova[5]
Charles University, Prague, Czech Republic
[1]*Prof. PhDr.*
[2]*Ph.D., MBA, PhDr.*
[3]*Ph.D., Mgr.*
[4]*Ph.D., PhDr.*
[5]CSc., MBA, Ing., Ph.D.

ABSTRACT

The main orientations of education policy with a view to the next decade include, inter alia, promoting educational innovation and verifying it through further professional development of teaching staff and exploring the effectiveness of learning. One of the possibilities of achieving this goal is co-teaching and its forms, which are constantly evolving. The aim of this study is to provide an overview of approaches not only to the actual implementation of co-teaching, but also to the whole process of preparation in order to evaluate the experience gained in a number of researches already carried out, in the form of an overview study. An inductive thematic analysis of published articles in 2005-2020, with a predominance of attention for the period 2019 and 2020, was used in 16 databases such as ERIC, Scopus®, Complementary Index, etc. As a result, 19 articles were finally included in the analysis of the issues examined. Inductive thematic analysis identified six themes: (1) "co-teaching effectiveness", (2) "problems and obstacles", (3) "methods of and with co-teaching", (4) "teachers' roles and relationships", (5) "teachers' cooperation", and (6) "special educational needs" (SEN). The scoping review study covers the theoretical basis of co-teaching issues, the results of research surveys or experiments on the procedures, advantages or barriers of various co-teaching models. The study serves as a basic framework supporting the creation and application of a virtual component as a new part of the educational method of co-teaching solved by the TAČR project.

KEYWORDS

Co-Teaching, Co-Teaching Efficiency, Co-Teaching Methods, Problems and Obstacles of Co-Teaching, Relationships and Cooperation of Teachers, Educational Needs

1. INTRODUCTION

Co-teaching as an innovative method is being given increasing attention in the international environment, especially through realized experiments. Several expert studies are being conducted with research-based knowledge. Research topics are specifically focused on other forms of professional development of teachers in relation to specific educational needs, on the development of social interactions, active learning, reflective thinking, cooperation and joint learning, with the aim of effective learning of pupils and acquisition of competences needed for active civic, professional and personal life.

Co-teaching defines Bacharach et al. (2010) as joint planning and teaching of two or more teachers. The co-teaching model, where the teacher-mentor and the starting teacher perform together, use strategies requiring shared authority, consistent involvement of both teachers, cooperation in teaching planning and evaluation of teaching. Co-teaching, as stated in e.g. Friend (2014, 2015) was originally based on cooperation between teachers of special and general education. Practical applications mention e.g. Ricci and Fingon (2017). However, in the course of co-teaching, research has revealed other benefits of such guided teaching (Friend, 2015; Ricci and Fingon, 2017; Sanchez et al., 2019; Walsh, 2012). When applying co-teaching, it is possible, for example, to divide students into groups according to their abilities and to take advantage of the opportunity to teach students in different ways, apply different methods, individualize teaching. The mentoring model makes it possible to improve cooperation in school environments, promote mutual learning among teachers (Baeten and Simons, 2014; Fraser and Watson, 2013; Rabin, 2020). In the framework of research into the cooperation of teachers in general education in co-teaching, better student learning outcomes, knowledge consolidation (Eckardt and Giouroukakis, 2018; Ronfeldt et al., 2015; Vescio et al., 2008). Experiments or case studies also focus on the effects of virtual co-teaching, e-learning (Chan et al., 2012; Puttonen, 2014; Takala and Wickman, 2019; Wilson and VanBerschot, 2014).

The key to co-teaching success, as Rexroat-Frazier and Chamberlin (2019) report, is the clearly defined purpose of joint teaching and the selection of partners in teaching, co-teacher education. The effectiveness of co-teaching is further influenced by teaching practices, together with the use of effective teaching strategies, effective practices, their balance. The research carried out shows that they focus mainly on teaching practices.

The aim of the scoping review is to analyze and summarize the most important knowledge on selected topics of co-teaching as a starting point for further research work within the project Technology Agency of the Czech Republic (TAČR: TL03000133) entitled *New Method of Education for the 21st Century: Virtual-Co-Teaching* solved in the period 2020-2023. This project focuses on virtual co-teaching and its effectiveness. Therefore, also our research question asked is: "What role does virtual environment play in co-teaching?"

2. BODY OF PAPER

2.1 Methods

2.1.1 Scoping Review Methodology

We chose scoping review as the research method. This method is suitable for the systematic search, selection, analysis and subsequent synthesis of the obtained information so that we can answer research questions responsibly. The methodological basis for our study was the work of Arksey and O'Malley (2005), which we followed in all steps of the research.

2.1.2 Identifying Relevant Studies

When searching for studies, we first used the keyword "co-teaching". The result was more than 2,000 studies. That's why we've added an advanced search that's consistent with our goal. Another string was the word "long-term", the results suddenly from 12 studies. We replaced the word long-term with "longitudinal" and the result was another 17 studies, different from the previous combination. Another combination was the search for "co-teaching" and virtual at the same time. The result was another 10 studies. We then used the same criteria in Google Scholar. For 5 records were found after the phrase "virtual co-teaching" was found. Next, we searched in the title of the article virtual and co-teaching and found 5 articles.

16 Databases (ERIC, Complementary Index, Academic Search Ultimate, Scopus®, Supplemental Index, APA PsycInfo, Social Sciences Citation Index, Directory of Open Access Journals, Gale eBooks, Springer Nature Journals, ScienceDirect, MEDLINE, JSTOR Journals, Library, Information Science and Technology Abstracts, Business Source Ultimate, Humanities Source Ultimate) and Google Scholar were searching to find as many relevant studies as possible. We limited your search to 1990-2020. The search tool was the system of Charles University UKAZ and separately the search engine Google Scholar. In Table 1, all the results are.[1]

2.1.3 Inclusion and Exclusion Criteria

We identified a total of 49 studies that we had to go through and manually sort. The inclusion and exclusion criteria were discussed by all authors together. We focused mainly on the period 1990-2020, as previous studies are not relevant to the virtual dimension. In the end, we selected 19 studies in our sample that meet the main criterion of long-term research and deal with the effects of co-teaching or its effectiveness. We have also included all studies that study the virtual possibility of co-teaching. PRISMA systematic evaluation (Moher et al, 2009) was used and our algorithm and results are described on Figure 1.

[1] Reference to the UKAZ system, which has access to all of the above databases:
http://eds.b.ebscohost.com/eds/search/advanced?vid=7&sid=b259143b-4e01-42db-8c7c-22f94f9d499f%40pdc-v-sessmgr04.

Table 1. Exact search string results in indexed databases with exact search string

Databases	Search String	Records Identified
ERIC, Complementary Index, Academic Search Ultimate, Scopus®, Supplemental Index, APA PsycInfo, Social Sciences Citation Index, Directory of Open Access Journals, Gale eBooks, Springer Nature Journals, ScienceDirect, MEDLINE, JSTOR Journals, Library, Information Science & Technology Abstracts, Business Source Ultimate, Humanities Source Ultimate	co-teaching	2162
	co-teaching AND virtual	10
	co-teaching AND long-term	12
	co-teaching AND longitudinal	17
Google Scholar	"virtual co-teaching"	5
Google Scholar	allintitle: virtual co-teaching	5

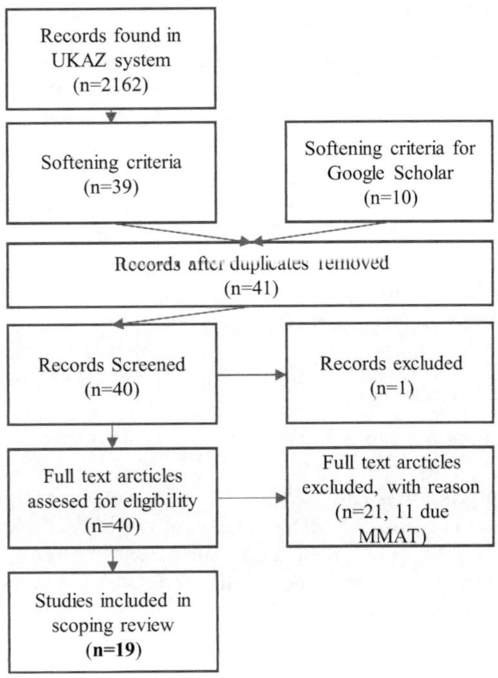

Figure 1. Search Flowchart

2.1.4 Critical Appraisal

When evaluating the quality of studies, we used the Mixed Method Appraisal Tool (MMAT), version 2018. According to this methodology, we were able to disable studies based on proven quality criteria for mixed research and study methodology. The MMAT follow-up was used independently by two authors from our group to promote independence and eliminate subjective concepts. Based on NMAT, 11 studies were excluded.[2]

[2] See http://mixedmethodsappraisaltoolpublic.pbworks.com/w/file/fetch/127916259/MMAT_2018_criteria-manual_2018-08-01_ENG.pdf.

2.1.5 Data Analyses

The method of inductive thematic analysis was used for data analysis (Corbin and Strauss, 2008). The articles were sorted by content into individual categories, the authors identified key topics in them, and then the articles were re-grouped according to selected key topics.

2.2 Results

A total of 19 articles were analyzed. The most frequently declared aim in these articles was "to analyze the experience with co-teaching" (n=5), "describe the impact and benefits of co-teaching for students" (n =4), "identify specifics and patterns of cooperation of teachers in the co-teaching process" (n = 4), "describe the advantages and disadvantages of co-teaching" (n =2), "describe specific possibilities of use" (n=2), "identify the strengths and weaknesses of the method and modify it" (n=1) and "describe the attitudes of teachers" (n=1). 10 of these 19 studies, used a qualitative design, 3 used a quantitative design and 6 studies used mixed methods. Most studies relied on multiple methods of data collection (n= 12). The most common method of collecting qualitative research data was interviews (n=7). This method was supplemented by written reflection of respondents (n=6), observation (n=4) and open question questionnaire (n=2). Statistical methods were mainly based on questionnaires and scaling (n=10). An overview of the methods used can be found in Table 2.

2.3 Themes

Based on thematic analysis, six themes mentioned by the respondents in the articles reviewed were identified in the studies: (1) "**co-teaching effectiveness**", (2) "**problems and obstacles**", (3) "**methods of and with co-teaching**", (4) "**teachers' role and relationships**", (5) "**teachers' cooperation**", and (6) "**special educational needs**". Individual topics cannot be completely separated from each other, because, for example, the topic of co-teaching effectiveness is mingled with virtually all the texts analysed and is always placed in another context related to another identified topic. Otherwise, effectiveness will be seen in combination with special educational needs and otherwise in the context of teacher cooperation, their roles and relationships. It is therefore clear that in the co-teaching process, individual topics are logically intertwined and always accentuate a certain aspect related to the specific context in which this method is implemented. The following section describes the identified topics in more detail, including the relationship or context with other co-teaching topics.

2.3.1 Co-Teaching Effectiveness

The effectiveness of co-teaching is a central identified topic, which in a way contains all the texts. It includes, on the one hand, a view of effectiveness by the teacher (e.g. Wilson and VanBerschot, 2014, Jurkowski and Müller, 2018, Neifeald and Nissim, 2019, Rabin, 2020) as well as a student view (e.g. Puttonen, 2014, Strogilos, King-Sears, 2019). The view of effectiveness by teachers is usually the basis for revision of the methods used or modification of a new co-teaching course. Based on a pilot study, the teachers reflect the entire teaching process, finding the positives and negatives on which it is based when adjusting the course or educational activity to its final form (Kim et al., 2007, Wilson and VanBerschot, 2014, Neifeald and Nissim, 2019).

In view of the research question asked, "What role does virtual environment play in co-teaching?", the technical readiness is essential in terms of efficiency (Chan et al., 2012, Wilson and VanBerschot, 2014). This factor lies (Chan et al., 2012) on the border between efficiency and problems, because with technical complications it is impossible to teach effectively with two people, the benefit of the method decreases and complications and negative impact on results dominate. This aspect is also essential from the point of view of students who perceive the readiness of a co-teaching pair (whether technical or human).

Table 2. Summary of individual studies

Author/Year	Aim	Research type	Study design and methods	Study Participants	Themes	Virtual
Chan et al. (2012)	Based on a three-month measurement, describe the positive impact of co-teaching on students, teachers and school principals.	Mixed methods	structured questionnaire with scale, personal interview after the lesson	3 full classes (A with leading teacher, B with supportive tacher and C observing)	problems and obstacles, teachers' cooperation, co-teaching effectiveness, teachers' roles and relationships	Yes
Eckardt et al. (2018)	Describe the impact of co-teaching in combination with situational learning on the teaching students.	Qualitative	analysis of anonymous reflection of students taught by co-teaching, observation during lessons and teacher's notes	21 teachers taking a co-teaching-led "teen literacy" course	teachers' cooperation, effectiveness of co-teaching, combination of methods	No
Rabin (2020)	Describe the process of implementing co-teaching in the co-work of a mentor and a novice teacher.	Qualitative	interviews, observations, qualitative analysis of co-teaching implemenatation	241 participants, 70 mentors and 171 novice teachers	teachers' cooperation, ethical dimension, co-teaching effectiveness, teachers' roles	No
Jurkovsky and Müller (2018)	Describe the development of the relationship of a co-teaching couple composed of a special educator and an ordinary teacher.	Quantitative	questionnaire, 3 measurements / year	36 ordinary teachers, 19 special educators, 184 students	teacher cooperation, teacher relationships, problems and obstacles, co-teaching effectiveness, special educational needs	No
The Park (2014)	Identify specific patterns of cooperation of teachers in class.	Qualitative	analysis of 5 videos from English lessons in one class	2 teachers (native and non-native speaker)	teachers' cooperation, teachers' roles and relationship	No
Neifeald and Nissim (2019)	Identify the benefits of the "Academia Class" programme and its impact on co-teaching practices.	Quantitative	questionnaire, statistical evaluation	participants in the Academia Class project, 125 (51 teachers, 26 teachers students, 18 primary school teachers, 20 early childhood teachers, 10 trainers)	teachers' cooperation, combination of methods, teachers relationship, co-teaching effectiveness	Yes
Ricci and Fingon (2017)	Based on the analysis of experience with co-teaching to create the basis for effective application of co-teaching at primary and secondary schools in teaching a class with pupils with SEN.	Mixed methods	evaluation and reflection of co-teaching training plans, analysis of experience; mathematical and statistical methods of data evaluation	34 postgraduate students, 14 special pedagogy, 20 literature	special educational needs, teachers' cooperation	No
Campbell et al. (2018)	Describe the pros and cons of co-teaching by looking at university students.	Mixed methods	structured questionnaire (online Likert scale), qualitative analysis of open responses	not stated	teachers' cooperation, problems and obstacles	No
Puttonen (2014)	Analyse new experience of students with online teaching led by two experts.	Quantitative	structured questionnaire (online)	32 graduates of virtual co-teaching course	co-teaching effectiveness, teachers' cooperation	Yes
Takala and Wickman (2019)	Describe the experience of rural teachers with co-teaching and identify problems in its application.	Mixed methods	questionnaire, content analysis of open answers	40 teachers from one municipality (29 ordinary , 11 special educators)	cooperation of teachers, problems and obstacles to co-teaching	No
Sanchez et al. (2019)	Analyse the pedagogical experience with a postgraduate course led by the co-teaching method in order to identify the strengths and weaknesses of this method.	Qualitative	case study, written reflection of participants and its content analysis	3 cooperating experts (university teacher), 2 directors	teachers' cooperation, problems and obstacles	No
Strogilos and King-Sears (2019)	Describe the experience and progress of students with and without SEN in co-teaching.	Qualitative	semi-structured interviews	3 students with SEN, 7 students without SEN	co-teaching efficiency, special educational needs	No
Wilson and VanBerschot (2014)	Analyse and subsequently modify the e-learning course for master's students.	Qualitative	case study, design thinking	2 teachers and course participants	teachers' cooperation, co-teaching effectiveness	Yes
Thompson and Dow (2017)	Describe the effectiveness of co-teaching of two experts from different disciplines compared to teaching led by one expert.	Mixed methods	action research, observation and measurement using a scale	24 science students	co-teaching effectiveness, combination of methods, teachers' cooperation	No
Kim et al. (2007)	Describe the possibilities of using the CACSR computer program in co-teaching lessons to promote reading among students with SEN.	Qualitative	evaluation and reflection of the method	2 teams of teachers (ordinary teacher and special educator)	special educational needs, teachers' cooperation, teachers effectiveness, teachers' roles	Yes
Duran et al (2020)	Analysis of attitudes of teachers towards co-teaching in the context of conceptual training.	Mixed methods	questionnaire, analysis of written reports	82 wells as co-teachers in two groups (with and without training)	teachers' cooperation, co-teaching effectiveness, problems and obstacles	No
Lohmus et al (2019)	Describe the benefits of co-teaching and identify its potential risks.	Qualitative	structured interviews	2 co-teachers. 4 students reflecting co-teaching at higher education	teachers' roles, co-teaching effectiveness, teachers' cooperation	No
Montgomery (2019)	Analyze co-teachers' collaboration.	Qualitative	reflection of experience	2 co-teachers reflecting on their practical teaching experience	teachers' cooperation, teachers' roles, co-teaching effectiveness	No
Bilican et al. (2020)	Analyse the use of co-teaching as a method of further teacher education.	Qualitative	VNOS-C questionnaire , analysis of recordings of educational activities, reflective interviews, participating observations	2 co-teachers (science teacher and university teacher)	teachers' cooperation, teachers' roles, co-teaching effectiveness	No

2.3.2 Problems and Obstacles

Problems and obstacles of co-teaching can be divided according to three identified potentially problematic factors – the factor of technical problems, the human factor and the lack of time – based on the texts analyzed. Technical problems are complicated mainly by co-teaching using a virtual environment. Chan et al. (2012) stated that the well-managed technical aspect of the whole process is essential for virtual co-teaching and therefore, after a pilot analysis of virtual learning, they made the necessary technical adjustments. For example, the problem of face imaging and face-reading had to be technically solved by installing additional audio/video technology and cameras on the move (specifically, mobile cameras on teachers' heads). Thanks to this effect, students in the classroom were able to synchronize and at the same time include a peer learning method, which was not possible without additional technical installation. Subsequent results have shown that if virtual co-teaching is technically handled well, it can lead to positive impacts on students (Chan et al., 2012).

The human factor is the most fundamental. If cooperation does not work, teachers do not plan and evaluate joint teaching, there are significant shortcomings and the method does not have the necessary benefits (Jurkowski and Müller, 2018). A specific area of the human factor is the approach of the school management to co-teaching. Takala and Wickman (2018) have identified the role of the headmaster as a significant obstacle in the implementation of co-teaching, since its implementation is directly dependent on the decision of the headmaster and not on the teachers, which logically leads to the fact that the headmaster who is not inclined to it will not support and implement it at the school.

It is clear that teaching one group of students with two people is challenging and necessarily requires time to prepare lessons, create a meaningful plan, split roles, set up cooperation and then reflect on teaching and translate it into further planning and other lessons (Ricci and Fington, 2017). However, teachers do not have enough time available (Park, 2014, Jurkowski and Müller, 2018) and therefore cannot devote themselves to preparation and reflection to the extent necessary. The lack of time factor was reported by most studies as the most important and most affecting overall effectiveness of co-teaching (Takala and Wickman, 2018, Jurkowski and Müller, 2018, Ricci and Fington, 2017, Sanchez et al., 2019).

2.3.3 Methods of and with Co-Teaching

Specific chosen methods, procedures and forms are different in different implementations. In the analyzed texts we encountered the following forms of co-teaching methods:

- One teach – one support, also supporting model (Park, 2014, Chan et al., 2012, Eckardt et al., 2018, Takala and Wickman,2018, Lõhmus et al., 2019, Montgomery, 2019, Duran et al., 2020, Rabin, 2020).
- Alternative Teaching, also complementary or complementary model (Ricci and Fington, 2017, Strogilos and King-Sears, 2019, Jurkowski and Müller, 2018, Kim et al., 2007).
- Team-teaching (Wilson and VanBerschot 2014, Puttonen,2014, Thomson and Dow, 2017, Campbell et al., 2018, Neifeald and Nissim, 2019, Sanchez et al., 2019, Bilican et al., 2020).

In the "one teach – one support" model, in addition to standard assistance to the head teacher, it is also a method of education for future or novice teachers. In fact, the head teacher becomes a mentor at the same time, listening and learning from each other based on a partnership, which is not entirely possible with classical mentoring (Montgomery, 2019; Rabin, 2020). Bilican et al. (2020) shows co-teaching as a possible way of further education. A team consisting of a university teacher and an ordinary teacher confirms that the professional development of teachers can be effectively based on a co-teaching strategy.

Furthermore, co-teaching was supplemented by other methods, which are used as standard even in classical teaching by one teacher. Eckardt et al. (2018) combine co-teaching with situational learning, resulting in more effective knowledge consolidation than teaching with one teacher. Chan et al. (2012) combines co-teaching in a virtual environment with peer learning by students, which increases the effectiveness of the positive impacts of co-teaching on students. The virtual part is involved in co-teaching in different ranges. It allows you to teach using e-learning courses (Wilson and VanBerschot, 2014), teach together and be different (Puttonen,2014, Chan et al. 2012) or take advantage of two teachers and digital technologies and special educational programs (Neifeald and Nissim,2019, Kim et al., 2007).

2.3.4 Teachers' Roles and Relationships

The division of roles is closely related to the chosen co-teaching method. As far as the "one teach – one support" model is concerned, it makes sense that the teaching will always have its head teacher (e.g. Lõhmus et al., 2019). Roles between the different co-teaching pairs can also result naturally from the education and approbation of individual teachers. It is logical that otherwise there will be divided roles in the teaching of pupils with special educational needs, where special educator and ordinary teacher teaches (Strogilos and King-Sears, 2019, Jurkowski and Müller, 2018, Kim et al., 2007) and otherwise in foreign language teaching, where a native speaker and teacher speaking the student's mother tongue is involved (Park, 2014). When using the virtual component of co-teaching, they are also the basis for the division of roles of digital competence of individual teachers (Kim et al., 2007). With regard to the various roles, it is also necessary to mention the ethical dimension of cooperation, where the balance of power, collegiality, the pursuit of the same goal at the same level of mutual consent should be maintained in relations between co-teachers and feedback on teaching should be shared (Rabin, 2020).

2.3.5 Teachers' Cooperation

The cooperation of teachers is also based on individual methods of co-teaching and their role in teaching. However, regarding the effectiveness of co-teaching, its development is important. Teacher cooperation is in three stages – planning, implementation and reflection. In this area, however, it also encounters the problem of the time factor, which is the most frequently mentioned obstacle to the quality implementation of co-teaching (Takala and Wickman,2019, Jurkowski and Müller, 2018, Ricci and Fington,2017, Sanchez et al., 2019). In preparation there is room for more creative methods of teaching and in implementation a faster and better response is possible, as well as space for improvisation (Eckardt et al., 2018). Based on joint reflection, it is possible to change and modify the work with students to make it more effective and impact on students greater (Wilson and VanBerschot, 2014, Thompson and Dow, 2017). In the preparatory phase of co-teaching, it is advisable for future co-teachers to use suitable workshops to help them set up mutual cooperation and lead to greater efficiency of the method (Rabin, 2020)

Cooperation co-teachers can also be based on mutual replenishment, where the pair consists of experts with different specializations. The results demonstrate the effectiveness of co-teaching led by two subjects, leading to a deeper understanding of the subject (Thompson and Dow, 2017).

Quality cooperation of teachers also brings reliability to students. If there are 2 teachers, students have answers from two different sources, which they consider more reliable. Furthermore, this association opens a new perspective for them at work, because the differences in teacher experience make students see the problem from multiple perspectives and there is constructive discussion (Eckardt et al., 2018). Co-teaching enables the application of a wide range of teaching practices, including partnerships between teachers and teachers, shared planning and evaluation of teaching. Without co-teaching, these procedures would be very difficult to implement, even completely unfeasible Neifeald and Nissim, 2019).

2.3.6 Special Educational Needs (SEN)

A specific thematic area consists of special educational needs, in which co-teaching is used as a method that helps to lead teaching in the class of intacted and SEN pupils. Studies show a positive experience (Strogilos, King-Sears, 2019) and pupils report that it was an effective "extra help" that allows them to feel valid members of the class (Strogilos, King-Sears, 2019). More flexibility of teachers and the ability to respond to individual needs have also been confirmed by these students (Strogilos, King-Sears, 2019). Jurkowski and Müller (2018) offer another look at the use of co-teaching in teaching students with SEN, which focuses mainly on the cooperation of an ordinary teacher and a special teacher, which is not always easy. Cooperating teachers encounter a lack of planning time, which in turn also affects the possibility of a positive impact on students and the effectiveness of teaching. This aspect is also mingled with other mentioned topics and is the overall dominant mentioned problem in the implementation of co-teaching (Chan et al., 2012, Takala and Wickman, 2019, Sanchez et al., 2019).

3. CONCLUSION

The overview study focuses on co-teaching as an innovative method, which is also given increasing attention in terms of professional development of teachers and especially with regard to social interactions, active and joint learning and, above all, to the development of the effectiveness of pupils' learning and the acquisition of their necessary competences for a successful and active civic, professional and personal life.

As already mentioned in the previous sections of this overview study, co-teaching is a topic whose importance is increasing over time, while virtual co-teaching is also part of the expert discussion. Co-teaching can be analyzed from different points of view. However, the different areas of co-teaching and the prospects for its use are intertwined and linked to specific contexts (e.g. virtual environments), with the issue of co-teaching effectiveness linking them. Given the research question asked ("What role does virtual environment play in co-teaching?") this co-teaching context is examined within the individual identified topics as and if it appears in the source documents.

Co-teaching efficiency, identified as a central and cross-cutting theme, includes both a view of effectiveness by the teacher (Wilson and VanBerschot, 2014, Jurkowski and Müller, 2018, Neifeald and Nissim, 2019, Rabin, 2020), and students (e.g. Puttonen, 2014, Strogilos and King-Sears, 2019). Technical readiness, standing on the border between the topic of efficiency and problems and obstacles, is crucial for the effectiveness of the virtual co-teaching process from the point of view of teachers. In addition to the mentioned technical readiness, the human readiness (cooperation) of the co-teaching two is also important for students in the virtual form of co-teaching, allowing students to orientate well in their teaching.

3.1 Application

The findings presented in this study and the lessons learned from previous research in selected six thematic areas can be used as a basic framework for the preparation, implementation and reflection of co-teaching as an innovative method using different methodological procedures and forms of teaching, in which two teachers are always involved in different roles and evolving cooperation. For the effectiveness of co-teaching (including virtual co-teaching), it is important to deal with its entire process (planning, implementation, reflection, including the choice of co-teaching type and its specific variant of virtual co-teaching). Other contextual conditions that affect the effectiveness of (virtual) co-teaching and are elaborated in sub-topics in this study include technical readiness, a time factor for considering the specific educational needs of pupils.

3.2 Limitations

English articles were included in the overview study. This can affect the overall validity of the results found and their portability into local education systems, which are shaped in accordance with each country's education policy strategy (subsidiarity principle). Grey literature was not included in the review.

The presented study provides an overview of the types of co-teaching (including virtual) and the basic topics to be addressed in order to make this innovative teaching method effective. The results of the study will also be used in the next phases of the TAČR project[3]

REFERENCES

Arksey H. and O'Malley, L., 2005. Scoping studies: towards a methodological framework. *International Journal of Social Research Methodology*, Vol. 8, Iss. 1, pp. 19-32.

Bacharach, N. et al., 2010. Changing the face of student teaching through co-teaching. *Action in Teacher Education*, Vol. 32, Iss. 1, pp. 3-14.

Baeten, M. and Simons, M., 2014. Student teachers' team teaching: Models, effects, and conditions for implementation. *Teaching and Teacher Education*, Vol. 41, pp. 92-110.

Bilican, K. et al, 2020. Learning by Teaching: a Case Study of Co-teaching to Enhance Nature of Science Educators, Successes, and Challenges. *International Journal of Science and Mathematics Education,* Vol. 18, Iss. 1, pp. 1-20.

[3] Funding/: This study was supported by Technology Agency of the Czech Republic (TAČR); Project No. TL03000133.

Campbell, E. L. et al., 2018. Better Together: Co-Teaching in Undergraduate Applied Psychology Courses. *Psychology Teaching Review,* Vol. 24, No. 2, pp. 3-11.

Chan, B. et al., 2012. Case study: Affordances of using multi-HD technology for distanced co-teaching in Hong Kong secondary schools. *2012 World Congress on Information and Communication Technologies, Information and CommunicationTechnologies*, Trivadrum, 2012, pp. 162-166.

Corbin, J. M. and Strauss, A. L., 2008. *Basics of qualitative research: techniques and procedures for Developing grounded theory.* Sage Publication, Los Angeles, USA.

Duran, D. et al., 2020. Student teachers' perceptions and evidence of peer learning through co-teaching: improving attitudes and willingness towards co-teaching. *European Journal of Psychology of Education: A Journal of Education and Development,* Vol. 35, pp. 1-16.

Eckardt, P. and Giouroukakis,V., 2018. The Impact of Co-Teaching on Pedagogical Approaches and Student Conceptual Understanding in a Graduate, Adolescent Literacy Course. *Journal for Leadership and Instruction*, Vol. 17, No. 2, pp. 40-43.

Fraser, J. and Watson, A., 2013. Bring student teaching into the 21st century. *Phi Delta Kappan*, Vol. 94, Iss. 7, p. 25.

Friend, M., 2014. *Co-teach! Building and sustaining effective classroom partnerships in inclusive schools.* 2nd ed. Author, Greensboro, USA.

Friend, M., 2015. Co-teaching versus apprentice teaching: An analysis of similarities and differences. *Teacher Education and Special Education*, Vol. 38, No. 2, pp. 79-87.

Jurkowski, S. and Müller, B., 2018. Co-teaching in inclusive classes: The development of multi-professional cooperation in teaching dyads. *Teaching and Teacher Education,* Vol. 75, pp. 224-231.

Kim, A. et al., 2007. Facilitating Co-Teaching for Literacy in General Education Classrooms through Technology: Focus on Students with Learning Disabilities. *Reading,* Vol. 22, No. 3, pp. 269-291.

Lõhmus, E. et al., 2019. Lecturer's and assistant's views on collaborative teaching at the university. *Estonian Journal of Education / Eesti Haridusteaduste Ajakiri,* Vol. 7, No. 2, pp. 231-233.

Moher, D. et al., 2009. Preferred Reporting Items for Systematic Reviews and Meta-analyses: The PRISMA Statement. PLoS Med Vol. 6 No. 7: e1000097. https ://doi.org/10.1371/journal.pmed.1000097.

Montgomery, M. and Akerson, A., 2019. Facilitating Collaboration through a Co-Teaching Field Experience. *Networks: An Online Journal for Teacher Research.* Vol. 21, Iss. 1, pp. 1-21.

Neifeald, E. and Nissim, Y., 2019. Co-Teaching in the "Academia Class": Evaluation of Advantages and Frequency of Practices. *International Education Studies,* Vol. 12, No. 5, pp. 86-98.

Park, J. 2014. English co-teaching and teacher collaboration: A micro-interactional perspective. *System,* Vol. 44, No. 1, pp. 34-44.

Puttonen, K., 2014. Information Specialist and ICT Lecturer Co-Teach an Online Course: A New Way and What Students Think About It. *Nordic Journal of Information Literacy in Higher Education,* Vol. 6, No. 1, pp. 52-64.

Rabin, C., 2020. Co-Teaching: Collaborative and Caring Teacher Preparation. *Journal of Teacher Education,* Vol. 71, No. 1, pp. 135-147.

Rexroat-Frazier N. and Chamberlin, S., 2019. Best Practices in Co-Teaching Mathematics with Special Needs Students. *Journal of Research in Special Educational Needs*, Vol. 19, No. 3, pp. 173-183.

Ricci, L. A. and Fingon, J. C., 2017. Faculty Modeling Co-Teaching and Collaboration Practices in General Education and Special Education Courses in Teacher Preparation Programmes. *Athens Journal of Education,* Vol. 4, No 4, pp. 351-362.

Ronfeldt, M. et al., 2015. Teacher collaboration in instructional teams and student achievement. *American Educational Research Journal*, Vol. 52, Iss. 3, pp. 475-514.

Sanchez, J. at al., 2019. Exploring the Co-Teaching Experience in a Graduate-Level, Principal Preparation Course. *InSight: A Journal of Scholarly Teaching,* Vol. 14, pp. 99-112.

Strogilos, V. and King-Sears, M., 2019. Co-Teaching Is Extra Help and Fun: Perspectives on Co-Teaching from Middle School Students and Co-Teachers. *Journal of Research in Special Educational Needs,* Vol. 19, No. 2, pp. 92-102.

Takala, M. and Wickman, K., 2019. Collaborative Case-Based Virtual Learning in Higher Education: Consultation Case in Special Education. *Journal of Digital Learning in Teacher Education*, Vol. 35, No. 4, pp. 236-248.

Thompson, K. W. and Dow, M. J., 2017. Co-Teaching to Improve Control Variable Experiment Instruction in Physical Sciences Education. *Electronic Journal of Science Education,* Vol. 21, No. 5, pp. 36-52.

Vescio, V. et al., 2008. A review of research on the impact of professional learning communities on teaching practice and student learning. *Teaching and Teacher Education*, Vol. 24, Iss. 1, pp. 80-91.

Walsh, J., 2012. Co-teaching as a school system strategy for continuous improvement. *Preventing School Failure*, Vol. 56, pp. 29-36.

Wilson, B. G. and VanBerschot, J. L., 2014. Co-Teaching an Online Action Research Class / Co-enseignement et classe de recherche-action en ligne. *Canadian Journal of Learning and Teaching,* Vol. 40, No 2, pp 1-18.

ON-LINE COLLABORATIVE KNOWLEDGE BUILDING IN HIGHER EDUCATION: TESTING A QUANTITATIVE MODEL

Ian S. McGowan
University of Technology, Jamaica

ABSTRACT

Upto now, the knowledge building influence of the fundamental communicative functions during an on-line collaborative learning (OLCL) session, i.e. argumentative, responsive, elicitative, informative and imperative have been mainly based on results from qualitative studies, results that could have been strengthened by quantitative approaches. Starting from a literature review, we formulate a dual quantitative model of an on-line collaboration knowledge building (OCKB) that described these communicative functions, and aim to validate this model in a computer science topic related OCKB with a total of n=44 participants. Corpuses are collected for manual dialog act coding and communicative function variable calculations. A regression analysis failed to provide for the hypothesized model on seven of the eight tests on the basis of quantitative data. Findings suggest the imperative communication function best explain the assessment results statistically alone and in some significance in combination with some of the other communicative functions.

KEYWORDS

Knowledge Building, Utterances, Collaborative, Participants, Communicative Functions

1. INTRODUCTION

On-line collaborative knowledge building (OCKB) is assuming an increased role in higher education. In this practice of dialogue supported by chat-room technology, groups of people with shared goals, share activities and experiences in the context of the practice (Nistor, 2012; Lave, 1991; Wenger, 1999). Participation in OCKBs is assumed to lead to the accumulation of experience, stimulation of the social construction of knowledge, and the development of expertise (Nistor, 2012; Bereiter, 2002; Boylan, 2010; Engestrom, 2010). Research in this form of participation often draws on a sociocultural perspective, that is one that emphasizes knowledge building through social and communicative processes. Nevertheless, despite this push towards on-line collaboration approach in both academia and in the workplace as a knowledge building enabler, the studies related to this approach are mainly qualitative which maybe missing or could be complimented by some of the strengths presented by quantitative approaches, including communicative activity investigations and testing hypotheses.

Conflicting views can be identified and resolved collaboratively when participants are working as a community of inquirers (Chan, 2012), but this form of participation often leads to problem solving through creative thinking and inquiry, is open-ended and crucially conducted with others in the group. In this process of joint knowledge building using interactions, participants are active rather passive through exploring, transforming, comparing, coordinating and analyzing different ideas (Hennessy, 2020; Elbers, 1996; Mercer, 2000; Rogoff, 1990). Through these interactions, participants usually make influential responses commonly through *elaborating*, *clarifying* and *building* on previous contributions made by themselves and others in the group (Hennessy, 2020; Elbers, 1996; Mercer, 2000; Rogoff, 1990). The quality of these interactions is therefore paramount (Hennessy et al, 2020).

Participation generally involves natural language dialogue, an essential element of OCKB, and dialogue in an OCKB generally generates a cluster of utterances from multiple participants (Traum, 2018). Identifying the speech acts of utterances (from amongst the cluster) is necessary to correctly classify the participant's intentions. According to (Traum, 2018), it remains a challenge in inferring speech acts (or dialogue) from a surface utterance since an utterance may represent more than one speech act according to the context.

Many researchers of classifying utterances in a knowledge building group, focus on the collective, reciprocal, cumulative and purposeful nature of dialogue (Hennessy, 2020; Alexander, 2008; Mortimer, 2003). This perspective (1) includes construction of meaning through pursuing common goals and chained lines of collaborative inquiry in which answers to questions give rise to new questions (Bakhtin, 1981; Kumpulainen, 2010; Wells, 1999), and (2) recognizes the importance of participants testing their ideas against other as a means of promoting participants' argument literacy ("evaluativist" epistemology) (Hennessy, 2020; Wilkinson, 2017).

The communication functions representing the utterances typed by participants in an OCKB are identified as "dialog acts" (Erkens, 2008). For instance, if participant A would like participant B to send off an email, A could use various utterances to achieve this goal, and these utterances would all share the same dialogue function, i.e. fulfil the same dialogue act. *A dialogue act therefore is a unit in the semantic description of communicative behavior produced by a sender and directed at an addressee, specifying how the behavior is intended to influence the context through understanding of the behavior* (Bunt, 2004). The developed coding system that identifies dialog acts with a long history of about twenty years is the [DAC] Dialogue Act Coding system (Erkens, 2008), therefore the main dialog acts used in this paper as independent variables in the proposed regression model of the OCKB, are *argumentative*, *responsive*, *elicitative*, *informative* and *imperative* in keeping with DAC. A sixth independent variable is pre-OCKB assessment grade (*Pre*). The dependent variable is the post-OCKB assessment grade (*Pst*). We begin with an examination of research literature to define these five (5) dialog act variables. Then we define the regression model of the OCKB.

2. DIALOG ACT VARIABLES OF THE OCKB MODEL

2.1 Argumentative (*Arg*)

Erkens (2008), Fraser (1999), and Heeman (1998) describe argumentative as dialogue acts that represent a temporal, causal, or inferential relation between utterances and use conjuncts such as "but", "because" and therefore as a discourse marker. Indicating a line of argumentation or reasoning, Walter (2012) explains that an argumentative utterance is meant to convince someone else and is aimed at proving (or disproving) some claim. Once both parties are committed to a claim, there is no point in arguing any further. Van Boxtel (2000) studied the effects of two different face-to-face collaborative tasks on upper secondary level students' interactions and found that students who scored high on a pretest formulated more arguments during interaction. In this sense, we build our quantitative regression model of the OCKB by regarding the argumentative dialog act as a contributory factor of positive learning.

2.2 Responsive (*Res*)

As part of a constructive argument between two parties, an explanation is usually followed by either a positive response or a negative response (Erkens, 2008; Walton, 2012). Erkens (2008) and Louwerse (2003) went on to argue that responsive dialog acts (e.g. confirmations, denials and answers) have a backward-looking relation to an earlier utterance while the other four communicative functions are forward looking and give new information. Responsive utterances (such as "right", "no", "yeah", "yep" and "uh-huh") react or refer to preceding utterances. (Stolcke, 2000) stresses that detecting these utterances (as answers) are also semantically significant since they are likely to contain new information. Agreement responses (such as "that's ok","right" and "okay") are verbal responses which minimally show that the speaker has heard (and often understood and accepted) the move to which it responds (Louwerse, 2006). In (Ribeiro, 2019), the automatic multilingual dialog act recognition study showed that agreements were among the most frequent set of dialogs in the datasets collected. We therefore regard responsive dialog acts as an influencing variable in our quantitative regression model of the OCKB.

2.3 Elicitative (*Eli*)

Elicitative dialog acts (such as questions or proposals) request a response from the dialogue partners and consists of proposal to act or a question for information (Erkens, 2008; Graesser, 1994; Lehnert 1978). Some of the utterances requiring or soliciting a response include "Agree?", " ....or....?", and "Why?". Stolcke (2000) took additional interest in the backchannel or elicitative short utterance "uh-huh". These utterances play discourse-structuring roles, e.g., indicating that the speaker should go on talking. These are usually referred to in the conversation analysis literature as "continuers" and have been studied extensively (Jefferson 1984; Schegloff 1982; Yngve 1970). Therefore elicitative dialog acts are included in our quantitative regression model of the OCKB.

2.4 Informative (*Inf*)

Informative dialog acts are statements or opinions transmitting new information. The utterances signal that the speaker intends the hearer(s) to acquire the given information (Eugenio, 2010). Eugenio went further to suggest statements (e.g. "that result makes no sense", "but household items are not supposed to be taxed") describe a psychological state of the speaker. Opinions often include such hedges as "I think", "I believe", "It seems", and "I mean". In the Stolcke (2008) study, it was shown that 26% of all statements elicit backchannels. In Eugenio (2010) it was disclosed that statements, across all three datasets, were the most frequent utterances. In this sense, we build our quantitative regression model of the OCKB by regarding the informative dialog act as a contributory factor of positive learning.

2.5 Imperative (*Imp*)

Imperative dialog acts (command utterances) request an action to be fulfilled by the dialog partner or other group members (Erkens, 2008). For example: "Just give me a call tomorrow by five.", "What was that again?", "Please say yes or no." and "Let me check. Just a second please.". Yu (2019) suggest commands are among the most crucial utterances as they direct the conversation towards a specific topic, and paired with answer utterances [(positive answer, command) and (negative answer, command)], are the most frequent co-occur tags in the conversations studied. Yu went on further to show that a (negative answer, command) pair usually implies an implicit request to change the topic. In (Mezza, 2018) (Louwerse, 2006) (Anderson, 1991), a map-task challenge in the form of a task-based dialogue corpus was collected. The dialogues involve two participants, one with an empty map and one with a route marked map which must instruct the other speaker to draw the same route. The corpus (collection of texts) was chosen for the study due to its abundance of command utterances (more than 30% of the overall corpus). We therefore include imperative dialog acts in our quantitative regression model of the OCKB.

3. DERIVING A QUANTITATIVE REGRESSION MODEL OF THE OCKB

$Pst = Pre + \text{Dialog Act}_g + \varepsilon$ (1)
$Pst = Pre + \text{Dialog Act}_{g1} + \text{Dialog Act}_{g2} + \varepsilon$ (2)

where $\text{Dialog Act}_{g|g(n)} = \text{Total Weight}_g$ comes from [1-*Arg*|2-*Res*|3-*Eli*|4-*Inf*|5-*Imp*]

Two versions of the quantitative OCKB model are proposed- version 1 and version 2. According to the first version of the model, a participant's performance on the post OCKB assessment is statistically explained by his/her pre OCKB assessment grade together with the corresponding total weight factor of dialog act_g considering the error ε. A total weight factor represents the total weight of the contribution made by the participant to the corpus for dialog act_g where g={1-*Arg*,2-*Res*,3-*Eli*,4-*Inf*,5-*Imp*}.

According to this second version of the model, a participant's performance on the post OCKB assessment is statistically explained by his/her pre OCKB assessment grade together with the corresponding total weight factors of dialog act_{g1} and dialog act_{g2} together considering the error ε.

4. AIM OF THE STUDY AND HYPOTHESIS

In correspondence with the quantitative model of the OCKB (versions 1 and 2), our research aims at validating the hypothesized quantitative OCKB model (one or both versions), which implies measuring the respective dialog act variables and verifying the following hypotheses:

$H_1$1. Argumentative dialog acts have an influence on the participant's performance.
$H_1$2. Responsive dialog acts have an influence on the participant's performance.
$H_1$3. Elicitative dialog acts have an influence on the participant's performance.
$H_1$4. Informative dialog acts have an influence on the participant's performance.
$H_1$5. Imperative dialog acts have an influence on the participant's performance.
$H_2$1. Argumentative dialog acts together with informative dialog acts have an influence on the participant's performance.
$H_2$2. Elicitative dialog acts together with imperative dialog acts have an influence on the participant's performance.
$H_2$3. Responsive dialog acts together with imperative dialog acts have an influence on the participant's performance [Yu (2019)].

5. METHODOLOGY

5.1 Design

Data from one study was used. During the study, participants collaborated in small groups in an online chatroom environment on query writing tasks for the computer science related subject of Database Management. As part of the study (1) participants undertook an assessment [Task 1 of 3] before the collaboration exercise [Task 2 of 3] ahead of the second assessment [Task 3 of 3], and (2) the collaborative process between the participants was captured in log files. These log files were manually coded (using the coding scheme in 5.7) for the calculations of the dialog act variable weights (see section 5.8). In terms of quantitative learning improvement through knowledge building as hypothesized (H1 – H3), we investigated the dialog act weights in combination that influenced the second assessment scores given the first assessment scores using a regression model.

5.2 Participants

Participants were second and third year computer science degree students in the Faculty of Engineering and Computing at the University of Technology, Jamaica in the capital city of Kingston, Jamaica. Both cohorts in full were invited to participate from which a total of 59 students accepted. From that group, 44 completed the mandatory three (3) tasks. Ranging from the age of 17 years to 28 years, this final group comprised of 24 males and 20 females. None of the participants had undertaken a formal course in database query writing prior.

5.3 Learning Objectives

The topic of the 3rd year level database management course is called SQL (Structured Query Language), a technique used to query a set of related data tables. At the end of the learning activities over the four (4) consecutive days, participants should be able to write efficient SQL scrips to solve complex queries.

5.4 Task 1

Day 1, 5 hours: Participants were asked to complete a five (5) question assessment individually given a set of related data tables. Each of the questions comprise of a complex query to solve with an SQL script.

5.5 Task 2

Days 2-3: Participants, in groups of 4-5 persons formed by themselves, collaborated exclusively using WhatsApp. WhatsApp is a text messaging, image sharing, video sharing and voice messaging app for mobile devices. With an additional feature of group chatting, this free service facilitated collaborative learning. Participants were given material on SQL to include a different set of related data tables and nine (9) complex query questions. Four of questions were already solved. In keeping with an evaluativist epistemology approach, groups were encouraged to brainstorm inside the group, ask each other probing questions, test each other's SQL scripts and ideas in solving the remaining five questions together. I made myself available to the groups to provide scaffolding support and at strategic points, posted tips from which the groups could generate news ideas.

5.6 Task 3

Day 4, 80 minutes: Participants were asked to complete a five (5) question assessment individually. In fact, this assessment was exactly the same given for the pretest (in Task 1).

5.7 Dialog Act Coding Scheme

The text data collected in Task 2 represented the individual group conversations thus constituted a corpus of participant collaboration. Table 1 shows an example how the DAC was used to code a fragment of four participants collaborating on the SQL script writing task in the same group. The derived functions (or dialog act variables) are counted towards the calculations of the weight factors (described in section 5.8)

Table 1. Example of a coded online collaboration protocol

Participant	Message	Dialog Act Code	Description	Function/Dialog Act Variable
302	Inner joins can solve it but I'm not familiar with them	InfEvlNeu	Neutral Evaluation	Inf
309	What ya talking abt	EliQstOpen	Open Question	Eli
315	We solved it I think	InfStmAct	Announcement of actions	Inf
307	Aite I'm done with this practice	InfStmAct	Announcement of actions	Inf
307	I solved them last night	InfStmAct	Announcement of actions	Inf
302	Explain. Pls	ImpAct	Order for action	Imp

5.8 Dialog Act Variable Weight Factor Calculations

Dialog act variable weight factors were calculated to be a representation of respective contribution level percentages of each participant in his/her group. Corpuses were sampled upto the first 60% per group.

n = size of the group corpus sampled (number of text conversations)

Arg_g = number of arguments (*Arg*) made by the participant
$Arg_p = Arg_g/n$ [*Arg* weighted factor for the participant]
Res_g = number of responses (*Res*) made by the participant
$Res_p = Res_g/n$ [*Res* weighted factor for the participant]
Eli_g = number of elicitative (*Eli*) dialog acts made by the participant
$Eli_p = Eli_g/n$ [*Eli* weighted factor for the participant]
Inf_g = number of informative (*Inf*) dialog acts made by the participant

$Inf_p = Inf_g/n$ [*Inf* weighted factor for the participant]
Imp_g = number of imperative (*Imp*) dialog acts made by the participant
$Imp_p = Imp_g/n$ [*Imp* weighted factor for the participant]

5.9 Regression

A regression analysis on the data was performed to indicate how effective the learning improvements were. The following hypotheses were tested:

H_11: $Pst = Pre + Arg + \varepsilon$
H_21: $Pst = Pre + Arg + Inf + \varepsilon$
H_14: $Pst = Pre + Inf + \varepsilon$
H_15: $Pst = Pre + Imp + \varepsilon$
H_13: $Pst = Pre + Eli + \varepsilon$
H_23: $Pst = Pre + Res + Imp + \varepsilon$
H_12: $Pst = Pre + Res + \varepsilon$
H_22: $Pst = Pre + Eli + Imp + \varepsilon$

6. RESULTS

Table 2. Regression results

	Variable	Coefficient	t Stat	p-Value	r^2	Standard Error	Based on the p-Value
H_11					0.23449	12.42861	*Rejected*
	Pre	0.65432	3.40989	0.00155			Sig
	Arg	0.90019	0.75664	0.45393			Not Sig
H_12					0.23849	12.39605	*Rejected*
	Pre	0.66201	3.44573	0.00140			Sig
	Res	0.64477	0.88055	0.38407			Not Sig
H_13					0.21807	12.24309	*Rejected*
	Pre	0.55457	2.86621	0.00673			Sig
	Eli	0.76571	1.32300	0.19374			Not Sig
H_14					0.22712	12.48829	*Rejected*
	Pre	0.63279	3.33412	0.00192			Sig
	Inf	-0.18805	-0.45247	0.65351			Not Sig
H_15					0.31792	11.73181	***Accepted***
	Pre	0.47698	2.51815	0.01613			Sig
	Imp	1.64957	2.30011	0.02703			**Sig**
H_21					0.24659	12.49546	*Rejected*
	Pre	0.67582	3.46707	0.00135			Good
	Arg	1.25196	0.97796	0.33444			Not Sig
	Inf	-0.34317	-0.77104	0.44558			Not Sig
H_22					0.31815	11.88731	*Rejected*
	Pre	0.47856	2.48664	0.01753			Sig
	Eli	-0.08113	-0.11118	0.91207			Not Sig
	Imp	1.71653	1.81898	0.07702			Not Sig
H_23					0.26804	11.84548	***Rejected***
	Pre	0.50354	2.54491	0.01523			Sig
	Res	0.37239	0.52367	0.60362			Not Sig
	Imp	1.58086	2.14815	0.03832			**Sig**

As shown in Table 2, regression model version one revealed that there was no strong statistical evidence to support H_11, H_12, H_13 and H_14. Communicative function *informative* with a p-value of 0.654 ($r^2 = 0.23$) showing the weakest down to *elicitative* at 0.94 ($r^2 = 0.22$). The model (version 1) however, showed a statistical significant evidence to support H_15 with a p-value of 0.027 and r^2 of 0.32. This further suggest that for every percentage gain on the second assessment, an average of 1.65 (coefficient) *imperative* dialog acts was helpful.

For regression model version two also shown in Table 2, it was revealed that the most statistically significant communicative function p-value was 0.04 (*imperative*) to the least p-value of 0.912 (*elicitative*), hence not enough evidence to support $H_2 1$, $H_2 2$ and $H_2 3$. The best r^2 from the version two model was 0.32 ($H_2 2$). Again however, communicative function *imperative* with p-values of 0.03 ($H_2 3$) and 0.77 ($H_2 2$), some evidence was shown to exist statistically that the function had some effect on the second assessment results in combination with another communicative function.

7. DISCUSSION & IMPLICATIONS

The purpose of this study was to validate a proposed dual quantitative model of an OCKB and to investigate (1) the knowledge building effects, if any, of the natural communicative functions between participants in small groups in a computer science related discipline, and (2) by how much these communicative functions individually and in combination, contribute to predicting participant assessment performances.

The results of the regression analysis didn't provide strong enough evidence for the hypothesized dual quantitative OCKB model for seven of the eight tests. The analysis failed to demonstrate statistically that all of communicative functions individually and in combination except those involving *imperative*, had an effect on the final assessment grades thus not supporting $H_1 1$, $H_1 2$, $H_1 3$, $H_1 4$, $H_2 1$, $H_2 2$ and $H_2 3$. The analysis therefore suggests that dialog acts that are *argumentative*, *responsive*, *elicitative* and *informative*, may not be effective towards a positive learning outcome during OCKB sessions. The analysis however provided a statistical significant support for $H_1 5$ suggesting that communicative function *imperative* has some effect on the learning outcome during OCKB sessions. Even in combination with *responsive* utterances as highlighted by (Yu, 2009) [$H_2 3$] and *elicitative* utterances [$H_2 2$] during OCKB sessions, a fairly strong statistical effect of the *imperative* dialog act was demonstrated. The findings therefore suggest that of the five communicative functions, *imperative* contributed most to knowledge building during on-line collaborative learning sessions.

A subsequent examination of some of the group corpuses was conducted to review fragments of the *imperative* utterances used and to learn to whom these utterances were attributed. Figure 3 (below) is an example:

Participant	**Message**
453	Let me see your code Gregory (*Participant 556*)?
453	Y'all are moving too quickly
634	Oh sorry
556	mek we move through together [*mek we* means *let us*]

Figure 3. Fragment of mostly imperative utterances from a group corpus

According to Yu (2009), imperative or command utterances (as demonstrated in Figure 3), are used to control the direction of a group discussion which can change at any moment especially if one of the members doesn't find the current conversation useful or appears to be negative. Command utterances are also used to set the mood of the conversation. Participants #453 & #556 in my face to face classes are considered by some of the others in the class as *authoritative* and usually dominate the conversations. Together, both were responsible for 92.50% of the *imperative* utterances made in their OCKB group.

This has implications for the blending in of or reliance on on-line collaborative learning (OLCL) to supplement campus-based or on-line courses. In a South Korean study (Lee, 2017), it was concluded that in face to face classes where the teacher (or lead) has gotten students' approval, the teacher (or lead) has an implicit form of power in the form of an authority which allows for the class lessons to be delivered more effectively. Lee stressed that approval is not given until the teacher (or lead) has demonstrated certain attributes or qualities: demonstration of qualifications, a strong background in content knowledge, demonstrated enthusiasm, and the ability to understand students. But this form of authoritative discourse according to Bakhtin (1981), is fixed in a learning setting, that gives the learners little or no space to personalize meaning or information received by inserting other meanings situated in their context. Therefore, in a group or classroom, learners or participants are forced to either uphold or disregard the discourse. Every learning group has or develops an implicit hierarchical social structure (Lee, 2017) that tends to be driven by or allows some form of authoritative discourse as a result, but for authoritative discourse to work in OLCL sessions and for the lead person(s) to be accepted and be approved by the other participants in the learning group, Lee (2017) suggests relationships between the group members in cultural meaningful ways be developed early, and that the lead takes the time to learn more about the other group members, their contexts of living and to respect their respective cultures and beliefs.

This research aimed at proposing a quantitative model of the OCKB model that describes or better statistically explain the relationship between dialog act variables and a positive learning outcome among the participants in the collaboration. Results from the research suggest this quantitative approach along with some explanatory qualitative analysis, provides a powerful framework for understanding OLCL. The importance of the imperative function was demonstrated necessary for knowledge building, however the function might be a product of influence and power dimensions which underscores interactions. Understanding the strong possibility of influence that can be generated during interactions, the OCKB model can provide valuable insights to teachers and researchers in understanding group dynamics during an OLCL.

This study has some limitations. First, while manual coding of the utterances may guard against coding in isolation, considering preceding or following utterances, the final codings are subjected to inconsistencies especially because analyzing interactions often requires an interpretation of the context within which the utterance was used (Erkens et al, 2008). Future research in this methodological issue in addressing reliability of the coding with some level of automation is needed. Second, the rejection of so many of the hypotheses, suggests a level of weakness in the proposed OCKB models. A key contributory factor is the fact that the dialog weight factor calculations used weren't founded in literature. Future research should seek to strengthen and validate these calculations.

The results of the study provide some evidence that knowledge building during OLCL sessions can be quantified statistically from the corpuses perhaps only from the *imperative* communicative functions as the proposed model proved. Instructors, in allowing students or participants to form groups to collaborate for learning, should be mindful of the hierarchical social structure that forms implicitly and the possible learning impact on the respective groups from the structures.

ACKNOWLEDGMENT

This research was undertaken as part of the PhD in E-research and Technology Enhanced Learning in the Department of Educational Research at Lancaster University. I am pleased to acknowledge the contribution of tutors and peers in supporting the development of this study and its report as an assignment paper.

REFERENCES

Alexander, R. J. (2008). Towards dialogic teaching. Rethinking classroom talk (4th Ed). Cambridge: Dialogos, UK.

Bakhtin, M. M. (1981). The dialogic imagination: Four essays (M. Holquist, Ed.; C. Emerson & M. Holquist, trans.). Austin, TX: University of Texas Press.

Bereiter, C. (2002). Education and mind in the knowledge age. Mahwah, NJ: Lawrence Erlbaum.

Bex, F., Walton, D. (2012) Combining Explanation and Argumentation in Dialogue. ECAI 2012 Workshop on Computational Models of Natural Argument (CMNA), Montpellier, France.

Boylan, M. (2010). Ecologies of participation in school classrooms. Teaching and Teacher Education.

Bunt, H. (2004). A Framework for Dialogue Act Specification.

Chan, C., Lam, I., Leung, R. (2012). Can Collaborative Knowledge Building Promote Both Scientific Processes and Science Achievement? International Journal of Educational Psychology, 1(3), 1 99-227.

Elbers, E. (1996). Cooperation and social context in adult-child interaction. Learning and Instruction.

Engestrom, Y., Sannino, A. (2010). Studies of expansize learning: Foundations, findings and future challenges. Educational Research Review.

Erkens, G., Janssen, J. (2008). Automatic coding of dialogue acts in collaboration protocols. International Journal of Computer-Supported Collaborative Learning.

Fraser, B. (1999). What are discourse markers? Journal of pragmatics, 31, 931-952.

Graesser, A. C., Person, N. K., (1994). Question asking during tutoring. American Educational Research Journal, 31, 104-137.

Heeman, P. A., Byron, D., Allen, J. F. (1998). Identifying discourse markers in spoken dialog. AAAI Spring Symposium on Applying Machine Learning & Discourse Processing.

Hennessy, S., Howe, C., Mercer, N., Vrikki, M. (2020). Coding classroom dialogue: Methodological considerations for researchers. Learning Culture and Social Interaction.

Jefferson, G. (1984). "Notes on some orderlinesses of overlap onset". In V. D'Urso & P. Leonardi (Eds.), Discourse Analysis and Natural Rhetorics (pp. 11–38). Padua: Cleup Editore.

Jeong-A, L., Chan-Jong, K. (2017). Teaching and Learning Science in Authoritative Classrooms: Teachers' Power and Students' Approval in Korean Elementary Classrooms. Res Sci Education.

Kumpulainen, K., Lipponen, L. (2010). Productive interaction as agentic participation in dialogic enquiry. Educational Dialogues: Understanding & Promoting Productive interaction. Abingdon, Oxon: Routeledge.

Lave, J., Wenger, E (1991). Situated Learning. Legitimate peripheral participation. Cambridge, UK: University Press

Lehnert, W. G. (1978). The process of question answering: A computer simulation of congnition. Hillsdale, NJ: Lawrence Erlbaum Associates.

Louwerse, M., Crossley, S. (2003). Dialog Act Classification Using N-Gram Algorithms.

Mercer, N. (2000). Development through dialogue. In N. Mercer (Ed.), words and minds: How we use language to think together.

Mortimer, E. F., Scott, P. H. (2003). Meaning making in secondary science classrooms. Maidenhead: Open University Press.

Nistor, N., Fischer, F. (2012). Communities of practice in academia: Testing a quantitative model. Learning, Culture and Social Interaction.

Ribeiro, E., Ribeiro, R., Martins de Matos, D. (2019). A Multilingual and Multidomain Study on Dialog Act Recognition Using Character-Level Tokenization. MDPI.

Rogoff, B. (1990). Apprenticeship in thinking: Cognitive development in social context, Oxford: Oxford University Press

Stolcke, A., Coccaro, N., Bates, R. (2000). Dialogue Act Modeling for Automatic Tagging and Recognition of Conversational Speech. Association for Computational Linguistics.

Traum, D., Henry, C., Lukin, S., Artstein, R. (2018). Dialogue Structure Annonation for Multi-Floor Interaction.Proceedings of the Eleventh International Conference on Language Resources and Evaluation.

Van Boxtel, C., Van der Linden, J., Kanselaar, G. (2000). Collaborative learning tasks and the elaboration of conceptual knowledge. Learning and Instruction, 10, 311-330.

Wells, G. (1999). Dialogic Inquiry: Towards a socioculturalpractice and theory of education. Cambridge: Cambridge University Press.

Wenger, E. (1999). Communities of practice. Learning, meaning and identity. Cambridge, UK: University Press.

Wilkinson, I. A. G, Reznitskaya, A., Bourdage, K. (2017). Towards a more dialogic pedagogy: Changing teachers' beliefs and practices professional development in language arts classrooms. Language and Education.

Yu, D., Yu, Z. (2019). MIDAS, A Dialog Act Annotation Scheme for Open-Domain Human-Machine Spoken Conversations. arXiv.org

DIGITAL SUPPORT FOR THE PRE-STUDENT PHASE IS SUCCESSFUL

Pia Drews and Alke Martens
University of Rostock, Institute of Computer Science
Albert-Einstein-Str. 22, 18059 Rostock, Germany

ABSTRACT

Juniorstudy is a concept of the University of Rostock, which can be used by school students before starting their time at the University. Thus, it is an instrument of supporting the choice of study direction. Moreover, we have been able to show in our last cohort, that using Juniorstudy courses also helps to significantly enhance the knowledge required to start the university study, thus our courses become an important tool for bridging the gap between school and University. In this paper we will show the results of our study which shows that our approach improves the students' knowledge and thus facilitates being successful in testes and exams in the basic courses in the first term.

KEYWORDS

Online Study, Digital Study, Junior Study Program

1. INTRODUCTION

Orientation programs for school students can be found at Universities since the 1970s (e.g. Solzbacher, 2018; Deutsche Telekom Stiftung, 2018). Initially, these programs stem from the support of highly gifted school students, and historically were launched as a side effect of allowing early performers to join University programs. Over the years, these kind of programs have been established at quite a lot of Universities worldwide (e.g. Falzer, 1987; Solzbacher, 2018; Gröber et al., 2018; Drews, Martens, 2019).

In Germany, such approaches are often called Juniorstudyprograms – thus, we have called our project the "Juniorstudium of the University of Rostock". In the following, when we say "Juniorstudium" we refer to our project. The students (who are still at school) will be called Juniorstudents, to distinguish them from the enrolled regular students. The project was started with an external funding in 2008. During this time, we have fine-tuned our approach and resulting in a project, which is outstanding in Germany. It is not developed for highly gifted students only, but is open for everyone who is a German school student.

As far as we know, there have been few studies on the learning success of Juniorstudents. Therefore, this study should show the first results of the success of the Juniorstudium. We focus on school students starting their 10th grade (the German system has 12 grades ending with the baccalaureate, phase of 10th to 12th grade is called Sekundarstufe II – Sek II in Germany). Our Juniorstudium consists of a program of three columns (Waßmann et al. 2015; Waßmann 2018). The first column consists of recording of first and second term lectures. These are life recordings, refined and prepared for the Juniorstudium afterward. Currently we have around 20 different lecture courses from various fields, including Medicine, STEM fields (STEM – Science, Technology, Engineering, Mathematics), but also topics like Psychology or Pedagogics. As side effect, in this column, we offer the Juniorstudents a variety of potential topics for their study decision, which is an aspect of our University's orientation program. The second column consists of homework, tests and interaction elements. Depending on the course the Juniorstudents have chosen, they have to solve homework tasks, they can participate on tests and in some cases can get credit points, which are re-usable after enrollment at University of Rostock.

Regarding the third column, we learned over the years that our best approach is a close connection between the Juniorstudents and student tutors. For us it is of major importance, that the Juniorstudents are not only accompanied during their participation on a digital lecture in form of homework support, but that they are accompanied by senior students, which can answer questions regarding the content of the topic, but also questions regarding student life, emotional feelings of being a student, and organizational aspects. Feedback from our Juniorstudents is that this combination is well received. The study materials, i.e. the digital lectures, additional digital material, tests and homework are organized on the platform Stud.IP (https://www.studip.juniorstudium.uni-rostock.de) by the student tutor, who is responsible for a group of 3 to 60 Juniorstudents. Additional functions like chat and forum can be used. In most cases, tutors and Juniorstudents are in contact via email.

We have participants from all over Germany, and we have several schools, which have made a close cooperation with our project and integrated this as a permanent offer in their Sek II program. Currently we have over 300 students (summer term 2020). Quite naturally, we have been a strong support for our Juniorstudents during the Corona Crisis.

Based on this background, a while ago we started with different research projects, one of which steers the research shown in this paper. In the following, we describe the basic idea, the study design and the results.

2. DESCRIPTION OF THE STUDY

We have an annual evaluation regarding the quality of our program. However, some terms ago, we started to take a closer look at our Juniorstudents. We wanted to find out which "type" of student starts in our program, as we are not focusing on highly gifted students, and we wanted to investigate, if different specified learner types exist in our courses (Kolb, 1981; Drews, Martens, 2019). For example, in one part of the study we asked for motivational aspects to take up a part-time study during school time, whether it was their own idea or the idea of teachers and/or parents, etc. Hidden behind this is the idea, that we have high performers, which don't fall into the psychological category of highly gifted (e.g. Stanley 1996; Möller, 2006), but which are nonetheless bright and eager to learn – as long as the material is interesting enough (McLeod, 2019). In the research shown in (Drews, Martens, 2019), we work together with psychologists and instructional designers. We have focused in that study, same as in the study described in this paper, on our students in the medicine tracks, as this is our largest group with over 200 participants annually.

The study, sketched in this paper, is based on the following background. Currently students in the Sek II in German schools have to choose few courses for intense study, and others for basic study. Often, courses overlap – thus, due to organizational aspects, in quite a lot of schools it is not possible to select for example all basic courses in all nature sciences to prepare for University. As a result, we find a lot of students entering the University without having Sek II courses in Chemistry or Biology or Physics (neither basic nor intense). The Universities in Germany reacted to this with establishing "Crash-Courses" in Chemistry, Biology and Physics for students in human medicine. With courses of actions like these, Universities try to give all students equal opportunities. However, in real life, these crash courses are really challenging, and come in a time where everything is demanding for the new students.

For the Juniorstudium it was an obvious idea to put these courses in the phase where the students are still at school and investigate, whether this might be more fruitful. Thus, we try to close the gap between school and University in an early stage and offer better start chances at the University. To the best of our knowledge, the extent to which young German students benefit from early studies has never been investigated. The aim of this study is to examine the learning success of Juniorstudents by the example "Chemistry for Medicine", also in comparison to regular students at the beginning of their studies.

The course "Chemistry for Medicine" in medical studies consists of 21 lectures, each of which takes 105 minutes working time. Additionally, the course offers 7 online practical training unit videos each of which takes 3 hours of time. This is too much for a full-time school student and part-time Juniorstudent, thus we have split the course in two halves and extended the time for working through the digital material over two terms which 14 videos and 4 practical exercises in each term. Moreover, the tutor offers a presence seminar at University of Rostock to practice exercises in preparation of the final exam – this takes place each term.

At the summer term 2019, we started with our chemistry course, which is only focused on anorganic chemistry, and repeated the course again starting in winter term 2019/2020. From the 210 enrolled

Juniorstudents in the summer term 2019, an amount of 26 Juniorstudents decided to choose the "Chemistry for Medicine" course. In winter term 2019/2020, we had 300 Juniorstudents enrolled, and 51 of those decided for "Chemistry for Medicine". We think that this large amount of Juniorstudents has two backgrounds: a) based on a survey at the start of the term we know, that quite a lot students learned from friends and teachers about the existence of the course, and b) school students are eager to take the opportunity, when they learn that they have the chance to participate on the real University exam (together with the enrolled students) after they have successfully passed the two tests required to finish the Juniorstudy Chemistry module.

3. METHODS

The module starts with a presence based pre-test (duration: 90 minutes), so that we had a chance to find out the knowledge gained from school. After seeing all the required material and tests, as described above, at the end of the term, the course is finished with a presence based post-test (duration: 90 minutes).

Both tests consist of a set of 35 questions, which have to be answered. Of these, this article only looks at 6 questions on mathematical principles and 6 questions on chemistry mathematics.

1. Solve the given equation for x: **(max. 2points)**

a) $\frac{60}{x} - 10 = \frac{120}{x} - 100$ *b)* $(10-x)3 + 9x = 90$

2. Solve the mathematical equation: **(max. 1point)**

a) $lg10^{-2} =$ *b)* $\sqrt{0{,}9 \cdot 10^{-9}} =$

3. Write the given numbers as power of ten: **(max. 1.5points)**

a) 310.000 = b) 22 = c) 0,00083 =

4. Transform the power of ten to the real number: **(max. 1.5points)**

a) $0.045 \cdot 10^{4} =$ *b)* $328 \cdot 10^{-2} =$ *c)* $2{,}9 \cdot 10^{3} =$

5. Reduce the given equation: **(max. 2points)**

a) $3 \cdot 10^{3} \cdot 4 \cdot 10^{-4} =$ *b)* $\frac{32 \cdot 10^{5}}{4 \cdot 10^{3}} =$ *c)* $\frac{32 \cdot 10^{5}}{4 \cdot 10^{-3}} =$ *d)* $18 \cdot 10^{4} - 3 \cdot 10^{5} =$

6. Tranform the numbers to the given unit: **(max. 2,5points)**

a) 10µ = … g *b)* 100nm = … mm *c)* 20L = … m^3

d) The DNA of a cell is 2m long and 2nm thick. An enlargement of 105 is made. Enter the dimensions of the DNA after this enlargement (length in km, density in mm).

23. Calculate the amount of the following substance: **(max. 2points)**

a) 1.2g carbon *b)* 3.94g gold *c)* 9g water *d)* 2.24ml hydrogen chloride (gas)

24. A chemical reaction is characterized at 10° Celsius by the following thermodynamic quantities:
$\Delta H = 270kJ/mol$ and $\Delta S = -140J/mol \cdot K$. Calulate the free reaction enthalpy. **(max. 1point)**

28. The solubility product of $CACO_3$ is $2.5 \cdot 10^{-9}$ mol^2/L^2. Calculate, how much CaCO3 must be solved in 100 ml solution. **(max. 2points)**

29. 13.6 g of NaHCOO are solved in water. Then the solution is mixed with water, till an amount of 2000 ml is reached. Calculate the ph-value of the solution. **(max. 2points)**

30. Give is an amount of 500 ml of a solution of formic acid cHCOOC = 0.1mol/L. To this solution, 100 ml of diluted caustic soda cNaOH = 0.25mol/L is added. Calculate the ph-value of the resulting solution. **(max. 2points)**

31. The following curves of a titration are given. Which one shows the titration of a weak base with a strong acid? How is the point 1 in figure x called? **(max. 2points)**

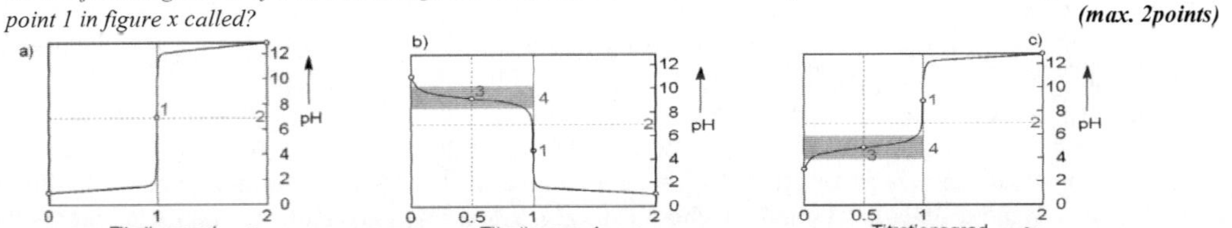

Figure 1. Questions 1 to 6 - mathematical basics. Question 23, 24, 29 to 31: chemistry mathematics

In the mathematical part of the test, no additional materials and no pocket calculators were allowed. For the other 29 questions, small (not programmable) pocket calculators, the table of periodic elements and small mathematical formularies are allowed to be used. All the questions are mapped to a competence matrix, containing information like "I am able to calculate the ph-value of anorganic acids." This competence matrix is needed, as different questions relate to different competences. The tests and the matrices have been developed by the responsible lecturer from the Chemistry Department at the University of Rostock.

The statistic of the collected data were evaluated in SPSS (Version 27, IBM Corp., 2020). Since there was no normal distribution, the Wilcoxon-Mann-Whitney-Test was used to compare the Juniorstudents pre- and post-tests and the Mann-Whitney-U-Test was used for the statistical evaluation the post-test of the Juniorstudents compared to the test of first term students.

4. EVALUATING THE RESULTS

In summer term 2019 and winter term 2019/20, we had an amount of 23 out of 77 Juniorstudents in the "Chemistry for Medicine" lecture, who participated in the study. Most of the participants are school students of the Sek II ($n = 16$), seven Juniorstudents are currently in the waiting phase for a place in medicine at any University in Germany. The average age of the Juniorstudents is 17,9 years. In the beginning of the term, 6 out of 23 of the Juniorstudents would have passed the test (with an overall score of 50% required). The mean score was 41% of the overall score. At the end of the term, the Juniorstudents achieved the mean total score of 66%. 19 of 23 Juniorstudents passed the exam.

As a control group, we used students of the first term enrolled in medicine at the University of Rostock, with $n = 22$. At the date of investigation, these 22 participants are between 17 and 28 years old, with an average age of 20,1 years. Four of the students are over 20 years old – this is due to the fact that waiting on a place to study medicine in Germany can take up to seven years. When those students enter the first term, they have often finished another medical qualification (e.g. care giver). However, as they are exemplary for those classical first term students, which did not get a place at the University directly after finishing school, we have integrated them in our study as well.

From first term medicine students participating on this study at their first week of study, we had three persons with a baccalaureate finished in 2017, five persons finished in 2018 and nine persons in 2019. From two persons, the information is missing, some have older baccalaureates as they had waited for a place for study medicine. Generally speaking, regarding the control group, the baccalaureate is not that far away to assume a complete loss of chemistry knowledge.

We also checked, whom of the Juniorstudy group and of the control group has or had chemistry at Sek II, or even chemistry as selected course in their baccalaureate. Regarding the control group, only two persons have had chemistry as part of their baccalaureate exams (i.e. intensive course), 13 persons have had chemistry in their Sek II. Seven of 23 Juniorstudents already passed their baccalaureate, seven Juniorstudents are in 11th grade, eight Juniorstudents are in their final school year.

Regarding our comparative study, we have been able to observe the following. We have made the tests with both groups, i.e. the Juniorstudy group and the new enrolled students of medicine. The Juniorstudents were questioned in summer term 2019 and winter term 2019/2020 both at the beginning and end of the term. The students were questioned in winter term 2019/2020 in the beginning of their studies.

In the post-test, the Juniorstudents succeeded in 24 of 35 tasks and reached 66% of the total. Taking the 50% benchmark for passing the exam, 19 of the 23 Juniorstudents would have passed the real exam. This is incredible, compared with the 1 (one!) person passing in the enrolled student group, mentioned above (there, one person out of $n = 22$ has passed the exam).

For our purpose, we wanted to look deeper into the details of this. Thus, we have analyzed the difference between pre- and post-test results based on the question types and the competence matrix. As mentioned in the above section, we had the pre- and post-test content separated in three parts: a) fundaments of mathematical calculation, b) anorganic chemistry, and c) chemical calculation (which again is mainly mathematics, but closely related to chemistry). The most significant differences in the results have been the differences between the pre- and the post-test related to the categories a) and c), i.e. both topics which are related to mathematics.

This can be seen in detail in the following figures. In figure 2 and table 1 the values for the Juniorstudy group can be seen. In figure 3 and table 2, the results of the enrolled first term students who never attended the Juniorstudium are compared with the Juniorstudents post-test results.

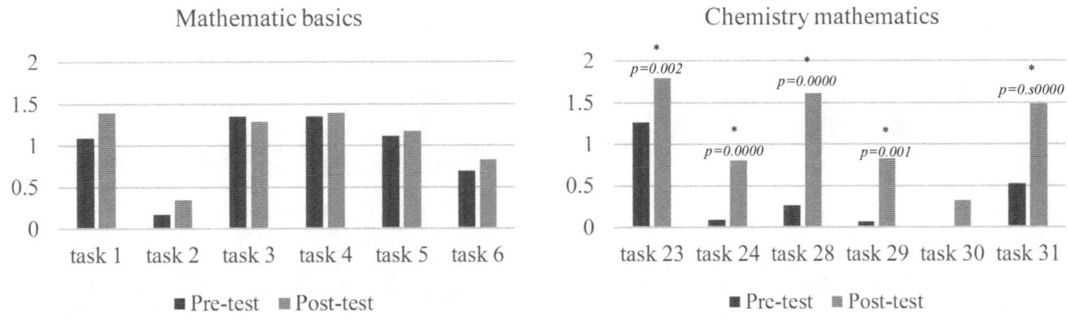

Figure 2. On the left side, the results the Juniorstudents reached in the basic mathematics is shown, on the right side are the results on chemistry mathematics. The darker columns show the results in the pre-test. The lighter columns show the results in the post-test. The p-values are rounded to the fourth position after decimal point

The related statistical results are shown in table 1.

Table 1. Results of Juniorstudents in pre- and posttest. Upper half: mean values and standard deviation of the tasks about basic mathematics, bottom half: mean values and standard deviation in chemistry mathematics

	Pre-test Juniorstudents						Post-test Juniorstudents					
task	1	2	3	4	5	6	1	2	3	4	5	6
average	1.09	0.17	1.35	1.35	1.11	0.70	1.39	0.35	1.28	1.39	1.17	0.83
standard deviation	0.73	0.32	0.32	0.44	0.71	0.89	0.78	0.35	0.42	0.34	0.75	0.72
task	23	24	28	29	30	31	23	24	28	29	30	31
average	1.26	0.09	0.26	0.07	0.00	0.52	1.79	0.80	1.61	0.83	0.33	1.47
standard deviation	0.58	0.29	0.69	0.23	0.00	0.59	0.39	0.60	0.72	0.82	0.63	0.73

It can be seen, that the Juniorstudents did have some problems in basic mathematics that persisted over the term (left side of figure 2).

Surprisingly, task 1, 2 and 6 were the most complicated for the Juniorstudents. At the beginning of the term, the Juniorstudents were told that basic mathematics is part of the final exam/post-test and that they are not taught in Juniorstudium lectures because they are assumed to have this knowledge from school mathematics education. So the problem that basic mathematic abilities are missing seems to be a problem in school teaching - we can only guess, whether this is simply too long ago at that point or whether they are too focused on pocket calculators. However, we had the impression, that it is also a lack of personal commitment to catch up on the basics as recommended, which should be an important general quality of a student!

Looking at the tasks about chemistry mathematics (for which a calculator could be used), we have achieved following results. It would have been expected that Juniorstudents, which have not yet finished their baccalaureate, perform similar but not better than students which have finished the baccalaureate (thus, assumingly had more knowledge). Surprisingly, we have been able to show, that the Juniorstudents perform significantly better in all the aspects of anorganic chemistry (21 of the 29 tasks have been answered significantly better!).

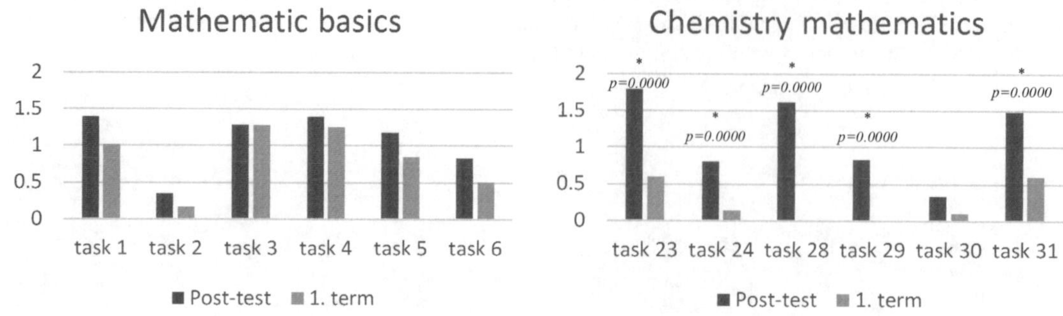

Figure 3. On the left side, the results of the Juniorstudents compared with the students reached in the basic mathematics is shown, on the right side are the results on chemistry mathematics. The darker columns show the results in the post-test with the Juniorstudents. The lighter columns show the results in the exam at the beginning of the 1st term medicine

The related statistical results are shown in table 2.

Table 2. Results of Juniorstudents posttest und students of their 1st term. Upper half: mean values and standard deviation of the tasks about basic mathematics, bottom half: mean values and standard deviation in chemistry mathematics

	Post-Test Juniorstudents						Test of students					
task	1	2	3	4	5	6	1	2	3	4	5	6
average	1.39	0.35	1.28	1.39	1.17	0.83	1.02	0.16	1.27	1.25	0.84	0.50
standard deviation	0.78	0.35	0.42	0.34	0.75	0.72	0.70	0.24	0.48	0.48	0.64	0.53
task	23	24	28	29	30	31	23	24	28	29	30	31
average	1.79	0.80	1.61	0.83	0.33	1.47	0.59	0.14	0.00	0.00	0.09	0.59
standard deviation	0.39	0.60	0.72	0.82	0.63	0.73	0.72	0.32	0.00	0.00	0.20	0.59

Juniorstudents performed better in both parts of the test: in mathematics, they are slightly better than the students at the beginning of their 1st term. Even more impressive are the results in the chemistry mathematics: here, the Juniorstudents performed significantly better than the 1st term students! Especially task number 28 has not been solved by the 1st term students, but by almost all Juniorstudents.

We observed the further results of the Juniorstudents. Out of 23 study participants, 20 Juniorstudents took part in the 2nd term. Of these, 13 were admitted to the final exam. In the end, 11 out of 23 Juniorstudents graduated successfully - the best result was an 97%. On average 80% were reached. According to the lecturer Dr. Gisela, some Juniorstudents achieve significantly better results than regular students who have completed the "Chemistry for Medicine" during their first term.

5. CONCLUSION AND OUTLOOK

In our study, we have compared the learning success of Juniorstudents with the state of knowledge that our first term students have. The result, as mentioned in the section above, clearly shows that in contrast to our expectations, Juniorstudents had an impressing learning success during the term and especially compared to students of the first term. This came unexpected, as the enrolled students are highly motivated and have finished their school time, hence our assumption has been that they would have an advantage. Thus, summing up the result of this investigation is that the course "Chemistry for Medicine", which is identical with the module offered at the first term, is a very good offer for school students.

What makes the Juniorstudium at the University of Rostock unique is the fact that everybody who is interested and who is still at school is allowed to participate on the courses – independent of any "highly gifted" attest. As the courses are digital, and the complete program is "digital with person-to-person support", we have participants from all over Germany. Courses like the "Chemistry for Medicine" offered in our Juniorstudium, are a significant element for preparing for University, especially as we have been able to show in this study that Juniorstudents significantly perform better than first term students, resulting in deeper knowledge in Chemistry after starting their University life. Thus they have lesser problems being successful in their study time. At least, it lies at hand that they have less problems in the above mentioned "Crash course" which is part of the first term.

Even if our first study offers surprising results, we are still working on broadening the evaluation. We are planning to repeat the study in the next years, plus we establish a test for the students, which will help us to learn whether they have developed a deeper understanding of chemistry and thus have lesser problems in chemistry during their study time.

We don't want to be so bold to say that as a result "digital" is better than "life" – which is really not our impression. And which does not reflect what the students tell us – they really love life lectures at the campus, especially in the first terms, and, given the choice, would have never swapped life courses against digital ones.

So summing up, our first study reveals that in the case of medicine study programs, the integration of Juniorstudyprograms in school is a valuable tool in two ways:

a) It was out of question in the past time, that Juniorstudy program are very valuable for finding the fitting study direction while still visiting school. Quite a lot of school students decide for a study direction which is well known to them, either from their family or from their own experience. This has been revealed for medicine in (Drews, Martens, 2019). Often, these students find out after their first two terms that they have made the wrong decision and swap study directions. Whatever the reasons are, these are counted as drop outs for each study direction.

b) Our first study shows, that – if temporal resources allow it – Juniorstudy programs are a valuable additive for students at the Sek II in Germany.

Interesting for us – as a side track – has been the question, whether the chemistry module is simply too difficult for the students. This is also a usual assumption for student drop out in the first terms (e.g. Waßmann et al., 2015; Egetenmeier, 2018). We started with this as a pre-assumption from the medicine lecturer staff. However, our chemistry lecturer had the impression, that chemistry simply overburdens the University starters, and as they want to become physicians, and have problems to accept that basic chemistry is a necessary part of the study program. We can observe a similar situation in computer science, where most students have problems with the mathematics required (which has been shown in another study running for several years now in the Computer Science Department – not published, yet, but also observed in (Bildungsministerium, 2017)). The result of the detailed analysis and comparison between pre- and post-test related to the question categories (i.e. mathematic, anorganic chemistry, and chemical mathematics) revealed that the main problem seems to be the mathematics! This leads us to think about a finer grained approach for the Juniorstudents and the enrolled full-time students, who seemingly have both the same problem – and it is not acquiring the knowledge related to anorganic chemistry. We have asked several students and Juniorstudents about this in our competence matrix, and learned, that they were themselves completely unaware of their lack of mathematical knowledge.

As a next step, it would also be very interesting to support this insight with additional material, e.g. Juniorstudents and students from other topics, which require basic mathematical knowledge – which are mainly all topics related to the field of STEM. Also, it might be fruitful to investigate how the school curriculum is related to the expected University curriculum. We are currently working in this direction together with instructional designers (in German: Didaktiker) from the field of Mathematics and Computer Science.

ACKNOWLEDGEMENT

We want to thank Dr. Gisela Boeck for her support and for being a brilliant lecturer of the course, and the students working in her lab and acted as tutors in our Juniorstudy. We thank the University of Rostock, which is financing this project.

REFERENCES

Bundesministerium für Bildung und Forschung. Pressemeldung, https://www.bmbf.de/de/studienabbrecher-beginnen-haeufig-eine-berufsausbildung-4283.html (2017) last accessed 2019/06/26.

Deutsche Telekom Stiftung, Solzbacher, C.: Frühstudium - Schüler an die Universität. Osnabrück (2008).

Deutsche Telekom Stiftung: Frühstudium Telekom Stiftung, Bonn (2011).

Drews, Pia, Martens, Alke: Juniorstudium – Study Digital while Going to School. In: Herzog, M.A., Kubincova, Z., Han, P., Temperini, M. (Eds): Advances in Web-Based Learning ICWL 2019, pp. 313 (2019).

Egetenmeier, A. Analyse des fachlichen Studienabbruchs an einer Hochschule. eleed, Iss. 12. (urn:nbn:de:0009-5-46635) (2018).

Fatzer, G.: Ganzheitliches Lernen. Humanistische Pädagogik und Pädagogik und Organisationsentwicklung, Junfermann-Verlag, Paderborn (1987).

Gröber, S., Müller, T., Kuhn, J.: The early entrance physics program FiPS. Physik und Didaktik in Schule und Hochschule, 1-12 (2018).

Kolb, D. A.: Learning styles and disciplinary differences. In: The modern American college, 232-255. Jossey-Bass, San Francisco (1981).

McLeod, S. A.: Kolb - learning styles, https://www.simplypsychology.org/learning-kolb.html last accessed 2019/08/11.

Möller, H.: Die Lernstilanalyse nach Kolb und ihre Konsequenzen für die Hochschul- und Schuldidaktik und die berufliche Aus- und Weiterbildung. In: 1. Innsbrucker Bildungstage, pp. 88-94. Univ. Press Insbruck (2006).

Stanley, Julian C.: In the Beginning: The Study of Mathematically Precocious Youth. Intellectual Talent: Psychometric and Social Issues, 225-235 (1996).

Waßmann, I.; Dharma - Dynamic, Heuristic & Adaptive Peer Recommendation in Social Learning Environments. In: International Technology, Education and Development (INTED) Conference Proceedings. pp. 3515-3525 (2018).

Waßmann, I., Müller, M., Tavangarian, D.: Adaptive Lehrvideos. In: DeLFI 2015, 13. E-Learning Fachtagung Informatik, pp. 131-144. GI Edition, Bonn (2015)

AI PLANNING AND REASONING FOR A SOCIAL ASSISTIVE ROBOT

Bilal Hoteit[1], Ali Abdallah[2], Ahmad Faour[2], Imad Alex Awada[1], Alexandru Sorici[1] and Adina Magda Florea[1]
[1]*Politehnica University of Bucharest, Splaiul Independentei 313, Bucharest, 060042, Romania*
[2]*Lebanese University, Badaro, Museum, Beirut, 6573/14, Lebanon*

ABSTRACT

Social robot in service is radically changing the ways of performing tasks and it becomes a distinct and valuable nascent. To achieve persist autonomy, robotic systems implement a closed-loop consisting of at least planning, reasoning and acting phases. From the continual loop perspective, this paper presents the ROSPlan framework, as a task planning and executing platform, and it introduces the integration of the ROSPlan framework in a service robotic system. Moreover, it discusses the planning, observing, monitoring, and executing processes in detail.
A use case scenario is proposed which is suitable for the experiment requirements, and it presents a service robot accomplishing an assistant task in educational campus. Considering the implementation of the ROSPlan framework, TurtleBot3 robot using Gazebo simulates the execution phase of the proposed scenario.

KEYWORDS

Service Robot, Robotic Control System, Automated Planning, Task Planning, Artificial Intelligence

1. INTRODUCTION

A service robot is earning more interest in the field of scientific research, because it enables the robot to achieve complex tasks that could assist staff in carrying out their jobs. Service robot could be asked to achieve several tasks where every task is attached with a predefined plan consisting of several basic behaviors, as demonstrated in (Gavril, 2019). In practice, a plan for any mission could not be easily scripted due to the variance of the environmental conditions, the initial position of the robot, the goals, and other dynamic factors. For instance, to navigate to various landmarks, robot should deal with a proper ordering of landmarks based on his initial location every time. On the one hand, to accomplish a mission, robot should handle several heterogeneous actions or skills. On the other hand, a plan construction becomes tedious and, in some cases, arbitrarily complex.

Planning approach increases the self-management property of the control system (Belta, 2007). Planning requires a domain model representing the states and actions which supports the planner to generate a causally valid structure that composed of organized actions. AI planning (Long, 2005) could be used to manage the robotic control system, and it could rebuild the structure to optimize cost or to fix execution failure. Several planning techniques have been applied to different types of robots and in several domains.

AI planning and robotic control approaches have different mechanisms and representations that consider as a big challenge for integrating planning and robotics systems. In particular, service robot must adapt to their dynamic environment. Robotic control systems should handle uncertainty and consider exogenous events to successfully achieve their goals. Thus, classical planning is not adequate to the robotic systems. Task planning (Hanheide, 2017). which is related to the robotics domain, is in growing interest. Task planning has been proposed to support a robot, resulting in a more intelligent behavior. Several tools and frameworks have been proposed to facilitate the integration of robotics systems and planning approaches, and increased reliance on AI systems in various fields. Most of the proposed frameworks faced several problems, and even they have implemented a non-adopted mechanism or non-standard language.

Robot operating system (ROS) (Quigley, 2009) integrates the architecture components seamlessly and serves as a middleware between the higher and lower-level architecture layers. ROS embodies several packages that provide robot-specific skills to support the robot accomplishing several tasks such as navigation, manipulation, etc. External ROS-based planning systems can be integrated with ROS through specific wrapper interfaces.

ROSPlan framework (Cashmore, 2015) has been proposed as a modular and common framework, and it adopts two standards: ROS platform and PDDL language (Aeronautiques, 1998). Presently, ROSPlan has been limited to temporal planning and deterministic approach. ROSPlan is not appropriate for neither Probabilistic nor Conditional planning without a proper extension, as described in section 2.

Historically, classical planning is classified as an intractable problem. AI Planning might not guarantee to generate plans in a reasonable time. Moreover, the probabilistic or conditional planning requires a computational demand and might be not scale to handle huge and complex tasks as demonstrated in Kaelbling et al. (1998) and Pryor et al. (1996) respectively. Regardless of the required knowledge about either the probability distribution over the domain space or the history of the observation, modeling a dynamic space is a serious challenge.

For the above, we adopt to use the ROSPlan framework as a generic symbolic planner or a task planner for our service mobile robot. Taken into consideration: 1) the present ROSPlan drawback; 2) the planning issues; and 3) our proposed scenario. We push towards a deterministic approach to somehow decrease the planning generation time and to facilitate domain modeling. Therefore, we adopt a re-planning strategy during execution failure considering the unexpected state and the original goals. The main contribution of this paper is: 1) to present the ROSPLAN framework; 2) to generate a reasonable plan to achieve somehow a complex mission; 3) to adapt for a dynamic environment in a more intelligent way than using pre-compiled plan; 4) to update or advise the plan due to either the inaccuracy of the sensors or during execution failure.

2. RELATED WORK

Historically, a domain-specific planner is integrated into several types of systems. On the contrary, several architectures have been proposed and integrated a domain independent planning system with their robotic control systems. Planning depends on a representational model that provides the available actions, the prediction of the action's effects, and where the actions are applicable. The Planning Domain Description Language (PDDL) is a standard modeling language and is used to represent the planning domain. PDDL presented in 1998 (Aeronautiques, 1998) and extended through several variants (Pinto, 2012).

Planning component (Gavril, 2019) has been proposed to control a pepper-type robot by implementing a hand-coding plan composing of several basic behaviors. In (Pinto2012), the authors extended T-Rex (Teleo-Reactive Executive) to a goal-oriented system architecture for autonomous underwater vehicles (AUVs) to enhance ocean science. Automated planning is embedded in T-Rex to provide on-board planning and execution processes. The planning module has a specific look-ahead which decides how far ahead it can plan, and a bounding time which decides the available planning period. In (Jim, 2013), the authors proposed PELEA (Planning and Execution LEarning Architecture) as a flexible modular architecture. The PELEA incorporates several processes like sensing, planning, executing, monitoring, re-planning and even learning from past experiences. Inspired by the Human Autonomic Nervous System, the authors in (Jimoh, 2013) proposed an architecture that incorporates a symbolic AI planning to enhance the self-management property. The architecture extends the Traditional control loop of UTC (Urban Traffic Control) by introducing deliberation that allows the system to reason and generate effective plans, in addition, to reduce traffic congestion. In (Dornhege, 2013), the authors integrate a Temporal Fast Downward/Modules (TFD/M) in the Tidyup-Robot system to facilitate the required tasks composing of both the navigation and manipulation processes. Moreover, the system extended the standard PDDL to PDDL/M which supports semantic attachments to provide the applicability testing for abstract actions.

In fact, there is a need for a standard planning and execution framework to be used in developing robotic architectures. The authors in (Cashmore, 2015) proposed the ROSPlan framework that provides a generic method for task planning in the (AUV). They highlight on how to integrate ROSPlan with the ROS ecosystem of AUVs. In (Cashmore, 2016), the authors introduced an opportunity planning to achieve additional utilities during the execution of AUV missions. The proposed system inserts opportunistic plan fragments into an existing robust plan. The execution of the original plan is suspended and pushed to a stack, whereas the tail of the original plan is re-executed only after the opportunistic plan execution is finished. In contrast of HTN planning (Erol, 1994), using a bottom-up approach, authors in (Cashmore, 2016) decomposed the problem into a strategic and a tactical layer. whilst, similar to an HTN model, the strategic plan composes of macro actions that encapsulate the tactical plans which are constructed from the original actions of the domain. The system plans for each task at the tactical layer independently, then it finds a valid execution order of the tactical plans. The aforementioned systems adopt the temporal planning technique, use POPF (Coles, 2010) as a planner, and relie on an extension version of PDDL to describe their domain.

On the contrary, conditional planning (Sanelli, 2017) and probabilistic planning (Canal, 2019) techniques have been used with an extended version of the ROSPlan framework. In the former, Sanelli et al. proposed a framework to generate a robust conditional plan. Based on a multi-layered architecture, the framework composed of a Planning System, a Plan Translator and a Plan Executor. The extended ROSPlan framework relies on the Contingent-FF (Hoffmann, 2015) and formulates the short term HRI as a conditional planning problem. Then, the conditional plan is translated into a Petri-Net Plan which is executed by the PNP executor module. In the latter, authors in (Canal, 2019) extended the ROSPlan framework to handle probabilistic planning domain and problems which are written in Relational Dynamic Influence Diagram Language (RDDL) (Sanner, 2010). They implement a custom interfaces to link the RDDL planner, PROST planner (Keller, 2012), that uses the RDDLSim server with the KB that represents an RDDL ontology. Moreover, they implement an online plan dispatcher that provides RDDL Client/Server protocol to interleave the plan execution and the deliberation process.

3. ROSPLAN FRAMEWORK

Since ROSPlan framework provides an innovative action and sensing interfaces that are compatible with ROS, it could be integrated easily with any ROS-enabled robotic system to automate the planning process and coordinate the activities of lower level controllers. ROSPlan is capable to reason with any version of PDDL and can easily wrapped several planners such as Temporal Fast Downward (Eyerich, 2012), UPMurphi (Della, 2012). With an extended approach, a non-standard models and planners can be used. ROSPlan consists of several components and interfaces where each component is an atomic module that performs a single function. ROSPlan is a scalable platform where components can be integrated in different manners to construct different set of architectures, whereas any component could be replaced by a more advanced one.

Knowledge Base node launches with two parameters, a domain and problem file. The node implements many services to fetch and update the domain and state variables. Problem generator node produces a new problem instance, and it relies on KB services to get the domain and state details. The problem instance is published as a message to a ROS topic, or it can be written to a file. The planner node is a wrapper for the AI planner, and it publishes the generated plan to a ROS topic or writes the solution to a file. The parsing node translates the plan into a ROS representation that is ready for execution through transforming each PDDL action into a ROS action message. These ROS messages are collected into a structure specifying the execution details. The dispatching node executes the parsing plan through publishing the action messages at the right time. This node is restricted with the same representation of the parsing node, whereas a custom algorithm is implemented to provide a simple plan dispatcher or an esternal plan dispatcher. Also, the dispatching node provides a service informing whether the plan is executed successfully. Action interface node simplifies the linking of PDDL action and ROS action message.

4. OUR PROPOSED ARCHITECTURE

Relying on several agents, service robot could perform several functions as vision recognition, speech recognition, and navigation. The overall performance of the robotic system becomes highly contingent on the proper architecture design due to the expanding of the application domains and the increasing number of components. Pepper (Gavril, 2019) is a social assistive robot interacting with and supporting administrative staff in their daily tasks. Pepper is focused on social interactions such as: speaking, guiding, reminding, observing. The robotic system implements a planning component that manages and controls several components (navigation, vision, speech), whereas each component is supported the robot to achieve a specific task. The planning component provides somehow a hard-coding plan that consists of several basic skills or behaviours.

This paper aims to replace the planning module with a symbolic task planner specifically the ROSPlan framework. It investigates the integration of the ROSPlan framework with ROS-enabled robotic system. The proposed system implements a closed-loop between the ROSPlan framework and ROS ecosystem. The loop drives the planning, observing, monitoring, and executing processes to enable the robot accomplishing a complex mission and adapting with the dynamic environment. We describe the implementation phase, and we present the domain model, the problem instance, the generated plan, in addition to the plan execution. Also, we implement a specific strategy for the re-planning phase.

Our proposed scenario entails a robot having the speech and navigation skills. Figure 1(a) illustrates the domain model for the proposed scenario, where the domain has been represented in aextended PDDL format.

```
(:requirements :strips :typing :fluents :disjunctive-preconditions :durative-actions)
(:types
        waypoint
        robot
)
(:predicates
        (robot_at ?v - robot ?wp - waypoint)
        (connected ?from ?to - waypoint)
        (visited ?wp - waypoint)
        (notified ?wp - waypoint)
)
;; Move between any two waypoints, avoiding terrain
(:durative-action goto_waypoint
        :parameters (?v - robot ?from ?to - waypoint)
        :duration ( = ?duration 10)
        :condition (and
                (at start (robot_at ?v ?from)))
        :effect (and
                (at end (visited ?to))
                (at start (not (robot_at ?v ?from)))
                (at end (robot_at ?v ?to)))
)
(:durative-action notify_waypoint
        :parameters (?m - robot ?loc - waypoint)
        :duration ( = ?duration 20)
        :condition (and
                (at start (visited ?loc))
                (at start (robot_at ?m ?loc)))
        :effect (and
                (at end (notified ?loc))
                 (at end (robot_at ?m ?loc)))
)b
```

(a)

```
(:objects
   wp0 wp1 wp2 wp3 - waypoint
   kenny - robot
)
(:init
   (robot_at kenny wp0)
   (connected wp0 wp0)
   (connected wp1 wp0)
   ------------------------
)
(:goal (and
   (notified wp0)
   (visited wp1)
   (notified wp1)
   (visited wp2)
----------------------
```

(b)

Figure 1. (a) the Domain File. (b) the Problem File for the Reminder Task

A problem file is used to insert the objects and their attributes, the facts such as the real coordinates of the landmarks, the available paths, and the goals into KB. A part of the planning problem for our scenario is shown in Figure 1 (b). The problem file is re-generated during either a first attempt of planning or during a re-planning phase, considering information that are available in KB. This process re-formulates the initial state and the remaining goals.

The planner POPF, a temporal and metrical planner, solves the planning problem, and generates the temporal plan. Figure 2 (a) illustrates the generated plan. The sequence of the generated actions is converted into ROS action messages that are closely tied and compatible with our ROS ecosystem as shown in Figure 2 (b). In addition, Figure 2 (c) illustrates a part of the Esternal parsed plan that considers the action timeout and is published through the parsing node. Sequentially, the dispatching node, denoted as the executor, executes each ROS action message in the parsed plan by relying on their relevant node which encapsulate the lower-level robot controllers.

4.1 Execution Phase

An action interface node implements an abstract execution method to connect ROS action message to an existing library through ROS service or ROS action-lib mechanisms. The action interface node, denoted as a controller, subscribes to an action dispatch topic that is published by the executor, whereas the controller publishes a feedback messages on an action feedback topic to inform the executor about the execution status.

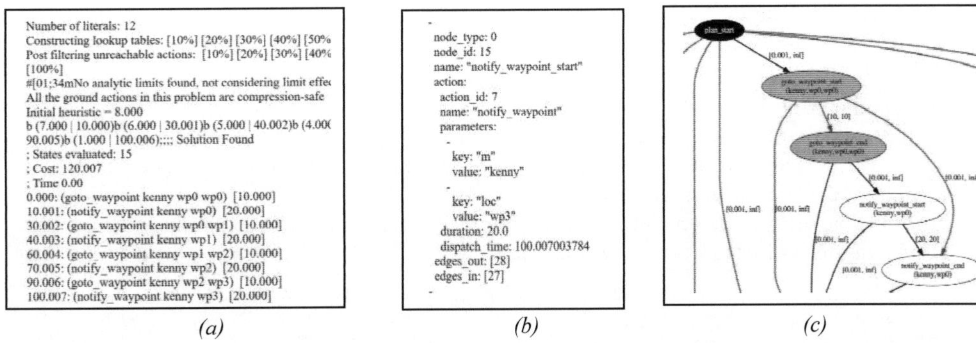

Figure 2. (a) A Fragment of the Plan. (b) A ROS notify_action Message. (c) Esternal Parsed Plan

Then, the executor can make a decision about the next step of the plan execution. For instance, the controller that matches the *goto_waypoint* action, communicates with the *move_base* node using a SimpleActionClient mechanism. So, the controller implements a *move_base* action client to connect with a *move_base* action server. First, the controller fetches the real values of the target location from the KB to create a valid *move_base* goal. Then, *move_base* action client sends the goal to *move_base* action server to navigate to the goal, and waits for the result. Based on the response of the *move-base* action server, namely the action client *goalstate*, and optionally on a monitoring phase that is described in more detail in the next section, the controller publishes an action feedback message that could be either positive (*action achieved*) or negative (*action failed*) feedback message.

Furthermore, the controller publishes action enabled as an initial feedback informing the executor that the action has been picked up. The controller, based on a *durative-time* parameter, could cancel the execution and publishes a time out feedback message to inform the executor that the action has exceeded the time and it is aborted. The duration time parameter of the controller is different from the timeout action of the planner. The executor, based on the schedules time of the planned action, could cancel the action without waiting for the feedback of the controller. In this case, the executor will send a cancel request to the controller that is continuously monitored an action cancellation message to stop the execution process at any time.

4.2 Monitoring Phase

KB supports the controller to implement a monitoring process. The controller checks the PDDL parameters to reveal if the action is applicable. For instance, the controller, that matches the *goto_waypoint* action, checks the preconditions of the action based on the *robot_at* predicates of the KB. When the action is not applicable, the controller publishes a negative feedback message to inform the executor that the action could not be executed.

In general, ROS-enabled robotic system consists of several libraries that provide ROS action messages previously, while also provide interpreted sensors data that are somehow a prerequisite for various robot functions. These interpreted sensors data that is provided through the observation process, supports another type of monitoring. This monitoring process checks the final status of the action execution and reveals if the real environment matches the expected one. This monitoring is implemented for the *notify_waypoint* action.

We implement a custom action interface matching the *notify_waypoint* action with their associated ROS action messages. This controller is supported by either the monitoring phase to check its real effects or the knowledge base to check its applicability. The controller is simply inherited from the *goto_waypoint* action interface. On-contrary, the controller is linked to a ROS library that provides the TTS operation through a ROS service mechanism. In this case, the controller could not solely depend on the response of the TTS service to validate the execution process. So, another monitoring process is implemented to check if the execution is achieved successfully. A node holding a speech recognition capability should be run. This node converts the speech into text and publishes the text on a specific topic. Thus, the controller is subscribed to this topic to reveal the execution's status. For instance, to enhance the NLP capabilities, the proposed system relies on *baidu_asr* and *sound_play* ROS packages. The former provides the *recognizer* node that converts the voice to a text and publishes a string message on the output topic. While, the latter provides a *sound_play* node that translates the text on the *robotsound* topic into sounds. The *notify_waypoint* controller publishes a text to the *robotsound* topic and scans the output topic to check the execution.

4.3 Re-Planning Phase

In general, when the action is executed successfully, the controller updates the knowledge base with the action effects and publishes the action achieved feedback message. In this case, the executor is continuing the dispatching process. On the other hand, the executor could trigger a re-planning phase due to several issues, such as: the dispatching time is over, the action is not applicable, the action duration is exceeded, or even the action is failed. In the re-planning case, the system re-formulates the mission as a new problem considering the new information such as the unexpected state, the remaining goals, as well as the predicates and facts in KB. The problem is constructed with new initial state and the new plan is generated for the remaining goals.

```
Run – Plan (D, KB, P)
   GenerateProblem (D, P);
   GeneratePlan (D, P);
   FilterPlan (π, KB);
   while Loop (If A exists in π)
      While Loop Execute (A)
         If CheckApplicability (A, KB) = Failure Then Run – Plan (D, KB, P);
         If Execute (A) = Failure Then Run – Plan (D, KB, P);
         If Monitor (A) = Failure Then Run – Plan (D, KB, P);
         Return;
      End Loop
      Return;
   End Loop
End
```

(a)

```
Run – Plan (D, KB, P)
   GenerateProblem (D, P);
   GeneratePlan (D, P);
   FilterPlan (π, KB);
   while Loop (If A exists in π)
      If AdvisePlan (D, KB, P, π) = Failure Then Run – Plan (D, KB, P);
      While Loop Execute (A)
         If CheckApplicability (A, KB) = Failure Then Run – Plan (D, KB, P);
         If Execute (A) = Failure Then Run – Plan (D, KB, P);
         If Monitor (A) = Failure Then Run – Plan (D, KB, P);
         Return;
      End Loop
      Return;
   End Loop
End
```

(b)

Figure 3. (a) re-plan only when necessary. (b) re-plan could be done before any action execution

We implement two re-planning strategies, the first approach only considers the execution failure, whereas the second approach responds to a plan validation mechanism, as illustrated in Figure 3 (a) and (b) respectively. Both approaches can break the continual closed-loop and trigger a re-planning phase. In the case of algorithm 1, the re-planning is triggered only when necessary, during any execution failure. On contrary, algorithm 2 implements an advice and validate process, where the plan is checked before any action execution. With such implementation, the executor can trigger the re-planning process if either the plan is invalid or the plan may cause failure in future.

Based on our proposed scenario, the environment is somehow predictable since it is a partial specified environment, in addition, this paper adopts an active sensing approach that is only updating the KB after a successful action execution. However, there is no continuous updating for the KB that could be occurred based on a passive sensing approach. Thus, the plan validation only considers the intersection of the facts and predicates of the KB with the preconditions of actions in the plan.

5. IMPLEMENTATION AND RESULTS

We evaluate our approach with a case scenario that presents a complex mission for a service robot interacting with humans. The robot navigates to five exam rooms and alert students about the remaining time for the exam. We run the proposed mission in the Gazebo simulation using TurtleBot3 robot. Gazebo works smoothly along with ROS, and can import Maps easily. Based on the map, we choose 5 real values as a valid location whereas the navigation program could run efficiently on the TurtleBot3 in the Gazebo simulation. We installed two out of box ROS packages, *sound_play* and *baidu_asr* to provide the NLP capabilities.

The system initializes the KB by inserting the initial states and several facts from the domain and problem file, such as the locations and the connected way-points. We assumed a 'most likely' duration for each action based on our scenario, such as 10 seconds for the navigation action and 20 seconds for the notification action. The same duration is used for the controller. The planner, POPF, is used to generate a temporal plan. Then, the cycle is continue as presented in the previous section. Two custom action interfaces have been implemented to support the robot to move and say. The *goto_waypoint* action controller relies on the *move-base* node to navigate the points, while the *notify_waypoint* action controller relies on the *sound_play* node to play sounds on the sound card. Denotes as to grounding process, the controllers fetch the state variables and predicates from KB, which are required for both PDDL actions. For instance, way-point *wp1* is changed to its real value [0.0, -0.5, 0.0]. Then, the controllers check the preconditions of their associated actions such as, for the *notify_action*, the *visited (wp1)* predicate in the KB should be true. Moreover, the controller optionally checks the current position of the robot through subscribing the *amcl_pose* topic.

The *notify_waypoint* action controller invokes the *say* service that is provided through the *sound_play* node, to accomplish the *notify_waypoint* action. Note that, the input argument is just a small notification message. To validate the execution, the controller scans the *output* topic propagating a message from the *baidu_asr* node. On the other hand, the *goto_waypoint* action controller handles the execution of the *move_base* action service by sending a goal to the *move_base* action server and waiting for the result message. When the execution is succeeded, the controllers update the knowledge base with the predicates such as, *notify(wp1)* and *visited(wp1)* are updated to true. Then, the controllers inform the executor that the execution is accomplished. The executor will handle another action. Figure. 4 illustrated the whole execution.

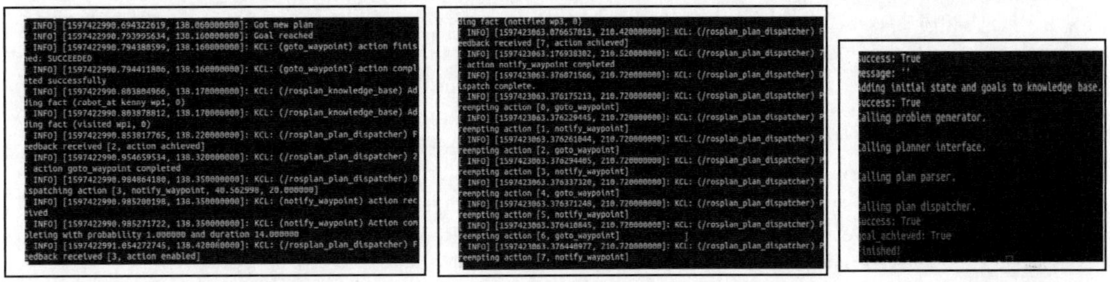

(a) *(b)* *(c)*

Figure 4. (a) Presents the Controllers Execution. (b) Presents the Actions Execution. (c) Presents Final Result

Otherwise, during any failure, the system will trigger a re-planning phase. The proposed scenario is implemented considering algorithm 1. Note that, based on our proposed scenario, the original plan is always valid. The implementation of algorithm 2 is out of scope from this paper.

6. CONCLUSION AND FUTURE WORK

This study is implemented in a simulated environment, and it used the ROSPlan framework to integrate in one unit the robotic (lower-level) and planning (higher-level) approaches in order to control the behaviour of the robot. Since the approach is basic on the ROS platform, it can be a general one and can be deployed for several tasks and in several domains. This paper highlights on how to implement the interleaving between acting and planning, and it presents the challenging of the integration process to increase the persist autonomy. An innovative approach is introduced to implement the closed loop that manages different operations in details. In particular, it highlights on the planning, sensing, monitoring, and execution operations.

In the future work, this framework will be implemented in a real world using the pepper robot. A scripted system is needed to match the specified mission written in a high-level or human-like language into a symbolic one. For the navigation task, we need to construct the goals based on the domain, locations, and map. Moreover, the system can implement a custom sensing interface that subscribes to a sensor node and continuously updates KB with the current data. We can adopt the visual sensing as a passive technique where KB is updated continuously through the sensors and speakers by implementing a new or separate node. Consequently, considering another complex scenario, we will implement the second approach of the re-planning mechanism, as demonstrated in algorithm 2.

REFERENCES

Aeronautiques, C., 1998. PDDL| The Planning Domain Definition Language.

Belta et al., 2007. Symbolic planning and control of robot motion: Finding the missing pieces of current methods and ideas.

Canal et al, 2019. Probabilistic planning for robotics with ROSPlan. Proceedings of Annual Conference Towards Autonomous Robotic, pp. 236- 250

Cashmore et al, 2015. Rosplan: Planning in the robot operating system. Proceedings of the Twenty-Fifth International Conference on Automated Planning and Scheduling, Jerusalen, Israel, pp. 333-341.

Cashmore et al, 2016. Strategic planning for autonomous systems over long horizons. Proceedings of ICAPS.

Cashmore et al, 2016. Opportunistic planning for increased plan utility. Proceedings of ICAPS.

Coles et al., 2010. Forward-chaining partial-order planning.

Della p. et al, 2012. A universal planning system for hybrid domains. In Applied intelligence, Vol. 32, No. 4, pp 932-959

Dornhege, C. and Hertle, A., 2013. Integrated Symbolic Planning in the Tidyup-Robot Project. Proceedings of AAAI Spring Symposium: Designing Intelligent Robots.

Erol, K. et al, 1994. HTN planning: Complexity and expressivity. Proceedings of AAAI, pp. 1123-1128.

Eyerich p. et al, 2012. Using the context-enhanced additive heuristic for temporal and numeric planning. Springer.

Fox et al., 2011. Modelling Mixed Discrete-Continuous Domains for Planning. In arXiv, p 1110.

Gavril, A. et al, 2019. Towards a Modular Framework for Human-Robot Interaction and Collaboration. Proceedings of 22nd International Conference on Control Systems and Computer Science (CSCS), pp. 667- 674.

Hanheide et al. 2017. Robot task planning and explanation in open and uncertain worlds. In Artificial Intelligence, Vol. 247, pp 119-150.

Hoffmann, J. and Brafman, R., 2005. Contingent planning via heuristic forward search with implicit belief states. Proceedings of ICAPS.

Jim et al, 2013. Integrating planning, execution, and learning to improve plan execution. In Computational Intelligence, Vol. 29, No. 1, pp 1-36.

Jimoh, F. et al, 2013. Autonomic system architecture: An automated planning perspective. Proceedings of IFIP International Conference on Artificial Intelligence Applications and Innovations.

Kaelbling et al., 1998. Planning and acting in partially observable stochastic domains. In Artificial intelligence, Vol. 101, No. 1-2, pp 99-134.

Keller, T. and Eyerich, P., 2012. PROST: Probabilistic Planning Based on UCT. Proceedings of ICAPS, pp. 119-127

Long, D., 2005. Automated planning: Theory and practice. In Assembly Automation

Pinto, J. et al, 2012. Experiments with deliberative planning on autonomous underwater vehicles. Proceedings of IROS 2012 Workshop on Robotics for Environmental Monitoring, Vilamoura, Portugal.

Pryor et al., 1996. Planning for contingencies: A decision-based approach. In Journal of Artificial Intelligence Research, Vol. 4, pp 287-339.

Quigley, M. et al, 2009. ROS: an open-source Robot Operating System. Proceedings of ICRA workshop on open source software, Kobe, Japan, p. 5.

Sanelli et al., 2017. Short-term human-robot interaction through conditional planning and execution.

Sanner S. et al, 2010. Relational dynamic influence diagram language (rddl): Language description. In Unpublished ms.

PERFORMANCE EFFECTS OF STRUCTURAL AND BEHAVIOURAL DEBRIEFINGS IN TRANSPARENT SIMULATIONS

Carlos Capelo[1], Renato Pereira[2] and João Ferreira Dias[3]
[1]Universidade Europeia, Estrada da Correia, 53, 1500-210 Lisboa, Portugal
[2]Iscte Business School, Instituto Universitario de Lisboa, Avenida das Forças Armadas, 1649-026 Lisboa, Portugal
[3]Independent researcher, Rua Luis Pedroso de Barros, 26, 1400-238 Lisboa, Portugal

ABSTRACT

Simulation-based learning environments are used extensively to support learning in complex business systems. Nevertheless, studies show that subjects have great difficulty in understanding and managing dynamic systems, mainly due to cognitive processing difficulties. Previous research has addressed some aspects of model transparency and instructional strategy and produced inconclusive results about their impact on learning effectiveness. This study explores the learning and performance effects of using transparent simulations (that is, showing users the internal structure of models) and applying structural and behavioural debriefings focussed respectively on the critical variables and relations and on the relation between model structure, patterns of actions, and system behaviour. We present a set of hypotheses about the influence of the model transparency and debriefing conditions on participants' performance and comprehension of the system dynamics. In a simulation experiment, participants interacted with a system dynamics model, representing the growth of a business venture. Participants provided with the more transparent strategy and exposed to structure and behavioural debriefings achieved higher performance and demonstrated better comprehension of the model dynamics. However, our findings indicate that while these conditions are beneficial for understanding the business system dynamics, making only the simulator transparent, even combined with structural debriefing, is more limited in its effect. Three out of the six hypotheses were confirmed. Structural debriefing (in conjunction with model transparency) positively influences performance, behavioural debriefing (combined with model transparency) positively influences both model dynamics comprehension and performance.

KEYWORDS

Management Education, Simulation-Based Learning, System Dynamics, Model Transparency, Simulation Debriefing

1. INTRODUCTION

Simulation-based learning environments (SBLEs) are promising tools for teaching in the business management domain. However, whilst the benefits of SBLEs are often discussed in the literature, evidence regarding the impact of their utilisation remains scarce. Furthermore, a need exists for more research addressing how the learning potential of such environments might be enhanced (Davidsen & Spector, 2015). According to the literature, the effectiveness of SBLEs depends on many factors related to the learning context, e.g., simulation task, prior knowledge, interest, instructional method, and type of assessment. The present study focusses on two aspects: simulator model transparency and simulation debriefing.

Simulator transparency refers to the extent the structure of the underlying computational model is shown to students using the simulation. In black-box model or opaque simulations, students can explore a system's behaviour, but the underlying computational models remain hidden and can only be inferred by what appears on the screen. Studies have suggested that this type of ''black-box'' situation could lead students to form wrong mental models, interfering with proper learning. "Glass-box model'' or ''transparent'' simulations have alternatively been proposed to obviate the above-described problems, as the relations among their variables are accessible to students. Transparent simulators have been used in system dynamics (SD) learning environments, detailing through their stocks-and-flows diagram (SFD) the causal structure of the underlying system. By using this approach, students may trace the cause and effect structure and understand the relationships between structure and behaviour, and they are in a position of understanding even counterintuitive system behaviours (Groesser, 2012).

Research shows that structural knowledge provided by transparent simulations has the potential to improve leaning and task performance (Größler et al., 2000). Kopainsky and Alessi (2015) found that participants provided with the more transparent strategy demonstrated better understanding of the underlying model, but their performance, however, was equivalent to those in the less transparent situation. More recently, Capelo and Silva (2020) analysed the learning effects of using transparent simulations (that is, showing participants the model SFD) and exploratory guidance (that is, guiding learners so they are able to explore the simulation by themselves) and found that while the transparent strategy combined with the exploratory guidance is a beneficial method for understanding both model structure and behaviour, making the model transparent alone is more limited in its effect. The implication of the previous studies is that students must not only identify the structure of the simulator model but also have to recognise the relationship between structure and behaviour.

According to many scholars, debriefing is a critical step in any SBLE. A debriefing session is characterized as a facilitated or guided reflection in the experiential learning cycle, structured around a set of questions that encourages students to reflect on their simulation experience. The debriefing method may be incorporated in the instructional support, by asking and discussing with students (at the end or between simulation runs) their difficulties related to the comprehension of the model structure and behaviour. Such approach can motivate learners to reflect on the simulation experience in the quest to comprehend the game behaviour and its causes. In other words, debriefing may help learners to overcome misconceptions about dynamic and complex tasks and make it possible to improve mental model construction thereby (Qudrat-Ullah, 2014). Thus, debriefing influences the potential of SBLEs in such way that students may improve their task performance and learning in dynamic tasks.

Previous research on debriefing in simulation studied the effects on learning and performance (Qudrat-Ullah, 2014) and discussed how to design debriefing sessions (Grund & Schelkle, 2019). In the simulation experiments conducted by Qudrat-Ullah (2014), in order to facilitate the comprehension of the structure and behaviour of the underlying model, students were involved in different combinations of pre-task, in-task, and post-task discussions. Those discussions generally improved students' mental models and task performance. However, subjects provided only with pre-task facilitation performed poorly. Grund and Schelkle (2019) tested two different versions of a simulation game: one integrating debriefing into the game itself, whereas the other version used classical post hoc debriefing. Results indicate that it is favourable to integrate debriefing into the game in terms of motivation and learning outcomes.

2. RESEARCH HYPOTHESES

This study investigates whether model transparency combined with an instructional approach that includes structural and behavioural debriefing can improve the learning potential for teaching the dynamics of venture growth, leading to enhanced student understanding of their main concepts and performance.

Under a model-based learning perspective, students use the simulation program to form an initial mental model and develop it into a target conceptual model (the same one underlying the simulation model). Thus, the learnings outcomes refer to the students' understanding of the simulated system, in terms of structure and behaviour, and to their performance in the simulation task.

The analysis of subjects' learning is based on their actions related to specific dynamic aspects of the simulator model. As students deal with the simulator dynamics, (they interpret the situation and mentally simulate the consequences of selected actions) they define and implement courses of action which reflect their comprehension about the structure and behaviour of the simulator model.

The expected relations and hypotheses are based on the following variables: (i) Level of model transparency (LMT). This variable represents the transparency level of the simulator. LMT indicates the extent to which students have access to the variables and relations included in the simulation model when they perform the simulation task. (ii) Level of structural debriefing (LSD). This variable indicates in what extent the instructional method includes a debriefing session focussed on the variables and relations of the simulation model. (iii) Level of behavioural debriefing (LBD). This variable indicates in what extent the instructional method includes a debriefing session focussed on the behaviour of the simulation model and relation to its structure. (iv) Comprehension of model dynamics (CMD). This variable reflects how students comprehend the structure of the simulation model (representing the growth of a business venture) and are able to infer its dynamical behaviour. (v) Performance. The performance of this simulation task is measured in terms of the financial value created by the venture.

The following hypotheses are defined: H1 - LMT positively influences CMD, H2 - LMT positively influences Performance, H3 - LSD positively influences CMD, H4 - LSD positively influences Performance, H5 - LBD positively influences CMD, and H6 - LBD positively influences Performance.

3. METHOD

3.1 Simulator, Participants, and Procedure

The SBLE incorporates the same mathematical model based on SD that was used in previous research (Capelo et al., 2018), which represents the growth of a business venture. By using this SBLE, students would be able to appreciate the dynamical complexity involved in a business venture and the performance effects caused by system misconceptions. The simulator provides two alternative interfaces. One represents an opaque simulator and the other a transparent one. The interface includes six screens. The first screen (the panel control) allows participants to adjust simulation parameters and includes tables presenting critical measures. In the transparent interface, the panel control provides the information included in a stock and flow diagram. The second and third screen present the historical behaviour over time for key variables. The other screens, only available in the transparent interface, show the causal loop diagram (CLD) and selected SFDs of the model.

Participants run a realistic simulator of a n business venture by making critical decisions every six months until the end of the third year and every year onwards for a simulation period of ten years. They analyse the business status and make decisions related to the development of key resources. The participant objective was to develop those critical and interrelated resources at appropriate rates and levels in order to maximize value creation.

In order to test the hypotheses, we conducted a laboratory experiment using three treatment groups: a group (A) of students who interacted with an opaque simulator and did not participate in debriefing sessions - low LMT, low LSD, and low LBD; a group (B) of students who used a transparent simulator and did not participate in debriefing sessions - high LMT, low LSD, and low LBD; and a group (C) who used a transparent simulator and participated in debriefing sessions - high LMT, high LSD (in the second and third simulation runs), and high LBD (in the third simulation run).

This research was conducted at Iscte Business School in Lisbon, Portugal. The experiment involved three classes of entrepreneurship courses with 67 students in total. One of the authors acted as instructor in these classes. Each of the three different treatments was assigned randomly to one of the three classes: groups A (with 23 students), B (with 22 students), and C (with 22 students). As participants from group A were submitted to the basic conditions (low LMT, low LSD, and low LBD), this group was assigned the role of control group. Participants did not know the business game and had no previous experience with the simulator.

The present experiment was carried out individually in class with one participant per computer. All participants were given a full experimental guide including: description and objective of the simulation task; case text; instructions for accessing and starting the simulator; instructions for interacting with the simulator; simulation guide; and instructions for interpreting CLDs and SFDs (only for participants using a transparent simulator). The decisions made on the simulation and its results were automatically stored in a protected spreadsheet on the participant's computer.

To succeed in this simulation task, participants needed to identify and understand the cause-and-effect relationships among critical variables, particularly those included in the CLD and selected SFDs provided in the transparent interface. That model complexity has been demonstrated to negatively influence both formation of accurate mental models and tasks. Moreover, subjects who are not familiarized with systems dynamics have additional difficulties in recognizing and comprehending dynamical structures as they are not able to properly read and interpret causal-loop-diagrams and stocks-and-flows diagrams (Alessi, 2000; Davidsen & Spector, 2015). In order to obviate these problems, we complemented model transparency with structural and behavioural debriefings. The students from group C participated in a debriefing session (after the first simulation run) focused on the model variables and relations. Then (before the third simulation run) they were involved in discussions about the relation between model structure, courses of action, and behaviour.

The experiment procedure involved two sessions and had the following steps (Figure 1).

Session 1. This session involved only the participants from experimental groups B and C. The literature (Groesser, 2012) pointed out that the extra information provided by the transparency of SD models can only benefit learners who are able to read and interpret stocks-and-flows diagrams (SFDs). Thus, the students received a lecture on CLDs and SFDs, so that they were able to read and interpret the CLD and SFDs available in the simulator interface.

	Experimental Procedure							
Treatment	a) Lecture on CLD and SFD	b) Objectives and task description	c) Instructions about the simulator	d) First simulation run	e) Structural debrifing	f) Second simulation run	g) Behavioural debrifing	h) Third simulation run
A Low LMT, low LSD, low LBD		●	●	●		●		●
B High LMT, low LSD, low LBD	●	●	●	●		●		●
C High LMT, high LSD[a], high LBD[b]	●	●	●	●	●	●	●	●

(a) low LSD in the first simulation run; (b) low LBD in the simulation runs 1 and 2

Figure 1. Experimental procedure

Session 2. In this session, students performed the simulation task using three simulation runs. They read the introduction with the overall description and the objectives of the simulation task. Participants then read the instructions for accessing, starting and running the simulator. Some simulation rounds were conducted to familiarised participants with the game interfaces and commands. In groups A and B, the three simulation runs were performed sequentially (for approximately 20 to 25 minutes each). During the simulation task, the participants from experimental groups B and C were encouraged to read and interpret the CLD and SFDs available in the game interface.

Participants from group C, after performing the first simulation run, participated in a structural debriefing (lasting approximately 35 minutes). The instructor described the CLDs and SFDs in the game interface in a form of a step-by-step guided tour and cleared all the doubts raised by students concerning the model variables and their relations. Participants then performed the second simulation run followed by a behavioural debriefing. This debriefing (lasting approximately 50 minutes) focused on the relation between the model structure, courses of action, and corresponding dynamical behaviour. The instructor first described the main challenge of this simulation task, which is how to successfully manage the growth of the venture in order to overcome the dead valley of negative financial performance and start a value creation process. The reference modes for the critical variables and corresponding desirable and "fear" scenarios were explained. Then, a debate on how certain model structures (included in the model CLD and SFDs) can support a sustainable growth was moderated by the instructor. Finally, students from group C performed the third simulation run.

3.2 Research Variables

This section summarises the use of the variables that were defined in the research model.

Level of model transparency (LMT). This variable features two degrees. In the low degree (low LMT), students perform the simulation task without accessing any structural information of the simulator model. In the high degree (high LMT), students, during the simulation task, have access to the CLD and selected SFDs of the simulator model.

Level of structural debriefing (LSD). This variable features two degrees. In the low degree, students perform the simulation task without prior structural debriefing. In the high degree, students have participated previously in a structural debriefing.

Level of behaviour debriefing (LBD). This variable features two degrees. In the low degree, students perform the simulation task without prior behavioural debriefing. In the high degree, students have participated previously in a behavioural debriefing.

Comprehension of the model dynamics (CMD). This variable indicates how students understand the structure and behaviour of the simulation model. The measurement of this variable is based on students' patterns of action throughout the simulation task, by analysing how they consistently deal with certain dynamical structures of the simulation model. This variable is calculated as the average of four components that are rated in a continuous scale (from 0 to 1) against reference values.

Performance. The performance of this simulation task is measured in terms of the financial value created by the venture, indicated by the final value of the parameter MVA (market value added). This variable is rated in a continuous scale (from 0 to 1) against reference values of MVA.

4. RESULTS AND DISCUSSION

Table 1 presents the mean values, standard deviations, and sample sizes for the variables CMD and Performance corresponding to the three experimental treatments. Table 2 presents the results of a paired-samples t-test of significance for differences in means between pairs of simulation runs within treatment groups. The differences in means for the pair SR3-SR1 (which compares the mean values of the third to the first simulation run) are significant for all the three treatment groups, suggesting that, on average, all the treatment groups enhance CMD and Performance as they progress in the task, from the first to the last simulation run. A similar conclusion can be derived from the results found for the pair SR2-SR1 (which compares the second to the first simulation run). However, the differences in means for the pair SR3-SR2 are only significant for group C (transparent simulator with debriefings), which means that, on average, the groups A (opaque simulator) and B (transparent simulator without debriefing) do not significantly improve their CMD and Performance from the second to the third simulation run.

Table 1. Means and standard deviations for variables CMD (comprehension of model dynamics) and Performance for each simulation run and treatment group

			CMD – Comprehension of Model Dynamics		Performance	
Treatment	Description	N	Mean	SD	Mean	SD
Simulation Run 1						
A	Low LMT, low LSD, low LBD	23	0.214	0.120	0.093	0.105
B	High LMT, low LSD, low LBD	22	0.231	0.123	0.104	0.101
C	High LMT, low LSD, low LBD	22	0.197	0.123	0.096	0.123
Simulation Run 2						
A	Low LMT, low LSD, low LBD	23	0.282	0.130	0.146	0.124
B	High LMT, low LSD, low LBD	22	0.294	0.155	0.191	0.209
C	High LMT, high LSD, low LBD	22	0.312	0.134	0.254	0.153
Simulation Run 3						
A	Low LMT, low LSD, low LBD	23	0.275	0.154	0.184	0.135
B	High LMT, low LSD, low LBD	22	0.304	0.172	0.205	0.199
C	High LMT, high LSD, high LBD	22	0,458	0.144	0.455	0.196

LMT - Level of Model Transparency; LSD - Level of Structural Debriefing; LSD - Level of Behavioural Debriefing.

In order to analyse and compare the degree of improvement in participants' comprehension and performance between treatment groups, we computed the variables ICMD (improvement in comprehension of model dynamics) and IP (improvement in performance), as the differences for CMC and Performance between simulation runs for each participant. Table 3 displays the results of an independent-samples t-test of significance for differences in means for the variables CMD, Performance, ICMD, and IP between pairs of treatment groups within simulation runs.

Table 2. Paired-samples t-test of significance for differences in means for the variables CMD and Performance between pairs of simulation runs within treatment groups

	CMD - Comprehension of Model Dynamics			Performance		
Treatment	Mean Difference	SD	p-value	Mean Difference	SD	p-value
Simulation Run 2 vs Simulation Run1						
A	0.069**	0.032	0.044	0.053*	0.031	0.099
B	0.063*	0.035	0.090	0.087**	0.041	0.044
C	0.115***	0.030	0.001	0.158***	0.043	0.001
Simulation Run 3 vs Simulation Run1						
A	0.062*	0.034	0.081	0.091**	0.034	0.013
B	0.073*	0.035	0.052	0.101**	0.042	0.025
C	0.261***	0.045	0.000	0.360***	0.058	0.000
Simulation Run 3 vs Simulation Run 2						
A	-0.007	0.023	0.776	0.038	0.024	0.124
B	0.010	0.024	0.675	0.014	0.028	0.628
C	0.146***	0.045	0.004	0.202***	0.059	0.003

***p<0.01, **p<0.05, *p<0.1

Table 3. Independent-samples t-tests of significance for differences in means for the variables CMD, Performance, ICMD, and IP between pairs of treatment groups within simulation runs

	CMD		Performance		Improvement in CMD		Improvement in Performance	
Pair	Mean (SD)	p-value	Mean (SD)	p-value	Mean (SD)	p-value	Mean (SD)	p-value
	Simulation Run 1				Simulation Run 3 vs Simulation Run 1			
B-A	0.018 (0.036)	0.628	0.010 (0.031)	0.737	0.011 (0.049)	0.822	0.010 (0.053)	0,852
C-A	-0.016 (0.036)	0.650	0.002 (0.034)	0.946	0.199** (0.056)	0.001	0.269** (0.066)	0,000
C-B	-0.034 (0.037)	0.362	-0.008 (0.034)	0.813	0.188** (0.057)	0.002	0.259** (0.072)	0,001
	Simulation Run 2				Simulation Run 2 vs Simulation Run 1			
B-A	0.012 (0.043)	0.785	0.045 (0.051)	0.386	-0.006 (0.048)	0.900	0.034 (0.051)	0.503
C-A	0.030 (0.039)	0.447	0.107* (0.041)	0.013	0.047 (0.044)	0.294	0.105* (0.052)	0.050
C-B	0.019 (0.044)	0.673	0.063 (0.055)	0.261	0.053 (0.046)	0.261	0.071 (0.059)	0.236
	Simulation Run 3				Simulation Run 3 vs Simulation Run 2			
B-A	0.029 (0.049)	0.556	0.020 (0.050)	0.688	0.017 (0.034)	0.615	-0.024 (0.037)	0.512
C-A	0.183** (0.044)	0.000	0.271** (0.050)	0.000	0.153** (0.050)	0.004	0.164* (0.062)	0.012
C-B	0.154** (0.048)	0.002	0.251** (0.060)	0.000	0.135* (0.051)	0.012	0.188** (0.065)	0.006

**p<0.01, *p<0.05

The lowest mean values for the variables CMD and Performance were found in the first simulation run. As displayed in Table 1 and Table 3, the mean values for those variables are not significantly different between treatment groups. That means that participants from groups B and C, with access to information concerning the structure of the simulator model, did not show better model comprehension and performance. This result may be explained by the lack of experience with the simulator. In order to start the process of building and calibrating their mental models about the simulated system, students need to complete a first simulation run. These results are somehow consistent with the findings reported by Qudrat-Ullah (2014) that subjects only submitted to pre-task facilitation perform poorly. In simulation run 2, participants in group C showed on average the best CMD (mean=0.312) and the best Performance (mean=0.254), but, according to Table 3, only the mean Performance value is significantly different from the equivalent value for group A. For the simulation run 3, the best values for the variables CMD (mean=0.458) and Performance (mean=0.455) were also exhibited by participants from group C. The statistical testing presented in Table 3 provides evidence that the average results from group C are significantly different from the equivalent values for groups A and B. These results suggest that students learn and perform more effectively if the simulation approach combines model transparency with structural and behavioural debriefings. These processes combined gave participants from group C a significant cognitive aid that accelerated their learning about the relationships between structure and behaviour of the simulated system, thus resulting in an improved performance.

As shown in Table 3, groups A and B show similar improvements from the first to the third simulation run, as the differences in means for the variables ICMD and IP are not significant. These results indicated that by increasing only transparent simulation, students did not learn and perform more effectively.

As presented in Table 2, participants from group C show, on average, the highest improvements in CMD and Performance as they progress in the task throughout the simulation runs. Additionally, the following results can be observed in Table 3. (i) From the first to the second simulation run, the differences in means for ICMD between groups are not significant, and a significant difference in means for IP is only found between group C and group A. These findings indicate that, on average, participants who combined model transparency with structural debriefing improved more their performance than those using the opaque simulation. Consequently, the variable LSD seems to positively moderate the impact of LMT on Performance. (ii). From the second to the third simulation run, the differences in means for ICMD and IP between group C and other groups are significant, while the differences in means for those variables between groups A and B are not significant. These results suggest that, on average, participants who combine model transparency with structural and behavioural debriefings improved more their model comprehension and performance than those using only transparent simulation. Consequently, the variable LBD seems to positively moderate the impact of LMT on CMD and Performance.

Even though students from group B benefitted from a more transparent interface (showing the causal-loop-diagram and some stock-and-flow diagrams of the simulator model), they were not more successful than those from control group (A) in comprehending the model dynamics and performing the simulation task. On the other hand, as students from group C were engaged in a structural debriefing (after the first simulation run), they had the opportunity to clear their misinterpretations about the diagrams provided by the transparent interface, they improved their structural knowledge, and they were more able to identify the key variables and relations. Nevertheless, however, comparing to group B students, on average, group C participants did not significantly improve more their comprehension and performance. After the second simulation run, participants from group C were involved in a behavioural debriefing where they discussed and resolved their doubts about the relation between model structure, patterns of action, and corresponding expected behaviours. This helped them to improve even more their comprehension about the model dynamics and enhanced their performance in the simulation task.

Table 4 shows the results of multivariate regression analyses of CMD and Performance on the independent variables. The regressions were ran on standardised values for all the variables to directly compare the relative effects of each independent variable on the dependent variable. As presented in Table 4, regression analysis for CMD on the independent variables shows no significant effects for LMT and LSD, and significant effects for LBD and SR. Regression analysis of Performance shows no significant effects for LMT and significant effects for LSD, LBD, and SR.

Table 4. Regression results for all Independent variables

	Dependent Variables			
	Comprehension of Model Dynamics		Performance	
Independent Variables	Standardized Beta	p-value	Standardized Beta	p-value
LMT - Level of Model Transparency	0.030	0.670	0.052	0.415
LSD - Level of Structural Debriefing	0.122	0.175	0.207*	0.013
LBD - Level of Behavioural Debriefing	0.212*	0.019	0.255**	0.002
SR - Simulation Run	0.215**	0.003	0.228**	0.001
Adjusted R^2	0.187		0.314	

**p<0.01, *p<0.05

5. CONCLUSION

This study is based on an educational experiment aimed at testing hypotheses about the impact of simulator transparency and debriefing sessions on students' learning and task performance. The simulation experience involves a simulator based on SD, designed to teach the dynamics of venture growth.

It was predicted that (1) making the simulator more transparent (by showing students the causal-loop and stocks-and-flows diagrams of the simulator model) and (2) providing debriefing sessions focussed on the structural (discussions about the variables and relations included in the model) and behavioural (discussions about the relation between the model structure, patterns of actions, and corresponding expected behaviours) aspects of the simulation model would benefit learning and task performance.

The results from regression analysis confirm three of the six hypotheses. The hypotheses H1 (the level of transparency of the simulation model positively influences the level of comprehension of the model dynamics) and H2 (the level of transparency of the simulation model positively influences performance) are not supported, thus suggesting that only by showing students the model diagrams, they do not learn and perform any more effectively than they would otherwise. We can conclude that a simulator does not become more transparent to subjects just by showing the model diagrams. As point out by Groesser (2012), the extra information provided by the transparency of SD models can only benefit learners who are able to read and interpret SFDs. Thus, one possible explanation is that as participants were not familiarized with the system dynamics approach (even though they have received a lecture on CLDs and DFDs), they were not completely enabled and motivated to read and interpret the model diagrams.

Executing the task with a transparent simulator after being submitted to a structural debriefing session significantly improved the students' performance, supporting hypothesis H4 (The level of structural debriefing positively influences performance). This finding is consistent with some of the literature on learning from transparent models. For example, Grobler et al. (2000) also reported that a presentation about the structure of a business simulator improved participants ability to control the system and had a positive influence on their task performance. However, our research does not provide support of hypotheses H3 (the level of structural debriefing positively influences the level of comprehension of the model dynamics). As participants enhanced their knowledge on the model variables and relations, they took more advantage of the more structured information provided by the transparent interface (e.g., the stock levels and flow rates in the prospect pipeline) and improved their ability to control and manage the task, which led to better performance. Nevertheless, however, courses of action of students submitted to that condition did not show that they consistently improved their comprehension of the model dynamics. This result is consistent with the findings reported by Capelo and Silva (2020) that subjects submitted to transparent conditions are able to acknowledge certain cause-and-effect relations, but they fail to mentally infer the model behaviour. This conclusion is in line with a learning difficulty frequently mentioned in system dynamics literature (Davidsen & Spector, 2015): that it is difficult to develop an understanding of how the behaviour of a complex system emerges from its underlying causal structure.

Regression results support hypothesis H5 (the level of behavioural debriefing positively influences the level of comprehension of the model dynamics) and hypothesis H6 (the level of behavioural debriefing positively influences performance). As we hypothesised, the results strongly show that the behavioural debriefing gave participants a powerful mean to reflect on the relation between model structure and behaviour, which accelerated their learning about the dynamics of the simulated system and enhanced performance. These results reinforce an assumption already articulated in previous research (Kopainsky & Sawicka, 2011; Qudrat-Ullah, 2014) that is important to provide facilitation in order to improve subject's performance and their understanding of system dynamics.

REFERENCES

Capelo, C., Dias, J., & Pereira, R. (2018). A system dynamics approach to analyse the impact of energy efficiency policy on ESCO ventures in European Union countries: a case study of Portugal. *Energy Efficiency, 11*, 1-33.

Capelo, C. & Silva, A. (2020). Optimizing the learning potential of simulations through structural transparency and exploratory guidance. *Simulation & Gaming.*

Davidsen, P. & Spector, J. (2015). Critical Reflections on System Dynamics and Simulation/Gaming. *Simulation & Gaming*, *46,* 430-444.

Größler, A., Maier, F. H., & Milling, P. M. (2000). Enhancing learning capabilities by providing transparency in business simulators. *Simulation & Gaming: An International Journal*, 31, 257-278.

Groesser, S. N. (2012). Model-Based Learning with System Dynamics. In N. Seel (Ed.), *Encyclopedia of the sciences of learning*, pp 2303–2307. New York: Springer.

Grund, C. & Schelkle, M. (2019). Developing Serious Games with Integrated Debriefing. *Bus Inf Syst Eng, 62*, 87–101.

Kopainsky, B. & Alessi, S. M. (2015). Effects of Structural Transparency in System Dynamics Simulators on Performance and Understanding. *Systems, 3*, 152-176.

Kopainsky, B. & Sawicka, A. (2011). Simulator-supported descriptions of complex dynamic problems: experimental results on task performance and system understanding. *System Dynamics Review 27* (2), 142-172.

Qudrat-Ullah, H. (2014). Yes we can: Improving performance in dynamic tasks. *Decision Support Systems 61*, 23-33.

TIME TO ACCLIMATE: EXAMINING THE INFLUENCE OF COGNITIVE ABILITY ON SITUATING TO A VIDEO GAME

Michael P. McCreery[1], Danielle L. Head[1], Joseph P. Fiorentini[1], Sam A. Leif[1], S. Kathleen Krach[2], Le Quanda L. Cole[1], Catherine A. Bacos[1] and Jeffrey Laferriere[3]
[1]*Univeristy of Nevada, Las Vegas, Las Vegas, NV, USA*
[2]*Florida State University, Tallahassee, FL, USA*
[3]*Lebanon Valley College, Annville, PA, USA*

ABSTRACT

The current study was designed to examine the relationship between cognitive ability and player experience in shaping how players think within, and acclimate to, video games as complex systems. Specifically, researchers examined the relationship between player's cognitive ability and gameplay outcomes within a video game (i.e., *The Deed*). Outcomes were evaluated and contrasted after two discrete playthroughs, each lasting approximately 30 minutes. Logistic regression indicated that cognitive ability predicted individual outcomes for both the first and second playthrough, but did not predict growth between playthroughs (i.e., outcome change). Findings are then discussed in terms of an acclimation stage.

KEYWORDS

Acclimation Stage, Cognitive Ability, Player Experience, Video Games

1. OBJECTIVES AND PURPOSE OF THE STUDY

It has long been recognized that individuals vary in their abilities to process information, construct meaning from that information, and apply it to real-world situations. Broadly speaking, that variability manifests through individual differences (e.g., cognitive ability) intersecting with contextualized experiences to produce an outcome (Goh et al, 2019; Jonassen & Grabowski, 2012). For this reason, researchers have begun to surmise that the complexity of video games, coupled with content embedded in narrative, may provide a contextualized experience through which individual differences shape learning (Schrader et al, 2019).

In line with this idea that meaning making is a complex and contextualized experience, Alexander and colleagues (2004) define expertise as a developmental process, broadly consisting of knowledge, interest, and strategic processing that grows with active engagement in a field or domain. From this perspective, previous research examining expert/novice differences within a video game have demonstrated that the situated understanding of the game itself also plays a significant role in how that contextualized experience manifests (McCreery et al, 2011). Not only do novices demonstrate difficulty with spatial navigation but also with navigating the graphical user interface (GUI) and associated information. This last point is of particular importance in that researchers and practitioners alike are unlikely to achieve their goals or outcomes if players are unable to discern how to use the system on a fundamental level. As such, McCreery and colleagues (2011) have not only suggested that an acclimation period is warranted when teaching or conducting research with video games, but also called for further research into how intra-individual differences may shape the acclimation period. Despite this call, little clarity exists with regard to how cognition shapes acclimation. For this reason, the current study set to explore the role of cognitive ability in shaping how students (players) think within, and acclimate to, a complex system (i.e. video games).

2. THEORETICAL FRAMEWORK

Briefly, complex systems are multifaceted (multiplicity of components), dynamic (interaction of multiple components), and emergent (evolving over time) (Hilpert & Marchand, 2018). Video games are complex systems consisting of a variety of elements (e.g., dimensional space, GUI, world objects) that afford interactions with each other and the player over time (Schrader et al, 2019). The player must possess a basic level of skill and understanding within this complex system in order to attend to and accurately interpret the feedback provided by interactions with the rules, goals, and objectives (McGonigal, 2011). These system characteristics not only interact with user characteristics (i.e., individual differences) in highly complex, dynamic, and emergent ways (Hilpert & Marchand, 2018), but they also do so in a cyclical manner, whereby game structures shape player behavior and player behavior shape game structures (McCreery et al, 2015).

Considering such complexity, researchers have sought to understand the implications individual differences have on research and instruction from, with, and within video games. For example, while examining expert-novice differences, time-series data revealed that an acclimation stage was warranted for players new to complex video game environments (McCreery et al, 2011). Defined as an orientation period that is typically represented by limited domain knowledge and problem-solving strategies (Alexander et al, 2004), the acclimation stage is of chief importance to new players. This stage allows for the opportunity to orient to the game space, navigate the GUI, and prioritize information about how feedback is presented. Without this time to acclimate, some players may miss important content intended to further game goals, which may negatively impact their ability to succeed in the game (McCreery et al, 2011).

Exploring intra-individual differences may provide context for conceptualizing the acclimation stage within video games. One such intra-individual difference that may influence acclimation is cognitive ability, as it is tied to both knowledge and strategic processing associated with a developmental perspective of expertise. Cognitive ability is characterized as both *crystallized* (when knowledge is acquired through education and experience) and *fluid* (when logic and skills are used in learning and acquiring new information) (Shipley et al, 2009).

Generally, the relationship between cognitive ability and video games can be examined through three lenses: (1) whether video games can be used as cognitive training tools to influence cognitive ability (Bediou et al, 2018; Fikkers et al, 2019), (2) whether video games can be used as a valid psychometric measure of cognitive ability (Buford and O'Leary, 2015; Quiroga et al, 2019), and (3) whether cognitive ability can influence video game performance. The first lens is interested in the use of digital games to influence or improve cognitive ability over time. Positive gains were found in the areas of attention, spatial cognition, and fluid intelligence (Bediou et al, 2018; Fikkers et al, 2019). The second lens is interested in the ability to leverage games as an environment within which to measure cognitive ability. Significant, moderate to strong correlations between in-game measures and general mental ability, fluid reasoning, and visuospatial ability shows promise that these methods are capturing the same latent cognitive factors (Buford and O'Leary, 2015; Quiroga et al, 2019). However, the current study is interested in examining the third lens, as little is known about how cognitive ability influences game play behavior and outcomes. At the time of this writing, no literature was found that explicitly used the construct of crystallized intelligence to examine its predictive relationship to video game performance. However, literature does exist that indirectly aligns with the above definition of crystallized intelligence (i.e., knowledge acquired through education and experience). For example, research examining previous video game experience and performance has demonstrated significant differences in how experienced players navigate the GUI and associated information within the game Defense of the Ancients 2 (DOTA 2) (Castaneda et al, 2016). Specifically, the more experienced the player, the less effort was spent monitoring in-game tools, and the more automated usage became. Alternatively, there is existing research that has directly examined fluid intelligence as a predictor of performance with video games (Baniqued et al, 2013; Kranz et al, 2017). For example, fluid ability was found to be positively correlated with video game performance across a variety of multiplayer online battlefield games (Kokkinakis et al, 2017). In discussions associated with this correlation, the researchers raise the possibility "that rather than games modifying cognition, learning to play video games depends on the same cognitive resources underlying performance on intelligence tests" (Kokkinakis et al, 2017, p. 7-8).

Reframing performance in video games to allow for an acclimation stage facilitates the examination of whether cognitive ability shapes how the acclimation stage emerges for players new to a particular game. Specifically, the current investigation was designed with two overarching questions as guides: a) how do individual differences in cognitive ability impact outcomes associated with a video game; and b) if players were given the opportunity to play the game more than once, would any changes in the predictive nature of cognitive ability on outcomes suggest the need for an acclimation stage? As such, the following research questions were designed:

RQ1. Does cognitive ability (Shipley-2 scores) predict gameplay outcomes for the first attempt of a new game (*The Deed*)?

RQ2. Does cognitive ability (Shipley-2 scores) predict gameplay outcomes for the second attempt of the same game?

RQ3. Does cognitive ability (Shipley-2 scores) predict the learning growth (outcome change) scores between gameplay one and two?

3. METHOD

3.1 Subjects

One hundred and forty-four ($N = 144$) participants completed the study (see Table 1). The gender breakdown included 39 males and 105 females. The racial makeup of the sample was as follows: 47% White, 7% Black or African American, 17% Hispanic or Latino, 16% Asian, 2% Native Hawaiian or Pacific Islander, 10% two or more races, and 1% other. The mean age was approximately 24 ($SD = \sim 6$) years old.

Table 1. Demographics

$N = 144$		Frequency	Percent
Race			
	White	68	47.2%
	Black or African-American	10	6.9%
	Hispanic or Latino	24	16.7%
	Asian	23	16.0%
	Native Hawaiian or Pacific Islander	3	2.1%
	Two or More Races	15	10.4%
	Other	1	0.7%
Gender			
	Male	39	27.1%
	Female	105	72.9%

3.2 Procedures

3.2.1 Game Selection

The Deed (Grab the Games, 2015) was selected as part of a more extensive study examining forced-choice games as a model for stealth assessment. The game is considered a reverse murder mystery with problem-solving elements where the desired outcome is to gather information (i.e., evidence and weapons) to get away with a crime, rather than gathering information to solve a crime. If players are successful, they evade prison by implicating another character for their crime and may even receive the family inheritance. If they are unsuccessful, they are sentenced to prison once their crime is discovered. *The Deed* is an appropriate choice for studying the effect of cognitive ability on gameplay outcomes. Firstly, the entire game can be completed in 20-30 minutes, falling within the acclimation time period (approximately 30 minutes) outlined by McCreery and colleagues (2011). Secondly, success in the game is predicated on player ability to interact with the content and narrative.

3.2.2 Data Collection

Data were collected during the 2017-2018 academic year from subject pool participants within a college of education in the southwestern United States. Participants were asked to complete a demographic questionnaire, followed by a first playthrough of *The Deed* (Grab the Games, 2015) video game. Participants were not provided verbal gameplay directions; rather the game provided a built-in introduction prior to gameplay. Following the first playthrough, participants completed the Shipley-2, and then completed a second playthrough of *The Deed.* All gameplay was captured for later coding and analysis using Fraps (Version 3.5.99) (Beepa Pty Ltd., 2013). The summative outcome was determined by reviewing the game capture footage.

3.3 Instruments

3.3.1 Deed Outcome Data

Outcome data were calculated by creating a dichotomous score based on video observations of the players' activity. Specifically, overall outcome scores were coded as failure (prison and no inheritance = 0) or success (no prison with or without inheritance = 1). Further, learning growth scores were coded as nongrowth (do the same or worse from Playthrough One to Playthrough Two = 0) or growth (do better on Playthrough Two compared to Playthrough One = 1).

3.3.2 Shipley-2

The Shipley-2 (Shipley, et al., 2009) is a brief measure of crystallized (e.g., prior knowledge) and fluid intelligence (e.g., problem-solving). Subtest scores are provided for Vocabulary (crystallized intelligence), Abstraction (fluid intelligence), and Block Patterns (fluid intelligence). Composite scores are labeled as: Composite A (Vocabulary with Abstraction) and Composite B (Vocabulary with Block Patterns). Composites A and B also each provide an Impairment Index score (not used in this study). Reviews for the Shipley indicate solid reliability and validity data to support its use (Hayes & Thorndike, 2010).

4. RESULTS

Prior to analyses, the Box-Tidwell (1962) test was conducted to check that the assumption of linearity was upheld. For all analyses, interaction terms were found to be nonsignificant, $p_{min} = .092$. We then proceeded to the main analyses of interest. The Shipley-2 subscales were used as continuous predictor variables (see Table 2). Gameplay Outcome was coded as a dichotomous nominal variable, with "0" denoting a failed outcome and "1" denoting a successful outcome. Gameplay Growth was also coded as a dichotomous nominal variable, with "0" denoting nongrowth and "1" denoting growth between the first and second playthrough outcomes. Although logistic regression allows for the classification of outcomes, that was not the purpose of this study.

Table 2. Descriptives

N = 144	Mean	SD
Shipley-2 Subscales		
Vocabulary	104.431	11.021
Abstraction	107.194	15.008
Block Patterns	107.556	14.599

4.1 RQ1

Analyses containing cognitive ability should maintain the structure of the composite scales (Sattler, 2008). Therefore, two separate binary logistic regression analyses were conducted to address the first research question: a) Vocabulary and Abstraction (Composite A) as the predictors of Playthrough One Outcome; and b) Vocabulary and Block Patterns (Composite B) as the predictors of Playthrough One Outcome (see Table 3).

4.1.1 RQ1a

The logistic regression model with Vocabulary and Abstraction as predictors was statistically significant, $\chi^2(2) = 13.864$, $p = .001$. The model explained 13.3% (Nagelkerke R^2) of the variance in outcome and showed good fit, Hosmer-Lemeshow: $\chi^2(8) = 6.948$, $p = .542$. Vocabulary was a significant predictor of gameplay outcome ($B = .062$, SE = .021, $e^B = 1.064$, Wald $\chi^2(1) = 8.787$, $p = .003$) whereas Abstraction was nonsignificant (Wald $\chi^2(1) = .784$, $p = .376$). As participants' vocabulary scores increase, there is as an associated increase in the likelihood of attaining a successful outcome on Playthrough One.

4.1.2 RQ1b

The logistic regression model with Vocabulary and Block Patterns as predictors was also statistically significant, $\chi^2(2) = 16.269$, $p < .001$. The model explained 15.5% (Nagelkerke R^2) of the variance in outcome and showed good fit, Hosmer-Lemeshow: $\chi^2(8) = 10.793$, $p = .214$. Vocabulary was again a significant predictor of gameplay outcome ($B = .063$, SE = .020, $e^B = 1.065$, Wald $\chi^2(1) = 9.581$, $p = .002$) while Block Patterns was nonsignificant (Wald $\chi^2(1) = 3.069$, $p = .080$). As participants' vocabulary scores increase, there is as an associated increase in the likelihood of attaining a successful outcome on Playthrough One.

Table 3. Logistic regression of cognitive ability predicting outcomes on playthrough one

Variable	B	SE B	e^B	Wald χ^2 (1)	p	% Success (1)
Vocabulary	.062	.021	1.064	8.787	.003	
Abstraction	.013	.014	1.013	.784	.376	
Nagelkerke R^2	.133					
$\chi^2(2)$	13.864				.001	27.1
Vocabulary	.063	.020	1.065	9.581	.002	
Block Patterns	.025	.014	1.026	3.069	.080	
Nagelkerke R^2	.155					
$\chi^2(2)$	16.269				.000	27.1

Note: e^B = Odds Ratio

4.2 RQ2

Following the same structure as above, two separate binary logistic regression analyses were conducted to address the second research question: a) Vocabulary and Abstraction (Composite A) as the predictors of Playthrough Two Outcome; and then b) Vocabulary and Block Patterns (Composite B) as the predictors of Playthrough Two Outcome (see Table 4).

4.2.1 RQ2a

The logistic regression model with Vocabulary and Abstraction as predictors was statistically significant, $\chi^2(2) = 6.365$, $p = .041$. The model explained 5.8% (Nagelkerke R^2) of the variance in outcome and showed fair fit, Hosmer-Lemeshow: $\chi^2(8) = 13.684$, $p = .090$. However, while the overall model was significant, neither of the individual predictors was significant (Vocabulary: Wald $\chi^2(1) = 2.666$, $p = .103$; Abstraction: Wald $\chi^2(1) - 1.898$, $p = .168$).

4.2.2 RQ2b

The logistic regression model with Vocabulary and Block Patterns as predictors was also statistically significant, $\chi^2(2) = 12.278$, $p = .002$. The model explained 10.9% (Nagelkerke R^2) of the variance in outcome and showed good fit, Hosmer-Lemeshow: $\chi^2(8) = 5.334$, $p = .721$. Block Patterns was a significant predictor of gameplay outcome ($B = .034$, SE = .012, $e^B = 1.034$, Wald $\chi^2(1) = 7.439$, $p = .006$) while Vocabulary was again nonsignificant (Wald $\chi^2(1) = 3.384$, $p = .066$). As participants' Block Patterns scores increase, there is as an associated increase in the likelihood of attaining a successful outcome on Playthrough Two.

Table 4. Logistic regression analysis of cognitive ability predicting outcomes on playthrough two

Variable	B	SE B	e^B	Wald χ^2 (1)	*p*
Vocabulary	.027	.016	1.027	2.666	.103
Abstraction	.017	.012	1.017	1.898	.168
Nagelkerke R^2	.058				
$\chi^2(2)$	6.365				.041
Vocabulary	.030	.016	1.030	3.384	.066
Block Patterns	.034	.012	1.034	7.439	.006
Nagelkerke R^2	.109				
$\chi^2(2)$	12.278				.002

Note: e^B = Odds Ratio

4.3 RQ3

To address research question three, a learning growth score was created wherein the outcome score from Playthrough One was subtracted from the outcome score from Playthrough Two. All nonpositive values were coded as a "0" for nongrowth and all positive values were coded as a "1" for growth. Binary logistic regression models were then analyzed (Vocabulary and Abstraction as predictors of Growth; Vocabulary and Block Patterns as predictors of Growth). Results indicated that neither regression model was significant ($\chi^2(2) = 1.334$, $p = .513$; $\chi^2(2) = 3.116$, $p = .211$, respectively; see Table 5).

Table 5. Logistic regression analysis of cognitive ability predicting outcome growth

Variable	B	SE B	e^B	Wald χ^2 (1)	*p*
Vocabulary	.008	.016	1.008	.228	.633
Abstraction	.011	.012	1.011	.758	.384
Nagelkerke R^2	.012				
$\chi^2(2)$	1.334				.513
Vocabulary	.009	.016	1.009	.341	.559
Block Patterns	.019	.012	1.019	2.489	.115
Nagelkerke R^2	.029				
$\chi^2(2)$	3.116				.211

Note: e^B = Odds Ratio

5. DISCUSSION

Previous research has shown the importance of both individual differences (Goh et al, 2019; Jonassen & Grabowski, 2012) and an acclimation stage (Irizarry & Kleyn, 2011; McCreery et al, 2011) for successful interactions with complex environments. In an effort to expand our understanding, the current study set out to examine the relationship between cognitive ability and player experience on gameplay outcomes. Based on the results of research question one, Vocabulary (i.e., prior knowledge) was predictive of success for the first playthrough. As players' vocabulary scores increased, the likelihood of attaining success in the game on the first playthrough also increased. Results of research question two indicated that Block Patterns (i.e., problem-solving) was predictive of success for playthrough two. As players' block pattern scores increased, the likelihood of attaining success in the game on the second playthrough also increased. Results of research question three indicated cognitive ability was not predictive of growth between playthroughs.

These findings illustrate several important points. Players rely on prior knowledge and experience (crystallized intelligence) when initially navigating a complex video game environment. During the acclimation stage (i.e., first playthrough), players develop situated knowledge and experience contextualized by the video game content and narrative. However, over time, the reliance on extant knowledge diminishes. Once players acclimate to the system, they are able to better rely on problem-solving (fluid intelligence) to more deeply engage in the experience, rather than having to integrate prior knowledge with a new experience. These results align with previous findings that indicate the presence of, and need for, an acclimation stage (Irizarry & Kleyn, 2011; McCreery et al, 2011; Schrader et al, 2011).

Findings suggest that the situated understanding of context and narrative is critical when designing a research study that examines game-based outcomes. Situations and storylines often provide clues and distractors that can influence outcomes (McCreery et al, 2019). For researchers, this means it would be prudent to understand how those situations and storylines may shape study findings prior to conducting game-based research. For example, if the purpose of the study is to examine content knowledge, but situations and storylines are vague, then it is quite possible the study is testing problem-solving rather than content knowledge. Research design also should account for an acclimation stage in which respondents gain a situated understanding of the game. In the context of the current study, the lack of situated understanding in the first playthrough demonstrated the importance of intra-individual differences in players' prior knowledge and experience. We recommend that study design be considerate of sampling procedures, particularly where novice gamers or new gaming environments are concerned, as this lack of experience could be a confound in outcome studies. Therefore, it may be helpful to use a gamer experience measure to more closely normalize sample experience levels or perhaps provide a tutorial to participants when introducing them to a novel game space. In both cases, this may strengthen the researchers' ability to control for how prior knowledge impacts outcomes.

In the second playthrough, the presence of situated understanding was demonstrated by the statistically significant increase in success rates, from 39 to 73 successes, from the first to second playthrough ($t(143) = 4.375$, $p < .001$). In order to assess the impact of problem-solving, participants should possess a situated understanding of content and narrative to draw from and apply to the contextualized experience. The inclusion of an acclimation time period is integral to providing participants a chance to develop an understanding of the system. This last point is of particular importance to researchers, in that rather than examining study outcomes, the lack of an acclimation time period may shift the focus toward unintentionally studying participants developing a familiarity with the system, and therefore increasing Type II errors.

Finally, the lack of significance associated with the third research question was expected based on the findings of research questions one and two. Specifically, each experience with the game highlighted separate cognitive abilities needed to acclimate and progress within the video game. As crystallized and fluid intelligence are related yet distinct ($r = .38$) (Shipley et al, 2009), they play substantially different roles. The reliance on crystallized intelligence in playthrough one highlights the reliance on prior knowledge and experience; while findings associated with fluid intelligence in playthrough two suggest that the player is becoming situated and engaging in more problem-solving activities. Taken together, this suggests that rather than contributing to growth, they appear to be demonstrating that acclimation is a process. The current study does come with limitations. Specifically, it sits within a sparse body of literature. As such, these findings need to be both replicated and expanded across different game contexts and genres. Cognitive ability was also examined in isolation of other constructs of interest. Future research may look to include these constructs within extant theoretical frameworks in order to interpret their significance within a more comprehensive model.

REFERENCES

Alexander, P. A. et al, 2004. Modeling Domain Learning: Profiles from The Field of Special Education. *Journal of Educational Psychology*, 96(3), pp. 545-557.

Baniqued, P. L. et al, 2013. Selling Points: What Cognitive Abilities Are Tapped By Casual Video Games?. *Acta psychologica*, 142(1), pp. 74-86.

Bediou, B. et al, 2018. Meta-analysis Of Action Video Game Impact on Perceptual, Attentional, And Cognitive Skills. *Psychological bulletin*, 144(1), pp. 77-110.

Beepa Pty Ltd. (2013). Fraps [Computer software]. Retrieved from http://www.fraps.com

Buford, C. C. and O'Leary, B. J., 2015. Assessment of Fluid Intelligence Utilizing A Computer Simulated Game. *International Journal of Gaming and Computer-Mediated Simulations (IJGCMS)*, 7(4), pp. 1-17.

Castaneda, L. et al, 2016. Game Play Differences by Expertise Level in Dota 2, A Complex Multiplayer Video Game. *International Journal of Gaming and Computer-Mediated Simulations (IJGCMS)*, 8(4), pp. 1-24.

Fikkers, K. M. e tal, 2019. Child's Play? Assessing the Bidirectional Longitudinal Relationship Between Gaming and Intelligence in Early Childhood. *Journal of Communication*, 69(2), pp. 124-143.

Gee, E. and Gee, J. P., 2017. Games as Distributed Teaching and Learning Systems. *Teachers College Record,* 119(12).

Glaser, R., 1985. *Thoughts on Expertise.* Pittsburgh Univ Pa Learning Research and Development Center.

Goh, J. et al, 2019. Exploring Individual Differences as Factors to Maximize Interactive Learning Environments for Future Learning. *Interactive Learning Environments*, 27(4), pp. 497–507.

Grab the Games, 2015. *The Deed [Computer software].* Retrieved from http://store.steampowered.com/app/420740/The_Deed/

Hayes, T. L. and Thorndike, T. (2010). 'Review of Shipley-2', in R. A. Spies, J. F. Carlson, and K. F. Geisinger (Eds.), *The Eighteenth Mental Measurements Yearbook.* Omaha: Buros Institute, University of Nebraska.

Hilpert, J. C. and Marchand, G. C., 2018. Complex Systems Research in Educational Psychology: Aligning Theory and Method. *Educational Psychologist*, 53(3), pp. 185-202.

Holzman, T. G. et al, 1983. Cognitive Variables in Series Completion. *Journal of Educational Psychology*, 75(4), pp. 603-618.

Irizarry, J. G. and Kleyn, T., 2011. Immigration and Education in the "Supposed Land of Opportunity": Youth Perspectives on Living and Learning In The United States. *The New Educator*, 7(1), pp. 5-26.

Jetter, H. C. et al, 2014. Blended Interaction: Understanding Natural Human–computer Interaction in Post-wimp Interactive Spaces. *Personal and Ubiquitous Computing*, 18(5), pp. 1139-1158.

Jonassen, D. H. & Grabowski, B. L., 2012. *Handbook of Individual Differences, Learning, and Instruction*. Hillsdale, NJ: Erlbaum.

Kokkinakis, A. V. et al, 2017. Exploring the Relationship Between Video Game Expertise and Fluid Intelligence. *PloS one*, 12(11), pp. 1-15.

Kranz, M. B. et al, 2017. Examining the Roles of Reasoning and Working Memory in Predicting Casual Game Performance Across Extended Gameplay. *Frontiers in psychology*, 8.

McCreery, M. P. et al, 2011. Navigating Massively Multiplayer Online Games: Evaluating 21st Century Skills for Learning Within Virtual Environments. *Journal of Educational Computing Research*, 44(4), pp. 473-493.

McCreery, M. P. et al, 2015. Social Interaction in A Virtual Environment: Examining Socio-spatial Interactivity and Social Presence Using Behavioral Analytics. *Computers in Human Behavior*, 51, pp. 203-206.

McCreery, M.P. et al, 2019. Can Video Games Be Used as a Stealth Assessment of Aggression? A Criterion-Related Validity Study. *International Journal of Gaming & Computer Mediated Simulations*, 11(2), pp.40-49.

McGonigal, J., 2011. *Reality Is Broken: Why Games Make Us Better and How They Can Change the World.* New York, NY: Penguin.

Murias, K. et al, 2016. The Effects of Video Game Use on Performance in A Virtual Navigation Task. *Computers in Human Behavior*, 58, pp.398-406.

Quiroga, M. A. et al, 2019. Intelligence and Video Games: Beyond "Brain-games". *Intelligence*, 75, pp. 85-94.

Sattler, J. M., 2008. *Assessment of Children: Cognitive Applications* (5th ed.). San Diego, CA: Author.

Schrader, P. G. et al, 2011. Training by Gaming: Preparation Teachers of Today for Tomorrow's Learning Environments. *Journal of Technology and Teacher Education,* 19(3), pp. 261-286.

Schrader, P. G. et al, 2019. 'Assessing Learning From, With, And in Games Revisited: A Heuristic For Emerging Methods And Commercial-off-the-shelf Games', in D. Ifenthaler and Y. J. Kim (eds.) *Game-based Assessment Revisited*, New York, NY: Springer.

Shipley, W. C. et al, 2009. *Shipley Institute of Living Scale, Second Edition (Shipley-2).* Torrance, CA, Western Psychological Services (WPS).

Squire, K., 2006. From Content to Context: Videogames as Designed Experience. *Educational Researcher*, 35(8), 19-29.

Yan, E.Q. et al, 2015. Masters of Control: Behavioral Patterns of Simultaneous Unit Group Manipulation in Starcraft 2. *Proceedings of the 33rd Annual ACM Conference on Human Factors in Computing Systems,* pp. 3711-3720.

IMPACT OF PROGRAMMING WORKSHOP ON IMPRESSION REGARDING COMPUTER PROGRAMMING

Yukiko Maruyama
Tokai University
Hiratsuka Kanagawa, Japan

ABSTRACT

To investigate the effects previous experience on the impressions of parents regarding computer programming, a survey was carried out before and after parent–children workshops were conducted. The results of the survey showed that the impressions of the participants regarding computer programming after the workshops became more positive than before the workshops.

KEYWORDS

Computer Programming, Elementary School, Parent Impression, Semantic Differential Method, Programming Workshop

1. INTRODUCTION

There have been widespread attempts to introduce computational thinking into K–12 education (Barr 2011, Grover 2013). The term “computational thinking” was first used by Papert (1993) and was popularized by Wing (2006). According to Wing, “computational thinking involves solving problems, designing systems, and understanding human behavior, by drawing on concepts that are fundamental to computer science” (p. 33). In addition, the author stated that computational thinking is a fundamental skill and should be added to every child’s analytical ability. The article caught the attention of many educational researchers and educators, and many research studies related to computational thinking in K–12 education have since been carried out. In the United Kingdom, a new subject, “computing,” was introduced to primary and secondary schools. In the primary teachers’ guide for this subject, the importance of computational thinking is repeatedly stated.

As computational thinking continues to receive an increasing amount of attention, programming education is also receiving attention as one of the ways for teaching computational thinking. Lye and Koh (2014) stated that “programming is more than just coding; for, it exposes students to computational thinking which involves problem-solving using computer science concepts, and is useful in their daily lives” (p. 51). In Japan, the central council for education in the Ministry of Education, Culture, Sports, Science, and Technology submitted a report mentioning the introduction of programming education to elementary schools. Another council report stated that programming education in elementary schools should not aim to teach students how to code, but rather to foster programming thinking (translated by the author). Programming thinking is considered to be a concept similar to computational thinking and is considered to be a part of computational thinking. However, the idea of programming education has not adequately infiltrated the public. Misconceptions and anxieties concerning programming education seem to have spread among parents. Parents play a significantly important role in elementary education, and their attitudes toward education have a considerable influence on their children’s attitudes. Indeed, some researchers have investigated parent–child collaboration in robotics education (Cuellar et al. 2013, Roque et al. 2016) and in learning programming (Lin and Liu 2012, Hart 2010). These studies showed that the experiences of parent–child collaboration affect the parents’ attitudes toward such education. Maruyama (2019) suggested that experiences in programming workshops for parents and children improved the parents’ attitudes toward, and their confidence in, supporting their children in learning computer programming. Moreover, it is conceivable that experiences at programming workshops will have an effect on changing the parents’ impression of programming itself.

This paper provides the results of a preliminary investigation into the influence of participation in a programming workshop for children and parents on changes in parent impressions of computer programming.

2. RELATED STUDIES

2.1 Research Studies on Parents' Role in Education Involving New Technologies

As mentioned above, the attitudes of parents toward education have a considerable influence on the attitudes of their children.

Hart (2010) carried out a computer science-based workshop that targeted fourth through sixth graders, mainly female students, and their parents. The participants took part in an attitudinal survey during the first and last sessions of the workshop. The results of this survey show their perceptions regarding general computer use and their potential for developing a career as a computer scientist and that the perceived differences in ability based on gender became positive during the last session. Moreover, much of the feedback from parents was positive.

Lin and Liu (2012) observed three parent–child pairs at a computer camp where they used MSWLogo. They found that parent–child collaboration during programming naturally fell into a special form of "pair programming" and that children wrote programs in a more systematic and disciplined manner. Moreover, they reported that the programs produced by these participants were relatively more compact, well-structured, and error-free.

Cuellar et al. (2013) conducted a robotics education workshop in which parents and children interacted by experimenting with the concepts of robotics and by developing problem solving skills. They expected the students to become more interested in technology and their parents to encourage them to pursue engineering and science majors. As a result, they observed enhanced teamwork and interaction as well as a positive attitude toward the initiative over the course of the workshop.

Thus, parent involvement in education significantly impacts the attitudes and outcomes of the children. However, it seems that some parents have low confidence in their involvement in education, particularly regarding new technology.

Feng et al. (2011) regard parents as important influencers in their children's decision to attend a robotics course and the use of educational robots among children. Therefore, they investigated the parent perception of edutainment products, including programmable bricks. They sent questionnaires to 55 parents and received 26 valid responses. The questionnaires included questions about the usefulness of programmable bricks and the respondent's confidence in teaching using such devices. The results showed that parents considered programmable bricks to be useful for their children; however, they were not confident in using them to teach their children. Taking this into account, Feng et al. alluded to future research into customized courses for both parents and children as a means of improving the confidence of parents in teaching their children.

Lin et al. (2012) investigated parent perceptions regarding educational robots. The results of the responses to self-reported questionnaires from 29 parents indicated that the parents had a positive attitude toward educational robots and considered learning about such robots to be beneficial for their children. In addition, they found that parents had little confidence in using educational robots to teach or play with their children. Therefore, they suggested that it was crucial to train or teach the parents about such robots.

As mentioned in these two research studies, participation in educational workshops can be a promising method for improving parent attitudes and confidence.

Maruyama (2019a) examined the impact of different types of workshop activities on parent concerns regarding their children's programming education. Three types of workshops were organized, each characterized by a particular activity, including a wooden robot with coding blocks, a robotics toy with visual programming language, and visual language. Data were collected from the parents before and after their participation in these workshops. The results from the data analysis revealed that the impact of the three activities on the parents varied, with all three activities and workshops having a positive impact on the attitudes and confidence levels of the parents in supporting their children at home with technology-related education in addition to enhancing their understanding of programming education.

As described above, participation in workshops with their children is likely to improve the attitudes of parents and provide them with confidence regarding programming education. However, the effect on parent impression of the learning material itself has yet to be investigated in depth. The impressions of the learning materials are considered to influence the attitude of parents toward supporting their children. By investigating changes in impressions, we can gain insights on how to encourage parents in this area.

2.2 Research Studies on Impression toward Computer Programming

Ando et al. (2017) conducted surveys to investigate the impressions of teachers and students regarding computer programming based on a semantic differential (SD) method (Osgood 1952). The subjects of these surveys included 146 elementary school teachers, 242 university students, and 35 elementary school students.

Overall, the results showed the following trends:

1) The subjects believe that computer programming is modern and cool.

2) The subjects feel highly motivated to acquire computer programming skills and believe that it is necessary to acquire such skills.

3) The subjects feel that computer programming is difficult.

4) The subjects are aware that they are not good at computer programming.

Maruyama (2019b) conducted a survey before and after parent–child workshops to investigate the effects of computer programming experience on parent impressions of computer programming. The respondents to this study appeared to be relatively familiar with computers but were not very skilled. The results of the survey showed that their impressions regarding computer programming after the workshops were more positive than they were before the workshops. However, the number of participants in this survey was limited, and it was suggested that a survey with more participants and a detailed analysis of the results be conducted.

This paper reports the results of a further investigation into the impressions of parents toward computer programming. The details of the changes in impression of computer programming before and after the workshop are examined.

3. METHOD

The survey used for this study was carried out in programming workshops conducted for children and their parents, which were organized by the author.

3.1 Programming Workshops

The programming workshops took place in August 2018 and in March and August 2019. The participants were recruited through brochures distributed at 19 local elementary schools in Kanagawa, near Tokyo. The children were required to attend the workshops with their parents or guardians. Three types of workshops were held 42 times each in total over a period of 21 days. Each parent–child pair took part in one workshop. Each workshop lasted for 2 h with a break in the middle. Each workshop was moderated by an instructor (author) and an assistant (university student). At the beginning of each workshop, a short lecture on computer programming was presented. After a short lecture, the workshop activities were conducted.

In workshop 1, a Cubetto (Primo Toys, https://www.primotoys.com/) was used. Cubetto is an educational and screenless coding toy for children aged 3–6. Users can make a program that controls Cubetto's movements using coding blocks by placing them on a control board. The workshop targeted first and second grade students. During the workshop, each group used one Cubetto set.

In workshop 2, a toy robot, i.e., a BB-8™ App-Enabled Droid™ (Sphero, https://www.sphero.com/), and the visual programming language SpheroEdu (https://edu.sphero.com/) were used. The workshop targeted third–sixth grade students. During the workshop, each group used one BB-8.

In workshop 3, the visual programming language Scratch (The Lifelong Kindergarten Group at the MIT Media Lab, https://scratch.mit.edu/) was used. The workshop targeted first through sixth grade students. In the workshop, parents and children used a computer on their own.

A total of 398 groups (83 in August 2018, 149 in March 2019, and 166 in Aug 2019) took part in the workshop.

3.2 Investigation

The survey was carried out using questionnaires. The participants of the workshops were handed two questionnaires at reception and were asked to voluntarily fill them out before and after the workshops. A total of 293 valid responses were obtained. Among the 293 respondents to the survey, 176 were mothers, 112 were fathers, and 2 were grandfathers of elementary school children. The average age of the respondents was 42.4.

The questionnaires had the following sections: 1) demographics of the participants and their children (only for the questionnaire administered before the workshop), 2) the impression of the participants toward computer programming, 3) the interest of the participants in programming education, 4) attitudes of the participant toward programming education in elementary schools, 5) the expectations from introducing programming education to elementary schools, 6) anxieties regarding the introduction of programming education, 7) attitudes toward and confidence in supporting children's programming education at home, and 8) the computer experience of the participants (only in the questionnaire administered before the workshop). There were other questions that sought responses from the children.

This paper focuses on section 2. In this study, the SD method was used. The measurement items in section 2 were based on a study by Ando et al. (2017). Nineteen pairs of Japanese adjectives, the meanings of which are listed in Table 1, were used. Originally, each item was a one-word Japanese adjective; however, in Table 1, some items were translated into multiple English words such that their meanings were as close as possible to the original Japanese. For each pair of words, the word on the left side has a positive connotation, whereas the word on the right side has a negative connotation, with a few exceptions. The participants were asked to evaluate on a 5-point scale which of the two words in each pair was closer to their impression of the computer programming workshop. The answers were converted into values of 1–5, where a value of 1 is closest to the left-side word in each pair and 5 is closest to the right-side word. That is, small values indicate a relatively positive impression.

Table 1. Measurement items for impression of computer programming

No.	Item meanings	No.	Item meanings
1	New - Old	11	Enjoyable - Dull
2	Cool - Not cool	12	Cheerful - Gloomy
3	Necessary - Unnecessary	13	Quick - Slow
4	Want to acquire - Do not want to acquire	14	Stand out – Does not stand out
5	Want to try – Do not want to try	15	Want to use – Do not want to use
6	Like a play - Like a study	16	Soft - Solid
7	Good at - Bad at	17	Easy to understand - Difficult to understand
8	Easy - Difficult	18	Adult-like - Child-like
9	Fun - Hard	19	Amazing - Average
10	Like - Dislike		

4. RESULTS AND DISCUSSION

Figure 1 shows the average values of each item for all respondents, the respondents in workshop 1, the respondents in workshop 2, and the respondents in workshop 3. In each figure, the solid lines represent the values before the workshops, whereas the dashed lines represent the values after the workshops. For the results of all respondents, after the workshops, the average values decreased compared with before the workshops except for item 3 (Necessary – Unnecessary), item 13 (Quick – Slow), and item 18 (Adult-like – Child-like). As mentioned above, small values indicate a positive impression; thus, the general impressions of the respondents toward computer programing after the workshop were more positive than those before the workshop. The results of a Wilcoxon signed-rank test (Table 2) indicate statistically significant differences before and after ($p < 0.05$) the workshops for all items except items 4 and 13. With regard to item 4 (Want to acquire – Do not want to acquire), the average value was 1.69, which was originally high. This suggests that participation in a programing workshop had a positive impact on the impression of parents toward computer programming. This result is consistent with the author's previous research (Maruyama 2019b). Furthermore, similar tendencies can be seen in the graphs of each workshop. However, compared with the results of all respondents, the number of items with a statistically significant difference was slightly smaller.

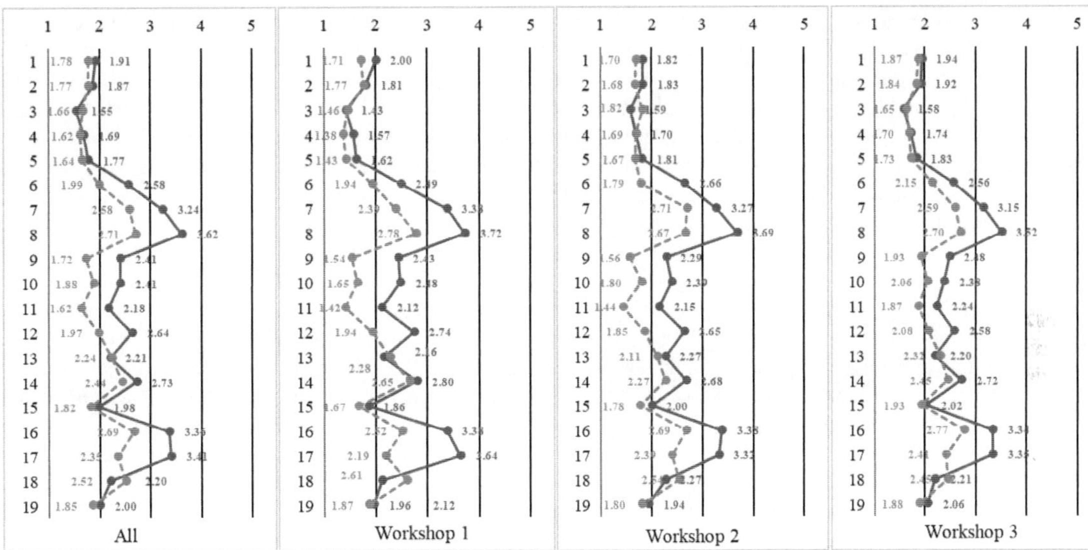

Figure 1. Average values of each item for impression

Table 2. Measurement items for impression of computer programming

	1	2	3	4	5	6	7	8	9	10
All	0.005	0.018	0.013	0.104	0.004	< 0.001	< 0.001	< 0.001	< 0.001	< 0.001
Workshop 1	0.005	0.559	0.833	0.026	0.035	< 0.001	< 0.001	< 0.001	< 0.001	< 0.001
Workshop 2	0.152	0.036	0.016	0.881	0.136	< 0.001	< 0.001	< 0.001	< 0.001	< 0.001
Workshop 3	0.391	0.191	0.285	0.472	0.122	0.001	< 0.001	< 0.001	< 0.001	< 0.001
	11	12	13	14	15	16	17	18	19	
All	< 0.001	< 0.001	0.708	< 0.001	0.003	< 0.001	< 0.001	< 0.001	0.004	
Workshop 1	< 0.001	< 0.001	0.345	0.281	0.047	< 0.001	< 0.001	0.001	0.370	
Workshop 2	< 0.001	< 0.001	0.118	< 0.001	0.025	< 0.001	< 0.001	0.003	0.126	

$p < 0.05$

A factor analysis was conducted on the impressions before and after the workshops for all respondents. In addition, a factor analysis was applied on the impressions after the workshop for the respondents in each workshop. To determine the number of factors and eliminate inappropriate items, three preliminary analyses were applied to all datasets. From the results of the preliminary analyses, the number of factors was determined to be three. In addition, items 6 and 18 were eliminated from further analysis because their factor loadings were smaller than 0.35. Finally, all datasets were analyzed through a factor analysis using a Promax rotation. Table 3 shows the factor loadings matrixes before and after the workshops for all respondents.

With regard to the results before the workshops, items 7, 8, 9, 10, 11, 16, and 17 were extracted as the first factor. All items except item 16 were considered as words regarding feelings produced from the experience. Because these are the answers before going through the workshop, it is probable that the respondents answered in anticipation of how they felt. Three of the items, Easy – Difficult, Good at – Bad at, and Easy to understand – Difficult to understand, are considered as feelings related to the difficulty of computer programming. Three other items, i.e., Like – Dislike, Enjoyable – Dull, and Fun – Hard are considered feelings of enjoyment. The factor loadings for Easy – Difficult and Good at – Bad at were 0.800 and .0723, respectively, which were high. This suggests that difficulty was more relevant to the feelings of the participants than enjoyment. The average values of items related to difficulty were all over 3, which implies that the participants seemed to expect that programming was difficult before the workshops. It is conceivable that participants were worried regarding whether they could program well and, thus, they were not sure if they were able to enjoy it. Their impression seemed to depend on the difficulty rather than their enjoyment. The factor loading of item 16, which was Soft – Solid, was 0.406, which is not too high.

As the second factor, four items, i.e., Want to acquire – Do not want to acquire, Want to try – Do not want to try, Want to use – Do not want to use, and Necessary – Unnecessary, were extracted. These items are considered as expressing the motivation for computer programming and appear to reflect the interest and importance of participants in computer programming. The average values of these items are all under 2. This suggests that the participants have a high motivation for trying to learn how to program. In particular, the value for item 3 (Necessary – Unnecessary) was 1.55, which indicates that participants strongly felt its importance, and might be an importance-led motivation. Six items, i.e., Cool – Not cool, New – Old, Stand out – Does not stand out, Amazing – Average, Cheerful – Gloomy, and Quick – Slow, were extracted as the third factor. The items in the first and second factors are feelings obtained from performing an activity, and the items in the third factor are not necessarily feelings based on performance.

However, the factor structure changed after the workshops were conducted. Seven items were extracted as the first factor. Three were included in the first factor before the workshops, which were related to a feeling of enjoyment. The other four items were consisted the second factor before the workshops, and were items related to motivation. The second factor consisted of the same items as in the third factor before the workshops. The third factor consisted of four items from first factor before the workshops. Three of them are related to the level of difficulty.

Before the workshop, items related to difficulty and items related to enjoyment were included within the same factor; however, after the workshop they were included within different factors. It seems that the difficulty came to have less influence on the enjoyment of the participants. After the workshops, the average values of the items related to difficulty became smaller than before, which suggests a decrease in the idea of the participants that programming is difficult. Therefore, it seems that the participants came to become less concerned about programming difficulties. However, items related to enjoyment were included in the same factor as items related to motivation. The experience of fun at the workshop may have helped further motivate them.

Table 3. Factor loading matrixes before and after workshops for all respondents

Before workshop	1	2	3	After workshop	1	2	3
Easy – Difficult	.800	−.155	−.222	Want to acquire – Not want to acquire	.947	−.038	−.116
Good at – Bad at	.723	.093	−.346	Want to try – Not want to try	.901	.007	−.124
Like – Dislike	.660	.294	.077	Want to use – Not want to use	.725	.055	.047
Fun – Hard	.637	.116	.302	Necessary – Unnecessary	.645	.117	−.142
Easy to understand – Difficult to understand	.626	−.116	.089	Like – Dislike	.632	−.073	.343
Enjoyable – Dull	.574	.220	.181	Enjoyable – Dull	.553	.101	.270
Soft – Solid	.406	.058	−.103	Fun – Hard	.476	.090	.373
Want to acquire – Not want to acquire	−.070	.932	−.078	Cool – Not cool	.100	.868	−.177
Want to try – Not want to try	.057	.803	−.035	New – Old	.039	.759	−.170
Want to use – Not want to use	.186	.631	.097	Amazing – Average	.084	.718	−.070
Necessary – Unnecessary	−.043	.621	−.025	Cheerful – Gloomy	.023	.566	.283
Cool – Not cool	−.206	.220	.631	Stand out – Not stand out	−.087	.535	.238
New – Old	−.266	−.015	.606	Quick – Slow	−.104	.448	.401
Stand out – Not stand out	.181	−.119	.600	Easy – Difficult	−.185	−.079	.918
Amazing – Average	−.338	.087	.589	Easy to understand – Difficult to understand	−.040	.159	.693
Cheerful – Gloomy	.496	−.261	.562	Good at – Bad at	.189	−.318	.641
Quick – Slow	.130	−.031	.381	Soft – Solid	−.020	.100	.490

Similar factor structures were obtained from the analysis after each workshop. With regard to workshop 2, the factor structure was the same as the factor structure of all respondents. With regard to workshop 3, although items included in each factor were the same as the result for all respondents, the factor order changed. Items related to difficulty were extracted as the first factor, items related to motivation and enjoyment were extracted as the second factor, and other items were extracted as the third factor. With regard to workshop 1, only two items, i.e., Easy – Difficult and Good at – Bad at, were extracted as the third factor. It is necessary to further examine whether the difference in the teaching materials has an effect.

Table 4. Factors after each workshop

Workshop 1	Workshop 2	Workshop 3
Want to acquire – Not want to acquire	Want to acquire – Not want to acquire	Easy – Difficult
Want to try – Not want to try	Want to try – Not want to try	Good at – Bad at
Like – Dislike	Want to use – Not want to use	Easy to understand – Difficult to understand
Want to use – Not want to use	Like – Dislike	Soft – Solid
Enjoyable – Dull	Necessary – Unnecessary	Want to try – Not want to try
Fun – Hard	Enjoyable – Dull	Want to acquire – Not want to acquire
Necessary – Unnecessary	Fun – Hard	Necessary – Unnecessary
New – Old	Cool – Not cool	Want to use – Not want to use
Cool – Not cool	New – Old	Enjoyable – Dull
Amazing – Average	Amazing – Average	Like – Dislike
Easy to understand – Difficult to understand	Cheerful – Gloomy	Fun – Hard
Cheerful – Gloomy	Stand out – Not stand out	Cool – Not cool
Stand out – Not stand out	Quick – Slow	Amazing – Average
Soft – Solid	Easy to understand – Difficult to understand	New – Old
Quick – Slow	Easy – Difficult	Stand out – Not stand out
Easy – Difficult	Soft – Solid	Cheerful – Gloomy
Good at – Bad at	Good at – Bad at	Quick – Slow

5. CONCLUSION

To investigate the effects of experience with computer programming on the impressions of parents of elementary school children, a survey was carried out before and after parent–children computer programming workshops were conducted.

The results of the survey showed that the impressions of the participants regarding computer programming after the workshops became more positive than they were before the workshops. Before the workshops, the impressions of the participants seemed to depend on difficulty rather than enjoyment. After the workshops, the participants seemed to become less concerned with programming difficulties. Moreover, the experience of fun at the workshop may had helped further their motivation.

However, the effects of the different activities of the workshop could not be confirmed, and it will be necessary to examine this further. Furthermore, an investigation into how the changes in the impressions of the parents affected their children should be conducted.

ACKNOWLEDGMENT

This work was supported by JSPS KAKENHI, Grant Number JP18K02832.

REFERENCES

Ando, A., Sugawara, K., Sakari, S., Torii, T., Shiga, H., Tan, Y., and Manda, A., 2017, The comparison between teachers' and students' attitudes to computer programming. *Proceedings of the 33rd Annual Conference of JSTE (Japan Society for Educational Technolo-gy)*, Shimane, Japan, pp. 257–258 (in Japanese).

Barr, V. and Stephenson, C., 2011. Bringing computational thinking to K-12: What is involved and what is the role of the computer science education community? *Acm Inroads*, Vol. 2, No. 1, pp. 48–54.

Cuellar, F., Penaloza, C. and Kato, G., 2013, Robotics education initiative for parent-children interaction. *The 22nd IEEE International Symposium on Robot and Human Interactive Communication*, Gyeongju, Korea, pp. 364–365.

Feng, H.C., Lin, C.H. and Liu, E.Z.F., 2011. Parents' perceptions of educational programmable bricks for kids. *British Journal of Educational Technology*, vol. 42, No. 2, pp. E30–E33.

Grover, S., and Pea, R., 2013. Computational thinking in K–12: A review of the state of the field. *Educational Researcher*, Vol. 42, No. 1, pp. 38–43.

Hart, M. L., 2010, Making contact with the forgotten K-12 influence: Are you smarter than YOUR 5th grader? *Proceedings of the 41st ACM Technical Symposium on Computer Science Education*, Wisconsin, USA, pp. 254–258.

Lin, C.H., Liu, E.Z.F. and Huang, Y.Y., 2012. Exploring parents' perceptions towards educational robots: Gender and socio-economic differences. *British Journal of Educational Technology*, Vol. 43, No. 1, pp. E32–E34.

Lin, J. M.-C., and Liu, S.-F., 2012, An investigation into parent-child collaboration in learning computer programming. *Educational Technology & Society*, Vol. 15, No. 1, pp. 162–173.

Lye, S. Y., and Koh, J. H. L., 2014, Review on teaching and learning of computational thinking through programming: What is next for K-12? *Computers in Human Behavior*, Vol 41, pp. 51–61.

Maruyama, Y., 2019a, The impact of workshop activities on parents' concerns about computer programming education in elementary school. *IADIS International Journal on Computer Science and Information Systems*, Vol. 14, No. 1, pp.1–16.

Maruyama, Y., 2019b, Investigation into parents' impressions of computer programming with comparisons before and after a programming workshop. *Smart Education and e-Learning*, Vol. 144, pp. 421–431.

Osgood, C. E., 1952, The nature and measurement of meaning. *Psychological Bulletin*, Vol. 49, No. 3, pp. 197–237.

Papert, S., 1993. *Mindstorms: Children, Computers, and Powerful Ideas*, 2nd ed, Basic Books, New York.

Roque, R., Lin, K. and Liuzzi, R., 2016. "I'm Not Just a Mom": Parents developing multiple roles in creative computing. Singapore: International Society of the Learning Sciences.

Wing, J.M. 2006. Computational thinking, *Communications of the ACM*, Vol 49, No. 3, pp. 33–35.

TEACHER SUPPORT IN COVID-19 PANDEMIC TO DEVELOP BLENDED LEARNING DISRUPTIVE MODELS IN HIGHER EDUCATION

Francesco Floris, Alessio Genovese, Marina Marchisio, Fabio Roman and Matteo Sacchet
Department of Molecular Biotechnologies and Health Sciences, University of Turin, Italy

ABSTRACT

Covid-19 pandemic has created significant changes in higher education institutions. After university lockdown, a transition from face-to-face learning to distance learning was unavoidable and several teachers and students had to approach new technologies. The DELTA (Digital Education for Learning and Teaching Advances) Research Group provided support to six degree programs at the University of Turin: each professor received specific trainings and the group constantly helped and checked the implementation of the online courses. In this paper the support provided during the emergency period has been analysed in order to evaluate the improvements in teaching methodologies, and to assess professors' transition to future blended learning disruptive models. The results show an important change in methodology for some courses, aiming at improving the online learning processes. The research data analysis and qualitative study about the usage of the Digital Learning Environment describe the courses' disruptive models. They are useful to understand which elements of the emergency response turned out to be positive and which ones to be unfavourable, in order to be able to redesign post-Covid higher education.

KEYWORDS

Blended Learning, Digital Learning Environment, Distance Teaching, Higher education, Online Teaching

1. INTRODUCTION

Over the last few years, education in universities and in schools has been characterized by a gradual introduction of new technologies and teaching methodologies based on blended learning, combining therefore a face-to-face component with digital and online learning (European Commission/EACEA/Eurydice, 2019).

The Covid-19 pandemic in Italy forced the implementation of emergency measures because of the lockdown of brick-and-mortar schools and universities since March, 5th 2020. To provide continuity of teaching activities, it became necessary to promote the transition from face-to-face or blended learning to a fully digital emergency approach. The implementation of new directives necessarily sped up the ongoing digitalisation process in schools and universities, binding all the users to an immediate and exclusive use of online learning tools. On one hand, the adoption of new ways of learning and teaching promoted the distribution of new technologies, while on the other hand, it often brought backlashes due to the sudden emergency situation, where both teachers and students had to deal with the acquisition of new digital skills. University professors needed to rapidly adapt whole courses to the new - and not yet mastered - educational approaches, while students had to adapt to new learning processes, little experienced before.

It should be noted that the new technologies introduced over time in university programs, such as Learning Management Systems (LMS), Interactive Whiteboard (IWB), digital laboratories, are not enough to guarantee the quality and effectiveness of teaching. They should be backed up with appropriate learning methodologies. Moreover, in Italy online learning plays a marginal role in university landscape, because only in a few cases online learning activities are officially allowed and approved, and this usually comes with some limitations. The degree programs are divided into four types defined by the Ministry of University and Research (MUR, 2019): conventional study programs, delivered entirely face-to-face with a maximum 10% of online learning; study programs with mixed modalities, for a maximum of 60% of online learning; study programs mainly at distance, with more than 60% of online learning; and study programs fully delivered online. The degree programs regarding some specific disciplines, such as Medicine and Architecture, must be by law conventional study programs, and almost all the degree programs of the public university fall into the first case.

At the University of Turin, during the Covid-19 crisis, the DELTA (Digital Education for Learning and Teaching Advances) Research Group, who does research in the field of Digital Education, provided support in this transition to professors of the Department of Molecular Biotechnologies and Health Sciences (DMBHS) and of the Interdepartmental University School of Strategic Sciences (SUISS), with a total of 6 degree programs, falling within the conventional study program typology. Before the pandemic, every degree program was already provided with a Digital Learning Environment (DLE), i.e. an online space shared between teacher and students for the availability and use of training (Badoni et al., 2011). Even if DLE was available to all the professors, it was rarely used effectively to improve learning processes or proposing online activities. The DLE provided to degree programs during the pandemic is based on a Virtual Learning Environment, a Moodle-Learning platform, combined with a web conference system, an Advanced Computing Environment (ACE) and an Automatic Assessment System (AAS). Concerning the courses belonging to the DMBHS, professors had required the addition of external tools integrated into the platform, which boasts several virtual laboratories. The DLE was already in use within SUISS (Spinello et al., 2019) and it was introduced within the DMBHS at the beginning of the academic year 2019-2020, to replace a former system: in November, two trainings on the usage of the AAS were provided, but the transition from the former platform to the new DLE was still ongoing. The support started with the setup of a number of specific trainings on the use of the DLE accompanied with a constant monitoring of the quality of the educational offer. The support was not only aimed to guarantee the teaching continuity using the DLE, but also to train the teachers to allow permanent and effective use of the new learning approaches.

In this paper we answer the following research questions:

- RQ1: How the support provided to the university professors in transition from a face-to-face approach to distance teaching and learning during Covid-19 emergency has been exploited to promote and spread the evolution from a traditional educational model to a blended learning disruptive model?
- RQ2: Which learning models were widely adopted by professors and how does the use of technology influence learning approaches?

In order to answer these questions, the research analysis data about the usage of the DLE and qualitatively study describes the courses disruptive approaches. The specific use of the technology in some courses offered by the 6 degree programs will be described through the SAMR model, and the most relevant methodologies will be identified, with reference to the classification proposed by the Christensen Institute. Section 2 describes the theoretical framework about blended learning models. Section 3 illustrates the research methodology and the support model adopted. Qualitative and quantitative results are presented in Section 4.

2. THEORETICAL FRAMEWORK

Even before the universities lockdown the use of technologies had been encouraged within the 6 degree programs to promote and spread blended learning approaches. Blended learning has been variously defined over time, due to the high number of different interpretations of this topic (Ossiannilsson, 2017). This paper relies on the characterisation proposed by the Christensen Institute, and in particular we use the different models described here to better analyse the activities proposed by professors. In this paper, we will adopt the definition of Blended learning as "a formal education program in which a student learns, at least in part through online delivery of content and instruction, with some element of student control over time, place, path, and/or pace, and at least in part in a supervised brick-and-mortar location away from home. The modalities along each student's learning path within a course or subject are connected to provide an integrated learning experience" (Christensen et al., 2013 p. 8).

2.1 Theory of Hybrid Models in Blended Learning

With reference to definition of blended learning mentioned above, it is possible to determine different models depending on different teaching approaches. These models are (Christensen et al., 2013):

- Rotation Model (which includes Station Rotation Model, Lab Rotation Model, Flipped Classroom, Individual Rotation)

- Flex Model
- À la Carte Model
- Enriched Virtual Model

The first model can be considered as a blended learning approach as long as the educational activities switch between different learning methods, at least one being carried out online. This rotation can take place within the classroom itself (Station Rotation Model), between a classroom and a laboratory (Lab Rotation Model), between face-to-face guided activities and online contents available from the students outside the school (Flipped Classroom). The rotation can be personalised for each student, so that they do not need to approach to every option included in the rotation of the learning activities (Individual Rotation).

The Flex Model online learning is considered as the backbone, optionally referring to offline activities, and face-to-face component with the trainer is limited to the support activities. In the À la Carte Model instead there is the possibility for the student to take some online courses in addition to the regular ones which take place in the brick-and-mortar school. In the last approach (Enriched Model) each course requires mainly fruition of online contents, but a periodical class attendance to lectures is required, too.

Which of these models can describe the learning activity before and during the Covid-19 emergency? Researchers are looking for disruptive models to propose for the future. The distinction between different blended learning models can be inserted in the more general theory of hybrid and disruptive models, coming from the economic field. A hybrid model upgrades old models through inclusion of new technologies, but it still represents a sustaining innovation, with the purpose of serving customers according to the original definition of performance. Disruptive innovations, unlike the sustaining ones, substantially transform the traditional idea of performance. Disruptive models have therefore several advantages compared to hybrid ones, such as the opportunity to approach new users excluded from the old system, the redesign of traditional models and the simplification of the quality of services. By analysing blended learning in the perspective of hybrid and disruptive models, blended learning might be considered as a hybrid model preceding the transition to the actual disruptive innovation of fully online learning. It is therefore important to point out that blended learning is considered here as a potential disruptive innovation in the field of education: relying on the different blended learning models described above, different teaching methods can assume both hybrid and disruptive characteristics.

2.2 SAMR Model in Blended Learning

The analysis of educational methodologies also concerns the role of technologies in planning the learning activities. We adopted the SAMR model to classify educational materials provided during Covid-19 emergency according to the technologies involved. This model includes 4 different approaches to new technologies (Puentedura, 2013):

- Substitution: technology acts as a direct substitute to traditional methods and resources
- Augmentation: technology acts as a direct substitute with functional improvements in the design of teaching activities
- Modification: technology affects the redesign of the learning task, with a significant modification
- Redefinition: technology allows to create new tasks, inconceivable in the traditional face-to-face model

As in the former theory of hybrid and disruptive models, also the SAMR model is characterized by a progression, with every step representing an improvement in learning outcomes and students' engagement.

3. METHODOLOGY

We adopted two different research work methods: the first one concerning quantitative data, the second one concerning qualitative analysis. We initially extracted the most relevant data on the use of the DLE: in fact, it allows to collect different typologies of reports on the activities of the platform, such as views, usage and interaction with the different types of resources or of activities. Our group exploited these reports both while monitoring teachers in distance learning activities and, subsequently, in the elaboration of the collected data.

Data analysis was guided by the identification of different indicators: accessibility, availability, interactivity, flexibility, personalisation, completeness. The research group classified each type of resource according to such indicators in order to define the general trend of teachers' choices. Quantitative analysis has been deepened by a qualitative approach considering the supervision activity. In fact, support activities and constant monitoring of professors and courses on the DLE provided this study with relevant examples of distance learning approaches. A qualitative analysis of courses with reference to the SAMR model was performed, with the same purpose of detecting the suitability of different distance learning methodologies to a fully online approach. The consistent dialogue with professors gave us further elements to consider.

It was possible to recognize the main critical issues while analysing courses during the emergency. In critical cases, the support activity often influenced the choice of different materials, opting, for instance, for more interactive ones.

3.1 Support Activity Provided

The support group is composed mainly of researchers and instructional designers who are used to online learning methodologies and to the management of DLE (Marchisio et al., 2019). All components are administrators of the two platforms of DMBHS and SUISS and have the possibility to check all the courses and to manage users' accreditation. The group trained and supported professors to develop necessary digital skills and capability in planning an online course and in implementing it.

We provided training courses inside the DLEs, where self-learning materials and recorded online lectures dedicated to the teachers were uploaded. During the first days after university and school lockdown, free access basic trainings were scheduled. From March to June more than 15 hours of synchronous training were provided, concerning the management of the DLE, the creation of multimedia and interactive materials, the usage of the AAS. However, support was provided to professors mainly individually, through synchronous assistance (via call phone or VoIP systems) and asynchronous assistance (via e-mail or dedicated forum on the platform): more than 50 cases of synchronous assistance and more than 300 cases of asynchronous assistance. The former scheduled plan for face-to-face lectures was adapted into a new format which includes the distinction, specified by the teacher, between synchronous lectures (held via web conference system) and asynchronous modules (such as fruition of materials or activities uploaded). The adaptation of the schedule, especially in the cases of asynchronous activities, required attention to the correspondence between the hours required by the plan and quality and quantity of materials uploaded on the platform. In order to do so, a constant monitoring of every course, with in-depth periodical checks, was a relevant part of the work. Lastly, further reflections took place within internal meetings as departmental councils, with the aim to receive immediate feedback on the problematic aspects of DLE management by professors.

Training moments, personal support, course monitoring and classification of methodologies were not considered as different and subsequent phases. In fact, these aspects influenced each other: in particular, course monitoring improved support activities. Classification of use of technology and support events were two inseparable aspects of the research group activity.

4. RESULTS

Last February, before the emergency period, platforms of DMBHS and of SUISS registered 321 professors and 2028 students logged in. In a couple of weeks since the introduction of distance learning, after the creation of the missing courses, users counted 369 professors and 2355 students. The number constantly increased during the following months, due to the creation of new courses (sometimes external to the reference departments, like in the case of interfaculty courses). In July 2020, the DLE registered 201 active courses, 403 professors, 2763 students logged in. It should be noted that the growth is not exceptional, because many students and professors logged in just a few times in the first semester of a.y. 2019-2020.

Professors can choose among different types of resources and activities to share on the online platform, such as interactive lessons, books, automatic tests for formative and summative assessment, textual files, slides, videos, URLs to external links, forums, concept maps, folders of pictures, etc. It is interesting to have a look at the main types of resources and activities uploaded (Table 1 and Figure 1). The number of resources and activities uploaded on the two platforms during a.y. 2019-2020 totals 5094 in 201 active courses: only the most spread and significant typologies are reported.

Table 1. Main resources and activities uploaded during a.y. 2019-2020 by the 6 degree programs

Resources/Activities	Courses involved	Total numbers
Resources (PDF files, PowerPoint, etc)	112	2376
Moodle Pages (videos, web pages, etc)	42	514
Labels (videos, section titles, etc)	37	355
URLs to external online contents (Youtube, news, etc)	35	344
Forums	201	315
Web Conference Sections	56	219
Test with Automatic Assessment	51	169
Assignments	38	169
Chats	9	11

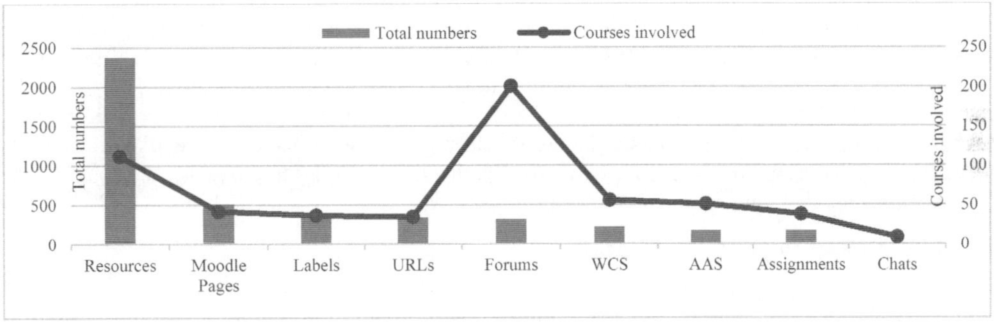

Figure 2. Main resources and activities uploaded during a.y. 2019-2020 by the 6 degree programs

In a few cases questionnaires, feedback tools, glossaries or other activities for collaborative learning were created. Interactive materials sometimes are created too, but in general this type of resources is less used than other ones, despite their relevance in online teaching, especially in STEM disciplines (Barana et al., 2019b). As it can be noticed, almost half is represented by static resources, mostly documents and slides. Video lessons can be uploaded on the platform through the tools Moodle page or labels. A relevant use of external resources can as well be observed in the number of URLs. many links refer to videos uploaded on platforms dedicated to multimedia materials sharing, significant of a quite spread use of the Open Educational Resources (OERs). This is very positive, because professors were trained on the importance of the use of OERs and the use of Creative Common Licences in order to share their materials.

An important specification is needed with regards to synchronous activities: even if they seem to be present in a low number of courses (a total of 219 activities in only 56 courses), these numbers do not take into account different systems external to the DLE, used by some of the teachers to virtually meet their students, and the fact that most professors used the same activity for all the live moments. Another interesting data concerns the use of forums: each course includes a default chat system for asynchronous communications, but the actual number of forum activities shows the importance of this system beyond the automatic announcement.

Through a comparison of the resources and activities provided in SUISS platform in a.y. 2019-2020 and the ones of a.y. 2018-2019, it can be noticed that while the total number of materials has more than doubled, the number of static resources has increased by 88%. This is the smaller increase among the typologies presented in Table 1: for example, the use of OER through external URLs has increased by 460%, video resources by 260%. These data refer only to SUISS due to lack of data of previous years in DMBHS, and they show a change of needs and, during the emergency, support activities tried to understand and to answer new necessities.

4.1 Different Approaches to the use of Technology for Distance Learning

In order to better analyse the methodologies adopted in online courses, it is first necessary to discuss how technology was used. Some typical examples of use of DLE during the emergency period seem useful to better describe the resources provided to the students through distance learning. With reference to the SAMR model, it should be noted that a significant case of "redefinition" model has not yet been identified: this achievement needs in fact a long and phased process of transition, difficult under extreme circumstances like Covid-19 emergency period.

4.1.1 Online Learning as "Substitution"

In certain cases, teachers initially did not upload any resource, while they only scheduled synchronous web conference activities, simply substituting face-to-face lectures with online live meetings where students are able to interact. These online sections do not cause any actual change in the educational offer, since they do not involve any improvement in the teaching methodology: the traditional setting simply shifted from the physical class to the online platform together with the synchronous explanation of the teacher. Technology acts therefore as a direct tool to substitute face-to-face lectures, without causing any change or improvement in the learning activity. The overlap between online teaching and synchronous activities also implies some recurrent disadvantages, such as the unavailability of a strong connection or the impossibility to use an appropriate device during classes, due to the schedule, for a part of the students. Training and support activities were therefore aimed at pointing out and discussing similar cases and highlighting other functions of DLE, monitoring the actual upload of the resources used in the synchronous meetings in order to guarantee the right to education to those students who were unable to attend classes.

4.1.2 Online Learning as "Augmentation"

In most part of the courses, students were provided, together with the resources, with uploaded video recorded lectures specifically projected for asynchronous fruition. These didactic materials allow the students to autonomously access resources with the further advantage of the teacher's oral explanation, which promotes a more effective comprehension and mastery. This use of DLE can be seen as a direct substitute to the face-to-face model but, in this case, resources and activities are projected to improve student's fruition through the possibility of self-management of materials and time and individualization of the learning process. To promote and spread the use of video lessons, decreasing the high number of synchronous activities, an important part of training activities was dedicated to video making and audio recording to be attached to slides presentation.

Other relevant examples of online learning as "augmentation" are the use of forum for questions and doubts about the disciplines to which students themselves were able to answer, and the use of an Automatic Assessment System for the formative evaluation, provided as online drills and followed by personalized feedback. This model of online learning brings about actual and relevant improvements to the learning processes, the most significant being the increase of students' engagement (Barana et al., 2020).

4.1.3 Online Assessment as "Modification"

The issue of distance exams and the necessity of new forms of assessment have been largely discussed during the lockdown of universities, and it would deserve an appropriate in-depth discussion. The University of Turin immediately provided professors with guidelines on the best evaluation systems, among which stands written testing and webcam checks. In our support and training professors were invited to redesign examination procedures in order to avoid cheating or other issues: some exams previously structured in open questions or multiple choice questions were redesigned as open book exams, focused on papers or works to be submitted. The advantage of open book exams, which allow the students to freely access educational materials and manage the execution time, consists in the possibility to avoid the difficulties presented by simultaneous tests, such as cheating or technical issues caused by synchronous use of online tools. Moreover, the use of specific tools which allow professors to add comments and assess students submissions was promoted. Since the assessment phase fully involves the didactic planning of a course, this is a relevant example of technology acting not only as direct substitute with functional improvements, but also as actual "modification" of traditional methodologies. Professors were invited to use also formative assessment and to use the examples of final assessments available on the platform in order to help students to better prepare for them (Barana et al., 2019a).

4.2 Adopted Methodologies towards a Flex Model

With reference to the former analysis, which blended learning model better fits the learning methods proposed before and during the Covid-19 emergency? Before March 2020, digital support activities were already provided, but they were not very appealing: most of the courses were structured with the traditional face-to-face model and the use of technology often did not effectively influence learning methodologies. This marginality did not of course affect all courses: exceptions are represented by Mathematics and Physics modules of the three master's degree programs offered by DMBHS and SUISS. These courses were based on face-to-face teaching but a key point of the educational offers concerned also the use of the ACE and included a large use of interactive resources and activities in the DLE: several lectures were dedicated to practicing in a computer lab, and the study of a real problem through the ACE is required and evaluated. Courses presenting similar learning methodologies can actually be ascribed to the blended learning Lab Rotation Model, with some points in common with the Flipped Classroom model, such as the follow-up activities proposed by some teachers. Blended learning models mentioned above can be described as functional hybrid models, since they combine traditional elements (face-to-face learning activities) with innovative components (online learning through the use of a DLE), and involve the same users of the traditional system.

With reference to the methodologies proposed during distance teaching, it is necessary to specify that they clearly cannot be defined exactly as blended learning models, since the face-to-face component is absent. However, it is useful to adopt these models to classify the online learning activity, in order to choose future methodologies. The use of DLE, as we observed, shares common aspects with the traditional face-to-face approach, in particular by transposing physical lectures to online learning through synchronous lessons: courses based on the use of technologies as a direct substitute tool can be ascribed to traditional models.

In order to classify methodologies in distance teaching, it is important to understand how traditional methods (synchronous activities substituting face-to-face lectures) and innovative methods are related. As observed, one of the results of support activities was to avoid a simple transposition of the face-to-face schedule into only synchronous moments. In fact, most of the courses provided the students with autonomous study resources uploading online materials and video lessons. However, we observed an actual need from both students and professors for moments of discussion. Different tools can meet this need: forum activities were strongly recommended, and also a periodic (moderate) use of synchronous meetings, via chat or via web conference, was suggested. Therefore, almost all the courses included activities and resources available to students for autonomous learning, with the possibility of discussion moments with the teacher. Synchronous sections were a moment of discussion. With regards to the resources, with the help of training activities we were able to encourage professors to reconsider the phase of elaboration of educational material: a relevant example concerns the use of video lessons, mentioned above, not only delivered as a single video recorded but divided into shorter and well-structured unities, more accessible to students.

The blended learning model that better represents the methodology described above is the Flex model: students have maximum autonomy in planning and personalising learning processes, but they can benefit from necessary moments of discussion with the professor. In the characterization of the Christensen institute, the Flex Model is a disruptive model: it evolves the idea of students sitting in a brick-and-mortar classroom and not being able to manage their time, place, and path of learning. Even when considering it with its actual face-to-face component, including offline activities and discussions with the teacher, this model is still suitable for possible students who might encounter difficulties in attending face-to-face or hybrid courses.

A necessary component for an effective fruition of this methodology by students is a strong personal layout planning of the online course, together with a general well-structured organisation of the activities and resources, and with a desirable aware use of OERs. The support group contributed to the development of such skills in professors, with some significantly positive feedback.

With the help of instructional experts' suggestions, many professors managed to design their modules according to Flex Model methods. Someone took it even further: the teachers who learned how to use the AAS are able to use innovative assessment methodologies, such as the formative ones. As we observed, drills were provided, not only based on automatic assessment but also on multiple attempts and personalized feedback: in courses that provided such activities, students' participation was very high. An example is the Molecular Immunology course, where at least 60% of students took part in the latest optional tests. Some professors promote formative assessment for supporting autonomous studying and training in view of the exam. In such cases, personal assistance proved to be fundamental for positive outcomes.

5. CONCLUSION

Through the support and training provided to the academic staff of 6 degree programs during the Covid-19 emergency, we observed different approaches to the use of technology (using the SAMR model), and we promoted a common disruptive model of blended learning in the courses provided. The forced and immediate use of new technologies caused some relevant changes in teaching methodologies: synchronous activities were initially largely spread and tended to maintain the structure of traditional face-to-face lectures as much as possible. After the support activities, both professors and students developed important skills about new methodologies, which can be ascribed to the Flex Model, which was eventually the most used learning model (RQ2). Thus, support activity was able to promote and spread the evolution of the educational model not only through technical assistance, but also, as we observed, through the proposal of innovative tech and confrontation with professors (RQ1).

It can be stated that almost all the teaching staff has acquired an open-minded approach and awareness in the use of disruptive teaching methods. It is appropriate to wonder how the emergency will influence the following months of stabilization and the future of learning methods, and what the better strategies are in order to provide necessary support and training for the gradual development of functional learning models for the best learning outcomes. In this perspective, it is conceivable and desirable to maintain disruptive mixed teaching models by providing constant support. For the development of disruptive learning methods in schools, the creation of "a team within the school that is autonomous from all aspects of the traditional classroom" is indicated by Christensen as the first step (Christensen et al., 2013p. 38). During the emergency, the DELTA Research Group actually played the role of an independent support group. The experience described in this paper shows how beneficial and effective an instructional team can be, not only for technical assistance but also for monitoring the activities and for suggestions concerning possible improvements of the online components of the courses, with potential benefit on students' outcomes and engagement. The cases presented in this paper are relevant examples of a support and research work aimed at achieving a deeper awareness.

Finally, it would be useful to deeper investigate feedback and issues concerning students' and professors' experience of management of distance learning: structured questionnaires dedicated to both professors and students are already available on DLE, and the analysis of results is still ongoing.

REFERENCES

Baldoni M. et al., 2011. *HAP-Moodle: una soluzione open-source per l'High-Availability e la performance applicata a Moodle. E-learning con Moodle in Italia: una sfida tra passato, presente e futuro*. Seneca Ed., Torino, pp. 213-226.

Barana A. et al., 2019a. Empowering engagement through automatic formative assessment, *Proceedings of 2019 IEEE 43rd Annual Computer Software and Applications Conference,* Milwaukee, Wisconsin, USA, pp. 216-225

Barana A. et al., 2019b. The role of an advanced computing environment in teaching and learning mathematics through problem posing and solving, 2019, *eLearning and software for Education Conference*, Bucharest, Romania, pp. 11-18

Barana A. et al., 2020. Empowering Engagement in a Technology-Enhanced Learning Environment, *Project and Design Literacy as Cornerstones of Smart Education*, Vol. 158, Springer, pp. 75-77

Christensen C. et al., 2013. *Is K-12 blended leaning disruptive? An introduction to the theory of hybrids*. Retrieved from: https://www.christenseninstitute.org/wp-content/uploads/2014/06/Is-K-12-blended-learning-disruptive.pdf

European Commission/EACEA/Eurydice, 2019. *Digital Education at School in Europe*. Eurydice Report. Luxembourg: Publications Office of the European Union

Marchisio et al., 2019, Instructional design to "train the trainers": the start@unito project at university of Turin, 2019, *Multi Conference on Computer Science and Information System, MCCSIS 2019 - Proceedings of the International Conference on e-Learning 2019*, pp. 195-202

MUR, 2019. Decreto Ministeriale n. 989 del 25/10/2019 relativo alle Linee Generali di indirizzo della programmazione delle università 2019-2021

Ossiannilsson E., 2017. Blended Learning State of the Nation. *Proceedings of the 10th International Conference on Computer Supported Education (CSEDU 2018),* Funchal, Portugal, pp. 541-547

Puentedura R. R., 2013. *SAMR: Moving from enhancement to transformation*. Retrieved from http://www.hippasus.com/rrpweblog/archives/000095.html

Spinello E. et al., 2019. A full spectrum lifelong e-learning project for the army, *15th International Scientific Conference eLearning and Software Education,* Bucharest, Romania, pp. 152-158

INTERACTIVE ONLINE PATH FOR ENGLISH REMEDIAL WORK AT SECONDARY SCHOOL

Elisa Corino[1], Cecilia Fissore[1] and Marina Marchisio[2]
[1]*Dipartimento di Lingue e Letterature Straniere e Culture Moderne*
Via Giuseppe Verdi Fronte 41, 10124 Torino TO, Italia
[2]*Dipartimento di Biotecnologie Molecolari e Scienze per la Salute*
Via Nizza 52 - 10126 Torino TO, Italia

ABSTRACT

According to the annual report of the EF EPI (Education First - English Proficiency Index), the level of fluency in English by Italians is among the lowest in Europe. It is important that young people acquire language skills at school, especially during secondary schools, so as not to be penalized at university or when looking for work. However, English is one of the most difficult subjects for students and remedial work interventions are often necessary. In this, but also in general in teaching and learning English, technologies can offer important support. The University of Turin has designed and implemented innovative methodologies for remedial work, based on the use of an integrated Digital Learning Environment. The context of this research is an interactive online course for the remedial work of English which involved 11 classes of a secondary school for a total of 265 students. Our research questions concerning the design and implementation of activities and resources to involve students and what utility and interest they have induced in students. To answer the research questions, the paths on the platform and the activities and resources created by the tutors were analyzed. To understand if students and teachers appreciated the remedial work path and if they considered it useful, their answers to the final questionnaire, completed at the end of the remedial work path, were analyzed.

KEYWORDS

Adaptive Interactive Lessons, Digital Learning Environment, English Remedial Work, Feedback, Interactive Teaching Materials, Tests with Automatic Assessment

1. INTRODUCTION

According to the annual report of the EF EPI (Education First - English Proficiency Index) which detects the level of knowledge of the English language, the level of fluency in English by Italians is among the lowest in Europe (EF EPI, 2019). This situation clashes with the globalized nature of the world and may preclude opportunities for future employment. School has a primary role in assuring a proper language education and the development of skills, which will allow students to successfully enter foreign universities or the labour market. Although the Italian National guidelines for secondary education state B2 as the exit level to be reached at the end of upper secondary school, according to data from the EF EPI, only 30% students have it. In addition, the percentage of students who reach B2 level falls from 40% in urban schools to 25% in provincial schools. Despite its universally acknowledged importance and pervasiveness in our everyday life, it appears that English is one of the subjects where students have most difficulties and motivation. This might be partly due to the persistence of traditional teaching, mainly focused on theoretical grammar skills and structural knowledge over functional competence and communication, which is still widely practiced despite the guidelines coming from research and good teaching practices. To face the difficulties in English, teachers and institutes, but also students and parents, devote many resources in terms of time and actions taken. As the research of the last two decades highlights, modern technologies and among them CALL (Computer Assisted Language Learning) and MALL (Mobile Assisted Language Learning) can offer valuable support for learning and teaching languages. They can be used by teachers to enrich lessons in the classroom, all the more to involve the least motivated or most struggling students (Wu, 2003; Alizadeh, 2016). The literature about the use of ICT in the language classroom is substantial and there are lots of projects focusing on good practices to integrate the active use of technology with the last waves of theoretical research about language teaching and learning - "ITIL2- Interactive Teaching in Languages with Technology" (http://www.itilt2.eu), "CATAPULT-Computer Assisted Training and Platforms to Upskill LSP Teachers" (http://catapult-project.eu) and "PETALL-Pan European Tasks for Language Learning" (http://petallproject.eu/petall/index.php/en/) among others - but little has been done about the specific needs of remedial work. In the light of that, the University of Turin has designed, studied and developed innovative methodologies to help remedial work and reduce school failures. These methodologies are characterized by the use of a Digital Learning Environment (DLE), a virtual space shared by students and teachers, both for face-to-face activities and for remote online activities. The DLE, implemented on a Moodle platform integrated with an automatic assessment system (AAS) and a web conference service, is based on constructivist theory, student-centered learning and collaborative learning. The context of this research is an interactive online course for remedial English classes which involved 11 classes of a secondary school for a total of 265 students. The school is the Amaldi Sraffa Higher Education Institute of Orbassano (in the province of Turin) and students from grade 9 to grade 11 were involved. The course should have included afternoon remedial activities in the classroom and remote online activities, both conducted by university tutors of the Master's Degree in Modern Languages and Literatures specially trained. However, due to the Covid-19 emergency and the consequent closing of the schools, the experience took place entirely online and the tutors only met their students through the platform. The course was organized within the integrated DLE and lasted about 3 months (from March 2020 until the end of the school year in May 2020). During this period, the tutors held weekly synchronous online meetings and they designed and created remedial activities and resources, always available to students on the platform. Our research questions are: "How were the activities and resources designed and implemented to involve students, given the emergency and the exclusively online nature of the experience?" and "What usefulness and satisfaction did the activities and resources have for the students and teachers, within the path of online remedial work?". To answer these questions, the interactive paths and the activities and resources created by tutors were analyzed in detail. The methodologies used by the tutors for the implementation, with the support of the trainers, of the platform activities were also analyzed. Students' and teachers' responses to the final questionnaire completed at the end of the remedial work process were also analyzed.

2. TECHNOLOGIES FOR ENGLISH TEACHING AND LEARNING: AN INTERACTIVE COLLABORATIVE LEARNING ENVIRONMENT

The development, the implementation and the assessment of language learning and teaching activities have significantly increased with the use of online technologies and mobile devices (Milthorpe et al., 2018). ICT and language education have been a fundamental combination and a precious resource for foreign language teachers since the 60s of the last century, when technologies started to be seen as a necessary support to language learning (Cuccurullo, 2012). Over the years, there have been different approaches to the use of technologies - often influenced by the theories of language acquisition - and numerous technological tools have been used in the teaching/learning processes of foreign languages. In recent years, CALL and MALL have contributed to forge paths to language learning in ways that do not replace the work of teachers in the classroom but complement it in significant manners.. The importance of ICT as components of the teaching-learning environment is generally acknowledged by literature (among the manifold works on the integration of technology and the language classroom, Chapelle & Sauro 2017 and Stanley 2013) in relation to all the benefits that this combination can have on the students' abilities, cognitive styles, learners' autonomy and motivation. Yet, online, blended, e-learning, or technology-enhanced learning remains an area of significant challenge for humanities that traditionally prize face-to-face pedagogical methodologies such as the lecture, and small group discussion and debate (Blended). A DLE, i.e. an online virtual space shared by teachers and students, can allow teachers to enhance the teaching and learning of foreign languages. Currently, various platforms are available (for example Padlet, Edmodo, Gsuite, Moodle), some free and some not, some simpler and more basic and some more complex with plug-ins and possible integrations with other software. What we mean by DLE integrated into teaching is much more than a platform. In a DLE it is important both the technological component and the human component, and how the activities are designed for the interactions between students, teachers and peers. Through a DLE one can propose many different types of activities in a single shared environment; it is important in an online teaching context, but it can also integrate the teaching experience into ordinary teaching in classroom-based or in a blended mode. And what is more, the availability of a platform on mobile devices can render even greater benefits for both language teachers and learners (Herrera Mosquera, 2017). A DLE foster the establishment and expansion of a community by offering a "real" context for interaction and support virtual communities, with no physical walls defining the borders of the place where the community resides and works (Ligorio and Van Veen, 2006). From the didactic and pedagogical point of view, DLEs should be designed to support and foster constructivist learning, thus enabling students to actively build their knowledge with the mediation of experiences and relationships with the environment and community (von Glasersfeld, 1989), stimulating motivation and autonomous investigation and, and redefining the role of teachers as facilitators rather than sources of knowledge. A central factor in the learning environment is feedback: frequent and well-structured feedback helps learners understand where they are, where they are going and what they should do in order to reach their goal, giving information not only about how the task was performed, but also about the process to be mastered, and enabling self-regulation and self-monitoring of actions (Hattie and Timperley, 2007). Digital technologies can support and expand feedback practices and, returning individualized information to students and teachers in real time, they can support and enhance learning processes. Among the requirements of an effective DLE that fulfils the constructivist and experiential ideal, there should be: the possibility for students to create and publish their own works, immediately usable and shared within the community, to compare it, and to actively collaborate with the teacher or other students; the implementation of activities that promote active exploration for students and that react to the user's action giving a feedback. Activities in which digital tools are used demonstrate ways that technology can be deployed to engage students, to look at texts in fresh ways, and to make learning more interactive and student driven (Milthorpe et al., 2018).

3. THE ONLINE PATH FOR ENGLISH REMEDIAL WORK

The University of Turin (Unito) has designed, studied and developed innovative methodologies for the reduction of school failures and has applied them in different contexts (Cavagnero et al., 2015; Fissore et al., 2019, In press). The Unito DLE is a Moodle platform (managed by the ICT services of the Department of Computer Science of the University of Turin), integrated with the AAS Moebius Assessment for the creation of online formative tests. This AAS allows the creation of adaptive questions that provide students another chance when they give an incorrect response and that can be adapted to: provide more information; let the student try a simpler version of the question; lead the student through the exercise one step at a time; and present whatever other approach the instructor feels is appropriate. This type of questions with interactive and immediate feedback is very suitable for automatic formative assessment (Barana et al., 2019; Marello et al., 2019). The platform (available at the link https://scuolapertutti.i-learn.unito.it/) is also integrated with a web conference system for online tutoring andfor all contents the EasyReading font with high readability is used. Using Moodle in teaching and learning is not innovative. The novelty of our work consists in the use of a DLE integrated with an AAS, to carry out activities that involve students, tutors and teachers (online or in the classroom when it is again possible) in a little explored and studied context such as that of recovery. For this reason, a qualitative and not quantitative analysis is proposed, which concerns the methodologies adopted for the recovery and not the numbers of how much the students have improved. The DLE allows to propose a remedial work intervention different from the traditional one, which in addition to the development of knowledge and skills related to learning English, is also concentrated on enhancing interest in the matter and trust in the possibility of success. The remedial work path of English took place within the third edition of the "Scuola per Tutti" (which in English means "School for Everyone") project. The project took place in the secondary school Amaldi-Sraffa of Orbassano in the province of Turin in order to recover school failures of 9th, 10th and 11th grade students in English, Mathematics, Latin and Physics (Barana et al., 2020). The goals of the project were to overcome learning difficulties, to reduce the phenomenon of early school leaving, to increase motivation in studying and to facilitate the transition between lower and upper secondary school. In this research we will focus exclusively on the third edition of the remedial work path for English, as the first two editions have been used to design and test methodologies for teaching English. The remedial work path lasted about three months in the second part of the 19/20 school year.. At the beginning of the project, the teachers selected the students with deficiencies in English (insufficiency between 4 and a half and 5 and a half). Throughout the period, students were followed by university tutors, specially trained on the project methodologies and on the use of the technologies involved. Initially the remedial work path included activities within the DLE of three types: synchronous face-to-face activities, synchronous online activities via web conference and online asynchronous activities. Due to the emergency from Covid-19 and therefore the closure of the schools, the remedial work activities took place exclusively online remotely via the DLE. This led to a redesign and reformulation of the remedial work path. On the one hand, synchronous online meetings have been enhanced to give tutors and students the opportunity to get to know each other and relate as much as possible to each other. On the other, asynchronous platform activities have been enhanced to give students the opportunity to carry them out when they could and when they wanted (compatibly with daily online lessons). A further consequence was that of deciding to involve all the students in the class, in addition to the students selected by the teachers, to offer everyone support during the emergency. The teachers were involved throughout the course and played a key role: they indicated to the tutor the topics to be addressed with the students, reminded the students to connect to the online meetings and carry out the activities and supported the tutor in creating the material. Conversely, the tutors constantly updated the teachers on the activities carried out with the students, on the results achieved and on the involvement of the students. Finally, the tutors received constant support from the researchers: in implementing the project methodologies, in the use of technologies, in making the materials more interactive and training and in relating with the students. The remedial work path involved 11 classes of 4 teachers for a total of 265 students. The classes were grouped into 5 groups and 5 interactive online courses were set up, to which students, their teacher and tutor always had access. Each path was managed by one of the three tutors (two tutors followed two paths). The use of the platform makes it possible to track all student activities within the course. The remedial work path was organized in this way: during the online meetings the tutor reviewed the disciplinary topics indicated by the teacher, after which they created and made available material that students could explore and do during the week before the next meeting. Students could also use the course forum at any time to ask questions to the tutor of a theoretical nature, on the materials made available or on the use of the platform.

4. RESULTS

Our research questions concern the design and implementation of activities and resources to involve students and what utility and interest they have induced in students. To answer the research questions, the five remedial work paths on the platform and the activities and resources created by the tutors were analyzed in detail. The activities and resources were analyzed according to their characteristics and the type of interactivity they offer. All the activities and resources created by the tutors have been classified according to the following categories: tests with automatic assessment, interactive lessons, interactive resources, submissions of tasks, recordings/podcasts and static resources (pdf files, URLs, images). The methodologies adopted by tutors were analyzed to make digital materials as interactive as possible, to involve students more and give them immediate and interactive feedback. Some representative examples will be shown. To understand if the students and teachers appreciated the remedial work path and if they considered it useful to recover their gaps, their answers to the final questionnaire, completed at the end of the remedial work path, were analyzed. In particular, the following questions were analyzed: the relationship of the students with the English subject before and after the course; their main difficulties; reflections on their progress; reflections on interactions with tutors and on the support they have given; reflections on the platform used for the course and on the activities and resources created by the tutors. The questionnaire was optional for the students and, having to fill it in at the end of the school year, not everyone replied. In total 101 students replied.

4.1 Analysis of the Activities and Resources

A total of 217 activities and resources for students on multiple topics were created in the various courses. Figure 1 shows a summary of the classification of the activities and resources in the various categories. At the beginning of the course, tutors shared many static resources such as theoretical pdf files, concept maps, power point presentations, images or URLs for further information. This can be explained in several ways: at the beginning of the course, the tutors were not skilled enough to exploit the potential of the DLE and chose to use tools that they were already familiar with; it is very easy to find very valid and interesting open static resources on the net; in some cases the tutors used references to textbooks that all students had.

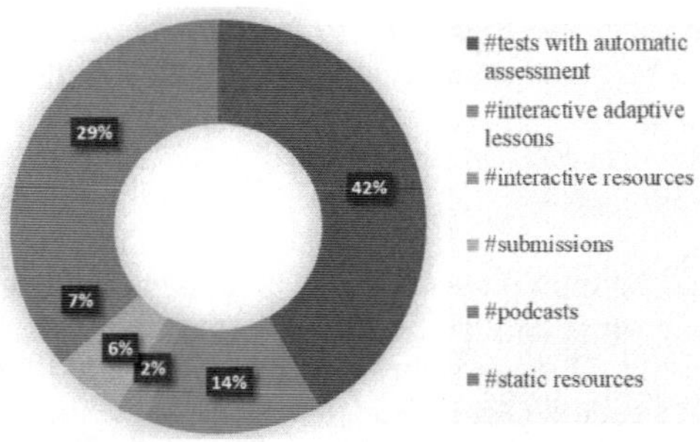

Figure 1. Summary of the classification of the various activities and resources in the remedial work paths

These contents can be very useful, such as videos or podcasts to practice listening or pages and conceptual maps for review, however making them available to students may not be enough. The researchers then suggested to tutors to create adaptive interactive lessons: a collection of customizable html pages. Each page can have content (video, audio, image, text, concept map, etc.) or questions. Student can navigate between the various pages and view different contents according to the choice (answer given, go to the next page, go to the previous page, select a specific page, etc.). Different comments/answers can be presented depending on the choice and students can be directed to navigation. For example, a lesson on the infinitive of purpose was proposed. In the first part of the lesson, students were asked to watch and listen to a video of a very famous English song ("The Scientist" by Coldplay) with English subtitles, in which the construct was often used. In the second part of the lesson a summary explanation was proposed through a concept map and a narrative explanation. After this explanation, students could choose whether to watch the video again or try to take a short quiz. In the quiz different sentences were presented and the students had to understand if the "to" in the sentence represented an infinity of purpose. For example, in the sentence "I went to the cinema to watch The Avengers!" students could choose from the answers: only the first, only the second, or both. Students had personalized feedback depending on the response, for example if they selected "only the first" they had the feedback "Pay attention! The first “to" is a prepositions of movement", if they selected "both" they had the feedback "Try to reason, where is the purpose in this sentence?". Students who answered all questions correctly concluded the lesson, while students who made mistakes were presented with an additional page of explanation. The lesson could also be repeated several times. This type of adaptive presentation of content and questions makes students the protagonists of their learning, forces them to think about what is required and stimulates them to be active in building their knowledge. Often, at the end of an interactive theory review lesson, students were offered tests with automatic assessment and immediate feedback. These tests, as shown in Figure 1, represent 42% of the activities carried out. For the creation of the tests, the tutors took inspiration from exercises in the textbooks, from open material on the web or from exercises provided by teachers. Initially tutors tended to reproduce the exercises by transcribing them with some modifications within the AAS. In the example question in Figure 2, students had to think about using "some" and "any" and complete sentences correctly.

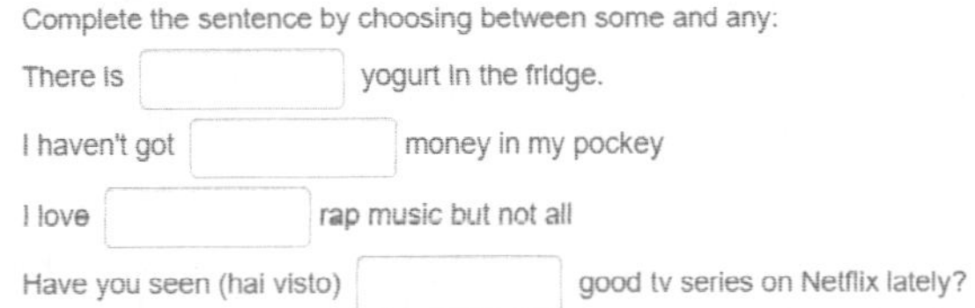

Figure 2. Example of initial question created by tutors with the AAS

In this case, the students had the assessment after having submitted the whole test, they did not have immediate and the simple "wrong answer" feedback does not give students information about their mistake and how to overcome it. It is possible to add final feedback, but students hardly look at it after submitting the test and seeing the score. Furthermore, they are probably no longer focused on this request because they answered the other questions as well. Trainers guided the tutors to create adaptive questions, more effective for formative assessment.. For example, the question seen above can be transformed into a question for formative assessment with immediate feedback. As in figure 3, the four cases can be proposed sequentially. After completing the first request, students can click on the "verify" button (which means "check" in Italian) and check the accuracy of the answer given, obtaining immediate feedback. In this way, if students make a mistake at the first request, they can rethink the reasoning and try to correct themselves, having experienced the previous result. After that, it is possible to insert feedback on the review of the theory directly within the question. In this way, students can actively review the rule, thinking about the answers entered and having more attempts available. By having immediate feedback, they can better acquire the general rule and put it into practice immediately. Finally, other requests are presented in the last part of the question to see if the student has internalized the rule correctly. The possibility of having more attempts available through a guided and interactive path is very important for the self-confidence of the students and can help to overcome the errors due to the correct insertion of the written answer. This type of activity allows students to practice independently when they prefer and to have immediate feedback on the activity carried out. Students can retry the test as many times as they wish and ask questions to the tutor or classmates in the forum if necessary. The tutor can view the students' answers and all attempts to answer, to be aware of the most frequent errors and any difficulties encountered. During synchronous online meetings, students can compare each other on the activity carried out and the tutor can give general feedback. In both activities, lessons and tests, adaptive teaching is proposed to activate effective formative assessment strategies, to give different feedbacks according to the level and responses of the students and to activate self-regulated learning.

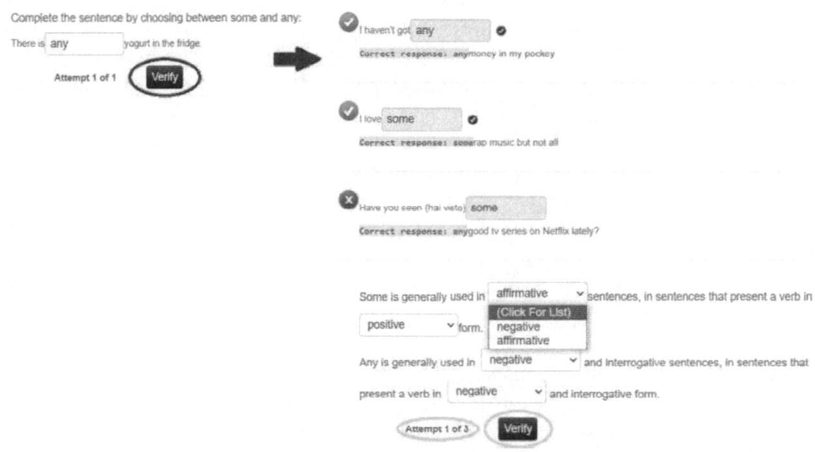

Figure 3. Previous example transformed for a more formative assessment

For other types of activities, such as writing a text or pronunciation exercises, tutors used the submission activity: the students submitted an online task and tutors returned feedback after a few days. In online education it is important to give continuous feedback to students but at the same time it can be important to receive it from students. For example, after a phonetic activity, a tutor submitted short surveys to students in order to get feedback on the usefulness and appreciation of the activities carried out. A student wrote that she really enjoyed the activity and that the most stimulating aspect was: "Knowing that there is no need to pronounce words like a native Englishman would do". This confirms that speaking in English is one of the activities in which students have the most difficulties. The latest types of activities shared by the tutors are SCORM (Shareable Content Object Reference Model) activities, a collection of specifications that enable interoperability, accessibility and reusability of web-based learning content. All activities and resources within the DLE were accessible to students at any time, via computer or mobile device. All students could choose when to dedicate themselves to the review activities. The activity with students gave the tutors the opportunity to receive very useful feedback and to reflect on the prepared activities.

4.2 Students' and Teachers' Satisfaction with the Remedial Work Path

In the final questionnaire, students had to give themselves a score from "1=insufficient" to "5=excellent" in different aspects of English included in the Table1. The results are good because in all aspects the scores have improved (except for the participation in the class lesson, but this could be difficult to assess given the emergency). The teachers also confirm these results. They were asked to give a score to each student, with the previous scale, before and after the course. All aspects have improved. In particular, the average score increased from 2.84 to 3.35 in the knowledge of the subject, from 2.85 to 3.36 in the study at home and from 2.88 to 3.38 in the confidence in the possibility of being able to recover. 90% of teachers thought the course was useful. The most significant reasons given by the teachers regarding the success of the course were: "the course proposed the discipline in a different and alternative way"; "the student has improved a lot thanks to the course"; "The course allowed the student to consolidate elementary contents that could no longer be reviewed in the class"; and "The course changed the student's attitude to study". As regards the reasons for the failure of the course, the reasons were: "the student generally showed little interest in the subject, despite having acquired knowledge thanks to the course" and "In the latter part of the school year, too many commitments and too many hours spent in front of the screen prevented a profitable". Students appreciated the course modalities in the following aspects (which they rated with the same scale as before): the number of meetings (3.78), the explanations of the tutor (3.65), relationship with the tutor (3.88), online dating as a support during an emergency (3.30). The students also appreciated the fact that they have interactive materials always available on the platform with an average value of 3.57 and the interactivity of these materials with an average value of 3.41. To the question "Do you think that interactive theory and review materials can be more useful and interesting than static ones?" 81% of students answered yes. The most significant responses to the request to explain why were: "interactive materials stimulate interest in the material treated"; "students are more involved"; "I find it useful to receive the correction immediately"; "with interactive materials you apply your knowledge and understand better"; "they can be more fun"; "because they stimulate you to be always concentrated and at a distance it is a necessary thing because at home we are constantly distracted". Most of the students who answered no reported that "taking lessons in class is irreplaceable" or that they prefer classical study to technology. Regarding the tests with automatic assessment, the students appreciated the following aspects indicating a score from "1= not at all" to "5=very much": perform the tests on the computer (3.53); always have access to tests with the possibility to try them several times (3.60); have immediate feedback (3.80); have multiple attempts to respond (3.41); have questions of different types available (3.43). The students were asked "If you had difficulties in the course subject, did you manage to recover them?", with the same scale as before. The answer is very positive because the average value of the answers was 4.47 with a standard deviation of 1.47.

Table 1. Comparison of students' answers on various aspects of English between before and after the remedial work path

	Mean before	Dev.St. before	Mean after	Dev.St. after
Interest in the subject	3.59	0.85	3.72	0.92
Knowledge of the subject	3.27	0.85	3.57	0.83
Participation in the class lesson	3.73	0.87	3.64	0.94
Study at home	3.22	0.92	3.35	0.88
Confidence in the possibility of being able to recover	3.54	1.04	3.78	0.92

5. CONCLUSIONS

In this paper an interactive path for the remedial work of English has been presented. The course was carried out online through an integrated DLE, which allows to propose student-centered learning in which students are active and responsible participants in their own learning. Students can choose between the different types of activities and resources proposed by the tutors and carry them out independently when they prefer, get feedback on the work done and actively collaborate with the tutor or with the other students. The tutors, with the support of the researchers, were able to design and create interactive activities and resources, especially tests with automatic assessment with immediate and interactive feedback. The university tutors had the opportunity to have a first experience of teaching support with secondary school students, which is also useful to understand if this can represent their future work. Furthermore, during the experience, they were able to train and put into practice the innovative teaching methodologies proposed. At the end of the experience the tutors have gained skills and we think that this type of training could also be very useful for pre-service teachers. Students appreciated the remedial work path and the interactive character of the course. Most of the students overcame their initial difficulties with the subject. In the coming months, students' participation in online meetings and their responses in different types of activities will be analyzed in detail. The opinion of the teachers was also positive. Most of the teachers felt that the course was useful and that, despite the difficulties due to the emergency period, most of the students took advantage of the experience. This remedial work path could be extended to more students and could last the whole school year in the order of giving greater and constant support. The teaching materials created by tutors could be used by the teacher for normal lessons, with some additions or modifications. In this regard, it could be interesting to enhance the training of teachers on the use of the methodologies and technologies proposed in order to use them in their daily teaching. Finally, taking inspiration from this experience, an online remedial work path for English could be designed and implemented to help students in the transition from lower to upper secondary school.

REFERENCES

Alizadeh, M, 2016. The impact of Motivation in English Language Learning, in *International Journal of Research in English Education*, Vol. 1, No. 1, pp. 11-15.

Barana, A. et al., 2019. Adapting STEM Automated Assessment System to Enhance Language Skills, in: *Proceedings of the 15th International Conference ELearning and Software for Education*. Bucharest, pp. 403–410.

Barana, A. et al., 2020. An online math path to foster the transition of students between lower and upper secondary school, in: *Proceedings of the 16th International Scientific Conference ELearning and Software for Education*. Carol I National Defence University Publishing House, Bucharest, pp. 568–575.

Cavagnero, S.M., Gallina, M.A., Marchisio, M., 2015. School of tasks. Digital didactics for the recovery of scholastic failure. *Mondo Digitale,* Vol. 14, pp. 834–843.

Chapelle, C., Sauro, S., 2017. Introduction to the the Handbook of Technology and Second Language Teaching and Learning, *Wiley*, pp. 1-9.

Cuccurullo, D., 2012. La didattica delle lingue straniere con le ICT. *ANSAS 2012*, pp. 1-83.

EF EPI, 2019. *Indice di Conoscenza dell'Inglese EF*, 100 Paesi e regioni classificati in base alla padronanza dell'inglese.

Fissore, C. et al., 2019. University tutoring actions using an integrated online platform, in: *6th International Conference on Cognition and Exploratory Learning in the Digital Age (CELDA 2019)*. IADIS Press, pp. 69–76.

Fissore, C., Marchisio, M., Rabellino, S., In press. Online tutoring through an integrated platform to support learning Mathematics at lower secondary school. *Proceedings of the 14th International Conference on e-Learning*.

Graham, S., 2013. *Language learning with Technology*, Cambridge University Press.

Hattie, J., Timperley, H., 2007. The Power of Feedback. *Review of Educational Research*, Vol. 77, No. 1, pp. 81–112.

Herrera Mosquera, L., 2017. Impact of Implementing a Virtual Learning Environment (VLE) in the EFL Classroom. *Íkala Revista de Lenguaje y Cultura,* Vol. 22, No. 3, pp. 479–498.

Ligorio, M.B., Van Veen, K., 2006. Constructing a Successful Cross-National Virtual Learning Environment in Primary and Secondary Education. *AACE Journal*, Vol. 14, No. 2, pp 103–128.

Marello, C. et al., 2019. Automatic assessment to enhance online dictionaries consultation skills, in: *6th International Conference on Cognition and Exploratory Learning in the Digital Age (CELDA 2019),* IADIS Press, pp. 331–338.

Milthorpe, N. et al., 2018. Blended English: Technology-enhanced teaching and learning in English literary studies. *Arts and Humanities in Higher Education*, Vol. 17, No. 3, pp. 345–365.

Stanley, G., 2013. *Language learning with technology: Ideas for integrating technology in the classroom*. Cambridge University Press.

Von Glasersfeld, E., 1989. Constructivism in Education, in: *Husen, T., Postlethwaite, T.N. (Eds.), The International Encyclopedia of Education*. Pergamon Press, Oxford/New York, pp. 162–163.

Wu, X., 2003. Intrinsecò Motivation and Young Language Learners: The Impact of the Classroom Environment, in *System*, Vol. 31, No. 4, pp. 501-517.

DISTRIBUTED RETRIEVAL PRACTICE ENHANCES PRIMARY SCHOOL STUDENTS' RETENTION OF COMPUTATIONAL THINKING CONCEPTS

Lydia Casanova, Emily Theophilou, Marc Beardsley, Patricia Santos and Davinia Hernández-Leo
Universitat Pompeu Fabra – Barcelona, Spain, 08018

ABSTRACT

Efforts are being made to add Computational Thinking (CT) to the curriculum of primary schools in order to develop student abilities to use computational tools to solve problems and better prepare them for an increasingly digital society. Distributed Practice (DP) and Retrieval Practice (RP) are evidence-based practices that have shown to lead to efficient and durable learning. Studies investigating Distributed Retrieval Practice (DRP), a combination of the two evidence-based practices, have found positive effects of DRP on university student learning of anatomy and vocabulary items. As CT is considered to be a complex thinking skill, one that is acquired over time with practice, we investigated whether DRP had durable effects on primary student learning of CT concepts. We conducted a quasi-experimental study involving 20 primary school students between 11 and 12 years of age. The students participated in 6 weekly sessions on CT and completed two tests – one at the end of the fifth session (immediate) and the other a week later (delayed). At the end of each of the first 4 sessions, students performed DRP by completing a class-wide review quiz consisting of 5 multiple-choice questions. The results of the study show that students attained higher scores on the delayed test (72.6% ± 19.2) in comparison to the immediate test (67.9% ± 20.7). However, the difference in scores was not significant. The results suggest that DRP may play a role in helping students overcome the natural decay of memory, however, studies with a larger sample size are required. Further, this study demonstrates that DRP can be applied in an authentic classroom environment that involves primary school student learning of a complex subject such as CT.

KEYWORDS

Distributed Retrieval Practice, Computational Thinking, Distributed Practice, Retrieval Practice

1. INTRODUCTION

Computational Thinking (CT) is shorthand for thinking like a computer scientist. In other words, it is "the ability to use the concepts of computer science to formulate and solve problems" (European Commission, 2019) and involves logical thinking, pattern recognition, and decomposition skills. Recent initiatives such as (EU) CompuThink, designed and funded by the Joint Research Centre of the European Commission, aim to introduce CT to primary and secondary school students (Bocconi et al., 2016). A key objective behind teaching CT is to develop student abilities to use computational tools to solve problems and better prepare students for an increasingly digital society (Yadav et al., 2016). To fulfill the objective of it being a useful skill for the future, students need to develop and retain a level of proficiency in CT. As it is considered to be a complex thinking skill, that is acquired over time with practice (Denning, 2017), appropriate teaching practices need to be explored to allow the acquired knowledge and skill to persist over time. However, learning can quickly become forgotten as demonstrated by the work of Ebbinghaus almost 135 years ago (Murre and Dros, 2015). With the rapid loss of memory over time, long-term or durable learning is hindered (Davis and Zhong, 2017).

Distributed Practice (DP) and Retrieval Practice (RP) are two evidence-based practices that have been shown to lead to efficient and durable learning. DP consists of distributing or spacing reviews over time instead of massing them in a single session (Murray and Udermann, 2003). RP consists of recalling information from memory instead of relying on information in hand. It is a strategy that spurs the learner to produce an effort from within to induce better retention (Roediger & Butler, 2011). Distributed Retrieval Practice (DRP) is a combination of the two evidence-based practices. Studies investigating DRP have found positive effects of DRP on university student learning of anatomy (Dobson et al. 2017) and vocabulary items (Nakata et al., 2020).

In our study, we looked to explore the effects of DRP on primary school student learning of a complex subject such as CT in an authentic classroom setting.

This paper is structured in the following manner. First, we present a review of literature related to the concepts that motivate our research question and support our hypothesis. This is followed by a description of the methods used for our study and the results. Finally, we discuss the results, limitations of the study, and present a conclusion of the overall work.

2. STATE OF THE ART

2.1 Durable Learning

An objective of formal education is for students to be able to apply the skills and knowledge acquired in the classroom to future contexts outside of the classroom. To achieve this, student learning needs to be durable and remain beyond immediate assessments (Halpern and Hakel, 2002). In writing about learning, Davis and Zhong (2017) explain that the process of learning involves the creation of memories. Memories are created by a symphony of different neurons that work together to create, store, and later allow us to retrieve information. Within this process, there is an ongoing balance between the strengthening forces of acquisition and consolidation and the weakening forces of forgetting in forming a memory. These weakening forces are referred to as the process of active forgetting which, along with acquisition and consolidation, are parts of the brain's biological system for managing memories. In other words, active forgetting contributes to the eroding of memory traces. These forces of forgetting were demonstrated in Ebbinghaus' seminal work on the forgetting curve almost 135 years ago. Work that has recently been reproduced by Murre and Dros (2015) shows that on average we remember as little as 30% of what we learned after one day has passed.

Research on evidence-based learning practices also demonstrates that much of what we learn is forgotten, unless appropriate learning practices are used to strengthen the memories of what we have learned. A study in 2006 (Roediger et al., 2006), investigated whether testing promotes longer retention than rereading in a comparison of study strategies. Subjects in both the testing and rereading conditions completed an immediate (same day) and delayed test (1 week later). The results of the study showed that both conditions performed worse on the delayed test in comparison to the immediate test. However, subjects in the testing condition only saw their performance decrease by 14%, whereas participants in the rereading condition saw a decrease of 52%. The study demonstrates that the retrieval of information can benefit memory retention and also provides an example of how much forgetting occurs over time. Interestingly the results of some studies suggest that DP can help learners circumvent the natural decay of memories. For example, the results of a study conducted by Rawson and Kintsch (2005) showed that students reviewing the target material following a distributed pattern performed better on the delayed test in comparison to an immediate test.

2.2 Distributed Retrieval Practice

Studies investigating Distributed Retrieval Practice (DRP), a combination of the two evidence-based practices, have found positive effects of DRP on student learning. For example, a study involving university students' learning anatomy information investigated whether the benefits of RP varied between massed and distributed learning conditions. Study results revealed that distributed strategies produced a significantly better recall of anatomy information than massed strategies (Dobson et al. 2017). Another study involving university students' learning vocabulary investigated the effects of cumulative and noncumulative quizzes taken across 9 weeks. The study found that cumulative tests (i.e. DP) are as much as three times more effective than noncumulative tests when comparing the results of a delayed test taken 3 weeks later (Nakata et al., 2020).

This leads to our research question: Does DRP positively affect primary student learning of a complex subject such as CT? Based on current research related to DP, RP, and DRP, we hypothesize that DRP will positively affect primary student learning of CT with students scoring higher on a delayed test of CT concepts in comparison to an immediate test.

3. METHODS

3.1 Study Context and Participants

The present study was conducted in the context of the project "Makers a les Aules" (Makers in the Classroom), an initiative carried out by a public university (providing the instructors of the sessions) and the Barcelona City Council. The goal of the project was to support primary school teachers in introducing maker activities to their students. Participating schools were public primary schools from Barcelona, Spain. In total 10 schools participated in the project with one group of students per school completing the Makers a les Aules activities across 5-6 sessions. Of the 10 groups of students, three with similar profiles were selected to participate in the study. However, due to the COVID-19 pandemic, only one of the groups (11 to 12-year-olds) was able to complete the study. The study was conducted in Catalan.

3.2 Experimental Design and Materials

We designed a quasi-experimental study that took place in an authentic classroom setting. The participating students attended 6 weekly sessions on CT (see Table 1) and completed two tests – one at the end of the fifth session (immediate) and the other a week later (delayed). Further, at the end of each of the first 4 sessions, students performed DRP by completing a class-wide review quiz consisting of 5 multiple-choice questions. A more detailed explanation of the experimental design and materials follows.

For the study, the following approach was used to teach students about CT via maker activities (Papavlasopoulou et al., 2017). Students participated in 6 weekly sessions. The first 5 sessions were learning sessions in which students were taught CT concepts and applied them toward creating a working prototype of an interactive mockup using Makey Makey (Silver et al., 2012). The final sixth session was a demonstration session in which groups of students showed demos of their prototypes. The 90-minute learning sessions taught programming with Scratch, as programming has been found to be an effective way to teach CT (Rich et al., 2013). Scratch is a simplified coding environment in which learners drag visual coding blocks in a canvas to control characters, images, sounds, and text to create different animations, games, stories, and art (Resnick et al., 2009). Despite having a simplified coding environment, Scratch still allows students to become familiar with the logic and structures involved in programming (Kelleher and Pausch, 2005). Table 2 shows the design of each classroom session. In the first learning session, the opening 20 minutes were spent on a pre-questionnaire, 15 minutes on theoretical content, 40 minutes for hands-on practice, and 15 minutes for a session review. In learning sessions 2-4, 15 minutes were allocated to theoretical content delivered at the beginning of the session, 60 minutes for practical hands-on applications such as Scratch programming or interconnecting elements using Makey Makey, and 15 minutes for a session review. In learning session 5, the only differences to the previous learning sessions were that the hands-on practice was 5 minutes shorter and an immediate test was given to students during the final 20 minutes of the session instead of the session review. The theoretical content which covered basic concepts from CT such as identification and understanding of loops, conditions, inputs, and outputs (see Table 1 for all topics) were introduced by an instructor from the university, using visual presentation slides combined with oral explanations. For the demonstration session no new material was introduced. The session was 60 minutes with the first 40 minutes spent on group demos. During the final 20 minutes students took the delayed test.

To apply DRP, students participated in a class-wide review quiz during the final 15 minutes of each of the first 4 sessions. The quiz provided an opportunity for RP. Further, the quiz questions were drawn from both the immediate and preceding sessions which permitted DP. A previous study applied DP (Rohrer, 2009) to a mathematics course by including a daily assessment for students with exercises from different chapters covered in earlier lessons mixed in. This approach improved the long-term performance of students. We followed a similar approach by mixing up the questions used in the 5-question, multiple-choice class review quiz. Table 1 shows how the questions were distributed per session. Kahoot!, a free online software that allows teachers to create quizzes and share them with students creating a contest-like environment, was used to deliver the review quiz to the class. Studies have shown that Kahoot! can have a greater positive effect on learning when compared to other tools and approaches (Wang and Tahir, 2020). Studies have also shown that receiving prompt feedback after RP can help improve student learning by allowing learners to reflect on their given answers and improve on them (Butler and Roediger, 2008; Pashler et al., 2005). Accordingly, after each review quiz question, students received immediate feedback on their answers.

Two tests were used to assess student learning of CT concepts. One test was given at the end of the final fifth session (immediate test) and the other test was given a week later (delayed test). Both tests contained 10 true or false questions (2 questions from each session) that needed to be answered within 20 minutes. Each question was presented with 3 possible answers: 'True', 'False', and 'I don't know'. These answers were scored as +1, -1, and 0 respectively. This formula scoring method gives students the opportunity to acknowledge that they do not know the correct answer instead of forcing them to guess (Muijtjens et. al 1999). Formula scoring offers an individualized way of correction for guessing and may reduce random guessing to as low as 2% of the items (Cecilio-Fernandes et al 2017). It should be noted that students were not warned in advance about the tests in an effort to reduce the likelihood of students reviewing the materials prior to the tests.

Note that in session 1, students also completed a 5-question pre-questionnaire. The pre-questionnaire explored student familiarity and prior knowledge related to CT, Scratch, and Makey Makey. The questionnaire consisted of two sections. The first section asked students about their prior experience with Scratch and Makey Makey. It consisted of binary answers which were quantified in order to average students' overall experience with the tools (Yes=1, No= 0). The second section aimed to gauge student competence related to CT. It consisted of pseudo-code and an exercise related to it. This question was scored as 1 if answered correctly or 0 answered incorrectly.

Table 1. Overview of classroom sessions

DRP	**Week 1**	**Week 2**	**Week 3**	**Week 4**	**Week 5**	**Week 6**
Sessions	S1	S2	S3	S4	S5	S6
Concepts	Introduction to Makey Makey Algorithm definition	Inequality symbols Variables definition	Identification and understanding of conditions	Identification and understanding of loops	Identification and understanding of inputs and outputs	No content provided Demonstration of prototypes
Experimental activities	Pre-questionnaire 5 questions S1	3 questions S2 2 questions S1	3 questions S3 2 questions S2	3 questions S4 1 question S3 1 question S1	Immediate test	Delayed test

Table 2. Design of the classroom sessions

Learning sessions	**Session 1**	**Session 2-4**	**Session 5**	**Session 6**
Duration	90 minutes	90 minutes	90 minutes	80 minutes
Time distribution	Pre-questionnaire [20 minutes] Theoretical content [15 minutes] Hands-on practice [40 minutes] Session review [15 minutes]	Theoretical content [15 minutes] Hands-on practice [60 minutes] Session review [15 minutes]	Theoretical content [15 minutes] Hands-on practice [55 minutes] Immediate test [20 minutes]	Student demos [60 minutes] Delayed test [20 minutes]

4. RESULTS

A total of 20 out of 25 eligible students completed the study. Five participants needed to be removed from the study as they did not complete both the immediate and delayed tests. Participants (11 boys, 9 girls) were between the ages of 11 and 12 (M = 11.15, SD = 0.37). Further, the results of the pre-questionnaire revealed that all students had previous knowledge of Scratch, few were familiar with Makey Makey (4.0 %), and 88% of the students answered the CT-related problem correctly.

4.1 Immediate and Delayed Test

To determine whether students scored higher on a delayed test of CT concepts in comparison to an immediate test, we conducted a dependent t-test. Firstly, the Kolmogorov-Smirnov Test for normality was conducted and results supported our choice of the next statistical measure. Subsequently, a dependent t-test was conducted with the following null hypothesis: average scores from immediate and delayed tests are the same. Students attained higher scores on the delayed test (M = 72.6, SD = 19.2) in comparison to the immediate test (M = 67.9, SD = 20.7). However, the difference between the immediate and delayed test scores was not significant ($t(18) = -0.91$, $p = 0.19$). The distribution of scores and statistics from the immediate and delayed tests can be seen in Figure 1 and Table 2.

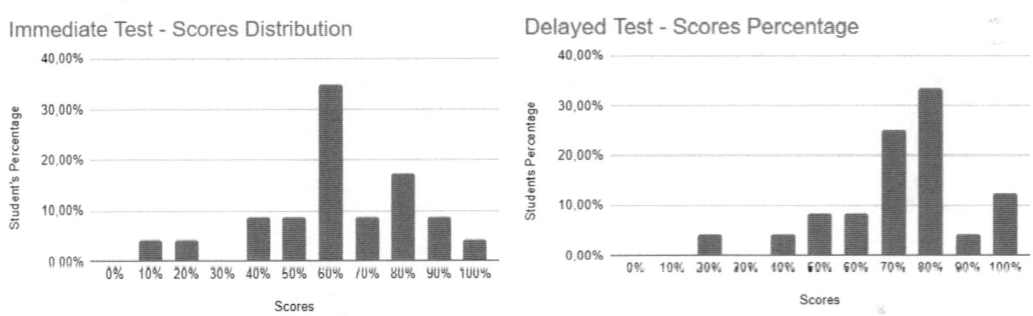

Figure 1. Distributions of Immediate and Delayed Test Scores

Table 2. Analysis of Immediate and Delayed Test Scores

Statistics	Immediate Test	Delayed Test
Average Score	67.90%	72.60%
Standard Deviation	20.7	19.2
Variance	450.9	387.1
Min score	20%	20%
Max score	100%	100%
% Fails (<50%)	15%	5%
% Pass (50% or 60%)	35%	20%
% Remarkable (70% or 80%)	30%	55%
% Excellent (90% or 100%)	20%	20%

5. DISCUSSION

5.1 Interpretation and Implication of Results

We hypothesized that students would attain significantly better results on the delayed test when compared to the immediate one. However, the p-value of the t-test showed that there was no significant difference between the two tests. Despite not obtaining significantly higher scores on the delayed test, the results of the delayed scores were not worse than the immediate scores suggesting that DRP helps learners overcome the natural decay of memory and this is consistent with Rawson and Kintsch´s study in which the performance of students following a DP pattern improved and did not worsen on a delayed test (Rawson & Kintsch, 2005). Nevertheless, our results are inconsistent with the study by Roediger et al. (2006) in which the performance of students under the RP condition performed worse on the delayed test compared to the immediate test. Thus, the enhanced results on the delayed test might be related to DP rather than RP. According to our results, DRP seems to be an educational method that could improve long-term memory retention and not hinder it. As DRP can be easily applied at the end of each session (only 15 minutes were used in this case) to review past content, it is worth exploring further to see if it can help the knowledge and skills students acquire in class to persist over longer durations.

Studies have reported that prior knowledge is a key factor that must be considered in order to evaluate the learning process (Pazzani, 1991) and to control for prior knowledge as a possible confound. Accordingly, we had students complete a pre-questionnaire. The results of the pre-questionnaire showed that there were no significant differences in students' prior knowledge related to CT or the tools being used in the sessions. All the participating students had previous experience with Scratch; few (4%) had experience with Makey Makey; and almost 90% answered the CT problem correctly. Hence, prior knowledge was unlikely to be a confounding factor in the study.

5.2 Limitations

There are some limitations to our study. Firstly, due to the study design, it is not clear whether the demonstration of prototypes or DRP had a greater effect on the improved delayed test performance. Despite no new instruction or explicit review of theoretical concepts in the final sixth session, students showed their prototypes. It is possible that the showing and viewing of demos acted as a review of the CT concepts and affected student performance on the delayed test. Future studies should control for this possible confound. Secondly, the validity and reliability of the immediate and delayed tests should be established. These were the main instruments used to measure the learning and future studies should look to either validate the current tests or use a validated measure for assessing CT knowledge in primary school students such as the Computational Thinking Test (CTT) for middle school students by Bati and Kaan (Bati and Kaan, 2018). Thirdly, a control condition and a larger sample size would increase the reliability of the results. The control condition and sample size were affected by COVID-19 which prevented additional groups of students from completing the study. Additionally, it is unclear whether the enhanced retention of CT concepts persists for longer periods. Having students complete tests given at greater intervals would be beneficial. Finally, it is unclear whether these results can be generalized beyond the specific context of the study (i.e. with younger or older students).

5.3 Future Work

To overcome the limitations of the current study, a similar study could be conducted with a validated CT assessment, larger sample size, and an updated study design that holds the delayed test as an isolated activity occurring days or weeks after the last session, be it a learning or demonstration session, has taken place. Future work could also include a control condition, additional patterns for distributing the reviews, and tests given over longer periods of time in order to determine which DRP pattern performs better. Furthermore, alternatives to class-wide multi-choice tests using Kahoot! used for reviews could be explored.

6. CONCLUSION

To explore the effects of DRP on primary school student learning of a complex subject, in an authentic classroom setting, we conducted a quasi-experimental study involving 20 primary school students (ages 11-12). For the study, students participated in six weekly sessions on CT. To apply DRP, at the end of the first four classes, students took part in a class-wide Kahoot! review quiz that included material from previous classes. To assess student learning, a test was given at the end of the fifth session (immediate test) and another test was given a week later (delayed test) at the end of the demo class. The students were not warned about the tests to reduce the likelihood of students reviewing the materials prior to the tests. Although, students did perform 5-minute demos of their prototypes prior to the delayed test. Students attained higher scores on the delayed test in comparison to the immediate test. However, the difference in scores was not significant. The results suggest that DRP may play a role in helping students overcome the natural decay of memory, however, studies with a larger sample size are needed to examine if the proposed DRP scheme is effective.

In addition, due to limitations in the study design it is not clear whether the demonstration of prototypes or DRP had a greater effect on the improved delayed test performance. Overall, the study shows a simple implementation of DRP in an authentic classroom environment that involves primary school student learning of a complex subject such as CT. This simple implementation involves setting aside the final 15 minutes of a session for a class-wide multiple-choice review. To better support durable learning, further research involving simple, yet effective teaching practices conducted in authentic classroom settings is needed. Such research can both illustrate the benefits of using evidence-based practices and provide educators with an example of how such practices can be applied in their classrooms.

ACKNOWLEDGEMENT

We thank the school, teachers and students participating in this study. We also thank the Barcelona City Council and Barcelona Activa for trusting us to carry out this initiative. This work has been partially funded by the European Regional Development Fund, Erasmus+, and the National Research Agency of the Spanish Ministry of Science, Innovation and Universities under project grants TIN2017-85179-C3-3-R, 2017-1-ES01-KA201-038220 and MDM-2015-0502. Dr. Hernández-Leo acknowledges the support by ICREA under the ICREA Academia programme.

REFERENCES

Bati, K., 2018. Computational Thinking Test (CTT) for Middle School Students. Mediterranean Journal of Educational Research, Vol. 12. pp. 89-101. doi: 10.29329/mjer.2018.138.6.

Bocconi, S. et al. 2016. Exploring the Field of computational Thinking as a 21st Century Skill, EDULEARN16 Proceedings, pp. 4725-4733.

Butler, A. C. and Roediger, H. L., 2008. Feedback enhances the positive effects and reduces the negative effects of multiple-choice testing, Memory and Cognition, Vol. 36, No.3, pp. 604–616. doi: 10.3758/MC.36.3.604.

Cecilio-Fernandes, D. et al, 2017. Comparison of formula and number-right scoring in undergraduate medical training: A rasch model analysis. BMC Medical Education Vol. 17, pp. 192.

Davis, R. L. and Zhong, Y., 2017. The Biology of Forgetting—A Perspective, Neuron. Elsevier Inc., Vol. 95, No. 3, pp. 490–503. doi: 10.1016/j.neuron.2017.05.039.

Denning, P. J., 2017. Remaining trouble spots with computational thinking. Communications of the ACM, Vol. 60 No. 6, pp.33-39.

Dobson, J. L., et al, 2017. Distributed retrieval practice promotes superior recall of anatomy information, Anatomical Sciences Education. John Wiley and Sons Inc., Vol. 10 No. 4, pp. 339–347. doi: 10.1002/ase.1668.

European Commission (2019) The Computational Thinking Study | EU Science Hub, EU Science Hub. Available at: https://ec.europa.eu/jrc/en/computational-thinking (Accessed: 24 July 2020).

Halpern, D. F. and Hakel, M. D., 2002. Learning That Lasts a Lifetime: Teaching for Long-Term Retention and Transfer. New Directions for Teaching and Learning. John Wiley & Sons, Ltd, Vol. 89, pp. 3–7. doi: 10.1002/tl.42.

Kelleher, C. and Pausch, R., 2005. Lowering the Barriers to Programming: a survey of programming environments and languages for novice programmers. ACM Computing Surveys - CSUR.

Muijtjens, A. et al, 1999. The effect of a "don't know" option on test scores: number-right and formula scoring compared. Medical Education, pp.267–275.

Murray, S. R. and Udermann, B. E., 2003. Massed versus Distributed Practice: Which is Better?, CAHPERD Journal. Vol. 28, No. 1.

Murre, J.M. and Dros, J., 2015. Replication and analysis of Ebbinghaus' forgetting curve. PloS one, Vol. 10, No. 7.

Nakata, T. et al, 2020. Effects of Distributed Retrieval Practice Over a Semester: Cumulative Tests as a Way to Facilitate Second Language Vocabulary Learning, TESOL Quarterly. Wiley Blackwell, p.596. doi: 10.1002/tesq.596.

Papavlasopoulou, S., et al, 2017. Empirical studies on the Maker Movement, a promising approach to learning: A literature review.' Entertainment Computing, Vol.18, pp. 57-78.

Pashler, H. et al, 2005. When Does Feedback Facilitate Learning of Words? Journal of Experimental Psychology: Learning, Memory, and Cognition, Vol 31, No. 1, pp. 3-8

Pazzani, M. J., 1991. Influence of prior knowledge on concept acquisition: Experimental and computational results. Journal of Experimental Psychology: Learning, Memory, and Cognition, Vol. 17 No.3, pp. 416–432 doi:10.1037/0278-7393.17.3.416.

Rawson, K. A. and Kintsch, W., 2005. Rereading effects depend on time of test, Journal of Educational Psychology, Vol. 97 No. 1, pp. 70–80. doi: 10.1037/0022-0663.97.1.70.

Resnick, M. et al, 2009 Scratch: Programming for All, Communications of the ACM, Vol. 5 No. 11. doi: 10.1145/1592761.1592779.

Rich, P. J., et al, 2013 Convergent cognition, Instructional Science. Springer, Vol. 41, No. 2, pp. 431–453. doi: 10.1007/s11251-012-9240-7.

Roediger III, H.L. and Karpicke, J.D., 2006. Test-enhanced learning: Taking memory tests improves long-term retention. Psychological Science, Vol. 17, No. 3, pp. 249-255.

Rohrer, D., 2009. The Effects of Spacing and Mixing Practice Problems, Journal for Research in Mathematics Education, Vol. 40, No. 1, pp. 4–17. doi: 10.2307/40539318.

Silver J, et al., 2012. Makey Makey improvising tangible and nature-based user interfaces. In Proceedings of the ACM tangible embedded and embodied interaction, Kingston, Ontario, Canada, pp 367–370.

Wang, A. I. and Tahir, R., 2020. The effect of using Kahoot! for learning – A literature review, Computers and Education. Elsevier Ltd, Vol. 149, p. 103818. doi: 10.1016/j.compedu.2020.103818..

Yadav, A. et al, 2016. Computational Thinking for All: Pedagogical Approaches to Embedding 21st Century Problem Solving in K-12 Classrooms. TechTrends Vol. 60, pp. 565–568doi: 10.1007/s11528-016-0087-7.

TOOL SUPPORT FOR LEARNING COMPUTER AND ROBOT PROGRAMMING

Obe O. Olumide[1] and Tiko Iyamu[2]
[1]*Federal University of Technology, Akure, Nigeria, Computer Science Department, School of Computing*
[2]*Cape Peninsula University of Technology, Cape Town, South Africa*

ABSTRACT

Computer Programming is believed to have effect on creativity, reasoning, analytic and mathematical skills. This cognitive development is at a cost from both ends of students and teachers of computer programming. Its abstractive nature makes it difficult to teach and learn hence, the enormous hours spent in teaching, learning and developing solutions. Consequently, the less interest among the students at all levels of education. Studies have shown various attempts to ease its teaching and learning by developing user friendly interfaces and use of course video teaching clips from seasoned programmers. However, learning and teaching programming skills remains a herculean task for student and teachers respectively. It is believed that interacting with a more tangible object can improve students' interest in developing computer programming skills. A mobile robot- a situated and embodied electronic device serves this purpose hence, the use of the device that students have more interest in interacting with in this study. In this work, an interactive program evaluation framework was developed that interact with a simulated e-puck robot on V-Rep simulator platform. The study shows an increased interest and improved performance in computer programming among Computer Science students.

KEYWORDS

Simulator, Programming, Mobile Robot, Learning, Python, Artificial Intelligence, V-Rep, Collaboration

1. INTRODUCTION

Computer programming becomes boring to new Computer programming students due to lengthy time spent in testing and debugging. It was estimated that software testing takes about 45% of time spent in software development (Obe, 2017). In order to sustain technological development that adopts more of software integration and encourage more participation in software development; methods, tools and techniques must be developed to simplify teaching, learning and development of computer software across all platforms among students at all levels of education. Siegfried et al. (2017) identified mobile robot as a veritable tool for teaching computer programming among school children because they are embodied and situated. These tangibility and sociability features of the mobile robots are necessary for assisting in conveying and impacting knowledge and skill sets.

Asides using mobile robots to assist teaching and learning computer programming, there exist needs to meet up with the minimum bench mark requirements in tertiary institutions for Computer Science students in Artificial Intelligence curriculum where robot programming is encouraged. A real-time program assessment framework for robot programming must be developed to assess the level of comprehension of various subject matters of the curriculum. Invariably, while the students are mastering computer programming fundamentals, they would as well be mastering the fundamentals of robot programming and the students can also implement more complex data structures for executing more complex tasks as necessitated by the robotic environments.

The use of mobile robot in teaching and learning especially, computer programming has been explored and researched on by many researchers using different tools, methods and techniques. Some of which were discussed in the next section. The research question is: what is the relevance of Robot programming application tool in teaching and learning Computer programming?

2. RELATED RESEARCH

The research findings of Pugnali et al., (2017) suggest that type of user interface does have an impact on children's learning, but is only one of many factors that affect positive academic and socio-emotional experiences. Different kinds of learning qualities are obtainable through graphical interfaces and tangible devices like robot.

Esteve-Mon et al., 2019 established the effectiveness of adoption of educational robotics in the growth of computational thinking of students, especially among male students. Mather, (2015) explored a mixed-method approach for evaluating technology-enhanced learning environments for Computer programming in early stage students. The finding shows an enhanced productive collaborative behavior and improved learning among learners by creating a learning environment and use of 3D animated Ceebot. *Nourbakhsh et al.* (2004) explicitly evaluated the educational impact of robotics on secondary level students by presenting statistically significant evidence of broad learning. Robert (*Róbert et al.,* 2010) designed method to help students acquire the essential programming structures visually with the help of LEGO NXT robots. In Major *et al.* (2011), the research was directed towards effort to help teach novices programming using physical robots. The effectiveness of using robots as tools in the teaching of introductory programming was investigated, and the impact of the technology in helping to overcome the current barriers for leaners was assessed. *Ernest et al* (2011) researched on the effectiveness of integrating Educational Robotic Activities into higher education Computer Science Curricula: A Case Study in a Developing Country. Marina et al, (2013) worked on: Computational thinking and tinkering: Exploration of an early childhood robotics curriculum. This research was motivated by the needs to expand robot programming in early student curriculum. CHERP (Creative Hybrid Environment for Robotic Programming) was developed that enabled children to dedicate their time building robot, planning its actions, using a physical wooden block or the computer screen to construct programs, and iteratively improving the robot and programs according to initial goals and subsequent discoveries. Attila et al. (2013) developed a tool to make the learning process of programming languages more concrete, practical and interesting for students, with an optimal environment and strongly limited set of statements. Park et al. (2015) developed systematic and effective robot-based learning with programming to improve learner's creativity and understand class satisfaction at the elementary school level in Korea.

Carina et al. (2016) worked on enhancing the Engagement of Intelligent Tutorial Systems through Personalization of Gamification. Tocháčeka et al. (2016) worked on identifying the potential and aspects of exploitation of educational robotics project in education at secondary schools and training teachers. Simon et al. (2017) in 'An exploration of the role of visual programming tools in the development of young children's computational thinking' explored the impact of young children's programming approaches to programming in two tools with contrasting programming interfaces, ScratchJr and Lightbot on developing computational thinking.

In this work, a program assessment framework for robot programming based on running navigation simulations in a known environment through a real-time implementation which provides score feedback and gamified hints to the students was developed.

3. RESULTS AND DISCUSSION

3.1 Research Method

This section presents the system architecture showing the interactions between the main components of the system.

The system trains a new user on robotics programming through detailed documentation and analysis on each user input. It achieves this by providing the user with tasks related to areas in robotics e.g. actuation, computer vision, real time logic decision making etc and analyzing each user input in real time. The user's performance is graded and the resulted is displayed at the end of each task. The system consists of five levels each consisting of four tasks or more.

3.1.1 System Architecture

The robot programming assessment system is composed of a test library, a simulator, and the user interface as depicted in figure 1. The python test library provides the user with the set of task to be executed, with each task containing a script describing the actions to perform during simulation.

The V-rep simulator loads the scenes that would be presented on the user's interface, which is connected together by the python remote API.

The GUI displays scenes loaded from the V-rep simulator, displays tasks to be executed at each level/stage within a specified time, then, it output scores feedbacks to the user at the end of each stage.

Implemented in each stage are set of tasks to be completed by a player. Therefore, the overall assessment is computed based on the feedback score gotten at the end of each stage.

This section presents the system architecture (Figure 1) showing the interactions between the main components of the system. The system is a desktop application written in the python programming language leveraging the framework for its graphical user interface (GUI).

The system was designed to interface with an existing simulation environment called VREP. The system starts up VREP in a server mode with the address '127.0.0.1' and establishes a connection as a client on the port '19998' as depicted in figure 2.

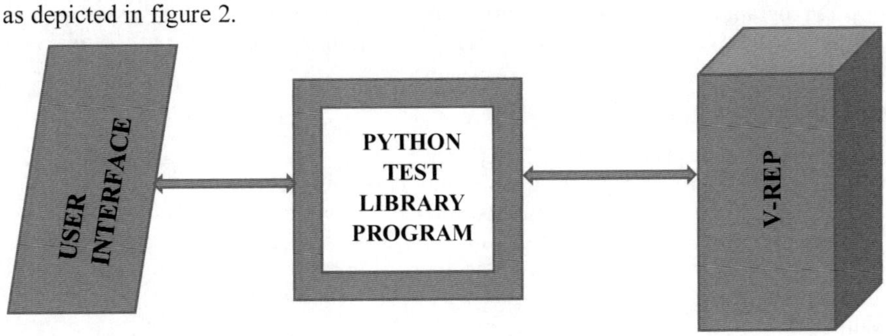

Figure 1. System Architecture of the Application

3.1.2 How the Application Interacts with the User

Figure 2 depicts how the desktop application will interact with the users of the system and the overall behavior of the system.

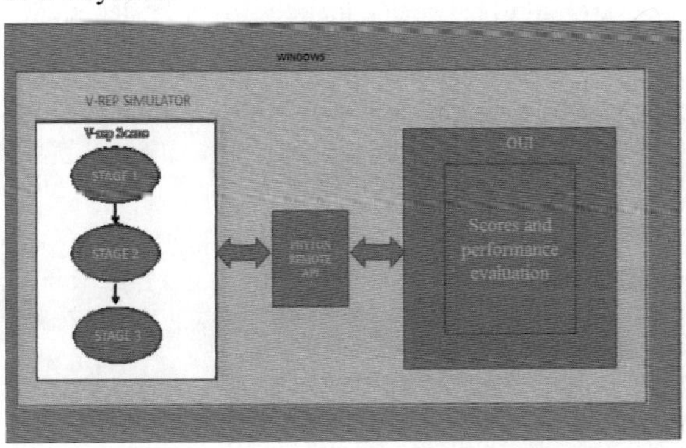

Figure 2. Breakdown of the System Architecture of the Application

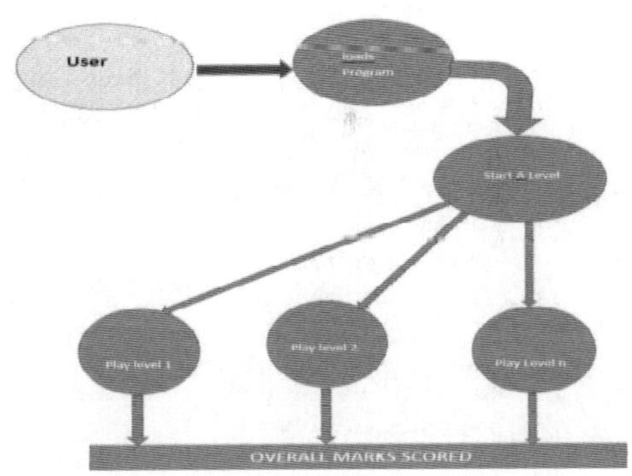

Figure 3. Application Interaction flow with the User

The robot program evaluation system was implemented with the E-puck robot in a V-REP (Virtual Robotic Experimentation Platform) simulator programming environment embedded with Lua scripts by defaults. V-REP is a comprehensive CAD-based application that can be used to simulate, test and program a robot from a 3D CAD environment, allowing users with basic robot programming skills to generate robot programs off-line.

The assessment system is composed of a test library, simulator, and the graphical user interface. The test library is built using a python programming language to provide the set of task to be executed, with each task containing a script describing the actions to perform during simulation. While the simulator contains scenes formulated on the V-REP simulator.

The remote API used for this work is extended by custom Lua functions which are recognized from their simx*, -prefix. The remote API is part of the V-REP API framework which supports remotely loading a scene, starting, pausing or stopping a simulation. The remote API functions are interacting with V-REP via socket communication (or, optionally, via shared memory) in a way that reduces lag and network load to a great extent. All this happens in a hidden fashion to the user.

The Graphical user interface (Game Play) is designed with PyQt, to implement the play button, Points gotten at each stage, the overall points, and countdown time. Then, python remote API functions was used to load the scenes from the V-REP simulator, corresponding to a particular stage of the game. When the time required to complete a task finishes, the script automatically rank the player and loads the next stage of the game. This repeats until the game is over.

Building on the evaluation framework, several hints for a task in which the students must program a robot (using control flow instructions) to navigate in a known environment within a specified time is given. Therefore, the assessment is based on the feedback score and hint gotten at the end of each test scenarios.

To test the program in a different environment of increasing complexity, the task is split into 3 stages, each containing navigating round an empty space, navigating from a certain point to the goal, and path following respectively.

3.1.3 Programming Language

There exists hundreds of programming languages but very few of them are applicable in programming robot. Python programming language, C/C++ and Java are the best languages for robot programming. Technically, C & C++ **are most appropriate start point for a new** roboticists, **because they contain a lot** of the hardware libraries which **allows** low-level hardware interaction resulting in time performance. They present very rich data structures and helps in learning other programming languages (i.e Java, Python, etc) in their categories. This work attempt teaching C/C++ languages using simulated e-puck robot on V-Rep simulator.

3.1.4 Task and Level

Robots are programmed to carry out tasks. Each task carries out a well-defined operation that impact the robot environment using its actuators. To carry out a mission, there may be need to carry out a number of tasks. There are low level task with low computational complexities. Complexity of the task dictates the kind of data structures, control structures, library functions/methods and algorithm to be implemented and invariably affect the mission. In a mission, a robot may have to switch several times between a numbers of tasks depending on the context as presented by the environment. Having the robot to successfully and efficiently perform depends on the kind on optimization algorithm implemented to optimize the robot movement and to perform the desired tasks. These tasks and algorithms implement data structures and control structures which are fundamental in learning computer programming. In this work, we classify these structures according to some level of difficulties and stages/lessons to be learned by the students (in their various curricula) and integrate them into tasks and levels.

Tasks Categories: in this work, we only consider elementary tasks for educational mobile robot which includes the following: wandering; moving on a straight line; drawing of shapes; following a line; following an object; obstacles avoidance; moving to a target position; follow leader; cooperative behavior; and swarm intelligence etc.

3.1.5 Tasks Levels

The tasks are classified as shown in Table 1. There are several number of tasks questions/problems formulated using problem solving and critical thinking approaches (Morin et al., 2015) under same level. Questions of the same difficulty level are randomly generated under the same level while difficulty increases across levels.

Table 1. Task Classification

Level 1 tasks	Level 2 tasks	Level 3 tasks
Wandering in free space Using simple commands	Drawing of shapes (circle, triangles etc.)	Target reaching
Line following (straight, curves, loops etc.)	Object following	Leader following
Obstacles avoidance		Implementing swarm behaviour algorithms

3.1.6 Mathematical Representation of the Assessment System

At each level, a number of tasks are assigned. Six tasks are randomly assigned at each level except for the first level where only four tasks are assigned. For each successful tasks assignment completion, a corresponding score is assigned. The accumulated score from each tasks completed successfully over a number of levels are summed up using the following mathematical expressions:

Level 1 (score) :

$$\sum_{i=1}^{n=4} X_i (t)$$

...

Level n (score) =

$$\sum_{i=1}^{n=6} X_i (t)$$

where;

X_i=marks for each task

n=number of tasks in each level

NB: Countdown time (t) is constant

Total Marks= $\sum$ ((level 1) + (level 2) + … (level n))

3.2 Results

How the Application Starts: The user launches the application and the system displays a screen with a loader and loads important modules into memory as shown in figure 4.

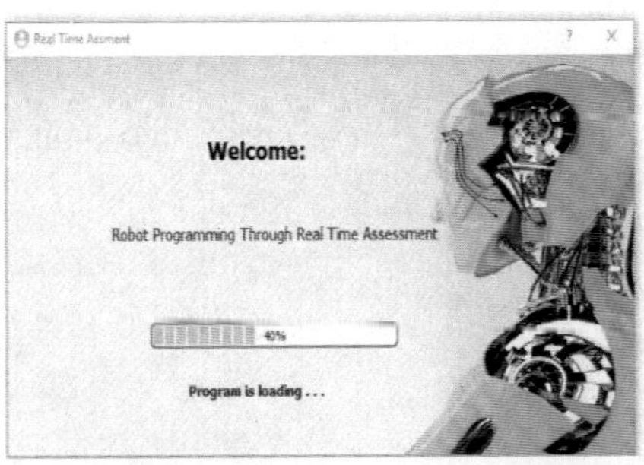

Figure 4. System Loading

Figure 5. Home Screen

The system finish loading modules and displays home screen (see figure 5). The user then clicks the start button to begin play. On click, the python remote helps to connect the GUI with the V-Rep simulator, then, several scenes will be loaded from the VREP simulation environment.

The game has 3 stages. In each stage, the player is expected to complete a task of programming e-puck robot with Python scripts inside V-Rep simulator to perform a single robotic control task.

How the Game Begin: User clicks start button on the home screen and the system loads screen for level 1 where the user starts level 1 by clicking on "level 1" (figure 6).

On Click, the system loads screen for level 1 where the user starts level 1 by clicking on "level" and a countdown timer starts

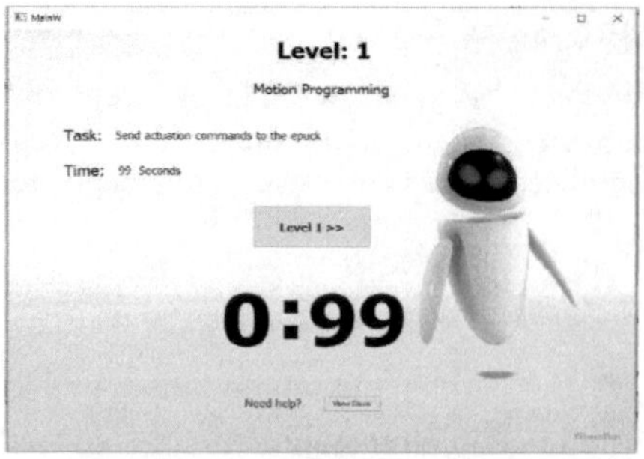

Figure 6. Level 1 GUI Screen with countdown timer

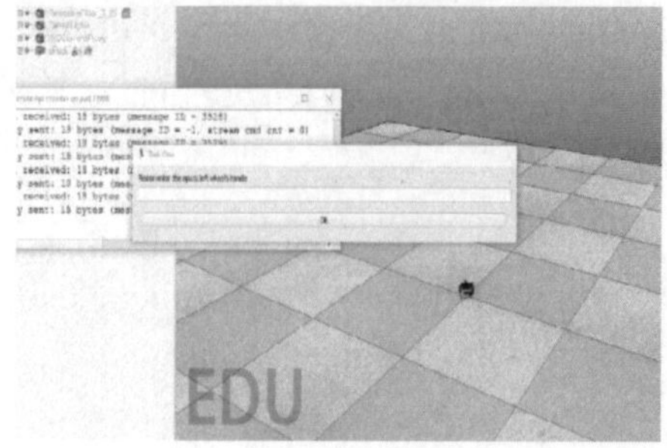

Figure 7. Level 1 V-Rep code Input Screen

The system then displays tasks for level 1 and accepts code inputs from the user as depicted in figure 7. The system displays success message if input is correct and error otherwise (figure 8).

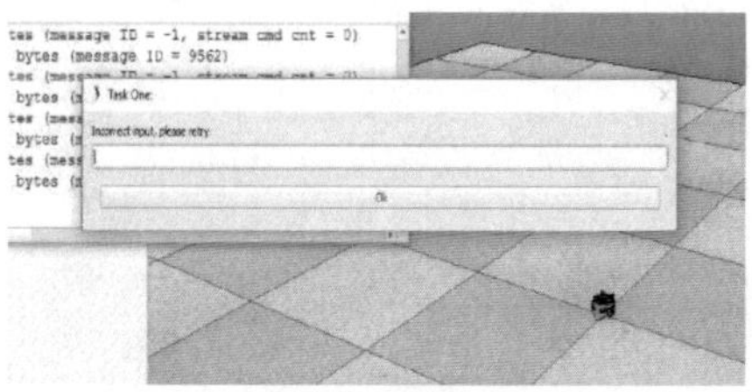

Figure 8. Wrong input entered

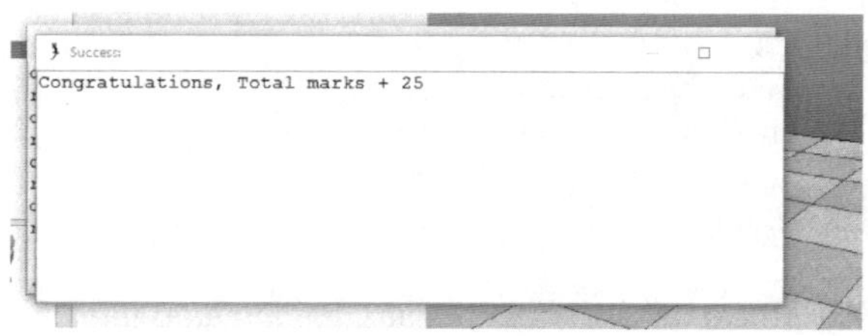

Figure 9. Right Input Entered

Once the user input the right code, a congratulation messgae will be displayed and the required score(marks) will be awarded for the level completion as shown un figure 9.

This process continues until the three levels are completed and the overall score is displayed. Therefore, at the end of a level, the tasks done will be combined together, and the simulation will be displayed for the user to see work progress. The user may also decide to take test only at any of the levels depending on the area of the curriculum of the programming language covered. Figures 10a and 10b depicts some of the results at level 1.

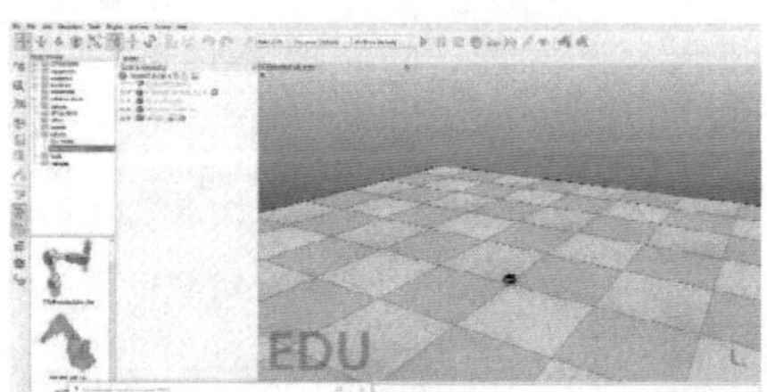

Figure 10a. Simulation of level 1- free wandering

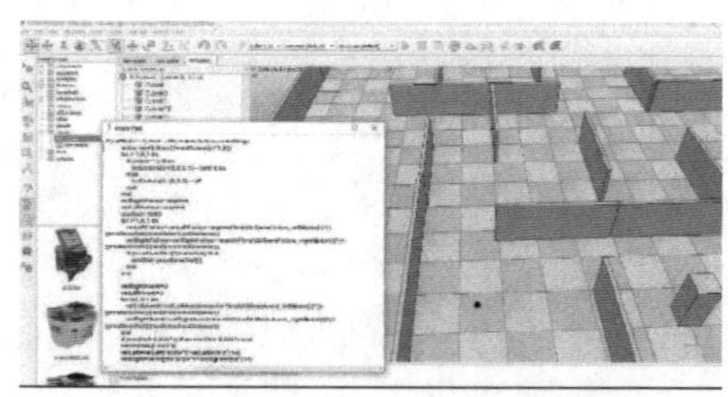

Figure 10b. Simulation of level 1- Obstacle Avoidance and wall following

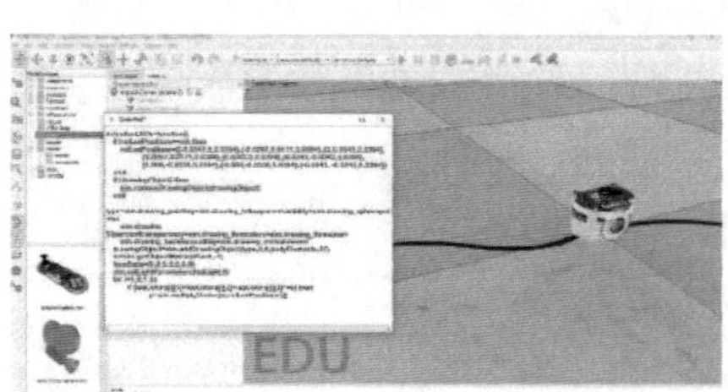

Figure 10c. Simulation of level 1- Line following

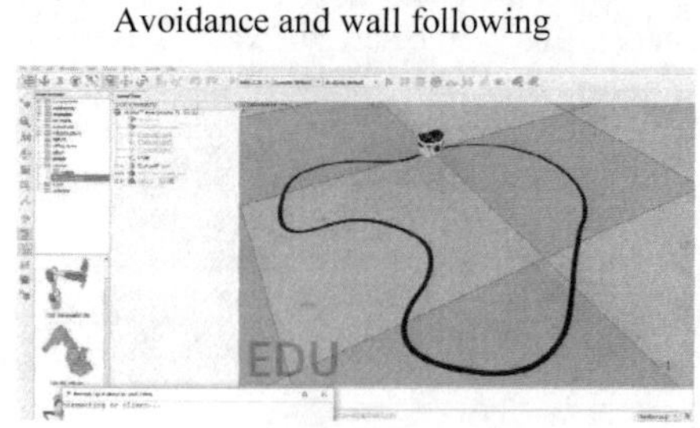

Figure 11. Simulation of Level 2-Shape drawing

Figure 11 shows one of the results at the level 2 of the training. The robot was programmed to draw shapes.

Figures 12a and 12b shows the result at the Level 3. The robot was programmed to move from a starting point to a target point (figure 12b) in the simulated robotic environment.

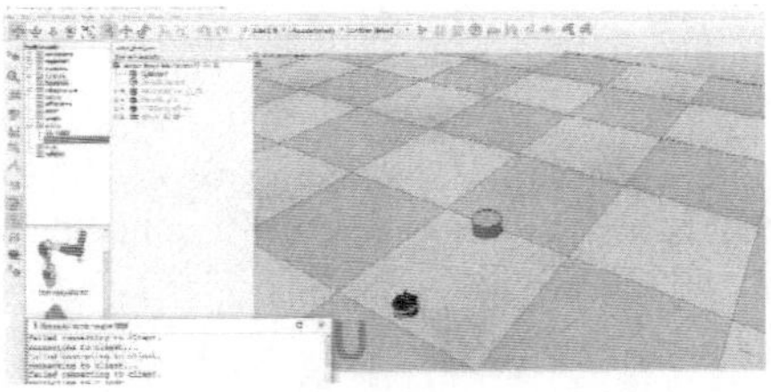

Figure 12a. Simulation of Level 3-Target Reaching

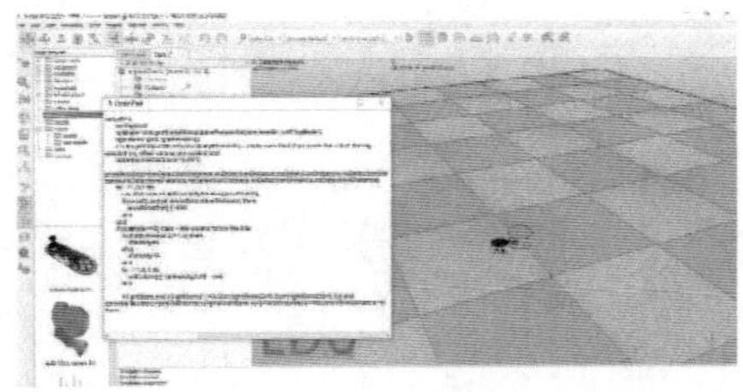

Figure 12b. Simulation of Level 3-Target Reaching

3.2.1 User Documentation

To aid user learnability, the game is embedded with a documentation which explain how each level works, how to learn basic python codes for Robot programming, and how to successfully work around various V-REP scene.

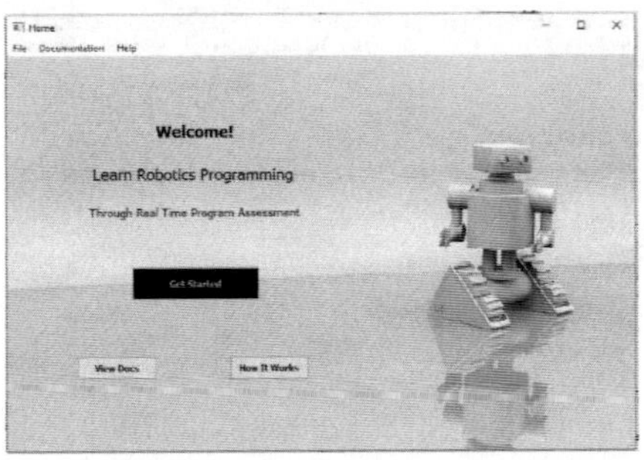

Figure 13. Documentation Button

Figure 14. Documentation Window

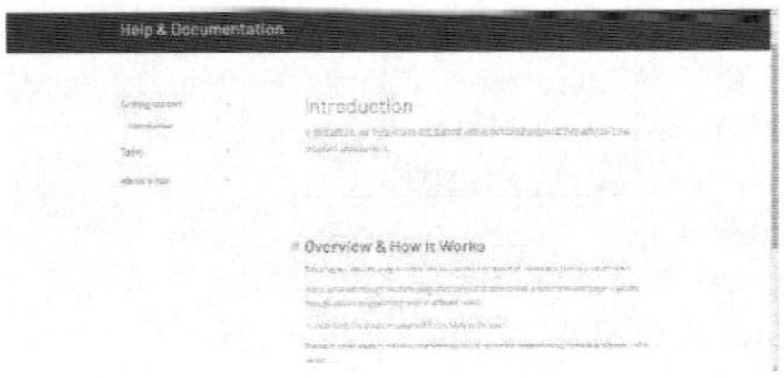

Figure 15. How the Game System Works Documentation

4. CONCLUSION

This work has presented an assistive system to aid novice computer and robot programming students to learn how to program and at the same time learn how to program a robot. It demonstrated a gamified hint system based on the assessment of robot programs. The system is able to evaluate students' programming skills in real time. By running the program inside the simulator, several scenarios were tested using the basic robot control functions.

However, by providing tutorials and hints to the students, they are eager to learn how to program and the awarding of grades at the end gives them the urge to take robot programming serious because every student would want to put in his best in order to score great points in the end.

5. CONTRIBUTION TO KNOWLEDGE

This work has developed an educative tool for teaching and learning computer programming through the use of robot programming. The real-time programming assessment tool will serve as an effective teaching aids to improve teaching and learning process of computer and robot programming.

REFERENCES

Attila P., Robert P., & Erika T. (2013) 'Mobile Robots in Teaching Programming for IT Engineers and Its Effects' International Journal of Advanced Computer Science and Applications, Vol. 4, issue 11, pp. 162-168 Doi: 10.14569/IJACSA.2013.041123

Carina S., Pedro T., & Vanesa M. (2016) 'Enhancing the Engagement of Intelligent Tutorial Systems through Personalization of Gamification' International Journal of Engineering Education Vol. 32, issue 1(B), pp. 532–541

Ernest B., Hanheide M., & Cielniak G. (2011) 'The Effectiveness of Integrating Educational Robotic Activities into Higher Education Computer Science Curricula: A Case Study in a Developing Country' A conference proceeding from the book 29 Effective Ways You Can Use Robots in the Classroom. (pp. 73-87) DOI: 10.1007/978-3-319-55553-9_6

Esteve-Mon, F. M., Adell-Segura, J., Llopis Nebot, M. A., Valdeolivas Novella, G., & Pacheco Aparicio, J. (2019). The development of computational thinking in student teachers through an intervention with educational robotics. Journal of Information Technology Education: Innovations in Practice, 18, 139-152. https://doi.org/10.28945/4442

Major L., Kyriacou T., & Brereton O. (2011) 'Systematic literature review: Teaching Novices Programming using Robots' School of Computing and Mathematics, Keele University, Staffordshire, UK Vol. 6, Issue 6, pp. 502 – 513. Doi: 10.1049/iet-sen.2011.0125

Marina U., Louise F., Elizabeth R., & Amanda S. (2013) 'Computational thinking and tinkering: Exploration of an early childhood robotics curriculum'. A journal of Computer & Education Vol. 72, pp. 145-157. https://doi.org/10.1016/j.compedu.2013.10.020

Mather, R. (2015). A mixed-methods exploration of an environment for learning computer programming. *Research in Learning Technology, 23*. https://doi.org/10.3402/rlt.v23.27179

Morin, D., Thomas, J. D. E., & Saadé, R. G. (2015). Fostering problem-solving in a virtual environment. Journal of Information Technology Education: Research, 14, 339-362. https://doi.org/10.28945/2273

Nourbakhsh I, Hamner E., Crowley K., & Wilkinson K. (2012) 'Formal measures of learning in a secondary school mobile robotics course' A Conference Proceedings in the IEEE International Conference on Robotics and Automation Vol. 2: pp. 1831 - 1836 DOI: 10.1109/ROBOT.2004.1308090

Obe (2017). Test Data Generation Using Intelligent Geno-Neuro Technique. International Journal of Scientific & Engineering Research Volume 8, Issue 8, 650-655.

Park I., Kim D., Oh J., Jang Y., & Lim K. (2015) 'Learning Effects of Pedagogical Robots with Programming in Elementary School Environments in Korea' Indian Journal of Science and Technology. Vol. 8, Issue 26. DOI:10.17485/ijst/2015/v8i26/80723

Pugnali, A., Sullivan, A., & Bers, M. U. (2017). The impact of user interface on young children's computational thinking. Journal of Information Technology Education: Innovations in Practice, 16, 171-193. Retrieved from http://www.informingscience.org/Publications/3768

Siegfried R., Klinger S., Gross M., Sumner R. W., Mondada F., & Magnenat S. (2017) Improved Mobile Robot Programming Performance through Real-time Program Assessment. In ITiCSE '17: Proceedings of the 2017 ACM Conference on Innovation and Technology in Computer Science Education, pp. 341-346 https://doi.org/10.1145/3059009.3059044

Simon P., Jacob P., & Tim J. (2017) 'An exploration of the role of visual programming tools in the development of young children's computational thinking' An Electronic Journal of e-Learning Vol.15, Issue 4, pp. 297-309.

Tocháčeka D., & Lapesa V. (2016) 'Developing technological knowledge and programming skills of secondary school students through the educational robotics projects' A conference proceeding on Social and Behavioral Sciences. Vol. 217, pp. 377 – 381. Doi: 10.1016/j.sbspro.2016.02.107

NEED OF EDUCATIONAL TECHNOLOGY TOOLS FOR COGNITIVE DEVELOPMENT IN INTELLECTUALLY DISABLED CHILDREN

Savitha Korattikkara Kumaran[1] and Renumol Vempalively Govindapillai[2]
Cochin University of Science and Technology, Kerala, India
[1]Research Scholar
[2]Professor

ABSTRACT

Research on special education has showed that the use of digital technology for the special need children can help to simplify their educational process. Intellectual disability (ID) is a kind of developmental disorder. ID children need some kind of scaffolding during their learning process. Hence, as part of our ongoing research to design and develop an AR-based educational technology (ET) tool for ID children, we have conducted 3 studies. This paper describes our findings from these studies. Initially we have conducted a pilot study to investigate how Augmented Reality (AR) based educational application would help the mild and moderate ID children in learning English alphabets. Then we have conducted a survey to know the concern of special teachers about technology tools for ID children. In the third study, we have visited some of the special schools in Kerala to know more about the issues pertaining to the ID children. The results of these 3 studies warrant the need to design and develop some kind of AR/VR application for educating ID children.

KEYWORDS

Special Need Children, Augmented Reality (AR), Intellectual Disability (ID), Educational Technology (ET) Tool, Virtual Reality (VR)

1. INTRODUCTION

Typically, education is the primary process to gain knowledge, skills and moral values for school-going children. Like ordinary children, Special Education Needs (SEN) children also deserve inclusion into the education system. Studies in the field of special education show that the learning difficulties of the children with disabilities are tough to recognize in the initial stage. They may show extreme impatience, deficiency in thinking capacity, lack of concentration on studies etc. at various stages. Initially we need to find their academic, social and behavioral problems and take appropriate measures to design suitable didactic settings (Bakken et al, 2017). There are many hurdles in providing didactic settings for the special need children, such as designing and developing interventions to facilitate their learning process, dedicated teachers to scaffold, developing the habit of using technology etc. (Jadán-Guerrero and Guerrero, 2015). Investigations in the education arena showed that the deficiency of time and resources led to the shortage of technology tools usages in schools (Schoepp, 2005). However, the use of digital technology for the special need children can help to simplify their educational process.

In our study we have focused only on the children with intellectual disability (ID). ID is a developmental problem. It consists of genetic and atmospheric factors (Daily, 2000). It is described by an IQ test. If the IQ test value is under 70, it is confirmed as intellectual disability. If the value is in the range from 51 to 70, then it is considered as mild ID and from 35 to 50 is recognized as moderate ID ("Mental Retardation", 2020). Mild group of children are poor in their educational activities whereas children with moderate ID require more specific attention even in their social life. Since the academic talent of ID children is limited, they need some kind of scaffolding during their learning process.

From the literature, it is learned that the learning process of the ID children is very challenging and they require more supportive and attractive learning materials. In this circumstance, it is found that there is a lot of scope for the innovative technology tools. So the recognition of various procedures and informative applications is important for the innovative development in the education system for SEN children (Edyburn, 2013). Educators are more responsible for integrating technologies into such informative applications (Baglama et al, 2017). Researchers assured that, using technological applications for the students with special needs is more influential in their educational progresses (Michaels and McDermott, 2003) (Schlosser and Wendt, 2008). A study on Information and Communication Technology (ICT) in special education has mentioned that ICT has the potential to balance and bring SEN children to the mainstream (Istenic Starcic and Bagon, 2014). Integration of ICT as an innovative mechanism in the classroom can improve the teaching learning practice (Sangrà and González-Sanmamed, 2010) and also the student's responsiveness in class (Hennessy et al, 2005). However, there are lot of obstacles in integrating ICT, such as teacher training, different viewpoints associated with the assessment process and organization of the resources, time limitations of the instructors etc. (Copley and Ziviani, 2004). Even though, the situation will be changed by the optimistic educational improvements associated with the incorporation of technology-based tools for the students with diverse population (Connor et al, 2010). And also the effective usages of ICT tools will inspire the special need children in the classroom atmosphere (Williams, 2006). One such technology is Augmented Reality (AR). It is a developing technology that may support students to acquire information through the collaboration of computer-generated entities in the actual atmosphere. AR has the capacity to engage and inspire students in the controlled, school environment. It permits students to realize the physical objects, which means that it complements realism than entirely changing it (Agarwal and Thakur, 2014).

AR provides the life-like experience for the students by the 3D hallucination of various things, which helps them to visualise things. Using AR as the instructional method, a teacher can demonstrate 3D/4D interpretation of entities to students, different from the conventional method in the classroom (Saidin et al, 2015). AR has the ability to support students to accomplish subject awareness and endure that knowledge uninterruptedly by the communication with a smartphone. AR in portable devices proposes a countless potential in the teaching learning process (Hwang et al, 2016). So in this paper we describe our studies conducted to understand the necessity of technology based tools for the cognitive development of ID children.

2. METHODOLOGY

We have conducted three studies to understand the need of technology tools for improving the social and academic activities of the Intellectually Disabled (ID) children. First one was a pilot study to investigate how Augmented Reality (AR) based educational application would help the mild and moderate ID children in learning English alphabets. The second was a survey to know the concern of special teachers about technology tools for the ID children. The third study was conducted to know more about the issues pertaining to the ID children. For this we have visited some of the special schools in Kerala and interacted with the teachers and parents. The following sections describe these studies, our observations and findings.

2.1 A Pilot Study Using AR-Based Educational Application

As mentioned earlier, in order to achieve the required learning outcome, the ID children need some kind of cognitive support. So we have conducted a pilot study to investigate how Augmented Reality (AR) based educational application would help the mild and moderate ID children in learning English alphabets (Savitha and Renumol, 2019). A comparative study was conducted to check the impact of the application. Eight ID children were participated in this study. They were divided into two groups. Children with hyperactivity were grouped as the experimental group, and they had more backing from AR-based tool via smartphone, whereas the control group learners have learned in the traditional mode. After assessing the parameters such as the learning outcome, response to the learning material, learning time and the memory capacity, it has been observed that the students from the experimental group showed progress in all the parameters than those in the control group. So we got an insight that the AR-based application has a hopeful influence on ID children. With the usage of this innovative technology, the resource teachers and parents could develop their children's responsiveness and curiosity to the class session compared to the traditional way of coaching. By using the AR tool, the resource teacher could prove that the topics incorporated with the smartphone could influence the children's concern in the learning activities. After this pilot study, we can say that AR has enough potential to be integrated in to the education system of the students with ID. Hence the upcoming expansions of the AR technology can be incorporated into the special education.

2.2 A Survey Based Analysis

Listening to the end users is important in software development to collect the requirements. Since our aim is to design and develop an AR-based tool for the ID children, we wanted to hear the concerns of the special teachers about technology use in the classroom. We consider teachers as our clients because we can understand the concerns and collect the requirements about technological tools for the ID children only through the interaction with the teachers. So we have conducted a survey among a set of special teachers from Kerala. The aim of the survey was to know the concern of those teachers about technology tools for ID children.

The instrument for the survey was based on the Stages of Concern Questionnaire (SoCQ) and it was designed by referring the paper "Measuring the stages of concern about an innovation: A manual for use of the stages of concern questionnaire" (Hall et al, 1977). It is a manual for the use of the SoC Questionnaire. The questionnaire included 35 items related to technology and 6 items related to demographic information. The questionnaire is available for reference in **Appendix**.

Each question was represented in a 7 point Likert scale (0-6 points) as shown below:

Unconcerned (0), Informational (1), Personal (2), Management(3),Consequence(4), Collaboration(5) and Refocusing(6).

Hundred and four resource teachers from different schools have participated in this survey. They were educationally trained teachers (B.Ed. and M.Ed. in Special Education) for handling special need children. Their responses indicated that, they are interested to learn more about technological tools to teach ID children. They expressed that they need an alternative method of teaching as well as teaching materials apart from which they are currently using.

2.3 Visit to Special School

Apart from these studies, we have also visited some of the special schools in Kerala to know more about the issues pertaining to ID children. Visits were mainly concerned about interacting with the teachers and parents to know the daily activities of ID children. From these visits we came to know that, children with ID have complicated problems in their daily life. In some schools, we have noticed that there are anecdotal evidences of positive impact on ID children while using technological tools for training. Teachers from one of the schools we have visited informed that, by using a Virtual Reality (VR) application one of the ID children improved his gross motor skill. Through the daily usage of that particular application he was able to climb stairs, which was an impossible task for that child. He was not able to take a step without the help of somebody. With the help of that VR application he could walk independently. From the interaction, we have observed that the teachers and the parents are more enthusiastic about AR/VR applications and generally, the possibility of integrating technological tools for the disabled children.

3. CONCLUSION

This study focuses on the necessities and advantages of ET tools for the special need children, specifically for the ID children. ID children need some kind of scaffolding during their learning process. They need some kind of cognitive support to achieve the learning outcome. Researchers in the field of special education stated that the learning process of ID children is very challenging and they require more cooperative and attractive learning materials. In this condition, using AR as an educational tool may make much more improved results in their motor skills and also in their cognitive abilities. So we have conducted 3 studies to know about the relevance and concerns of integrating ET tools in special education. Our observations from these studies indicated the relevance of ET tools for developing the cognitive skills of the ID children. From the observed results, we have reached a conclusion that, development of AR based educational applications for the ID children has potential to explore further.

ACKNOWLEDGEMENT

We express our sincere gratitude to the participants and their parents who have patiently participated in our pilot study. We wholeheartedly appreciate the support given by the District Program Officers, the Block Program Officers and the Heads of various Schools from the districts Kozhikode, Ernakulam and Thrissur of Kerala, India, to carry out our studies. We also thank the teachers from various schools of Kerala, who have participated in our survey.

REFERENCES

Agarwal, C., & Thakur, N. (2014). The evolution and future scope of augmented reality. International Journal of Computer Science Issues (IJCSI), 11(6), 59.

Baglama, B., Yikmis, A., & Demirok, M. S. (2017). SPECIAL EDUCATION TEACHERS'VIEWS ON USING TECHNOLOGY IN TEACHING MATHEMATICS. European Journal of Special Education Research.

Bakken, L., Brown, N., & Downing, B. (2017). Early childhood education: The long-term benefits. Journal of research in Childhood Education, 31(2), 255-269.

Connor, C., Snell, M., Gansneder, B., & Dexter, S. (2010). Special education teachers' use of assistive technology with students who have severe disabilities. Journal of Technology and Teacher Education, 18(3), 369-386.

Copley, J., & Ziviani, J. (2004). Barriers to the use of assistive technology for children with multiple disabilities. Occupational Therapy International, 11(4), 229-243.

Daily, DK, Ardinger, HH, & Holmes, GE (2000). Identification and evaluation of mental retardation. *American family physician*, *61*(4), pp. 1059-1067.

Edyburn, D. L. (2013). Critical issues in advancing the special education technology evidence base. Exceptional Children, 80(1), 7-24.

Hall, G. E., George, A. A., & Rutherford, W. L. (1977). Measuring the stages of concern about an innovation: A manual for use of the stages of concern questionnaire. Austin: Research and Development Center for Teacher Education, The University of Texas.

Hennessy, S., Ruthven, K., & Brindley, S. U. E. (2005). Teacher perspectives on integrating ICT into subject teaching: commitment, constraints, caution, and change. Journal of curriculum studies, 37(2), 155-192.

"Mental Retardation." International Encyclopedia of the Social Sciences. Retrieved August 11, 2020 from Encyclopedia.com:https://www.encyclopedia.com/social-sciences/applied-and-social-sciences-magazines/mental-retardation-0

Hwang, G. J., Wu, P. H., Chen, C. C., & Tu, N. T. (2016). Effects of an augmented reality-based educational game on students' learning achievements and attitudes in real-world observations. Interactive Learning Environments, 24(8), 1895-1906.

Istenic Starcic, A., & Bagon, S. (2014). ICT-supported learning for inclusion of people with special needs: Review of seven educational technology journals, 1970–2011. British Journal of Educational Technology, 45(2), 202-230.

Jadán-Guerrero, J., & Guerrero, L. A. (2015). A virtual repository of learning objects to support literacy of SEN children. IEEE Revista Iberoamericana de Tecnologias del Aprendizaje, 10(3), 168-174.

Michaels, C. A., & McDermott, J. (2003). Assistive technology integration in special education teacher preparation: Program coordinators' perceptions of current attainment and importance. Journal of Special Education Technology, 18(3), 29-44.

Saidin, N. F., Halim, N. D. A., & Yahaya, N. (2015). A review of research on augmented reality in education: Advantages and applications. International education studies, 8(13), 1-8.

Sangrà, A., & González-Sanmamed, M. (2010). The role of information and communication technologies in improving teaching and learning processes in primary and secondary schools. ALT-J, 18(3), 207-220.

Savitha, K. K., & Renumol, V. G. (2019) Effects of Integrating Augmented Reality in Early Childhood Special Education, *International Journal of Recent Technology and Engineering,* 8(3), pp. 7864-7867.

Schlosser, R. W., & Wendt, O. (2008). Effects of augmentative and alternative communication intervention on speech production in children with autism: A systematic review. American journal of speech-language pathology.

Schoepp, K. (2005). Barriers to technology integration in a technology-rich environment. Learning and teaching in higher education: Gulf perspectives, 2(1), 1-24.

Williams, P., Jamali, H. R., & Nicholas, D. (2006, July). Using ICT with people with special education needs: what the literature tells us. In Aslib Proceedings. Emerald Group Publishing Limited.

APPENDIX

0	1 2	3 4 5	6 7
Irrelevant	Not true of me now	Somewhat true of me now	Very true of me now

1.	I am concerned about students' attitudes toward the technology.	0	1	2	3	4	5	6	7
2.	I now know of some other approaches that might work better.	0	1	2	3	4	5	6	7
3.	I am more concerned about another technology.	0	1	2	3	4	5	6	7
4.	I am concerned about not having enough time to organize myself each day.	0	1	2	3	4	5	6	7
5.	I would like to help other faculty in their use of the technology.	0	1	2	3	4	5	6	7
6.	I have a very limited knowledge of the technology	0	1	2	3	4	5	6	7
7.	I would like to know the effect of reorganization on my professional status.	0	1	2	3	4	5	6	7
8.	I am concerned about conflict between my interests and my responsibilities.	0	1	2	3	4	5	6	7
9.	I am concerned about revising my use of the technology.	0	1	2	3	4	5	6	7
10.	I would like to develop working relationships with both our faculty and outside faculty using this technology.	0	1	2	3	4	5	6	7
11.	I am concerned about how the technology affects students.	0	1	2	3	4	5	6	7
12.	I am not concerned about the technology at this time.	0	1	2	3	4	5	6	7
13.	I would like to know who will make the decisions in the new system.	0	1	2	3	4	5	6	7
14.	I would like to discuss the possibility of using the technology.	0	1	2	3	4	5	6	7
15.	I would like to know what resources are available if we decide to adopt the technology.	0	1	2	3	4	5	6	7
16.	I am concerned about my inability to manage all that the technology requires.	0	1	2	3	4	5	6	7
17.	I would like to know how my teaching or administration is supposed to change.	0	1	2	3	4	5	6	7

18.	I would like to familiarize other departments or persons with the progress of this new approach.	0	1	2	3	4	5	6	7
19.	I am concerned about evaluating my impact on students.	0	1	2	3	4	5	6	7
20.	I would like to revise the technology's approach.	0	1	2	3	4	5	6	7
21.	I am preoccupied with things other than the technology.	0	1	2	3	4	5	6	7
22.	I would like to modify our use of the technology based on the experiences of our students.	0	1	2	3	4	5	6	7
23.	I spend little time thinking about the technology.	0	1	2	3	4	5	6	7
24.	I would like to excite my students about their part in this approach.	0	1	2	3	4	5	6	7
25.	I am concerned about time spent working with nonacademic problems related to the technology.	0	1	2	3	4	5	6	7
26.	I would like to know what the use of the technology will require in the immediate future.	0	1	2	3	4	5	6	7
27.	I would like to coordinate my efforts with others to maximize the technology's effects.	0	1	2	3	4	5	6	7
28.	I would like to have more information on time and energy commitments required by the technology.	0	1	2	3	4	5	6	7
29.	I would like to know what other faculty are doing in this area.	0	1	2	3	4	5	6	7
30.	Currently, other priorities prevent me from focusing my attention on the technology.	0	1	2	3	4	5	6	7
31.	I would like to determine how to supplement, enhance, or replace the technology.	0	1	2	3	4	5	6	7
32.	I would like to use feedback from students to change the program.	0	1	2	3	4	5	6	7
33.	I would like to know how my role will change when I am using the technology.	0	1	2	3	4	5	6	7
34.	Coordination of tasks and people is taking too much of my time.	0	1	2	3	4	5	6	7
35.	I would like to know how the technology is better than what we have now.	0	1	2	3	4	5	6	7

Please complete the following:

1. How long have you been involved with the technology, not counting this year?

   Never ___ 1 year ___ 2 years ___ 3 years ___ 4 years ___ 5 or more ____

2. In your use of the technology, do you consider yourself to be a:

   non-user ___ novice ___ intermediate ___ old hand ___ past user ____

3. Have you received formal training regarding the technology (workshops, courses)?

   Yes ____ No ____

4. Are you currently using any technology tools?

   Yes ____ No ____

   If yes, please specify the names of the tools:

   ____

   ____

   ____

5. If you have any suggestions about technology usage towards special children, please describe briefly:

   ____

   ____

   ____

THE ROLE OF GENDER IN LEARNERS' DIGITAL INTERACTION PREFERENCES

Muhittin Şahin[1] and Dirk Ifenthaler[2]
[1]*University of Mannheim, Germany; Ege University, Turkey*
[2]*University of Mannheim, Germany; Curtin University, Australia*

ABSTRACT

A major criticism brought to digital learning environments was that the individual learning activities cannot be monitored consistently. However, recent advancements of educational data mining and learning analytics allow a precise tracking of learner activities. Previous studies focused on learners' navigation profiles, academic achievements, or motivation, while missing a closer look a gender differences. This study focusses on the interaction preferences of $N = 161$ Bachelor students in a digital learning environment based on their gender. Within the scope of this research, interactions of the learners are defined as (a) learner-content, (b) learner-discussion (learner-learner), (c) learner-tutorial, (d) learner-video, and (e) learner-assessment. interaction preferences of the students were examined based on log data and evaluation data collected through digital instruments administered through a learning analytics system. For this purpose, adjusted residuals analysis has been conducted. Findings show that the interaction preferences of students differ throughout the study periods according to their gender. The findings obtained in this research can provide some initial suggestions for instructional designers of digital learning environments. Future research will include students' psycho-educational structures, such as learning strategies, motivational dispositions, and prior knowledge.

KEYWORDS

Interaction Preferences, Digital Learning Environment, Educational Data Mining, Learning Analytics, Gender Differences, Adjusted Residuals Analysis

1. INTRODUCTION

The advances of Information and Communication Technologies (ICT) provides multiple opportunities to support learners, teachers, and digital learning environments. One goal of using ICT in the field of education is to develop and improve learning processes without time and space constraints (Ji, Park, Jo, & Lim, 2016). In this context, many digital learning environments have been developed and implemented in higher education institutions around the world. A major criticism brought to these digital learning environments was that the individual learning activities cannot be monitored consistently (Graf, Kinshuk, & Liu, 2009). Since then, many approaches have been used to understand learners' learning profiles and to predict their future development based on such digital educational data and assessments (Ifenthaler, Pirnay-Dummer, & Seel, 2010). However, recent advancements of educational data mining and learning analytics allow a precise tracking of learner activities, i.e., trace data in digital learning environments (Şahin, Keskin, Özgür, & Yurdugül, 2017). Still, recording only trace data does not support a holistic perspective toward learning with regard to learners context and background (Ifenthaler & Widanapathirana, 2014).

One strategy of educational data mining is the identification and classification of interaction profiles and patterns of learners in order to optimize digital learning environments within the context of learner needs and preferences. As such, it is possible to offer more appropriate and customizable learning environments to the learners. Successful applications have been studied with a focus on learners' navigation profiles (Blagojević & Milosević, 2013; Graf, Kinshuk, & Liu, 2009), academic achievements (Jo, Yu, Lee, & Kim, 2015; Macfadyen & Dawson, 2010), or motivation sources and cognitive strategies (Şahin et al., 2017; Keskin & Yurdugül, 2019).

Within the scope of this research, the interaction preferences of students in a digital learning environment were examined based on their gender. In addition, the interaction preferences of the students were examined according to different phases of learning during a 12-week semester at a higher education institution.

2. BACKGROUND

2.1 Learning Management Systems and Learners' Preferences

In recent years, it is possible to see that the education paradigm has shifted from one size fits all to an adaptive and customizable approach (Brusilovsky & Henze, 2007). In this context, it is also seen that digital learning environments are used extensively by higher education institutions. Especially, Learning Management Systems (LMS) are used remarkably (Brown, Dehoney, & Millichap, 2015). LMS is a software designed to help instructors in order to achieve their pedagogical goals by presenting learning content to the students and managing users and rights on the platform (Ifenthaler, 2012; Machado & Tao, 2007). LMSs are used to manage the learning process and learning content (Ji et al., 2016; Ifenthaler & Pirnay-Dummer, 2011) and include several opportunities for stakeholders such as presenting the learning content, conducting exams, collecting assignments, and documenting students' learning process. One of the key features of such digital learning environments are the collection of various interaction types. Interaction has become even more valuable, especially with the emergence of new distance education programs that promote interaction at various levels and types (Brown & Long, 2006). It is possible to consider these types of interactions mainly as learner-content, learner-instructor and learner-learner interactions, which are put forth by Moore (1989). In addition, recent developments focus on the learner-assessment interaction type (Şahin et al., 2017). Within the scope of this research, the LMS interactions of the learners are defined as (a) learner-content, (b) learner-discussion (learner-learner), (c) learner-tutorial, (d) learner-video, and (e) learner-assessment.

Data of learners' interactions are stored unstructured in LMS environments (Šimić, Gašević, & Devedžić, 2004). This log data may contain multiple ways for determining learning profiles and patterns of learners. The learners' learning profile must be determined in order to support the learning process and present appropriate artefacts and actions in a digital learning environment (Ifenthaler, 2015). Current studies focusing on learning profiles of learners in digital learning envirnments focus on log data (Keskin, Şahin, & Yurdugül, 2019; Blagojević, M., & Milosević, 2013; Macfadyen & Dawson, 2010) or self-report data (Northrup, 2009; Rhode, 2009). In this research, interaction preferences of the students were examined based on log data and evaluation data collected through digital instruments administered through a learning analytics system. The interactions of students with the learning environment were considered as the number of clicks on the themes and the total frequencies were used in the standardized residual analysis. Detailed information about the analysis is presented in the method section.

2.2 Research Questions

This research focusses on interaction preferences of students in a digital learning environment with a specific focus on the influence of their gender. In addition, the learning experiences of the students were divided into three periods of study during the course of the semester. Accordingly, three research questions have been investigated:

1. Do the interaction preferences differ between females and males in the first study period?
2. Do the interaction preferences differ between females and males in the second study period?
3. Do the interaction preferences differ between females and males in the third study period?

3. METHOD

3.1 Context and Participants

The study followed an evidence-centered design approach (Behrens, Mislevy, Dicerbo, & Levy, 2012). Student and evaluation data were collected while implementing the learning analytics system LeAP (Learning Analytics Profile; Klasen & Ifenthaler, 2019) into the productive university systems, such as the learning management system and the student management system. The descriptive information about the participants is presented in Table 1.

Table 1. Descriptive information about the participants

Gender	Frequency	Ratio
Female	106	66%
Male	55	34%
Total	161	100%

As seen in Table 1, participants of the study were 161 students (106 female, 55 male) enrolled in a Bachelors program focusing on Economic and Business Education at an European university. The average age of the participants was 22.97 years (SD = 2.92) and their average course load in the semester of data collection was six courses (SD = 2.11). Participants received one credit hour for participating in the study.

The course of study focused on quantitative research methods and included weekly face-to-face lectures as well as online materials through a learning management system such as lecture slides and video recordings, self-assessments, reading assignments and discussion forums. In addition, students worked in small groups (max. 5) on a research project. The course concluded with a written exam at the end of the semester.

3.2 Data Collection Tools

Data used in this research consists of log data recorded through the universities LMS and learning analytics system LeAP. Data includes nine-week interactions of students with the digital learning environment. There are five different interaction themes: student-content, student-discussion, student-tutorial, student-video, and student-assessment. First, data pre-processing was applied. All data were cleaned while pre-processing and data quality checks were conducted. Then, the data were converted into contingency tables.

3.3 Data Analysis

Chi-square analysis is used when both the dependent and independent variables are discrete. However, in chi-square analysis, the number of categories in the variables is limited with two. Adjusted residuals analysis is used when the dependent and independent variables have more than two categories (Cornell Statistical Consulting Unit, 2018). Within the scope of this research, since there are contingency tables of 5 * 2, the standardized residual analysis was used as the Chi-square post-hoc test. The standardized residual value should be a < .05 + -1.96 (Field, 2018). Bonferroni adjustment is made in order to test the significance level in these contingency tables. Bonferroni adjustment is carried out to maintain a sufficient error rate for contingency table dimensions (MacDonald & Gardner, 2000).

4. RESULTS

The semester included twelve weeks of study, however, students lived experience in the digital learning environment was limited to nine weeks as through administrative constraints of the university. The learning experiences of students were examined as three different study periods. Each period is considered as three weeks (first period 1-3; second period 4-6; third period 7-9). The findings are presented based on these periods following the above mentioned research questions.

4.1 First Period Interaction Preferences of Students

The first period includes the first three weeks (1-3 weeks) of students' digital learning environment interactions. The observed and expected interaction frequencies of the students in this period are presented in Table 2.

Table 2. Students' observed and expected interaction preferences in the first period

	Gender	Content	Discussion	Tutorial	Video	Assessment
Observed	Male	6558	1168	23	464	659
	Female	16782	1142	7859	5291	710
Expected	Male	5093.28	504.09	1720.02	1255.86	298.74
	Female	18246.72	1805.91	4499.14	4499.14	1070.26

As shown in Table 2, students interact intensely with the content. On a descriptive level, female students show higher interact male students. In order to test for significant differences, adjusted residuals analysis has been conducted. The findings obtained from this analysis are presented in Table 3.

Table 3. Results of adjusted residuals analysis about interaction preferences for the first period

Gender	Content	Discussion	Tutorial	Video	Assessment
Male	**20.52**	**29.57**	**-40.92**	**-22.34**	**20.84**
Female	**-10.84**	**-15.62**	**21.62**	**11.81**	**-11.01**

Adjusted $p < .005$; z threshold > 2.81

As seen in Table 3. the interaction preferences of students significantly differ based on their gender. The values which are seen in Table 3 are z scores. After Bonferroni adjusted in the analysis phase, the z threshold value was obtained as 2.81. Accordingly, it was determined that male students preferred to interact with content, discussion, and assessment in the first period. It can be said that female students prefer to interact with tutorials and videos compared to female students.

4.2 Second Period Interaction Preferences of Students

The second period includes weeks 4-6 of the semester. The observed and expected interaction frequencies of the students' interactions in this period are presented in Table 4.

Table 4. Students' observed and expected interaction preferences in the second period

	Gender	Content	Discussion	Tutorial	Video	Assessment
Observed	Male	52025	976	47940	3488	1435
	Female	66439	5472	59485	59292	19549
Expected	Male	39674.26	2159.47	35977.24	21025.37	7027.66
	Female	78789.74	4288.53	71447.76	41754.63	13956.34

As shown in Table 4, students interact intensely with the content. On descriptive level, female students interact with tutorials and videos. Likewise, male students interact with not only content but also the tutorial. In addition, female students interact more frequently than male students. In order to test for significant differences, adjusted residuals analysis has been conducted. The findings obtained from this analysis are presented in Table 5.

Table 5. Results of adjusted residuals analysis about interaction preferences for the second period

Gender	Content	Discussion	Tutorial	Video	Assessment
Male	**62.01**	**-25.47**	**63.07**	**-120.95**	**-66.71**
Female	**-44.00**	**18.07**	**-44.75**	**85.82**	**47.34**

Adjusted $p < .005$; z threshold > 2.81

As shown in Table 5, the interaction preferences of students significantly differ between female and male students. Accordingly, male students preferred to interact with content and tutorial in the second period. Further, female students prefer to interact with discussion, video, and assessments.

4.3 Third Period Interaction Preferences of Students

The third period includes the last three weeks (7-9 weeks) of students' digital learning environment interactions. The observed and expected interaction frequencies of the students in this period are presented in Table 6.

Table 6. Students' observed and expected interaction preferences in the third period

	Gender	Content	Discussion	Tutorial	Video	Assessment
Observed	Male	33311	291	18106	6783	2014
	Female	80178	5838	37020	54967	2574
Expected	Male	28482.64	1538.21	13835.12	15497.56	1151.46
	Female	85006.36	4590.79	41290.88	46252.44	3436.54

As shown in Table 6, students interact intensely with the content. On a descriptive level, female students interact with tutorials and videos. In addition, female students interact more frequently than male students. Adjusted residuals analysis was applied to test for significant differences. The findings obtained from this analysis are presented in Table 7.

Table 7. Results of adjusted residuals analysis about interaction preferences for the third period

Gender	Content	Discussion	Tutorial	Video	Assessment
Male	**28.61**	**-31.80**	**36.31**	**-70.00**	**25.42**
Female	**-16.56**	**18.41**	**-21.02**	**40.52**	**-14.71**

Adjusted $p < .005$; z threshold > 2.81

As shown in Table 7, the interaction preferences of students significantly differ based on their gender. Accordingly, male students preferred to interact with content, tutorial and assessment in the third period and female students prefer to interact with discussion and video. After the students' interaction preferences for three different periods are given based on gender, the interaction preferences for each gender are presented in Table 8.

Table 8. Student interaction preferences based on their gender

Gender	First period	Second period	Third period
Male	Content	Content	Content
	Discussion	Tutorial	Tutorial
	Assessment		Assessment
Female	Tutorial	Discussion	Discussion
	Video	Video	Video
		Assessment	

As shown in Table 8, the interaction preferences of students differ throughout the study periods according to their gender. For example, male students preferred to interact with content, discussion and assessment in the first period. However, in the second period, male students chose to interact with content and tutorial. According to these findings, it is possible to say that students have different interaction preferences in different periods. Another point that draws attention to the findings is that female students consistently prefer to interact with video and male students to interact with content.

5. DISCUSSION

In this study, interaction preferences of students in a digital learning environment were examined based on their gender. According to the findings, it was concluded that students' online interaction preferences are different based on both their gender and study period. The interaction preferences of male students are as follows: a) for the first period; content, assessment, and discussion b) for the second period; content ant tutorial and c) for the third period; content, tutorial, and assessment. The interaction preferences of female students are as follows: a) for the first period; tutorial and video b) for the second period; discussion, video, and assessment and c) for the third period; discussion and video.

Another finding obtained within the scope of the research points toward a the preference of male students being the interaction with the textual content and female students prefer to interact with the video content. This finding is consistent with Ching and Hsu (2015) who found that female students prefer to interact with audio/video discussions and male students prefer text-based discussions. Female students seem to prefer to interact with video content because of including more personal and emotional forms of language (Ching & Hsu, 2015). However, more studies are needed to foster these findings on large-scale.

Findings obtained in this research can provide some initial suggestions for instructional designers of digital learning environments (Ifenthaler, 2017). However, in this study, interaction preferences of students are limited by gender. In further research, it is planned that students' psycho-educational structures will be examined, such as learning strategies, motivational dispositions, and prior knowledge. In this way, it is thought that further recommendations can be obtained for researchers and learning designers in order to design appropriate digital learning environments.

6. CONCLUSION

Epistemological changes in the 1990s led to the emergence of student-centered innovative approaches of learning environments (Land & Hannafin, 2009). With learner-centered learning approach learning environments that are designed based on the interests and needs of individuals are provided and thus more complex tasks can be done and understanding can be deepened (Land & Hannafin, 1997). Within the scope of this research, the interaction preferences of the students who are one of the most important stakeholders of student-centered approaches were determined. Learning environments can be designed in accordance with the needs and individual characteristics by determining the preferences of the students (Ifenthaler, 2015). According to the findings, it was found that the interaction preferences of students become different based on their gender. Besides, adjusted residuals analysis was performed in order to determine the interaction preferences. It is thought that the use of adjusted residuals analysis in discovering learning patterns from interaction data will be an example for researchers.

REFERENCES

Behrens, J., Mislevy, R., Dicerbo, K., & Levy, R. (2012). Evidence centered design for learning and assessment in the digital world. In M. Mayrath, J. Clarke-Midura, D. Robinson, & G. Schraw (Eds.), *Technology-based assessments for 21st century skills* (pp. 13–54). Charlotte, NC. Information Age Publishers.

Blagojević, M., & Milosević, M. (2013). Collaboration and learning styles in pure online courses: an action research. *Journal of Universal Computer Science*, *19*(7), 984-1002.

Brown, M., & Long, P. (2006). Trends in learning space design. *Learning Spaces*,*9*, 1-9.

Brown, M., Dehoney, J., & Millichap, N. (2015). The next generation digital learning environment. *A Report on Research. ELI Paper. Louisville, CO: Educause April.*

Brusilovsky, P., & Henze, N. (2007). Open corpus adaptive educational hypermedia. In P. Brusilovsky, A. Kobsa, & W. Nejdl (Eds.), *The adaptive web: Methods and strategies of web personalization* (pp. 671–696). Berlin: Springer. LNCS 4321.

Ching, Y. H., & Hsu, Y. C. (2015). Online graduate students' preferences of discussion modality: Does gender matter? *Journal of Online Learning and Teaching*, *11*(1), 31-41.

Cornell Statistical Consulting Unit. (2018). Adjusted standardized residuals for interpreting contingency tables (Report No. 95). Retrieved from https://www.cscu.cornell.edu/news/statnews/stnews95.pdf

Field, A. (2018). Discovering Statistics Using IBM SPSS Statistics.

Graf, S., Kinshuk, & Liu, T. C. (2009). Supporting teachers in identifying students' learning styles in learning management systems: An automatic student modelling approach. *Journal of Educational Technology & Society*, *12*(4), 3-14.

Ifenthaler, D. (2012). Learning management systems. In N. M. Seel (Ed.), *Encyclopedia of the sciences of learning* (Vol. 12, pp. 1925-1927). New York, NY: Springer.

Ifenthaler, D. (2015). Learning analytics. In J. M. Spector (Ed.), *The SAGE encyclopedia of educational technology* (Vol. 2, pp. 447–451). Thousand Oaks, CA: Sage.

Ifenthaler, D. (2017). Learning analytics design. In L. Lin & J. M. Spector (Eds.), *The sciences of learning and instructional design. Constructive articulation between communities* (pp. 202–211). New York, NY: Routledge.

Ifenthaler, D., & Pirnay-Dummer, P. (2011). States and processes of learning communities. Engaging students in meaningful reflection and learning. In *Social media tools and platforms in learning environments* (pp. 81-94). Springer, Berlin, Heidelberg.

Ifenthaler, D., & Widanapathirana, C. (2014). Development and validation of a learning analytics framework: Two case studies using support vector machines. *Technology, Knowledge and Learning*, *19*(1-2), 221-240.

Ifenthaler, D., Pirnay-Dummer, P., & Seel, N. M. (Eds.). (2010). *Computer-based diagnostics and systematic analysis of knowledge*. New York: Springer.

Ji, H., Park, K., Jo, J., & Lim, H. (2016). Mining students activities from a computer supported collaborative learning system based on peer to peer network. *Peer-to-Peer Networking and Applications*, *9*(3), 465-476.

Jo, I. H., Yu, T., Lee, H., & Kim, Y. (2015). Relations between student online learning behaviour and academic achievement in higher education: A learning analytic approach. In G. Chen, V. Kumar, Kinshuk, R. Huang, & S. C. Kong (Eds.), *Emerging Issues in Smart Learning* (pp. 275-286). Berlin: Springer.

Keskin, S., & Yurdugül, H. (2019). Factors Affecting Students' Preferences for Online and Blended Learning: Motivational vs. Cognitive. *European Journal of Open, Distance and E-learning*, *22*(2), 72-86.

Keskin, S., Şahin, M., & Yurdugül, H. (2019). Online Learners' Navigational Patterns Based on Data Mining in Terms of Learning Achievement. In *Learning Technologies for Transforming Large-Scale Teaching, Learning, and Assessment* (pp. 105-121). Springer, Cham.

Klasen, D., & Ifenthaler, D. (2019). Implementing learning analytics into existing higher education legacy systems. In D. Ifenthaler, J. Y.-K. Yau, & D.-K. Mah (Eds.), *Utilizing learning analytics to support study success* (pp. 61–72). New York, NY: Springer.

Land, S. & Jonassen, D.H. (2009). Student-centered learning environments. (Eds: Jonassen, D.H & Land, S.). In *Theoretical foundations of learning environments*. Routledge.

Land, S. M., & Hannafin, M. J. (1997). Patterns of understanding with open-ended learning environments: A qualitative study. *Educational Technology Research and Development*, *45*(2), 47-73.

MacDonald, P. L., & Gardner, R. C. (2000). Type I error rate comparisons of post hoc procedures for I j Chi-Square tables. *Educational and Psychological Measurement*,*60*(5), 735-754.

Macfadyen, L. P., & Dawson, S. (2010). Mining LMS data to develop an —early warning system for educators: A proof of concept. *Computers & Education, 54*, 588-599.

Machado, M., & Tao, E. (2007). Blackboard vs. Moodle: Comparing user experience of learning management systems. In *2007 37th annual frontiers in education conference-global engineering: Knowledge without borders, opportunities without passports* (pp. S4J-7). IEEE.

Moore, M. G. (1989). Three types of interaction. *The American Journal of Distance Education, 3*(2), 1-7.

Northrup, P. T. (2009). Online learners' preferences for interaction. *The perfect online course: Best practices for designing and teaching*, 463-473.

Rhode, J. (2009). Interaction equivalency in self-paced online learning environments: An exploration of learner preferences. *The International Review of Research in Open and Distributed Learning*, *10*(1), 1-23.

Şahin, M., Keskin, S., Özgür, A., & Yurdugül, H. (2017). Determination of interaction profiles based on learner characteristics in e-learning environment. *Educational Technology Theory and Practice, 7*(2), 172-192.

Šimić, G., Gašević, D., & Devedžić, V. (2004). Semantic web and intelligent learning management systems. In *Workshop on Applications of Semantic Web Technologies for e-Learning*.

WHAT IS THIS SOUND IN DECIBEL? − WE TRIED TO DETERMINE STUDENTS' COMPREHENSION OF SOUND LEVELS, ONLINE VER−

Mari Ueda and Tetsuo Tanaka
Faculty of Information Technology, Kanagawa Institute of Technology
1030 Shimo-ogino, Atsugi, Kanagawa, 243-0292, Japan

ABSTRACT

To examine the appropriate information disclosure method of noise as the final goal, we firstly set the goal to grasp the degree of understanding of the dB values of the sound sources among people other than acoustic experts. In this paper, first, in order to measure the degree of understanding of the dB in university students without expert knowledge, we developed a loudness chart kit and evaluated the understanding of loudness in the classes. As a result, they commonly regarded the sound volumes of the rocket and the take-off of the airplanes as first or second loudest, but the subjective ranks of other sound sources were completely different among them. Some of the students who seem to have no knowledge at all about the sound source answered unreality values entirely. Furthermore, since the university class was brought online due to the influence of the new coronavirus, we developed an online version of this teaching material. In the future, we will measure the changes in the evaluated dBs after learning the dB values. Then, we also accumulate more data about the differences of the understanding degree in dB values among the individual characteristics including their university, nationality, and whether they are environmental officials, to discuss the diagnostic criteria of the volume of the sound. Moreover, we will discuss how to learn a sense of loudness and dB. This reports on the online version of the teaching materials developed as university class are now online due to the impact of the novel coronavirus.

KEYWORDS

Sound Level, Education in Acoustics, University Students, Teaching Materials for Acoustics, Online

1. INTRODUCTION

The needs for the disclosure of environmental information, including the conditions of noise as well as air pollution, are increasing in the world (Ueda, 2015). In response to the needs, Also, information on environmental noise is becoming progressively more available, as exemplified by the availability of noise maps related to an airplane, traffic, and construction site activity as well as the release by local governments of environmental noise maps (Bellucci, 2017). Particularly, the positive information disclosure of the Environmental Noise Directive (hereinafter, END) in the EU countries is one of the good examples (Maisonneuve, 2009). Also, in addition to the general index of noise level L_{Aeq}, such the cases of information disclosure increasingly display L_{den} (day-evening-night sound level) that weighted the noise level of nighttime (Directive 2002/49/EC).

In European countries, where information disclosure of environmental conditions is becoming ordinary, the current problem is how to provide environmental information, including noise level that anyone cannot understand. As an example of the current studies, there are examinations of indicators other than decibel (hereinafter, dB): a heat map of blue-to-red and size of icons corresponding to low-to-high volumes.

However, these cases did not mention the degree of the citizen's understanding of the sound level dB. To begin with, the degree of understanding remains unclear when the general public who does not specialize in acoustics, physics, environmental studies, and related academic area. How many decibels do people who are not experts feel sounds? Thus, in this paper, for proposing appropriate information disclosure method of noise conditions, the objective is to grasp the degree of understanding to the size of the sound in the persons except the experts of acoustics. In particular, as an attempt to measure the degree of understanding of the loudness of university students, we measured the degree of understanding using the loudness chart kit developed by ourselves in lecture courses. This reports on the online version of the teaching materials developed as university class are now online due to the impact of the novel coronavirus.

2. SOUND VOLUME CHART KIT: OFFLINE VERSION

2.1 Overview

In order to measure the degree of understanding of the dB, we developed a sound volume chart kit that is illustrated in Figure 1 (Ueda, 2019). This kit consists of a sheet with several grid lines without values (Figure 1 (a)), and 18 sound source stickers. In particular, the sound source stickers consist of 17 images of sound sources, as well as blank ones describing favorite sound sources. Participants are asked to paste the stickers on the board at the position of the scale that corresponds to the size of the sound they imagine.

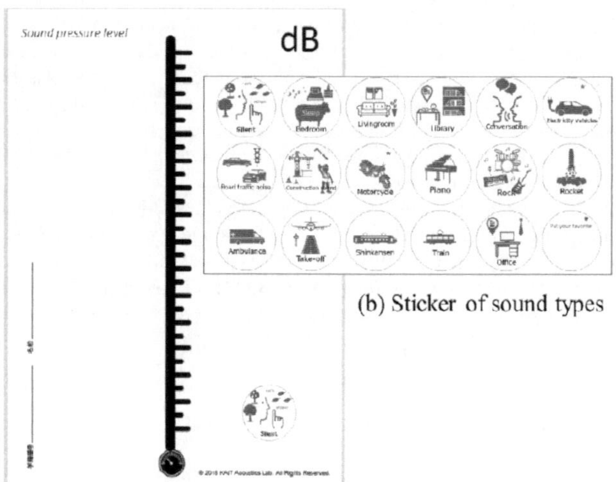

(b) Sticker of sound types

(a) Sheet of sound level chart

Figure 1. Detail of the sound level chart kit. (a) Sheet and (b) sticker set of 18 sound types

2.2 Procedure

Using the kit, we evaluated the degree of understanding of the dB in university students. This evaluation was conducted in the classes of (a) Introduction to speech communication, which is an elective course at Kanagawa Institute of Technology, and (b) Applied acoustical engineering seminar, which is a compulsory elective course at the same institute. In total, fifty-one students, including forty-two sophomores (34 males and eight females) and nine juniors (9 males) participated in these classes.

In either class, to begin with, we explained the brief introduction about feeling the volume of the sound. First, the agenda of the class were outlined based on the syllabus, and then the participants were asked to judge the volume of each sound source using a kit as if they heard near the sound source. At this time, we also asked them to intuitively judge the volume without talking to each other and looking at any references. The working time was about 15 minutes, including the explanation.

2.3 Results

Figure 2 shows an example of the response to the kit. Since we did not specify how to describe the dB values of the sound sources, some people entered numerical values for all sound sources, but some also entered only the maximum and the minimum values.

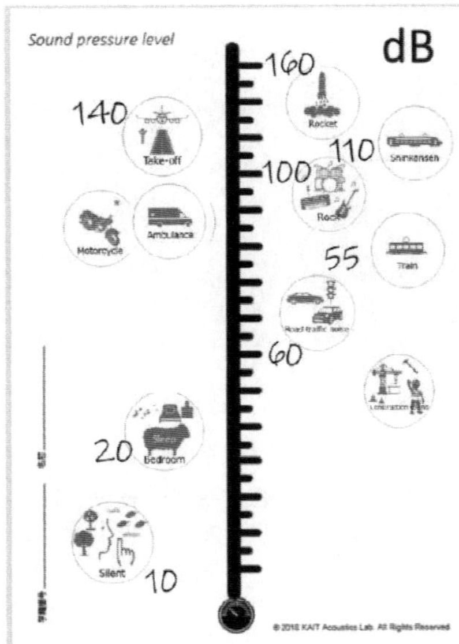

Figure 2. Detail of the sound level chart kit. (a) Sheet and (b) sticker set of 18 sound types

Figure 3 shows the confusion matrix of the actual order of the volumes of sound sources and the rank of the sound source volumes evaluated by the participants. The a—r on the x axis indicates the type of sound source (r means the sound source freely answered by the individuals), and the y-axis indicated the actual descending order of dB values from 1 to 18. As the frequency is higher, the color of the cell becomes more reddish, and when the frequency was zero, the corresponding cell turns into green.

According to the students' responses, 96 % of the student regarded a. Rocket as the loudest in dB value among the sound sources. Next, 94 % of them answered b. A take-off of a plane as the second loudest. For other sound sources, the variation among individuals is considerable, which suggests that there are individual differences in how people feel the volume of the sound sources.

Table 1 shows the values of each sound source ±50 dB from the reference level (Bellucci, 2017), in addition to the mean, standard deviation, maximum and minimum values of the dB values judged by the students. Among the students who seemed to have no knowledge at all about the sound source, for example, those who answered the sound volume of the rocket as 3,000,000 dB, which was completely unreality. Therefore, the mean values and standard deviations in Table 1 are far from reality. On the other hand, those who answered relatively near realistic values (Reference levels ±50 dB) accounted for around 35~60% for each sound source.

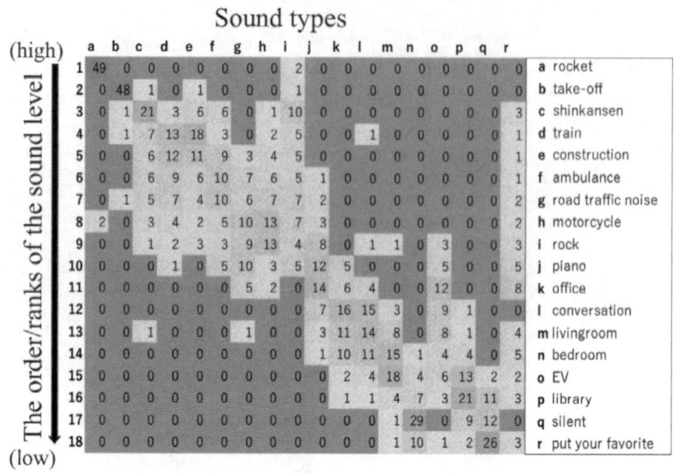

Figure 3. Confusion matrix of the ranks of actual and subjective volumes of sound sources

Table 1. Experimental results by the participant

Sound types	a	b	c	d	e	f	g	h	i	j	k	l	m	n	o	p	q
REF※	**180**	**120**	**110**	**100**	**90**	**80**	**80**	**70**	**120**	**100**	**60**	**60**	**60**	**40**	**50**	**40**	**20**
AVE	59778.4	61573.2	57827.3	53916.1	25232.3	24164	22834	23273	17973	163	139	102	91.9	62.2	62.1	40.8	23.1
SD	419952	390341	366929	343541	158077	153009	146555	144084	119228	371	318	244	239	188	138	94.6	50.1
MAX	3000000	2500000	2350000	2200000	1000000	980000	950000	900000	800000	2100	1800	1500	1500	1200	900	600	300
MIN	100	80	35	30	50	40	40	29	30	10	20	20	5	0	1	5	0
REF±50	43.1	35.3	45.1	47.1	49.0	41.2	47.1	37.3	39.2	37.3	35.3	54.9	39.2	52.9	47.1	51.0	60.8

3. SOUND VOLUME CHART KIT: WEB VERSION

3.1 Overview

We developed the online version of the teaching materials developed as university lessons are now online due to the impact of the novel coronavirus (db-spl, 2020).

As shown in Figure 4, this application consists of five screens: sign-in, explanation, face sheet, sound volume chart, and history. On the sign-in screen, the user can register the email address, name, and password in advance and sign in with that information or with the user's Google account. Next, after reading and understanding the explanations for this application on the explanation screen, the affiliation, name, age, gender, occupation, etc. is entered on the face sheet input screen. Filling out the face sheet allows one to create a sound volume chart.

In creating the sound volume chart, a chart is created using the screen in Figure 5. On the left side of the screen are sound source stickers representing 18 types of sound sources such as bedrooms, locks, bullet trains, and rockets, and on the right side are empty charts. The user first enters 1) four values on the scale of the chart. Then performs 2) drag and drop the sticker and place it where desired. The 18th sound source is designed so that the user can enter an arbitrary sound source in characters. The magnitude of the sound source is entered. The created chart is recorded every time, and the user can refer to the created chart at any time on the history screen.

Also, the instructor (administrator within the organization) can refer to the chart created by the user of the organization to which one belongs. Further, the administrator of this application can also acquire chart and face sheet data in CSV format.

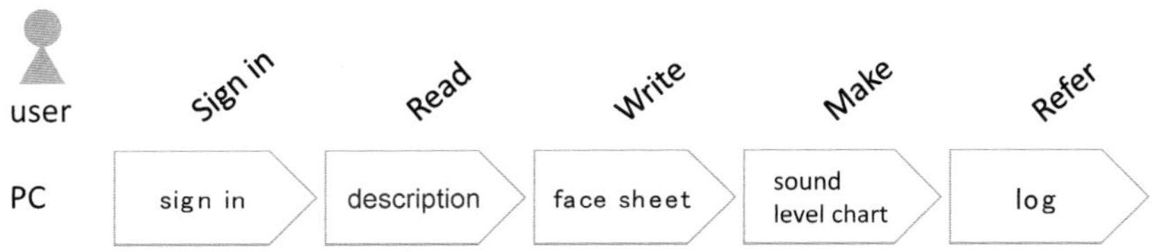

Figure 4. Application screen and flow of use

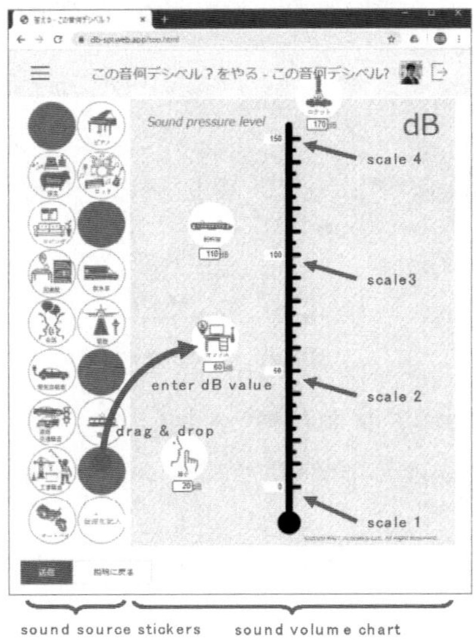

Figure 5. Online version of the sound level chart kit

3.2 Application Configuration

This application is implemented as a Web application, as shown in Figure 6. Firebase (Firebase) is used for server implementation. Firebase is a backend service (BaaS: Backend as a Service) for mobile and web applications offered by Google and consists of multiple product groups. Among them, the authentication service Firebase Authentication, NoSQL document-oriented database Cloud Firestore, and web hosting service Firebase Hosting are used. HTML, JavaScript, and CSS are used for implementation by the client, similar to general Web applications. In addition, Firebase SDK is used for accessing Firebase services and UIKit, a front-end framework (CSS and JavaScript library) widely used for web production. Further, HTML5 Drag&Drop API is used for dragging and dropping the sound source sticker, and the Web Storage API is used for temporarily storing data by the client.

The Cloud Firestore used in this application is a NoSQL document-oriented database. Contrary to relational databases, there are no tables or records, and data is stored in documents, which are organized into collections. Collections and documents correspond to tables and records in relational databases, respectively. Each document consists of multiple key/value pairs. The value can be a simple type, such as Boolean, number, string, or a map type (array or nested object). Maps allow one to structure the data in documents.

This application uses collection users, which stores user information, and answers, which stores information about the audio intensity chart (answer) created by the user. The structure (data model) of the document stored in users and answers. In the web application that uses Cloud Firestore, the database is accessed directly from the client (web browser). As the code of the client may be referenced or tampered with by a malicious user, user authentication/authorization is managed by rules stored on the server.

In this application, users are divided into three types: end-users, in-house administrators, and administrators, and the following rules are applied.

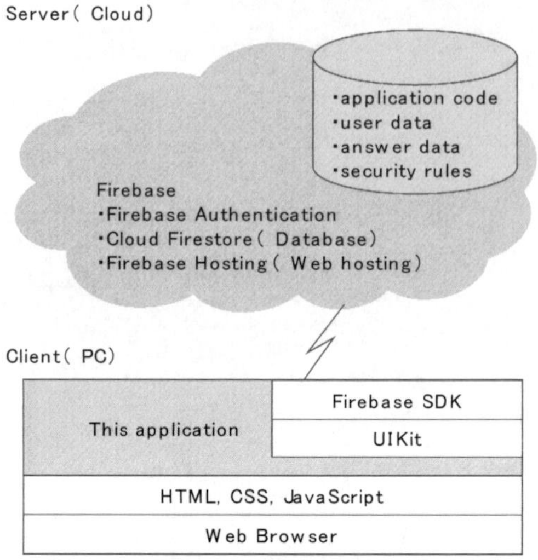

Figure 6. Application configurations

·The user can read/write own user data and answer data.

·The organization manager can read/write all user data and answer data of the organization to which one belongs.

·The administrator can read and write all user data and answer data.

3.3 Usability Evaluation of Application

3.3.1 Procedure

An experiment was conducted to measure the comprehension of sound volume chart using this application. The experiment was conducted with the students of the second class (May 19, 2020) of the Kanagawa Institute of Technology Faculty of Information Science second-year "Introduction to Acoustics" elective course as subjects. On the day of the experiment, which was held during an online lesson due to the novel coronavirus, the experiment and application were explained. If one could not register during the lesson, registration was to be performed within one week. As with the offline version, through the explanation screen and verbal directions, instructions were given to "not look at anything or speak with anyone, use your intuition," and "assume listening to each sound close to the sound source."

Of the 118 participants on the day of the experiment, 100 of them prepared and submitted answers. The respondents were students aged 19 to 23, with 86 males and 14 females. The task time of each respondent (the time from the beginning of preparing the sound volume chart to the registration) was about 10 minutes. More specifically, the average task time of 97 persons excluding three persons who discontinued preparation (appears chart preparation was discontinued when more than six hours was expended) was 588 seconds, the standard deviation was 389, and the median value was 464 seconds.

3.3.2 Results

Table 2 indicates the four values on the scale of the audio intensity chart. From the bottom of the axis, in the sequence of 1, 2, 3, and 4, the realistic values, average values, standard deviations, maximum values, minimum values, median values, and realistic values ±50 dB frequency, 200 dB and higher frequencies are listed.

A few students seemed to have no knowledge of the dB value, as they entered values higher than 200 on the four scales. For example, 18 students entered values higher than 200 dB on scale 3, and 25 students on scale 4. Along with this, the average value and standard deviation are also values that are not realistic. On the contrary, students who entered a value of ±50 dB consisted of more than 90% for scale 1 and 2, approximately 70% for scale 3 and 4, and the median value was realistic for all scales.

Figure 7 indicates the frequency distribution on the scale for the four values. Since dB itself is a unit of a logarithmic scale, it is not realistic to set the scale to logarithmic values such as 10, 100, 1000, 10000. However, as shown in Figure 7, 12 students entered the logarithmic scale or values close to the logarithmic scale. It appears that while students had a vague understanding that values were to be expressed in logarithm, those who did not fully understand responded in this way.

Figure 8 indicates the color map of the frequency of how many persons ranked the volume of the sound source filled in by the user. On the x-axis, a to q are sound sources, and on the y-axis, 1 to 17 are in sequence of increasing volume. The higher the frequency, the darker the color, and if lower than three, the color is white. The 18th sound source is the user's favorite sound source and is not included in the figure as it differs for each user.

Table 2. Outline of the experimental results by the participant

	scale1	scale2	scale3	scale4
standard value(ref)	0	50	100	150
ave	14.1	97.9	282.4	1403.0
sd	28.5	155.3	708.4	8078.3
max	250	1000	5000	80000
min	0	10	20	30
median	5	50	100	150
reference level±50	99	90	73	68
over 200 dB	1	7	18	25

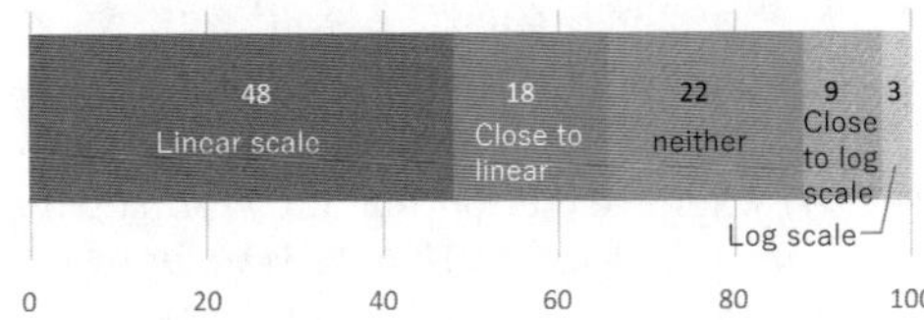

Figure 7. Frequency distribution of 4 scales

	a	b	c	d	e	f	g	h	i	j	k	l	m	n	o	p	q
1	99	6	0	0	0	0	2	0	0	0	0	0	0	0	0	0	0
2	1	83	6	3	0	0	7	3	0	1	0	0	0	0	0	0	0
3	0	6	12	40	11	0	21	6	5	7	0	0	0	0	0	0	0
4	0	2	9	16	28	0	20	16	7	8	0	0	0	0	0	0	0
5	0	1	6	12	15	2	19	20	10	12	0	0	0	1	0	0	0
6	0	2	18	9	16	2	15	18	15	14	0	0	1	1	0	0	0
7	0	0	13	4	16	4	8	16	15	15	0	0	0	1	0	0	0
8	0	0	12	4	5	9	3	10	21	19	0	0	0	1	0	0	0
9	0	1	16	6	3	14	2	6	16	16	1	0	1	5	0	0	0
10	0	0	3	4	3	26	1	1	6	4	13	3	1	28	0	1	0
11	0	0	0	0	1	26	0	0	0	0	12	10	10	30	1	0	0
12	0	0	2	1	0	6	0	1	1	1	27	21	25	12	0	2	0
13	0	0	1	0	0	3	0	0	0	0	18	27	26	6	5	0	0
14	0	0	0	0	0	1	0	0	0	1	13	18	22	4	13	2	1
15	0	0	0	0	1	0	1	0	2	1	5	8	2	1	53	17	14
16	0	0	1	1	2	0	0	2	1	1	0	1	0	0	13	38	31
17	0	0	0	0	0	0	0	0	0	0	0	0	0	0	1	25	39

a rocket
b take off
c rock
d shinkansen
e train
f piano
g construction sound
h ambulance
i road traffic noise
j motorcycle
k office
l livingroom
m conversation
n electricity vehicles
o library
p bedroom
q silent

Figure 8. Confusion matrix of the ranks of actual and subjective volumes of sound sources

The sound source a, the rocket, had the most responses from 99 students, and 83 students answered that b, the aircraft, which was second in frequency of responses. For other sound sources, it can be observed that there are significant variations among individuals, and there are differences in how one perceives the size of the sound source. Table 3 indicates the reference level(realistic value) of each sound source, the average of dB values entered by the user, the standard deviation, the maximum value, the minimum value, the median value, and the number of persons who responded with a value of reference level ±50 dB.

Some respondents entered unrealistic values, similar to the scale value, with the rocket sound of 50,000 dB. On the contrary, more than half of the users answered with a realistic value of ±50 dB as the reference value. Particularly for relatively low intensity sounds with a reference value of 60 dB or lower, more than 80% responded with realistic values.

Table 3. Experimental results by the participant

	a	b	c	d	e	f	g	h	i	j	k	l	m	n	o	p	q
	rocket	take off	rock	shin-kansen	train	piano	const-ruction sound	ambu-lance	road traffic noise	motor-cycle	office	living room	conver-sation	elect-ricity vehicle	library	bed room	silent
ref	180	120	120	110	100	100	90	80	80	70	60	60	60	50	40	40	20
ave	1104.3	590.3	173.9	265.1	195.6	83.0	237.2	190.2	132.3	192.8	48.3	41.1	48.8	77.1	26.9	18.3	11.8
sd	5135.3	1851.6	412.7	593.7	355.1	97.1	565.8	467.6	154.6	605.6	50.9	36.4	67.3	103.9	50.5	40.4	12.1
man	50000	15000	4000	5000	3000	800	5000	4500	900	6000	400	250	600	700	500	400	50
min	30	25	-1	18	19	5	17	11	10	15	3	-1	2	-1	-1	0	0
median	180	132.5	90	100	90	60	100	90	80	81.5	38	37.5	40	50	20	10	10
ref±50	50	61	59	67	70	66	69	77	80	78	86	86	89	86	98	99	100

4. CONCLUSION

To examine the appropriate information disclosure method of noise as the final goal, we firstly set the goal to grasp the degree of understanding of the dB values of the sound sources among people other than acoustic experts. In this paper, first, in order to measure the degree of understanding of the dB in university students without expert knowledge, we developed a loudness chart kit and evaluated the understanding of loudness in the classes. As a result, they commonly regarded the sound volumes of the rocket and the take-off of the airplanes as first or second loudest, but the subjective ranks of other sound sources were completely different among them. Some of the students who seem to have no knowledge at all about the sound source answered unreality values entirely.

Also, as university classes are now online due to the impact of the recent novel coronavirus, online versions of the teaching materials for about 100 students in the university lecture have been developed using web application with Firebase. The task was conducted using the app. As a result, the acoustic results, such as the dB value obtained, did not seem to be significantly different from the offline version of the kit. As comments from students from the minute paper session held in each class, students that experienced the offline version of the sticker noted: "I enjoyed pasting the stickers," "It was easy to do, and it was nice to be able to change the numbers and the position of the stickers," "For the implementer/administrator, the offline version requires additional work such as preparation for printing the sticker and data entry of the result, so I felt that the online version would be easier to implement once the application was created." Currently, the advantages and disadvantages of the offline and online versions of the teaching materials are being compared. After clarification, there is a plan to develop teaching materials that are further adapted to the individuality of students and the current social situation.

Furthermore, in the future, by measuring the changes in the evaluation results after learning of the dB value, and by further accumulating data (differences in universities and nationalities, whether an administrative officer involved in the environment is engaged or not), the volume of the sound, degree of understanding of dB is measured. Then, there is a plan to study how to more effectively understand the volume, dB of the sounds, perceptually and physically.

REFERENCES

Bellucci, P. and Peruzzi, L., 2017, Implementing the harmonica in the dynamap project, *ICSV24*, London, UK, 8 pages.

db-spl, 2020, https://db-spl.web.app/

European Parliament and Council, Directive 2002/49/EC relating to the assessment and management of environmental noise.

Firebase, https://firebase.google.com/.

Maisonneuve N. et al, 2009, Noise Tube: Measuring and mapping noise pollution with mobile phones. *In Information technologies environmental engineering*, Springer, pp. 215-228.

Ueda, M. et al, 2015, How to establish a better information disclosure system on noise and environment around the airport, *Inter Noise 2015*, San Francisco, USA, 5 pages.

Ueda, M. et al, 2019, What is this sound in dB? Pilot study on measuring the degrees of understanding of sound level in university students, *IEEE TALE 2019*, Yogyakarta, Indonesia, 6 pages.

TEACHING ROBOTICS DURING COVID-19: MACHINE LEARNING, SIMULATION, AND AWS DEEPRACER

Peter Holowka
West Point Grey Academy, Vancouver, British Columbia, Canada

ABSTRACT

COVID-19 presented a challenge to the traditional methods of teaching programming and robotics in a secondary school environment. When campuses were closed around the world in the spring of 2020, it was not possible for students to access the computer labs nor the robotics equipment that was traditionally used to facilitate the instruction of robotics programming units. This paper presents a design research project in which two secondary institutions in Canada and Turkey collaborated to teach computer science and robotics programming, specifically reinforcement learning, through the use of an online simulation environment. The two student cohorts in the study both were successful in developing reinforcement learning models for autonomous vehicles, despite not having any prior experience in machine learning nor artificial intelligence. The implications of this work are that physical robotics kits and dedicated robotics spaces are not essential to the teaching of programming and robotics. This is especially relevant to marginalized communities that do not have the resources to support robotics instruction, further exacerbating the digital divide.

KEYWORDS

Machine Learning, Artificial Intelligence, AWS DeepRacer, COVID-19, Simulation, Education

1. INTRODUCTION

The concept of Just in Time Learning (JITL) was initially primarily found in the context of professional and/or technical knowledge (Boese, 2016). The academic literature on this topic has recently expanded to include more formal education, including primary, secondary, and tertiary education (Khamis et al., 2019). JITL is defined as the acquisition of knowledge in response to an imminent problem or context requiring that knowledge. This paper will discuss the application of JITL as a means of educating and motivating secondary school students to learn Artificial Intelligence (AI) and Machine Learning (ML) during COVID-19. This work was conducted in the spring of 2020, during the height of the COVID-19 outbreak, within the challenging context of emergency remote instruction when access to physical robotics resources and computer labs was prohibited. Novice computer science students were successful in programming autonomous robotics vehicles, as well as learning the fundamentals of the Python programming language through the JITL approach. Moreover, the simulation environment enabled students to explore advanced topics in AI and ML as the simulation environment was free of many of the challenges that are characteristic of teaching with physical robotics kits. The advantages of using a simulation environment over physical robotics kits in a computer lab will be discussed further later in this paper.

1.1 Building upon a Foundation of Cloud Computing

In the spring of 2020, in response to the COVID-19 pandemic, physical school campuses were closed and students were required to attend school remotely. For many students, attending school meant interacting teachers through an online environment over the internet. This was the experience of the two cohorts in this design-based research project (Design-Based Research Collective, 2003; Zydney et al., 2020). One cohort was from a secondary school in Vancouver, Canada and consisted of seven students in the ninth grade. The other cohort was from a secondary school in Istanbul, Turkey and consisted of five students in the tenth and eleventh grades. The robotics and computer programming instruction for these two cohorts was delivered exclusively online using cloud computing. All students worked from their homes without access to school computers, robotics equipment, or specialized/licensed software. A combination of cloud computing tools was used to facilitate instruction. Zoom was used for synchronous video communication, hosted by the teacher. Google Classroom, Google Drive, and Google Docs were used for asynchronous document sharing and collaboration. The AI and ML simulation environment, AWS DeepRacer, was hosted on Amazon's public cloud platform as well.

This paper extends upon the author's earlier work concerning cloud computing in education within a Western Canadian context. The foundational work was an exhaustive study of all 75 large K-12 districts in Canada's three western-most provinces (Holowka , 2018). The study employed a data transformation mixed-methods triangulation design and captured the educational IT infrastructure serving over 1.14 million students (Creswell et al., 2003). The findings of the study revealed that Western Canada was a leader in the adoption of cloud computing globally with every school district employing several forms of cloud computing for their IT infrastructure. This early adoption of cloud computing now enables future cloud computing technologies, such as the online simulation environment for teaching AI and ML discussed in this paper. Moreover, the ubiquity of cloud computing in Western Canadian K-12 underscores the broad adoption possibilities for this simulation technology due to the existing IT infrastructure already available to students and their institutions. Similarly, the consistent internet access of the Istanbul cohort, as well as their success with this project, suggest that a shift to cloud computing-enabled instructional tools is an option for many schools around the world.

1.2 AWS DeepRacer

Amazon Web Services (AWS) AWS DeepRacer consists of two components: a physical 1/18th scale race car and an online simulation environment for programming the self-driving performance of the small scale race car (Balaji et al., 2019). Using AI and ML, users of the AWS DeepRacer console customize self-driving reinforcement learning models which they develop in the online simulation environment. These models can be transferred to the physical car for real-world testing, though this real-world testing is not required. Figure 1 shows the physical 1/18th scale race cars that contain a Linux operating system and a computer vision camera, in addition to a typical toy car electric motor drivetrain. Within the context of this paper, the use of AWS DeepRacer will refer to programming within the online simulation environment. This work did not use the physical race cars as they were inaccessible at the school due to COVID-19 restrictions. A discussion of the use of the physical cars occurs in the concluding section on future opportunities for research.

The AWS DeepRacer service incorporates multiple AWS services in order to create an environment for the development and testing of autonomous vehicles. These multiple AWS services include storage (AWS S3), compute (EC2), virtual environment creation tools (AWS Robomaker), and so forth (Balaji et al., 2019; Suenaga & Morioka, 2020). The integration of these discrete services into the single AWS DeepRacer service helps students learn complex AI and ML concepts with greater ease. If learning to program AI and ML can be likend to learning to drive a real car, then the use of AWS DeepRacer allows students to concentrate on their use of the brake pedal, rather than first trying to have them understand the theory behind how disc brakes work. The use of AWS DeepRacer in a secondary school educational setting embodies the JITL approach. Using AWS DeepRacer and JITL, students can focus on an immediate outcome they are trying to achieve, rather than being overwhelmed by the wide-ranging supporting individual components.

The use of AWS DeepRacer and JITL can be viewed as an alternative or modification of the conventional scaffolding approach used by educators. The classic use of scaffolding consists of students being guided through increasingly complex concepts and skills, with earlier work serving as a scaffolding for latter work (Hogan & Pressley, 1997). In this AWS DeepRacer application of JITL, students began with the seemingly complex task of programming a self-driving car. At the beginning, students had only a rudimentary understanding of how the multiple underlying AWS technologies functioned. However, with experience using the AWS DeepRacer environment, students gained familiarity with the integrated systems of the AWS DeepRacer plaform. Students are then encouraged to further optimize their cars' performance by more deeply investigating the individual supporting components of the integrated system. Similar to reverse engineering, students were invited to experiment by adjusting the underlying components. This AWS DeepRacer project revealed that once students gained an understanding of the basic operation of their model and the simulation environment, they were then motivated to investigate how the modification of individual supporting components could enhance their work.

Figure 1. Physical AWS DeepRacer cars that can run ML models trained in an online simulator

2. PROJECT GOALS AND STUDENT SKILLS

2.1 Cloud Computing Infrastructure

The purpose of the AWS DeepRacer unit was to introduce students to the fundamentals of computer science. This included an overview of cloud computing infrastructure and programming languages. The project began with the creation of individual student accounts, by the students themselves, in the AWS Console. Students created full AWS accounts and were introduced to the login process and the various services available by the instructor. Students were also given a lecture on ethics and the importance of cost management when using cloud computing services. The configuration of AWS DeepRacer was an authentic lesson about cloud computing using cloud computing.

2.2 Programming Languages and Python

The underlying motivation for the course and the AWS DeepRacer unit was to introduce students without prior programming experience to the fundamentals of computer science, namely to develop an understanding of programming languages such as Python. AWS DeepRacer provides a low-code environment where students can achieve success by using pre-populated reward function code. Students were first encouraged to pursue success by any approach, including the use of the pre-populated code library. This would serve as a baseline for student learning. Students were able to successfully complete the course task without fully understanding programming languages. This was the baseline and the aim for students was the mere completion of a simple oval track within the AWS DeepRacer simulator. Figure 2 presents the simulation environment for a simple oval track. Figure 3, in contrast, presents the simulation environment for a more complex track that students later used.

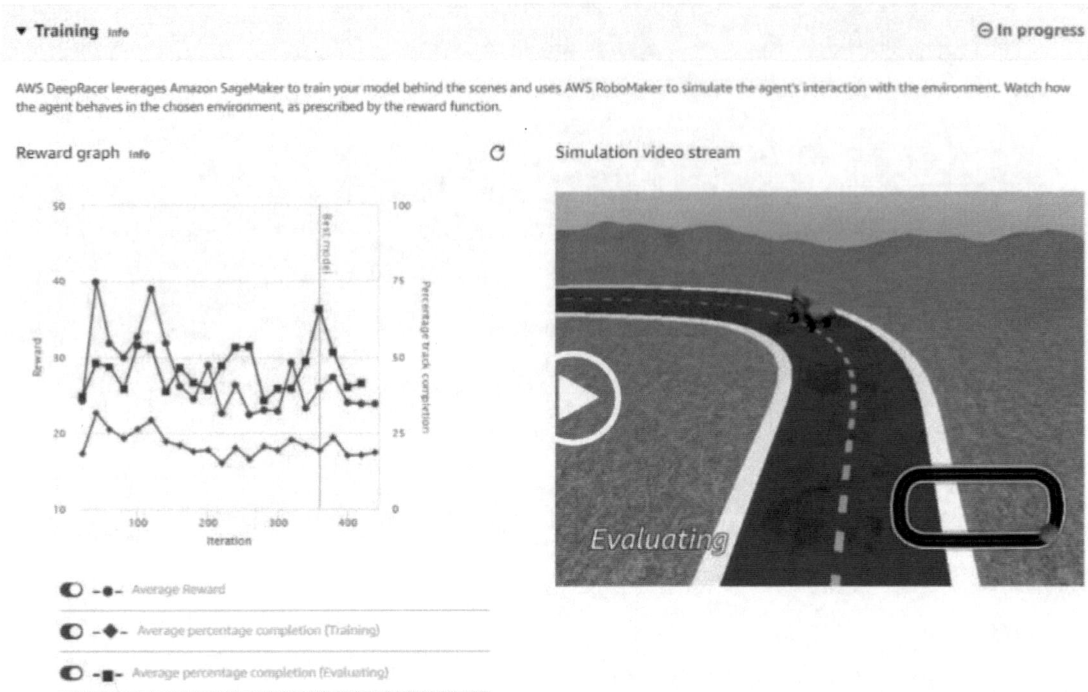

Figure 2. AWS DeepRacer model training and evaluation within simulation on a simple oval track

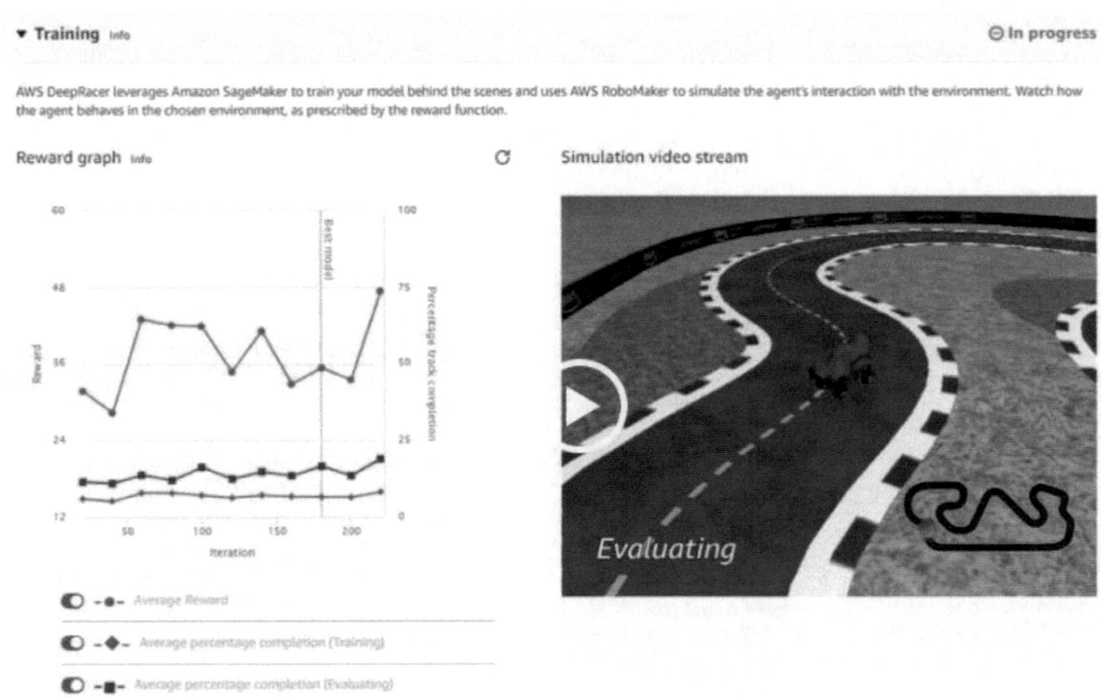

Figure 3. AWS DeepRacer model training and evaluation within simulation on a complex track

Using the synchronous and asynchronous cloud computing collaboration tools outlined earlier, students in the Vancouver and Istanbul cohorts exchanged ideas concerning how to improve their models and how to more quickly complete the simple oval track. Students reviewed the sample reward function code provided in the Python programming language and began to understand the code's structure. Similarly, they identified variable that they could change. An example of the Python reward function code for a successful reinforcement learning model is found in Figure 4. This code was initially developed for the simple oval track in Figure 2 but was then transferred to the more complex track in Figure 3.

Reward function

```
def reward_function(params):
    '''
    Example of rewarding the agent to follow center line
    '''

    # Read input parameters
    all_wheels_on_track = params['all_wheels_on_track']
    track_width = params['track_width']
    distance_from_center = params['distance_from_center']
    steps = params['steps']
    progress = params['progress']

    # Calculate 3 markers that are at varying distances away from the center line
    marker_1 = 0.01 * track_width
    marker_2 = 0.08 * track_width
    marker_3 = 0.2 * track_width
    marker_4 = 0.3 * track_width
    marker_5 = 0.5 * track_width

    #if all_wheels_on_track and (0.5*track_width - distance_from_center) >= 0.05:
    #     reward = 1.0

    # Total num of steps we want the car to finish the lap, it will vary depends on the track length
    TOTAL_NUM_STEPS = 10

    if (steps % 100) == 0 and progress > (steps / TOTAL_NUM_STEPS) * 100 :
        reward += 10.0

    # Give higher reward if the car is closer to center line and vice versa
    if all_wheels_on_track and distance_from_center <= marker_1:
        reward = 1.0
    elif all_wheels_on_track and distance_from_center <= marker_2:
        reward = 0.5
    elif distance_from_center <= marker_3:
        reward = 0.2
    elif distance_from_center <= marker_4:
        reward = 0.1
    elif distance_from_center <= marker_5:
        reward = 0.001
    else:
        reward = 1e-3  # likely crashed/ close to off track

    return float(reward)
```

Figure 4. An example of a successful AWS DeepRacer model reward function written in Python

2.3 Student Collaboration, Competition, and Success

The underlying goal of the AWS DeepRacer unit was to teach students robotics and programming skills. This was successful as each student in the course was able to iterate upon their reinforcement learning models and demonstrate an increased understanding of the Python programming language. By the end of the AWS DeepRacer unit, students were required to complete the following three tasks: 1) to successfully complete five virtual races on five different tracks within the simulation environment, 2) to develop a log of changes to their reward functions written in Python, and 3) provide an optional video reflection on their experience collaborating with peers, both locally and internationally. All students successfully completed the first two tasks and the majority of students completed the third.

The students demonstrated considerable growth in their understanding of the Python programming language and pursued advanced topics beyond the course's scope in order to achieve a higher position on the races' leaderboards. When students completed a track, their lap times were recorded automatically within the AWS DeepRacer Community Race Leaderboard. The competitive element of the activity, even though it did not have any relation to the course mark, provided added motivation and engagement for the students. Students took pride in leapfrogging each others' performance as they learned more advanced reinforcement learning strategies. Moreover, the leaderboards indicated the completion lap times for the students and was a helpful tool for showing the improvements in the performance of their AI/ML models.

An enabler of students' success was the open, collaborative nature of the activity. Students were required to produce a shared development log which detailed both successful ML models, as well as models which resulted in failure. The instructor modeled this activity by providing an open example for students to view using a shared Google Doc. The instructor included both working reward functions and reward functions that were unsuccessful. This openness modeled the collaborative scholarly process of research, as well as provided students with time-saving insights as to what strategies to avoid. The collaborative and social nature of this activity was often described as a positive aspect of the AWS DeepRacer exercise by the students in their reflection videos.

3. REIMAGINING ROBOTICS INSTRUCTION

COVID-19 exacerbated existing challenges pertaining to teaching robotics within a secondary school context. Prior to COVID-19, teaching computer programming for robotics was problematic because of the physical space required for the use of traditional robotics kits. When schools were moved to fully online instruction in the spring of 2020, access to such kits was further restricted. Prior to COVID-19, the Vancouver school shifted away from traditional robotics kits towards a cloud-based simulation environment for teaching programming and robotics. This approach resolved many of the challenges associated with teaching programming and robotics and made possible the international collaboration described in this paper. The success of this collaboration now serves as a guide, informing the teaching of programming and robotics in upcoming academic years.

3.1 Proprietary Physical Robotics Kit Limitations

The conventional means of teaching computer programming and robotics in many primary and secondary schools involves the use of physical robotics kits. These kits often contain proprietary components and kit/vendor-specific software that is not widely used in the IT industry (Vandevelde et al., 2013). Examples of such proprietary robotics kits include those made by VEX Robotics and Lego Mindstorms (Habib, 2012). Such kits are problematic for some schools in that they require a considerable initial financial outlay, physical storage space within the school, computers with licensed software through which to update the proprietary robotics controller hardware, maintenance of the computers which are used for the licensed software, maintenance/replacement of the robotics kits' parts, and consistent access to physical space for students to experiment with the physical robots. In many schools, the availability of physical space for such robotics activities would be at the expense of space for the enrollment of students. The challenges associated with physical robotics kits are considerable and can present a barrier to schools having any kind of robotics program and/or programming club.

3.2 Benefits of an Online Simulation Environment for Robotics Instruction

An online simulation environment for robotics instruction is free from all of the challenges associated with physical robotics kits outlined in the previous section. The shift from physical robotics kits towards virtual robots within an online simulation hosted in the cloud also yields benefits pertaining to instructional design. In addition to the space and equipment required for physical robotics kits, a considerable percentage of an activity's time involving such kits is often dedicated to the management of the physical components of the robot (e.g., plastic gears, wheels, etc.). The students' efforts go towards assembling and repairing the pieces of the robot, rather than developing and refining the code. In such an example, a considerable amount of time is spent by students on low-level assembly work rather than on the intended higher-level analysis of their code. The use of an online simulation environment means that students work nearly entirely on the programming of their vehicles and the code of their reward functions.

The use of an online simulation environment using cloud computing also allows students to work on their robotics projects at any time from any location with internet access. Students are able to log into the simulation environment from a web browser, such as Google Chrome, without the need for any other specialized software. Students can then experiment with the code of their model and run virtual training/evaluation sessions where they test the code. Educational initiatives by vendors, such as AWS Educate, give students free computational credits/hours resulting in no additional cost to students or their institutions.

As the testing of the code can take hours, students can also run these training/evaluation sessions unattended. Students can create a model training/evaluation, turn off their computer, and then review the results hours later. This is possible because the simulation runs entirely in the cloud, independent of the students' computer. This allows students to advance their robotics work at home and at school. This was a critical benefit during COVID-19 when schools were inaccessible. The simulation environment allowed students to engage fully in the robotics unit, in spite of not being able to access the school buildings.

3.3 Online Simulations Leading to Physical Robotics Testing

The use of online simulations for teaching students programming and robotics is meant to expedite the students' learning and not to serve as a complete replacement for physical robotics programming. The reality gap in robotics refers to the differences between simulations and reality (Collins et al., 2019; Koos et al., 2012). The AWS DeepRacer simulation environment is a training environment for reinforcement learning models which can later be downloaded to a robust physical small race car (Figure 1). Though this project did not involve the use of these physical cars, it is important to clarify that the online simulation environment is an accelerant for the development of student skills with robotics, rather than a purely virtual replacement with no connection to the real world. When students are ready, they can transfer their reinforcement learning models to the physical cars. The ability to explore and address the reality gap will be a valuable opportunity to extend their learning in the fields of robotics and programming.

4. CONCLUSION

The use of AWS DeepRacer during COVID-19 within a secondary school context was an emergency initiative that revealed the viability of using a simulation environment to teach a non-expert audience robotics, programming, AI, and ML. The initiative was successful in that all students were able to program working models for their simulation environments and complete multiple races/tracks. Students who had no prior experience with the Python language were able to modify/create the reinforcement learning code to improve their AI/ML car models. Students also engaged with concepts outside of the course's core curriculum in efforts to improve their models. This included modifying AI/ML hyperparameters and researching senior-level calculus to optimize the reward functions they had written in Python. As the majority of the students were in the ninth grade, this early effort to understand senior-level concepts in mathematics will hopefully allow them to make connections to the more advanced/abstract mathematical concepts they will encounter in future courses.

Limitations of this work pertain primarily to this project's relatively small size. As this was a pilot project, conducted in an emergency setting during the COVID-19, there are opportunities to expand upon this work in the future. Future studies can focus on replicating and expanding this study to better understand the efficacy of robotics instruction within a simulation environment. For example, a more experimental research design can be implemented where two cohorts of students are taught similar concepts of AI and ML. One cohort could be taught using a simulation environment such as AWS DeepRacer, while the other could be taught using more conventional, on-site-only methods with physical robotics kits. Quantitative analysis could be applied to examine the differences between the two groups, especially if multiple large cohorts can be engaged. Similarly, future research can be conducted into the reality gap and the challenges associated with transferring self-driving models from the AWS DeepRacer simulation environment to the physical cars.

A further opportunity for a future study may involve a simple replication of this work with a different cohort of students. It is possible that the success of this project was enabled by the very positive and perhaps exceptional nature of the students in this initial study's cohort. Future studies with different students, schools, and teachers would also yield valuable insights into the efficacy of using simulation environments to teach foundational robotics programming concepts.

ACKNOWLEDGEMENT

The author would like express his sincere gratitude to the two schools that participated in this project: West Point Grey Academy in Vancouver, British Columbia and Bahçeşehir Koleji in Istanbul, Turkey.

REFERENCES

Balaji, B., Mallya, S., Genc, S., Gupta, S., Dirac, L., Khare, V., Roy, G., Sun, T., Tao, Y., Townsend, B. and Calleja, E., 2019. AWS DeepRacer: Educational autonomous racing platform for experimentation with sim2real reinforcement learning. *arXiv preprint arXiv:1911.01562*.

Boese, E., 2016, February. Just-In-Time learning for the just Google it era. In *Proceedings of the 47th ACM Technical Symposium on Computing Science Education* (pp. 341-345).

Collins, J., Howard, D. and Leitner, J., 2019, May. Quantifying the reality gap in robotic manipulation tasks. In *2019 International Conference on Robotics and Automation (ICRA)* (pp. 6706-6712). IEEE.

Creswell, J.W., Plano Clark, V.L., Gutmann, M.L. and Hanson, W.E., 2003. Advanced mixed methods research designs. *Handbook of mixed methods in social and behavioral research*, *209*(240), pp.209-240.

Design-Based Research Collective, 2003. Design-based research: An emerging paradigm for educational inquiry. *Educational Researcher*, *32*(1), pp.5-8.

Habib, M.A., 2012. Starting a robotics program in your county. *Journal of Extension*, *50*(2), p.20.

Hogan, K.E. and Pressley, M.E., 1997. *Scaffolding student learning: Instructional approaches and issues*. Brookline Books. Cambridge, MA.

Holowka, P., 2018. 'IT leadership and cloud computing adoption in western Canadian K-12 school districts', doctoral dissertation, University of Calgary, Calgary, AB, DOI:10.11575/PRISM/32649.

Khamis, T., Gyn, G.V. and Rarieya, J., 2019. Introduction to the special issue of SOTL in the South: advancing student engagement in learning–experiences from Pakistan.

Koos, S., Mouret, J.B. and Doncieux, S., 2012. The transferability approach: Crossing the reality gap in evolutionary robotics. *IEEE Transactions on Evolutionary Computation*, *17*(1), pp.122-145.

Suenaga, R. and Morioka, K., 2020, January. Development of a Web-Based Education System for Deep Reinforcement Learning-Based Autonomous Mobile Robot Navigation in Real World. In *2020 IEEE/SICE International Symposium on System Integration (SII)* (pp. 1040-1045). IEEE.

Vandevelde, C., Saldien, J., Ciocci, M.C. and Vanderborght, B., 2013. Overview of technologies for building robots in the classroom. In *International Conference on Robotics in Education* (pp. 122-130).

Zydney, J.M., Warner, Z. and Angelone, L., 2020. Learning through experience: Using design based research to redesign protocols for blended synchronous learning environments. *Computers & Education*, *143*, p.103678.

THE EFFECTS OF AUGMENTED REALITY ON LEARNING PERFORMANCE AND COGNITIVE LOAD USING THE SPATIAL CONTINUITY PRINCIPLE

Xuewang Geng[1] and Masanori Yamada[2]
[1]*Graduate School of Human-Environment Studies, Kyushu University*
[2]*Faculty of Arts and Science, Kyushu University*
744 Motooka, Nishi-ku, Fukuoka 819-0395, Japan

ABSTRACT

In recent years, several studies have provided evidence for the positive impact of augmented reality in language acquisition. In particular, augmented reality as a multimedia learning environment has been found to be potentially more effective than learning using traditional methods, such as paper-based textbooks. According to the cognitive theory of multimedia learning, it can help reduce the extraneous cognitive load and improve learning by employing the spatial continuity principle. In this paper, the impact of the spatial continuity principle on the augmented reality learning system was tested by comparing the cognitive load and learning performance of two separate learning systems. The experimental results showed that the explanation integration system, which applies the principle of spatial continuity to the augmented reality learning system, was more effective in terms of knowledge retention. However, the results on the cognitive load contrasted previous research findings on the spatial continuity principle approach, as no differences were found in the extraneous cognitive load of the learners in the two systems.

KEYWORDS

Augmented Reality, Spatial Continuity Principle, Cognitive Load, Compound Verbs, Mobile Learning, Japanese Acquisition

1. INTRODUCTION

Advances in technology and the widespread use of smart mobile devices have transformed learning methods, making a variety of new approaches possible. Whereas traditional learning materials like textbooks are usually based on a static approach, visual technologies like augmented reality (AR) and virtual reality (VR) can interact with learners and make them experience learning contents directly (Ibáñez et al., 2016). By applying a combination of real world and virtual objects through the use of mobile devices, AR allows learners to experience them quickly and effectively without the need to wear specialized devices such as head-mounted displays.

Recently, research on the use of AR technology in education has received increasing attention and has been shown to promote motivation, increase satisfaction, make abstract or complex concepts easier to understand, and improve students' learning performance (Walczak et al., 2006; Ibrahim et al., 2018; Cabero-Almenara et al., 2019). In language acquisition, AR facilitates language learning by using more meaningful cues for the learner to see in the real world, while also integrating haptic and visual learning contents. As a multimedia learning environment, AR has been verified as being more effective for learning than text alone (Mayer, 2009). Santos et al. (2013) stated that AR learning by annotating objects is better than learning the same objects using paper-based textbooks. Therefore, AR systems have the potential to improve learning performance and knowledge retention compared to traditional learning methods, such as textbooks, in language acquisition.

The spatial continuity principle is one of the instructional design techniques for multimedia learning (Schroeder & Cenkci, 2018). Schroeder and Cenkci (2018) indicated that the spatial continuity design helps to reduce the extraneous cognitive load and improve learning. AR can easily integrate learning contents and additional information by attaching virtual content to learning objects. In contrast, other ineffective instructional designs may lead to distraction effects and thus increase the extraneous cognitive load (Sweller,

2010). This paper compares the learning performance and cognitive load of two AR systems to verify the effect of the spatial continuity principle.

This paper is organized as follows: a literature review on AR systems in language learning and the spatial continuity principle is conducted in Section 2. Section 3 presents the two AR learning systems and describes the research questions of this study. Section 4 justifies the methodology of this research. Section 5 describes the results and discusses these findings. Section 6 concludes the paper and proposes future lines of research.

2. LITERATURE REVIEW

2.1 AR Systems in Language Acquisition

Azuma (1997) defined three features of an AR system: the combination of real and virtual, real-time interaction, and being registered in 3D. In education, these features provide three main advantages: annotations of the real world, visualizations of context, and visualizations of vision-haptic (Santos et al., 2013). In turn, these advantages have the potential to facilitate employing AR in language acquisition. Boonbrahm et al. (2015) developed an AR application for learning the spellings and meanings of animal words. In the application, the learners can arrange letters to form a word that matches the name of the animal, and the 3D animal will be displayed on the application. Santos et al. (2016) developed and designed the two handheld AR systems for foreign vocabulary learning by using the surrounding spatial information. Moreover, Hsu (2017) developed the AR educational game to help third grade students learn English vocabulary. As such, many studies have concluded that AR systems have the potential to improve learning performance, as well as knowledge retention in language acquisition (e.g., Ibrahim et al., 2018; Hsu, 2017; Santos et al., 2016; Boonbrahm et al., 2015).

AR systems can be categorized into location-based and image-based systems. Location-based systems refer to the use of mobile devices' location services in relation to the recognition function. Image-based AR systems focus on image-recognition technology, and use real images as marks to identify objects that virtual information is attached to. Whether using the location-based or image-based AR system, Santos et al. (2013) stated that AR facilitates interaction with information, which assists learners in perceiving and remembering information.

In the specific case of the Japanese language, compound verbs are difficult learning items even for advanced learners (Matsuda, 2000). Japanese compound verbs are similar to phrasal verbs in English, and they are formed from two single verbs (see Figure 1; e.g., the compound verb *tori-hazusu* is formed from the single verbs *toru* and *hazusu*). The AR learning system was designed and developed to facilitate learning Japanese compound verbs based on the difficulties of compound verb acquisition (Geng & Yamada, 2019). It is an image-based AR system that displays the meaning of the verb with virtual information on the real verb characters.

2.2 The Spatial Continuity Principle

According to the cognitive theory of multimedia learning, since human working memory is limited, learners should have the cognitive ability to select information, organize relevant information, and integrate it within prior knowledge structures (Mayer, 2014). Consistent with the cognitive load theory (Sweller, 2010), Mayer (2014) indicated that there are three types of cognitive loads that arise when learners engage in cognitive processing during multimedia learning, namely, extraneous cognitive load, intrinsic cognitive load, and germane cognitive load. The intrinsic cognitive load is related to the complexity of information, the extraneous cognitive load is related to the design of materials, and the germane cognitive load is related to the acquisition of knowledge (Sweller, 2010).

Instructional design and learning materials affect learners' cognitive processes, thus interacting with the learning environment and the cognitive load experience (Paas & Sweller, 2014). The spatial continuity principle is one of the instructional design techniques developed using the cognitive theory of multimedia learning as a theoretical foundation (Schroeder & Cenkci, 2018). The principle of spatial continuity proposes that people learn more from multimedia messages when the corresponding words and pictures are close to each other on the page or screen rather than far away from each other, as this avoids the split-attention effect (Mayer & Fiorella, 2014). To solve the spatial separation, the physical distance between relevant information should be reduced by displaying the relevant information near the learning contents. In language acquisition, since the

AR features real-world annotations, words and visual information can be easily integrated to display them in the spatial vicinity. However, there are some contradictory results in terms of the spatial continuity principle. Schroeder and Cenkci (2018) indicated that spatial continuity design helps to reduce extraneous cognitive load and improve retention of learning. In spite of this, there are some studies that did not find the benefits of the spatial continuity principle (e.g., Florax and Ploetzner, 2010). Therefore, it is crucial to probe the cognitive load and learning performance of the AR learning system design based on the spatial continuity principle.

3. THE AR COMPOUND VERB LEARNING SYSTEM

In our previous research (Geng & Yamada, 2019; 2020), an AR learning system was designed and developed to facilitate the acquisition of Japanese compound verbs. Chen (2007) indicated that there are some difficulties in Japanese compound verb acquisition such as opacity in meaning: learners have difficulties understanding the meaning of compound verbs, and distinguishing between the meaning of compound verbs and the single verbs that form them. Therefore, the system is grounded on marker-based AR and shows learners the meaning of the verbs through 3D animations. In this system, learners can scan the verb cards and the animations of the verbs' meanings will be displayed on the card via the smartphone screen (see Figure 1). There are 11 cards printed with the characters of the single verb, which can be combined to form 8 compound verbs. In other words, learners learn single verbs by scanning the verb cards first, and then learn compound verbs consisting of two single verbs by correctly combining the two verb cards. This allows them to distinguish between a single verb and a compound verb by scanning and combining the cards to compare their meanings.

Regarding the meaning of verbs, animations as well as explanations and example sentences of the verbs are used to supplement verb learning in the system. Since the animations of verbs in this AR system (explanation separation system, hereafter referred to as ES) are spatially separated from the verb explanation materials, there are spatial split-attention effects in the system. We also developed a new system (explanation integration system, hereafter referred to as EI) based on the spatial continuity principle using the ES system to display verb explanations and animations on the same screen.

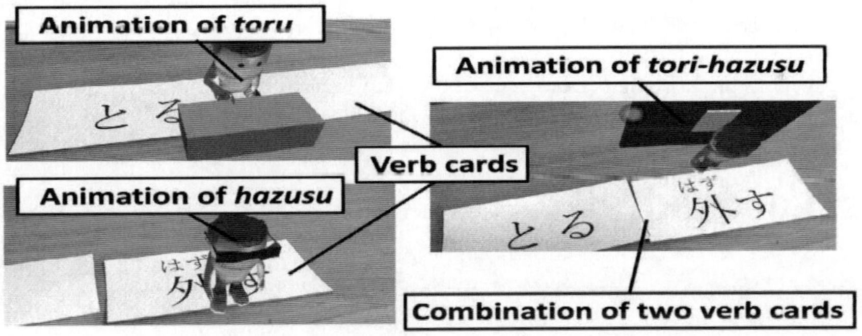

Figure 1. The verb card combinations of the AR learning system

3.1 ES System

In the ES system, verb explanations are provided to learners as paper-based learning materials to help them better understand the animation of verbs, and thereby learn compound verbs. As there is a spatial separation between the verb explanations and the animations, it is necessary to keep the verb cards on the screen while seeing the animations (see the image on the left in Figure 2). However, it is difficult for learners to refer to the learning materials while seeing the animations. In practice, learners tend to read the learning material before or after viewing the animations.

3.2 EI System

In contrast to the ES system, the EI system displays explanations of meanings on the screen of the smartphone. When the learners correctly scan the cards or combine the verb cards to form compound verbs, the explanations and animation of the compound verb meaning will be displayed on the screen (see the image on the right of Figure 2). The explanations of the verbs in the EI system is identical to the content of the paper-based learning materials in the ES system. The explanations and animations are both triggered at the same time. Therefore, learners must keep the verb cards on the screen while seeing the animations and explanations.

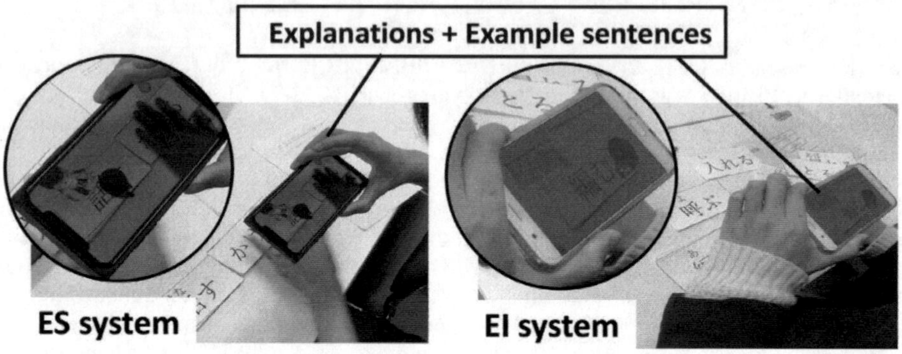

Figure 2. The usage of the ES system and the EI system

3.3 Research Questions

In this study, we investigated the effect of the spatial continuity principle by comparing the learning performance and cognitive load of these two AR language learning systems. For this purpose, we set the following two research questions.

RQ1: How does the learning performance of the EI system compare to the ES system?

RQ2: How does the perceived cognitive load of the EI system compare to the ES system?

4. METHODOLOGY

4.1 Participants

Two experiments were conducted in this study on the ES system and the EI system, respectively. The first experiment recruited ten participants and the second recruited thirteen participants, such that there were 23 participants in total. The participants were non-native Japanese speakers from China, Korea, Vietnam, Thailand, Cambodia, and other countries. However, they had an upper intermediate level of Japanese language proficiency, which meant that they could understand the explanations of the verbs provided in the experiments. Five male and five female participants took part in Experiment 1 and seven males and six females were included in Experiment 2. The age of all participants ranged from 18 to 30 years old.

4.2 The Experimental Procedure

Both Experiments 1 and 2 were 90-minutes long, and Experiment 2 was implemented a few months after Experiment 1. Both experiments were conducted using the same learning content and aimed to facilitate Japanese compound verb learning.

The procedure was basically the same for both experiments as shown in Figure 3. First, all participants were tested prior to the learning activity in order to assess their knowledge of compound and single verbs. All participants performed the learning activity for 40 minutes. However, participants in Experiment 1 used the learning material and the ES system to learn by scanning and combining cards, whereas participants in Experiment 2 did not need paper-based learning material during the learning activity. At the end of the learning activity, all participants took another test and the cognitive load questionnaire. Four weeks later, participants took a delayed test in Experiment 1. Due to COVID-19, participants in Experiment 2 took the delayed test only one week after the post-test.

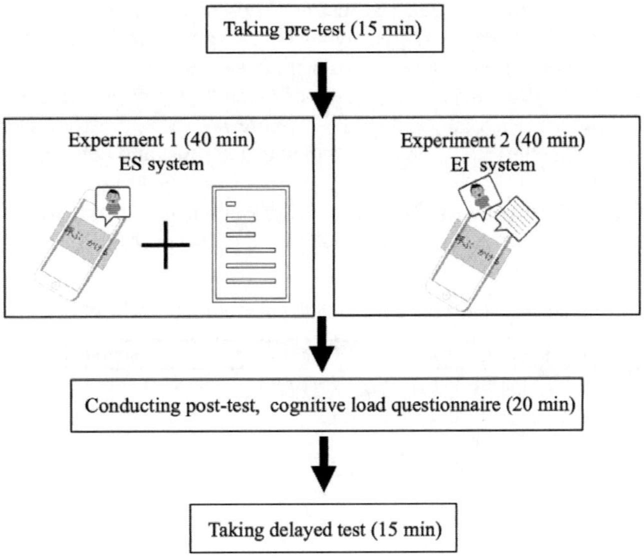

Figure 3. The procedure of the two experiments

4.3 Measuring Tools

The measuring tools in the study were composed of the pre-test, post-test, delayed test, and the cognitive load questionnaire. The pre, post, and delayed tests contained the same questions and options, but were presented in a different order. The tests consisted of two parts including fifteen true-or-false questions to judge the correct or incorrect options of the compound verbs and twenty-six multiple-choice questions to test the meaning of verbs. Each question was worth 1 point, and the total score for each test was 41 points.

The cognitive load questionnaire employed in this study was created by Leppink et al. (2013). The questionnaire measures the perceived cognitive load during the learning activity: intrinsic cognitive load, extraneous cognitive load, and germane cognitive load. It was performed using an 11-level Likert scale for ten questions (0 for completely disagree and 10 for completely agree). The intrinsic cognitive load consisted of three items on whether the compound verbs covered in the activity were complex. The extraneous cognitive load consisted of three questions on whether the explanations and AR system were clear and effective learning materials. Furthermore, there were four questions on the germane cognitive load (e.g., "The activity really enhanced my knowledge and understanding").

5. EXPERIMENTAL RESULTS AND DISCUSSION

5.1 How does the Learning Performance of the EI System Compare to the ES System?

The summary statistics for mean values, median values, and standard deviations of the two experiments' total scores on the pre-test, post-test, and delayed test are shown in Table 1. From Table 1, it appears that the pre-test scores of Experiment 1 were slightly higher than Experiment 2. Since the sample size was small and not normally distributed, non-parametric analyses were conducted in this study. Therefore, the Mann-Whitney U test was performed on the pre-tests of the two experiments to examine whether there was a difference in the participants' prior knowledge of compound verbs. There was no statistically significant difference of the pre-tests of the two experiments ($|Z| = 1.367$, n.s.). In addition, post and delayed test scores were higher in both experiments than in the pre-test.

The results of the two experiments showed that learners who used the AR learning systems of ES and EI improved their learning performance. These results further support the idea that the AR system is able to facilitate learning Japanese compound verbs.

Table 1. Mean, median, and SD values of the total scores in the three tests of the two experiment

Tests (total score: 41)	Experiment	Mean	Median	SD
Pre-test	Experiment 1	29.10	29.00	5.80
	Experiment 2	25.85	26.00	4.63
Post-test	Experiment 1	34.20	35.50	4.08
	Experiment 2	33.08	34.00	1.98
Delayed test	Experiment 1	31.90	32.00	5.22
	Experiment 2	33.69	34.00	4.25

We also conducted Mann-Whitney U tests on the change in test scores between the two experiments in order to verify the differences in learning performance using the ES and EI systems. The results of the Mann-Whitney U tests are shown in Table 2. Regarding the changes of scores between the post-test and the pre-test (post-test minus pre-test), no statistically significant differences were found between the two experiments. Conversely, there were significant differences in score changes between delay-pretests, and post-delay tests (changes in delayed test and pre-test scores : $|Z| = 2.434$, $p<.05$; changes in post-test and delayed test scores : $|Z| = 2.190$, $p<.05$).

Table 2. The Mann-Whitney U test results on changes in test scores

Changes in test scores	Experiment 1 (n=10)		Experiment 2 (n=13)		|Z|	p-value
	Mean	SD	Mean	SD		
Post - Pre	5.10	3.54	7.23	3.96	1.249	0.223
Delay -Pre	2.80	3.43	7.85	4.95	2.434^{*}	0.016
Post- Delay	2.30	2.79	-0.62	3.25	2.190^{*}	0.031

†p<1,*p< .05, **p < .01

As such, the current study found that learners using the EI system had greater changes between the delay-pretest, and smaller changes between post-delay test than learners using the ES system. Regarding the results of the change in test scores, it can be concluded that the EI system is more effective in terms of learners retaining knowledge. This finding supports evidence from the spatial continuity principle (Mayer, 2014). The EI system physically integrates the text into the visual display, reducing the split attention on the two information sources of verb explanation and animation compared to the ES system. This finding is contrary to previous studies which noted that interactive learning materials using the spatial continuity principle do not benefit as much as static and dynamic materials from spatial continuity design (Schroeder & Cenkci, 2018). However, the most important limitation lay in the different time intervals between the post-test and delayed test of the two experiments, due to the COVID-19 outbreak. Further research should control the time interval for consistency.

5.2 How does the Perceived Cognitive Load of the EI System Compare to the ES System?

The cognitive load questionnaire employed in this study measured the intrinsic cognitive load, extraneous cognitive load, and germane cognitive load, which the learners perceived using the ES or EI system. We analyzed the collected questionnaires and calculated three types of cognitive loads according to the answers of the related questions. The Mann-Whitney U-tests were performed to investigate the influence of ES and EI systems on the perceived cognitive load. The results are shown in Table 3. No statistically significant difference was found between the two experiments in terms of extraneous and germane cognitive load. However, it was found that the intrinsic cognitive load of Experiment 2 was higher than Experiment 1 at the significance value of 0.1.

Surprisingly, no differences were found between the extraneous cognitive load of the ES and EI system. Therefore, this finding was incompatible with the spatial continuity principle (Mayer, 2014). This study was unable to demonstrate that learners perceive less extraneous cognitive load using an AR system designed on the principle of spatial continuity. In contrast, there was a significant trend on intrinsic cognitive load of ES and EI system learners. The intrinsic cognitive load is determined by the complexity of the learning content and the learner's prior knowledge (Sweller, 2010). Based on a review of existing literature, Mayer and Fiorella (2014) concluded that the spatial continuity principle is most effective for learners with low prior knowledge. Although there was no difference between pre-test scores, there is indirect evidence supporting the fact that learners using the EI system retain knowledge better, as the intrinsic cognitive load of EI system learners was found to be higher. However, these results need to be explored further, because our experiments involved a low sample size. Furthermore, there is still a limitation in psychometric measures of cognitive load, since it is difficult for learners to clearly distinguish between different types of cognitive load (Schnotz & Kürschner, 2007).

Table 3. The Mann-Whitney U test results on cognitive load

Cognitive Load	Experiment 1 (n=10)		Experiment 2 (n=13)		|Z|	p-value
	Mean	SD	Mean	SD		
Intrinsic cognitive load	4.67	2.23	6.31	1.54	1.926†	0.058
Extraneous cognitive load	1.43	1.48	2.13	1.89	1.068	0.300
Germane cognitive load	7.66	1.63	7.27	1.29	0.281	0.803

†p<1,*p< .05, **p < .01

6. CONCLUSION AND FUTURE WORK

In this study, researchers explored the effects of the spatial continuity principle on the AR learning system by comparing the cognitive load and learning performance of two learning systems. We developed the EI system design based on the spatial continuity principle using the ES system. Two experiments were conducted to separately verify each system. The results of the experiments confirmed that learners using the EI system are more effective at retaining knowledge than learners of the ES system. This study also showed that there was a significant trend on intrinsic cognitive load, and no differences were found in the extraneous cognitive load of ES and EI system learners. However, the results need to be explored further by testing over a longer period of time and with a larger sample size. Furthermore, instead of relying on questionnaires to measure the cognitive load, other approaches should be used in future research. For example, behavioral assessments using learning analytics is a useful approach to investigating the relationships between learning processes and learning performances in terms of learner behaviors (e.g., Okubo et al, 2016; Kaneko et al, 2018).

ACKNOWLEDGEMENT

This research was supported in JSPS kaken-hi, Grant.No. JP18K18657, JP19H01716.

REFERENCES

Azuma, R. T., 1997. A survey of augmented reality. *Teleoperators & Virtual Environments*, Vol .6, No. 4, pp. 355-385.

Boonbrahm, S. et al, 2015. Using augmented reality technology in assisting English learning for primary school students. *In International Conference on Learning and Collaboration Technologies*, pp. 24-32.

Cabero-Almenara, J. et al, 2019. Adoption of augmented reality technology by university students. *Heliyon*, Vol. 5, No. 5, pp. 1-9.

Chen, X. 2007. Nihongo fukugoudousi no syutokujyoukyou to shidou hei no mondaiteiki (The acquisition of Japanese compound verbs and implications for teaching: An examination of "au" and "komu" at Xi'an Foreign Language University). *Forum of International Development Studies*, Vol. 35, No. 1, pp. 93-102.

Florax, M., and Ploetzner, R., 2010. What contributes to the split-attention effect? The role of text segmentation, picture labelling, and spatial proximity. *Learning and instruction,* Vol. 20, No. 3, pp. 216-224.

Geng, X., & Yamada, M., 2020. An augmented reality learning system for Japanese compound verbs: study of learning performance and cognitive load. *Smart Learning Environments*, Vol.7, No.1, pp. 1-19.

Geng, X., and Yamada, M., 2019. Development and design of a compound verb AR learning system employing image schemas. *In 15th International Conference on Mobile Learning 2019, ML 2019*, pp. 73-80.

Hsu, T. C., 2017. Learning English with augmented reality: Do learning styles matter? *Computers & Education,* Vol. 106, pp. 137-149.

Ibáñez, M. B. et al, 2016, The acceptance of learning augmented reality environments: A case study. *In 2016 IEEE 16th International Conference on Advanced Learning Technologies (ICALT)*, Austin, USA, pp. 307-311.

Ibrahim, A. et al, 2018. Arbis pictus: A study of vocabulary learning with augmented reality. IEEE Transactions on Visualization and Computer Graphics, Vol. 24, No. 11, pp. 2867-2874.

Kaneko, K. et al, (2018). Does physical activity enhance learning performance?: Learning effectiveness of game-based experiential learning for university library instruction. *The Journal of Academic Librarianship,* 44(5), pp. 569-581

Leppink, J. et al, 2013. Development of an instrument for measuring different types of cognitive load. *Behavior research methods*, Vol. 45, No. 4, pp. 1058-1072.

Matsuda, F. 2000. Fukuguodoushi no imi rikai houryaku no jittai to syutoku konnanten (Acquisition of compound verbs in Japanese by advanced learners of Japanese: Learners' strategies of comprehending the meanings of compound verbs). *Japanese Language Education*, Vol. 20, No. 1, pp. 52-65.

Mayer, R. E. 2014. *The Cambridge handbook of multimedia learning* (2nd ed.). Cambridge University Press, New York, USA

Mayer, R. E., 2009. *Multimedia learning* (2nd ed.). Cambridge University Press, New York, USA.

Mayer, R., and Fiorella, L., 2014. *Principles for Reducing Extraneous Processing in Multimedia Learning: Coherence, Signaling, Redundancy, Spatial Contiguity, and Temporal Contiguity Principles.* In R. Mayer (Ed.), The Cambridge Handbook of Multimedia Learning (Cambridge Handbooks in Psychology, pp. 279-315). Cambridge University Press, Cambridge, UK.

Okubo, F. et al, 2016, Learning Activity Features of High Performance Students, *Proc. of the 1st International Workshop on Learning Analytics Across Physical and Digital Spaces (Cross-LAK 2016),* Edinburgh, UK, pp. 28-33

Paas, F., and Sweller, J., 2014. Implications of cognitive load theory for multimedia learning. *The Cambridge Handbook of Multimedia Learning*, vol. 27, pp. 27-42.

Santos, M. E. C. et al, 2013. Augmented reality learning experiences: Survey of prototype design and evaluation. *IEEE Transactions on Learning Technologie*s, Vol. 7, No. 1, pp. 38-56.

Santos, M. E. C. et al, 2016. Augmented reality as multimedia: The case for situated vocabulary learning. *Research and Practice in Technology Enhanced Learning*, Vol. 11, No. 4, pp.1-23.

Schnotz, W., and Kürschner, C., 2007. A reconsideration of cognitive load theory. *Educational psychology review*, Vol. 19, No. 4, pp. 469-508.

Schroeder, N. L., and Cenkci, A. T. 2018., Spatial contiguity and spatial split-attention effects in multimedia learning environments: A meta-analysis. *Educ Psychol Rev,* Vol. 30, pp. 679-701

Sweller, J. 2010., Element interactivity and intrinsic, extraneous, and germane cognitive load. *Educational Psychology Review*, Vol. 22, No. 2, pp. 123-138.

Walczak, K. et al, 2006. Dynamic interactive VR network services for education. *In Proceedings of the ACM symposium on Virtual reality software and technology,* pp. 277-286.

PROTOTYPING A RETROSPECTIVE REVIEW SUPPORT FUNCTION FOR A FILL-IN WORKBOOK SYSTEM

Kousuke Abe[1], Tetsuo Tanaka[2] and Kazunori Matsumoto[2]
[1]*Course of Information and Computer Sciences, Graduate School of Engineering, Kanagawa Institute of Technology*
[2]*Dept. of Information and Computer Sciences, Faculty of Information Technology, Kanagawa Institute of Technology*
1030 Shimo-ogino, Atsugi, Kanagawa, 243-0292, Japan

ABSTRACT

The authors are developing and using a fill-in workbook system that allows faculty members to ascertain the attitude of all students to classes including students who are not active, and to improve lectures through well-timed and appropriate actions. In this paper, in order to help teachers improve lessons and teaching materials, and to help students review their own learning attitude, we propose functions for retrospective review. We focus on unfocused time, page transitions, number of keyboard operations and number of mouse clicks to extract the learning attitude of each student during the class. This function divides student's learning attitude into five categories, i.e. following the class and concentrated on it, following but not concentrated, jumping ahead, falling behind, and not participating. The system also provides visualization of changes in learning attitude during the class. It can be used for teacher's and students' retrospective review after the lecture.

KEYWORDS

Lecture Support, Fill-In Blanks, Learning Attitude, Log Analysis, Learning Analytics

1. INTRODUCTION

The computerization of higher education is progressing in, for example, the spread of LMSs (Learning Management Systems), which manage lecture materials and student reports on the Internet. In conjunction with this, learning analytics, which analyzes operation logs in LMSs and e-learning systems, is attracting attention. Learning analytics involves collecting a log of the learning process, to identify items such as which part of the material the student is learning, and when and for how long the student is learning. Analyzing this can contribute to class improvement and the provision of learning support(Ferguson, 2012, Kumar, 2018, Viberg, 2018, Diana, 2019, Verbert, 2020). Particularly in recent years, a real-time learning analysis environment that supports teachers and students in classrooms has been made possible by the development of wireless LANs in classrooms and the practice of "bring your own device" (BYOD), in which students bring their own laptops and other devices into the classroom (Shimada, 2018, Shimada, 2017, Fu, 2017).

The operation logs used in learning analytics mainly contain data on time and content such as turning the pages of teaching materials, underlines, memos, and questions. Therefore, it is possible to ascertain the status of engaged learners who actively underline, take notes, or ask questions. However, it is difficult to ascertain the status of many other students who attend classes but do not participate actively in learning.

Based on this background, the authors are developing a fill-in workbook system that will both allow faculty to ascertain the learning attitudes of all students, including those who are not active, and improve lectures through well-timed and appropriate actions, and also help students to understand lectures in an efficient manner. In a class using this system, students are provided with materials containing blanks to be filled in, and they engage in the lesson while filling the blanks in the materials. The operation logs are collected and analyzed and teachers and students receive feedback. This system compels students in class to interact with the system and makes it possible to collect the learning activities of students who are not active in class.

The authors have already reported on the function and configuration of the system (Abe, 2018), and the results of a trial using the system in a small class. A trial of about 90 students engaged in one lesson and extraction of class attitudes and the degree of understanding from system logs were reported in (Abe, 2019).

In (Abe, 2020), we reported the results of using this system continuously over multiple lessons of a single course.

On the basis of the results of the analysis so far, and in order to help teachers improve lessons and teaching materials and to help students review their own learning attitude, in this paper we propose specific functions for retrospective review. In Section 2, we summarize the operation logs and analysis target. Section 3 describes a method of extracting changes in each student's learning attitude for each lesson and for each time interval / each slide in the lesson for the entire class. Prototype retrospective review support functions are described Section 4.

2. ANALYSIS TARGET

In this study, in order to collect the learning behavior logs, we use a fill-in workbook system that the authors are developing. Before a lesson using this system, teachers create teaching materials by uploading PDF documents to which blanks are added in important sentences. In the lesson, teachers peel off the blank revealing the answer with the relevant explanations.

Students fill in the blanks while referring to these materials in a screen like that shown in Figure 1. The blanks filled with correct answer are opened. The operation logs are recorded in the database. In the teacher's screen (see example Figure 2) the results of analyzing the operation logs and extracting the learning attitudes are shown visually and presented to the teacher in real time.

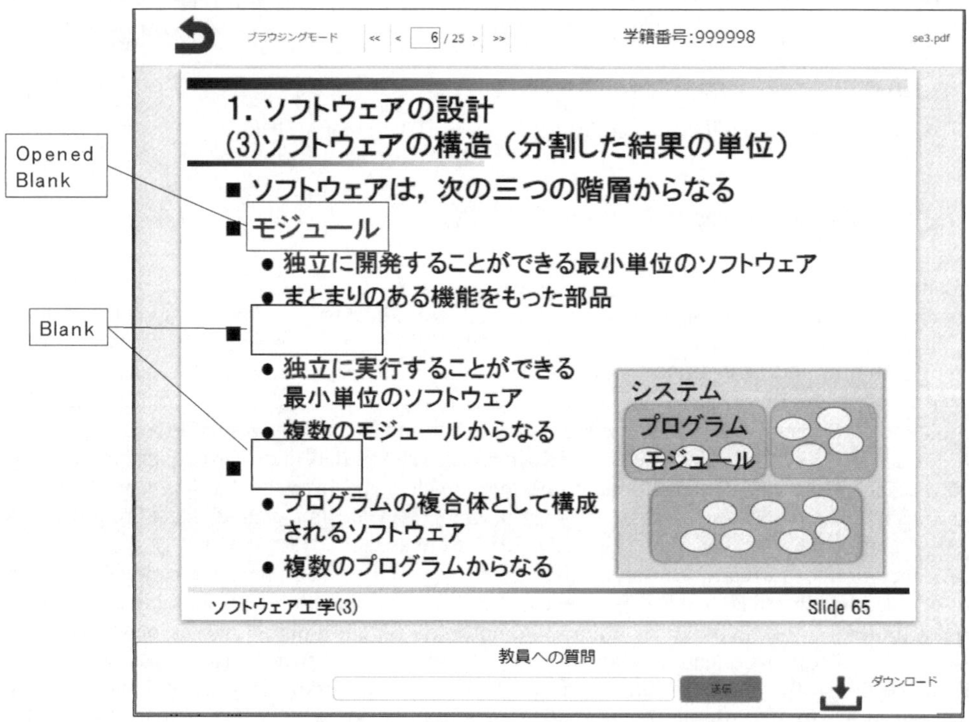

Figure 1. Example of student's screen

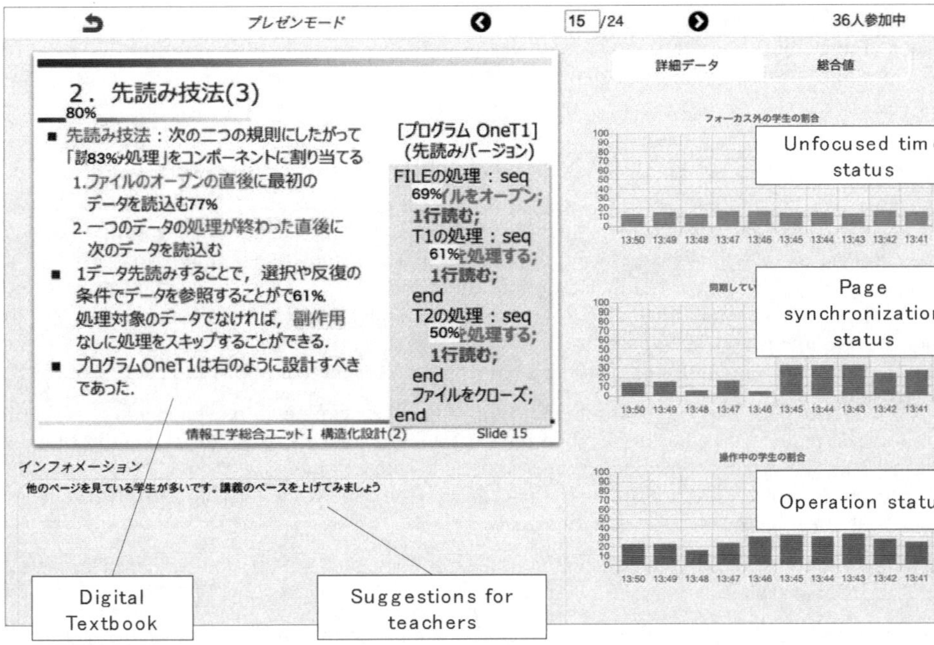

Figure 2. Example of teacher's screen

By using the system, students are compelled to interact with the system, and the operation logs of inactive students (students who do not actively participate in learning activities by, for example, underlining and writing notes) can be acquired. If teachers can effectively assess the student's learning attitude in real time during class, they can then take actions that encourage students to concentrate whenever the number of students with a poor learning attitude is seen to increase.

The items in the operation logs collected using this system are as follows:

- Fill-in blanks: Content and time of each answer written in the blank space, and whether answers are correct or incorrect
- Underlining: Underline position
- Notes: Note position and content
- Operation logs: Page focus time, number of mouse operations, number of keyboard operations per minute
- Page turning details: Time and destination page numbers
- Question details: Content of questions asked by students during class

In addition, a log of the teacher's operations is also compiled and can be used to compare course progress with the student's operation log. The teacher's operation log includes the following items:

- Page turning details: Time and destination page numbers
- Blanks peeled off (displaying correct answer): Peel-off times and identifiers of blanks peeled off

In analyzing the results of this study, we focused on the degree of synchronization between the teacher's slide transition and the student's slide transition, the number of keystrokes and mouse clicks, and unfocused time that is the time during which the student does not focus on the system – as collected by the learning behavior log as an indicator of overall class attitude.

The analysis was based on data collected during 90 minutes of actual lectures conducted by one faculty as follows:

- Software Engineering
  subject related to software development methods
  90 students from the Department of Information and Computer Sciences 2nd grade

- Introduction to Software
  subject related to algorithms and data structures
  130 students from the Department of Information and Computer Sciences 1st grade

3. METHOD OF EXTRACTING LEARNING ATTITUDES

In order to support the teacher's and the student's review of the class, changes in the attitude of each student during the class are extracted. We focus on unfocused time, page transitions, number of keyboard operations and number of mouse clicks to extract the attitude of each student during the class as follows:

- A student who is synchronized with the teacher's page transition most of the time and there is no unfocused time is considered to be attentive. unfocused time is the time during which the student does not focus on the system, for example, a student is opening another application such as to check email.
- The reference page may be synchronized with the teacher's explanation even in a time period with many unfocused periods. In addition, keyboard operations are also being performed a short time after page transition. The student at this time seems to be in a state of looking at the material without listening to the teacher's explanation, and filling in the blanks on the page while looking at the teacher's presentation material immediately after turning the page.
- Students jumping ahead are not listening to the teacher's explanation, that is, their learning attitude can be regarded as bad.
- Students falling behind can also be considered as not being able to keep up with the pace of the lecture, or sleeping or doing other things and not listening to the teacher's explanation. These can be distinguished by the presence or absence of operations.
- There may be a time period during which there is no page transition or operation for an extended period. During this time, the pages being explained by the teacher contain blanks, so it is necessary to fill in the gaps, but there are no operations and no page transition. It can be assumed that during this time the student is doing other things or sleeping without paying attention to the lecture.

To summarize the above, students' learning attitudes can be divided into the five categories shown in Table 1 based on unfocused time, page transitions, keyboard operations, and mouse clicks.

Table 1. Correspondence between operation log and learning attitude

	Learning Attitude	Unfocused time	Keystroke, Mouse click	Page transition
1.Excellen	Following and concentrated	Less than 30 seconds per minute	-	Synchronized
2.Good	Following but not concentrated	30 seconds or more per minute	-	Synchronized
3.Fair	Jumping ahead	-	-	Jumping ahead
4.Poor	Falling behind	-	Yes	Falling behind
5.Bad	Not participating	-	No	Falling behind

4. RETROSPECTIVE REVIEW FUNCTION

4.1 Function for Students

By presenting the transition of learning attitude to the students in the form of a retrospective review after the lecture, they can be made aware of the problems during the lecture and become more conscious of their learning attitude. We prototyped the retrospective review function.

Figure 3 shows an example of the retrospective review screen. The horizontal axis is the time from the start of the lesson, measured every minute. The bar graph at the top shows the unfocused time; the green line graph is the page being explained by the teacher, and the gray line graph is the page being referenced by the student. The left vertical axis corresponds to a line graph with page numbers, and the right vertical axis corresponds to a bar graph showing unfocused time (seconds). The middle part of Figure 3 is a line graph showing the learning attitude. The bottom bar graph shows the total number of mouse clicks and keyboard operations per minute.

This allows students to look back on their class attitude after class. For example, the students can find out in which part of the lesson they could not keep up with the teacher's explanation, or if they had a lapse in concentration. Thereby they can focus on reviewing that part, or ask other students/teachers about that part.

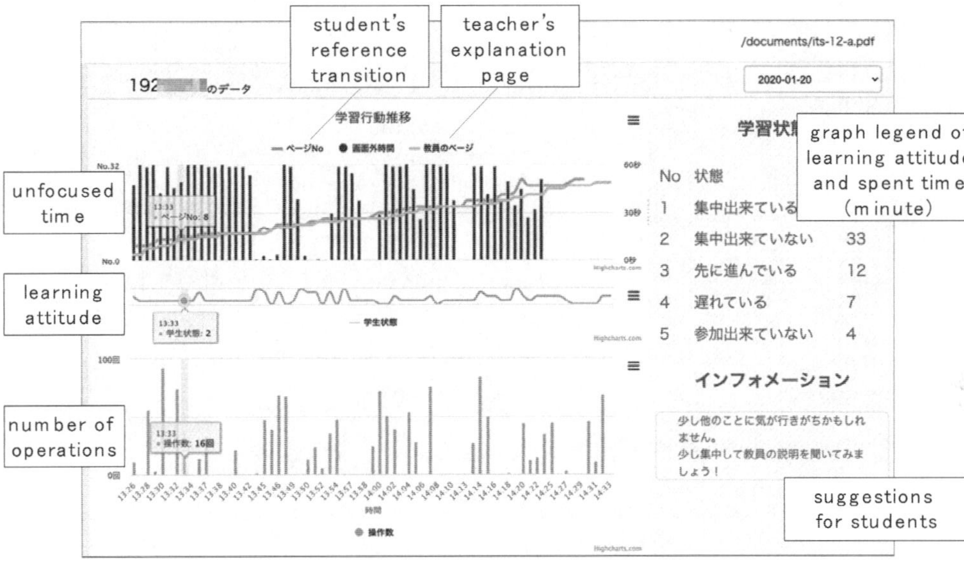

Figure 3. Example of retrospective review screen for students

4.2 Function for Teachers

This system provides the function of creating a time sequence aggregate learning attitude chart by totaling the learning attitudes of all students described in the previous section, and the function of presenting it to the teacher. This will allow teachers to improve their lessons. For example, if many students are late in class, the teacher can slow down the class or explain the material in more detail. After class, the teacher can improve teaching materials during the time when many students are late. In addition, individual guidance can be given such as selecting students who tend to be late and giving them advice.

Figure 4 shows a review screen for teachers. The horizontal axis is time. The upper bar graph shows the ratio of the five learning states at each time. This allows the teachers to understand how the student's learning status is changing. The lower bar graph shows the value of the learning attitude index (LAindex) expressed by the following formula at each time.

$$\text{LAindex} = \frac{(LA_2 + 2LA_3 + 3LA_4 + 4LA_5)}{4N} \times 100$$

$$LA_i : number\ of\ students\ of\ status\ i\ in\ Table1$$

$$\text{N: number of students}$$

Furthermore, the points where the LA index sharply rises are displayed in yellow, and the points where the high LA index continues are displayed in pink. These are the points that teachers should pay attention to.

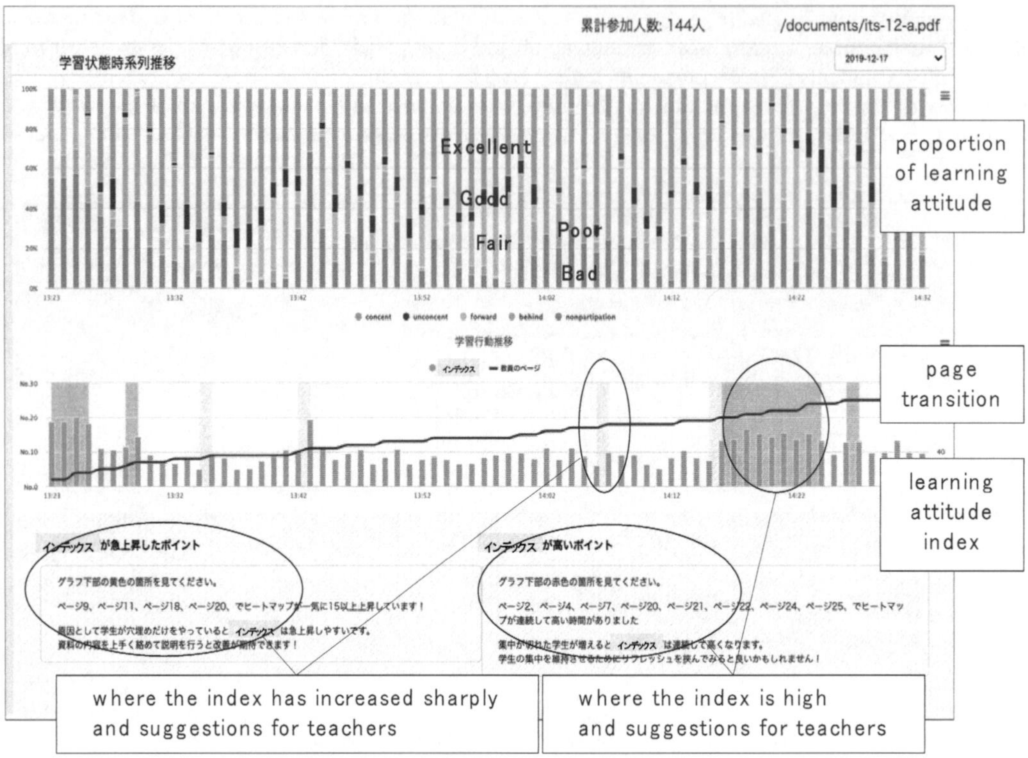

Figure 4. Example of retrospective review screen for teachers

5. CONCLUSION

In order to help teachers improve lessons and teaching materials, and to help students review their own learning attitude, we propose functions for retrospective review. We focus on unfocused time, page transitions, number of keyboard operations and number of mouse clicks to extract the learning attitude of each student in the class. This function divides student's learning attitude into five categories: following the class and concentrated; following but not concentrated; jumping ahead; falling behind; and not participating. It also visualizes changes in learning attitude during the class. It can be used for the teacher's and the students' retrospective review after the lecture.

The verification of the validity of the relationship between the operation log and the learning attitude is a future task. The learning attitude judged from the operation log will be presented to the students, and it will be verified by questionnaire whether or not they agree with the students' own senses. Furthermore, the results will be compared with the results of the method of estimating class attitudes proposed in other studies.

ACKNOWLEDGMENT

This work was supported by JSPS KAKENHI Grant Number JP20K03078.

REFERENCES

Abe, K. et al, 2018. Lecture Support System using Digital Textbook for Filling in Blanks to Visualize Student Learning Behavior, *In International Journal of Education and Learning Systems*, Vol.3, pp. 138-144.

Abe, K. et al, 2019. Analysis of Learning Behavior Logs based on a Fill-in Workbook System - Toward Real-time Learning Analytics -, *In International Journal of Education and Information Technologies*, Vol. 13, 2019, pp. 154-159.

Abe, K. et al, 2020. Learning Attitude Analysis based on Operation Log of Fill-in Workbook System, *Proceedings of IIAI 9th International Congress on Advanced Applied Informatics,* Online, to appear.

Diana, M. et al, 2019. A Visual Dashboard to Track Learning Analytics for Educational Cloud Computing, *In Sensors*, 19.

Ferguson, R., 2012. Learning analytics: drivers, developments and challenges. *In International Journal of Technology Enhanced Learning*, 4(5/6) pp. 304–317.

Fu, X. et al, 2017. Real-time learning analytics for C programming language courses, *Proceedings of the Seventh International Learning Analytics & Knowledge (LAK '17)*, Vancouver in Canada, pp. 280-288.

Kumar, K. and Vivekanandan, V., 2018. Advancing learning through smart learning analytics: a review of case studies, *In Asian Association of Open Universities Journal*, Vol. 13 No. 1, pp. 1-12.

Shimada, A. and Konomi, A., 2017. A Lecture Supporting System Based on Real-time Learning Analytics, *Proceedings of CELDA2017*, Vilamoura, Algarve, Portugal, pp. 197-204.

Shimada, A. et al, 2018. Real-time learning analytics system for improvement of on-site lectures, *In Interactive Technology and Smart Education*, Vol.15, No. 4, pp. 314-331.

Verbert, K. et al, 2020. Learning analytics dashboards: the past, the present and the future, *Proceedings of the Tenth International Conference on Learning Analytics & Knowledge (LAK '20)*, Cyberspace, pp. 35–40.

Viberg, O. et al, 2018. The current landscape of learning analytics in higher education, *In Computers in Human Behavior* 89, pp. 98-110.

THE ANALYSIS OF PISA TEST 2018 ON STUDENT PERCEPTION OF READING OBJECTIVE, HOW IS INDONESIAN STUDENTS?

Safari Safari, Asrijanty Asrijanty, Rahmawati Rahmawati and Bagus Hary Prakoso
Center for Assessment and Learning, Ministry of Education and Culture
Jl. Gunung Sahari Raya No. 4, Jakarta, 10710, Indonesia

ABSTRACT

The purposes of the study are to know the students' perceptions of reading objective among students, which have above and below the average score of the OECD countries, and to know the Indonesian'student achievement among other countries. The study uses a quantitative method as a research method, and to determine the position of Indonesian students, it used M-Plus and Winsteps program. PISA 2018 data which has been released are used for research development purposes. The data were taken from questionnaires who were answered by 15th-year-students of 80 countries. The data consist of 612.004 international students and 12.098 Indonesian students. The results of the Analysis of Variance states that there was a significant difference (P <0,000) of students' perceptions of reading objectives among students in countries which have above and below the average score of the OECD. While based on the analysis of Rasch Model, the reliability of Indonesian students was 0.36 while international data 0.51. Although they both are low, the reliability of Indonesian students is lower. The study concludes that the most students' states both (upper and below group) "Disagree" if the purpose of reading is only to fulfill obligations, merely hobbies, and spend time. Afterwards, students state "Agree" to discuss books with others and obtain the required information.

KEYWORDS

Perception, Students, Reading Objective, PISA

1. INTRODUCTION

Literacy problems in assessing Indonesian education can refer to the results of the Program for International Student Assessment (PISA). The science and mathematics literacy index of Indonesian students increased significantly by 21 and 11 points respectively: 382 points in 2012 to 403 in 2015, and 375 points in 2012 and 386 in 2015. Meanwhile, the reading literacy index only increased by one points: 396 in 2012, 397 in 2015, and dropped to 371 in 2018 (ranked 72nd out of 78 countries). Therefore, this study focuses only on the position of Indonesia.

This achievement dissatisfaction occurs due to several reasons related to test content, student competence, computer-based models, and learning models that do not encourage exploratory reading strategies (Kompas News, 2017). Other findings support the importance of reading habits for academic achievement (Owusu-Acheaw & Larson, 2014), Wan Dollah et al. (2017). To identify reading habits, certain investigations are needed, such as how students perceive reading goals in the PISA test. Guay et al. (2010) found that girls have higher intrinsic motivation to read and write than boys. The results of this study are the same as the research results of other experts. Reardon, et al. (2018) conducted research on gender disparities in United States school districts and reported that gender attainment gaps exist among school districts. Sindik (2011) conducted a study on gender differences in the use of learning strategies for adult foreign language learners at the American Academy of Management and Technology. This study reported significant gender differences in the use of learning strategies. Fergusson and Horwood (1997) study of gender differences in educational achievement in the New Zealand birth cohort reported statistically significant gender differences in academic achievement. Igbudu (2015) conducted a study on the influence of gender on student academic achievement in government subjects in public high school schools in the Oredo Regional Government area of

Edo State. All of these studies show that there is a significant gender difference in academic achievement, namely that women perform better than men.

In the PISA questionnaire 2018, questions related to the reading objective are code ST160 (ST160Q011A, ST160Q021A, ST160Q031A, ST160Q041A, and ST160Q051. How much do you agree or disagree with the statement about the objective of reading e.g.: (1) reading only for obligations, (2) is a favorite / hobby, (3) discussing books with others, (4) just wasting time, (5) to obtain the required information. Actually the reading objectives are more than five. In PISA 2018, it focuses on those five objectives only. According to Grabe (2009), there are 9 objectives of reading, namely: reading to find information, reading for rapid understanding, reading to learn, reading to integrate information, reading to evaluate, criticizing and using information, and reading for general understanding, cases, reading for interest or reading to entertain.

The reading objective is "the intention to combine complex processes" (Grabe, 2004, p. 14), which combines understanding: text, parts, paragraphs even books and the ability to understand and find out information presented in written text (Nasri & Namaziandost, 2019). The understanding of reading between students is different due to the different process … (Brantmeier, 2005). Every student has different goals in reading activities. This goal is important because it is closely related to the level of completeness of student competencies that must be possessed by each student. The level of completeness of competencies (knowledge, skills, and attitudes) can mostly only be obtained through reading activities. The results of Par's study (2020) showed there was a significant correlation between overall use of reading strategies and student reading achievement. The more students apply problem solving strategies in reading activities, the better their ability to understand texts. Therefore, this study only focuses on the variable students' reading objectives which were asked in the 2018 PISA test questionnaire.

Abidin (2017: 56) argues that reading was very helpful for students to obtain or meet their needs in the form of knowledge, information, experience, skills, and so on. Talwiasih (2019: 61) suggests that reading was an activity or cognitive process that seeks to find various information contained in writing. Putra, Purwadi, and Wulandari (2017: 234) explained that reading was a language skill that is related to other language skills. But the main object of the purpose of reading is the book. Books were a storehouse of knowledge, reading was the key, (Tosepu, 2018). Most curricula in schools do not provide sufficient time to develop reading skills, (Grabe, 2002). Its implementation in classroom learning must use a strategy of "reading efficiency" (Lin, 2008, 2009b). The efficiency of reading depends on the strategies and the reading method models used.

Parents of students and teachers in schools were the main supporters of students in providing motivation to read. Pachtman and Wilson (2006) stated that it was very important to motivate students to read by giving them the opportunity to choose their material of interest because one of the most important factors that helps learners read further was reading motivation and has an important impact on reading comprehension (Hairul, Ahmadi , and Pourhosein, 2012). According to Guthrie and Wigfield (2000), reading motivation was the great enthusiasm of students in learning who must consider positive or negative ideas about reading.

Referring the various descriptions, the study focuses on whether there are differences on perception of reading objective between students come from countries with above and below the average score of the PISA 2018 test.

2. RESEARCH METHOD

The method used is quantitative method. The basis for using this method is adjusted to the main purpose of this study, namely obtaining facts from existing symptoms and factually finding facts based on research data. This research uses PISA 2018 data that has been released to the public and has been permitted. The study population was 15 year old students taking the 2018 study, while the sample was 15 year old students who took PISA tests in 80 countries. The reason for choosing the sample was students who took the PISA test in 2018.

The data used is in the form of a questionnaire with four choices (strongly disagree, disagree, agree, and strongly agree) which were answered by 6,124 students from 80 countries, and answered by 1,2098 Indonesian students. The questions in the questionnaire related to the purpose of reading are (1) obligations, (2) hobbies / interests, (3) like talking about other people's books, (4) wasting time, (5) just to get the information needed.

There were 22 countries on PISA test results for reading tests have above an average score of the OECD (487) are: Canada, Switzerland, Czech Republic, Germany, Denmark, Estonia, Finland, France, United Kingdom, Hong Kong, Ireland, Japan, Korea, Macao, Norway, New Zealand, Poland, Portugal, BSJZ (China), Singapore, Sweden, Chinese Taipei, and the United States. While the countries with below the average score of the OECD are 58 countries: Albania, United Arab Emirates, Argentina, Austria, Belgium, Bulgaria, Bosnia and Herzegovina, Belarus, Brazil, Brunei Darussalam, Chile, Colombia, Costa Rica, Dominican Republic, Spain, Georgia, Greece, Croatia, Hungary, Indonesia, Iceland, Islael, Italy, Jordan, Kazakhstan, Kosovo, Lebanon, Lithuania, Luxembourg, Latvia, Morocco, Moldova, Mexico, North Macedonia, Malta, Montenegro, Malaysia, Netherlands, Panama, Peru, Philippines, Qatar, Azerbaijan, Moscow Region, Tatarstan, Romania, Russian Federation, Saudi Arabia, Serbia, Slovak Republic, Slovenia, Thailand, Turkey , Ukraine, Uruguay and Vietnam (Gurria, Secretary General OECD, 2019).

The analytical method used in this research is analysis of variance. This analysis is used to calculate differences in the perceptions of students, both women and men, on all reading objective between the countries with have above and below average score of the OECD. So that the results of the analysis of this study can be obtained accurately, then all data in this study are processed or analyzed using the SPSS 22.00 program. In addition, to determine the position of Indonesian students, the data were analyzed by using M-Plus and Winsteps Programs.

3. RESEARCH RESULT

Here are the percentage of students (612.004 people) from 80 countries who have filled out the PISA questionnaire.

Table 1. Percentage of Students on Reading Objective Both Groups (above and below group)

N	Aspect	I read only if I have to		My favourite hobbies		Talking about books with other people		Reading is a waste of time		Get information that I need	
		F	%	F	%	F	%	F	%	F	%
1.	Strongly disagree	129886	21,2	124665	20,4	125491	20,5	211385	34,5	97585	15,9
2.	Disagree	186853	30,5	183939	30,1	183241	29,9	227256	37,1	181240	29,6
3.	Agree	173651	28,4	180841	29,5	191778	31,3	86087	14,1	206311	33,7
4.	Strongly agree	83841	13,7	81307	13,3	68932	11,3	46280	7,6	87113	14,2

Table 1 informs that most students state "Disagree" if the purpose of reading is only to: (1) fulfill obligations, (2) merely hobbies, (3) spend time, but most students' state "Agree" to: (1) discuss books with people others and (2) obtain the required information. However, statements of students who are in countries above the OECD average (insufficient data shown here), most stated "Agree" if the purpose of reading to: (1) fulfill obligations, (2) channel hobbies, (3) discuss books with other people, (4) spending time, and (5) obtaining the information needed. Statements of students who are in the countries below the OECD average, most say "Agree" if the purpose of reading is to: (1) hobbies, (2) discuss books with others, and (3) get the necessary information, but most students state "Disagree" to: (1) fulfill obligations and (2) spend time.

Table 2. Results of Analysis of Variance on Students' Reading Objectives Differences in Countries Above and Below the OECD Average Value

No.	Source	Type III Sum of Squares	df	Mean Square	F	Sig.
1.	I read only if I have to	952,258	1	952,258	976,300	,000
2.	My favourite hobbies	5077,764	1	5077,764	5349,222	,000
3.	Talking about books with other people	4022,488	1	4022,488	4440,938	,000
4.	Reading is a waste of time	1793,262	1	1793,262	2138,060	,000
5.	Get information that I need	617,904	1	617,904	690,852	,000

Table 2 informs that based on the results of the analysis of variance shows that there are differences in the perceptions of students to reading objective between the countries above and below the average score of the OECD (P <0.05).

4. DISCUSSION

The results showed that the difference in students' perceptions of reading goals between countries that had a mean score above and below the OECD was evident (P <0.05). Most students stated "Disagree" if the purpose of reading was only to: (1) fulfill an obligation, (2) just a hobby, (3) spend time, but most students stated "Agree" to: (1) discuss books with other people and (2) obtain the necessary information. Let's take a look at the following examples of Indonesian students analyzed with Mplus. The main objective is to determine the relationship between variables in this study.

Figure 1 is PISA 2018 data for Indonesian students analyzed by the Mplus program version 8.2 which aims to determine the position of Indonesian students.

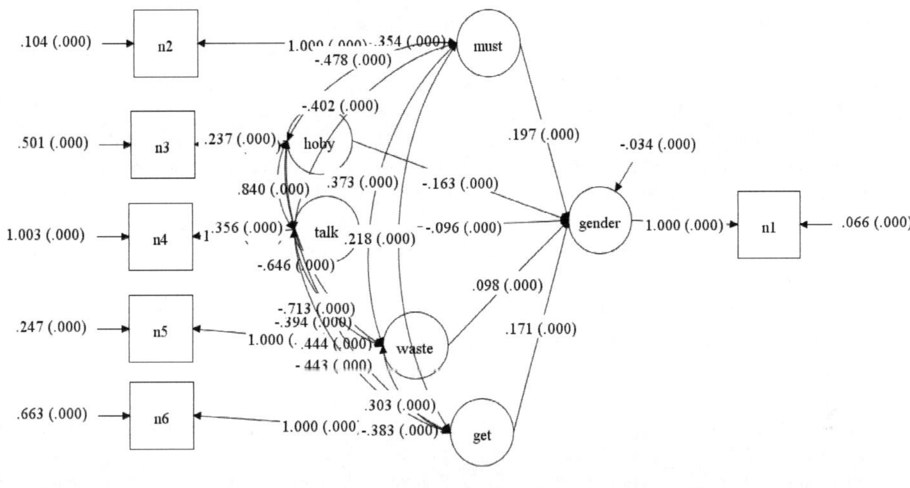

Figure 1. Relationship between Reading Objective and Gender (Indonesian Students)

Based on Figure 1, the reading objectives of Indonesian students (male and female) start from the smallest because: (1) a hobby or hobby (hobby) with a loading factor of -0.163; (2) discussing other people's books (talk) with a loading factor of -0.096; (3) lazy to read books because they spend time (wasteful) with a loading factor of 0.098; (4) reading only looking for the information needed to lead (get) with a loading factor of 0.171; (5) reading due to obligation (must) with a loading factor of 0.197. To determine the reliability of items and people from the perception data of international and Indonesian students, they were analyzed using the Rasch Model (see Table 3 and Table 4).

Table 3. Results of Rasch Model Analysis on Indonesian Student Data

PERSON	12025 INPUT	12025 MEASURED			INFIT		OUTFIT	
	TOTAL	COUNT	MEASURE	REALSE	IMNSQ	ZSTD	OMNSQ	ZSTD
MEAN	12.6	5.0	-1.56	.70	.96	-.2	1.02	-.1
S.D.	4.0	.0	.91	.19	1.10	1.2	1.31	1.4
REAL RMSE	.73	TRUE SD	.54	SEPARATION	.75	PERSON RELIABILITY		.36
ITEM	5 INPUT	5 MEASURED			INFIT		OUTFIT	
	TOTAL	COUNT	MEASURE	REALSE	IMNSQ	ZSTD	OMNSQ	ZSTD
MEAN	30237.6	12025.0	.00	.01	1.21	5.1	3.76	8.0
S.D.	4851.7	.0	.78	.00	.25	3.2	2.79	3.8
REAL RMSE	.01	TRUE SD	.78	SEPARATION	57.66	ITEM	RELIABILITY	1.00

Table 4. Results of Rasch Model Analysis in International Data

PERSON 599780 INPUT 599780 MEASURED					INFIT		OUTFIT	
	TOTAL	COUNT	MEASURE	REALSE	IMNSQ	ZSTD	OMNSQ	ZSTD
MEAN	12.9	5.0	-1.20	.57	1.00	-.2	1.01	-.2
S.D.	6.2	.0	.85	.19	.94	1.4	.99	1.4
REAL RMSE	.60 TRUE SD		.61 SEPARATION	1.02	PERSON RELIABILITY			.51
ITEM 5 INPUT 5 MEASURED					INFIT		OUTFIT	
	TOTAL	COUNT	MEASURE	REALSE	IMNSQ	ZSTD	OMNSQ	ZSTD
MEAN	1551669.6	599780.0	.00	.00	1.05	2.0	1.01	1.8
S.D.	106661.8	.0	.20	.00	.18	9.7	.18	9.6
REAL RMSE	.00 TRUE SD		.20 SEPARATION	140.6	ITEM RELIABILITY			1.00

Refering to Table 3 and Table 4, the reliability of Indonesian students is 0.36, and international students is 0.51. Although both are low, the reliability of Indonesian students is lower. Based on the two results of this analysis, there were students who have reading objective were only to fulfill obligations. Although most of the students (30.5%) expressed disagreement and 21.2% stated strongly disagree, however the second most statement that were 28.4% of students stated agree and 13.7% students stated strongly agree. There were two groups here who agree. This means that this group agrees that the reading objective is to fulfill obligations. The second group stated that they did not agree if the reading objective was only to fulfill obligations. Both should be to fulfill the obligation or not that the reading objective takes precedence.

It shows that most students have begun to realize that reading objective is not just to fulfill obligations such as reading assigned by the teacher at school but for personal or individual needs. It could be students who agree and strongly agree because at school they rarely get an explanation from their teacher, so interest in reading is still limited or depends on the assignment at school. This is in accordance with Rohman (2017) research results that the lack of independence of reading students, in learning at school because teachers rarely foster the interest in reading in children and the obstacles that are often faced in learning in children.

The results of Par's study (2020) also stated emphatically that most students rarely read because the majority of them spend less than 2 hours each day for reading. They were content to read only when were given an assignment or when an exam was near. Students were not given a problem solving strategy in reading so many students were incomplete in reading. The more students who applied problem solving strategies in reading activities, the better their ability to understand texts. So, in order to be successful in learning, students must read widely and apply effective reading strategies to construct the meaning of texts, (Denton et al., 2015).

Such conditions will affect other reading goals, such as reading purposes only for pleasure / hobbies. Even though most of the students (30.1%) and (20.4%) stated that they disagreed and strongly disagreed, many students (29.5%) and (13.3%) who agreed and strongly agreed. Another example is the purpose of reading to discuss books that are read with others. Although most students (31.3%) and (11.3%) agreed and strongly agreed, many students (29.9%) and 20.5%) stated that they did not agree and strongly disagreed. There were also students who have the notion that reading activities only consume time. Most students (37.1%) and (34.5%) expressed disagreement and strongly disagree, but many students (14.1%) and (7.6%) stated agreed and strongly agreed. In general, the reading objective was only to obtain important information. Although most of the students (33.7%) and (14.2%) agreed and strongly agreed, many students (29.6%) and (15.9%) stated that they did not agree and strongly disagreed.

What's more with the continued development of technology. Students also really need guidance in reading strategies with computers because the exams are now all computer based. Although the research of Mangen et al. (2020) shows that students who have read text in printed form were significantly better at reading comprehension tests than students who read text digitally (Mangen, et al., 2020). Many students were slower when reading from a screen than from paper (Muter et al., 1982; Mayes, Sims, & Koonce, 2001). But current technological developments show that the digital revolution has greatly influenced daily life. Proven in the existence of mobile devices and seamless integration of technology into general tasks such as shopping, reading, and finding direction (Anderson, 2016; Smith & Anderson, 2016; Zickuhr & Raine, 2014). The use of computers, mobile devices, and the internet are at the highest level to date and are expected to continue to increase because technology is becoming more accessible, especially for users in developing countries (Poushter, 2016).

5. CONCLUSION

The study has some conclusions that (1) Most students state "Disagree" if the reading objectives are only: (a) to fulfill obligations, (b) merely hobbies, (c) spend time, but most students state "Agree" to: (a) discuss book with other people and (b) obtain the required information. (2) Students come from countries with above average of the OECD, most state "Agree" if the reading objective are to: (a) fulfill obligations, (b) channel hobbies, (c) discuss books with other people, (d) spending time, and (e) obtaining the information needed. While students come from countries with below average the OECD, most state "Agree" if the reading objective are to: (a) hobbies, (b) discuss books with others, and (c) get the necessary information, but most students state "Disagree" to: (a) fulfill obligations and (b) spend time.

Based on the results of variance analysis, there are differences in the perceptions of students both women and men towards all reading objective between the countries with above and below the average score of the OECD. Indonesian students have a common sequence of reading objective (hobbies or favorites, discussing other people's books, spending time, and when searching for the information needed, and because of obligations at school). The reliability of Indonesian students is 0.36 while the international data is 0.51. Although both are low, the reliability of Indonesian students is still lower.

5.1 Suggestions

The study has some suggestions are as follows. First, teachers should be familiar with reading independence with students, and provided with problem solving strategies in reading. Second, teachers should reflect the benefits of reading in everyday life. Third, parents should teach their children to start reading from an early age and should provide reading material. Forth, government should introduce reading literacy of the PISA Test model for students at school.

ACKNOWLEDGMENT

The authors would like to thank the OECD for releasing PISA data every period for which the data used for this study. In addition, the authors would like to thank colleagues at the Center for Assessment and Learning, Agency of Research and Development, Ministry of Education and Culture who have provided input, suggestions, and comments in order to be contributive article.
Note. Safari is main contributor of the study in research method and discussions.

REFERENCES

Abidin, Z., 2017. Meningkatkan Keterampilan Membaca Siswa Kelas XI IPA~6 melalui Metode SQ3R SMA Negeri 1 Bontonompo, Kecamatan Bontonompo, Kabupaten Gowa. *Jurnal Nalar Pendidikan, 5(1), hal. 55-63.*

Ahmadi, M. R., & Pourhosein Gilakjani, A., 2012. Reciprocal Teaching Strategies and Their Impacts on English Reading Comprehension. Theory and Practice in Language Studies, 2(10), 2053-2060.

Anderson, M. (2016). More Americans using smartphones for getting directions, streaming TV. Washington, D.C.: Pew Research Center. Retrieved from http://www.pewresearch.org/fact-tank/2016/01/29/us-smartphone-use/.

Brantmeier, C., 2005. Effects of readers' knowledge, text type and test type on L1 and L2 reading comprehension in Spanish. *The Modern Language Journal, 8 (9), 37–53.* https://doi.org/10.1111/j.0026-7902.2005. 00264.x

Carrell, P. L., 1989. Metacognitive Awareness and Second Language Reading. *Modern Language Journal, 73, 120– 133.*

Denton, C. A., Wolters, C. A., York, M. J., Swanson, E., Kulez, P. A, & Francis, D. J. (2015)., Adolescents' use of reading comprehension strategies: Differences related to reading proficiency, grade level, and gender. Learning and Individual Differences, 37, 81-95. DOI: 10.1016/j.lindif.2014.11.016.

Dollah, W. A. K. W., Fakeh, S. S. K.W, Kamal Rafedzi, E. R., Ibrahim, A., Rahim, H., Masron, M. Z. A & Ibrahim, M. R. (2017). Inculcating reading habits among secondary school students. *Journal of Scientific and Engineering Research, JSAER, Pageno: 407, vol: 4, issues: 8*

Fergusson, D.M. & Horwood, L.J. (1997). Gender differences in educational achievement in a New Zealand birth cohort. New Zealand Journal of Educational Studies 32(1), 83 -96.Köymen, B., & Tomasello, M. (2018). Children's meta-talk in their collaborative decision making with peers. Journal of Experimental Child Psychology, 166, 549–566. https://doi.org/10.1016/j.jecp.2017.09.018

Grabe, W., 2004. Research on the teaching reading. *Annual Review of Applied Linguistics, 24(5), 44–69.* https://doi.org/10.1017/S0267190504000030.

Grabe, W., 2009. Reading in a second language: Moving from theory to practice. Cambridge University Press.

Guay, F., Chanal, J., Ratelle, C. F., Marsh, H. W., Larose, S., & Boivin, M. (2010). Intrinsic, Identified, and Controlled Types of Motivation for School Subjects in Young Elementary School Children. *British Journal of Educational Psychology*, 80(4), 711–735.

Guria, A. (2019). PISA 2018: Insights and Interpretations, Andreas Schleicher. OECD.

Guthrie, J. T., & Wigfield, A., 2000. Engagement and Motivation in Reading. In M. L. Kamil, P. B. Mosenthal, P. D. Pearson, and R. Barr (Eds.), Handbook of Reading Research. (Vol. III, pp. 403-22). Mahwah, NJ: Lawrence Erlbaum Associates.

Igbudu, U. (2015). Influence of gender on student academic achievement of government subject in public secondary schools in Oredo Local Government of Edo State, Nigeria. *Journal of Educational and Social Research* 5(2), 2015. Doi: 10.5901/jesr. 2015.v5n2p101.

Joseph, B.O., 2020. Evaluating Reading Habit among Junior Secondary School Students in Ekiti State in Nigeria. IJOLE: *International Journal of Language Education, Vol. 4, No. 1, 2020.* ISSN (Print) 2548-8457, ISSN (Online) 2548-8465.

Mangen, A.; Walgermo, BR.; and Bronnick, KK., 2020. Reading Linear Texts on Paper versus Computer Screen: Effects on Reading Comprehension. *International Journal of Educational Research, 58:61-68*·December 2013 *with* 28,670 Reads, DOI: 10.1016/j.ijer.2012.12.002

Mayes, D. K., Sims, V. K., & Koonce, J. M., 2001. Comprehension and workload differences for VDT and paper-based reading. *International Journal of Industrial Ergonomics, 28, 367-378.*

Muter, P., Latremouille, S. A., Treurniet, W. C. & Beam, P., 1982. Extended reading of continuous text on television screens. *Human Factors, 24 (5), 501-508.*

Nasri, M., & Namaziandost, E., 2019. The impact of topic choice on descriptive writing ability among Iranian advanced EFL learners. *International Journal of English Language Studies (IJELS), 1(1), 1–9.* http://ijels.one/wpcontent/uploads/2019/11/The-Impact-of-TopicChoice-on-Descriptive-Writing-Ability-Among-IranianAdvanced-EFL-Learners-converted.pdf.

Owusu-Acheaw, M., & Larson, A. G. (2014). Reading habits among students and its effect on academic performance: a study of students of Koforidua polytechnic. Library Philosophy and Practice, 0_1.

Pachtman, A. B., & Wilson, K. A., 2006. What Do the Kids Think? The Reading Teacher, 59(7), 680-684.

Par, L., 2020. The Relationship between Reading Strategies and Reading Achievement of the EFL Students. *International Journal of Instruction, 13(2), 223-238.* https://doi.org/10.29333/iji.2020.13216a.

Putra, W.A.P, Purwadi, A.J., Wulandari, C., 2017. Pembelajaran Keterampilan Membaca di Kelas VII B SMP Negeri 9 Kota Bengkulu Tahun Ajaran 2016/2017. *Jurnal Ilmiah Korpus, 1(II), hal. 233-247.*

Reardon, S.F., Fahle, E.M., Kalogrides, D., Podolsky, A., & Zarate, R.C. (2018). Gender achievement gaps in U.S School Districts (CEPA working paper No. 18-13). Retrieved from Stanford Centre for Education Policy Analysis http://cepa.stanford.edu/wp18-13.

Rohman, S., 2017. Membangun Budaya Membaca Pada Anak Melalui Program Gerakan Literasi Sekolah. TERAMPIL *Jurnal Pendidikan dan Pembelajaran Dasar, Volume 4 Nomor 1 Juni 2017 p-ISSN 2355-1925 e-ISSN 2580-8915.*

Sindik, J. (2011). Gender differences in the use of learning strategies in adult foreign language learners. *Metodicki Obzoni* 6(1), 2011. Doi:10.32728/mo.06.1.2011.01.

Smith, A., & Anderson, M., 2016. *Online Shopping and E-Commerce*. Washington, D.C.: Pew Research Center Retrieved from http://www.pewinternet.org/2016/12/19/online-shopping-and-e-commerce/.

Stanovich, K. E., 1980. Toward an Interactive-Compensatory Model of Individual Differences in the Development of Reading Fluency. *Reading Research Quarterly, 16(1), 32-71.*

Talwiasih, S., 2019. Peningkatan Keterampilan Membaca Permulaan melalui Media Big Book SD Negeri 2 Karangsoko Kecamatan Trenggalek. *Jurnal Pendidikan: Riset dan Konseptual, 3(1), hal. 61-64.*

Tosepu, YA. (2018). Membaca yang Menjadikan Buku Bermanfaat. http://yusrintosepu.wixsite.com/yoes/single-post/2018/10/10/Membaca-yang-Membuat-Buku-Bermanfaat.

Zickuhr, K., & Raine, L. (2014). *E-reading rises as device ownership jumps*. Washington, D.C.: Pew Research Center Retrieved from http://www.pewinternet.org/2014/01/16/e-reading-rises-as-device-ownership-jumps/.

A GRAPHIC ORGANIZER FOR SUPPORTING SUMMARY WRITING IN WEB-BASED INVESTIGATIVE LEARNING

Oriko Harada and Akihiro Kashihara
Graduate School of Informatics and Engineering, The University of Electro-Communications
1-5-1, Chofugaoka, Chofu, 182-8585, Tokyo, Japan

ABSTRACT

Web-based investigative learning is a form of learning where learners investigate Web resources to construct knowledge on a question. In our previous work, we have designed a learning model and a cognitive tool named iLSB to support learners in expanding the initial question into sub-questions so as to deepen and widen their investigation, and in creating their own learning scenario. The learning model consists of two processes of "knowledge construction" and "knowledge linearization". Learners are expected to construct knowledge using iLSB in the former process, and to linearize their knowledge to prepare a paper for report on their investigation in the latter process In this paper, we focus on how to help learners to make a summary of the paper by means of graphic organizers, which embed five types of information structure in expository text. This paper demonstrates how iLSB allows learners to build text structure of a summary with graphic organizers. We also report a case study whose purpose was to assess the effectiveness of it. The results suggest that graphic organizers function effectively as a scaffold for building comprehensive summary with fewer efforts.

KEYWORDS

Web-Based Investigative Learning, Summary Writing, Graphic Organizer, Learner-Created Learning Scenario

1. INTRODUCTION

The Web opens people to new opportunities for knowledge acquisition, and the skill in exploring information effectively is becoming ever more important. As such, learning systems that targets searching information on the Web are becoming more widespread in educational settings (Chen et al, 2006). On the other hand, unstructured information on the Web poses a challenge for learners to explore and select relevant information to restructure in a meaningful manner (Lawless et al, 1997). While learners have more freedom over navigation between information they explore (Lawless et al, 1997), they are required to constantly keep a mental model of the navigation path in order to effectively learn and build knowledge (Henze and Nejdl, 2001).

Recent related work on navigation on the Web to construct knowledge has been focused on modeling learners (Jeong, 2016; Lau et al, 2017). On the other hand, little is done on modeling navigational learning on the Web, with which this paper deals. Given this background, we have defined Web-based investigative learning (WBIL for short) as a form of learning where learners use search engines to investigate any question with Web resources to construct knowledge. We have also considered ways to support learners by designing a learning model and a cognitive tool named interactive Learning Scenario Builder (iLSB for short).

In our previous work, two main challenges for learners to conduct WBIL were identified (Kashihara and Akiyama, 2016). First, learners tended to use a single search query to investigate on a given question, and looked no further than several prioritized Web resources/pages of the search results. Investigation in this manner leads to a narrow viewpoint for the question, and induces learners to construct superficial and shallow knowledge. To construct comprehensive knowledge on the question, learners must deepen and widen their investigation by expanding the initial question into related sub-questions, and constructing knowledge for each sub-question. In navigating between Web resources for each sub-question, in addition, learners also need to keep track of the path between sub-questions. This suggests the lack of a learning scenario in investigating on the Web (Kashihara and Akiyama, 2016). While traditional learning resources such as textbooks and lectures provide a linearly organized information (Lawless et al, 1997), there is no pre-defined sequence for exploring information on the Web. Learners must accordingly create their own learning scenario while navigating Web resources, which is the second challenge in WBIL.

To address these challenges, we have designed a learning model for WBIL consisting of "knowledge construction process" and "knowledge linearization process", and developed iLSB (Kashihara and Akiyama, 2016). In the learning model, learners begin with an initial question to investigate, expand it into sub-questions from knowledge constructed from the initial question, and cyclically repeat their investigation for each sub-question. iLSB encourages learners to make a wider and deeper investigation in a systematic way, and to build their learning scenario in a self-directed way. Our previous work with iLSB has confirmed that iLSB could help learners create their own learning scenario while navigating Web resources, and linearize their knowledge by creating a table of contents for a paper for reporting their findings (Kashihara and Akiyama, 2016; Hagiwara et al, 2019; Kashihara et al, 2020; Morishita et al, 2020). On the other hand, support for writing the actual contents of the paper and assessment of the paper have not been done yet.

To address these, this paper proposes a systematic method of writing a summary of the paper. The summary is intended to act as an advance organizer for the paper. It could inform the readers (instructors or peers) what to expect from the paper, which is necessary for learners to clearly convey their findings to the readers. However, writing a summary in a comprehensive and concise way is not an easy task.

A summary of WBIL is one example of an expository text. Compared with narrative text, expository text is a non-fiction text whose objective is to convey information. According to Roehling et al. (2017), an expository text embeds information structure that can be categorized into one of the following five types: *description*, *sequence and order*, *cause and effect*, *compare and contrast*, and *problem and solution*. Roehling et al. (2017) also introduces graphic organizers as a way to teach learners to make expository text with the five types, which graphically represent the corresponding information structure with nodes and edges.

In this paper, we use graphic organizers to help learners make a summary of the paper for their learning scenario created with iLSB. We also propose a method for learners to construct text structure to be embedded into a summary with graphic organizers, which is implemented within iLSB. This paper also describes a case study with it. The results suggest that graphical organizers function effectively as scaffold for constructing comprehensive summary with fewer efforts.

2. WEB-BASED INVESTIGATIVE LEARNING

2.1 Learning Model

This paper proposes a learning model for Web-based investigative learning (WBIL), which consists of the following two processes: (1) knowledge construction process and (2) knowledge linearization process. Each process further has several learning phases. The learning model designed in our previous work (Kashihara and Akiyama, 2016; Kashihara et al, 2020; Hagiwara et al, 2019) corresponds to (1). In our subsequent work (Morishita, 2020) and this paper, we are attempting to extend this model to include (2).

2.1.1 Knowledge Construction Process

In the knowledge construction process, learners investigate a question (initial question), which is often represented such as "What is X?" They are then expected to search and explore Web resources by means of search engine with keyword (called q-keyword) representing the question and to build comprehensive knowledge. Such knowledge construction process is composed of the following three phases (Kashihara and Akiyama, 2016): (1-a) search for Web resources, (1-b) navigational learning, and (1-c) question expansion.

In (1-a), learners are expected to search Web resources with the initial q-keyword. Using the searched results, they are next expected to compare multiple resources to find out Web pages suitable for understanding the initial question. In (1-b), learners are expected to navigate and learn the Web pages, and to combine the contents learned at each page and construct their knowledge. In the model, learners extract keywords from the Web pages representing the contents learned to make connections among these keywords in constructing their knowledge for the corresponding q-keyword. In (1-c), learners are expected to find out sub-questions to be further investigated from knowledge constructed. In other words, learners expand the initial question into sub-questions. They are expected to cyclically repeat the three phases for each sub-question until no further question expansion occurs. The question expansion results in a tree structure called question tree as shown in Figure 1, which represents learning scenario for learners' WBIL. The root node corresponds to the initial q-keyword, and the other nodes correspond to q-keywords representing the corresponding sub-questions.

2.1.2 Knowledge Linearization Process

In the knowledge linearization process, learners are expected to write a paper from their learning scenario (question tree) created in the knowledge construction process. It includes findings in their investigation and its summary. In writing a paper, they are allowed to use their question tree to linearize their knowledge constructed. We have developed a support for learners to generate table of contents (TOC) from question tree (Morishita, 2020). TOC has a hierarchical structure, in which each node corresponds to q-keyword in the question tree. The nodes represent chapters, sections, subsections, etc. of the paper to be written. The relationships between a chapter and its sections, and the ones between a section and its subsections are represented as a link in iLSB. Each link has one of the 14 attributes such as "class", "instance", and "effect". As for how TOC is generated, refer to (Morishita, 2020).

Learners are expected to write a summary of the paper in the following two phases: (2-a) text structuring with graphic organizers, and (2-b) text writing. In (2-a), learners are expected to use graphic organizers to structure a text to be included in the summary. In the model, they reorganize the nodes in TOC with graphic organizers to visually represent the text structure to be embedded in the summary of their paper. In (2-b), they are then expected to compose sentences from the text structure with graphic organizers. In writing the summary, learners are expected to make connections between individual q-keywords, which leads to a deeper understanding of the initial q-keyword, and which allows them to gain an overview of their knowledge from a perspective different from the question tree. Moreover, learners could effectively communicate the summary as for what they learned to their instructors. The instructors can use it to evaluate the learners' investigation.

Through the linearization process, learners could reflect on their knowledge constructed, and write a summary of the paper to report on their investigation. In this work, we focus on how to help learners build a summary for the paper with graphical organizers.

2.2 iLSB

iLSB is a cognitive tool developed as a Firefox add-on to scaffold WBIL as modelled. For the knowledge construction process, iLSB provides a search engine for searching Web resources, keyword repository for collecting keywords extracted from the resources during navigational learning, and question tree (Figure 1) for expanding questions into their sub-questions.

For the knowledge linearization process, iLSB scaffolds creation of TOC from the question tree created in the knowledge construction process. Figure 2 shows an example of TOC created from the learning scenario shown in Figure 1. iLSB displays nodes (represented as q-keywords) in the question tree as a list. Learners are expected to select several nodes as chapters of TOC from the list, and then to select nodes of sections (called section nodes) to be included in each chapter. They are next expected to make part-of relationships among the section nodes to define sub-sections in each section, and finally to sort the sections/sub-sections/chapters to define the order of nodes that is best suited for explaining the initial question.

In addition to these scaffolding functions, we are developing a scaffold of iLSB for helping learners write a summary with graphical organizers.

3. SUMMARY WRITING FOR WBIL

Let us next explain how we scaffold summary writing. We currently plan to scaffold summary writing as follows. The requirements for the scaffolding are 1) to help learners write a comprehensive and concise summary that follows the TOC, and 2) to reduce cognitive load of summary writing to enhance the quality of the summary.

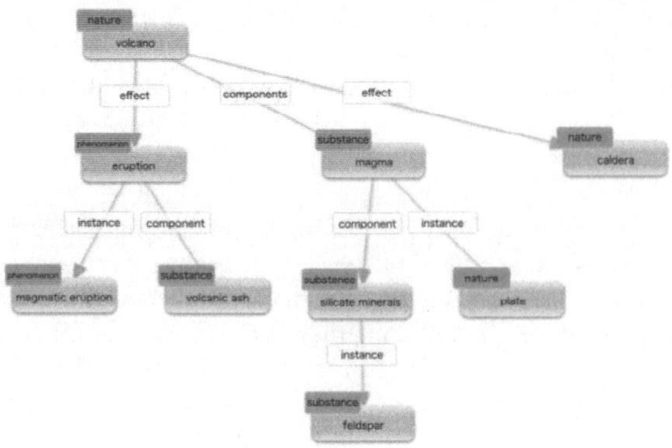

Figure 1. An example of question tree

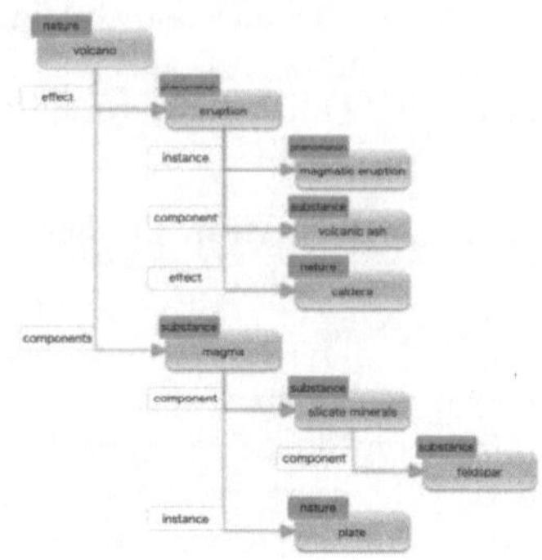

Figure 2. An example of TOC

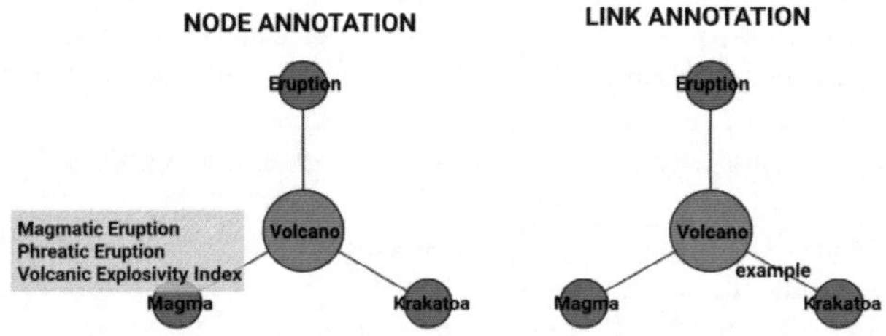

Figure 3. Text structures with node and link annotations

3.1 Framework

After completing TOC, learners use iLSB to write a summary. TOC includes nodes represented as q-keywords. Using TOC, iLSB first generates text structure involving the q-keywords, which are represented with graphic organizers. Graphic organizers have five basic structure types: *description*, *sequence and order*, *cause and effect*, *problem and solution*, and *compare and contrast* (Roehling et al, 2017). iLSB then allows learners to add two types of information to nodes and links in the generated text structure as **node** and **link annotations**. Node and link annotations enable them to supplement the contents of node and the relationships between nodes. They are expected to write the text of the summary using the text structure with annotations.

3.2 Representing Text Structure with Graphic Organizers

Using graphic organizers to help learners in reading or writing a text has been already a widely used method in conventional education (Roehling et al, 2017). In this work, we attempt to apply the same method to WBIL. Graphic organizers visually represent basic structures of expository text. The left structure in Figure 3 shows an example of graphic organizer for description about the subject of "Volcano", in which the keywords "Krakatoa", "Eruption", and "Magma" are objects used for describing the subject. It allows learners to compose a text such as "Volcano has eruption, and contains magma. An example of volcano is Krakatoa".

In this work, learners can annotate nodes and links in text structure represented with graphic organizers. Node annotations allow learners to add keywords to any node, which supplement the node. The left structure in Figure 3 shows the node "Eruption" has annotations including "Magmatic Eruption", "Phreatic Eruption", and "Volcanic Explosivity Index". Link annotations also allow learners to add keywords to any link, which supplement it. In Figure 3, the link between "Volcano" and "Krakatoa" is annotated with "example". These annotations allow learners to refer to the annotated keywords to write sentences for summary writing.

3.3 Summary Generation in iLSB

In accordance to the learning model, learners are expected to build text structure with graphical organizers after creating TOC, which will be divided into four steps. First, iLSB shows TOC to allow learners to review the nodes, relationships, and hierarchical order as shown in Figure 2. Second, iLSB automatically generates text structure of a summary from TOC to present. Let us explain the procedure for generating text structure with graphic organizer with an example of TOC shown in Figure 2 as follows.

iLSB groups q-keywords included in TOC into chapters/sections/sub-sections. In this example, the groups are: {volcano, eruption, magma} as chapters, {eruption, magmatic eruption, volcanic ash, caldera} and {magma, silicate minerals, plate} as sections, and {silicate minerals, feldspar} as sub-sections. Following the attributes attached between q-keywords in each group, iLSB then selects a basic structure of text corresponding to each group.

Table 1 shows the correspondence between attributes attached between q-keywords in TOC and types of basic structures. If there are multiple attributes in the group, iLSB splits the group for each basic structure. In the group {eruption, magmatic eruption, volcanic ash, caldera}, for example, the attribute attached between "eruption" and "caldera" is "effect", the one between "eruption" and "magmatic eruption" is "instance", and the one between "eruption" and "volcanic ash" is "component". The attribute "effect" corresponds to the basic cause and effect, while the attributes "instance" and "component" correspond to description. The group will be accordingly split into the two sub-groups {eruption, caldera} and {eruption, magmatic eruption, volcanic ash}. As a result, iLSB generates text structure embedding the six basic structures as shown in Figure 4 from TOC shown in Figure 2.

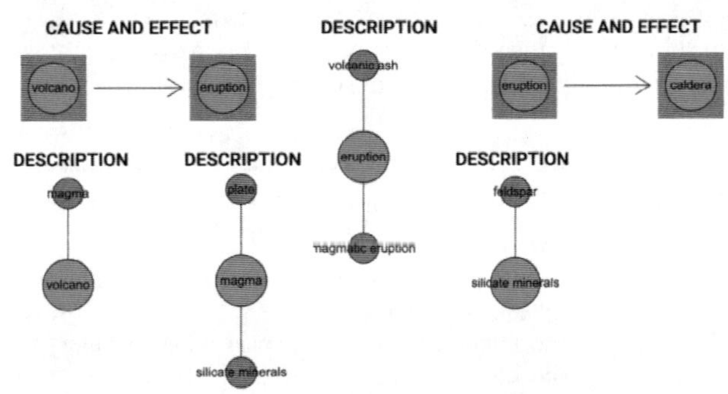

Figure 4. An example of text structure with graphic organizers

Table 1. Correspondence between attributes and basic structure

Attributes attached between q-keywords in TOC	Basic structure of text
class, instance, component, structure, characteristic	Description
origin, background	Sequence and Order
cause, effect, principle, action	Cause and Effect
measure	Problem and Solution
similar concept, contrasting concept	Compare and Contrast

When text structure generated are presented to learners, they are third expected to understand the basic structures to be used in their summary and the q-keywords included. Fourth, learners are expected to add node and link annotations to the basic structures. The keywords used for node annotations are selected from the keyword repository in iLSB, which stores keywords representing the contents learned about the node. As for link annotations, learners could use their own keywords.

Through these phases, iLSB finally shows learners the generated text structure. By clicking on any node, learners could see the node annotations. Link annotations are visible without any operation from the learners. After building text structure, learners are expected to start writing a summary.

4. CASE STUDY

We have conducted a case study whose purpose was to assess the effectiveness of building text structure with graphic organizers from TOC before writing a summary.

4.1 Methods

We had 8 participants, all of whom were undergraduate and graduate students majoring in computer science. This study was conducted with between-participants design, in which the participants were equally divided into the experiment group (4 participants) and the control group (4 participants).

The participants differed from the actual users of the iLSB in that 2 of the 8 participants used the system for the first time. The same instructions were given to the participants as would be given to the actual users.

All participants were first required to use iLSB for investigating as the initial q-keyword "Civil Lawsuit". They were next required to create TOC for the paper with iLSB to report on their investigation, and then to write a summary. In the summary writing, the experiment group was allowed to use graphic organizers to build text structure from their TOC. It was also allowed to look at the text structure to write a summary on paper. The control group, on the other hand, was required to write a summary on paper by means of TOC without graphic organizers.

In order to assess the effectiveness of summary writing with iLSB, we collected data from the following two sources: analysis of the resulting summary texts and peer assessment scores. As for the peer assessment, the participants were asked to review summaries written by other participants by means of the questionnaire including 5 questions shown in Table 2, each of which had a five-point scale. Q1-3 were the ones for confirming whether the summary generation promotes a comprehensive summary following TOC. Q4-6 were also the ones for confirming whether it enhances the quality of the summary.

Table 2. Peer assessment questions

Question number	Question
Q1	How exhaustively did the summary represent the keywords from the table of contents?
Q2	How well did the summary represent the relationships between keywords in the table of contents?
Q3	How accurately did the summary reflect the hierarchical relationship of the table of contents?
Q4	Was the summary coherent?
Q5	Was the information in the summary well organized and conveyed accurately what the learner learned?
Q6	Overall, how appropriate was the text as a summary for WBIL?

4.2 Results

As for the text analysis, we collected data about (1) exhaustiveness of summary, (2) length of summary, and (3) time taken to write summary. As for (1), we compared q-keywords in TOC with q-keywords included in summary. Table 3 and Table 4 show the ratios of q-keywords included in summary to the ones in TOC, the number of letters, and the average number of letters per q-keyword included in summary.

On average, the summary written in the experiment group covered about 89% (SD: 11) of q-keywords in TOC. On the other hand, the summary written in the control group also covered about 73% (SD: 16) of q-keywords in TOC. The coverage of q-keywords in the experimental group was higher than the one in the control group. As for the length of summary, the experiment group used 660 letters (SD: 328) on average, and the control group also used 273 letters (SD: 59). As for the average number of letters used per q-keyword, in addition, the experimental group used 45 letters (SD: 21) on average, and the control group used 21 letters (SD: 5.8). As for the time taken to write summary, it took 2.2 seconds per letter (SD: 0.40) on average in the experiment group. In the control group, it also took 3.1 seconds per letter (SD: 0.69). The time in the experimental group was shorter than the one in the control group.

Table 3. Results of summary analysis in experiment group

Participant	Ratios of q-keywords included in summary	Number of letters in summary	Average number of letters per q-keyword
B	17/17 (100%)	1010	59
C	16/17 (94%)	237	15
E	14/19 (74%)	795	57
F	12/14 (86%)	597	50
Average	89%	660	45

Table 4. Results of summary analysis in control group

Participant	Ratios of q-keywords included in summary	Number of letters in summary	Average number of letters per q-keyword
A	14/15 (93%)	270	19
D	12/19 (63%)	356	30
G	14/17 (82%)	228	16
H	12/22 (55%)	236	20
Average	73%	273	21

For Q1-3 in the peer assessment, the score for each participant was calculated by taking the average of scores given by all other subjects from both experiment and control group. On the other hand, evaluation for Q4-6 was considered dependent on which group the subject was assigned to. The scores were accordingly calculated by taking the average of scores from other participants in the same group. For example, the score for participant B (experiment group) in Q4 was calculated by averaging the scores given by other participants in the experiment group: C, E, F. The results for the experiment group and the control group for each question are shown in Table 5.

Table 5. Peer assessment results by group

Question number	Question	Experiment group average	Control group average
Q1	How exhaustively did the summary represent the keywords from the table of contents?	4.63 (SD: 1.09)	3.97 (SD: 1.09)
Q2	How well did the summary represent the relationships between keywords in the table of contents?	4.41 (SD: 0.66)	4.34 (SD: 0.75)
Q3	How accurately did the summary reflect the hierarchical relationship of the table of contents?	4.31 (SD: 1.06)	4.34 (SD: 0.83)
Q4	Was the summary coherent?	4.17 (SD: 0.83)	4.42 (SD: 0.67)
Q5	Was the information in the summary well organized and conveyed accurately what this person learned?	3.92 (SD: 0.90)	4.08 (SD: 1.24)
Q6	Overall, how appropriate was the text as a summary for WBIL?	3.83 (SD: 0.83)	3.75 (SD: 1.29)

4.3 Discussion

Due to the small number of the participants in this case study, we could not statistically assess significant differences between the experiment group and control group, but we will consider the differences between the two groups. From the results of the text analysis, the participants in the experiment group tended to use more q-keywords in their summary from their TOC than those in the control group. This suggests that graphical organizers allow learners to write a summary including more exhaustive contents of their TOC.

The experiment group also tend to explain more as to each q-keyword, which can be seen by comparing the number of letters per q-keyword between the experiment and control group. This can be attributed to the node and link annotation scaffolding function in iLSB. This suggests that iLSB allows learners to identify keywords for explaining each q-keyword. It is also suggested that text structure with graphic organizers has the effect of reducing cognitive load of writing a summary, as the experiment group took less time to write their summaries compared to the control group.

As for Q1 of the peer assessment, the experiment group on average scored higher than the control group, supporting the results of the text analysis. This suggests that summary built by the experiment group is considered comprehensive from a subjective point of view. In addition, although there was little difference between the experiment and control group, the scores for Q2-Q6 for the former ranged from 3.83 to 4.4 on the five-point scale, and this considerably high score implies that using iLSB to build text structure with graphic organizers is effective in writing a summary for WBIL.

5. CONCLUSION

This paper addressed the issue of summary writing in Web-based investigative learning, which has not been dealt with in our previous work. In this paper, we proposed a writing strategy using graphic organizers to help learners write a comprehensive and concise summary. Five types of graphic organizers corresponding to the five basic structures (*description*, *sequence and order, cause and effect*, *compare and contrast*, and *problem and solution*) were used to reorganize nodes included in TOC created during the knowledge construction process in WBIL. Results of the case study has shown that using GOs guaranteed a certain level of the quality of the summary. We were also able to collect data about summaries for WBIL, which should be further evaluated in more detail. In future, we will prepare templates for explaining concepts, order of GOs, structuring paragraphs in the summary in order to better promote summary writing.

ACKNOWLEDGEMENT

The work presented here is partially supported by JSPS KAKENHI Grant Number 17H01992.

REFERENCES

Chen, S. et al, 2006. Navigation in hypermedia learning systems: experts vs. novices. *Computers in human behavior*, Vol. 22, No. 2, pp. 251-266.

Hagiwara, M. et al, 2019. Adaptive recommendation for question decomposition in Web-based investigative learning, *The 2019 IEEE International Conference on Teaching, Assessment, and Learning for Engineering (TALE)*. Yogyakarta, Indonesia, pp.750-757.

Henze, N. and Nejdl, W., 2001. Adaptation in open corpus hypermedia. *International Journal of Artificial Intelligence in Education*, Vol. 12, No. 4, pp. 325-350.

Jeong, H. Y., 2016. UX based adaptive e-learning hypermedia system (U-AEHS): an integrative user model approach. *Multimedia Tools and Applications*, Vol. *75, No.*21, pp. 13193-13209.

Kashihara, A. and Akiyama, N., 2016. Learning scenario creation for promoting investigative learning on the Web, *The Journal of Information and Systems in Education*, Vol. 15, No. 1, pp. 62-72.

Kashihara, A. et al, 2020. A Microworld for Learning How to Learn with Web Resources. *Technical Report on SIG-ALST-B903-17, in Japanese.* Niigata, Japan, pp. 91-96

Lau, C. et al, 2017. Transitioning self-regulated learning profiles in hypermedia-learning environments. In *Proceedings of the Seventh International Learning Analytics & Knowledge Conference*, pp. 198-202.

Lawless, K. and & Brown, S., 1997. Multimedia learning environments: Issues of learner control and navigation. *Instructional Science*, Vol. 25, pp. 117-131.

Morishita, N. et al, 2020. Reconstructing Question tree in Web-based Investigative Learning. 44th Annual Conference of Japanese Society for Information and Systems in Education. *in Japanese*. Hamamatsu, Japan, pp. 169-176

Roehling, J. et al, 2017. Text structure strategies for improving expository reading comprehension. *The Reading Teacher*, Vol. 71, No. 1, pp.71-82.

LEARNING ANALYTICS TO EVALUATE THE EFFECTIVENESS OF HIGHER EDUCATION STUDENT FAILURE PREVENTION

Francesco Floris[1], Marina Marchisio[1], Matteo Sacchet[1] and Sergio Rabellino[2]
[1]*Department of Molecular Biotechnology and Health Sciences, University of Torino*
Via Nizza 52, 10126 Torino, Italy
[2]*Department of Computer Science, University of Torino*
Via Pessinetto 12, 10149 Torino, Italy

ABSTRACT

Open Online Courses can serve different purposes: in the case of Orient@mente at the University of Torino, they aim at facilitating the transition from secondary to tertiary education with automatic evaluation tests that students can try in order to understand their capabilities in - and their attitude towards - certain disciplines, and with remedial courses to fill the gaps in their knowledge. The university strategy of Orient@mente first started in 2014 and, after six years of deployment of the online platform, it has collected many data from students that were interested in starting a university course. The natural comparison and correlation analysis juxtapose the academic results of students who practice self-assessment in Orient@mente with the other university students. The measurable that we considered in this comparison is the average number of ECTS acquired during the first year, since this is a number that is considered for the university evaluation system - stakeholders in particular check the number of students who obtain more than 40 first-year ECTS. According to specific rules, we put together dataset from different origins, the platform logs, and users with the university record system. The results of this analysis, presented in this work, confirm the positive impact of Orient@mente on students, with statistical significance.

KEYWORDS

Data Analytics, Learning Analytics, MOOCs, Secondary to Tertiary Transition, University Guidance, University Orientation.

1. INTRODUCTION

Massive Open Online Courses (MOOCs) are a worldwide instrument to face diverse aspects in education: open education, open access, interactivity, and digital competencies. The education topics need many pedagogical studies on user interaction with online systems. MOOCs can pursue several goals, which are not necessarily strictly related to disciplinary contents. By using an automatic evaluation system, it is possible to enhance students' ability to self-evaluate and manage their self-regulated learning. By using computing environments, it is possible to enhance problem solving skills. By using web conference tools, it is possible to enhance collaborative competencies across different regions and countries.

In the 2010 report of the European Commission "Europe 2020" (European Commission, 2010) one of the objectives to be achieved for smart, sustainable and inclusive growth is the reduction of the abandonment rate (bringing it below 10%) and the increase in the percentage of young graduates up to 40%.

This objective is to lower the drop-out rate by five percentage points (in 2010 the European average was around 15%) in 10 years and increase the share of the population aged between 20 and 34 who successfully completes high school by approximately 10 percentage points.

The achievement of this goal is closely connected with the problems that students encounter in the transition phase from secondary to tertiary education, what is known as the Secondary to Tertiary Transition (STT). It is a decisive change in students' perspectives, since they need to be aware of the choice that will affect their future and be prepared to face the difference between expectations and reality. It is not surprising that first-year students are marked as unprepared, unable, or unwilling to cope with challenges of university-level education. From the student side, the STT experience looks differently. Students can face unexpected failures of the learning strategies they developed by previous education. The education system is responsible for making this challenging experience as positive and smooth as possible. Technologies and virtual environments are key components of the support to students, because multimedia resources give students an overview of what they will face at university in advance, communication technologies allow university students to interact with professors, online tests containing feedback allow students to check whether their preparation is adequate to attend first year courses, and interactive learning materials can help them fill their gaps.

Through various initiatives, universities have tried to adapt to the situation, developing different guidance activities, covering the various study programs. The main objective of university orientation is the reduction of the dropout rate, which directly impacts on the evaluation of the university itself, both in quantitative and qualitative terms. Another objective of universities is the balance between the education of new professionals and the demand of the job market. Because of this, many degree programs require students to take an admission test in order to assess the minimum requirements and provide a restriction on the numbers of new students, according to the score they get from questions about different topics related to the degree program. Orientation days, job fairs and open days are the most common initiatives promoted by universities, education offices and secondary schools. In addition to these orientation initiatives, new technologies offer a solution for the mass dissemination of information and assessment to facilitate the orientation of students, mediated by Learning Management Systems (LMS), which contains multimedia resources, interactive components, and online tests.

University of Torino proposes several strategies and actions to facilitate the transition from secondary school to university through the use new technologies. The common model consists in an open online platform, integrated with an Advanced Computing Environment (ACE), an Automatic Assessment System (AAS) and a Web Conference tool, that delivers self-paced Open Online Courses (OOC), even if not Massive since the main focus of these strategies is on the student. Moreover, there is no restriction on when to access courses: students can start them anytime. Considering the users of the various actions, more than 80,000 users are involved. Some of them can be duplicate across the platforms, but around 60,000 distinct students subscribed, from the most populated platform. On average, every month there are around 2,000 unique logins which correspond to more than 60,000 sign-ins per month.

Thus, the online environments collect a lot of data, which are very useful to analyze and evaluate the initiatives and improve and enhance their effect. The main criterion for assessing the effectiveness of these actions is the number of ECTS obtained by students in their first year of academic career, in relation to the online activity. In the present work, we will discuss the analysis of data collected from different sources of the action Orient@mente, with a methodology that can be applied to various strategies adopted at university level.

2. STATE OF THE ART

Every student failure is a failure of the whole education system, at any level this may occur. Thus, preventing failures and enhancing success are key objectives of all the institutions. The various strategies that can be adopted address evaluation, grouping, motivation, practices, responsibility, and relationships. The possible interventions can be divided into two main branches (Krull and Duart, 2018): academic support, which deals with the development of cognitive and learning skills, and non-academic support, which deals with emotional and organizational aspects such as counselling and guidance services. Both aspects have a positive impact on the students' experience.

The decision on which changes or strategies are good for preventing failure and enhancing success is driven by descriptive analytics, but in a fast-changing world predictive and prescriptive models. The ability to detect possible failures in advance allows preventive interventions. There are many experiences of prediction algorithms: the latest trends use data mining techniques (Marquez-Vera et al., 2013) and Learning Analytics (LA), as one can see from the trend topics in related conferences (Ochoa and Merceron, 2018). These approaches also make use of machine learning algorithms, which are generally used as black boxes which provide an output without any information on the decision process. More research needs to be devoted to the ethical aspects, since they need to be thoroughly examined in terms of fairness (Riazy et al., 2020), given that predictions of a student's performance have an impact on the student's success. Researchers developed methods and tutorials to detect discrimination (Hajian et al., 2016), which is endemic even when there is no discrimination intention in the developer of the algorithm.

These strategies for preventing failure and improving success find a strong point of support in the decision to use numerous guidance strategies by University of Torino through Learning Management Systems, even if this is not the standard for Italian universities. In fact, from the OECD (OECD/European Union, 2020) emerges the present perspective about Higher Education (HE) in Italy, and the various priorities of HE institutions. From the OECD HEI Leader Survey, to the question “Taking into account the HEInnovate dimensions/components listed below, please indicate the three that are most prominent in your strategy”, none of the survey respondents considers the enhancement of digital transformation as one of the top three priorities for the HEI. This is made worse by the allocation of most recent investments in digital technologies and systems performed by Italian HEIs, the lowest amount of which is devoted to developing digital skills of professors and researchers, who are directly responsible for the education of students. It is worth mentioning that the survey was not administrated to online universities. In this context, the following orientation actions of the University of Torino take place.

Orient@mente (https://orientamente.unito.it) consists of OOCs for the interactive exploration of courses, for the preparation for tests for the recovery of gaps in many courses, from natural sciences to humanities. It serves as an effective dematerialized orientation for secondary school students who will enroll to university. After a proper training and support in the use of the technologies, university professors select and arrange the materials in the courses, as a guarantee of quality (Barana et al., 2017).

Start@unito (https://start.unito.it) promotes and facilitates the transition from secondary school to the university system through the creation and dissemination of a series of OOCs, which are full university modules in many different first year disciplines. As a second effect, it helps students make a responsible choice about academic studies by offering interactive paths for university guidance and preparation for admission tests. Moreover, Start@unito addresses two non-traditional types of learners, namely university professors and high school teachers. These non-standard learner groups are considerably smaller than the traditional student population, but they have a large impact in the education sector (Marchisio et al., 2019).

Foundation Programme (https://foundationprogramme.unito.it) facilitates the integration of pre-university students with less than 12 years of education. The additional semester or year allows the achievement of the corresponding ECTS, according to international students’ needs. Since it is delivered completely online, students can attend the program from their home country, without the need of a permission or visa and without travelling. Only the final exam that allows to certify the ECTS has to be taken at the university, right before enrollment (Floris et al., 2019).

3. RESEARCH QUESTIONS AND METHODS

The goal of our analysis is to understand the impact of the Orient@mente platform on the career of students. Summing up previous research, with Orient@mente (Barana et al., 2017) the strategies to prevent student failure concern both the learning experience, with automatic assessment and courses, and the organizational one, with information on courses and interviews to older students or professors.

RQ1. How to evaluate the impact of the orientation action of Orient@mente on students' careers?

RQ2. How to use Learning Analytics (LA) in order to obtain a suitable evaluation of the impact of Orient@mente action?

All the university actions take place in a fully online environment, addressing the increasing need of digitalization of HE institutions. Data about the usage and the advantages of the online platform have already been studied in previous works: the originality of this research lies in the direct measurement of the correlation between academic results of students who used Orient@mente, tested against students who did not. It is important to measure the possible improvement of students who used the platform in admission tests and exams. The analysis considers data about the careers of students enrolled at the University of Torino from the degree programs that have a course in the Orient@mente platform, and students’ data arising from the interaction with the platform.

Hypothesis (H0): is there a significant difference in students’ academic performance in relation to their activity on the Orient@mente platform?

Data about academic performance consist in the weighted average grade and the number of University Credits (ECTS) acquired by students at the end of each exam session and at the end of the first year of university. This measurables are the most relevant, since the University evaluation system makes use of similar indicators: in particular, it evaluates the number of students that gain more than 40 ECTS, which is in fact an excellent aggregator for the dimensions of students who continue their studies and productivity. The analysis considers the previous education of students, such as the type of school attended, the city, the region, and the graduation mark. Data about the platform are divided into two main areas: the first one comes from students interaction with the LMS, while the other data source is the database of the AAS, which contains all the necessary information about tests, such as grades, number of attempts, time, and other data.

RQ2 will be investigated more qualitatively, analyzing which aspects of the adopted analysis methods provided useful insights and which one were avoidable, according to precise indicators (Marchisio et al., 2019; Scheffel et al., 2014).

4. ANALYSIS PROCESS

Data analysis was divided into different phases.

- Phase 1 (P1). The first action on the various datasets was merging them and creating a unique large database. The connecting point between the different databases is given by the email field, which may not be unique. The data about the students' career at the university contain two email addresses, the private and the institutional ones.
- Phase 2 (P2). The second action on the merged dataset was cleaning and transforming. This is an important phase which gives an overview of the whole population and prepares the data for the further phases (grouping and statistical analysis).
- Phase 3 (P3). Statistical hypothesis testing, with t-test and chi-square test, to verify the validity of the hypothesis (H0).
- Phase 4 (P4). The clean dataset can be grouped according to some variables expressing the use of the platform, like the number of logs and the number of tests, in correlation with the student's achievement at university level.

Two software were used for this analysis: "KNIME Analytics Platform 4.1.1" and "SAS 9.4". "KNIME", used in (P1), allows, with the node system, easy access to different data sources (career data, platform database), and the use of SQL language to access the necessary information and prepare the dataset for next phases. The merged dataset was imported to "SAS" for (P2) and (P3), for cleaning, transformation of database and statistical analysis. Last phase (P4) was performed on "KNIME" again. In this paper we will focus on the first three phases.

5. RESULTS

The analyzed sample consists of students who enrolled at the University of Torino from 2010 to the academic year 2017/2018.

The size of the dataset is 29256 observations, divided into two subsamples: the first one (SS1) composed of students that are Orient@mente users, too, containing 22.38% of the global sample, while the second one (SS2) consists of students who are not Orient@mente users. There are no significant differences in the proportionality of genders in both subsamples. Table 1 describes the percentage of users over the global number of observations, divided into (SS1) and (SS2) and grouped by the leaving certificate grade, for which the maximum grade is 100.

From Table 1 we can see that the distribution of students across the various ranges of grades is quite uniform, with percentages around 20% and 30%. Even inside (SS1) and (SS2) the same global proportion is respected. A similar procedure was carried out about gender, with no statistically significant difference in the proportion of males and females (Table 2).

Data do not show the same proportionality about the educational origin (Table 3), because it emerges that students from the "Liceo Scientifico" high school are less interested in attending Orient@mente, and this can be explained with the fact that most of the MOOCs available are about science, which is a pivotal discipline in that kind of school.

Table 1. Percentages and numbers of users according to the subsample and grouped by the leaving certificate grade

Group	SS1 (freq, pct, pct col)	SS2 (freq, pct, pct col)	Row total
R1: First range of students with leaving certificate grade between 60 and 69	1366 students	5023 students	6389 students
Percentage	4.67%	17.17%	21.84%
Column percentage	20.86%	22.12%	
R2: Second range of students with leaving certificate grade between 70 and 79	2029 students	6851 students	8880 students
Percentage	6.94%	23.42%	30.35%
Column percentage	30.99%	30.17%	
R3: Third range of students with leaving certificate grade between 80 and 89	1747 students	6081 students	7828 students
Percentage	5.97%	20.79%	26.76%
Column percentage	26.68%	26.78%	
R4: Fourth range of students with leaving certificate grade between 90 and 100	1406 students	4753 students	6159 students
Percentage	4.81%	16.25%	21.05%
Column percentage	21.47%	20.93%	
Column total	**6548 students 22.38% 100%**	**22708 students 77.62% 100%**	**29256 students 100%**

Table 2. Percentages and numbers of users according to the subsample and grouped by gender

Gender	SS1	SS2	Row total
Male	3246 students	11160 students	14406 students
Row percentage	22.53%	77.47%	100%
Column percentage	49.58%	49.15%	49.24%
Female	3302 students	11548 students	14850 students
Row percentage	22.24%	77.76%	100%
Column percentage	50.42%	50.85%	50.76%
Column total	**6548 students**	**22708 students**	**29256 students**
Row percentage	**22.38%**	**77.62%**	**100%**

Table 3. Percentages and numbers of users according to the subsample and grouped by educational origin

Educational origin	SS1	SS2	Row total
International	85	124	209
Percentage	0.29%	0.42%	
Row percentage	40.67%	59.33%	
Column percentage	1.30%	0.55%	0.71%
Professional School	437	1314	1751
Percentage	1.49%	4.49%	
Row percentage	24.96	75.04%	
Column percentage	6.67%	5.79%	5.99%
Istituto Tecnico	1638	4432	6070
Percentage	5.60%	15.15%	
Row percentage	26.99%	73.01%	
Column percentage	25.02%	19.52%	20.75%
Liceo	3977	14922	18899
Percentage	13.59%	51.00%	
Row percentage	21.04%	78.96%	
Column percentage	60.74%	65.71%	64.60%
Unknow	411	1916	2327
Percentage	1.40%	6.55%	
Row percentage	17.66%	82.34%	
Column percentage	6.28%	8.44%	7.95%
Column total	**6548 students**	**22708 students**	**29256 students**
Row percentage	**22.38%**	**77.62%**	**100%**

First access of 68.10% of (SS1) students was prior to enrollment at the university. 79% of (SS1) students did not use university institutional mail to access Orient@mente, even when the first access to the platform occurred after enrollment (16% of SS1). Thus, it is possible that in (P1) some (SS1) students do not correctly appear in the merged dataset, because it is possible that they used two different personal emails, one to subscribe to Orient@mente and one to enroll at the University of Torino. In cases like this one, the platform user cannot be traced back to the university student and will thus appear as a student in (SS2) in the dataset.

5.1 Hypothesis Tests

We performed a hypothesis test to check the equality between the average number of ECTS (which we will indicate with the Greek letter μ) achieved by the students at the end of the first academic year in the subsamples (SS1) and (SS2).

$$\begin{cases} H_0 : \mu_{SS1} = \mu_{SS2} \\ H_A : \mu_{SS1} > \mu_{SS2} \end{cases}$$

The p-value for the test much less than 0.0001, thus rejecting the hypothesis of equality, it is possible to state that there is statistical difference between the average number of ECTS achieved depending on the access to the Orient@mente platform.

The same Hypothesis test checked the equality of the weighted average grade of students between the subsamples (SS1) and (SS2). The p-value for the test is almost null, thus rejecting the hypothesis of equality. Thus, even for this second measurable there is statistically significant difference.

The behavior of the same measurables can be different according to the various groups of students. The same analysis was performed with a restriction of the sample to the four ranges (R1), (R2), (R3), (R4). There is statistically significant difference between the average number of ECTS of (SS1-R1), (SS2-R1) and of (SS1-R4), (SS2-R4) with p-value less than 0.005, while for (R2) and (R3) we cannot reject the hypothesis of equality. In particular, the case of (R3) is very significant, since difference between the two averages (SS1-R3) and (SS2-R3) is below 0.05

Thus, from the sample we analyzed, we can infer that Orient@mente action is more effective when it involves users with the highest and users with the lowest leaving certificate grades, two completely diverse kinds of students. Looking more closely at the behavior of students in these two ranges, 35% of (R1) students log in after enrollment, against 25% of (R4) students, showing that (R1) students use the platform to fill the gaps that emerge during the first year of studies. There is no particular evidence regarding the various platform activities carried out by these students, whose study regards both the test area and the realignment courses in the same way.

5.2 Focusing on Two Courses

There could be a strong difference between the various courses. Two cases were of interests for their different behavior. Case 1 (C1) concerns students in Mathematics (1271 students), for whom the average number of ECTS achieved by SS2 students is even 3.5 points higher (p-value < 0.02). This result is not surprising since a student who enrolls in the course Mathematics is usually someone who is aware of his own interests. Moreover, it is a student with no need to attend courses to remediate gaps in the discipline.

On the other hand, Case 2 (C2) concerns students in Biological science (2041 students), for whom the average number of ECTS earned by (SS1) students is 4 points higher compared to (SS2) students (p-value < 0.0001). This result is very important because 4 ECTS more mean an extra exam during first year. This is particularly relevant for courses where mathematics, physics, chemistry are not the main topics, but basic disciplines anyway. They often represent first-year stumbling blocks because they are the first modules that students encounter, but of less specific interest.

5.3 Features of the Adopted LA

There are different indicators that can be used to evaluate LA. We will briefly describe and summarize Structure, Background, Statistic methods, Population, Procedure, Availability, Outcomes, Intervention.

From the point of view of Structure, we have provided a full description of the kind of analysis that we adopted, pointing out the various phases which delineate the Procedure. The Background is provided by the Orient@mente action, which involved a large Population of prospective students that became university students afterwards, in comparison with students that did not use the orientation tool. The Statistic methods are given by the descriptive statistics of the sample and the hypothesis test to evaluate the equality between the average number of ECTS in the subgroups. The Availability of this analysis is a little bit restrictive, because it uses data from different sources that may require official procedure to access. Moreover, new data arises after years of activity. The Outcomes provide clear information: acceptance or rejection of the hypothesis, with statistical significance. These provides information to the institution in order to take data driven decision.

In this particular setting, given the results, the analysis and the evaluation of the impact of Orient@mente, the University of Torino took immediately action and has decided to invest in this initiative: new Orient@mente courses and new test areas are currently under development for more than 85% of the university degree programs and will soon become available to prospective students.

6. CONCLUSION

From the analysis, it emerges that the research hypothesis has statistical significance in the case of both the weighted average grade and the average number of first-year acquired ECTS, thus proving that there is a positive impact on students' outcome thanks to the OOC orientation actions, especially in the case of Orient@mente. In this work we provided a method which can be useful to analyze other systems and platforms in order to assess effectiveness (RQ1). Apart from the different sources of data, the method could be refined in order to be automatically executed and return real time results.

These results guide future university orientation actions (RQ2). In fact, the Orient@mente platform is going to be further enlarged with new courses, which are currently under development and will be available to students who are thinking about or going to enroll to one of the numerous degrees at the University of Torino. As described in subsection 5.3, the institution invested in new courses and new test areas, that are currently under development.

There are many more parameters that can guide the evaluation process over the guidance service and which can be included in close future research:

- Students' information in their personal profile to provide a personalized orientation experience, suited to their needs, to offer them quickly the content they need most.
- Design personalized learning paths using Machine Learning techniques to differentiate students' learning paths, adapting them to their attitudes and their learning speed.
- Cluster analysis to identify "behavior" patterns within the platform and study their effects. In this way, once recognized non-productive behaviors by new users, it is possible to intervene to suggest a more effective learning path.
- Learning Analytics techniques to connect the results of tests carried out with the automatic assessment system to improve the implementation of automatic formative assessment strategies and provide immediate and personalized feedback to students.
- Analysis of other variables, such as the region of the school, the type of school attended, the chosen program.

ACKNOWLEDGEMENT

The authors would like to thank the bank foundation Compagnia di San Paolo, which financially supports many of the initiatives at the University of Torino, in particular the project OPERA Open Program for Educational Resources and Activities, in which this research took place. The authors would like to thank Dr. Massimo Bruno, Director of the Didactics office at the University of Torino and his staff for the support they gave to the action Orient@mente.

REFERENCES

Barana, A., Bogino, A., Fioravera, M., Marchisio, M., & Rabellino, S. (2017). Open Platform of Self-paced MOOCs for the continual improvement of Academic Guidance and Knowledge Strengthening in Tertiary Education. Journal of E-Learning and Knowledge Society, 13(3). https://doi.org/10.20368/1971-8829/1383

Barana, A., Conte, A., Fissore, C., Marchisio, M., & Rabellino, S. (2019). Learning Analytics to improve Formative Assessment strategies. Journal of E-Learning and Knowledge Society, 15(3), 75-88. https://doi.org/10.20368/1971-8829/1135057

Floris, F., Marchisio, M., Marello, C. & Operti, L. (2019). Bridge the gap between high school systems with less than twelve years of schooling and European Universities. Proceedings of the 5th International Conference on Higher Education Advances (HEAd'19), Valencia (Spain), 1207-1216. https://doi.org/10.4995/HEAd19.2019.9494

Krull, G., & Duart, J. (2018). Meeting the Needs of Digital Learners: Learner Support Patterns and Strategies. In 13th International Conference on e-Learning (ICEL 2018), At Cape Town, South Africa.

European Commission (2010). EUROPE 2020 A strategy for smart, sustainable and inclusive growth, https://eur-lex.europa.eu/legal-content/EN/TXT/PDF/?uri=CELEX:52010DC2020&from=en

Hajian, S., Bonchi, F., & Castillo, C. (2016). Algorithmic Bias: From Discrimination Discovery to Fairness-aware Data Mining. In Proceedings of the 22nd ACM SIGKDD International Conference on Knowledge Discovery and Data Mining (KDD '16). Association for Computing Machinery, New York, NY, USA, 2125–2126. https://doi.org/10.1145/2939672.2945386

Marchisio, M., Rabellino, S., Roman, F., Sacchet, M., & Salusso, D. (2019). Boosting up Data Collection and Analysis to Learning Analytics in Open Online Contexts: an Assessment Methodology. Journal of E-Learning and Knowledge Society, 15(3), 49-59. https://doi.org/10.20368/1971-8829/1135048

Marquez-Vera, C., Morales, C. R., & Soto, S. V. (2013). Predicting School Failure and Dropout by Using Data Mining Techniques, in IEEE Revista Iberoamericana de Tecnologias del Aprendizaje, vol. 8, no. 1, pp. 7-14, Feb. 2013, https://doi.org/10.1109/RITA.2013.2244695

OECD/European Union (2019), Supporting Entrepreneurship and Innovation in Higher Education in Italy, OECD Skills Studies, OECD Publishing, Paris, https://doi.org/10.1787/43e88f48-en

Ochoa, X., & Merceron, A. (2018). Quantitative and Qualitative Analysis of the Learning Analytics and Knowledge Conference 2018. Journal of Learning Analytics, 5(3), 154–166. https://doi.org/10.18608/jla.2018.53.10

Riazy, S., Simbeck, K., & Schreck, V. (2020). Fairness in Learning Analytics: Student At-risk Prediction in Virtual Learning Environments. In Proceedings of the 12th International Conference on Computer Supported Education - Volume 1: CSEDU, ISBN 978-989-758-417-6, pages 15-25. https://doi.org/10.5220/0009324100150025

Scheffel, M., Drachsler, H., Stoyanov S., Specht, M.(2014). Quality Indicators for Learning Analytics. Educational Technology & Society, 17(4), 117–132.

GEOGEBRABOOK: PRELIMINARY RESEARCH WITH PRIMARY SCHOOL STUDENTS

Sara Cruz[1], Marco Bento[2] and José Alberto Lencastre[2]
[1]*Instituto Politécnico do Cávado e do Ave, Portugal*
[2]*Universidade do Minho, Portugal*

ABSTRACT

GeoGebraBook is a pedagogical resource in the form of a digital book created and developed for free on the GeoGebra online page. This paper presents preliminary research using GeoGebraBook to support explaining the area of a flat figure and the volume of a solid. The study was based on qualitative and quantitative research and involved forty-four Primary school students. Findings suggest that students are receptive to an exploration of GeoGebra applets, get involved in tasks and declare advantages using GeoGebraBook for their learning. The students identified the problem, investigated, debated, interpreted and produced possible justifications and solutions. We observed that the students collaborated to solve the proposed questions in a playful way. This didactic proposal proved to be an enriching experience for students. It served as a basis for the development of a new procedure for the consolidation of mathematical concepts based on the GeoGebra dynamic geometry app.

KEYWORDS

Mathematic, GeoGebra, Learn by Doing, Problem-Based Learning

1. INTRODUCTION

Geometry is present in our lives when we visualize what surrounds us. Geometry is essential not only for its numerous practical applications but also for the development of vital skills in the 21st century. It constitutes a powerful tool from the visualization that allows the connection with the surroundings. Teaching geometry aims to develop in the student these skills (Breda, Serrazina, Meneses, Sousa & Oliveira, 2011). The teaching and learning processes of geometry are complex and multidimensional. The reason why it is common to find students who manifest difficulties with geometric concepts and with your representations or your meaning (Seabra, Barros, Pires & Martins, 2019). Learning geometry benefits from the use of dynamic software (NCTM, 2009; Breda, et al., 2011). Currently, students in the digital age are receptive to the use of technology (Lencastre & Araújo, 2007), so it should be used to improve skills in geometry. The goals that guided this preliminary research were formulated as follows: i) To understand the pedagogical relevance of simulators in understanding the concept of volume and area; ii) To foster student's curiosity in area and volume concepts.

The article begins by introducing the GeoGebraBook as a feature of the online GeoGebra application. Then the methodology adopted in the study and its description is presented. Finally, we offer a discussion of the results and main conclusions. It ends with some proposals for future studies.

2. CONCEPTUAL FRAMEWORK

2.1 GeoGebraBook

The mathematical understanding capacity improves with the experimental capacity of the GeoGebra software (Rohaeti, E. E., & Bernard, M. (2018). A dynamic geometry software GeoGebra is a powerful technological tool for teaching mathematics (Hohenwarter, Hohenwarter, Kreis & Lavicza, 2008), being an open-source software available for free. GeoGebra is intended to be used by teachers and students for mathematics teaching and learning that offers geometry, algebra (Hohenwarter, Hohenwarter, Kreis & Lavicza, 2008), being very efficient in mathematics education (Seloraji & Kwan, 2017). GeoGebra is a significant dynamic geometry software for meaningful student learning (Hohenwarter, Hohenwarter, Kreis & Lavicza, 2008; Zhou, 2012), that improves teaching and learning of mathematics (Hohenwarter, Hohenwarter, Kreis & Lavicza, 2008; Zhou, 2012; Seloraji & Kwan, 2017).

A GeoGebraBook is a type of online book, the educational product being an interactive material, containing proposals of activities, questions, figures, videos, problem situations and learning objects developed in GeoGebra, among other resources, with the aim of providing a dynamic approach to teaching (Lemke & Siple, 2018). It is a resource accessible through any device, easy to share and view, works as an editable and interactive digital book. The basic idea of the software is to combine geometry, algebra, and calculus, which other packages deal with separately, in a single easy-to-use package for learning and teaching math from elementary to university (Hohenwarter, et al., 2008).

The GeoGebraBook can be shared through a link and can be accessed sequentially by order of chapters and sections, or at random, or just by going to the topic of interest (Lemke & Siple, 2018). The GeoGebraBook is a free educational tool available for online use and therefore accessible through any device with internet access. In a GeoGebraBook it is possible to insert several resources (Figure 1), such as text, video, an applet, a GeoGebra file, a pdf, a web page, an image or simply a question.

Figure 1. Type of GeoGebraBook activities

A GeoGebraBook is shareable through a simple link, it has an intuitive navigation that allows teaching to be adapted to the student.

2.2 Problem-Based Learning

There is the tradition in research on mathematical thinking that has focused on procedural knowledge, or on how to solve problems and implement procedures. Lately, there has been a paradigm shift, and there is a growing concern not only in problem-solving but also in the development of conceptual knowledge (Crooks & Alibali, 2014). The focus has been also on developing more creative and effective learning environments with the implementation of ICT (Poikela et al., 2009). Throughout the process of learning based on problem-solving, students acquire knowledge based on experiences. For developing creativity in education, it is important to help students realize their creative potential, understand what is known about creativity, and increase confidence in their own knowledge (Zhou, 2012). Experiences that promote the development of logical, analytical, systematic thinking and the critical capacity to deal with a problem (Eviyanti, Surya, Syahputra & Simbolon, 2017).

Problem-based learning is a student-centered pedagogical strategy, where students are sought to learn for themselves, and active learning improves student learning outcomes in education (Ng, Ting, Lam, and & Liu (2020). Development in today's society increasingly demands the community in general to have the capacity to think creatively and mathematically. Improving the quality of teaching is also improving the ability to think creatively and quality education can be promoted to train thinking (Maskur, 2020). In an educational context, there are several organized approaches to learning from experiences that can enhance and complement the learning that takes place in everyday work. In problem-based learning, students organize information to solve problems. It is a method that uses everyday problems to make students think, communicate, analyze information to conclude. A method that leads students to think scientifically and learn scientific thinking skills (Eviyanti, Surya, Syahputra & Simbolon, 2017).

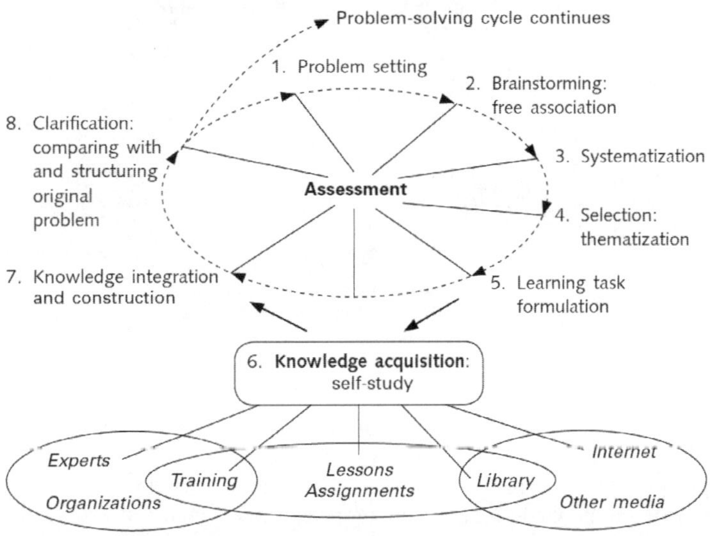

Figure 2. Problem-Based Learning cycle

According to Poikela et al. (2009), the problem-based learning consists in a process of eight steps (Figure 2). In this process, students began by working toward a shared understanding of the problem presented to them. Subsequently, their knowledge and prior experiences originate ideas. Then, similar types of ideas are grouped, and important information is categorized. They take a tutorial, look for information, work individually or in groups depending on the tasks and learning objectives, as well as the strategy considered to be the best. Then, they apply the new knowledge acquired, to tackle the learning tasks, and to reconstruct the problem in a new way, clarifying doubts, reflect on the process of finding solutions to problems to achieve deep learning. Self-assessment is also necessary to close the tutorial with feedback about students' own learning.

3. METHOD

This study took place during the COVID-19 pandemic, where classes were mostly remote. This work main objective is to understand the pedagogical relevance of simulators (applets of GeoGebra) in understanding the concept of volume and area. We also intend to foster student's curiosity in these concepts. We intend to build a new paradigm in the teaching and learning process for the understanding of concepts using the GeoGebra application. The intervention will be made with 44 students from the 1st CEB of a school in the central region of Portugal. We articulate the activities based on the problem-based learning methodology to promote the understanding of mathematical concepts. In this method, the student is the protagonist in the learning process, being the teacher a facilitator between the student and the knowledge. In the beginning, we collected concepts from the student's regular teacher, and then we guided students through the following process:

Step 1, students made a diagnosis about basic knowledge;
Step 2, we introduced students to the problematic scenario and students were engaged with the situation
Step 3, students identified the facts, students investigated the situation and new knowledge was applied;
Step 4, students generated hypotheses and explain the situation;
Step 5, students clarified doubts with teachers or students;
Step 6, students solved problem situation and applied their knowledge on the new situation;
Step 7, students reflected about their knowledge with teacher and other students.

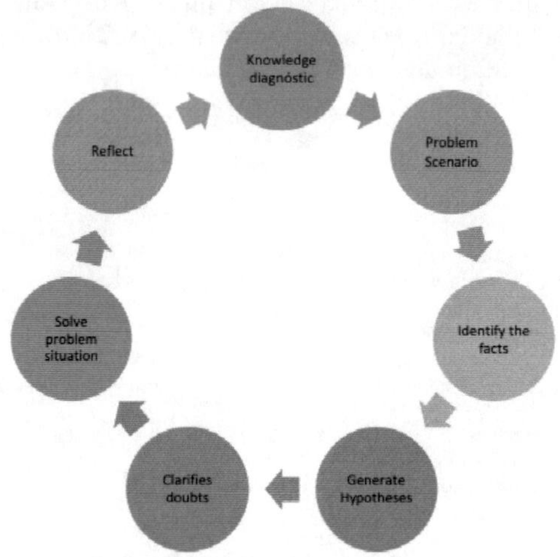

Figure 3. Learning process

Process (Figure 3) was mediated by the Google Classroom platform and by the GeoGebra.org platform, which served as support in all phases of the process described above to communication with students. GeoGebra is a powerful tool to create interactive online learning environments (Hohenwarter et al., 2008), which led us to create on the GeoGebra.org online platform a GeoGebraBook for the theme of the area and volume in primary-school students.

Different methods were applied in order to collect the data: (i) system logs on the platform, (ii) a diary to collect direct observations, (iii) a diagnostic questionnaire and a diagnosis of final reflection and (iv) a final focus group with the students to get a qualitative assessment and to understand their perceptions about the whole process. The questionnaires were subjected to a statistical analysis based on techniques of data collection, analysis and subsequent presentation (Lima & Pacheco, 2006; Coutinho, 2014), and it seeks to establish relationships and explain causes of changes in measurable social facts (Mc Millan & Schumacher, 1997). To code the students' responses, we use the designation Si for student i, with i = 1,…44. With the focus group, a qualitative analysis of the data was carried out, which allows describing the data (Bogdan & Biklen, 1994; Lima & Pacheco, 2006), to understand and interpret them in a context (Mc Millan & Schumacher, 1997). For the analysis of the data of the focus group on the opinion of the students, we considered two dimensions: the understanding of the concept and the visualization of the concept, using GeoGebra.

3.1 Participants

Forty-four students of a Portuguese school (23 females and 21 males), with ages between 8 and 10 participated in this study. Most students showed affection for mathematic, despite facing some difficulties in the subject, especially in certain contents. Initially, students did not mention mathematical experiences previously lived with GeoGebra in their classes. None of the students knew about the GeoGebra application and had never worked with it. Regarding the use of the computer, it was noted that most students had access to this resource at home.

4. RESULTS

The activity took place throughout two classes. At the beginning, a diagnosis questionnaire of the students' knowledge was made, which they did again at the end of each class to verify knowledge. From the initial questionnaire to the end, we found that everyone improved some aspect, with 25 registering that they got all questions right at the end of the process. We presented the scenario of the problem to solve and the students identified the facts and generated hypotheses individually or in groups and answered questions essentially by video call. The students result (Figure 4) are displayed as a graphic chart, which makes it easy to identify the progress.

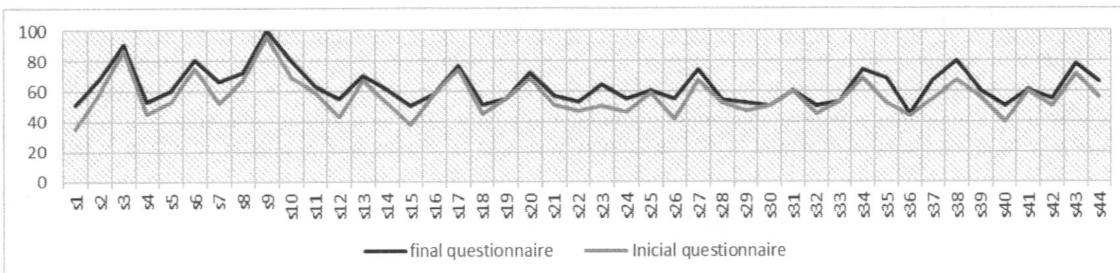

Figure 4. Learning process

Regarding the subject of mathematics, of the 44 students, 8 reported that they did not like the subject and only 5 admitted that they did not felt difficulties in calculating the area of a figure and the volume of a solid. All students except 3, admitted during the work of exploring the GeoGebraBook that GeoGebra helped them to better understand the concept of area and volume. All students were enthusiastic about the task, some referred to "how cool" (S6 & S15), "this is really cool" (S2, S23 & S28), others observed carefully what happened while manipulating the mobile points of the applet. The area and volume applets (Figure 5) available in the GeoGebraBook are fully dynamic, meaning that points can be moved along function graphs, parameters are changeable using sliders, and text adapts automatically to changes.

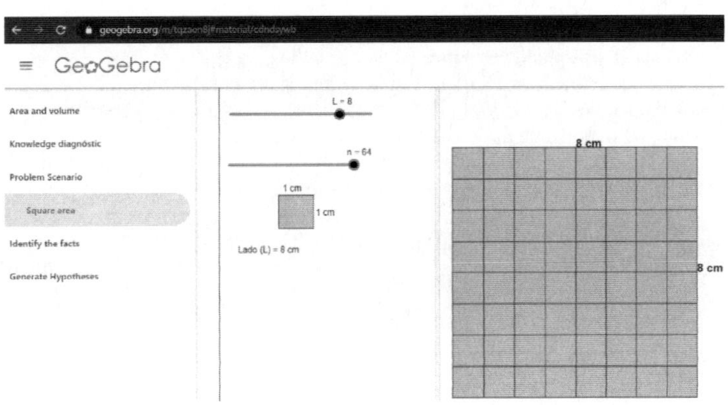

Figure 5. GeoGebraBook Area and Volume

Regarding the interaction mechanism, students interacted with the teacher and colleagues through Google Hangout on asynchronous lessons and video call in the synchronous lessons. Of the 44 students 20 were joining the class through computer and the rest through tablet.

All students were able to view the resources through the link to the GeogebraBook that was placed in the classroom, a place where they were used to access classes every day. The use of the Classroom platform allowed, throughout this new challenge, to shorten distances and streamline the planned learning activities. Children's learning, benefit from activities that involve gesturing in the development of mathematical concepts, the learning by doing (Novack, Congdon, Hemani-Lopez & Goldin-Meadow, 2014). So, we structured the work on GeoGebraBook by tasks that allowed, in a very interesting way, to give accurate feedback on the evolution and acquisition of knowledge by the students.

All students managed to reach to the end of the process successfully. Regarding the use of GeoGebra to explain mathematical concepts, none of the students considered it insufficient or sufficient, 12 considered that GeoGebra was good to help them understand the concepts, 12 considered it to be very good and 20 that GeoGebra was great. Still on the use of GeoGebra, most (27 students) found GeoGebra very easy to use and manipulate, 10 students considered it was easy and the remaining 7 considered that it was moderately easy to use. It should be noted that no student found the manipulation of GeoGebra applets difficult.

At the end of the process, students reflected on the advantages and difficulties they encountered in the process. All admitted that the manipulation of the applets helped them to perceive better the concepts covered. We present the students' speeches in the final focus group below (Table 1):

Table 1. Categories of analysis from student responses

Dimension	Student
GeoGebra helped understanding concepts	it made me understand the story better! (s1)
	it clarified some doubts that I had (s2)
	it was much easier to see (s3)
	learning like this is fun (s9)
	it helped me to understand the area and the volume faster (s11)
	it is easier to learn when we have fun (s12)
	it helps me achieving more easily (s13)
	it is interactive and allowed me to move, see and understand it better (s14).
	it is interactive and when I moved, I realized how it works (s15).
	i saw it, we put measurements, and then it gives us the answers (S17).
	it is very cool and fun (s19)
	it helped me to understand (s21)
	it lets me visualize and interact with the concept of area and volume (s28).
	it helped me to understand, I was able to put the squares and count to check if I was right (s30).
	simplified perceiving and calculating (s42)
GeoGebra helped visualizing concepts	Because it explains me the steps on how can I do it (s2)
	Because it demonstrates how it works and I see it (s4)
	Because it helps us memorizing (s5)
	Because it makes complicated things look simply (s7).
	Because it's more fun (s13)
	When I have difficulty thinking, I go there to understand better and see the result (s15).
	because we can put several measures to see the area (s16)
	It helps me to memorize and to visualize better than other times (s20).
	with GeoGebra it is easier to use because you can immediately see the answer and understand (s21)
	Because I understand and visualize better how it works (s23).
	I think GeoGebra helps me to understand the subject better because I can practice (s31).
	Because it lets me visualize the material and it's fun (s33).
	Because it teaches us things we don't know and reminds us of things we know (s34)
	It allows me to do a lot of things with math (s35)
	Because it is very practical and simple, as we just need to move those little pieces, and I think it is also a lot of fun (s37).
	Because you can see very well when we move (s38).
	Because we see better, and it makes calculations easier to do (s40).

Most students considered that the use of GeoGebra makes classes more attractive. In the opinion of the students, the presentation of the problem and exploration of GeoGebra helped them to understand the concept of area and the concept of volume. It allowed "*perceiving*" (s1), "*clarifying doubts*" (s2), "*moving, seeing and understanding*" (s14) the "*area and the volume faster*" (s11). Through the manipulation of the applets, it was possible to "*make mathematical concepts easier*" (s12), to learn in a fun and interactive way, visualizing the result of their experimentation. They consider that GeoGebra, besides helping to better understand the concepts, helped to visualize what they mean mathematically, since in their opinion, it "*explain steps and how to do it*" (s2), "*demonstrate how it works*" (s4), "*help decorate*" (s5) the contents. The fact that they are able to investigate a phenomenon, promote learning by doing, create ideas and apply "*the contents makes complicated concepts simple*" (s7), allows "*better visualization* "(s20; s23) and makes learning mathematics "*more fun*"(s13). They admit that GeoGebra helped them to "*better understand the subject because they can practice*" (s31), in addition "*it makes calculations easier to do*" (s40).

5. DISCUSSION AND CONCLUSION

Results showed that the manipulation of the simulators promoted the student's motivation to work on mathematical concepts and that the GeoGebra application, namely the GeoGebraBook, can help the teacher to support learning for his students.

The use of the problem-based learning methodology allowed students to develop independence, responsibility, and their ability to work. Additionally, results suggest that these software packages can be used to encourage discovery and experimentation in classrooms, and their visualization features can be effectively employed in teaching. Students admit the advantages of using the GeoGebraBook for their learning but find it difficult to explain why. Our results meet the results of Seloraji and Kwan (2017) when they indicate that the use of the GeoGebra software promotes good learning outcome in geometric transformations, especially in the topic of reflection. NCTM (2009) suggests that the learning of geometry can be done using dynamic software with the use of concrete models through activities and tools that allow students to explore conjectures about geometry and reflect carefully about geometric concepts. The students identified the problem, investigated, debated, interpreted, and produced possible justifications and solutions or resolutions. We observed that students collaborated to be able to solve the proposed problems playfully, meeting what Ng, Ting, Lam and Liu (2020) wrote. According to these authors, problem-based learning is a strategy that allows improving the dynamics of the classroom and the relationship between teacher, student, and content. Our students used video calls preferentially to clarify doubts in line with the study of Poikela et al. (2009), according to which students prefer to use online collaboration to get reassurance for being correct than thinking about solving the problem. Like in Zhou (2012) study, our students developed the ability to solve problems creatively which is essential to think scientifically.

The use of the GeoGebra application, and in particular the Geogebrabook, made it possible to clarify the instructions for students less autonomous, to improve their ability to work online. GeoGebraBook has attracted students' attention since the first minute, engaging them for the activities, motivating them to explore and solve the proposed problems. We observed that the students asynchronously worked with their peers, but we noticed that they preferred synchronous calls with the teacher to clarify doubts. These results are in line with what Poikela et al. (2009) say, according to which on problem-based learning method there is a focus on synchronous learning to achieve shared understanding and knowledge. For students, the Open-source packages are an opportunity to use them in the teaching-learning process, but for the community it also represents an opportunity to collaborate and evolve (Hohenwarter, et al., 2008). We have provided an example on how GeoGebraBook can be used to promote mathematics learning. We found that the area and volume simulators contributed very positively to "understanding the concept of the volume area" (S2, S5, S34 & S38). For the teaching of geometry, GeoGebraBook is more advantageous than a paper or an animation that takes the figures in different directions, because it is interactive, dynamic, and sequentially structured. GeoGebraBook was a useful resource to assist students of primary school in solving problems, but also for checking regularities.

As an exploratory research, this study allowed us to draw some conclusions that constitute suggestions for future studies: the use of Geogebrabook can be revealing to help students understanding threshold concepts, as the sharing of results by students can contribute to the establishment of connections. We live in an environment where the technological tools can be employed for recording, constructing, and visualizing the shared understanding and knowledge in face-to-face tutorials. In an online teaching environment, it seems relevant to us to consider in future studies the implications that, video lessons combined with Geogebrabook, can have for mathematical education. Problem-based learning follows the structure of problem solving within shared or individual learning. It also seems relevant to understand the impact of this teaching model on the development of transversal skills and interdisciplinary content, because it can influence guidelines for education.

ACKNOWLEDGEMENT

We would like to thank the Directorship of Colégio Santa Eulália (Santa Maria da Feira - Aveiro), in particular Dr. Madalena Malta for the possibility of carrying out data collection, but also to the Pedagogical Directorship of Colégio Santa Eulália (www.colegiosantaeulalia.pt), to the teachers and students of the Primary school involved.

REFERENCES

Bogdan, R., & Biklen, S. (1994). *Investigação Qualitativa em Educação*. Uma introdução à teoria e aos métodos. Porto Editora: Porto.

Breda, A., Serrazina, L., Menezes, L., Sousa, L., & Oliveira, P. (2011). Geometria e Medida no Ensino Básico. Lisboa: Ministério da Educação, Direcção Geral de Inovação e Desenvolvimento Curricular.

Crooks, N. M., & Alibali, M. W. (2014). Defining and measuring conceptual knowledge in mathematics. Developmental Review, 34(4), pp. 344–377.

Eviyanti, C. Y., Surya, E., Syahputra, E., & Simbolon, M. (2017). Improving the students' mathematical problem-solving ability by applying problem-based learning model in VII grade at SMPN 1 Banda Aceh Indonesia. *International Journal of Novel Research in Education and Learning*, *4*(2), pp. 138-144.

Hohenwarter, M., Hohenwarter, J., Kreis, Y., & Lavicza, Z. (2008). Teaching and learning calculus with free dynamic mathematics software GeoGebra. In *11th International Congress on Mathematical Education. Monterrey, Nuevo Leon, Mexico*.

Lemke, R., & Siple, I. Z. (2018). Funções reais de duas variáveis e Geogebrabook: recursos dinâmicos para o ensino de Cálculo. *Revista BoEM*, *6*(11), pp. 18-36.

Lencastre, J. A., & Araújo, M. J. (2007). Impacto das tecnologias em contexto educativo formal. In Libro de *Actas do Congreso Internacional Galego-Portugués de Psicopedagoxía*, A. *Coruña/Universidade da Coruña: Revista Galego-Portuguesa de Psicoloxía e Educación*, pp. 624-632.

Lima, J. A., & Pacheco, J. A. (2006). *Fazer investigação*. Porto: Porto Editora.

McMillan, J., & Schumacher, S. (1997). *Research in Education: a conceptual introduction*. New York: Longman.

National Council of Teachers of Mathematics (2009). *Princípios e Normas para a Matemática Escolar*. APM: Lisboa.

Ng, O. L., Ting, F., Lam, W. H., & Liu, M. (2020). Active learning in undergraduate mathematics tutorials via cooperative problem-based learning and peer assessment with interactive online whiteboards. *The Asia-Pacific Education Researcher*, *29*(3), pp. 285-294.

Novack, M. A., Congdon, E. L., Hemani-Lopez, N., & Goldin-Meadow, S. (2014). From action to abstraction: Using the hands to learn math. *Psychological Science*, *25*(4), pp. 903-910.

Poikela, S., Vuoskoski, P., and Kaerna, M. (2009) 'Developing creative learning environment in problem-based learning', in Tan, O. S. (eds.) Problem-based Learning and Creativity, Cengage Learning, Singapore, pp. 67-85.

Rohaeti, E. E., & Bernard, M. (2018). The students mathematical understanding ability through scientific-assisted approach of geogebra software *Infinity Journal*, *7*(2), pp. 165-172.

Seabra, M., Barros, P. M., Pires, M. V., & Martins, C. (2019). Projeto EGID3: ensino da Geometria, investindo no diagnóstico, dificuldades e desafios. *In International Conference on Innovation*, Documentation and Education: Innodoct/19, pp. 1089-1097. Universitat Politècnica de València.

Seloraji, P., & Eu, L. K. (2017). Students' Performance in Geometrical Reflection Using GeoGebra. *Malaysian Online Journal of Educational Technology*, *5*(1), pp. 65-77.

Zhou, C. (2012). Teaching engineering student's creativity: A review of applied strategies. *Journal on Efficiency and Responsibility in Education and Science*, *5*(2), pp. 99-114.

DEFINING PROCESS STRUCTURE FOR PROJECT RESOURCE ALLOCATION

Mihaela Carmen Grigore, Sorin Ionescu and Doina Marina Stefan
University Polytechnic of Bucharest – Faculty of Entrepreneurship, Business Engineering and Management
Bucharest, Romania

ABSTRACT

Resource allocation has become an activity with high criticality and impact on product delivery, going to transformation into a process involving multiple stakeholders.

The purpose of this paper is to present the results of a PhD research with defined resource allocation diagram, process and subprocesses, based on previous work results analysis and interpretation, having input from local project management community through online surveys and propose those for a larger input and implementation as process improvement in project management.

Availability of resources in projects has definitive impact on product delivery. Key function resources allocated to multiple projects within an organization create dependencies to all involved projects, therefore risks coming along to all involved products and organization's strategic targets.

Contribution of this paper is foreseen as important to large project management-oriented individuals and organizations, providing a guidance and good practice for designing and implementing improved processes with focus on resource allocation.

KEYWORDS

Resource Allocation, Process, Subprocess, Diagram, Product

1. INTRODUCTION

Projects can be considered as a set of activities that must be completed in accordance to specific objectives which involves the utilization of a company's resources (Alias et al, 2014).

Project development is done through project management processes.

A process may be defined as a sequence of activities completed by participants with the scope of meeting targets and deliver increased value to an organization (Ionescu, 2017).

Product delivery is done with the participation of all compartments, each compartment having its own contribution. As each product has its own value, it results that each activity contributes to obtain value (Ionescu, 2017).

Project focused organizations have defined and implemented processes around mostly of the project management areas. Thus, in a multicultural large program environment, project resource allocation has become a great challenge to program/project managers and product owners, dedicated processes for resource allocation becoming mandatory for program/project success.

Resource allocation has become an activity with high criticality and impact on product delivery, going to transformation into a process involving multiple stakeholders.

The purpose of this paper is to present the results of a PhD research with defined resource allocation diagram, process and subprocesses, based on previous work results analysis and interpretation, having input from local project management community through online surveys and propose those for a larger input and implementation as process improvement in project management.

Availability of resources in projects has definitive impact on product delivery. Key function resources allocated to multiple projects within an organization create dependencies to all involved projects, therefore risks coming along to all involved products and organization's strategic targets.

Contribution of this paper is foreseen as important to large project management-oriented individuals and organizations, providing a guidance and good practice for designing and implementing improved processes with focus on resource allocation.

2. DEFINING PROCESS STRUCTURE

From a Project Management perspective, critical success factors, are characteristics, conditions or variables, that can have a significant impact on the success of the project when properly sustained, maintained or managed (Alias et al, 2014).

Organizational and project success factors are influenced by the inside and outside perception as well.

Stakeholders' perception defines the organizational image.

Various assumptions over an organizational image have been approached and brought into attention by Richard W. Scott that contributes to understanding the essential organizational characteristics. The system rationale: the organizations are collectively focused on tracking certain specific targets and high formalized structures (Scott, 1998).

Managing a multi-project environment requires a different method than managing a single project. The main challenge of managing a multi-project environment is the allocation of the scarce human resources over the projects in execution (Ponsteen and Kusters, 2014). That results in a need of process definition for resource allocation.

Project resource allocation represent a challenge to all project managers, especially in the IT Software Development area, where project outcome is not very well known in most cases.

A resource problem in one project can easily create problems in many other projects. Therefore, solving the resource allocation problem is crucial for the performance of the organization (Ponsteen and Kusters, 2014).

Allocation of resources to multiple projects creates dependencies between projects or even programs. The need of designing and implementing a resource allocation process, shared and agreed with all involved stakeholders has become mandatory in large project-oriented organizations to ensure projects success.

The process represents a sequence of activities that generates a desired outcome (Ionescu, 2017).

In order to propose best practices in resource allocation, as process improvement in project management, a diagram for resource allocation process has been developed, based on research analysis and surveys results interpretation.

Following our research results, we have designed the resource allocation process diagram, which in detail, may be explained as follows:

The resource allocation process is managed by the program manager together with the involved project managers. The current year book of work is decomposed by the program manager in projects. The project managers build the work breakdown structure for those projects they are responsible for. Based on the detailed work breakdown structures, the resource estimations are done, as well as definition of roles and needed skills within each project. Depending on determined resource availability, the program manager consulting project managers will decide the allocation of resources to projects. For those cases where lack of resources for project completion is identified, the program manager consulting the sponsor/ product owner will step to prioritizing projects and/or project activities and/or asking for new positions permanent/ temporary to be created/ approved, so that resource allocation may be completed. Resource allocation percentage is defined within same process.

The resource allocation process diagram proposed for guidance and implementation is presented in Figure 1:

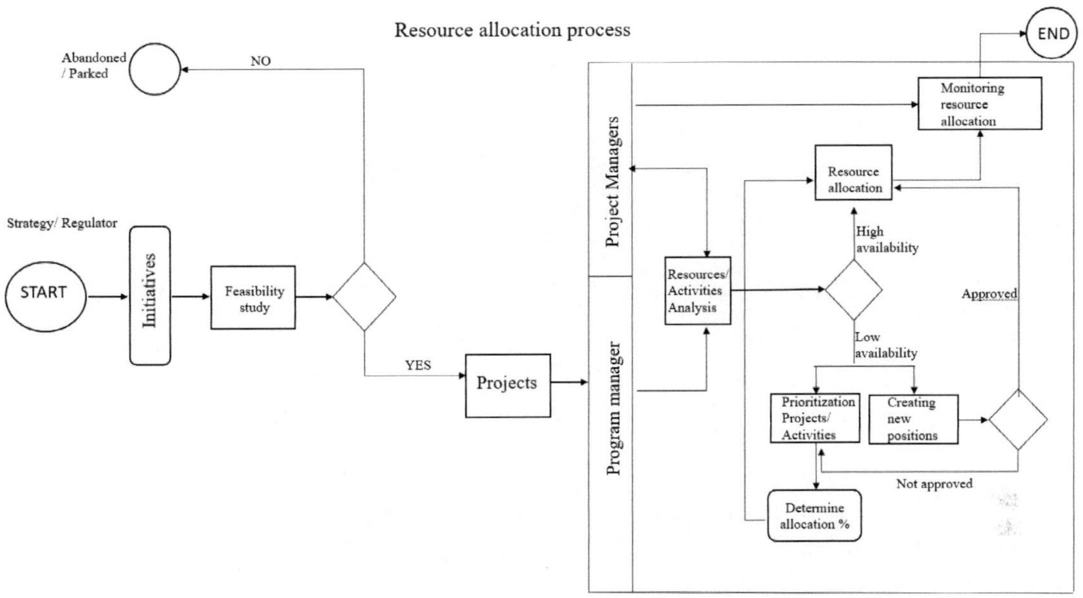

Figure 1. Resource allocation process diagram

The proposed resource allocation process is composed of subprocesses. A subprocess is represented by a sequence of activities that ensure the completion of a process.

The subprocesses of the resource allocation process are defined as follows:

1. Resources/ Activities Analysis
2. Prioritization Projects/ Activities
3. Creating New Positions
4. Resource Allocation
5. Monitoring Resource Allocation

The detailed list of subprocesses activities are presented in Figures 2-6.

1. Resources/ Activities Analysis:

Resource/ Activities analysis subprocess

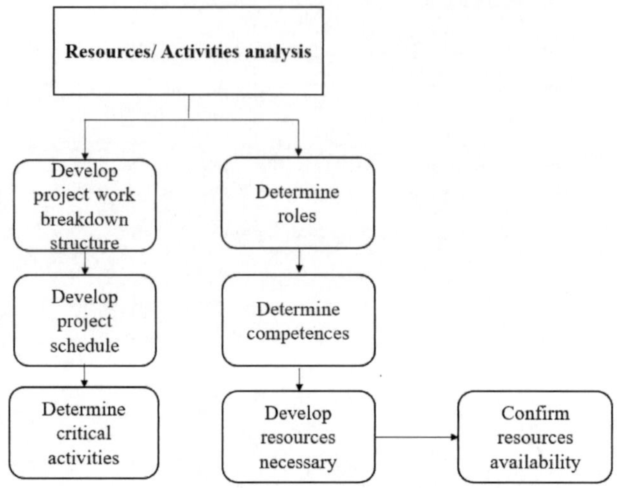

Figure 2. Resources/ Activities analysis subprocess diagram

2. Prioritization Projects/ Activities

Prioritization Projects/ Activities subprocess

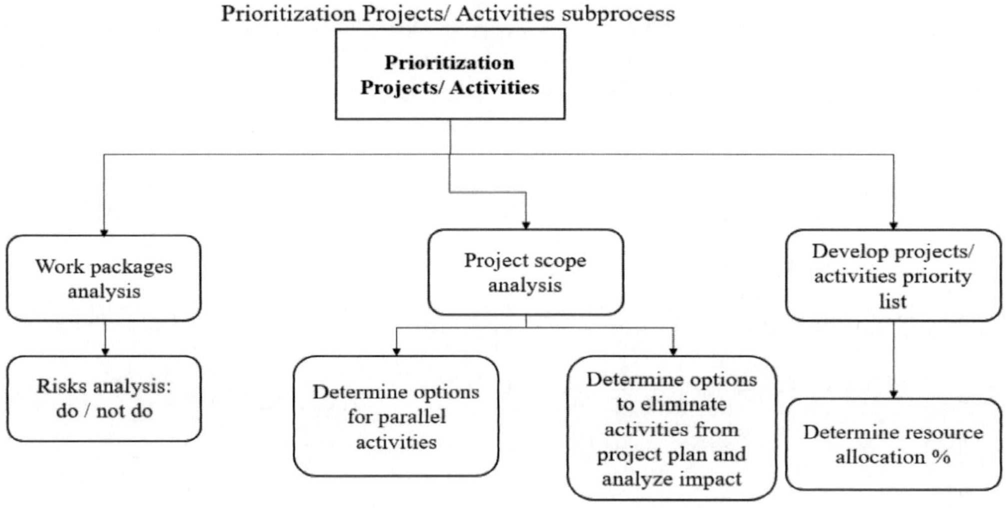

Figure 3. Prioritization Projects/ Activities subprocess diagram

3. Creating New Positions

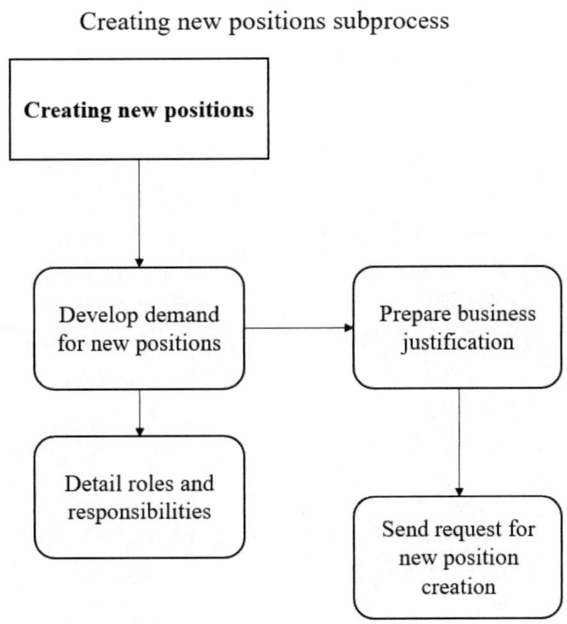

Figure 4. Creating new positions subprocess diagram

4. Resource Allocation

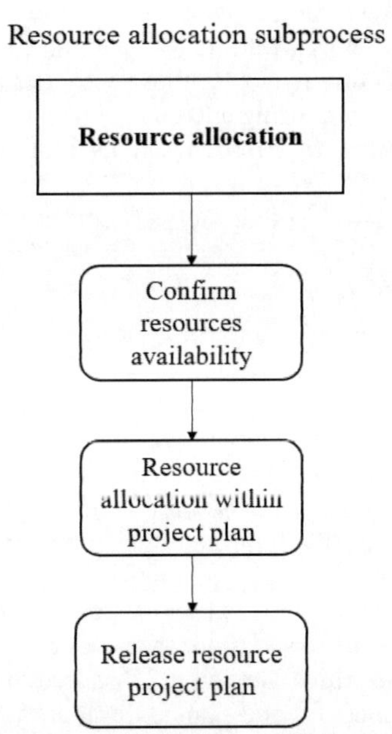

Figure 5. Resource allocation subprocess diagram

5. Monitoring Resource Allocation

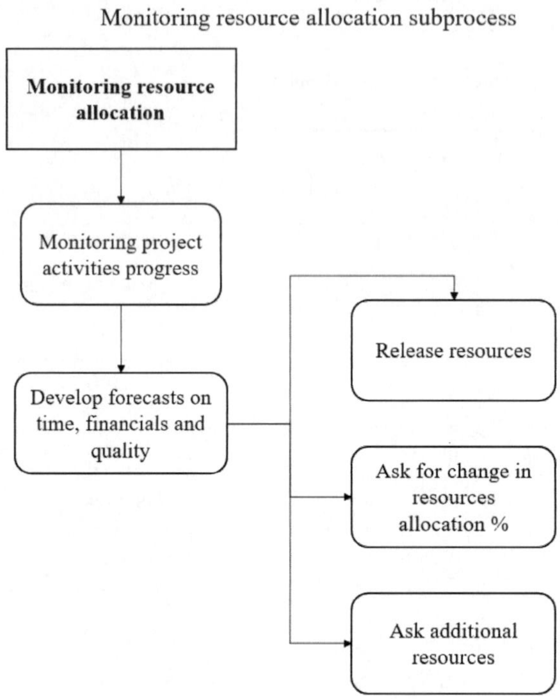

Figure 6. Monitoring resource allocation subprocess diagram

The resource allocation process incorporates in its flow the activities identified through PhD research as being critical for project delivery. According to the research study and author's recommendations, criticality of activities is extended to those activities with direct impact on delivery, highlighting the risk of not having product acceptance from the product owner in case these activities are missing from the project plan and not considered during project execution, monitoring and control phases.

The developed process is intended to be proposed as best practice for project management process improvement.

A best practice is a proven process that delivers measurable improvements in efficiency and/or effectiveness.

3. CONCLUSION

High complexity and focus on project development worldwide have brought even more into the attention of practitioners and researchers the need of designing a context to resource availability for product delivery.

Efficient planning is crucial for project success and it involves planning of those activities required in order to obtain the scope of the project. Criticality of the activities is widely discussed in the context of their existence on the critical path of the project. Author's research points out the need and justification to extend the rationale of activities criticality to those activities whose absence from the project plan would have direct impact on deliverables of the project, creating a high risk of non-acceptance of the product.

The advantage of introducing the critical activities illustrated in the resource allocation process flow is to significantly reduce the risk of product non acceptance. In addition to this, the implementation of a resource allocation process adapted to project's scope and utilized project management methodology ensures transparency for main stakeholders within complex programs/ portfolios with shared key resources and meeting project milestones.

The resource allocation process including subprocesses may be applied in Waterfall based developed projects as well as Agile fashioned.

Possible limitation would appear in case of large portfolios with teams located in several world regions, communication between project managers utilizing shared resources being essential for the successful implementation of the resource allocation process.

The data on resource allocation process presented in this paper will be considered for further investigation in order to help define the state of the art within the PhD research mentioned in the Acknowledgement section and will stay as basis of development for a Good Practices in resource allocation for project monitoring framework, with focus on IT Software Development projects.

ACKNOWLEDGEMENT

This paper has been developed as part of an ongoing PhD research at the Polytechnic University of Bucharest, related to resource allocation and quality assurance in project monitoring. The title of the thesis is "Development of modules for resource allocation and quality assurance in project monitoring".

REFERENCES

Alias, Z., et al, 2012, *Project Management towards Best Practice*, ASIA Pacific International Conference on Environment Behavior Studies, Giza, Egypt, pp. 108-120.

Alias, Z., et al, 2014, *Determining Critical Success Factors of Project Management practice: A conceptual framework*, AMER International Conference on Quality of Life, Sabah, Malaysia, pp. 61-69.

Ionescu, S.C., 2017, *Introduction in Management*, POLITEHNICA PRESS, Bucharest, Romania.

Ponsteen, A. and Kusters, R.J., 2014, *Classification of Human and Automated Resource Allocation Approaches in Multi-Project Management*, 28th IPMA World Congress, Rotterdam, The Nederlands, pp. 165-173.

Scott, W. Richard, 1998, Organizations: rational, natural and open systems, Canadian Journal of Sociology/ Cahiers canadiens de sociologie, pp. 29(1).

PROMOTING FORMATIVE ASSESSMENT IN MATHEMATICS TEACHER EDUCATION: AN EXPERIENCE OF DISTANCE TEACHING

Annalisa Cusi[1], Francesca Morselli[2] and Agnese Ilaria Telloni[3]
[1]*Mathematics Department, Sapienza University of Rome, Piazzale Aldo Moro 5, Rome (Italy)*
[2]*Mathematics Department, University of Genoa, Via Dodecaneso 35, Genoa (Italy)*
[3]*Dep. of Industrial Engineering and Mathematical Sciences, Polytechnic University of Ancona Via Brecce Bianche 12, Ancona (Italy)*

ABSTRACT

We discuss a distance teaching-learning approach, developed within two courses for prospective mathematics teachers, exploiting digital technologies to activate formative assessment practices. In particular, we analyse excerpts, from synchronous and asynchronous activities within the courses, to highlight the formative assessment processes that were activated, the feedback provided by prospective teachers to each other and their meta-reflections that testify learning in the domain of teacher education.

KEYWORDS

Distance Teaching-Learning, Teacher Education, Formative Assessment, Feedback

1. INTRODUCTION

Distance teaching-learning at university level has become an important focus for research in Mathematics Education. Many researchers (see, for instance, Albano & Ferrari, 2008; Silverman & Hoyos, 2018) stressed that e-learning, which combines face-to-face lectures and online activities by using synchronous or asynchronous tools of communication, could support students at different levels (cognitive, metacognitive and affective). Moreover, research highlighted the effectiveness, at university level, of a method aimed at activating, through digital environments, formative assessment (in the following, FA) processes, which foster collaborative work between students and effective interactions between the teacher and the students (Cusi & Telloni, 2019; Albano et al., 2019).

In this paper we discuss an approach developed in the context of distance teaching (due to the COVID-19 emergency) within courses for prospective mathematics secondary teachers (in the following, PT). This approach, an adaptation of the one presented in Cusi & Morselli (2018), exploits digital technologies to activate FA practices. The aim of the paper is to analyze the processes of FA developed thanks to this approach. Specifically, the paper aims at highlighting the kind of feedback that students provide to each other in relation to a task focused on the design of teaching-learning activities aimed at characterizing the key-role played by the teacher.

2. THEORETICAL FRAMEWORK

The theoretical framework is constituted by two main components that guided both the design of the approach adopted within our courses and the analysis of the data collected during the courses.

2.1 Formative Assessment in Mathematics and Key-Role of Feedback

FA represents a fundamental element of the frame within which we develop our approach. Indeed, we think that FA could represent an effective tool to foster comparison of ideas and reflections and to the develop an effective assessment of learning in the complex domain of teacher education.

We conceive FA as a method of teaching where "[...] evidence about student achievement is elicited, interpreted, and used by teachers, learners, or their peers, to make decisions about the next steps in instruction that are likely to be better, or better founded, than the decisions they would have taken in the absence of the evidence that was elicited" (Black & Wiliam, 2009, p.7). This method is characterized by the activation, by the three main agents within the FA processes (the teacher, the learners and their peers) of specific key-strategies that Wiliam and Thompson (2007) have identified: (A) Clarifying and sharing learning intentions and criteria for success; (B) Engineering effective classroom discussions and other learning tasks that elicit evidence of student understanding; (C) Providing feedback that moves learners forward; (D) Activating students as instructional resources for one another; (E) Activating students as the owners of their own learning.

Within the European Project FaSMEd, Wiliam and Thompson's framework has been extended, considering a further dimension, that is the functionalities of technology that could support FA (Cusi, Morselli & Sabena, 2017): (a) sending and displaying; (b) processing and analyzing; (c) providing an interactive environment.

In FA, providing feedback represents a key-strategy to support students in reflecting about their learning processes to find out ways of overcoming their difficulties. We refer in particular to the four main levels of feedback identified by Hattie and Timperley (2007): (1) feedback about the task, which includes feedback about how well a task is being accomplished or performed; (2) feedback about the processing of the task, which concerns the processes underlying tasks or relating and extending tasks; (3) feedback about self-regulation, which addresses the way students monitor, direct, and regulate actions toward the learning goal; (4) feedback about the self as a person, which expresses evaluations and affect about the student.

2.2 The Dialectic Theory-Practice in Teacher Education

Our research may be inserted into the stream that focuses on mathematics teacher education, with a special focus on the need for teachers' reflection about their own practice (Jaworski, 2001) and the role of awareness in teaching (Mason, 2008). Mason claims that teacher educators should lead teachers to become aware "not simply of the fact of different ways of intervening, but of the fact of subtle sensitivities that guide or determine choices between types and timings of interventions" (p. 49), thus promoting teachers' shifts of attention toward constructs, theories, and practices that can inform and guide their future choices. As a consequence, it is important to focus on the complex interplay between theory and practice within teacher education programmes.

We refer here to the work by Cusi and Malara (2016), who propose a method for in-service teacher education that, in a former work (Cusi & Morselli, 2018), we adapted to the case of PT. Adopting a narrative approach, already used in the field of teacher education (Lloyd, 2006; Zazkis, Sinclair and Liljedahl 2009), we asked PT to imagine and narrate what could happen in the class when the activities are implemented. As advocated by Zazkis, Sinclair and Liljedahl (2009), the activity of lesson play, that is writing a virtual dialogue between teacher and students, may foster PT' focus on the process of teaching, and finally promote their awareness. In the present contribution we present a further evolution of our method for PT education in the context of distance teaching, namely the activation of FA processes, by means of digital technologies, to support the PT' design of fictional classroom discussions and subsequent reflections on this design.

3. RESEARCH CONTEXT AND QUESTIONS

The study documented in this paper was carried out during the academic year 2020-21, within two courses of Mathematics Education for the master-degree in Mathematics developed at the University of Genova and at Sapienza University of Rome. Totally, 35 students attended the courses. More specifically, there were 7 students attending a laboratory course in Mathematics Education (16 hours) within the master-degree in Mathematics at the University of Genova (3 of them are enrolled in a degree in Science) and 28 students attending a course in Mathematics education (48 hours) within the master-degree in Mathematics at Sapienza

University of Rome (3 of them enrolled in the master-degree course in Physics and 1 enrolled in the master-degree course in Aerospace Engineering).

The students (in the following PT) were attending their fourth year of degree course (5 years totally). They did not yet experience practicum, since this is usually done during the fifth year. Then, when they participated to the course, they did not have any experience in teaching.

Within the course the teacher educators (two of the authors) presented theoretical tools useful to frame the classroom activities and to analyze the roles played by the teacher during classroom discussions (one of the theoretical tools was the $M_{AE}AB$ construct, see Cusi & Malara 2016). Initially the teacher educators (TE) guided the PT to use the tools to analyze excerpts from real classroom discussions. Afterwards, PT were involved in these FA activities:

a. they were given tasks, and were asked to perform their a-priori analysis and to analyze some solutions of these tasks produced by students during teaching experiments;
b. they were asked to create fictional classroom discussions focused on the same tasks, explicitly referring to theoretical tools;
c. the fictional discussions were shared among the PT and each of them was asked to provide a written peer-review of at least one fictional discussion (in asynchronous mode by means of the Moodle platform);
d. the TE collected both the fictional discussions created by PT and the peer reviews to organize synchronous collective discussions, by means of the Zoom platform, aimed at sharing and analyzing the work of PT;
e. PT were asked to work in small groups and develop, during the last part of each course, the design of a complete activity, that is to create their own task, develop an a-priori analysis of the task itself, make hypothesis of possible students' answers and create the related fictional discussion starting from the students' answers;
f. the final lessons of the courses were devoted to synchronous presentations, by means of the Zoom platform, of the activities designed by groups of PT, during which a group of reviewers was asked to comment the whole design process, referring to specific guidelines provided by TE, who themselves gave feedback to the designed activities during the collective synchronous discussions.

Most of the activities were performed in small groups. Only activities b and c were performed individually. In this paper, we are focusing on the FA that is developed through the adaptation of our method for PT education to the context of distance teaching. More specifically, we aim at studying the feedback that are provided to PT during some of the activities of the courses.

4. ANALYSIS

In this paragraph we analyze, drawing from our framework, data collected from the phases c (asynchronous peer review on the creation of fictional classroom discussions), d (synchronous collective discussions focused on the fictional discussions created by PT and guided by TE) and f (synchronous collective discussions focused on the presentation of the activities designed by group of PT, during which other PT acted as reviewers).

4.1 Analysis of Excerpts from Phase C

The starting point of the activity was the analysis of data from a teaching experiment carried out by one of the authors in grade 9. The task ("*Prove that the sum of a number and its square is always an even number*") referred to the first approach to algebraic proof. PT were given four solutions produced by groups of students and were asked to write down a fictional classroom discussion, starting from the data at disposal. The discussions were to be presented in a word document and accompanied by the analysis of the roles played by the teacher (referring to the $M_{AE}AB$ construct). Students organized their product in a table: one column contained the fictional discussion, the second column contained the justification and explanation of the fictional interventions within the discussion, in terms of the theoretical tools at disposal.

PT uploaded their fictional discussions (in non-anonymous form) in a "Workshop" activity in Moodle. Afterwards, each of them was assigned randomly as a reviewer to another discussion. The task for PT was explained by the TE in a post on Moodle: "I just assigned to each of you a discussion created by one of your classmates, you have to "evaluate" it by next week. The "evaluation" that you are asked to do is not a "correction", rather an analysis by means of theoretical tools that we presented during the course: do you think that in the fictitious discussion the teacher is playing the roles of the $M_{AE}AB$ construct? If possible, please indicate those interventions that you consider very efficient, and finally write a brief concluding remark".

In this way, a process of peer review (FA strategy D) was realized. Reviewers provided feedback (FA strategy C) at different levels. When commenting, they showed to the TE and their mates their degree of understanding of the theoretical tools, thus becoming responsible of their own learning (FA strategy E). Here we present some comments from the peer review and analyze them in terms of level of feedback (Hattie & Timperley, 2007) provided to the author of the fictional discussion.

The first comment is from Alessia to Flavia and represents a *feedback about the task*. Alessia acknowledges that Flavia accomplished the task in a correct way, making the teacher play the expected roles: "I think the most common role played by the teacher is "investigating subject": the teacher always tries to elicit students' attitude of research and listens to the different proposals without judging them, even too much in my opinion".

The second comment, again from Alessia to Flavia, contains a *feedback about the processing of the task*: Alessia observes that the teacher imagined by Flavia should have intervened more, in order to promote the understanding of the meaning of proof. Alessia points out other roles that the teacher should have played in order to promote students' understanding. Besides referring to the roles of the teacher, Alessia comments in reference to the learning objective (proof): "The teacher, although saying that Group 1 just described one case, doesn't underline that "doing one example" is not sufficient as a proof. [...] The discussion seems a mere "show" of the groups' strategies, only in the shift to group 4 there is some assessment of the efficiency of the solution. What is missing is, for instance, the role of "guide in promoting a balance between semantic and syntactic dimensions": the teacher presents both verbal and algebraic approach, but does not compare them, then the students are not led to see similarities and differences between the approaches".

The third comment, from Livia to Simone, represents a *feedback about the self as a person*: Livia recognizes that Simone "acted" as a good teacher: "I think that Simone worked well; if it had been a real discussion, he would have involved the students in a correct way".

In some cases, reviewers wrote also some reflections that were inspired by the fictional discussion. Such reflections were intended to be shared and discussed by the whole class in a subsequent moment. We underline that the presence of these reflections is a promising fact, in terms of efficacy of the activity (discussion creation and peer reviewing) for PT education.

4.2 Analysis of an Excerpt from Phase D

Within this activity, the PT were asked to organize a fictional classroom discussion to be conducted during a lesson developed in the context of early algebra in grade 7, starting from a set of real answers to a task collected during a teaching experiment. The PT were asked to design a discussion aimed at a reflection on mistakes and on the different strategies carried out by students.

The following excerpt refers to a moment in the synchronous discussion, during which the TE displays three written texts from PT' fictional discussions connected to different approaches to the introduction of the discussion. In the third approach, proposed by Federica, the teacher writes at the blackboard the symbolic expressions that summarize the main students' strategies and guides the class to discuss the strategies. This approach is the one which is less in tune with the $M_{AE}AB$ construct, so the TE, with the aim of making PT focus on strengths and weaknesses of the proposed approaches, asks to the whole group of PT to comment on them.

1. Federica: I wrote the third one and in fact I thought it was initially correct to clarify what the right answer was and to identify the wrong answers. Then each group would go to the blackboard to explain the reasoning because, at that point, it is clear what the right answer is, so there would have been a discussion from each group to understand how they reached the answer. …The important thing is that I wanted the correct solution to be clear first, then to think about how to get there.
2. TE: Why did you choose to reformulate the solving approaches of the groups of students?
3. Federica: Because I wanted to write them mathematically to explain, verbally, how students reasoned.

4. TE: From the choices you made, maybe you think that, if the students are those who speak at first in a discussion aimed at comparing their ideas, the risk is that the discussion will not follow the direction planned by the teacher. So, you prefer to anticipate and reformulate students' answers.
5. Federica: Yes, since I never experimented, in my experiences as student, a different kind of discussion. In my experience, it was the teacher that used to say "it is right" or "it is wrong", then each student could speak, but all the students already had the idea of what was right and what was wrong. If they do not know what is right or wrong, they do not question their answers and so they do not listen to their mates. Instead, if they know that they made a mistake and that there are different right answers, they try to understand how to reach the correct answer.
   Giulio asks to comment what Federica said.
6. Giulio: I would like to say that, within an activity of this kind, I think that immediately having an idea of what the correct and incorrect answers are is demotivating because this approach establishes a hierarchy immediately. I find this approach, in general, wrong in the case in which the aim is to share strategies because it prevents the students who gave a wrong answer to reflect on the good parts of their answer.
7. Luca: I agree with Giulio. I would not say what is right and what is wrong at the beginning, since also those who gave a wrong answer could have started their reasoning in a correct way.
8. TE: I also think that, in this kind of discussions, it is better to leave some doubts, so that the class gets used to the fact that discussing their answers means learning by listening to others' point of view. This approach minimizes, in my opinion, the risk of situations in which everyone wants to defend his idea and does not listen to others. It is a matter of creating a classroom culture, in which students do not feel the need that the teacher, at the beginning, legitimizes or not their thinking processes.

Within this excerpt, the TE is activating important FA strategies. First of all, she has designed the collective synchronous discussion to make PT reflect on the approaches proposed by their colleagues, activating FA strategy B. In this excerpt, in particular, the focus is on the teaching approach proposed by Federica, in which the teacher declares what is the correct answer before activating a classroom discussion. As a result of this design, also FA strategies C and D are activated, since the other PT intervene in the discussion, proposing feedback to Federica. Both Giulio and Luca propose a feedback *about the processing of the task*, stressing on the limitations of Federica's approach and suggesting the positive effects of an approach in which students start to develop a classroom discussion without a-priori knowing if their answer is correct. In this discussion also the TE provides feedback to Francesca. The first feedback is *about self-regulation*, since the TE (line 4) interprets Federica's approach in relation to the possible reasons underlying her choice: the fear of not being able to follow a clear direction in the discussion if students are free to intervene from the very beginning of the discussion. This feedback enables Federica to explicit the deep reasons that led her to choose this approach. As a result, Federica proposes a meta-reflection focused on her past experiences, stressing that the limited experiences she had as a student influenced her choices and also her vision of classroom interaction.

The TE gives also a feedback *about the processing of the task* (line 8) addressed not only to Federica, but to the whole group of PT, in which she confirms Giulio and Luca's feedback, providing them with a meta-feedback (that is a feedback on the feedback) and stressing on the importance of creating a classroom culture in which students are real protagonists of discussions.

4.3 Analysis of an Excerpt from Phase F

We present an excerpt from the collective synchronous discussion on the activity designed by two PT, Alice and Miriam. Since Alice and Miriam's design was widely not in line with the theoretical perspectives discussed during the course, the two reviewers, Federica (the same protagonist of the excerpt analyzed in paragraph 4.2) and Clara, have identified different weaknesses of the activity in their revision work. In the following excerpt, in particular, Federica and Clara focus on the weaknesses highlighted in Alice and Miriam's design of the fictional discussion.

1. Clara: It seemed to us that the teacher uses too often expressions like "good" or formulates direct judgments to students' answers. We think that, in this way, students can become demotivated. We think it is better that students themselves assess their classmates' answers. Moreover, we think that the teacher guides too much the discussion and does not listen enough to students' proposals.

2. Federica: You have planned to leave students time to reflect on the task before the discussion. In what way does the teacher refer to the work developed by students before the discussion? It seems that she does not consider what they did before.
3. Clara: Maybe it would be better to make students speak more, make them participate from the beginning, even in proposing the examples.
4. Miriam: We think that, in order to develop a lesson in a certain way, there is the need that the teacher is not only a participant, but that she also tries to put order within the discussion.
5. Alice: And we must consider that it is not the typical task proposed at school. This is the main reason why we decided that the teacher should guide more the discussion.

Giulia asks to intervene in the discussion.

6. Giulia: I would like to ask why expressions like "good" are considered negative within this fictional discussion. I think they could encourage students, so I cannot understand why they are negative.
7. Federica: In my opinion, it is not negative. What we wanted to say is that, as we always said during the course, if the teacher makes judgments from the very beginning, the students says "Ok, my answer is correct" or "My answer is wrong".
8. Clara: And those that gave a wrong answer could feel demoralized.
9. Giulia: But I think that, as Miriam said, in a real class, the classroom dynamics are those described by Miriam and Alice.
10. TE: The classroom dynamics are those chosen by the teacher! What Federica and Clara wanted to say is that "good!" should not be said too early in order to avoid that students do not intervene anymore. Sometimes it is better to leave a doubt and to stimulate different interventions from the students, than making a judgement that blocks the discussion.

This excerpt, like the previous one, is rich in terms of FA strategies activated and highlights the effectiveness of the choice of providing PT with specific guidelines to carry out the review process. In this way, PT were activated as resources for their classmates (FA strategy D), giving them important feedback (FA strategy C). Clara and Federica's interventions at the beginning of the excerpt (lines 1, 2, 3), in fact, represent feedback *about the processing of the task* since they criticize the approach chosen by Miriam and Alice, highlighting the problems connected to a too guided approach, in which the teacher, since the very beginning, makes judgements about students' answers. In particular, Federica (line 2) shows the contradictions behind the choice of giving time to students to work on the task and then not considering the work they have developed.

When reacting to this feedback, Miriam and Alice (lines 4 and 5) propose meta-reflections that explicit the deepest beliefs that guided their design, stressing that they think that this kind of activity (a problem solving activity involving students' exploration, formulation of conjectures and proof) is not usual in "normal school" and that the only way, for the teacher, of carrying out a discussion on this activity is to pose herself as a guide, not in the sense of the $M_{AE}AB$ construct, but in the sense of someone who directs the discussion in a strict way. This point of view is shared also by another student, Giulia, who intervenes (lines 6 and 9) to defend Miriam and Alice's choice, stressing that, in her opinion, real classes are not those on which the design of fictional discussion is focused. When reacting to Giulia' interventions, Federica and Clara (lines 7 and 8) propose meta-reflections in which they explicit the new awareness reached thanks to the previous activities of the course. As in the previous transcript, the meta-reflections are about a previous experience lived by the PT who propose them: in the case of Miriam, Alice and Giulia, they refer to a vision of teaching that collides with the theoretical tools introduced during the course, a vision strictly linked to past experiences (as students); in the case of Federica, the meta-reflection refers to a new vision of teaching that she has developed thanks to her experience within the course. We can highlight a change in Federica's vision about the effective way of designing a classroom discussion and we interpret this change in terms of Federica's professional learning.

Finally, we stress that also in this excerpt the TE intervenes, only at the end (line 10), to reformulate Clara and Federica's comments in order to legitimize the feedback they give (therefore providing a meta-feedback), so that they can really become resources for Miriam, Alice and Giulia and for the whole group of PT in general.

5. CONCLUSIONS

In this paper, we discussed a distance teaching-learning approach, developed within two courses for PT. The wide range of FA processes highlighted through our analysis of excerpts testifies the effectiveness of this approach in exploiting the functionalities of digital technologies to activate FA practices. In fact, the *sending and displaying* functionality of technology supported the TE in collecting, organizing and sharing students' written materials, making these materials become fundamental objects of reflections for PT. Moreover, our adaptation of the method for PT education to the context of distance teaching massively exploited the *providing an interactive environment* functionality, since the designed asynchronous and synchronous activities enabled TE and PT to effectively interact, contributing, thanks to the feedback provided to each other, to their own development of new awareness about the processes in which they were involved.

Thanks to our analysis, we adapted the use of Hattie and Timperley's levels of feedback to the context of teacher education, where the tasks are at a professional level: (1) *feedback about the task* refers to an effective use of the theoretical tools for the design of fictional discussions; (2) *feedback about the processing of the task* concerns the choices made within the design process and their effects in terms of learning objectives; (3) *feedback about self-regulation* refers to the factors that influence the design process; (4) *feedback about the self as a person* projects the PT in their future profession.

We also discussed the key-role of the teacher educator in both designing effective discussions to reflect on PT' fictional discussions and in legitimating, through meta-feedback, the different types of provided feedback. Moreover, we highlighted PT' meta-reflections during the discussions carried out within the courses, interpreting their reactions to the feedback as both evidences of their deepest beliefs about teaching and hints of the growing awareness they developed through their participation into the courses' activities.

As a further development, we plan to deepen this last part of our analysis to identify categories of meta-reflections.

REFERENCES

Albano, G. and Ferrari, P.L., 2008. Integrating technology and research in mathematics education: the case of e-learning. In F.J. Garcia Peñalvo (Ed.), *Advances in E-Learning: Experiences and Methodologies*. IGI Global, Hershey, PA, pp. 132-148.

Albano, G., Pierri, A. and Sabena, C., 2019. Enhancing formative assessment practices in undergraduate courses by means of online workshop. *Proceedings of ICTMT 14*. Essen, Germany, pp. 155-162.

Black, P. and Wiliam, G., 2009. Developing the theory of formative assessment. Educational Assessment, *Evaluation and Accountability*, Vol. 21, No. 1, pp. 5-31.

Cusi, A. and Telloni, A. I., 2019. The role of formative assessment in fostering individualized teaching at university level. *Eleventh Congress of the European Society for Research in Mathematics Education*. Utrecht, Netherlands, pp. 4129-4126.

Cusi, A. and Malara, N.A. 2016. The Intertwining of Theory and Practice: Influences on Ways of Teaching and Teachers' Education. In L. English, & D. Kirshner (Eds.), *Handbook of International Research in Mathematics Education 3rd Edition*. Taylor & Francis, London, pp. 504-522.

Cusi, A. and Morselli, F., 2018. Linking theory and practice: prospective teachers creating fictional classroom discussions. *Proceedings of PME 42.* Umeå, Sweden, pp. 323-330 (Vol. 2).

Cusi, A., Morselli, F. and Sabena, C., 2017. Promoting formative assessment in a connected classroom environment: design and implementation of digital resources. ZDM Mathematics Education, 49 (5), 755-767.

Hattie, J. and Timperley, H., 2007. The power of feedback. *Review of Educational Research*, Vol. 77, No. 1, pp. 81–112.

Jaworski, B., 2004. Grappling with complexity: Co-learning in inquiry communities in mathematics teaching development. *Proceedings of PME 28*. Bergen, Norway, pp. 17–36 (Vol. 1).

Lloyd, G.M., 2006. Preservice teachers' stories of mathematics classrooms: explorations of practice through fictional accounts. *Educational Studies in Mathematics*, Vol. 63, pp. 57-87.

Mason, J., 2008. Being mathematical with and in front of learners. In B. Jaworski & T. Wood (Eds.), *International handbook of mathematics teachers education*. Sense Publishers, Rotterdam, Vol. 4, pp. 31–55.

Silverman, J & Hoyos, V. (Eds.), 2018. *Distance Learning, E-Learning and Blended Learning of Mathematics*. ICME-13 Monographs. Springer, Cham, Switzerland.

Wiliam, D. and Thompson, M., 2007. Integrating assessment with instruction: What will it take to make it work?. In C. A. Dwyer (Ed.), *The future of assessment: Shaping teaching and learning*. Erlbaum, Mahwah, NJ, pp. 53–82.

Zazkis, R., Liljedahl, P., & Sinclair, N., 2009. Lesson Play – A vehicle for multiple shifts of attention in teaching. In B. Davis &S. Lerman (Eds.), *Mathematical Action & Structures of Noticing: Studies inspired by John Mason*. Sense Publishers, Rotterdam, pp.165-177.

FACTORS OF THE USE OF LEARNING ANALYTICS DASHBOARD THAT AFFECT METACOGNITION

Li Chen[1], Min Lu[2], Yoshiko Goda[3], Atsushi Shimada[4] and Masanori Yamada[2]
[1]*Graduate School of Human-Environment Studies, Kyushu University[1], 744, Motooka, Nishi-ku, Fukuoka 819-0395, Japan*
[2]*Faculty of Arts and Science, Kyushu University, 744, Motooka, Nishi-ku, Fukuoka 819-0395, Japan*
[3]*Research Center for Instructional Systems, Kumamoto University, 2-39-1, Kurokami, Chuo-ku, Kumamoto, 8600862 Japan*
[4]*Faculty of Information Science and Electrical Engineering, 744, Motooka, Nishi-ku, Fukuoka 819-0395, Japan*

ABSTRACT

In this study, we used a learning analytics dashboard (LAD) in a higher education course to support students' metacognition and evaluated the effects of its use. The LAD displays students' reading path and specific behaviors when viewing digital learning materials. The study was conducted on 53 university students to identify the factors that affected metacognition changes in terms of their awareness and behavior dimensions when using the LAD. In terms of results, first, the students' perception of visual attraction for the LAD, and behaviors related to reflection such as deleting annotations they had previously added, positively affected the changes in the *knowledge of cognition* dimension of metacognition. Second, students' perception of behavioral changes by using the LAD had positive effects on the *regulation of cognition* dimension of metacognition. However, the behaviors of using some cognitive tools, negatively affected *knowledge of cognition*, which indicated the necessity to provide more guidance or feedback to students.

KEYWORDS

Metacognition, Self-Regulated Learning, Learning Analytics Dashboard, Learning Behaviors

1. INTRODUCTION

Self-regulated learning (SRL) is a self-directive process that is important for learners to gain academic achievements such as good grades and academic skills (Zimmerman, 1998, 2002). In SRL, which includes the metacognition and motivation dimension, learners apply their cognitive learning strategies when conducting specific tasks, during which time they also monitor and reflect on their own learning processes (Tobias & Everson, 2009). Metacognition, the self-perception of the cognitive learning process, is an important dimension of SRL in which it is essential for learners to make sense of their own learning processes and regulate their learning effectively and efficiently (Tobias & Everson, 2009).

In order to support learners' metacognition, visualization is a useful tool to make learners aware of their learning processes and learning behaviors by providing specific information regarding their learning activities (Yen et al., 2018). As technology advances, various types of data can be collected through a learning analytics (LA) approach, including learning log data to represent learning behaviors. In SRL, the LA approach is useful for recording and collecting learners' learning processes and informing learners and instructors in a salient way such as with the dashboard. In this paper, we used a learning analytics dashboard (LAD) to support students' metacognition and examined the effects of the use of LAD on awareness and behavior dimensions on metacognition changes; this is useful to identify the factors that should be considered in the design of the use of the LAD.

2. LEARNING ANALYTICS APPROACHES FOR METACOGNITION

Metacognition includes two dimensions: *knowledge about cognition* and *self-regulation of cognition* (e.g., Hofer et al., 1998; Jacobs & Paris, 1987). The *Knowledge about cognition* dimension concerns learners' awareness and perceptions of their cognitive processes, which generally includes declarative knowledge, procedural knowledge, and conditional knowledge (Jacobs & Paris, 1987). *Self-regulation of cognition*, which refers to the plan and control of these cognitive processes, generally includes three metacognitive phases: planning, monitoring, and regulating (Hofer et al., 1998). When learners engage in metacognition-related activities during their learning, they usually need to use relevant knowledge and awareness about how to conduct cognitive processes, as well as plan, control, and monitor these processes.

However, these cognition and metacognition-related processes are complex and include several learning strategies; this causes difficulties in measuring metacognition (Zimmerman, 2002). As one of the most widely used metacognition measurements, 'self-reported inventory' showed some limitations regarding validity and accuracy. For example, it is difficult for learners to remember all their behaviors during the learning process, which would influence their answers during measurement (Tobias & Everson, 2009). Therefore, in addition to self-reporting inventory, other metacognition measurements capable of recording learners' learning processes are expected. The LA approach has demonstrated great potential in collecting and recording learning log data from the whole learning processes in a continuous and automatic way, without the interference of learners' perceptions or the external environment (Shimada et al., 2015; Yamada et al., 2016; Yin et al., 2015). As such, this can effectively minimize the limitations of self-reported inventory.

However, effectively providing and displaying learning information to learners and instructors remains a challenge. LAD is the integration of the LA approach with the concept of a dashboard, which visualizes the specific information regarding learning data, learning patterns, and behaviors in a concise, direct way (Teasley, 2017). LAD can help learners monitor and reflect on their learning processes, particularly in terms of recognizing what they have been doing and what they should be doing based on their learning goals (Klerkx et al., 2017).

Previous research has focused on the design and development of LAD and the effects of its use in educational environments, aiming to improve instructors' teaching and learners' learning. For example, in higher education, student-facing LADs have often been used to support online learning (e.g., Bodily et al., 2018; Kim et al., 2016) by visualizing students' operations on LADs during the online course. As a result, the positive effects of LADs on final scores (Kim et al., 2016), and the positive perceptions of LAD, were confirmed (Bodily et al., 2018). However, in spite of the findings, both of these studies indicated a necessity to motivate students to use LADs consistently. In this regard, it is necessary to take students' expectations into consideration and provide them with a personalized dashboard, statistical data information, feedback, and advice on how to improve and how to interpret the results (Teasley, 2017).

Based on the insights from previous research, we designed and developed an LAD to support metacognition. The purpose of this study is to explore the effects of LAD on supporting metacognition. Specifically, in order to improve the design and practical use of the LAD, we aim to identify the factors that impact metacognition changes in terms of students' awareness and behavior dimensions while using the LAD.

3. METHODS

3.1 Design Overview

This study was conducted in an education course where 79 undergraduate students participated. The course was conducted over a 7-week period, with one 90 minute lecture per week. During the course, students studied some basic topics regarding the challenges of modern education and learning, as well as a theoretical background in education. Orientation, which aimed to help students become familiar with the theme and the procedure of the course, was held in the first week. In Week 2~Week 8, before each lecture, the teacher distributed advanced learning materials on BookRoll, which was used as an e-book reader system. Students were asked to review the learning materials before lectures and access the learning materials during lectures.

Meanwhile, students were provided another system, the LAD named "Metaboard," to support their metacognition. On the Metaboard, students could see their own information and the class average of BookRoll learning behaviors, in an attempt to help them contextualize their learning situation relative to the class average.

3.2 BookRoll System and Metaboard

In this study, two systems were used throughout the course. First, the BookRoll system was used as an e-book reader system to store and distribute digital lecture materials. Students read this material by using functional tools such as highlighting contents, adding annotations, and posting bookmarks within the materials (Ogata et al., 2017). All the operations of these functional tools were recorded and collected as learning logs to represent students' learning behaviors in terms of reading and learning the material.

Second, an LAD named Metaboard was used to support students' metacognition. The Metaboard was designed to display details about how students read digital lecture materials on BookRoll (Chen et al., 2019a). The Metaboard consisted of two parts, a reading path overview and a detailed view. In the reading path overview (Figure 1), students could view their own score (left) and the class average (right) in the reading path of the lecture materials, including the time they spent reading each page and whether markers (highlights) or memos (annotations) were used on each page. All the information was divided into in-class and out-of-class view. The meaning of each element is as follows (Lu et al., 2020a, b):

- The node represents the page number, and the color intensity of a node indicates the reading duration for that page (the darker the color, the more time the learners spent reading).
- The thickness of the link indicates the frequency of viewing the page (the thicker the link, the more learners read on that same path).
- The color of the links indicates the direction of the reading path (light gray: turn to the next page; dark gray: turn to the previous page; mint: jump forward; orange: jump backward).
- The smaller circles (circles with the letter H and M) indicate highlight markers (H) or memo annotations (M) included on that page, and the color intensity indicates the total number of tools used.

When students click a page node, a detailed view of this page is provided (Figure 2), including the specific numbers of highlight markers and memo annotations, as well as the reading time for that page.

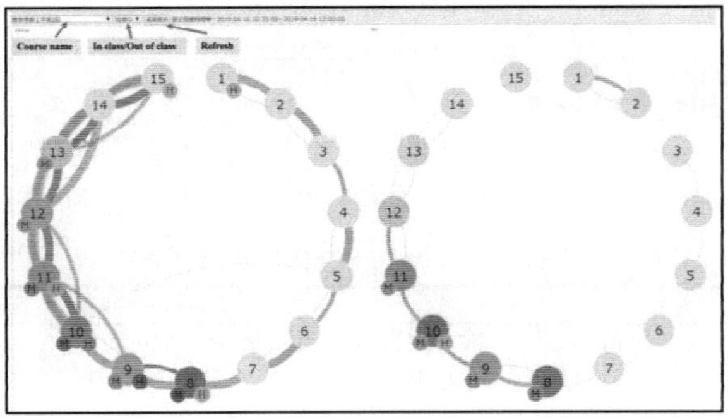

Figure 1. Reading path overview of Metaboard

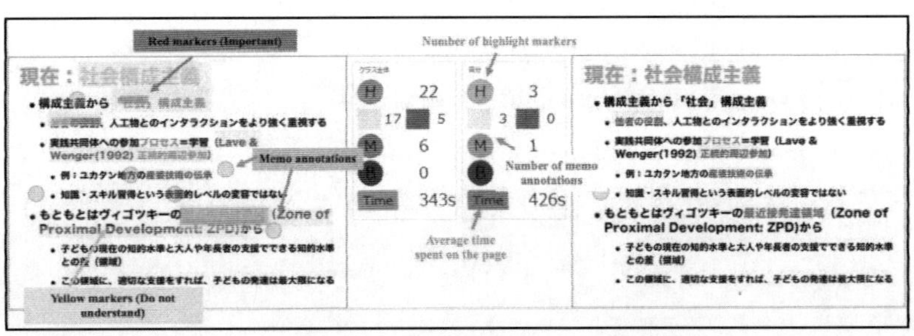

Figure 2. Detailed view of Metaboard

3.3 Data Collection and Analysis

Data was collected using two methods: questionnaires and learning logs. Before and after the whole course, students were asked to answer the Metacognitive Awareness Inventory (MAI) (Harrison & Vallin, 2018) to assess any changes in their awareness of metacognition. After the course, students completed the LAD success questionnaire (Park & Jo, 2019) to evaluate the effectiveness of the Metaboard. Both MAI and LAD success questionnaire were translated into Japanese and the items were revised minorly to suit Japanese university students. In addition, all learning logs from BookRoll and Metaboard were collected. Although 79 students initially enrolled in this course, due to absences and missing data from the questionnaires, 53 students' data were collected and analyzed for this study.

3.3.1 Metacognitive Awareness Inventory (MAI)

As presented in Table 1, the pre-post MAI consists of two dimensions: ***knowledge of cognition*** (what cognitive knowledge students are using) and ***regulation of cognition*** (how students regulate their learning by using cognitive and metacognitive strategies). The dimensions contained a total of 19 items.

Table 1. The descriptions of pre-post MAI

Dimension	Factors	Description
Knowledge of cognition dimension	*Declarative knowledge*	Knowledge of learning contents and concepts (for example, what learning contents should be acquired)
	Procedural knowledge	Knowledge of effective methods and learning strategies (for example, what learning strategies are effective)
	Conditional knowledge	Knowledge of learning conditions, such as which strategy is useful for certain contents, and when and how to use this strategy
Regulation of cognition dimension	*Planning*	Organizing what is needed to learn and make a learning plan before performing a task
	Information management strategies	Organizing the information, and connecting already known information to new information
	Monitoring	Regularly reviewing learning contents to understand the important relationships between what has been learned
	Evaluation	Summarizing and confirming what has been learned
	Debugging strategies	Reflecting on learning contents, revising, or changing learning strategies according to outcomes

3.3.2 LAD Success Questionnaire

As Table 2 shows, the LAD success questionnaire consisted of five dimensions: ***visual attraction***, ***usability***, ***understanding level***, ***perceived usefulness***, and ***behavioral changes***, and contained a total of 28 items.

Table 2. The descriptions of the post-LAD success questionnaire

Dimension	Description
Visual attraction	Conciseness of the LAD's visual elements (e.g., graphs), the way information was presented, and the appropriate amount of presented information
Usability	Ease of access and use of the LAD
Understanding level	Degree of understanding of the information presented by the LAD
Perceived usefulness	Degree of usefulness of the information presented in the LAD for learning activities
Behavioral changes	Tendency to change learning behaviors such as improving learning motivation, setting learning plans, and managing learning activities through the use of the LAD

3.3.3 Learning logs of BookRoll System and Metaboard

Table 3 presents descriptions of the learning logs, which recorded the students' operations on BookRoll (ten types) and Metaboard (two types). The learning logs on the BookRoll system were collected and analyzed because Metaboard visually presented the data from BookRoll.

Table 3. The descriptions of learning logs

System	Learning logs	Description
BookRoll system	*Next*	Turn to next page
	Prev	Turn to previous page
	Add_Ant	Add an annotation
	Del_Ant	Delete an annotation
	Add_Bm	Add bookmarks to learning material
	Del_Bm	Delete a bookmark
	Add_red_Mk	Add markers (highlight text) within a page in red when students think the text is important
	Del_red_Mk	Delete red markers
	Add_yel_Mk	Add markers (highlight text) within a page in yellow when students do not understand the text
	Del_yel_Mk	Delete yellow markers
Metaboard	*Open_Mb*	Access to Metaboard
	Open_tool	Click the page icon to view the specific information of each page slide

3.3.4 Variables and Data Analysis

In order to explore the factors that affect changes in students' metacognition in terms of the awareness and behavior dimensions of using the LAD, a stepwise multiple regression analysis was conducted. The abovementioned ten types of learning behaviors on BookRoll and two types of learning behaviors on Metaboard, as well as the results of the post-LAD success questionnaire, were used as independent variables to predict the two dependent variables of metacognition changes: the changes in ***knowledge of cognition*** and ***regulation of cognition*** in the MAI. Regarding multicollinearity, the Variance Inflation Factor (VIF) values were checked. The VIF values ranged from 1.00 to 2.65, indicating no problems in terms of multicollinearity.

4. RESULTS AND DISCUSSION

4.1 Descriptive Data of Dependent and Independent Variables

Table 4 presents the descriptive data of the two dependent variables (DVs) (i.e., the difference in ***knowledge of cognition*** and ***regulation of cognition*** of the pre-post MAI) and independent variables (IVs), which are the sum of the scores from the five dimensions of the post-LAD success questionnaire, ten learning behaviors on BookRoll system, and two learning behaviors on Metaboard.

Table 4. Descriptive data of dependent and independent variables (N=53)

Data collection method	Variable	Average	SD	Minimum	Maximum
Pre-post MAI (DVs)	Difference in ***knowledge of cognition***	-0.72	3.03	-9	8
	Difference in ***regulation of cognition***	0.04	4.85	-15	10
Post-LAD success questionnaire (IVs)	***Visual attraction***	29.26	3.80	20	35
	Usability	15.62	2.40	10	20
	Understanding level	15.87	2.93	8	20
	Perceived usefulness	15.81	2.66	10	20
	Behavioral changes	35.62	5.65	22	45
Learning logs on BookRoll system (IVs)	*Next*	1285.92	797.55	177	3546
	Prev	475.34	364.72	26	1517
	Add_Ant	12.13	24.71	0	132
	Del_Ant	0.55	1.15	0	6
	Add_Bm	0.58	1.34	0	6
	Del_Bm	0.36	0.88	0	4
	Add_red_Mk	75.96	87.6	0	438
	Del_red_Mk	6.75	12.86	0	59
	Add_yel_Mk	33.3	36.54	0	160
	Del_yel_Mk	3.42	5.99	0	28
Learning logs on Metaboard (IVs)	*Open_Mb*	4.17	2.78	0	16
	Open_tool	4.06	3.68	0	15

4.2 Effects of the use of BookRoll and Metaboard on Metacognition Changes

4.2.1 Effects on the Changes in *Knowledge of Cognition*

As presented in Table 5, when the difference in ***knowledge of cognition*** was used as the dependent variable, the independent variables ***Understanding level*** (β = .300, p = .017) from the post-LAD success questionnaire, and *Add_Ant* (β = -.535, p = .006), *Del_Ant* (β = .632, p = .002), *Add_Bk* (β = -.306, p = .022), *Del_yel_Mk* (β = -.395, p = .002) from the learning logs accounted for 28.11% of test score variance: F(5, 47) = 5.07, p = .001. The results indicate that students' ***knowledge of cognition*** awareness increases in accordance with an increase in ***visual attraction*** of the LAD assessment and the deleting of annotations (*Del_Ant*). However, their ***knowledge of cognition*** awareness tends to decrease with an increase in the learning behaviors of adding annotations (*Add_Ant*), adding bookmarks (*Add_Bm*), and deleting yellow markers (*Del_yel_Mk*).

The awareness of ***knowledge of cognition*** is representative of the cognitive knowledge students use in their learning. According to the results, first, the higher assessment of the ***visual attraction*** of Metaboard and the learning behavior of *Del_Ant* showed positive effects on the change in ***knowledge of cognition***. ***Visual attraction*** means that a dashboard contains useful information in a concise, direct, and clear form (Park & Jo, 2019). In addition to providing appropriate graphical representations, it is also necessary to take users' needs and expectations into consideration (Teasley, 2017). Therefore, we required students to answer free-form questions regarding their perceptions and reflections on the use experience of the Metaboard. According to their answers, some students felt that "the provided information was easy to view in graphs," and they also provided some suggestions to improve the visual effects such as "adding functions to adjust the graphs" or "adjusting the thickness of the lines to make it clearer." This information indicates that many students pay attention to the visual attention of an LAD, and considered the visual elements to have an impact on the effective use of the Metaboard. Another factor, *Del_Ant* indicates students' deleting previously-added annotations. In previous studies, annotation tools were shown to be positively related to students' participation during a lecture (Chen et al., 2020). Students always deleted annotations after they reconsidered or reflected on the content, which is related to metacognition behaviors. Thus, actively deleting or revising annotations is considered effective in helping students reflect on the contents, and understand what content is important and what strategies should be used, which is the main point of ***knowledge of cognition***.

In contrast, the behaviors of *Add_Ant*, *Add_Bm,* and *Del_yel_Mk* had negative effects on the change in ***knowledge of cognition***. Using a cognitive tool such as a bookmark proved to be effective in helping students understand content, and was positively related to the learning performance (Van Horne et al., 2016). However, when using such functional tools to support students' cognitive and metacognitive strategies, it is necessary to provide students with guidance about the use of tools and related strategies (Chen et al., 2019b). The lack of guidance and feedback about the use of annotation tools seemed to be one reason for the negative effects on changes in ***knowledge of cognition***. *Del_yel_Mk* indicates students deleting yellow markers, which were the parts they did not understand well. This behavior can be related to reflection, which is proven to have a positive relationship with learning performance (Chen et al., 2019b) and is effective during discussion or communication with others (Chen et al., 2020). However, some previous studies also indicate occasions when marker tools were ineffective in terms of learning. When students re-read or reviewed content, it is possible that they ignored non-highlighted text, making it difficult to construct overall knowledge (Van Horne et al., 2016; Yue et al., 2015). Therefore, similarly to the use of the annotation and bookmark tools, some specific and direct marker tool guidance from instructors is essential (Van Horne et al., 2016).

Table 5. Results of the regression analysis predicting difference in ***knowledge of cognition*** with LAD success assessment and learning behaviors (N=53)

Variable	B	SE B	*β*	t
Visual attraction	0.311	0.125	0.300	2.48*
Add_Ant	-0.066	0.023	-0.535	-2.87**
Del_Ant	1.663	0.504	0.632	3.30**
Add_Bm	-0.696	0.293	-0.306	-2.37*
Del_yel_Mk	-0.200	0.061	-0.395	-3.30**

R^2 = .350, Adjusted R^2 = .281, **p < .01, *p < .05

4.2.2 Effects on the Changes in *Regulation of Cognition*

As Table 6 shows, when the difference in ***regulation of cognition*** was used as the dependent variable, the independent variable ***Behavioral changes*** (β = .393, p = .004) of the post-LAD success questionnaire accounted for 13.76% of the variance in test scores: F(1, 51) = 9.30, p = .004. The results indicate that students' ***regulation of cognition*** awareness increases along with an increase in the ***behavioral changes***.

The ***regulation of cognition*** concerns the metacognitive behaviors (such as planning or monitoring) of how to conduct cognitive processes during learning. The ***behavioral changes*** are the students' tendencies to change learning behaviors after using the LAD (Park & Jo, 2019). The learning behaviors in ***behavioral changes*** include some metacognitive behaviors such as setting learning plans, as well as managing and regulating learning activities based on monitored results. These results are understandable given that these two dimensions have referred similar metacognitive behaviors.

Table 6. Results of the regression analysis predicting differences in ***regulation of cognition*** with LAD success assessment and learning behaviors (N=53)

Variable	B	SE B	β	t
Behavioral changes	0.337	0.111	0.393	3.05^{**}

R^2 = .154, Adjusted R^2 = .138, $^{**}p < .01$

5. CONCLUSIONS

In order to support students' metacognition, we developed an LAD named Metaboard to visualize students' reading paths and specific information about learning behaviors while viewing digital learning materials. This formative evaluation was conducted on a university education course with 53 participants, to identify the factors that affect students' metacognition changes regarding their awareness and behavior dimensions by using the LAD. As the results indicate, first, students' perceptions of ***visual attraction*** for LAD assessment and learning behaviors were related to reflection; for example, the act of deleting annotations was found to have a positive effect on changes in the ***knowledge of cognition*** dimension. Second, the students' perceptions of ***behavioral changes*** for LAD had positive effects on the ***regulation of cognition*** dimension. This is easy to understand since these behaviors are all related to metacognitive activities such as planning and monitoring. However, the use of some cognitive tools, such as adding annotations and bookmarks, negatively affected ***knowledge of cognition***, which indicates the necessity to provide guidance or feedback for students. One main implication this study provides is that the Metaboard can be used to support students in reflecting on and making sense of their cognitive activities, based on the comparison with class average.

In a future study, we will revise and improve the Metaboard based on these results. The effects on learning performance should also be examined when evaluating its effectiveness in future research. Finally, the sample size of 53 students is relatively small for a multiple regression analysis; in order to increase the statistical power of our findings, a further study should be conducted with a larger sample size.

ACKNOWLEDGEMENT

This work was supported by a JST AIP, Grant No. JPMJCR19U1, and JSPS KAKENHI Grant Number JP19H01716, JP20H01727, JP20K19939, Japan.

REFERENCES

Bodily, R., Ikahihifo, T. K., Mackley, B., & Graham, C. R., 2018. The design, development, and implementation of student-facing learning analytics dashboards. *Journal of Computing in Higher Education*, Vol. 30, No. 3, pp. 572-598.

Chen, L. et al, 2019a. Design of learning analytics dashboard supporting metacognition. *Proceedings of 16th International Conference Cognition and Exploratory Learning in Digital Age* (CELDA 2019), Cagliari, Italy, pp. 175-182.

Chen, L. et al, 2019b. Direction of collaborative problem solving-based STEM learning by learning analytics approach. *Research and Practice in Technology Enhanced Learning*, Vol. 14, No. 1, pp 1-28.

Chen, L. et al, 2020. Exploring factors that influence collaborative problem solving awareness in science education. *Technology, Knowledge and Learning*, Vol. 25, pp. 337-366.

Harrison, G. M., & Vallin, L. M., 2018. Evaluating the metacognitive awareness inventory using empirical factor-structure evidence. *Metacognition and Learning*, Vol. 13, No. 1, pp. 15-38.

Hofer, B. et al, 1998. *Teaching college students to be self-regulated learners.* In: Schunk, D. H., and Zimmerman, B. J. (eds.), Self-Regulated Learning: From Teaching to Self-Reflective Practice, Guilford Press, New York, USA.

Jacobs, J. E., & Paris, S. G., 1987. Children's metacognition about reading: Issues in definition, measurement, and instruction. *Educational Psychologist*, Vol. 22, No. 3-4, pp. 255-278.

Kim, J. et al, 2016. Effects of Learning Analytics Dashboard: Analyzing the Relations among Dashboard Utilization, Satisfaction, and Learning Achievement, *Asia Pacific Education Review*, Vol. 17, No. 1, pp. 13-24.

Klerkx, J. et al, 2017. *Learning analytics dashboards*. In C. Lang, G. Siemens, A. Wise, & D. Gašević (Eds.), The handbook of learning analytics (pp. 143–150). Society for Learning Analytics Research (SoLAR).

Lu, M. et al, 2020a. *Visualizing Studying Activities for a Learning Dashboard Supporting Meta-cognition for Students.* In: Streitz N., Konomi S. (eds) Distributed, Ambient and Pervasive Interactions. HCII 2020. Lecture Notes in Computer Science, Vol. 12203. pp. 569-580. Springer, Cham, New York, USA.

Lu, M. et al, 2020b. Development of a learning dashboard prototype supporting meta-cognition for students, *Companion Proceedings of the 10th International Conference on Learning Analytics & Knowledge (LAK 2020)*. FrankFurt, Germany, pp.104-106.

Ogata, H. et al, 2017. M2B System: A Digital Learning Platform for Traditional Classrooms in University. *Practitioner Track Proceedings of the Seventh International Learning Analytics & Knowledge Conference (LAK 2017)*. Simon Fraser University, Vancouver, Canada, pp. 155-162.

Park, Y., & Jo, I.-H., 2019. Factors that affect the success of learning analytics dashboards. *Educational Technology Research and Development*, Vol. 67, No. 6, pp. 1547-1571.

Shimada, A. et al, 2015. Informal learning behavior analysis using action logs and slide features in e-textbooks, Proceedings of IEEE ICALT 2015, Hangzhou, China, pp.116-117.

Teasley, S. D., 2017. Student Facing Dashboards: One Size Fits All? *Technology, Knowledge and Learning*, Vol. 22, No. 3, pp. 377-384.

Tobias, S. and Everson, H. T, 2009. *The importance of knowing what you know: A knowledge monitoring framework for studying metacognition in education*. In: Handbook of Metacognition in Education, Routledge.

Van Horne, S. et al, 2016. The adoption of mark-up tools in an interactive e-text- book reader. Educational Technology Research and Development, Vol. 64, No. 3, pp. 407-433.

Yamada, M. et al, 2016. Learning Analytics in Ubiquitous Learning Environments: Self-Regulated Learning Perspective. *Proceedings of International Conference on Computers in Education 2016 (ICCE 2016)*, Mumbai, India, pp. 306-314.

Yen, M. H. et al, 2018. A Framework for Self-Regulated Digital Learning (SRDL), *Journal of Computer Assisted Learning*, Vol. 34, No. 5, pp. 580-589.

Yin, C. et al, 2015. Analyzing the Features of Learning Behaviors of Students using e-Books, *Proceedings of International Conference on Computers in Education 2015 (ICCE 2015)*, Hangzhou, China, pp.617-626.

Yue, C. L. et al, 2015. Highlighting and its relation to distributed study and students' metacognitive beliefs. Educational Psychology Review, Vol. 27, pp. 69-78.

Zimmerman, B. J, 1998. *Developing self-fulfilling cycles of academic regulation: An analysis of exemplary instructional models*. In: Schunk, D. H., and Zimmerman, B. J. (eds.), Self-Regulated Learning: From Teaching to Self-Reflective Practice, Guilford Press, New York, USA.

Zimmerman, B. J., 2002. Becoming a Self-Regulated Learner: An Overview, *Theory into Practice*, Vol. 41, No. 2, 64-70.

POST-DISASTER LEARNING MODEL: DESIGN OF DISTANCE LEARNING BASED ON LOCAL WISDOM PERSPECTIVE

Jaka Warsihna[1], E. Oos M. Anwas[2], Zulfikri Anas[2], Fauzy Rahman Kosasih[3] and Zulmi Ramdani[4]

[1]*Universitas Terbuka, Indonesia, Jalan Jendral Ahmad Yani, No 43, Jakarta*

[2]*Center of Curriculum and Book, Ministry of Education and Culture, Indonesia, Jalan Gunung Sahari No 4, Jakarta*

[3]*Universitas Terbuka, Indonesia, Jalan Jendral Ahmad Yani, No 43, Jakarta*

[4]*Faculty of Psychology, UIN Sunan Gunung Djati Bandung, Jalan AH Nasution, No 105, Cibiru-Bandung, Indonesia*

ABSTRACT

The occurrence of disasters in certain areas resulted in drastic changes in the lives of the affected communities. It also has an impact on learning process which may not work properly. Damage to learning infrastructure, loss of student interest and motivation, and limited human resources after a disaster may be the factors that determine how quickly the community can rise up and recover from this situation. This study aims to create an adaptive post-disaster learning model that can be used to maintain the learning process optimally. The study employed qualitative research method with a research and development model. Observation activities, semi-structured interviews, and focus group discussions were conducted on a group of respondents consistent with the characteristics of the study. The results show that the post-disaster learning model should focus on existing resources in evacuee camps (local wisdom). This learning model can be achieved through optimizing existing teaching materials in the affected areas or by carrying out social fun activities while maintaining the achievement of learner's competence in certain subjects. Thus, this study provides an initial framework for explaining a suitable learning model that can be used in disaster-stricken areas.

KEYWORDS

Disaster, Local Wisdom, Learning Media, Distance Learning, Post-Disaster Learning

1. INTRODUCTION

Being in a complex geological zone, makes Indonesia one of the countries with rich natural resources. This contradictory condition also creates a great potential for the threat of disasters that may occur at any time (Pek, Kang and Anantharaman, 2019). Disasters that come unexpectedly often result in various losses even under certain conditions capable of paralyzing various sectors of human life, one of which is the education sector (James, 2014). When a disaster occurs, the education aspect is often a big concern of policy makers where they try to optimize this part, because it is considered very fundamental to the sustainability of the lives of the affected community.

Various natural disasters that have occurred to date usually have a tremendous impact not only on a person's physical and cognitive development, they can also disrupt the person psychological condition (Forbes, Creamer and Wade, 2012; Thurston et al., 2017). In the realm of education, natural disasters that occur in an area result in several unpleasant conditions, including damage to existing educational facilities and infrastructure, hindering accessibility and community services in affected areas, the learning process stops, and more seriously disturbs emotional stability of learners who experience it. This condition is not only felt by learners, teachers and other related parties are also the parts who must feel such conditions as well. By looking at such limited conditions, it is very unlikely that learning is carried out normally, so an adaptive learning model is needed that can be used after a disaster.

Post-disaster learning is an absolute thing that must be fulfilled, especially for learners who live in disaster-prone areas. This is necessary to prepare individuals to remain optimal in the learning process even in conditions that are full of limitations. Several studies have shown that post-disaster learning is very effective in recovering motivation, feelings of enthusiasm, struggling attitudes, life resilience, and perspectives for learners who are affected (Rusilowati and Binadja, 2012; Rahman and Umam, 2018; Susiana, 2018). Post-disaster learning itself focuses on an adaptive and flexible process that can be carried out at any time by involving the resources owned by the affected areas and also taking into account the psychological conditions of the individuals who experience it. Post-disaster learning can only be achieved when each individual collaborates to find the best adaptive model with the enthusiasm and sincerity of everyone to help together (Li, Wu and Wong, 2016; Robertson *et al.*, 2019).

Studies that have been conducted in Indonesia show that the implementation of post-disaster learning is highly dependent on the model. Post-disaster learning is the main thing to pay attention to the psychological condition of the individual first so that when the individual is in a stable condition, this will make it easier for them to carry out post-disaster learning. Several examples of post-disaster learning are exemplified by Putri, Sanjoto and Sriyanto (2018) through a pocket book containing adaptive guidelines that can be carried out by disaster-affected communities. Kusmaryono (2012) also conducted a study that attempted to implement a technology-based learning that was able not only to contain learning content, but also to entertain the learners because of the content. In addition, post-disaster learning is carried out by identifying the advantages and possible benefits that can be obtained from the affected areas (Dewy, 2018).

The post-disaster learning model applies an open and distance learning (ODL) system. It refers to the flexibility of learning amid existing limitations (Hemsley, Holm and Dodd, 2013; Steinert et al., 2017). Learning can be effective in the midst of a disaster when everyone together helps each other according to their respective capacities. The flexibility that is present in the learning process does not allow individuals to learn without direction, in this case it is necessary to have individuals who really understand the advantages and disadvantages of the resources they have after a disaster. Ideal post-disaster learning not only gives learners the freedom to explore their environment just like that, but also prepares them to become agents of change in the future who will participate in volunteering for education in their environment. In addition, post-disaster learning has a broader urgency. In addition to providing local wisdom-based learning, it is also expected to be able to increase learner's participation to love their environment, form a stronger generation in the future, until the fulfillment of a control system that is fast and responsive to disasters around (Issa et al., 2019; Tsujiguchi et al., 2019).

Several previous studies have specifically explained that the post-disaster learning model is considered the most effective one to be used after a disaster (Li, Wu and Wong, 2016; Robertson *et al.*, 2019). The majority of studies describe the model in a limited application or innovative activity which require a lot of money and take longer time to execute. Meanwhile, the individual learning process is an absolute thing that must be addressed immediately after a disaster, so that a more appropriate learning model is based on the potential and local wisdom in the affected areas. This study aims to focus on the potential of existing resources in disaster-affected areas, be able to provide effective and fun learning media, and become an integrated system with existing policy makers. Thus, the study aims to conduct an in-depth exploration of (1) Government and local community efforts in implementing education for learners affected by disasters; (2) Description of potential resources in the disaster-affected area; (3) The most suitable teaching resources model for learners in disaster-affected areas, and (4) The most effective learning model used after a disaster.

2. METHOD

The study was conducted using a research and development model. It is used to develop, refine, and validate the learning model which in this study focuses on a post-disaster learning design (Wang and Hannafin, 2005). The study adopted several steps for implementing this method by referring to several previous studies (Gall, Borg and Gall, 1996; Joseph, 2004; Wang and Hannafin, 2005), which can be seen in Figure 1.

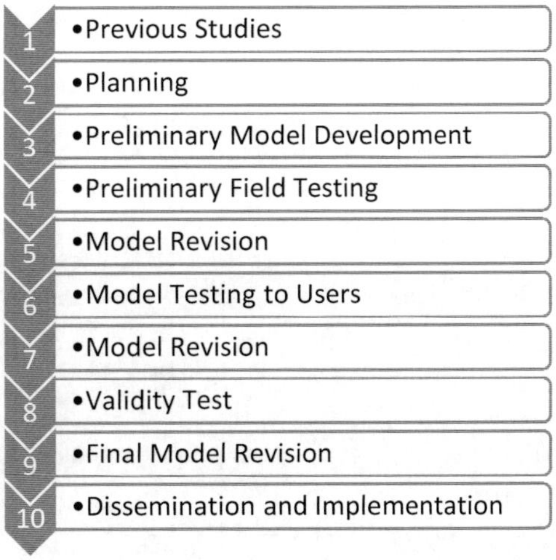

Figure 1. Post-Disaster Learning Development Procedure

Referring to the procedures in Figure 1, each procedure must certainly consider the validity and objectivity of the data collected so that it will affect the accuracy of the results. This study used a comprehensive frame of mind by providing a model built by a suitable method. The researchers conducted a case study by focusing on data collection in two areas affected by the earthquake in Indonesia, namely Palu-Southeast Sulawesi and Lombok-West Nusa Tenggara. Respondents who are involved in research were theoreticians who were tasked with conducting focus group discussions related to the study carried out, the policy makers in the affected areas as the parties who have the authority in the affected areas, make direct observations of the activities of the learners in the disaster-affected areas, as well as volunteers from surrounding community, teachers, and other activists who work in the disaster-affected areas.

To collect objective data, the researchers validated the activity process by maintaining applicable ethics and upholding human right values. All respondents who were involved in the research consciously and voluntarily took part in the activity until it was finished. The process of data analysis and interpretation of research results is carried out by referring to thematic content analysis that focuses on achieving results according to the objectives (Ramdani, Amrullah and Felisima Tae, 2019; Tae, Ramdani and Shidiq, 2019; Prakoso, Ramdani and Rahmah, 2020).

3. RESULTS & DISCUSSION

To get a comprehensive picture of the facts in the field, the researchers present the results of the research by first giving the real conditions in the disaster-affected areas.

Figure 2. Post-Disaster Learning Infrastructure Condition

Figure 2 presents a real picture of the damage to school infrastructure as a result of the earthquake that occurred in the affected areas. Many schools are paralyzed and cannot be operated due to inadequate conditions and may result in other physical threats, so by seeing these conditions the learning process is transferred outside of school and uses areas that are safer from previous damage. Furthermore, in a certain period of time the government together with the community built emergency schools which were considered to be an effective alternative in carrying out the learning process (see Figure 3).

Figure 3. Learning Process in Emergency Schools

Emergency schools (see Figure 3), of course, were built to get an optimal learning process even though they were within the limitations. Emergency schools are an effective strategy that can be used as a place for individual development after a disaster. After the emergency school is built, post-disaster learning must certainly involve various stakeholders who are concerned about education development in the affected areas. One of them is to provide adaptive learning as shown in Figure 4.

Figure 4. Adaptive Learning Guidance

Furthermore, the learning media development process was carried out by exploring the potentials that might be used as learning media based on local wisdom. It was done by making observations in the affected areas and conducting FGDs with several related parties, in order to obtain several important points related to how the post-disaster learning process is carried out. The results are then presented in an indicator which can be seen in Table 1.

Table 1. Analysis of Needs and Potential of Disaster-Affected Areas

Disaster-Affected Areas	Learning Process Overview
Palu, Southeast Sulawesi	1. Post-disaster learning process is carried out collectively by utilizing available learning resources and facilities that can still be used. 2. Learning activities are prioritized to heal the learner's trauma and strengthen their mentality through fun learning. 3. The importance of disaster mitigation education which is still considered insufficient and has not taken advantage of what the disaster-affected areas have, so it still relies heavily on assistance from outside parties.
Lombok, West Nusa Tenggara	1. Learning process focuses on trauma healing by carrying out activities that made use of available materials. 2. All communities in the area work together to maintain the learning process by providing emergency schools while considering safety and feelings of happiness for all the learners. 3. Speedy post-disaster rehabilitation as one of the main indicators that functions to find an integrated system in learning process.

Table 1 describes some of the findings from observations, FGDs, and interviews with several related parties. If you look at the process carried out in restoring existing learning process, activities are carried out with a focus on the positive changes in the child's mental which are predicted to be very important and this should be put forward in post-disaster management. The researchers conducted further analysis to find effective learning designs that could be used after a disaster which can be seen in Table 2.

Table 2. Post-Disaster Learning Design

Aspects	Implementation of Learning Process Activities
Learning Principles	1. Learning without limits by considering the learner's development and without being limited by the paradigm of formal education 2. Creating a comprehensive learning atmosphere with sensitivity to the problems that exist around them 3. Doing social activities, learners build their own understanding, and make use of the resources around them
Learning Model	1. Based on the environment and local wisdom 2. Strengthening character and strengthening the five senses 3. Building togetherness and independent learning through good cooperation
Learning Process Scenario	1. Considering the conditions and needs of the learners 2. Using learning media effectively in emergency situations 3. Involving all the learners and using togetherness to carry out activities 4. Creating various learning activities and using learning resources openly and remotely with the help of available media

Table 2 explains what kind of lesson plans might be possible in post-disaster affected areas. This design is certainly based on in-depth exploration of the advantages and disadvantages that may be found in the post-disaster affected areas. In addition, it is possible for learning activities to form a study group that is divided based on the characteristics that best suit the learner's condition in the field. The concept of a post-disaster study group can be seen in Table 3.

Table 3. Post-Disaster Learning Process Groupings

No	Types of Study Groups	Description
1	Small Homogeneous Group	Fewer than 10 learners with similar education levels are accompanied by one or two adults
2	Small Heterogeneous Group	Fewer than 10 learners with various educational levels are accompanied by one or two adults
3	Medium Homogeneous Group	10-30 learners with almost the same education level are accompanied by one or two or more adults
4	Medium Heterogeneous Group	10-30 learners with various education levels are accompanied by one or two or more adults
5	Large Homogeneous Group	Over 30 learners with almost the same education level are accompanied by one or two or more adults
6	Large Heterogeneous Group	Over 30 learners with various educational levels are accompanied by one or two or more adults

Table 3 describes the grouping of study groups that might be formed after a disaster. The grouping is of course adjusted to the characteristics of the existing development in the learners so that the hope is that in post-disaster conditions, they can return to good emotions and survive better. Learning topics that can be done in the group can also vary greatly depending on what the they have in exploring their environment while being given directions by the supervisors who participate in the learning process.

Disaster is something that we cannot predict in advance. This situation can occur at any time without preparation and without planning, so what can be done is a process of anticipation and proper handling after the disaster occurs. Post-disaster learning process is an activity that should be implemented and used as a teaching subject, especially for disaster-prone areas. According to Mitani (2019), post-disaster learning process teaches the learners how they can survive and rise to achieve their dreams. Post-disaster learning process always prioritizes the value of local wisdom, meaning that everything in the disaster-affected areas must be a top priority as learning resources.

Post-disaster learning process certainly requires many parties to support one another. As found in this study, learning process can take place when many parties help one another in compliance with their respective competencies. The government as the main party with a centralized policy must be able to see learning process as an important aspect so that when a disaster occurs, they have prepared various things to restore it. The government must also provide targeted coordination so that the implementation of post-disaster learning process can be done optimally. In addition, there needs to be assistance from voluntary organizations and other communities that usually provide human resources to help restore the disaster-affected areas. These parties must become partners with the community to support post-disaster learning process (Fekete et al., 2020; Keating and Hanger-Kopp, 2020; Lightfoot, Lesen and Ferreira, 2020).

The study provides a disaster learning process framework that focuses on several key points. First, that the development of post-disaster learning process must prioritize the psychological and physical condition of the learners running normally. It means that the learners must be in the best and most pleasant condition because it will bring them to a high awareness to continue living and growing properly. Second, learning process must be based on the optimization of the disaster-affected areas. Utilizing all available resources at the disaster-affected areas is an important thing in implementing post-disaster learning process. The remaining natural resources must be optimized and used as learning resources, while the people in the disaster area can be the parties who help facilitate the learning process. Another side that must also be an important consideration for policy makers and researchers in the future is how to create a learning model that can be online based because this will be much more helpful, especially in conditions like the one we are currently facing. Furthermore, post-disaster learning process must also consider the use of effective study groups which are predicted to be one of the important activities that are effectively carried out. In addition, by considering the various other existing media, both those supported by outsiders, it will help spark motivation and diversity of activities to be more interesting. Thus, post-disaster learning process must consider these things.

4. CONCLUSION

The sustainability of the learners affected by disasters needs special attention. Through post-disaster learning process, they learn by grouping themselves into groups according to the level of needs required. The learning process is fulfilled by using various instruments such as textbooks, props, and other objects around, as well as carrying out various activities such as trauma healing, playing, exercising, telling stories, and watching educational and entertainment shows. In addition, the post-disaster learning model that is implemented includes the principles of independence, openness, and distance learning where all activities involve the closest community as parties who will encourage the learners and of course jointly get happiness by doing these activities.

ACKNOWLEDGEMENT

This study was conducted as a collaboration between Universitas Terbuka lecturers and researchers at the Center for Curriculum and Books of Ministry of Education and Culture of the Republic of Indonesia. Our highest appreciation goes to the Institute for Research and Community Service (LPPM) of the Universitas Terbuka for funding this study. We also thank all respondents who participated in this study.

REFERENCES

Dewy, C. (2018) 'Model pembelajaran berbasis masalah untuk mengatasi keterbatasan sumber belajar geografi pada pembelajaran kelas darurat pasca bencana sinabung', *Jurnal Kapita Selekta Geografi*, 1(September), pp. 39–45.

Fekete, A. *et al.* (2020) 'Pathways for advancing integrative disaster risk and resilience management in Iran: Needs, challenges and opportunities', *International Journal of Disaster Risk Reduction*, 49. doi: 10.1016/j.ijdrr.2020.101635.

Forbes, D., Creamer, M. and Wade, D. (2012) 'Psychological support and recovery in the aftermath of natural disaster', *International Psychiatry*, 9(1), pp. 15–17. doi: DOI: 10.1192/S1749367600002939.

Gall, M. D., Borg, W. R. and Gall, J. P. (1996) *Educational research: An introduction*. 6th edition. Longman Publishing.

Hemsley, G., Holm, A. and Dodd, B. (2013) 'Conceptual distance and word learning: Patterns of acquisition in Samoan-English bilingual children', *Journal of Child Language*, 40(4), pp. 799–820. doi: 10.1017/S0305000912000293.

Issa, F. S. *et al.* (2019) 'Effectiveness of children's disaster risk reduction (DRR) program on earthquake preparedness in Jordan', *Prehospital and Disaster Medicine*, 34(s1), pp. s42–s43. doi: 10.1017/s1049023x1900102x.

James, J. J. (2014) 'Education and training: Integrating the disaster cycle', *Disaster Medicine and Public Health Preparedness*, 8(4), p. 279. doi: 10.1017/dmp.2014.86.

Joseph, D. (2004) 'Methodological alignment in design-based research', *Educational Psychologist*, 39(4), pp. 203–212. doi: 10.1207/s15326985ep3904.

Keating, A. and Hanger-Kopp, S. (2020) 'Practitioner perspectives of disaster resilience in international development', *International Journal of Disaster Risk Reduction*, 42, p. 101355. doi: 10.1016/j.ijdrr.2019.101355.

Kusmaryono, I. (2012) 'Pengembangan pembelajaran matematika kontekstual edutainment berbasis budaya lokal di daerah bencana', in *Makalah Seminar Kemdikbud Dikti 'Designing Quality Learining Landscape in Indonesia'*, pp. 1–14.

Li, S.-J., Wu, C. S. T. and Wong, H. T. (2016) 'School safety and children health in a post-disaster community: Implications to collaborative care and service learning in school health', *Journal of Acute Disease*, 5(1), pp. 46–50. doi: 10.1016/j.joad.2015.08.005.

Lightfoot, E. S., Lesen, A. E. and Ferreira, R. J. (2020) 'Gender and resilience in Gulf Coast communities: Risk and protective factors following a technological disaster', *International Journal of Disaster Risk Reduction*, 50, p. 101716. doi: 10.1016/j.ijdrr.2020.101716.

Mitani, S. (2019) 'Learning effects of cross road game using a clicker-nano system', *Prehospital and Disaster Medicine*, 34(s1), pp. s145–s146. doi: 10.1017/s1049023x19003236.

Pek, J. H., Kang, H. M. and Anantharaman, V. (2019) 'Teaching disaster site medical support in Indonesia', *Disaster Medicine and Public Health Preparedness*, pp. 1–6. doi: 10.1017/dmp.2019.134.

Prakoso, B. H., Ramadani, Z. and Rahmah, B. (2020) 'Best Pratices of Character Education in Leading Schools in Bandung', *Indonesian Journal of Educational Assesment*, 3(1), p. 61. doi: 10.26499/ijea.v3i1.61.

Putri, N. A. E., Sanjoto, T. B. and Sriyanto (2018) 'Pendidikan mitigasi bencana tsunami dengan menggunakan media pembelajaran buku saku pada masyarakat pesisir desa karanggadung kecamatan petanahan kabupaten kebumen', *Edu Geography*, 6(1), pp. 72–79. Available at: http://journal.unnes.ac.id/sju/index.php/edugeo.

Rahman, F. and Umam, Q. (2018) 'Sena Sakti (Sekolah Bencana ; Siaga , Aksi dan Mitigasi)', *Jurnal Ilmiah Ilmu Sosial*, 4(1), pp. 6–11.

Ramdani, Z., Amrullah, S. and Felisima Tae, L. (2019) 'Pentingnya Kolaborasi dalam Menciptakan Sistem Pendidikan yang Berkualitas', *MediaPSI*, 5(1), pp. 40–48. doi: 10.21776/ub.mps.2019.005.01.4.

Robertson, B. W. *et al.* (2019) 'Using a combination of human insights and "deep learning" for real-time disaster communication', *Progress in Disaster Science*, 2, p. 100030. doi: 10.1016/j.pdisas.2019.100030.

Rusilowati, A. and Binadja, A. (2012) 'Mitigasi bencana alam berbasis pembelajaran bervisi science environment technology and society', *Jurnal Pendidikan Fisika Indonesia*, 8(1), pp. 51–60. doi: 10.15294/jpfi.v8i1.1994.

Steinert, C. *et al.* (2017) 'Psychodynamic therapy: As efficacious as other empirically supported treatments? A meta-analysis testing equivalence of outcomes', *American Journal of Psychiatry*, 174(10), pp. 943–953. doi: 10.1176/appi.ajp.2017.17010057.

Susiana, S. (2018) 'Peran pemerintah daerah dalam penyelenggaraan kesehatan reproduksi (Studi di provinsi jawa tengah dan provinsi kalimantan barat)', *Jurnal Aspirasi*, 7(1), pp. 1–16. doi: 10.22212/aspirasi.v7i1.1084.

Tae, L. F., Ramdani, Z. and Shidiq, G. A. (2019) 'Analisis tematik faktor-faktor yang mempengaruhi keberhasilan siswa dalam pembelajaran sains', *Indonesian Journal of Educational Assesment*, 2(1), p. 79. doi: 10.26499/ijea.v2i1.18.

Thurston, W. E. *et al.* (2017) 'Disaster management and farm family mental mealth: The BSE crisis as a case study', *Prehospital and Disaster Medicine*, 32(S1), pp. S185–S186. doi: 10.1017/s1049023x17004927.

Tsujiguchi, T. *et al.* (2019) 'The development of an active learning program for the medical responders in a nuclear disaster', *Disaster Medicine and Public Health Preparedness*, 13(5–6), pp. 853–858. doi: 10.1017/dmp.2018.168.

Wang, F. and Hannafin, M. J. (2005) 'Technology-enhanced learning environments', *ETR&D*, 53(4), pp. 5–23.

INFLUENCE OF ENGLISH AS A SECOND LANGUAGE ON THE TRAINEES' ACADEMIC PERFORMANCE AT EENHANA VOCATIONAL TRAINING CENTRE IN NAMIBIA

Hambeleleni Albertina Nepolo[1] and Ifeoma R. Eze[2]
[1]*Department of Education and Language Skills, Botho University, Botswana*
[2]*PhD, Department of Educational Management and Leadership, Botswana Open University, Botswana*

ABSTRACT

It has been observed that the low academic performance of trainees at the Windhoek Vocational Training Centre has been on the increase at an alarming rate without any proven reasons Malwa (2018). This may be the case in other vocational training centres. Thus, this study examined the influence of English as a Second Language on trainees' academic performance at Eenhana Vocational Training Centre in Namibia. The study, therefore, tried to answer these questions; **(a)** What factors in English influence trainees' academic performance? **(b)** How did the influence of English as a Second Language and medium of instruction affect other subjects? **(c)** How did the trainees comprehend their academic work? '.This is a qualitative study which used the snowball sampling method to select 5 trainers and 10 trainees as participants.'. The data were collected through face-to-face interviews, participants observations and documentexaminations. Narrative and thematic analysis were used in analyzing data. The study revealed that the performance of trainees in their academic work is determined by their ability to understand English as a Second Language. Their proficiency level in English influences how best or poorly they can perform in their academic work.,. It was also found that trainees who have poor English language proficiency find it difficult to understand their subjects content and also performing their best in academic work, while those who are good at the language perform well academically as they can understand what they are learning and they can handle the assessment activities appropriately. The study will inform the Higher Education policymakers, trainers, and trainees as it enhances an understanding of the influences of English as a medium of instruction on other subjects for them to employ the best teaching and learning strategies such as Access or bridging courses to improve the problem caused by the language barrier.

KEYWORDS

Eenhana Vocational Training Centre, English as Second Language, Trainees' Academic Performance

1. INTRODUCTION

Namibia is a multilingual country of at least 14 languages due to different ethnic groups such as Herero, Damara, Nama, Kwanyama, Ndonga and so forth, but with only one language as the official language and medium of instruction across the curriculum. This language got into use when the South West Africa People's Organisation (SWAPO) language policy decided English to be an official language and the only language of communication throughout all government sectors (Frydman, 2011).

English as a Second Language being an important and official language in the country, prompted the curriculum designers and education's national assessment and evaluation to set up the language promotional and admission requirements from primary level grades, Grade 1 to secondary level Grade 12, as well as to higher institutions of education. This implies that to pass grade 10, a pass with 23 points and Grade 12, a pass with 25 points with or at least E or better in English as a minimum entry requirement to tertiary education levels should be achieved, as it is said that a learner in Grade 10 or 12 should be promoted to another level if he or she has obtained an E grade or better in 5 five subjects out of six subjects including English (Hanse- Himarwa 2017). Some of the tertiary institutions where learners go to further their studies are vocational training centres, which train and prepare trainees with knowledge and skills to be used in technical aspects of the job market.

The vocational training centres admit those who have just ended up at or completed Grade 10 and do not meet the entry requirements for Grade 11 to 12. They also admit those who have completed Grade 12 and do not meet the admission requirements for universities and other institutions which focus on academic comprehension. In addition, the Namibian education policy has a provision of training the marginalized and vulnerable ethnic groups such as; the San and the Himba, despite not having schooled up to grade 10 or 12, which are the entry grades into vocational training centres.

Despite the school phases or grade levels achieved, for instance, Grade 10 or 12, when training or teaching is being done, it is always delivered in English language as the medium of instruction. All the trainees with different grade levels achieved, which are either Grade 10 or 12, or the marginalized and vulnerable ones who may not have done any of the two grade levels are all taught in the same classrooms, receiving the same subject content, and do the same assessments in English as a medium of instruction. As a prerequisite for graduation, these trainees are expected to pass all the modules they are doing in their trades, and get into the job market in which they can interact with speakers of different languages.

In India, it is also an inherited language and is used as a second language and a medium of instruction in most of the schools, and it is claimed that learners struggle to master the language skills which are listening, reading, speaking and writing. This results into the language anxiety among students, as it negatively affects the students' academic performance (Ujjwal 2018). Literature also revealed that foreign languages which are used as second languages in schools do not become effective predictor of the primary education's academic performance, but at the upper education levels like secondary and tertiary levels. It is regarded as the main contributor to the academic failure and importantly academic achievement (Tuncer & Dogan 2015).

2. THEORETICAL FOUNDATIONS

This study is focused on the influences of English as a Second language in academic performance. Nath (2010) defines language as a way in which thoughts are well arranged in a manner that meanings can be formed and understood. To provide an understanding of this practice, language and academic performance were studied by Vygotsky, as a theorist, and it was indicated that there is a correlation between the two. It was shown that academic performance depends on the ability to use the language of instruction. He explained this as a Zone of Proximal Development (ZPD). It explains that the gap between what the children can comprehend by themselves and what can be understood with assistance, indicating that a leaner needs to be supported quickly up a learning curve, and their ZPD can continuously be advanced with necessary help (Fry Ketteridge & Marshall, 2009). This idea is very much into scaffolding learning, which entails that for someone to learn something, help, and support should be provided. This is illustrated in the diagram below:

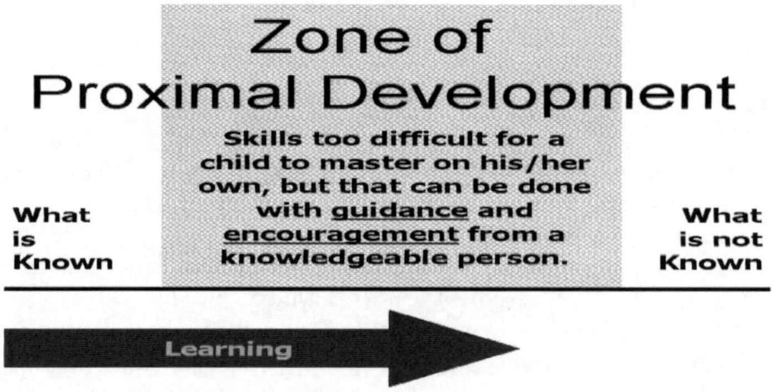

Figure 1. Source: McLeod (2019) The Zone of Proximal Development and Scaffolding
https://www.simplypsychology.org/Zone-of-Proximal-Development.html

Vygotsky claims that the cognitive development of students is driven by the use of language, as the student can only be able to learn how to think and internalize the complex concepts which may enhance understanding of the learned aspect (Dahms, Geonnotti, Passalacqua, Wetzel, Schilk & Zulkowsky, 2007). This implies that learning happens via the use of language, which enables the transformation of perceived experience into the internal processes. This promotes learning, which may enhance performance as what is being learned can be understood (Mlay 2010). Vygotsky further indicated that a language first acts as a social communication which enhances proper understanding of concepts, which leads to mental development that may promote learning.

It is further stated that the capacity to use mental functions at higher levels, such as in thinking, reasoning, and logical processing of memory are led by the usage of language (Culligan 2013). That means correct thinking and learning, which may enhance academic performance, mainly occurs if there is an understanding of the concepts being learned. Vygotsky also asserts that as language is used for communication, then it can be used in playing a significant role in the mental development of students, which may also indirectly transform what is perceived during communication into meaningful understanding (Culligan 2013). Vygotsky then suggests that students' understanding of what they are learning may become their mental resources, which they may later use in their academic activities (Culligan 2013).

3. STATEMENT OF THE PROBLEM

Most of the trainees at the vocational training centres are those who obtained low points in their previous grades which are grade 10 and 12, the points which may not qualify them to be able to do courses which require cognitive usage but rather technical subjects, which just require (hands-on) skills. They at least obtained an E or better in English as a Second Language. Obtaining an E or better in English is considered as one of the least grades a candidate can obtain in examination. The candidates who obtained such an E grade did not reach the good passing mark, which is 50. It indicates that some language learning aspects were required to be learned for better performance, either in English or other subjects, to be achieved.

Some trainees had never been in grade 10 or 12. These are the marginalized people who get admitted due to the Ministry of Education's provision that the marginalized and vulnerable tribe groups should be admitted to institutions of higher learning. Based on the types of trainees at vocational training centres, this study tried to examine the influences of English as a Second Language on trainees' academic performance at Eenhana Vocational Training Centre. This is because proficiency of English as a Second Language is the most influencing factor on the academic performance of trainees (Sadeghi, Kashanian, Maleki. & Haghdoost, 2013).

4. PURPOSE OF THE STUDY

Enter the text here. The study examined the influences of English as Second Language on the trainees' academic performances at Eenhana Vocational Training Centre in Ohangwena Region, Namibia. The investigation was guided by the following objectives, which were to:

- examine how English as a Second Language influences the academic performance of trainees
- identify how the influence of English as a Second Language and medium of instruction affects other subjects
- examine how trainees comprehend their academic work

5. SIGNIFICANCE OF THE STUDY

Finding out how English as a Second Language influences the trainees' academic performance at Eenhana Vocational Training Centre would enable the researcher to suggest teaching and learning strategies to promote the best performance among trainees. It would also contribute to the understanding of trainers about how the trainees' academic performance is affected by the medium of instruction.

6. RESEARCH METHODOLOGY

The study aimed to find subjective realities which helped in promoting understanding of real experiences from the chosen research population, the trainees and trainers, about how they perceive the influences of English as a Second Language on their academic performance. It also enabled interaction between the researcher and the research participants to give their own experiences and opinions. This method contributed much at getting a lot of ideas from individual trainees and trainers as participants through interviews, observation and report or activities checking. This was the best approach to use as no generalized information was given. Participants were openly expressing themselves, since it was conducted individually, between interviewer and interviewee.

Study partipants were obtained by the snowball sampling technique. '. Participants were trainees in the vocational training centre who had completed their basic education at different schools and were admitted with different entry requirements. Some only completed Grade 10, others went up to Grade 12, while the rest were admitted because of the policy which allows the disadvantaged tribes to be included in education training centres. As the centre has trainees of different academic abilities depending on the levels of basic education achieved, it was quite challenging for the researcher to find different participants according to their categories. Therefore, one participant was selected with the assistance of the trainer and was asked to refer another one to the researcher. This referral chain (snowball) continued until all nine participants were recruited. This sampling method contributed to obtaining the study population at a remarkably low cost (Devkota, 2020). The study population comprised 9 trainees from one class and one trade and 5 trainers. Participants were informed of all relevant rules regarding the study and how their wellbeing was to be protected in a way that they would not be exposed.

7. DISCUSSION AND INTERPRETATION OF FINDINGS

It is noted that their proficiency in the language of instruction determines the understanding and performance of trainees in their academic work. In this study, some participants indicated that they get to understand their academic work well, and that is promoted by the advantage of understanding English as the medium of instruction. Adequate understanding of the language of instruction contributes to best academic performance (Aina, Ogundele & Olanipekun, 2013).

English as a Second Language is noted to play a major role in the trainees' academic performance, as that when they find it difficult to express themselves in English. This also affects the way they perform in other subjects as well, as they may find it challenging to understand and answer academic questions. Some trainees were noted to have used few words when responding to the interview questions posed to them. It shows that they were unable to give detailed information, especially in content subjects which require explanations. This means that for the trainees to perform well academically, then they should be able to demonstrate adequate proficiency in the language of instruction.

It is also noted that trainees perform poorly in their academic work when they cannot understand what is asked, or understand the meaning of questions and the content studied. Trainees require a fairly extensive vocabulary to perform well in their academic work. A poor vocabulary may cause trainees to misinterpret the questions and fail to provide correct information, thus resulting in a poor academic performance (Wilson & Komba, 2012; Kagwesage, 2012).

7.1 Challenges Experienced in English as a Second Language by Trainees Across all their Subjects

Trainees found it difficult to understand some terms used in their subjects due to their low English proficiency levels, and this results in poor academic performance. It is imperative that trainees understand the meaning of words and other expressions used in their academic work for them to perform well. This is because an adequate understanding of the vocabulary aids the learner to interpret questions and provide correct answers. They may find it difficult to contextualize, resulting in undesired academic performance. This was in agreement with Amua-Sekyi, E.T. & Nti, S. K. (2015) as well as with Wilson & Komba (2012

7.2 Understanding or Comprehending of Academic Work

Some trainees indicated not being able to comprehend their academic work due to limited English proficiency which contributes much to poor academic performance. This can adversely affect academic performance in subjects studied in the English language because it is unlikely that a student will perform optimally in the subject if he does not understand the medium of instruction (Kagwesage, 2012). So, trainees need to understand the medium of instruction first for them to comprehend and perform well academically. This places trainees who may not understand the meaning of words or expressions at an academically disadvantaged position whereas those who demonstrate adequate proficiency in the language of instruction may be the best advantage to perform well in their academic work as alluded by Racca & Lasaten (2016).

7.3 Relationship between English as a Second Language and other Subjects

Being good at English as a medium of instruction makes the trainees' academic work easier and perform their best. This only happens when, for instance, they learn certain words in one subject, and they find them used in other subjects, then that would be helpful as it can make them understand the other content (Kagwesage, 2012). When they understand what they are learning, they can be able to understand the assessment activities, answer them correctly and as a result perform well academically.

7.4 Confidence and Competence in English as a Second Language

It was noted that trainees found it difficult to speak at length, and some were not at ease. They acted as if they were afraid of making errors. This is an indication that trainees were not confident in what they were saying. That could be caused by not having ideas of what to say, or not being able to express themselves due to limited proficiency in English as a Second Language. The trainees also opted just to be listeners and not be actively involved in a way that they could give answers or participate in class discussion. They were neither able to support nor clarify their points. They also overused or repeated some words in their responses.This indicates a state of inadequate proficiency in the language, and this can have a negative impact on the trainees' academic performance (Mlay, 2010).

7.5 Interview with Trainers as Participants

Trainers stated that trainees' competence in English was determined by their academic background and exposure to the language (English as a Second Language). It was noted that their exposure to the language at their previous grades or primary education affects the way trainnes express themselves in English. Trainees who got the best exposure to the language, confidently express themselves in English. This means that proficiency level in English determines their ability to participate, which may enhance best academic performance (Racca & Lasaten, 2016; Amua-Sekyi, et al 2015).

The trainees also experienced many spelling problems which in most cases affected their best academic performance, as they end up failing because of wrongly spelt answers. However, they perform well in Mathematics and technical subjects as compared to other theoretical subjects. The more uncomplicated structure and style of the English language used in technical subjects usch as Mathematics makes it easier to be understood by trainees (Wilson et al. 2012).

7.6 Factors in English as a Second Language that Influence Trainees' Academic Performance

The usage of mother tongues affects the trainee's academic performance negatively,as they try to translate some of their vernacular expressions into English, which may not literally translate into the same expression intended in the English Language. This makes the trainees misinterpret information, and results in academic failure (Wilson et al., 2012; Racca et al., 2016).

The use of grammar or tenses also affects the trainees' academic performance in theoretical subjects which often require extensive expressions in the language of instruction, as they find it challenging to present their answers correctly and in an understandable manner. Djihed (2018) posits that poor command or best command in English as a medium of instruction either makes them perform poorly or adequately in their academic work.

7.7 Relationship between English as a Medium of Instruction and other Subjects

Trainees were noted to have lacked the language basics which enables them to express themselves clearly and to understand and interpret the questions correctly. This means that if the trainees experience difficulties in understanding the subject content or assessment activities due to poor English skills. Trainees need to understand what they are learning for them to be able to comprehend their academic work and perform better (Aina et al., 2013).

7.8 How well Trainees Comprehend their Academic Work

Trainees' comprehension of academic work depend on their individual effort and understanding of the language of instruction, which can promote a better understanding of the content taught (Aina et al., 2013). This enhances better performance for those who are proficient in the language, as they can provide the required answers and follow the instructions as per assessments

Those trainees who have problems in the language of instructions end up memorizing what is taught, which may not promote comprehension of what they are learning. These trainees do not always perform well. For instance, if the structure or words they have memorized happens to be changed, they may get confused and be unable to provide correct answers, resulting in academic failure (Kagwesage 2012).

8. OBSERVATION REPORT

Some trainees reported difficulty in discussing academic material in their mother tongue, especially in technical work (practical). They only used English when talking to the instructor or trainer. This can be a burden to their academic work as they may find it challenging to understand the instructions and procedures that they may be given by the instructors during individual assessments (Komba 2012, Robelle et al 2016, Ekua et al 2015).

9. DOCUMENT ANALYSIS

The document analysis was done in HIV and AIDS module as well as in the assessment marks for English for Communication, HIV and AIDS as well as in Welding and metal fabrication. It was discovered that trainees who understood the questions because of adequate proficiency in English, answered the questions correctly. In assessment marks, those who performed well in English for communication also did well in other subjects. This provides evidence that, being good at the language of instruction, enhances best academic performance (Aina et al., 2013).

10. SUMMARY

The study was strengthened by the Zone of Proximal Development theory and guided by the qualitative data collected from the participants that provided information on how English as a Second Language influences trainees academic performance at Eenhana Vocational Training Centre. It was found that the trainees proficiency level in English as a Second Language determine how they perform academically.

11. RECOMMENDATIONS

It is recommended that participants for future studies be selected based on their Grade 10 or 12 school leaving certificates. Future studies will need to consider the grade obtained in English as a Second Language in order to get valuable information on the influences of medium of instruction plays in on trainees academic performance. The academic performance of those who graduated at Eenhana Vocational Training Centre can also a deeper understanding of the English as a Second Language' influence in the trainees' academic performance. The findings of the study are that the academic performance of trainees is highly influenced by their abilities to use the language. It is on the background of these findings that the following recommendations are made;

- VTCs should introduce a bridging course for trainees to attend before starting their main academic courses which will strictly be in English
- English as a medium of instruction for learning should be taken seriously in basic education and institutions of higher learning
- Trainees should read a lot and practise English activities to acquire vocabulary and improve their grammar
- All trainers should strictly consider the appropriate usage of the language
- There should be learning spots at the centres where trainees can go to learn and practise English besides just learning it in the lessons
- Lastly, as there is an integration of trainees with different school leaving certificates, the Ministry of Higher Education should also make provisions for improvements of different levels of English Language proficiency.

REFERENCES

Aina, J. K. et al. (2013). Students' Proficiency in English Language Relationship with Academic Performance in Science and Technical Education. *American Journal of Educational Research*, *1*(9), 355-358.

Amua-Sekyi, E.T. & Nti, S. K. (2015). Factors affecting students' performance in English at colleges of education in Ghana. IMPACT: *International Journal of Research in Humanities, Arts and Literature* (IMPACT: IJRHAL) ISSN(E): 2321-8878; ISSN(P): 2347-4564 Vol. 3, Issue 10, 29-44.

Culligan K. (2013). *The relationship between language and thought exploring Vygotsky and socialcultural approaches to second research. New* Brunswick, Canada.

Dahms, M. et al. (2007). *The Education Theory of Lev Vygotsky: An Analysis.* New Foundations Site. http://www.newfoundations.com/GALLERY/Vygotsky.html. Accessed 11-09-20

Devkota, B. R. (2020). *Snowball sampling.* Mathstopia. https://www.mathstopia.net/sampling/snowball-sampling. Accessed 25-08-20

Djilied A. (2013). Investigating the reading difficulties of Algerian. Est student with regards to their general English knowledge. *Arab world English Journal* 4 (1).

Fry, H. et al. (2009). *A Handbook for Teaching and Learning in Higher Education: Enhancing Academic Practice* 3rd edition. Routledge270 Madison Ave, New York, NY 10016

Frydman J. (2011). *A critical analysis of Namibian's English only language.* 40th Annual Conference on African Linguistics. Somerville, MA: Cascadilla proceedings project. https://www.lingref.com/cpp/acal/40/paper2574.pdfAccessed 03-03-20

Hanse – Himarwa K. (2017). *National promotion policy guide for junior and senior secondary school phases.* NIED, Okahandja https://www.simplypsychology.org/Zone-of-Proximal-Development.html. Accessed 14-01-20

Kagwesage, A. M. (2012). Higher education students'' reflections on learning in times of academic language shift. *International Journal for the Scholarship of Teaching and Learning, 6/2.* Retrieved December, 2015, from: http://academics.georgiasouthern.edu/ijsotl/v6n2.html Accessed 02-05-20

Malwa N.N.L. (2018). *Difficulties that level one trainees encounter in learning Mathematics.* Windhoek Vocational Training Centre. University of Namibia

McLeod, S. (2019) The Zone of Proximal Development and Scaffolding. Simply Psychology https://www.simplypsychology.org/Zone-of-Proximal-Development.html Accessed 02-08-20

Mlay N. (2010). *The influences of the language of instruction on students' academic performance in secondary schools in Africa: A comparative study of urban and rural schools in Arusha* –Tanzania, University of Oslo.

Nath. B. K. (2010). *Theories of language in learning of Mathematics: Major language theorists influencing learning of Mathematics.* University of Calicut, India.

Racca, R & Lasaten, R. (2016). English Language Proficiency and Academic Performance of Philippine Science High School Students. *International Journal of Languages, Literature and Linguistics*. 2. 44-49. 10.18178/IJLLL.2016.2.2.65.

Sadeghi, B. et al. (2013). *English Language Proficiency as a predictor of academic achievement among medical students in Iran.* Theory practice. Lang. stud. 3 (12):2315 -2321.

Tuncer M. and Dogan Y. (2015). Effect of foreign language classroom anxiety on Turkish University students' academic achievement in foreign language learning. *Journal of education and training studies*, 3 (6), 14 -19.

Ujjwal K.H. (2018). *English Language Anxiety and Academic Achievement*. University of Gour Banga, Malda, WB – 732103.

Wilson, J., & Komba, S. C. (2012). The Link between English Language Proficiency and Academic Performance: A Pedagogical Perspective in Tanzanian Secondary Schools. *World Journal of English Language, 2(4).* doi:10.5430/wjel.v2n4p1

DIGITAL TWIN: DECREASING THE COGNITIVE LOAD BY USING INDUSTRY 4.0 SIMULATION

Lukas Heschl, Thomas Dilger, Reinhard Bernsteiner and Christian Ploder
MCI – Management Center Innsbruck
Universitätsstrasse 15, 6020 Innsbruck, Austria

ABSTRACT

As the integration of teaching theory and the application of Digital Twin (DT) technology is a challenge in our study programs, the authors put an effort on finding a supporting industry simulation model for in-class use. With the Fischertechnik Industry 4.0 Simulation Unit. This paper describes the objectives and the theoretical background of why this would be used in a case-based teaching setting. Further on, the authors are interested in the measurement of the cognitive load for the students and the influence of better design the lectures based on the simulation. The methodology is clearly stated and it is described how the first implementation of the given scenario in October 2020 will be done.

KEYWORDS

Digital Twin, Case-Based Teaching, Simulation, Augmented Reality, Cognitive Load Measurement

1. INTRODUCTION

Industry 4.0 is an umbrella term promoted by the German government in 2011 to increase the digital transformation of manufacturing (Fuchs, 2018). This strategy was put forward to act on the new generation of information technologies as well as its integration and extensive applications (such as the Internet of Things - IoT, Big Data, Social Media, Cloud Computing, Sensors, and Artificial Intelligence which are used for physical goods). Furthermore, the purpose of this work is to achieve interoperability between the virtual and physical world of manufacturing. The communication and interaction of both fields can be one of the bottlenecks to accomplish this purpose (Tao, Zhang, Cheng, & Qi, 2017).

These virtual products are defined by Grieves (2015) as a depiction of products that are identical to their physical counterpart. Before a wide variety of sensing technologies digitalized data-collection, the rise of Manufacturing Execution Systems (MES) resulted in a richness of data collection (Grieves, 2015) which can also be seen in the current discussions about Low Code / No Code applications (Ploder et al., 2019). Through this technological progress, the concept of Digital Twin (DT) moved from an exciting approach to understanding the product with its environmental information to a demanding element of an enterprise-wide closed-loop product lifecycle. Fully implemented within a company, it can help to reduce costs and develop innovation for the quality of manufactured products (Grieves, 2015).

For students it can be hard to understand IT systems supporting an enterprise-wide product lifecycle. By creating an integrated learning scenario with the support of simulation, the hands-on experience will help to understand this big picture. With the Fischertechnik Industry 4.0, it is possible to simulate and present networked digital applications in a real production environment. This simulation enables us to digitalize the ordering, production, and delivery process. Through a network, the generated data of environmental sensors are synchronized to an IoT-Platform. With this data, a DT can be created and will help to decrease the cognitive load on students to understand this big picture of product lifecycles and Industry 4.0.

2. THEORETICAL BACKGROUND

One of the key drivers in Industry 4.0 is the digital transformation of value chains, as well as the creation of digital products. As a result of this digitalization, new business models can be created. The usage of technologies in Industry 4.0 is meant to gain an advantage from the high amount of collected data. With analysis and simulations, the collected data can be used for a better understanding of the limitations and environmental aspects of a product or process.

The digital transformation in companies with cloud-based technologies, high-performance computing, or the IoT led to the possibility of imitating and modeling the physical world. The DT is a virtual replica that enables advanced and complex simulation, which is used to understand the performance of the product in the present and future. With data collected from connected sensors combined with related information, predictive analysis can be performed. The technology of the DT is a combination of artificial intelligence, data analytics, and IoT. As a result of the increasing networking and acquisition of data by sensors, more and more data are being collected. This data can also be used in new ways to execute the DT approaches, allow the development of new digital products and consequently affect other areas of technology, such as the collection of large amounts of data.

2.1 Digital Twin

The concept of the DT was introduced in 2003 at the University of Michigan in the course of product life cycle management (PLM) (Grieves, 2015). Its vision includes the full physical and functional description of components, products, or systems (Boschert & Rosen, 2016). The approach of using twins is originated in the Apollo program of NASA. Two identical space vehicles were built to simulate conditions during the mission and mirror them in the twin vehicle that stayed on earth. In this understanding, a prototype to reflect the real operating terms for simulation can be defined as a twin (Rosen, von Wichert, Lo, & Bettenhausen, 2015).

Following this idea to digitalize all life cycles of the physical model into a complete digital model is the vision of a DT. In the last decades, simulation developed from a restricted technology for experts to a standard tool for engineers in their daily tasks and as a core function of systems (Boschert & Rosen, 2016). Prototyping and simulations to develop is nowadays a standard process to validate requirements and discover problems in advance and, hence, to realize failure prediction. Simulation is a conjunction of all life cycles in the physical and virtual world (Boschert & Rosen, 2016).

The core functionality of a DT is provided through the collected data from the physical model. In the significant data-driven manufacturing era at any stage of the product lifecycle, data is processed, gathered, and leads to increased creation of digital artifacts (Tao et al., 2018; Rosen et al., 2015). The objects can be seen as stored data, containing all information that is needed by different stakeholders, but the DT is more than a data storage. It has a structure where all components are connected (Rosen et al., 2015). From a technical point of view, the data volume is too vast, diverse, and unstructured (Boschert & Rosen, 2016). The product lifecycle is an iterative process, and as a consequence, lots of duplicate data in several phases can cause a waste of resources and lead to sharing problems (Tao et al., 2018). Grieves (2015) demonstrates three tools of human knowledge, which are supported by the capabilities of DT: (1) Conceptualization, (2) Comparison, and (3) Collaboration.

Conceptualization reflects that humans take in all data about a situation and then conceptualize it in their mind. During processing this visual information, it will be reduced to letters and symbols and then re-conceptualized visually. A loss of details and time is the result of this mechanism. The concept of DT eliminates this counterproductive mental step and builds a collective mindset of physical and virtual product information. As an alternative to looking at a bunch of numbers, the DT allows us to look at the progress of the physical product (Grieves, 2015).

Comparison is a natural habit of human beings, and it is done unconsciously and continuously with the desired and actual result to determine a difference. Working out the differences between physical and virtual product information is very inefficient. With a DT in place, the comparison of the ideal character with the actual measurement can be made quickly. Are the difference highlighted in colors, instantaneous decisions can be made (Grieves, 2015).

Collaboration brings more variability and perspectives on situations. Furthermore, the DT allows a shared model of conceptualization and solves the problem of individual concepts. To be at the same location is not needed anymore. The capabilities of DT additionally allow viewing physical products with overlaying their virtual counterpart at any stage in the factory, which could be extended across multiple factories across the globe (Grieves, 2015). The merge of information about how the product is manufactured and built can bring a contemporary perspective of how the process is meeting its specification goals. With this real-time information, digital factories can be created to predict how the product is to be manufactured. Emphasizing the connection between physical and virtual products will increase efficiency, the consistency and lead to higher quality of the product (Grieves, 2015).

2.2 Industrie 4.0 Simulation Unit

The Fischertechnik Simulation Units aim to create a factory simulation for a whole production chain with its modules and controller units that are connected and transfer their data to the cloud. Therefore, it allows us to develop a process that acts as a training model. It consists of an automated high-bay warehouse with a vacuum gripper robot, a multi-processing station with an oven, and a sorting line with detection. By connecting and controlling these stations, a complete production line can be demonstrated. The controllers are programmable with ROBO Pro, C-Compiler, PC-Library, and are preinstalled with similar programs.

In addition, through an environmental sensor and a pivoting camera, values of temperature, humidity, air pressure, and air quality are synchronized with the IoT-Platform via an MQTT broker. MQTT is based on industry standards, and all data can be immediately seen on the dashboard and used for further analysis. The traceability of the current status is enabled through the unique identification number of each workpiece.

The capabilities of smart and connected products and their resulting data are altering every activity in a manufacturing value chain. Traditional sources of data across the value chain are being supplemented by the product itself (Porter & Heppelmann, 2015). Handling a lot of information brings up the need to develop Human-Computer Interfaces for the DT, to overcome the problem of showing the necessary information to the right user (Schroeder et al., 2016). Therefore, new digital user interfaces are enabled and eliminate the need of controlling the product itself (Porter & Heppelmann, 2015). Augmented Reality as a critical enabling technology can display digital content onto the real world by using mobile devices that have proven to be accessible and highly versatile (Schroeder et al., 2016). Furthermore, Augmented Reality can support the connection between the physical object and the DT (Kritzler, Funk, Michahelles, & Rohde, 2017). An authoring tool (Vuforia Studio) is connected to the IoT-Platform that transforms and contextualizes the data to create meaningful experiences.

2.3 Cognitive Load Theory

To optimize mental performance, the cognitive load theory has been designed to provide guidelines about the presentation of information (Sweller, Van Merrienboer, & Paas, 1998). It was primarily developed for instructional design based on human's cognitive architecture. Without an appropriate framework of instructional techniques and knowledge about social cognitive processes, the evaluation of why instructional procedures do or do not work would be impossible (Sweller, Ayres, & Kalyuga, 2011). From the time of its initiation, the theory generated experimental and instructional effects when new and traditional procedures were compared through randomized, controlled experiments (Sweller, 2011). In the planning of the experiment, the limited accommodation of the learner has to be taken into consideration. Therefore, the task will be divided into small steps. In addition to that, Miller (1956) demonstrated in his research that people have limited capacity for processing information and can only memorize seven elements plus/minus two in their working memory. The limited capacity of the working memory with new information is also evaluated by Sweller, Ayres, and Kalyuga (2011). Therefore, instructions and the teaching materials need to consider these limitations that information can be stored effectively in long-term memory. Because to construct them, data must be processed in the working memory (Sweller et al., 1998). Successful transformation of information into long-term memory can trivially simplify tasks that were beforehand impossible (Sweller et al., 2011).

The main interest of cognitive load theory is the ease with which information is processed in working memory. The factors which affect the working memory load are (Sweller et al., 1998): (1) intrinsic load, (2) extraneous load, and (3) germane load. Intrinsic load is described as not alterable by instructional modifications because the material being dealt with is elementary (Sweller et al., 1998). Extraneous load, on the other hand, is an unnecessary cognitive load and is the presented material or activities of students. Therefore, it can be adjusted by instructional interventions (Sweller et al., 1998). Germane load is a further distinction of extraneous load and reflects the effort of contribution to transfer the knowledge from working memory to long-term memory (Sweller et al., 1998). The multidimensional character and the complex interrelationships between performance, mental load, and mental effort cause difficulties of how to determine cognitive load.

Generally, the cognitive load is considered as a construct that represents the execution of a specific task afflicting on the cognitive system. This construct can be drafted in a task-based dimension (mental load) and a learner-based dimension (mental effort) while affecting the performance of the learner. Mental load refers to the load that is needed for demands of the task, and mental effort refers to the amount of cognitive capacity to accommodate the task demands (Sweller et al., 1998).

Wierwille and Eggemeier (1993) are recommending three significant categories for measuring mental-effort techniques. These classifications are including subjective, physiological, and task-performance-based indicators. The evaluation of Paas and van Merrienboer (1993) of individual and physiological measurement techniques demonstrates that physiological measures based on heart-rate variability are unreliable, invalid, and only sensitive to significant variations of cognitive load. In contrast, subjective rating-scale measurement is valid and reliable and, therefore, the most promising technique for research in the context of cognitive load theory (Sweller et al., 1998).

3. OBJECTIVES AND METHODOLOGY

The focus of this paper lies on reducing the cognitive load by using the Fischertechnik Simulation Unit to train students on the concept of DT and Industry 4.0. In an integrated learning scenario, the cognitive load of students working with and without a Simulation Unit will be determined and compared. This study should answer the following research question: How will the cognitive load of students be influenced by the help of simulation to understand the concept and the application of DT technology?

To answer the question, the authors plan to use the methodology of an experiment with A/B testing. Therefore, two randomized groups will have the same problem situation, but only one will work with the Firschertechnik Simulation Unit. The measurement of the cognitive load will be performed by using the NASA task load index (NASA-TLX) (Hart, 1986; 2006). With this comparison, it can be determined which group has the lower cognitive stress level by performing the tasks necessary to understand DT.

The target group of the experiment will be students from a bachelor's degree course with no limitation in gender or age. As the authors are teaching the class on their own, it is easy to get the students for the empirical evaluation. The aim is to have 40 participants for each group in the experiment.

The main focus of the explained cognitive load theory lies in the instructional design (Sweller et al., 2011). Therefore, the approach will also be used for planning the integrated learning scenario.

4. CONCLUSION, LIMITATIONS AND FURTHER RESEARCH

The DT used in our paper is limited to specific implementation with the Fischertechnik 4.0. The virtual model will use the data from the sensors of the Fischertechnik Simulation Unit and is therefore limited in this context. The learning scenario will be created based on a real-world example, but it will be a simulation with a controlled environment.

This research is a first step of combining the Fischertechnik 4.0 Simulation Unit with the concept of DT to reduce the cognitive load for students. This practical approach can be used to improve the overall understanding of IT Systems over several layers (Koller et al., 2020). Parts of the outcome of the research will be used for developing a new teaching concept for the department of Management Communication & IT. It addresses the first two layers (shopping floor, manufacturing execution) of a six-layer model for integrated ERP lectures (Dilger, Ploder & Bernsteiner, 2020). The overall case-based teaching scenario with the DT and the Fischertechnik 4.0 can also be applied to the industry - as a showcase for digitalization. The haptic experience to see what is possible is an essential aspect for companies to indicate advantages, limitations, and potential applications.

ACKNOWLEDGEMENT

This research is made possible by the support of the Tyrolean Science Funding.

REFERENCES

Boschert, S., & Rosen, R. (2016). *Digital twin - the simulation aspect*. In Mechatronic futures (pp. 59–74). Springer.

Dilger, T., Ploder, C., & Bernsteiner, R. (2020). "Extensive"-Case Teaching as Means of Testing Comprehensive Learning Outcome? – a Pre-Study. INTED2020 Proceedings, 1(March), 4864–4868. https://doi.org/10.21125/inted.2020.1333

Fuchs, C. (2018). Industry 4.0: *The digital german ideology*. Triplec: Communication, Capitalism & Critique, 16(1), 280–289.

Grieves, M. (2015). *Digital twin: Manufacturing excellence through virtual factory replication*: A white paper by dr. micheal grieves.

Hart, S. G. (1986). *NASA Task load Index (TLX)*. Volume 1.0; Paper and pencil package.

Hart, S. G. (2006, October). *NASA-task load index (NASA-TLX); 20 years later*. In Proceedings of the human factors and ergonomics society annual meeting (Vol. 50, No. 9, pp. 904-908). Sage CA: Los Angeles, CA: Sage Publications

Kritzler, M., Funk, M., Michahelles, F., & Rohde, W. (2017, October). The virtual twin: controlling smart factories using a spatially-correct augmented reality representation. In Proceedings of the Seventh International Conference on the Internet of Things (pp. 1-2).

Koller, M., Ploder, C., Bernsteiner, R., & Dilger, T. (2020). *Algorithms in the IoT: An Evaluation Model for Predictive Maintenance of Cyber-Physical Systems*. In L. Gaur, A. Solanki, V. Jain, & D. Khazanchi (Eds.), Handbook of Research on Engineering Innovations and Technology Management in Organizations. https://doi.org/10.4018/978-1-7998-2772-6

Miller, G. A. (1956). *The magical number seven, plus or minus two: Some limits on our capacity for processing information*. Psychological Review, 63(2), 81.

Paas, F. G., & Van Merriënboer, J. J. (1993). *The efficiency of instructional conditions: An approach to combine mental effort and performance measures*. Human factors, 35(4), 737–743.

Ploder, C., Bernsteiner, R., Schlögl, S., Gschliesser, C. (2019). *The future use of LowCode / NoCode Platforms by Knowledge Workers - an Acceptance Study*. In Knowledge Management in Organizations: 14th International KMO 2019, Proceedings, Cham: Springer. July 2019, doi: 10.1007/978-3-030-21451-7_38

Porter, M. E., & Heppelmann, J. E. (2015). How smart, connected products are transforming companies. Harvard business review, 93(10), 96-114.

Rosen, R., von Wichert, G., Lo, G., & Bettenhausen, K. (2015). *About the importance of autonomy and digital twins for the future of manufacturing*. ifac papers online 48 (3): 567–572. In the 15th ifac symposium on information control problems in manufacturing.

Schroeder, G., Steinmetz, C., Pereira, C. E., Muller, I., Garcia, N., Espindola, D., & Rodrigues, R. (2016, July). Visualising the digital twin using web services and augmented reality. In 2016 IEEE 14th International Conference on Industrial Informatics (INDIN) (pp. 522-527). IEEE.

Sweller, J. (2011). *Cognitive load theory*. In Psychology of learning and motivation (Vol. 55, pp. 37–76). Elsevier.

Sweller, J., Ayres, P., & Kalyuga, S. (2011). *Explorations in the learning sciences, instructional systems and performance technologies, cognitive load theory*. London, UK: Springer Science+ Business Media.

Sweller, J., Van Merrienboer, J. J., & Paas, F. G. (1998). *Cognitive architecture and instructional design*. Educational psychology review, 10(3), 251–296.

Tao, F., Cheng, J., Qi, Q., Zhang, M., Zhang, H., & Sui, F. (2018). *Digital twin-driven product design, manufacturing, and service with big data*. The International Journal of Advanced Manufacturing Technology, 94(9-12), 3563–3576.

Tao, F., Zhang, M., Cheng, J., & Qi, Q. (2017). *Digital twin workshop: a new paradigm for a future workshop*. Computer Integrated Manufacturing Systems, 23(1), 1–9.

Wierwille, W. W., & Eggemeier, F. T. (1993). *Recommendations for mental workload measurement in a test and evaluation environment*. Human factors, 35(2), 263–281.

INTEGRATING MEDIA DIDACTIC COMPETENCES IN PSYCHOLOGY COURSES OF TEACHER EDUCATION

Sarah Lukas, Anna-Lisa Max and Holger Weitzel
Pädagogische Hochschule Weingarten
Kirchplatz 2, 88250 Weingarten, Germany

ABSTRACT

Internationally, ICT have become an integral part of school curricula in recent years. As a consequence, teacher education has the aim of imparting the necessary knowledge for the effective use of ICT. The TPACK framework is a frequently used theoretical basis to achieve this goal. In our study we investigate to what extent TPACK is promoted in a psychology course and how TPACK development correlates with other aspects of professional teachers. Results show that educational psychology courses can promote TPACK and that aspects of motivation or comprehension of constructivist learning settings should be considered in the conceptualization of courses with the aim to promote TPACK.

KEYWORDS

TPACK, ICT, Educational Psychology, Teacher Education, Motivation, Constructivist Learning Settings

1. INTRODUCTION

Psychology courses play an important role in teacher education. Traditional educational psychology includes issues like learning, development, motivation, classroom management, and assessment. However, in the recent years, also media psychological expertise becomes more and more important in teacher curricula, as the use of digital media for teaching and learning (ICT) is increasingly discussed (e. g., Gmundusdottir & Hatlevik, 2018). This development is reflected in research and set down in competence guidelines for teacher education (e.g. USDE, 2017, Redecker, 2017). Internationally, the TPACK framework (Mishra & Koehler, 2006, 2008) has received increasing attention for describing the knowledge teachers need to effectively integrate ICT into classroom teaching (e.g. Chai, Koh & Tsai, 2016; Rocha Fernandes et al., 2020). The TPACK framework defines seven technology-related knowledge domains, which extend subject knowledge and pedagogical knowledge as central dimensions of teacher knowledge by the technological aspect. TPACK describes the knowledge and skills required to teach the content of a subject in a didactically and pedagogically appropriate manner by means of ICT (Fig. 1). TPACK thus represents a context-related synthesis of teachers' professional knowledge for teaching domain-specific content through the use of digital technologies. Developing TPACK among teachers is considered a long-term process (Hofer & Grandgenett, 2012) that can take place in different areas of teacher education and is influenced by other variables such as the students' comprehension of constructivist learning settings (CCL), self-efficacy (Valtonen et al., 2020), and motivation (Holland & Piper, 2014).

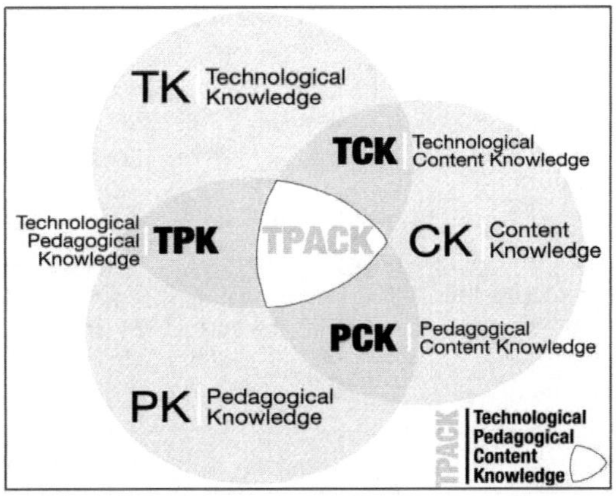

Figure 1. The TPACK model (own depiction, adapted from Koehler & Mishra, 2009)

With educational psychology being an important topic in teacher education and including media psychology as a rather recent important part of the discipline (for the current discussion see for instance Edling & Liljestrand, 2020), we argue here that psychology courses in preservice teacher education can be effectively used to convey TPACK, at least to a certain extent. It is not within the scope of psychology courses in teacher education to convey content knowledge and didactics. Hence, the C component of TPACK cannot be fully addressed in psychology courses and probably, rather TPK is developed. Lachner et al. (2019) suggested that for TPK especially pedagogic knowledge was important, which is in line of our hypothesis that educational psychology courses can effectively improve TPK/TPACK. Specifically, modern educational psychology includes media pedagogic contents. Accordingly, issues of the traditional educational psychology (like motivation) are intertwined with the modern media psychology (like how digital media can be used to improve motivation). Hence, we hypothesize that educational psychology courses can be important to convey TPACK. In the following, we will present an example of how this could be done and how the development of TPACK within one semester is changed in a psychology class of master teacher education. We additionally gathered data of motivation, self-efficacy with respect to using technology, and CCL, because the use of digital media can provide constructivist learning environments and it has been shown that constructivist beliefs correlate with use of computers in the classroom (Hermans et al., 2008).

2. METHOD

2.1 Course Content

The course in which this study was conducted was part of the project TPACK 4.0, which has the aim to foster TPACK in preservice teacher students. To this end, a TPACK-input was created and implemented in the teacher courses. The TPACK-input was based on the TPACK model, the DigCompEdu framework (Redecker, 2017), the Substitution Augmentation Modification Redefinition (SAMR) Model (Hamilton et al., 2016), principles of multimedia learning (Mayer, 2009), as well as criteria for good quality teaching (Steffensky & Neuhaus, 2018). The course "Visualisation of cognitive psychological theories" contained cognitive-psychological theories which might be relevant for teacher students (e.g., the working memory model, Baddeley, 2002; Language and simulation in conceptual processing, Barsalou et al., 2008). Each working group processed one self-selected theory by reading the basic literature and transferred it into the creation of a digital media teaching unit. Most of the students chose to create an explanatory video, but one group also decided to design an AR worksheet. Due to the Covid-19 pandemia, the TPACK-input as well as the other course units had to take place online. Also the creation of the teaching media, which were foreseen to be conducted in the pedagogical makerspace CoLiLab (see for further details Lukas et al., 2019; Max et al., 2020) had to take place at home.

2.2 Questionnaire

The pre-post questionnaire was developed on the basis of standardized scales in order to measure the influence of working on psychology related media projects in terms of TPACK (Schmidt et al. 2009; Handal et al. 2013) as well as in terms of the construct's intrinsic motivation (Wilde et al., 2009) and self-efficacy (Holden & Rada, 2011). Moreover, we collected data of the students' CCL. TPACK was measured with 13 items, which tested self-assessment of TPACK. The scale could be ranked between one and four. Motivation was tested with 12 items, ranging between one and five. Self-efficacy concerning the use of technology and digital was measured with ten items, ranging from one to four. CCL was tested with 12 items, ranging from one until four. The pretest was conducted at the beginning of the summer semester 2020 (march - july), the posttest was conducted at the end of this semester.

2.3 Sample

The sample consisted of 50 participants (male = 7; female = 40; not reported = 3) of a master's degree course in educational psychology. This course is a compulsory elective subject within the framework of their further basic-education-program, regardless of their chosen teaching subjects and later teaching level (primary or secondary school). Of the 50 participants, not all completed the pre- as well as the posttest. In some cases it was due to a dropout of the course. Only those who completed both questionnaires were included in the analysis, which resulted in a sample of 23 participants (male = 3; female = 20). Age ranged between 21 and 45 years, with a mean of $M = 24$.

2.4 Reliability Analysis

We measured reliability of the scales TPACK, motivation, CCL and self-efficacy of the pretest. Reliability of TPACK was $\alpha = .88$, of motivation $\alpha = .88$, of constructivist learning settings $\alpha = .67$, and of self-efficacy $\alpha = .66$. It can be rated as good for TPACK and motivation, but as rather dubious for CCL and self-efficacy.

3. RESULTS

First, the development of TPACK during the course was analyzed. The mean rating of the TPACK pretest was $M = 2.59$ and of the posttest $M = 2.9$. A t-test revealed that TPACK increased significantly during the semester, $t\,(22) = 2.91$, p = .008. With Cohen's $d_z = .6$, effect size was medium high. None of the other variables changed significantly in the respective timeframe (see Table 1 for the means of the pre- and posttest, respectively).

In a second step, we conducted a correlation analysis of the variables TPACK, motivation, CCL and self-efficacy. TPACK correlated significantly positive with motivation in the pretest ($r = .48$, $p = .001$), and even more in the posttest ($r = .64$, $p < .001$). Interestingly, TPACK correlated significantly negative with CCL in the pretest ($r = -.31$, $p = .036$). This correlation vanished in the posttest ($r = -.31$, $p = 0\ .12$). There was no significant correlation between TPACK and self-efficacy.

Table 1. Means and standard deviation (in brackets) of the measured constructs TPACK, motiviation, self-efficacy and students' comprehension of constructivist learning settings (CCL) in the pre- and posttest

	TPACK	Motivation	Self-efficacy	CCL
Pretest	2.59 (0.32)	3.47 (0.49)	2.03 (0.33)	2.81 (0.31)
Posttest	2.9 (0.48)	3.4 (0.58)	2.1 (0.29)	2.82 (0.4)

4. DISCUSSION

The aim of the study was to examine if educational psychology courses in teacher education can convey TPACK. Indeed, a significant increase of TPACK was found during the course. Integrating TPACK contents in educational psychology courses in teacher education seems to be successful for the development of TPACK. As a result, TPACK/TPK components should be integrated in educational psychology curricula in teacher education. Earlier findings were confirmed by showing a significant correlation between intrinsic motivation and TPACK. By developing courses with the aim to convey TPACK, the activation of intrinsic motivation of the learners should be taken into account. In the pretest an unexpected negative correlation between TPACK and CCL was found. This suggests that although student's might have a comprehension of constructivist learning settings, they were not able to clearly connect it with TPACK. This issue should be addressed in future TPACK courses as well.

Please note that the described psychology course rather addressed the TPK component, but the result in TPACK was measured. For a better understanding of the correlations between TPK and TPACK, and how teaching TPK is reflected in TPACK, further studies have to be conducted.

5. CONCLUSION

The presented study clearly shows promising indication that educational psychology courses can promote TPACK in teacher students. Given that developing TPACK is a long-term process and acquires various experience possibilities, it should be integrated interdisciplinarily in the teacher education and also be transferred by the basic subjects of educational sciences. The presented study is only a small part of the still ongoing project TPACK 4.0 and can thus only address limited aspects of a bigger picture. But it provides indications of the importance of educational psychology and its adaptation regarding ongoing debates and developments.

ACKNOWLEDGEMENT

This project is funded by the Ministry of Science, Research and Arts, Ministerium für Wissenschaft, Forschung und Kunst, Baden-Württemberg, digital@bw, Az.: 43-6700.-4/2/1/1.

REFERENCES

Baddeley, A. D., 2002. Is working memory still working? *European Psychologist, 7*, pp. 85-97.

Barsalou, L. W., Santos, A., Simmons, W. K., & Wilson, C. D., 2008. Language and simulation in conceptual processing. In: M. de Vega, A. Glenberg & A. Graesser (Eds.) *Symbols and embodiment debates on meaning and cognition.* Oxford University Press, Oxford, pp. 245-284. doi:10.1093/acprof:oso/9780199217274.003.0013.

Chai, C. S., Koh, J. H. L., & Tsai, C.-C. (2016). A Review of the Quantitative Measures of Technological Pedagogical Content Knowledge (TPACK). In M. Herring, P. Mishra, & M.J. Koehler (Eds.). *Handbook of technological pedagogical content knowledge (TPCK) for educators* (second edition), Routledge, New York, pp. 87–106.

Edling, S., Liljestrand, J., 2020. Let's talk about teacher education! Analysing the media debates in 2016-2017 on teacher education using Sweden as a case. *Asia-Pacific Journal of Teacher Education, 48*, pp. 251–266. https://doi.org/10.1080/1359866X.2019.1631255

Gudmundsdottir, G.B., Hatlevik, O.E., 2018. Newly qualified teachers' professional digital competence: implications for teacher education. *European Journal of Teacher Education, 41*, pp. 214–231. https://doi.org/10.1080/02619768.2017.1416085

Hamilton, E.R., Rosenberg, J.M., Akcaoglu, M., 2016. The Substitution Augmentation Modification Redefinition (SAMR) Model: A critical review and suggestions for its use. *TechTrends, 60,* pp. 433–441. https://doi.org/10.1007/s11528-016-0091-y

Handal, B., Campbell, C., Cavanagh, M., Petocz, P., & Kelly, N., 2013. Technological Pedagogical Content Knowledge of Secondary Mathematics Teachers. *Contemporary Issues in Technology and Teacher Education, 13(1)*, pp. 22-40

Hermans, R., Tondeur, J., van Braak, J., Valcke, M., 2008. The impact of primary school teachers' educational beliefs on the classroom use of computers. *Computers & Education 51*, pp. 1499–1509. https://doi.org/10.1016/j.compedu.2008.02.001

Hofer, M., Grandgenett, N., 2012. TPACK Development in Teacher Education: A Longitudinal Study of Preservice teachers in a Secondary M.A.Ed Program. *Journal of Research on Technology in Education, 45(1),* pp. 83–106.

Holden, H., & Rada, R. (2011). Understanding the Influence of Perceived Usability and Technology Self-Efficacy on Teachers' Technology Acceptance. *Journal of Research on Technology in Education, 43(4),* pp. 343–367. https://doi.org/10.1080/15391523.2011.10782576

Holland, D.D., Piper, R.T., 2014. A Technology Integration Education (Tie) Model: Millennial Preservice Teachers' Motivations about Technological, Pedagogical, and Content Knowledge (Tpack) Competencies. *Journal of Educational Computing Research 51,* pp. 257–294. https://doi.org/10.2190/EC.51.3.a

Koehler, M.J., Mishra, P., 2009. What is Technological Pedagogical Content Knowledge? *Contemporary Issues in Technology and Teacher Education 9,* pp. 60–70.

Lachner, A., Backfisch, I., & Stürmer, K. (2019). A test-based approach of Modeling and Measuring Technological Pedagogical Knowledge. *Computers & Education, 142,* 103645. https://doi.org/10.1016/j.compedu.2019.10364

Lukas, S., Müller, W., Huwer, J., Drüke-Noe, C., Koppel, I., Rebholz, S., Stratmann, J., Theilmann, F., Weitzel, H., 2019. Improving students' TPACK through learning labs: The implementation of IChemLab and STEAM Makerspace. *EDULEARN2019 Proceedings,* Palma, Spain, pp. 6718–6726. https://doi.org/10.21125/edulearn.2019.1611

Max, A.L., Schmoll, I., Uhl, P., Huwer, J., Lukas, S., Mueller, W., Weitzel, H., 2020. Integration of a teaching-learningn lab and a pedagogical makerspace into a module for media education for STEAM teacher students, *INTED2020 Proceedings*. Valencia, Spain, pp. 2050-2059. https://doi.org/10.21125/inted.2020.0645

Mayer, R.E., 2009. *Multimedia Learning,* 2nd ed. Cambridge University Press, Cambridge. https://doi.org/10.1017/CBO9780511811678

Mishra, P., Koehler, M.J., 2008. Introducing Technological Pedagogical Content Knowledge. Presented at the *Annual Meeting of the American Education Association*, pp. 1–16.

Mishra, P., Koehler, M.J., 2006. Technological Pedagogical Content Knowledge: A Framework for Teacher Knowledge. *Teachers College Rec 108*, pp. 1017–1054. https://doi.org/10.1111/j.1467-9620.2006.00684.x

Redecker, C., 2017. *European Framework for the Digital competence of educators. DigCompEdu*. (Policy Report No. EUR 28775 EN). Publication Office of the European Union, Luxembourg.

Rocha Fernandes, G.W., Rodrigues, A.M., & Ferreira, C.A. (2020). Professional Development and Use of Digital Technologies by Science Teachers: a Review of Theoretical Frameworks. *Res Sci Educ* 50, pp. 673-708.

Schmidt, D.A., Baran, E., Thompson, A.D., Mishra, P., Koehler, M.J., Shin, T.S., 2009. Technological Pedagogical Content Knowledge (TPACK): The Development and Validation of an Assessment Instrument for Preservice Teachers. *Journal of Research on Technology in Education 42*, pp. 123-149.

Steffensky, M., & Neuhaus, B. J., 2018. Unterrichtsqualität in der naturwissenschaftlichen Forschung. In D. Krüger, I. Parchmann, & H. Schecker (Eds.) *Theorien in der naturwissenschaftsdidaktischen Forschung,* Springer, Berlin, pp. 299–313.

U.S. Department of Education (2017). *Reimagining the role of technology in higher education: A supplement to the National Education Technology Plan*. Washington, D.C.: Office of Educational Technology. Retrieved July 20, 2020 from https ://tech.ed.gov/files /2017/01/Highe r-Ed-NETP.pdf.

Valtonen, T., Leppänen, U., Hyypiä, M., Sointu, E., Smits, A., & Tondeur, J. (2020). Fresh perspectives on TPACK: pre-service teachers' own appraisal of their challenging and confident TPACK areas. *Educ Inf Technol* 25, pp. 2823–2842.

Wilde, M., Bätz, K., Kovaleva, A., & Urhahne, D. (2009). Überprüfung einer Kurzskala intrinsischer Motivation (KIM). *ZfDN*, 15, pp. 31-45.

A KIT OF APPS TO IMPROVE AND ASSESS EXECUTIVE FUNCTIONS AND WORKING MEMORY CAPACITY IN PRESCHOOLERS

Sabrina Panesi, Laura Freina and Lucia Ferlino
Institute for Educational Technology of the CNR, Via de Marini, 6, Genoa, Italy

ABSTRACT

Several methods for the assessment and training of executive functions and working memory capacity in preschoolers have been developed over previous decades, but despite our digital era, new technologies are seldom addressed. To fill this gap, in the context of the "shareFUN" project, a set of digital games was designed, including measures and training activities for inhibition, shifting, updating and working memory capacity. The games were designed as a kit of apps since preschoolers show a deep interest and a high level of confidence in approaching digital games, mainly on tablets or smartphones. The current paper has the main aim to present this kit and outline further research activities, scheduled within the "shareFUN" project, for the validation of the apps used for assessment and their efficacy for training.

KEYWORDS

Executive Functions, Working Memory Capacity, Cognitive Training and Assessment, Preschoolers, App

1. INTRODUCTION

Executive Functions (EF) is an "umbrella term" that refers to a family of adaptive, goal directed, top-down mental control processes. According to Miyake and colleagues (Miyake et al., 2000; Miyake and Friedman, 2012) the three core EF components are: *inhibition*, the ability to suppress task-irrelevant cognitive processing and ignore salient yet irrelevant features of the situation; *shifting*, the ability to switch between different operations or levels of processing; and *updating*, the ability to encode, hold and monitor incoming information in the working memory (WM), replacing the no longer relevant information with new one. Furthermore, these authors argued that these three core EF components rely to some extent on WM capacity, i.e. the simultaneous maintenance and manipulation of information. In line with this perspective, a recent study highlighted a strong relationship between inhibition, shifting, updating and WM capacity in preschoolers (Panesi and Morra, 2020): a period of most remarkable changes (Garon et al., 2008; Morra et al., 2018).

In preschool years, EF and WM capacity seem to be associated with and predictive of other domains as self-regulation (Sokol and Müller, 2007), social cognition (Denham et al., 2014), and future academic outcomes (De Franchis et al,, 2017), as well as behavioral problems (Allan and Lonigan, 2014) and ADHD symptoms (Pauli-Pott et al., 2014). Furthermore, EF deficits have been found in children with specific impairments or disabilities, such as preschoolers with autism (Pennington and Ozonoff, 1996), Down Syndrome (Lanfranchi et al., 2009), language impairment (Vissers et al., 2015), and also in children whose development is hampered by their low socio-economic backgrounds (Miech et al., 2001).

Due to the strong relationship between EF, WM capacity and other developmental domains in preschoolers, specific interventions to improve them at an early age, as well as appropriate tools for their assessment are crucial. Recently, Scionti and colleagues (2020) conducted a meta-analysis and found that cognitive training for preschoolers produced both near and far transfer effects, and that in this age range, a cognitive intervention has similar effects in younger and older children. They found positive effects of EF training programs in children both with and without developmental risks, in particular preschoolers with ADHD symptoms and with socially disadvantaged conditions. This finding suggests that cognitive interventions in an educational context enhancing the early development of some cognitive skills and resources, such as EF and WM capacity, may prevent future developmental risks. Finally, they found that cognitive EF training programs are more effective when done in a group, which calls for educational and clinical settings. However, in order to develop an effective cognitive intervention to foster EF and WM capacity, an accurate assessment of the child's developmental level is needed. Several methods of assessing EF and WM capacity in young children were developed over the last decades (Howard and Melhuish, 2017), nevertheless, there still are conceptual and pragmatic issues in early measurement of young children's emerging cognitive abilities. Actually, there is often a lack of clarity in the construct being measured, due to the difficulty of investigating EF and WM capacity in isolation; in fact, usually the tasks used measure also other cognitive processes, as visual or motor processes. This issue, known as "task impurity", is usually solved by administering multiple tasks, but, with preschoolers, one of the main problems is the lack of age-appropriate EF and WM capacity tasks. New digital technologies allow the introduction of new methods of assessment and intervention, however, to the best of our knowledge, there are only a few studies focused on technology based interventions promoting EF and WM capacity in preschoolers (Thorell et al., 2009), or assessing EF and WM capacity young children (Howard and Melhuish, 2017). Furthermore, they are usually developed for clinical purposes (Thorell et al., 2009).

This paper presents a new kit of apps for training and assessing of early EF and WM capacity development. Specifically, the kit includes assessment tasks and training activities of the three core EF components (i.e. inhibition, shifting, updating) and WM capacity for preschoolers.

2. THE KIT OF APPS

Within the "shareFUN" project[1], a tool for improving and measuring EF and WM capacity in preschoolers was designed in the form of a kit of apps (for details: Freina and Panesi, 2020). The aim was to create an easy to use tool, available for clinicians, researchers, but also for teachers and parents, allowing them to monitor and support young children's cognitive development in different contexts. Such a tool is very important especially when children cannot move from home, as was the case during the COVID-19 health emergency.

Today, young children start using digital games, mainly on tablets or smartphones, at a very young age. They generally show a deep interest in games and a high level of confidence in approaching the digital tools. In order to capture their attention and get the most from all session, four games were developed using the Unity 3D (https://unity.com/) development platform. Three games are aimed at one specific EF component, and the fourth at WM capacity (see Table 1). Each was developed as a separate app, for a tablet or smartphone with a touch interface.

Table 1. The kit of apps for Android to measure and improve EF and WM capacity

App		Refers to
Basilio		Inhibition
The Farmer		Shifting
The Magic House		Updating
Evelyn		Working Memory Capacity

[1] "shareFUN" (https://www.sharefun.it) is a project of the Institute for Educational Technology of the Italian National Research Council (ITD-CNR), co-funded by the Operative Program POR FSE Liguria Region 2014-2020 Code: RLOF18ASSRIC/77/1.

Each game can be used as a test or training tool: in test mode, the game goes through a fixed sequence of tasks, while all the actions of the player are logged on a cloud database for later analysis. All the logged data is anonymous, children are identified with a code and the association between the code and the single child is external to the games. Furthermore, no feedback is given, and when the error rate gets higher than a threshold, the game finishes. When the games are used for training purposes, data from the game is not logged and a specific feedback is provided to correct errors and help the child reflect about his own performance.

All the games are designed to be used directly by the child under supervision of an adult. Instructions are spoken to make them accessible to the child, while, short written messages remind the adult about the task.

Basilio (inhibition). Basilio is a nice little ghost who invites the child to try to touch him. At first, only reaction times are logged, but later Basilio presents some friends of his and asks the player to touch him as quicky as possible, but to avoid touching the other characters. Then, one character appears on the screen for one second and the child has to touch it only if it is Basilio, while avoiding all the other characters.

The Farmer (shifting). In the game, a farmer presents his eight baby animals: a lamb, a chick, a kitten and a puppy with their mothers. Four animals are white and four are colored. On the scene there are a large white house and a little red one. The game asks the child to touch the house where each animal should go, using two different classification rules:

- Mother/baby: when the farmer is on site, babies go to the little house and mothers to the large one;
- White/colored: when the farmer is out of sight, white animals go to the white house, and colored animals to the red one.

After a set of trials where the two rules are presented separately, the child has to decide which rule to use depending on the presence of the farmer: when present, the mother/baby rule should be used, otherwise the color rule should be used.

The Magic House (updating). Eight little animals, after presenting themselves, want to play together in a little house, but the house is magic, and only the last two animals that enter the house can play together. A sequence of 3 to 6 animals entering the house one after the other is shown and then the child has to touch the last one that entered the house, and then the second-last one (Panesi and Morra, 2017).

Evelyn (WM capacity). Evelyn, a young puppy, challenges the child to remember a sequence of everyday objects. The objects are shown one at a time, and then the child is asked to touch the objects s/he has seen. At the beginning, the child can touch them in any order, later the objects have to be touched in the same order as they have been shown, and finally, (to test the WM capacity) they have to be touched in an inverse order, starting from the last one.

3. CONCLUSION AND FURTHER RESEARCH

In this paper we described a kit of apps developed for assessing and training EF and WM capacity in preschoolers. The apps, including tests and training activities, can be easily used by clinicians, teachers, families, and researchers. Moreover, the small games in the form of apps for tablets are easy to use and motivating for preschoolers.

All the apps were ready for a first evaluation from the end users in spring 2020, but, due to the lockdown caused by COVID-19, all schools, including nursery schools, were closed and it was not possible to get in touch with the children. At present, schools have just reopened, and lots of measures are in place to guarantee students' safety, it is therefore impossible to organize a wide scale validation.

In the next months, two different research actions are planned:

ACTION 1: (i) some professionals (clinicians, teachers and researchers) will test the four apps while filling in a questionnaire. After their test, a focus group will be organized to discuss their opinions and collect suggestions for further refinements; (ii) a limited set of children of the target age will be involved in playing with the game. All children will use the games in a supervised manner, involving directly the researchers. While children will be playing, a structured interview will be carried out and observations will be made in order to evaluate the ease of use and the child's appreciation.

ACTION 2: (i) a much wider validation of the apps in the test mode will be organized, administering the kit of apps and a battery of traditional tests to measure EF and WM capacity to a large sample of preschoolers; (ii) the efficacy of the training activities with the apps will be investigated by administering a battery of traditional tests to measure EF and WM capacity as pre- and post- test to a sample of preschoolers that will use the games for training (experimental group) and to another sample of preschoolers that will continue traditional activities (control group) in the educational context.

The kit of apps will be tested with children with typical development and with some young children with atypical development in the clinical context.

REFERENCES

Allan, N. Lonigan, C., 2014. Exploring dimensionality of effortful control using hot and cool tasks in a sample of preschool children. *Journal of Experimental Child Psychology*, Vol. 122, pp. 33–47.

De Franchis, V., Usai, M.C.,. Viterbori, P., Traverso, L., 2017, Preschool executive functioning and literacy achievement in Grades 1 and 3 of primary school: A longitudinal study. *Learning and Individual Differences*, Vol. 54, pp. 184-195

Denham, S.A., Bassett, H.H., Zinsser, K., Wyatt, T.M., 2014. How preschoolers' social–emotional learning predicts their early school success: Developing theory-promoting, competency-based assessments. *Infant and Child Development*, Vol 23, No. 4, pp. 426-454.

Freina, L., Panesi, S. (2020). ShareFUN project: Executive functions in pre-schoolers. *CNR-ITD Internal Report*. Available online at: http://bit.ly/IntRepPanesi .

Garon, N., Bryson, S. E., & Smith, I. M., 2008. Executive function in preschoolers: A review using an integrative framework. *Psychological Bulletin*, Vol. 134, No.1, pp. 31–60.

Howard, S. J., & Melhuish, E., 2017. An early years toolbox for assessing early executive function, language, self-regulation, and social development: Validity, reliability, and preliminary norms. *Journal of Psychoeducational Assessment*, Vol. 35, No. 3, pp. 255-275.

Lanfranchi, S., Jerman, O. Vianello, R., 2009. Working memory and cognitive skills in individuals with Down syndrome. *Child Neuropsychology*, Vol.15, No. 4, pp. 397-416.

Miech, R., Essex, M., Goldsmith, H.H., 2001. Socioeconomic status and the adjustment to school: The role of self-regulation during early childhood. *Sociology of education*, pp. 102-120.

Miyake, A., & Friedman, N. P. , 2012. The nature and organization of individual differences in executive functions: four general conclusions. *Current Directions in Psychological Science*, Vol.21, No.1, pp. 8-14.

Miyake, A., Friedman, N. P., Emerson, M.J., Witzki, A.H., Howerter A., & Wager, T.D., 2000. The unity and diversity of executive functions and their contributions to complex "Frontal Lobe" tasks: a latent variable analysis. *Cognitive Psychology*, Vol.41, No. 1, pp. 49-100.

Morra, S., Panesi, S., Traverso, L., & Usai, M. C., 2018. Which tasks measure what? Reflections on executive function development and a commentary on Podjarny, Kamawar, and Andrews (2017). *Journal of Experimental Child Psychology*. Vol. 167, pp. 246–258.

Panesi, S., & Morra, S., 2020. Executive functions and mental attentional capacity in preschoolers. *Journal of Cognition and Development*, Vol.21, No.1, pp. 72-91.

Panesi, S., Morra, S., 2017. La casetta magica. Uno strumento per indagare l'aggiornamento (updating) della memoria di lavoro in età prescolare [The magic house. A new measure of updating for preschoolers]. *Psicologia Clinica dello Sviluppo*, Vol. 21, No .3, pp. 443-462.

Pauli-Pott, U., Dalir, S., Mingebach, T., Roller, A., & Becker, K., 2014. Attention deficit/hyperactivity and comorbid symptoms in preschoolers: Differences between subgroups in neuropsychological basic deficits. *Child Neuropsychology*, Vol. 20, No. 2, pp. 230-244.

Pennington, B.F., Ozonoff S., 1996. Executive functions and developmental psychopathology. *Journal of child psychology and psychiatry*, Vol. 37, No.1, pp. 51-87.

Scionti, N., Cavallero, M., Zogmaister, C., & Marzocchi, G. M., 2020. Is cognitive training effective for improving executive functions in preschoolers? A systematic review and meta-analysis. *Frontiers in Psychology*, 10, 2812.

Sokol, B.W., & Müller, U., 2007. The development of self-regulation: Toward the integration of cognition and emotion. [Editorial], *Cognitive Development*, Vol. 22, No. 4, pp. 401–405.

Thorell, L.B., Lindqvist, S. Bergman Nutley, S., Bohlin, G., & Klingberg, T., 2009. Training and transfer effects of executive functions in preschool children. *Developmental science*, Vol. 12, No. 1, pp. 106-113.

Vissers, C., Koolen, S., Hermans, D., Scheper, A., Knoors, H., 2015. Executive functioning in preschoolers with specific language impairment. *Frontiers in psychology*, 6:1574.

MOBILE AUGMENTED REALITY: DESIGN PRINCIPLES FOR THE USE IN EDUCATIONAL SETTINGS

Luca Moser
University of St.Gallen
St. Jakob-Strasse 21, CH-9000 St.Gallen, Switzerland

ABSTRACT

Mobile Augmented Reality (MAR) is increasingly used in education. MAR has the potential to motivate and engage learners, increase learning effects and change the quality and quantity of interaction during the learning process. Therefore, MAR learning settings (MARLS) design principles are needed to provide teachers and researchers with orientation knowledge MARLS. However, there is a lack of frameworks and principles to guide the design of effective MARLS. Design principles for MARLS should include technical and pedagogical aspects. In a literature review we analyzed 12 studies on MAR design and application for education to identify the design principles: 1. Usability; 2. User centeredness; 3. Basic learning theories; 4. Conscious application; 5. Cognitive overload. The principles may guide researchers and practitioners to bridge the gap between MAR innovations and real-world classrooms.

KEYWORDS

Augmented Reality, Mobile Augmented Reality, Education, Design Principles

1. INTRODUCTION

Augmented Reality (AR) supplements and enriches the real physical space with digital elements (Wu et al., 2013). Especially Mobile AR (MAR) applications are increasingly used in education due to the possibility to apply them with any mobile device (smartphone or tablet computer) and their cost-efficiency. MAR might soon become standard in classrooms (Akçayır and Akçayır, 2017), therefore this contribution focuses on MAR. The literature on MAR for education identified considerable potential for MAR-learning settings (MARLS) to increase engagement, motivation, learning effects and the quality and quantity of interaction of learners (Akçayır and Akçayır, 2017). MARLS allow authentic, interactive and learner-centered learning experiences (Bacca et al., 2014), a deeper knowledge acquisition, and a better application of the acquired knowledge in different contexts (Radu, 2012).

However, there is a difference between a system that supports learning and the effective and sustainable implementation of such a system in real-world classrooms (Cuendet et al., 2013). Teachers often lack the necessary media-didactical skills to use MAR and design effective MARLS (Bucher et al., 2020). Even though, multiple design principles for the creation of MAR applications have been developed, the scientific discourse identified a shortage of principles illustrating how to effectively use MAR applications to design learning settings (Kerr and Lawson, 2020; Kourouthanassis et al., 2015).

This paper addresses the aforementioned research gap. Its main goal is to identify design principles for MARLS. Because isolated knowledge about a technology and isolated knowledge about pedagogy are not sufficient to effectively use new technologies in classrooms (Mishra and Koehler, 2006), design principles should combine technological and pedagogical considerations.

The following section aggregates recent metastudies to summarize the findings of MAR research. Thereafter, a literature review on MAR design and implementation principles lays the ground to develop the MARLS design principles applying the TPACK model (Mishra and Koehler, 2006).

2. MAR IN EDUCATION

Seven recent metastudies on MAR in education, condense the research of 346 studies conducted between 2006 and 2019. Because the technological advances in MAR continue and steadily change the possibilities and challenges of MAR (Cuendet et al., 2013) only metastudies conducted in the past five years were included for this overview. Table 1, however, illustrates that the included studies still date back to 2006.

Table 1. Seven metastudies on MAR in education

Metastudy	No of Analyzed Studies	Years of Analyzed Studies
(Akçayır and Akçayır, 2017)	68	2007 – 2015
(Altinpulluk, 2019)	58	2006 – 2016
(Chen et al., 2017)	55	2011 – 2016
(Garzón et al., 2019)	61	2012 – 2018
(Quintero et al., 2019)	50	2008 – 2018
(Sommerauer and Müller, 2018)	36	2010 – 2017
(Yuliono et al., 2018)	18	2009 – 2018

The metastudies draw a concise picture of the potentials and challenges of MARLS. MAR applications can increase the motivation and engagement of learners (Yuliono et al., 2018). Positive learning effects could be identified in multiple MAR studies (Altinpulluk, 2019). Particularly, the possibility to change the perspective on learning objects and to provide new ways for learners to interact with materials, teachers and other learners, offer new possibilities to design effective learning settings (Akçayır and Akçayır, 2017). The major challenges include technological difficulties and a high complexity for teachers and learners (Garzón et al., 2019). However, most of the studies investigated the introduction of a MARL. Therefore, a "novelty effect" might have increased the enjoyment and motivation and the lack of experience might have enlarged technical and instructional challenges (Akçayır and Akçayır, 2017). With only few MARLS that are applied repeatedly, the development of design principles appears to be of high relevance to implement and investigate sustainable MALRS that do not entail these novelty effects.

3. IDENTIFYING MARL DESIGN PRINCIPLES

3.1 Method

According to the TPACK model, the design and use of digital learning settings requires, content knowledge, technological knowledge, pedagogical knowledge and the combinations of the respective knowledge types (Mishra and Koehler, 2006). Teachers' core competences lie in pedagogical knowledge and content knowledge. The combination of content knowledge with technical and pedagogical knowledge varies with the content. Consequently, we focus on the combination of technical and pedagogical knowledge to identify general MARLS design principles.

The literature review therefore focuses on the pedagogical and technical aspects of MAR for education. In an online search using the library access of the University of St. Gallen, the BASE, ERIC, Science Citation Index, Science Direct, and Scopus databases were accessed. The Boolean phrase ("design principl*" OR "design framework" OR "usability principl*") AND (educat* OR learn* OR school OR teach*) AND ("augment* reality") was used on the 9th of July 2020. The search terms had to appear in the title or abstract. This initial search led to 155 results. After filtering for online available scientific journals published between 2010 and 2020, to exclude outdated and non-reviewed contributions, 77 articles entered the analysis. After reading the 77 contributions, the twelve studies that proposed design principles or frameworks for the construction or application of MAR applications for educational purposes were analyzed to identify the design principles (Table 2).

3.2 Results

Table 2. Literature review on MARLS design principles

Study	Theoretical Foundation	Design Principles	
(Altmeyer et al., 2020)	Spatial contiguity principle Cognitive load theory Cognitive theory of multimedia learning	1 Avoid split-attention effect 2 Use common technology and context	
(Bucher et al., 2020)	Learning technology by design Action-oriented didactics Basic of media pedagogy Basics of HCI (human-computer-interaction)	1 Learning activities 2 Teaching activities 3 Interdisciplinarity	
(Cuendet et al., 2013)	Usability of HCI settings Classroom orchestration Design whole learning settings, (AR only a part of the whole learning setting)	1 Integration 2 Empowerment 3 Awareness	4 Flexibility 5 Minimalism
(Dunleavy, 2014)	Intrinsic motivation	1 Enable than challenge (challenge) 2 Gamified story (fantasy) 3 See the unseen (curiosity)	
(Kerr and Lawson, 2020)	Digital storytelling Physicality of learning object Scaffolding Informal learning	1 Experiential theme/s 2 Unique narrative 3 Multisensory design	4 Design for gaps 5 Collaboration
(Ko et al., 2013)	Usability of mobile applications	1 User-information 2 User-cognitive 3 User-support	4 User-interaction 5 User-usage
(Kouroutha nassis et al., 2015)	Usability of mobile applications	1 Context 2 To-the-task content 3 Transparency	4 Feedback on infrastructure 5 Memory
(Messuti et al., 2015)	Basic learning theories Usability of mobile applications	1 Basis in learning theories 2 Simple interface and usability 3 Blend the environment	
(Sommerau er and Müller, 2018)	Lens of theory Cognitive, behavioral and constructivist learning theories	1 Mobile learning 2 Game based learning	3 Experiential learning 4 Situated learning
(Stefan and Moldovean u, 2013)	Game based learning	1 Playability 2 Emotional appeal 3 Player's contribution 4 Challenge 5 Curiosity	6 Control 7 Fantasy 8 Motivation 9 Iteration 10 Scaffolding
(Tuli and Mantri, 2020)	Usability of mobile applications Generic AR design principles	1 Cognition 2 Orientation	3 Design 4 Support
(Zhao, 2018)	Interactive interface design method Design analysis including user analysis, requirements analysis, task analysis, environmental analysis, and product analysis	1 User centeredness 2 Consistency 3 Rationality and clarity	4 Diversity 5 Interactivity

The 54 proposed design principles were clustered to five design categories by using the concepts that were most frequently referenced in the twelve papers as theoretical basis for the design principles– usability, user centeredness, cognitive (over)load – as starting points. Because all the principles dealing with general learning theories or the inclusion of MAR-elements in the overall MARLS could not reasonably be attributed to these three categories, two more were added. The resulting five clusters reflect dominant pedagogical and technical challenges of designing MARLS:

1. Usability: Similar to other learning-applications, the MAR application that is part of an overall learning design has to be easy and appealing to use for teachers and students (Cuendet et al., 2013). Common complaints about MARLS, concern the usability of the applied MAR applications (Ko et al., 2013; Garzón et al., 2019). A good usability of the MAR application appears to be a key success factor for effective learning with MAR and depends on an appealing interface containing only relevant information and functions to handle the application (Ko et al., 2013).

2. User centeredness: Because main advantages of MARLS lie in their potential to increase the learners' motivation and engagement, the MARLS should focus on the needs and requirements of the targeted learners (Stefan and Moldoveanu, 2013). Especially the overarching motivational design and a context relevant to the learning process appear important (Dunleavy, 2014; Kerr and Lawson, 2020). Because usually, a teacher acts as the gatekeeper or designer of a learning setting, MARLS have to cover the teachers' needs, too. Particularly an easy classroom management and an efficient use of the scarce learning time has to be considered when designing MARLS (Cuendet et al., 2013).

3. Basic learning theories: Most studies mentioned that the classical learning theories still apply for MARLS (Messuti et al., 2015). Especially, experiential and gamified learning theories seem to fit well with MARLS and help to create motivational and learner-centered MARLS (Bucher et al., 2020; Dunleavy, 2014).

4. Conscious application: The MAR application usually represents only one part of a learning setting including many non-augmented activities. Therefore, the MARLS designer has to decide which activities should be augmented (Cuendet et al., 2013). Similar to planning a blended learning design, the MARLS designer has to organize and scaffold the activities to use the learning time effectively (Stefan and Moldoveanu, 2013). The small screen size of smartphones limits the possible activities and forces the MARLS designer to restrict its use to the activities where MAR may support the learning process effectively (Tuli and Mantri, 2020). Therefore, the type of AR application and technology should be chosen thoughtfully – location- or picture based, 3D or 2D objects, sound or no sound, interactivity or not.

5. Cognitive overload: Preventing cognitive overload is a major challenge when designing MARLS (Altmeyer et al., 2020). The handling of the mobile device may distract learners from the content and other tasks. Although, the cognitive load depends on the usability, and sensible scaffolding, it deserves special attention. Most studies mentioned the danger of cognitive overload of MARLS and demand special consideration for the cognitive load of students (Garzón et al., 2019) and teachers (Cuendet et al., 2013). As the cognitive load, the amount of information a person can process in their working memory, is limited (Sweller, 2011), the handling of the MAR application should be easy to allow focus on the learning content and activities, to enable effective learning (Dunleavy, 2014).

4. CONCLUSION

The low number of studies outlining design principles that cover pedagogical and technological aspects of MARLS illustrates the need to intensify respective research. Furthermore, the variety of studies and applications of MARLS makes it difficult to identify general design principles. The MARLS that build the foundation of the analyzed studies and metastudies vary with regard to the applied type of MAR, the learners, the content, and the media-didactical knowledge of the teachers. Therefore, it is essential to investigate and further improve the technological and pedagogical design principles by conducting educational design research (McKenney & Reeves, 2014) projects and closely monitoring the developments in MAR technology.

The identified design principles may guide researchers and practitioners to bridge the gap between MAR innovations and real-world classrooms. However, the design principles cover only the pedagogical and technical dimensions and need to be supplemented with content specific expertise to create valuable MARLS.

REFERENCES

Akçayır, M. and Akçayır, G., 2017. Advantages and challenges associated with augmented reality for education: A systematic review of the literature. *Educational Research Review*, Vol. 20, pp. 1–11.

Altinpulluk, H., 2019. Determining the trends of using augmented reality in education between 2006-2016. *Education and Information Technologies*, Vol. 24 No. 2, pp. 1089–1114.

Altmeyer, K., Kapp, S., Thees, M., Malone, S., Kuhn, J. and Brünken, R., 2020. The use of augmented reality to foster conceptual knowledge acquisition in STEM laboratory courses—Theoretical background and empirical results. *British Journal of Educational Technology*, Vol. 51 No. 3, pp. 611–628.

Bacca, J., Baldiris, S., Fabregat, R., Graf, S. and Kinshuk, 2014. Augmented Reality Trends in Education: A Systematic Review of Research and Applications. *Educational Technology & Society*, Vol. 17 No. 4, pp. 133–149.

Bucher, K., Oberdörfer, S., Grafe, S. and Latoschik, M., 2020. Von Medienbeiträgen und Applikationen–ein interdisziplinäres Konzept zum Lehren und Lernen mit Augmented und Virtual Reality für die Hochschullehre. *Preprint*, pp. 225–238.

Chen, P., Liu, X., Cheng, W. and Huang, R., 2017. A review of using Augmented Reality in Education from 2011 to 2016. in Popescu, E., Kinshuk, Khribi, M.K., Huang, R., Jemni, M., Chen, N.-S. and Sampson, D.G. (Eds.), *Innovations in Smart Learning, Lecture Notes in Educational Technology*, Springer Singapore, Singapore, pp. 13–18.

Cuendet, S., Bonnard, Q., Do-Lenh, S. and Dillenbourg, P., 2013. Designing augmented reality for the classroom. *Computers & Education*, Vol. 68, pp. 557–569.

Dunleavy, M., 2014. Design principles for augmented reality learning. *TechTrends*, Vol. 58 No. 1, pp. 28–34.

Garzón, J., Pavón, J. and Baldiris, S., 2019. Systematic review and meta-analysis of augmented reality in educational settings. *Virtual Reality*, Vol. 23 No. 4, pp. 447–459.

Kerr, J. and Lawson, G., 2020. Augmented Reality in Design Education: Landscape Architecture Studies as AR Experience. *International Journal of Art & Design Education*, Vol. 39 No. 1, pp. 6–21.

Ko, S.M., Chang, W.S. and Ji, Y.G., 2013. Usability Principles for Augmented Reality Applications in a Smartphone Environment. *International Journal of Human-Computer Interaction*, Vol. 29 No. 8, pp. 501–515.

Kourouthanassis, P.E., Boletsis, C. and Lekakos, G., 2015. Demystifying the design of mobile augmented reality applications. *Multimedia Tools and Applications*, Vol. 74 No. 3, pp. 1045–1066.

McKenney, S. and Reeves, T. C., 2014. Educational design research. *Handbook of research on educational communications and technology*, Springer, New York, pp. 131-140.

Messuti, A., Wambeke, T. and Saltetti, F., 2015. Usability principles to design mobile workplace learning content. *Open Journal per la formazione in rete*, Vol. 15 No. 1, pp. 118-128.

Mishra, P. and Koehler, M.J., 2006. Technological pedagogical content knowledge: A framework for teacher knowledge. *Teachers college record*, Vol. 108 No. 6, pp. 1017–1054.

Quintero, J., Baldiris, S., Rubira, R., Cerón, J. and Velez, G., 2019. Augmented Reality in Educational Inclusion. A Systematic Review on the Last Decade. *Frontiers in psychology*, Vol. 10, p. 1835.

Radu, I., 2012. Why should my students use AR? A comparative review of the educational impacts of augmented-reality. *2012 IEEE International Symposium on Mixed and Augmented Reality (ISMAR)*, pp. 313–314.

Sommerauer, P. and Müller, O., 2018. Augmented reality for teaching and learning – a literature review on theoretical and empirical foundations. *Twenty-Sixth European Conference on Information Systems (ECIS2018)*, Portsmouth, UK, 2018, pp. 1–17.

Stefan, L. and Moldoveanu, F., 2013. Game-based learning with Augmented Reality-from technology's affordances to game design and educational scenarios. *The International Scientific Conference eLearning and Software for Education*, No. 2, pp. 105–114.

Sweller, J., 2011. Cognitive load theory. *Psychology of learning and motivation*, Vol. 55, pp. 37-76.

Tuli, N. and Mantri, A., 2020. Usability Principles for Augmented Reality based Kindergarten Applications. *Procedia Computer Science*, Vol. 172, pp. 679–687.

Wu, H.-K., Lee, S.W.-Y., Chang, H.-Y. and Liang, J.-C., 2013. Current status, opportunities and challenges of augmented reality in education. *Computers & Education*, Vol. 62, pp. 41–49.

Yuliono, T., Sarawanto and Rintayati, P., 2018. The Promising Roles of Augmented Reality in Educational Setting: A Review of the Literature. *International Journal of Educational Methodology*, Vol. 4 No. 3, pp. 125–132.

Zhao, Q., 2018. The Application of Augmented Reality Visual Communication in Network Teaching. *International Journal of Emerging Technologies in Learning (iJET)*, Vol. 13 No. 07, p. 57.

EDUCATIONAL APPROACHES TO ADDRESS FAKE NEWS – PRELIMINARY INSIGHTS FROM A SYSTEMATIC REVIEW

Christoph Eisemann and Christoph Pimmer
FHNW University of Applied Sciences and Arts Northwestern Switzerland
Peter Merian-Strasse 86, 4002 Basel – Switzerland

ABSTRACT

Fake and false news, an unfortunate hallmark of today's information society, have serious political and societal consequences. Little systematic knowledge is available about effective learning, teaching and awareness-raising strategies that help users in addressing fake news. This study reports preliminary results from a systematic literature review aimed at systematising different approaches and determining their effectiveness. Three main approaches emerged in the analysis: Firstly, the findings suggest that strategies to correct existing misconceptions caused by fake news have limited effectiveness and can be even counterproductive, particularly for polarising topics. Secondly, the evidence on the effectiveness of training on fake news detection methods is encouraging but inconclusive. Thirdly, despite the common perception that fake news detection needs to be linked to an understanding of the economic, ideological and cultural dimensions of media systems, the few empirical studies found in this area did little to support this claim. A tentative conclusion from these findings is the need to integrate education on false news and training on fake news detection strategies in educational programmes as early as children's media consumption starts.

KEYWORDS

Fake News, False News, Misinformation, Disinformation, Fake News Resilience, Education, Systematic Review

1. INTRODUCTION

The circulation of fake and false news has become emblematic for today's information society. To address this issue, Lazer et al. (2018) have called for a multidisciplinary effort in their recent article in the journal *Science.* This effort should include technical measures aimed at preventing the exposure of individuals to fake news. Secondly, it should also contain measures that empower internet users in dealing with fake news. With the goal of developing a better understanding of the effectiveness of different educational approaches and methods that can support users in tackling fake news, the present study focuses on the second aspect highlighted by Lazer et al. (2018). Despite the considerable number of individual studies about this topic and systematic reviews on media literacy (e.g. Jeong et al., 2012), the literature in this field is still fragmented. With reference to this gap, the following research question was addressed by a systematic literature review: How effective are educational approaches that help users in dealing with fake news?

2. METHODOLOGY

The search was conducted in April 2020 and included contributions from 2000-2020 in the databases ERIC, OVID Medline, APA PsycInfo and PsycARTICLES via the platform OVID (using title and abstract search) and in the Web of Science. The search combined the two domains of (1) fake and false news and (2) educational approaches in the following way: (Fake news OR false news OR misinformation OR disinformation) AND (Education OR training OR interventio* OR debunk* OR debias*). Upon deleting 179 duplicates, the two authors screened the abstracts of the remaining 955 articles against the following criteria: (1) educational interventions, i.e. instruction, training, or awareness-raising measures, which were (2) evaluated empirically, i.e. through quantitative, qualitative or mixed-methods studies; (3) articles aimed at the change of knowledge, behaviour or attitudes, i.e., excluding cross-sectional surveys or theoretical papers; (4) studies that report outcomes and/or users' experience of these interventions (reports that described technical designs only were excluded); (5) articles with a sound methodological design (including a detailed description of data collection and analyses methods according to established standards). After the independent review of this corpus of studies by the two authors against these criteria and a subsequent consensus discussion, a number of 14 articles was retained and summarised in the present short paper, alongside five articles that were identified through a selective search in Google scholar, resulting in a total 19 studies. In this short paper, we present tentative findings grouped around three emerging themes that were identified through thematic analysis.

3. FINDINGS

3.1 Reactive, Fact-Based Correction of Misinformation

A relatively large number of studies examined interventions aimed at correcting already internalized misconceptions (Cook et al., 2017; Hameleers and van der Meer, 2020; Murrock et al., 2018; Rich et al., 2017; Nyhan et al., 2014; Paynter et al., 2019; Pluviano et al., 2019, 2017; Tarchi, 2019). Correcting users' misbeliefs and misconceptions is a reactive strategy, which seeks to redress the negative impact of an individual's exposure to prior misinformation and disinformation. Although the provision of information about what is right and wrong in a fact-based manner might seemingly be the most intuitive and straightforward pedagogical approach, the literature suggests that it is linked to limited effectiveness. Some interventions were even counterproductive for some groups, in particular when the topic was polarising, such as vaccination (Nyhan et al., 2014; Paynter et al., 2019; Rich et al., 2017). An example is the study of Nyhan et al. (2014) who compared in their large, nationally-representative, randomised controlled trial four different instructive strategies aimed at reducing vaccine misperceptions. These strategies included the provision of: (1) an explanation of the lack of evidence between vaccines and autism; (2) information about the dangers of missing out on vaccinations; (3) images of children suffering from diseases that could be prevented by vaccines; (4) a dramatic narrative about an infant who almost died of a preventable illness. Whereas some misperceptions were reduced, none of these interventions increased parental intent to vaccinate a future child and even decreased the intent to vaccinate among parents with the least favourable vaccine attitudes (Nyhan et al., 2014).

What makes the correction of misinformation more effective is the combination of several strategies (Paynter et al., 2019), the provision of additional, explanatory information (Paynter et al., 2019; Rich et al., 2017), and the communication of scientific consensus. For example, Cook et al. (2017) found that highlighting scientific consensus on climate change was effective in neutralizing adverse effects of misinformation. This finding is similar to Van der Linden et al.'s (2017) study which showed that the communication of scientific consensus on human-caused climate change significantly increased the public perception of the expert consensus. However, also these approaches need to be treated with caution as some studies found that effects were not sustained over time (Paynter et al., 2019).

3.2 Proactive Training of Specific Fake News Detection Methods

The second main approach that emerged in the analysis was to equip users with specific methodological and technical repertoire, i.e. knowledge, skills and tools that can help them in recognising fake news (Basol et al., 2020; Jones-Jang et al., 2019; Katsaounidou et al., 2019; Kim and Dennis, 2019; Lutzke et al., 2019; McGrew, 2020; Murrock et al., 2018; Roozenbeek and van der Linden, 2019; Tsipursky et al., 2018a, 2018b; Velautham, 2017).

Within this pro-active approach, various methods can be differentiated. Making participants aware of guidelines and techniques on fake news detection was reported to be successful in two studies (Murrock et al., 2018, Lutzke et al., 2019). For example, prompting users with questions, for instance on the authorship or style of a Facebook post, decreased their likelihood to trust, like and share fake news – but not legit news – about climate change in comparison with a control group (Lutzke et al., 2019). Results from another study are more ambiguous, because the effect of nudging users to scrutinize the authorship of news articles made them more sceptical of all articles regardless of whether they were true of false (Kim and Dennis, 2019). More extensive course formats showed clearer effects: The majority of the participants of a digital literacy programme reported retaining their behaviour of cross-checking news even 1.5 years after the training. Their abilities of recognising fake news declined only slightly (Murrock et al., 2018). Another, more extensive, eight-lesson-course through which students were taught to evaluate digital content found that they demonstrated a significantly improved ability to investigate the source of a website, critique evidence and locate reliable sources during an open internet search (McGrew, 2020).

However, methodological-technical fake news detection training was no guarantee of success. In a large Indian field study, users were trained through an hour-long media literacy intervention. The training, which included the use of reverse image search and fact checkers, did not only show no increase in fake news detection skills; for some partisan groups, it even decreased their abilities to spot fake news (Tan, 2019).

A noteworthy approach is gamification (Basol et al., 2020, Roozenbeek and van der Linden, 2019, Katsaounidou et al., 2019, Urban et al., 2018). One example is a digital game that included the use of tools such as search engine search, reverse image research, image verification assistant and fact checkers (Katsaounidou et al., 2019). The analysis was restricted to self-perceived effects, and more than 60% of the participants reported that it enhanced their digital literacy (Katsaounidou et al., 2019). An interesting story-telling element was featured in the digital game Bad News, where users learned by assuming the role of fake news disseminators. The large-scale study with 15'000 participants found that fake news detection abilities increased between the pre-test and post-test (Roozenbeek and van der Linden, 2019). A second study found positive effects also in comparison to a control group (Basol et al., 2020). However, the findings from our own randomised controlled trial suggest that in higher education contexts the game had no meaningful effects (Pimmer et al., 2020, accepted). A tool that is often integrated in educational interventions is fact checkers (Hameleers and van der Meer, 2020, McGrew, 2020, Katsaounidou et al., 2019). Two large-scale experiments found that their use was successful because it decreased participants' agreement with attitudinally congruent political misinformation. However, fact-checkers were most likely used when they confirmed prior attitudes - and avoided when they were incongruent with previous beliefs, which points to a confirmation bias (Hameleers and van der Meer, 2020).

3.3 Development of a Critical Understanding of Media Systems

The third main approach identified in this review is the provision of users with knowledge of the wider, political economic, ideological and cultural fabric and the dynamics of media systems and media production with the goal of helping them to critically reflect and contextualise news. However, contrary to scholarly conceptions of the importance of a broader understanding of the overall media system (e.g. Buckingham, 2019), the very few studies identified in this area provided little evidence to substantiate this rationale. One exception that points to the potential linkage between knowledge of the wider media system and concrete fake news detection skills is a study from the Ukraine. Citizen were instructed through a learning programme which included content on the nature of information, manipulation, propaganda, fake news and their dangers, types of mass media and media ownership (Murrock et al., 2018). The curriculum considered also the contextual specificities of the news media environment in the Ukraine. The post-hoc evaluation found that participants in the programme, who were also instructed in fake news detection strategies, had in fact higher levels of knowledge of the news media environment and they were better in distinguishing false from correct news in comparison to a control group, which was not subject of any intervention. Interestingly, across intervention and control group, there was a linkage between fake news detection skills and knowledge about the workings of news media, although the research design did not permit the closer examination of this relationship. In addition, some digital games touch on the broader dynamics through which disinformation is being shared, albeit to a very limited extent (Urban et al., 2018, Roozenbeek and van der Linden, 2019, Basol et al., 2020). It was, in fact, suggested that a way to improve one game would be to integrate more information about underlying political motives and dynamics (Urban et al., 2018).

4. CONCLUSION, LIMITATIONS AND NEXT STEPS

The tentative results of this review show that there is a relatively convincing evidence base suggesting that pre-existing misconceptions can at best be removed with difficulties. This can be explained with the avoidance of cognitive dissonance and the concept of motivated reasoning, with people seeking to confirm what they already believe (Lewandowsky et al., 2012). Secondly, there is encouraging but inconclusive evidence that shows the effectiveness of interventions which train users in applying concrete fake news detection methods. However, some studies reported no or even adverse effects, and studies very rarely measured the mid-term and long-term impact. Moreover, many of these studies were carried out in artificial laboratory settings in which users were aware of their exposure to misinformation. Thirdly, despite the common understanding that fake news detection should be linked to the broader knowledge of the wider media system (Buckingham, 2019), the corpus of studies that focused on this aspect identified in the present review is very thin and inconclusive. The inconclusive nature of this relationship is also reflected by a cross-sectional study in which peoples' abilities to find reliable information online was linked to better fake news detection skills; however, news literacy, i.e. their knowledge about the news production system was not (Jones-Jang et al., 2019). The "missing link" between media system knowledge and fake news detection skills could result from our search strategy (see the limitation section) but also from the methodological challenges linked to measuring these linkages. Finally, an interesting strand to be followed is gamification, where results can be viewed cautiously optimistic. A proposition to be examined more thoroughly in the future could be that the less "authoritarian" and more subtle and playful ways of gamification could be more adequate in changing peoples' perception of and knowledge on fake news.

The tentative findings from this review need to be interpreted with caution. Firstly, because of limitations in the body of studies identified (such as the focus on short term effects), and secondly, due to specific scope of our search strategy, which was systematic but not comprehensive. A limitation was that there might be a potentially interesting corpus of media literacy studies which has already addressed similar concepts without using the terms that we have considered in our search. In the next step, we thus plan to enhance the scope of our search by further scrutinising media literacy and digital literacy studies in connection with fake and false news. However, we would argue that the current findings present some interesting insights. A tentative practical recommendation from this review is to anchor news analysis and fake news detection education as early as possible in education curricula to prevent misconceptions from striking roots and to equip users with the adequate methodological repertoire.

ACKNOWLEDGEMENT

We would like to thank the dean of BSc Betriebsökonomie Basel and the management board from the School of Business FHNW University of Applied Sciences and Arts Northwestern Switzerland for their support of this study. We are also very grateful for the students who agreed to participate in this research.

REFERENCES

Basol, M., Roozenbeek, J., van der Linden, S. 2020. Good News about Bad News: Gamified Inoculation Boosts Confidence and Cognitive Immunity Against Fake News. Journal of Cognition, 3.

Beker, K., Kim, J., Van Boekel, M., van den Broek, P., Kendeou, P., 2019. Refutation texts enhance spontaneous transfer of knowledge. Contemp. Educ. Psychol. 56, 67–78. https://doi.org/10.1016/j.cedpsych.2018.11.004

Cook, J., 2019. Understanding and countering misinformation about climate change. Handb. Res. Decept. Fake News Misinformation Online, Advances in media, entertainment, and the arts (AMEA) book series. 281–306. https://doi.org/10.4018/978-1-5225-8535-0.ch016

Hameleers, M., van der Meer, T.G.L.A., 2020. Misinformation and Polarization in a High-Choice Media Environment: How Effective Are Political Fact-Checkers? Commun. Res. 47, 227–250. https://doi.org/10.1177/0093650218819671

Jeong, S.-H., Cho, H., Hwang, Y., 2012. Media literacy interventions: A meta-analytic review. Journal of Communication, 62, 454-472.

Jones-Jang, S.M., Mortensen, T., Liu, J., 2019. Does Media Literacy Help Identification of Fake News? Information Literacy Helps, but Other Literacies Don't. Am. Behav. Sci. https://doi.org/10.1177/0002764219869406

Katsaounidou, A., Vrysis, L., Kotsakis, R., Dimoulas, C., Veglis, A., 2019. MAthE the Game: A Serious Game for Education and Training in News Verification. Educ. Sci. 9. Lazer, D. M., Baum, M. A., Benkler, Y., Berinsky, A. J., Greenhill, K. M., Menczer, F., Metzger, M. J., Nyhan, B., Pennycook, G., Rothschild, D., 2018. The science of fake news. Science, 359, 1094-1096.

Kim, A., Dennis, A. R., 2019. Says who? The effects of presentation format and source rating on fake news in social media. Mis Quarterly, 43(3), 1025-1039.

Lewandowsky, S., Ecker, U.K.H., Seifert, C.M., Schwarz, N., Cook, J., 2012. Misinformation and its correction: Continued influence and successful debiasing. Psychol. Sci. Public Interest 13, 106–131. https://doi.org/10.1177/1529100612451018

Linden, S. van der, Leiserowitz, A., Rosenthal, S., Maibach, E., 2017. Inoculating the Public against Misinformation about Climate Change. Glob. Chall. 1, 1600008. https://doi.org/10.1002/gch2.201600008

Lutzke, L., Drummond, C., Slovic, P., Arvai, J., 2019. Priming critical thinking: Simple interventions limit the influence of fake news about climate change on Facebook. Glob. Environ. CHANGE-Hum. POLICY Dimens. 58. https://doi.org/10.1016/j.gloenvcha.2019.101964

McGrew, S., 2020. Learning to evaluate: An intervention in civic online reasoning. Comput. Educ. 145. https://doi.org/10.1016/j.compedu.2019.103711

Murrock, E., Amulya, J., Druckman, M., Liubyva, T., 2018. Winning the War on State-Sponsored Propaganda: Results from an Impact Study of a Ukrainian News Media and Information Literacy Program. J. Media Lit. Educ. 10, 53–85.

Nyhan, B., Reifler, J., Richey, S., Freed, G. L., 2014. Effective Messages in Vaccine Promotion: A Randomized Trial. Pediatrics, 133, E835-E842.

Paynter, J., Luskin-Saxby, S., Keen, D., Fordyce, K., Frost, G., Imms, C., Miller, S., Trembath, D., Tucker, M., Ecker, U., 2019. Evaluation of a template for countering misinformation-Real-world autism treatment myth debunking. PLoS ONE 14. (1): e0210746. https://doi.org/10.1371/journal.pone.0210746

Pimmer, C., Eisemann, C., & Mateescu, M. (2020 (accepted)). *Fake news resilience through online games? Tentative findings from a randomized controlled trial in higher education.* Paper to be presented at the CELDA – 17th International Conference on Cognition and Exploratory Learning in Digital Age 2020, Lisbon, Portugal.

Rich, P.R., Van Loon, M.H., Dunlosky, J., Zaragoza, M.S., 2017. Belief in Corrective Feedback for Common Misconceptions: Implications for Knowledge Revision. J. Exp. Psychol.-Learn. Mem. Cogn. 43, 492–501. https://doi.org/10.1037/xlm0000322

Roozenbeek, J., van der Linden, S., 2019. Fake news game confers psychological resistance against online misinformation. PALGRAVE Commun. 5. https://doi.org/10.1057/s41599-019-0279-9

Tarchi, C., 2019. Identifying fake news through trustworthiness judgements of documents. Cultura Y Educacion, 31(2), 369-406. doi:10.1080/11356405.2019.1597442

Tsipursky, G., Votta, F., Mulick, J.A., 2018. A psychological approach to promoting truth in politics: The Pro-Truth Pledge. J. Soc. Polit. Psychol. 6, 271–290. https://doi.org/10.5964/jspp.v6i2.856

Urban A., Hewitt, C., Moore, J., 2018. Fake it to make it, media literacy, and persuasive design: Using the functional triad as a tool for investigating persuasive elements in a fake news simulator. Proceedings of the Association for Information Science and Technology, 55, 915-916.

Velautham, L., 2017. Designing an Intervention to Promote Critical Thinking about Statistics in the General Public. Berkeley Rev. Educ. 7, 113–119.

PEPPER: A HUMANOID ROBOT WITH PERSONALITY?

Josef Guggemos, Sabine Seufert and Stefan Sonderegger
University of St.Gallen, St. Jakob-Str. 21, 9000 St. Gallen, Switzerland

ABSTRACT

Perceived personality plays an important role in human-robot interaction. This paper uses the Big Five Inventory–2 (BFI-2-S) to assess the perceived personality of a type Pepper social robot. Pepper provided a sample of its capabilities during an introduction to academic writing university course. N = 462 students evaluated Pepper's personality by answering the BFI-2-S questions. A confirmatory factor analysis with the implied five-factor structure did not converge. A subsequent exploratory factor analysis yielded inconclusive results. Although we were not able to provide evidence for a Big Five personality structure of the social robot, perceived personality may be an important characteristic of a social robot: The latent correlation of a factor labeled 'positive characteristics' with the intention to use the robot equals .487.

KEYWORDS

Big Five, Personality, Social Robot, Pepper

1. INTRODUCTION

Social robots have the potential to become an integral part of the educational infrastructure (Belpaeme et al., 2018; Mubin et al., 2013): As tutors or teachers, robots might take over selected duties that human teachers carry out. By assisting the teacher, they free up resources. For instance, the robot can answer frequently asked questions, which allows the teacher to focus on other activities. As peers, social robots are companions of students and collaboratively learn with them. For example, they can act as time guards during group work and take the minutes. The aim of social robots is to communicate and interact with humans; most of them are designed to resemble humans to a certain degree (humanoid robots). Nao (see Figure 1), developed by SoftBank Robotics, may be a quasi-standard form in education (Belpaeme et al., 2018). In commercial settings, Pepper (see Figure 1), also a humanoid robot from SoftBank Robotics, is more widely used (Gardecki & Podpora, 2017).

Perceived personality plays an important role in human-robot interaction (Lee et al., 2008). It may depend on visual appearance, language, vocal features, eye contact, and movement (Mou, Shi, Shen, & Xu, 2020). Since these characteristics substantially vary among available social robots, this paper addresses the research question: *Do students attribute a personality to a type Pepper social robot?*

2. THEORETICAL PERSPECTIVE

2.1 State of the Art

Mou et al. (2020) reviewed the literature on personality of social robots. A definition or conceptualization of personality is often missing in the analyzed 40 studies. Personality is mostly captured with the psychoticism, extraversion and neuroticism (PEN) model or a Big Five inventory. The Big Five are an established concept for capturing the personality of humans; the five factors are usually labeled: Extraversion, Agreeableness, Conscientiousness, Neuroticism, and Openness (Goldberg, 1990). According to Mou et al. (2020), only one study has addressed the perceived personality of a type Pepper model: Craenen et al. (2018) used a Big Five inventory. The aim of this experimental study with 30 participants was to investigate the association between Pepper's gestures and the attributed personality. However, the authors did not present evidence for the quality of the personality measurement, i.e., if the Big Five can be captured in a valid and reliable manner.

2.2 The Present Study

The study at hand is in the realm of social robots in higher education (Guggemos, Seufert, & Sonderegger, 2020; Guggemos et al., 2020). It was carried out during a large-scale university course, 'Introduction to academic writing', which was mandatory for all the 1,552 freshmen at the University of St.Gallen. We drew on the work of Cooney and Leister (2019), who provided a list of tasks that social robots could carry out in higher education. Based on this, we developed samples that may fairly represent the capabilities of the social robot. Besides generic activities like greeting, we relied on our own experience regarding typical issues and questions in academic writing, e.g., how plagiarism is detected. A video that shows the performance of the robot can be found here: https://unisg.link/lexi2020. Overall, Lexi (name of the robot) supported the lecturer for about 45 minutes. We invited all students via the learning management system to fill in an online questionnaire. Students were asked to assess Lexi's personality by means of the short version of the Big Five Inventory–2 (BFI-2-S) that comprises 30 questions (Soto & John, 2017). The questions can be found in Table 1. N = 462 students (163 female) took part in our study. Their intended study subject was Business administration (n = 225), Economics (n = 102), International affairs (n = 71), Law (n = 28), and Law and economics (n = 36). On average, they were aged 19.78 years (SD = 1.42 years). Missing values did not occur.

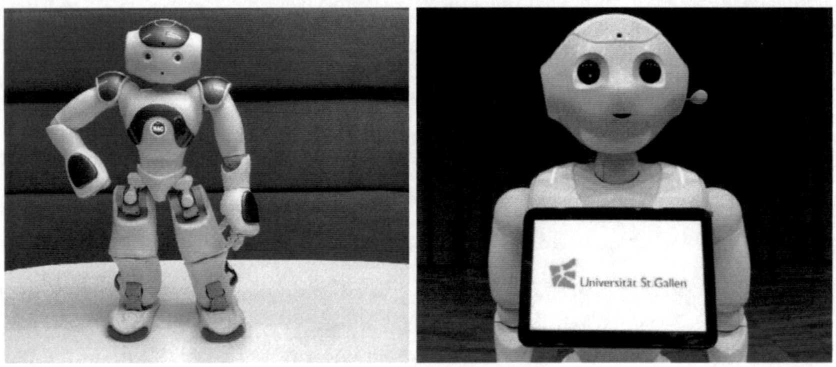

Figure 1. On the left, social robot 'Nao'; on the right, 'Pepper'

2.3 Analysis

Since (for human beings) there is strong evidence for a five-factor structure of personality, we first carried out a confirmatory factor analysis (CFA: R package 'lavaan' version 0.6-3). Each dimension is measured with six items on a five-point scale of rating (see Table 1). The CFA did not converge. Hence, we subsequently conducted an exploratory factor analysis (EFA: R package 'psych' version 1.8.12) and followed the guidelines of Goretzko, Pham, and Bühner (2019). The data showed slight deviations from a normal distribution. Thus, we used weighted least squares (WLS) as factoring method. Moreover, we applied a 'varimax' rotation (Soto & John, 2017). Afterward, we evaluated if the extracted factors show a sufficient internal consistency reliability. To this end, we used Revell's ω because it is superior to Cronbach's alpha α (McNeish, 2018). An ω greater than .7 may point to sufficient reliability. However, since Cronbach's alpha α is widely used, we report it along with ω.

The value and usefulness of the obtained factors should be judged by assessing the relationship with external criteria (Watkins, 2018). Against this backdrop, we correlated meaningful extracted constructs with the intention to use the robot for learning purposes, which is measured with three items, e.g., "I would rely on social robots like Lexi for learning purposes if they were available" ($\alpha = \omega = .92$).

3. RESULTS

The CFA with the five-factor structure implied by theory did not converge. Moreover, the reliability of the five factors are in most cases insufficient. Extraversion: $\alpha = .52$, $\omega = .58$, Agreeableness: $\alpha = .41$, $\omega = .63$, Conscientiousness: $\alpha = .52$, $\omega = .66$, Neuroticism: $\alpha = .62$, $\omega = .77$, and Openness: $\alpha = .45$, $\omega = .71$. In terms of the EFA, the Kaiser-Meyer-Olkin criterion equals .87 (> .50) and the Bartlett test was significant ($Chi^2 = 4{,}194$, $df = 435$, $p < .001$), which indicated the suitability of the data for EFA. We decided to extract three factors from the data because a parallel as well as a comparison data analysis revealed a three-factor structure as optimal. The results of the EFA can be found in Table 1. Based on this, we formed constructs using all items with a salient standardized loading on one factor ($\lambda > .5$) that at the same time do not load substantially on a second factor ($\lambda < .3$) (Watkins, 2018). Following this rule, the first construct operationalized by the items E3, A3, C3, O3, and E4 (see Table 1) shows sufficient reliability: $\alpha = .75$, $\omega = .76$. The second construct comprising the items N1, E2, N2 and N6 lacks reliability ($\alpha = .62$, $\omega = .62$). This is also true for the third factor with the items A4, C6, and O6 ($\alpha = .64$, $\omega = .64$). The latent correlation between the intention to use the robot for learning purposes and the first (only reliably measured) construct equals .487 ($p < .001$).

Table 1. Exploratory factor analysis for personality of social robot (N = 462)

		Descriptive statistics				Factor			
Item	Lexi ...	Mean	SD	Skew	Kurt.	F1	F2	F3	h^2
E1	"tends to be quiet." (r)	2.93	0.87	-0.08	-0.17	-0.13	-0.07	**0.31**	0.12
A1	"compassionate, has a soft heart."	2.84	0.97	-0.34	-0.44	**0.45**	**0.31**	0.14	0.32
C1	"tends to be disorganized." (r)	2.39	0.96	0.26	-0.38	0.14	**-0.53**	0.16	0.32
N1	"worries a lot."	2.49	0.88	-0.21	-0.31	0.07	**0.62**	-0.05	0.39
O1	"is fascinated by art, music, or literature."	2.76	0.93	-0.41	0.16	**0.35**	**0.43**	0.15	0.33
E2	"is dominant, acts as a leader."	2.50	1.02	0.10	-0.58	0.17	**0.50**	0.09	0.29
A2	"is sometimes rude to others." (r)	2.47	0.99	0.07	-0.65	0.06	**-0.56**	0.17	0.35
C2	"has difficulty getting started on tasks."	2.73	0.95	-0.11	-0.32	0.03	**-0.42**	**0.34**	0.30
N2	"tends to feel depressed, blue."	2.43	0.93	-0.17	-0.60	-0.07	**0.56**	-0.24	0.38
O2	"has little interest in abstract ideas." (r)	2.79	0.88	-0.13	0.45	-0.12	-0.30	0.30	0.20
E3	"is full of energy."	3.40	1.06	-0.36	-0.24	**0.63**	0.10	0.12	0.42
A3	"assumes the best about people."	3.24	0.85	-0.38	0.83	**0.67**	0.07	0.08	0.46
C3	"is reliable, can always be counted on."	3.13	0.94	-0.36	0.05	**0.59**	0.03	-0.04	0.34
N3	"is emotionally stable, not easily upset." (r)	3.47	0.96	-0.15	0.00	**-0.49**	0.24	0.23	0.35
O3	"is original, comes up with new ideas."	2.93	0.98	-0.28	-0.16	**0.54**	0.24	0.14	0.37
E4	"is outgoing, sociable."	3.11	0.96	-0.36	0.01	**0.58**	0.12	0.13	0.36
A4	"can be cold and uncaring." (r)	2.85	0.92	0.09	0.22	0.13	-0.22	**0.54**	0.36
C4	"keeps things neat and tidy."	3.39	0.80	0.05	0.67	**0.50**	-0.13	**-0.35**	0.38
N4	"is relaxed, handles stress well." (r)	3.42	0.86	-0.27	0.51	**-0.68**	0.20	0.25	0.56
O4	"has few artistic interests." (r)	3.02	0.75	-0.27	1.93	**-0.43**	-0.17	0.16	0.24
E5	"prefers to have others take charge." (r)	3.08	0.82	-0.01	0.95	-0.18	0.04	**0.46**	0.25
A5	"is respectful, treats others with respect."	3.58	0.92	-0.31	0.11	**0.61**	**-0.30**	-0.15	0.48
C5	"is persistent, works until the task is finished."	3.57	0.97	-0.20	-0.15	**0.62**	**-0.32**	-0.26	0.55
N5	"feels secure, comfortable." (r)	3.34	0.87	-0.25	0.69	**-0.67**	0.11	0.14	0.48
O5	"is complex, a deep thinker."	2.97	0.98	-0.22	-0.05	**0.49**	0.18	0.10	0.29
E6	is less active than people.[a] (r)	3.22	0.99	-0.09	-0.17	0.04	0.02	**0.44**	0.20
A6	"tends to find fault with others." (r)	2.89	0.77	-0.44	1.45	-0.12	**-0.31**	**0.38**	0.26
C6	"can be somewhat careless." (r)	2.89	0.81	-0.08	0.79	0.16	-0.18	**0.55**	0.37
N6	"is temperamental, gets emotional easily."	2.50	0.90	-0.33	-0.56	0.00	**0.55**	-0.07	0.31
O6	"has little creativity." (r)	3.11	0.94	0.01	0.12	0.00	0.05	**0.55**	0.30

[a] Original item: "is less active than other people." Note. Items from Soto and John (2017, pp. 79–80); measured on a five-point scale of rating ranging from disagree strongly to agree strongly. h^2 = communality. (r) = item is reversely scored. E = Extraversion, A = Agreeableness, C = Conscientiousness, N = Neuroticism, O = Openness. Factoring method = WLS. Rotation = varimax. Standardized loadings > |.3| in bold. Overall, 34% variance extracted: 16% F1, 10% F2, 8% F3.

4. DISCUSSION AND CONCLUSION

The perceived personality of Lexi, a type Pepper model, does not seem to follow the Big Five: the corresponding CFA did not converge. The EFA with three factors and varimax rotation yielded a loading matrix where items from all Big Five facets load on the three factors. The first factor (F1) may be labeled as perceived positive characteristics: "is full of energy", "assumes the best about people", "is reliable, can always be counted on", "is original, comes up with new ideas", and "is outgoing, sociable" (Soto & John, 2017, p. 80). The second factor (F2) could be labeled as negative characteristics: "worries a lot", "is dominant, acts as a leader", "tends to feel depressed, blue", "is temperamental, and "gets emotional easily" (Soto & John, 2017, pp. 79–80). The third factor (F3) may comprise characteristics hard to assess for the students: "can be cold and uncaring", "can be somewhat careless", and "has little creativity" (Soto & John, 2017, pp. 79–80). Only the first factor shows sufficient internal consistency reliability ($\omega > .7$). The construct 'positive characteristics' of the robot may be useful because it is moderately to highly correlated with the intention to use the robot for learning purposes ($r_{latent} = .487$, $p < .001$). Our results may lend support to Mou et al. (2020) who claim that inventories designed for capturing human personality may not be well suited for social robots. Hence, an undeniable limitation of our study is the use of a Big Five inventory. Conceptual research is necessary to gain a better understanding of the construct 'personality of social robots'. Empirical research should examine this construct much more comprehensively than our study.

REFERENCES

Belpaeme, T., Kennedy, J., Ramachandran, A., Scassellati, B., & Tanaka, F. (2018). Social robots for education: A review. *Science Robotics*, *3*(21), 1-9. https://doi.org/10.1126/scirobotics.aat5954

Cooney, M., & Leister, W. (2019). Using the Engagement Profile to Design an Engaging Robotic Teaching Assistant for Students. *Robotics*, *8*(1), 1–26. https://doi.org/10.3390/robotics8010021

Craenen, B. G.W., Deshmukh, A., Foster, M. E., & Vinciarelli, A. (2018). Shaping Gestures to Shape Personality: Big-Five Traits, Godspeed Scores and the Similarity-Attraction Effect. In M. Dastani, M. Sukthankar, E. André, & S. Koenig (Eds.), *Proceedings of the 17th International Conference on Autonomous Agents and Multiagent Systems* (pp. 2221–2223). Stockholm: International Foundation for Autonomous Agents and Multiagent Systems.

Gardecki, A., & Podpora, M. (2017). *Experience from the operation of the Pepper humanoid robots*. Piscataway, NJ: IEEE. https://doi.org/10.1109/PAEE.2017.8008994

Goldberg, L. R. (1990). An alternative "description of personality": The Big-Five factor structure. *Journal of Personality and Social Psychology*, *59*(6), 1216–1229. https://doi.org/10.1037/0022-3514.59.6.1216

Goretzko, D., Pham, T. T. H., & Bühner, M. (2019). Exploratory factor analysis: Current use, methodological developments and recommendations for good practice. *Current Psychology*. Advance online publication. https://doi.org/10.1007/s12144-019-00300-2

Guggemos, J., Burkhard, M., Seufert, S., & Sonderegger, S. (2020). Social Robots as Teaching Assistance System in Higher Education: Conceptual Framework for the Development of Use Cases. *Proceedings of the 12th International Conference on Computer Supported Education (CSEDU)*, 125–132. https://doi.org/10.5220/0009794801250132

Guggemos, J., Seufert, S., & Sonderegger, S. (2020). Humanoid robots in higher education: Evaluating the acceptance of Pepper in the context of an academic writing course using the UTAUT. *British Journal of Educational Technology*, 51(5), 1864–1883. https://doi.org/10.1111/bjet.13006

Lee, K. M., Peng, W., Jin, S.-A., & Yan, C. (2006). Can Robots Manifest Personality?: An Empirical Test of Personality Recognition, Social Responses, and Social Presence in Human–Robot Interaction. *Journal of Communication*, *56*(4), 754–772. https://doi.org/10.1111/j.1460-2466.2006.00318.x

McNeish, D. (2018). Thanks coefficient alpha, we'll take it from here. *Psychological Methods*, *23*(3), 412–433. https://doi.org/10.1037/met0000144

Mou, Y., Shi, C., Shen, T., & Xu, K. (2020). A Systematic Review of the Personality of Robot: Mapping Its Conceptualization, Operationalization, Contextualization and Effects. *International Journal of Human–Computer Interaction, 36*(6), 591–605. https://doi.org/10.1080/10447318.2019.1663008

Mubin, O., Stevens, C. J., Shahid, S., Mahmud, A. A., & Dong, J.-J. (2013). A Review of the applicability of robots in education. *Technology for Education and Learning, 1*(1), 1–7. https://doi.org/10.2316/Journal.209.2013.1.209-0015

Soto, C. J., & John, O. P. (2017). Short and extra-short forms of the Big Five Inventory–2: The BFI-2-S and BFI-2-XS. *Journal of Research in Personality, 68*, 69–81. https://doi.org/10.1016/j.jrp.2017.02.004

Walters, M. L., Syrdal, D. S., Dautenhahn, K., te Boekhorst, R., & Koay, K. L. (2008). Avoiding the uncanny valley: robot appearance, personality and consistency of behavior in an attention-seeking home scenario for a robot companion. *Autonomous Robots, 24*(2), 159–178. https://doi.org/10.1007/s10514-007-9058-3

Watkins, M. W. (2018). Exploratory Factor Analysis: A Guide to Best Practice. *Journal of Black Psychology, 44*(3), 219–246. https://doi.org/10.1177/0095798418771807

E-LEARNING SYSTEM FOR THE COMPREHENSIVE LEARNING OF ELECTRONIC CIRCUITS

Atsushi Takemura
Tokyo University of Agriculture and Technology
2-24-16, Naka-cho, Koganei-shi, Tokyo 184-8588, Japan

ABSTRACT

This paper proposes a novel e-learning system for comprehensive learning covering theoretical analysis, design, and experiments involving the construction of practical electronic circuits. The proposed system possesses technical novelty that enables a student to efficiently construct circuits according to an automated instruction of circuit design. Moreover, this system allows the student to select an appropriate type of circuit construction strategy, such as with/without soldering, depending on his purpose and ability. The effectiveness of the proposed system was verified by performing a comparison experiment using 40 undergraduate students at the Tokyo University of Agriculture and Technology. The comparison tests were done by two groups of students comprising students that used or did not use the proposed system demonstrated the effectiveness of the system.

KEYWORDS

e-Learning, Experiment, Electronic Circuit Construction

1. INTRODUCTION

In technology education, acquiring knowledge and skills of electronic circuit construction and practical applications (e.g., signal processing, and machine control) are important. Therefore, it is necessary to teach and learn electronic circuit construction and how to perform experiments with the constructed circuits. However, it is difficult to efficiently teach and acquire comprehensive skills relating to the field of electronic circuitry such as theoretical analysis, design, and experiments involving circuit construction. Further, several university students in the world are presently forced to receive online lectures instead of normal classroom lectures because of the spread of COVID-19 in 2020. In the first semester, many Japanese universities were forced to embark on online lectures and did not open courses that require face-to-face instruction, such as experiments in a laboratory. To deal with these problems, the development of an e-learning system for virtual experiments to substitute laboratory works is needed. Recently, in the technology field, several remote laboratory systems have been developed for learning field-programmable gate array (FPGA) using augmented reality (AR) (Andujar, 2011), system control (Chevalier, 2017), and virtual measurements of electric circuits (Garcia-Zubia, 2017). However, these remote education systems are limited in scope and are only suitable for specific circuits within a subject area. To realize a remote learning system applicable to a wide variety of electronic circuits, a learning system for supporting laboratory works involving circuit construction based on image processing techniques was proposed (Takemura, 2019). However, this system is not applicable to e-learning and comprehensive electronic circuit learning. To overcome these shortcomings, this study proposes an e-learning system for the comprehensive learning of electronic circuits that covers theoretical analysis, design, and experiments involving the construction of practical electronic circuits. This system also has the technical novelty that enables individual students to select an appropriate level of circuit construction, such as with/without soldering on a circuit board, depending on the ability and purpose of the student.

The rest of this paper is organized as follows. Section 2 presents the technical features of the proposed system. Section 3 presents the experimental methodology to evaluate the proposed system. Section 4 presents the quantitative evaluation of the proposed system based on the experiments performed by actual university students. Finally, Section 5 presents the conclusions of the study.

2. TECHNICAL FEATURES OF THE SYSTEM

To realize an e-learning system for the comprehensive learning of electronic circuits, this study develops two functions described in 2.1 and 2.2.

2.1 Function for Learning Design and the Workings of Circuits

Figure 1(a) shows a schematic of the function for learning circuit design and the workings of electronic circuits (F-1). The function F-1 helps the student in learning theoretical analysis, design, and understanding of the workings of electronic circuits through circuit simulation. F-1 translates a designed circuit into the general circuit description language, simulation program integrated circuit emphasis (SPICE) (Rabaey). F-1 possesses technical novelty needed in performing an automated translation technique involving cooperation with the function for virtual experiments (described in 2.2) and the evaluation of a designed circuit based on the SPICE information in the system's database. F-1 allows a student to learn design and the working of circuits in the following manner *A)–C)*.

A) Web-based Instruction

The proposed system provides individual students with manuals and the datasheets necessary for understanding the theoretical analysis of circuit design available through common databases in the system.

B) Circuit Design and Evaluation

Students can calculate the parameters of the circuit components (e.g., connected devices and equipment) based on the web-based instruction of theoretical analysis of the system. Following this, the student can use his PC to draw the circuit diagram using a general circuit simulator (e.g., LTspice) using the SPICE-based processing. The SPICE-based simulator translates the circuit designed by a student into SPICE. This function can automatically evaluate the designed circuit by analyzing the differences in the SPICE information between a designed circuit and the model circuit prepared in the database of the proposed system. Based on this evaluation, the system automatically indicates errors in the designed circuits and instructs the students to correct the errors.

C) SPICE-Simulation and Automated Evaluation

Based on SPICE information, students can simulate the working of the designed circuit. The system requires the students to check whether the simulated working of his designed circuit corresponds to the specification and working of the model circuit in the database.

2.2 Function for Virtual Experiments Involving Circuit Construction

Figure 1(b) schematizes the function for learning virtual experiments involving circuit construction (F-2). The function F-2 helps a student in web-based learning of circuit construction and measurements of the constructed circuits. To virtually construct a circuit, F-2 allows individual students to use general graphic editors in their PCs to virtually construct circuits and performs automated translation of the virtual circuits into SPICE. This study improves on the previous SPICE-translation technique (Takemura, 2019) by making it possible to perform automated evaluation of the parameters of circuit components. F-2 automatically evaluates the virtually constructed circuit by comparing it with the SPICE information of the model circuit in the database of the system. Further, F-2 possesses the technical novelty and wide usefulness that enables individual students to select an appropriate type of circuit board (a breadboard or universal circuit board) depending on their purposes and abilities. Circuit construction using a breadboard does not require soldering of the circuit components (e.g., devices and cables), and the components' terminals are only plugged into the holes on the upper surface of the breadboard. Therefore, breadboard-based construction is suitable for beginners' education because of the easiness of construction and reusability of circuit components. However, the solder-less circuit on a breadboard is inferior in terms of stability and practical use. Thus, the breadboard is only applicable to trial construction or construction of small-scale circuits for elementary education. On the other hand, circuit construction using a universal circuit board necessitates soldering on the lower surface of the circuit board; thus, circuit construction on a universal circuit board is suitable for students whose experiences and abilities of circuit construction are at intermediate level and above. Further, circuit construction on a universal circuit board with soldering is applicable to practical circuits and large-scale circuits. The approach for learning virtual circuit construction using F-2 is presented in the subsections *A)* and *B)* below.

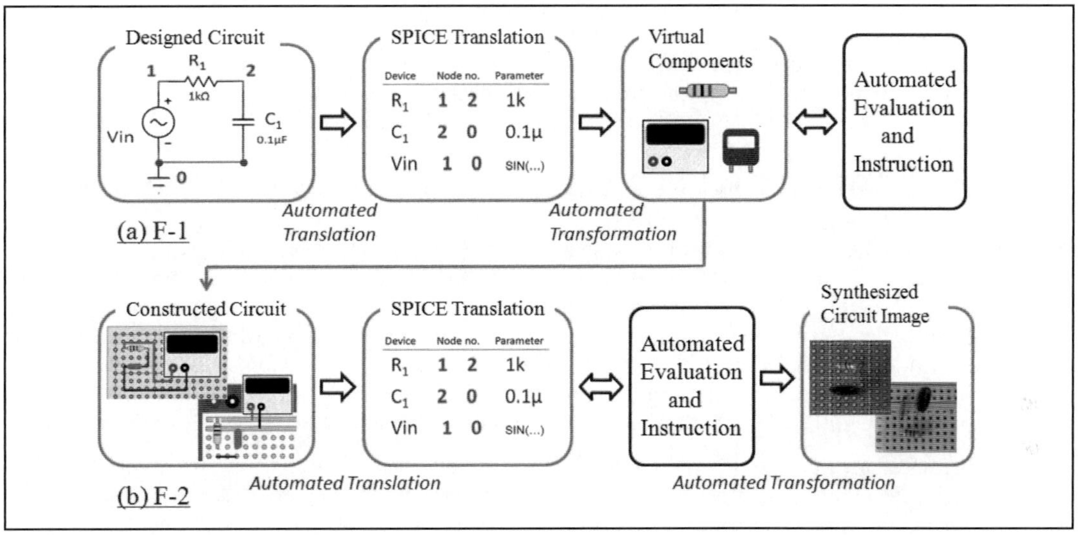

Figure 1. Schematic of the two proposed functions for experiments involving circuit construction; (a) function for learning design and workings of circuits (F-1) and (b) function for virtual experiments involving circuit construction (F-2)

A) Virtual Circuit Construction and Evaluation

The manner of experiments involving the virtual circuit construction using each circuit board is presented hereunder.

- *Virtual Circuit Construction on a Breadboard*

The function F-2 allows individual students to construct virtual circuits using general graphical editors in their PCs. F-2 automatically provides the student with the pictures of necessary circuit components corresponding to the SPICE information obtained from the circuit designed using F-1 (see Figure 1). To construct a virtual circuit, the student places the virtual components on a picture of the selected circuit board and draws lines to indicate the circuit connections. Following this virtual construction, F-2 automatically translates the composition of the virtual circuit into SPICE. This SPICE information allows the student to simulate the workings of the virtual circuit and learn measurements of the circuit. The presence and location of incorrect components in the virtual circuit are determined by analyzing the difference in SPICE information between the constructed circuit and the correct circuit in the database of the system. If faulty parts or incorrect behavior of the virtual circuit is observed, the system provides the student with instructions or warnings on the issue.

- *Virtual Circuit Construction on a Universal Circuit Board with Soldering*

F-2 allows a student to use a general graphic editor in his PC and enables him to design the layout of a circuit by placing the virtual circuit components obtained from F-1 on the image of the upper surface of a universal circuit board. The student draws colored lines to indicate the wiring of each device on the upper surface of the circuit board. Based on the circuit recognition of an image of the upper surface of the virtual circuit, the proposed system can automatically provide instructions for wiring and soldering on the lower surface of the circuit board. F-2 also simulates the circuit operation based on automated translation of the constructed circuit into SPICE and individual students can virtually learn measurements of their circuit. The presence and location of incorrect components in the virtual circuit are determined by analyzing the difference in the SPICE information between the constructed circuit and the correct circuit in the system's database. If faulty parts or incorrect behavior of the virtual circuit is observed, the system provides the student with instructions or warnings on the issue.

B) Image Synthesis for Learning a Physical Circuit

To learn physical circuit-construction using the proposed e-learning system, F-2 provides the students with a synthesized image of the physical circuit by using the images of physical circuit-components corresponding to the virtual components during the process *A)*. This synthesized image gives the student knowledge of the actual circuit construction using physical circuit components.

3. METHODOLOGY FOR EVALUATING THE PROPOSED SYSTEM

The effectiveness of the proposed e-learning system was evaluated via a comparison experiment by two groups of students aged 19–21 at Tokyo University of Agriculture and Technology. Group-1 comprised 20 students instructed to construct a DC voltage control circuit shown in Figure 2(a), by using conventional methods. Group-2 consisted of 20 students who performed the same circuit construction using the proposed e-learning system. Groups-1 and -2 were evaluated in 2019 and 2020, respectively. Before starting the experiments, questionnaires were provided to ascertain the degrees of individual students' experience in circuit construction with/without soldering. Based on this, the students were subdivided into three categories as listed below:

A: Experienced in circuit construction with soldering in addition to practice exercises at school
B: Experienced in breadboard-based circuit construction in addition to practice exercises at school but no experience in circuit construction with soldering except for practice exercises at school
C: No experience in circuit construction except for practice exercises at school

The number of students belonging to each experience category is shown in Figure 2(b) and indicates that more than half of the students belonged to Category C and the majority of the students have no experience in circuit construction on a universal circuit board with soldering except for practice exercises at school. All students had learned the construction of elementary circuits with soldering as a part of compulsory education in junior high schools in Japan and thus, there were no students with no experience in circuit construction.

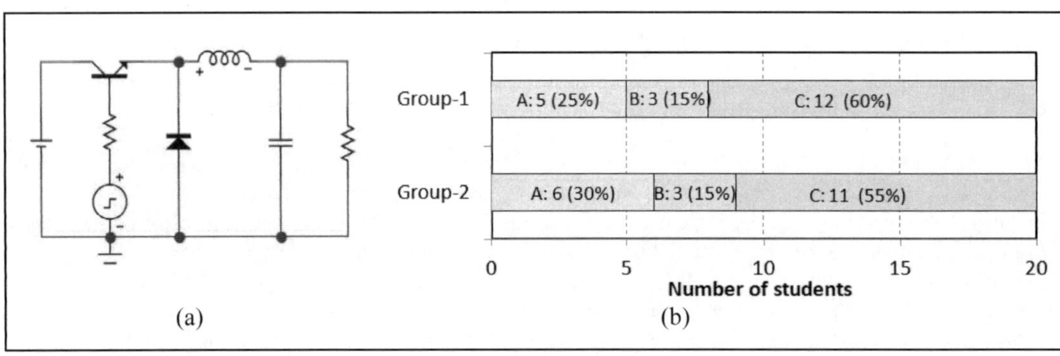

Figure 2. Circuit and grouping of students for evaluation of the proposed system; (a) circuit diagram to be constructed and (b) distribution of experience categories in circuit construction for each group

The students in Group-1 were tasked to construct circuits based on conventional methods listed below within a time limit of 4 h:

(G1-1) Lecture on the theory and analysis of a DC voltage controller circuit by an instructor (0.5 h)
(G1-2) Theoretical analysis and circuit design
(G1-3) The instructor inspects the result of (G1-2). If an incorrect part is discovered, the concerned student corrects it under the instructor's guidance (1 h for (G1-2) and (G1-3))
(G1-4) Physical circuit construction using the necessary circuit components and a breadboard provided by the instructor

(G1-5) The instructor inspects the constructed circuit. If an incorrect part is discovered, this student corrects it under the instructor's guidance (1.5 h for (G1-4) and (G1-5))
(G1-6) Measurement of the characteristics of the constructed circuit using experimental equipment (1 h)

The individual students in Group-2 were tasked to construct circuits using the proposed new system within 4 h according to the following processes.

(G2-1) Online lecture on the theory and analysis of a DC voltage controller circuit by an instructor (0.5 h)
(G2-2) Theoretical analysis and circuit design using F-1
(G2-3) The system automatically inspects the result of (G1-2). If an incorrect part is discovered, this student corrects it based on the instruction from F-1 (1 h for (G2-2) and (G2-3)).
(G2-4) Virtual circuit construction using F-2—each student can choose an appropriate circuit board (a breadboard or universal circuit board) depending on his purpose and ability.
(G2-5) The system automatically inspects the virtually constructed circuit. If an incorrect part is discovered, the concerned student corrects it based on the instruction from F-2 (1.5 h for (G2-4) and (G2-5)).
(G2-6) Measurement of the characteristics of the virtually constructed circuit using F-2 (1 h)

4. RESULTS AND DISCUSSION

In this section, the effectiveness of the proposed e-learning system is discussed based on the results of the comparison test between Group-1 and Group-2 as described in Section 3. Figure 3(a) shows examples of the web-based experiments on the virtual circuit construction using the proposed e-learning system obtained by a student in Group-2. This student was able to complete the two types of virtual circuit constructions using a breadboard and a universal circuit board with soldering and virtual measurements using these two circuits within the time limit.

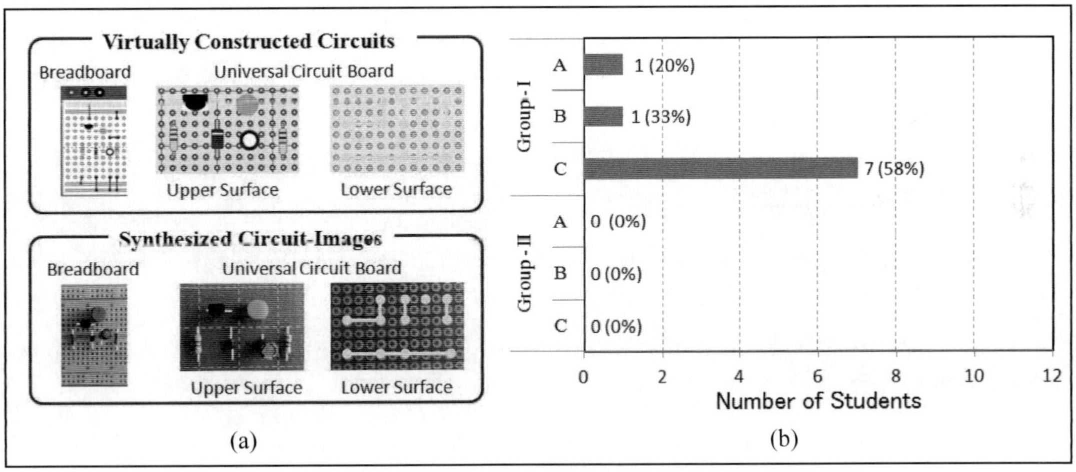

Figure 3. Results of the comparison test between Group-1 and Group-2; (a) virtual circuits constructed by a student in Group-2 using the proposed system and (b) the number of students whose circuits contained errors.

Figure 3(b) indicates the occurrence of errors in the constructed circuits that were discovered at the processes (G1-5) and (G2-5). As shown in this figure, nine (45%) students in Group-1 had errors in circuit construction that were observed by the instructor. Conversely, no errors in the circuits constructed by the students in Group-2 were noted. These results indicate the effectiveness of the proposed system for circuit construction. It is worthy of note that all students in Group-2 were able to complete two types of circuit construction using a breadboard and universal circuit board with soldering within the same time limit as Group-1.

Through the evaluation process, positive responses were obtained from the instructors, which provide further validation of the effectiveness of the proposed system. These comments show that:

- This new system enables e-learning for teaching and learning both theory and experiments.
- This system has wide usability because individual students can learn circuit construction using an appropriate type of circuit boards depending on their abilities and purposes.
- The web-based instructions decrease an instructor's load for instructing experiments involving circuit construction.

From the students in Group-2, positive responses indicating the usefulness of the proposed system were obtained, as follows:

- The system was helpful in checking whether the workings of designed and constructed circuits are correct or not and in removing errors in the circuit.
- Circuit design using F-1 has an important role for improving the efficiency of circuit construction.
- F-2 is useful because an appropriate circuit board is selectable depending on user's purpose and ability. This function helps beginners to challenge an advanced level of circuit construction (e.g., soldering and large-scale circuit).
- The synthesized imaging of this e-learning system provides useful knowledge of the real shape of a physical circuit.

To improve the applicability and usefulness of the system, the following studies should be implemented:

- Improvement of the graphic quality using 3D-CG
- Expansion of the applicability to various use cases by combining virtual reality (VR) and AR.

5. CONCLUSION

A novel e-learning system for comprehensive learning of electronic circuits covering theoretical analysis, design, and experiments involving circuit construction is proposed. The proposed system enables students to select an appropriate mode of circuit construction depending on their purposes and abilities. A comparison study between two groups of university students demonstrated the effectiveness of the proposed system for accurate circuit construction with and without soldering on a circuit board. This e-learning system is expected to be applicable to various use cases by improving graphics qualities such as 3D graphics, VR, and AR.

ACKNOWLEDGMENT

This study was partly supported by a Grant-in-Aid for Scientific Research (KAKENHI) 19K03079 from the Japan Society for the Promotion of Science.

REFERENCES

Andujar, J. M, et al., 2011, Augmented reality for the improvement of remote laboratories: an augmented remote laboratory, *IEEE Trans. Education*, vol.54, no. 3, pp. 492–500.

Chevalier, A., et al., 2017, A three-year feedback study of a remote laboratory used in control engineering studies, *IEEE Trans. Education*, vol. 60, no. 2, pp. 127–133.

Garcia-Zubia, J., et al., 2017, Empirical analysis of the use of the VISIR remote lab in teaching analog electronics, *In IEEE Trans. Education*, vol. 60, no. 2, pp. 149–156.

Rabaey, J. M., The Spice Page, <URL: http://bwrc.eecs.berkeley.edu/Classes/IcBook/SPICE/> (accessed Aug. 31, 2020).

Takemura, A., 2019, Education system for electronic circuit construction involving soldering on a circuit board, *Proc. IADIS Conference CELDA 2019*, pp. 447–452, Cagliari, Italy.

A HEALTHCARE SYSTEM TO SUPPORT WELL-BEING OF MIGRANTS: THE PROJECT PREVENZIONE 4.0

Veronica Rossano, Teresa Roselli and Flora Berni
Department of Computer Science, University of Bari Aldo Moro,
Via Orabona, 4, Bari, Italy

ABSTRACT

The paper presents one of the outcomes of a project in the context of the Asylum, Migration and Integration Fund (AMIF) 2014-20 financial program, named Prevenzione 4.0 (Prevention 4.0). The project has been proposed by Apulia Region in cooperation with the University of Bari and other private and public partners. The project aims to offer additional health services to migrant in order to reinforce the National Health Services and to promote the migrant's selfcare to prevent diseases and maintain health with the support of local health services. The proposed solution offers: some medical devices useful to measure fundamental biometric parameters, a mobile app to both store the measures and to offer microlearning contents for migrant's empowerment, and an information system to monitor all medical data collected in the various places which host migrants. The paper presents a healthcare system to support migrants in taking care of their health. The system is composed of a mobile app to supply information useful for well-being and to monitor biometric parameters, a locker in which a set of electronic devices will be available, and an information system to store data and to monitor migrants' health.

KEYWORDS

e-Health, Migrant, Mobile Application, Microlearning

1. INTRODUCTION

The migration flows are one of the hugest problems in Italy, which needs to be tackled from various point of views, to overcome cultural and bureaucratic barriers (Regional Committee for Europe, 2015). With the project Prevenzione 4.0, the Apulia Region addresses the issue of migrant's health. The idea is to enhance the effectiveness of the national health care system which could fail since the patient's medical history is lacking and since the monitoring of the health parameters is difficult because of the difference in cultural behaviour. The literature is full of examples of the use of technologies in medical context (Conrick, 2006), for example, to support diagnosis of serious diseases (Kamruzzaman, 2020) (Baek & Chung, 2020) but also to support the empowerment of patients (Di Bitonto et al, 2012) (Pesare et al, 2015). The study of the literature in this context has highlighted some similar applications, MigrAdvisor (http://inmigration.caritas.it/node/549), RefAid (https://refaid.com/blog/), Infostranieri (http://www.infostranieri.org) for example are addressed to get basic information to move around Italy or to get the permanent resident card. ImMigRant (https://www.migrantaid.eu), instead, provides migrants first-aid advices for the most common emergencies using only images. The proposed system in Prevenzione 4.0 (Buono et al, 2019) put together those aspects: give basic information and support individual's self-care. To acquire self-care ability, is the practice of individuals looking after their own health using the knowledge and information available to them (Cohen et al, 2007), is important. It is a decision-making process that empowers individuals to look after their own health efficiently and conveniently, in collaboration with health and social care professionals as needed.

This paper presents the healthcare system designed to help the migrant centres to provide medical and psychological support to their guests and to empower migrants to take care of their health without involving the National Health Service when not strictly necessary.

2. THE HEALTHCARE SYSTEM IN PREVENZIONE 4.0

As said before, one of the outcomes of the project Prevenzione 4.0 is to design and build a Healthcare system able to support prevention of diseases and self-care assessment of migrants hosted in First and Second Reception Centers. The system will be composed of three main components (Figure 1): a locker in which will be available a set of electronic devices to monitor the biometrical parameters (Fit bit, thermometer, personal scales, ...), a mobile app to register these parameters on migrants' smartphone, and an information system to store data and to allow the monitoring of physical and psychological health of individuals.

The locker will be placed in the reception facilities, called SIPROIMI - System of protection for holders of international protection and unaccompanied foreign minors, to support migrants' integration and inclusion in Italy.

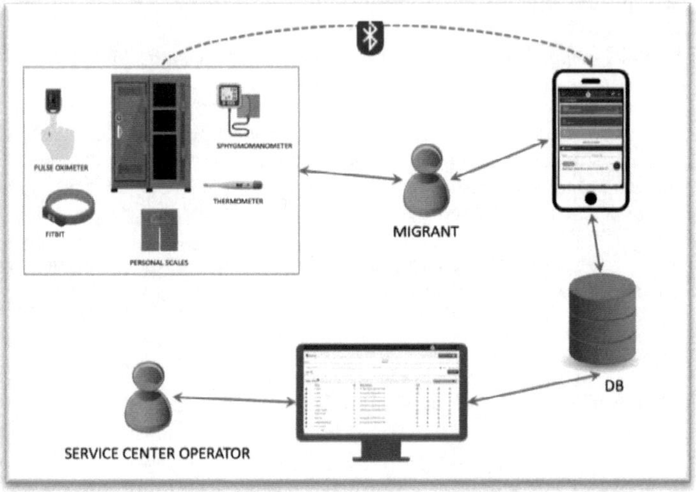

Figure 1. Healthcare system components

The system will be accessible to different user categories, for each of them it provides customized services and features:

(i) *Migrant* is a registered user able to access to all features offered by the system;

(ii) *Service Center Operator* (SCO) user will be the responsible for the management of both microlearning contents and users' accounts. Moreover, using the web app the SCOs can monitor data stored in the information system and define if it is necessary to contact health operators (physicians, nurses, phycologist, and so forth);

(iii) *Guest* (who has not logged in) is able to access the basic functionality of the mobile app, i.e. he will be able to access information and training contents (microlearning contents) but will not have access to any other service.

The mobile app is the main component of the healthcare system, it will be used by migrants both to record biometric parameters to take care of their health and to acquire knowledge about Italian laws, employment procedures, medical information and so forth.

The functionalities of the app are:

(iv) Dashboard (Figure 2): is the main page of the app, it displays the recent recorded measures and knowledge contents added in the management system;

(v) Library: using the approach of micro-learning (Job, & Ogalo, 2012), it supplies a set of knowledge contents addressed to promote healthy lifestyle, to patient's empowerment, to bureaucratic information, and so on;

(vi) Measures: where all graphs of the recorded biometric parameters are visualized (Figure 3). There is also the diary to see the numeric values of each parameter (Figure 4). The measurement can be entered either manually or automatically using devices with Bluetooth communication.

(vii)Chat: allows direct communication with the operators in the Service Center that can help migrants. When some specific problems occur, the SCO can contact specific professional figures (physician, phycologist, dietician, etc.) to support migrants.

(viii) Covid-19: an extra feature added to monitor migrants during the pandemic. The app will propose some simple questions about symptoms and travels. The answers are used to suggest the probability of being at risk for Covid-19.

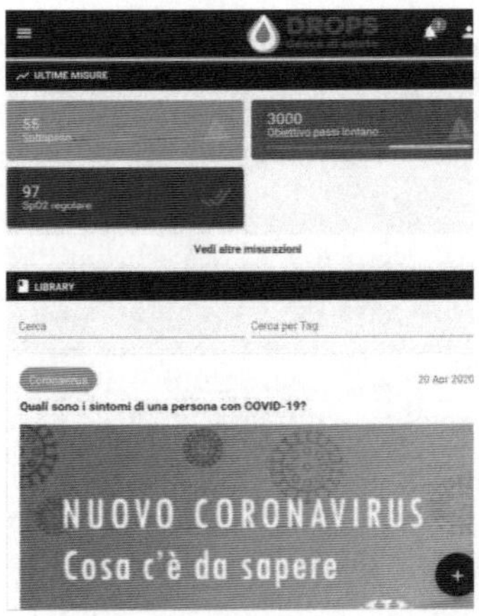

Figure 2. Dashboard

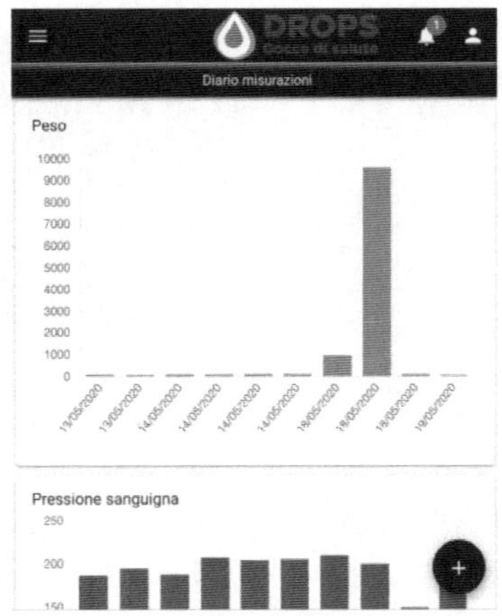

Figure 3. Diary of measures registered

Figure 4. Measures Graphs

In addition, when a biometric parameter is out of healthy range, an alert is visualised using a red number on a bell (see all figures above), and at the same time a message is sent in the chat to allow the user to pay attention. All data are stored in a DB to allow the Service Center to monitor the migrants' health and to intervene to prevent problems from occurring. The information system of the Service Center offers features to manage the users (add, delete, modify), to monitor the measurements of each migrant, and communicate with the migrant using the chat. When the users list is visualised a marker green, yellow or red is showed in order to allow the operators to see if some problems are occurring.

3. CONCLUSIONS AND FUTURE WORKS

Taking care of migrants' health is one of the issues that countries should be dealing with. The Prevention 4.0 project is one of the actions carried out by the Apulia Region to strengthen institutional health services by allowing reception centres for migrants to take care of the health of their guests. The app will be used also during Covid-19 pandemic in order to monitor the temperature of people in informal settlements. A first pilot study involving 5 migrants in a SIPROIMI placed in Molfetta, a city near Bari, was aimed to evaluate the users' perceived usefulness. A usability inspection based on the Nielsen heuristics was carried out. This inspection was important to evaluate the comprehensibility of the interface and the functionality provided by the app. During the test, language comprehension problems emerged because some of them were not able to read, some problems were related to the poor technological skills of migrants who have difficulties to understand the app's operational flow, others showed a low level of interest in health issues. To overcome these difficulties: audio was added to all microlearning information, some icons have been enlarged to make them more clearly visible, and currently we are thinking of building a core version of the app with only a few features, for example to store biometric parameters, and to give the option of downloading a richer app only to those users who are more technologically proficient.

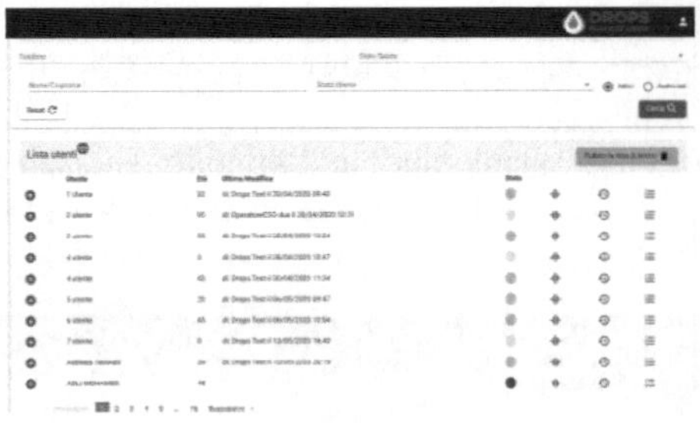

Figure 5. User list

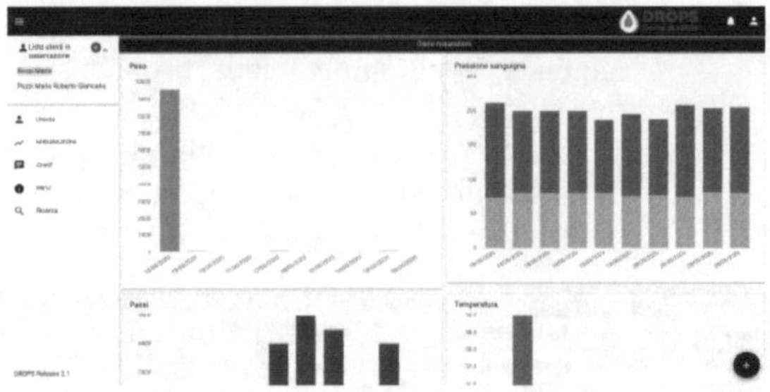

Figure 6. Graphs of all measures of a specific user

ACKNOWLEDGMENT

This work is partially funded by the project "Prevenzione 4.0" - Fondo Asilo Migrazione Integrazione 2014/2020 – OS 1/ON 1 - PROG_2301. Partner: Regione Puglia - Sezione Sicurezza del Cittadino, Politiche per le migrazioni e Antimafia sociale, AreSS Puglia, Università degli Studi di Bari Aldo Moro, NOVA onlus - Consorzio di cooperative sociali - società cooperativa sociale.

REFERENCES

Baek, J. W., & Chung, K., 2020, Context Deep Neural Network Model for Predicting Depression Risk Using Multiple Regression. *IEEE Access*, 8, pp. 18171-18181.

Buono, P., Cassano, F., Piccinno, A., Rossano, V., Roselli, T., and Berni, F., 2019, Multimedia technologies to support delivery of health services to migrants by enhancing their inclusion. *Proceedings of the 23rd International Conference Information Visualisation (IV),* IEEE, pp. 370-375.

Cohen, S., Nutt, W., and Sagic. Y., 2007, Deciding equivalences among conjunctive aggregate queries. J. ACM 54, 2, Article 5 (April 2007), 50 pages. DOI: https://doi.org/10.1145/1219092.1219093.

Conrick, M., 2006. *Health informatics: Transforming healthcare with technology*. Cengage Learning Australia.

Di Bitonto, P., Roselli, T., Rossano, V., Frezza, E., & Piccinno, E., 2012, An educational game to learn type 1 diabetes management. *Proceedings of DMS 2012: International Conference on Distributed Multimedia Systems*, pp. 139-143.

Job, M. A., & Ogalo, H. S. (2012). Micro learning as innovative process of knowledge strategy. *International journal of scientific & technology research*, *1*(11), pp. 92-96.

Kamruzzaman, M. M., 2020, July, Architecture of Smart Health Care System Using Artificial Intelligence. *Proceedings of 2020 IEEE International Conference on Multimedia & Expo Workshops (ICMEW)*, IEEE, pp. 1-6.

Pesare, E., Roselli, T., & Rossano, V., 2015, Intelligent Agent and Virtual Game to support education in e-health. *Proceedings of DMS 2015: 21st International Conference on Distributed Multimedia Systems*, pp. 204-21.

Regional Committee for Europe, 2015. Strategy and action plan for refugee and migrant health in the WHO European Region, http://www.euro.who.int/__data/assets/pdf_file/0004/314725/66wd08e_MigrantHealthStrategyActionPlan_160424.pdf

IMPLEMENTING AN ONLINE TRAINING PROGRAMME IN PRECISION MEDICINE FOR PRIMARY CARE PROFESSIONALS: A MULTI-METHOD APPROACH

Sharon Mitchell[1], Evrim Jaccard[2], Regula Cardinaux[2], Prune Collombet[3], Jacques Cornuz[4], Gérard Waeber[2], Idris Guessous[3] and Sissel Guttormsen[1]

[1]*Institute for Medical Education, Medical Faculty, University of Bern, Mittelstrasse 43, 3012 Bern, Switzerland (CH)*
[2]*Department of medicine, University Hospital CHUV-Lausanne, CH,*
[3]*Division and department of primary care medicine, Geneva University Hospitals and Faculty of Medicine, Geneva, CH*
[4]*Unisanté, Faculty of biology and medicine, University of Lausanne, Rue du Bugnon 44, 1011 Lausanne, CH*

ABSTRACT

Never before have expectations of healthcare professionals been more challenged by complex diseases and more educated patients in increasingly consumer driven healthcare systems. A new era of Precision Medicine (PM) is gaining momentum to bring tailored interventions to patients, informed by genomics, lifestyle and environment. The delivery of a more precision approach requires targeted training to frontline health care professionals. *The objective* of this paper is to report on the structured design and planning of online training modules for Primary Care Professionals (PCPs) specifically targeted at family doctors, pharmacists and advanced practice nurses. We report on initial findings of an ongoing *mixed-method approach* initiating applied research in a process where each method informs, guides and refines the design of the next step. Kern's 6 Steps method serves as development framework. Literature and experts' reviews supported clarification of learning objectives, focus groups, guided by Kirkpatrick's levels of evaluation supports refinements of content and form. *The findings* to date support the need to use methods that will challenge pre-existing assumptions, employ best practice approaches informed by evidence and ensure the development of a quality online training programme acceptable and applicable to the defined target groups.

KEYWORDS

Online Training, Precision Medicine, Primary Care Professionals, Needs Assessment, Blended Learning

1. INTRODUCTION

This approach for needs assessment, our first data on acceptance from PM experts and PCPs, and planned next steps. The target group identified within 'PCPs' include family doctors, pharmacists and advanced practice nurses, but also other groups of health professionals will be considered.

Precision Medicine (PM) as an era of 'precision' or 'personalisation' in patient care continues to gain momentum within the literature. While traditionally emerged in the study of genomics, PM is rapidly incorporating new domains including precision public health, environment and lifestyle, use of big data and health records (National Library of Medicine 2018) challenging previously conceived definitions of PM as the practice of genomics. Yet infiltration in the use and practice of bringing the right strategy to the right patient, particularly for frontline professionals is needed (Feero 2017). Adapting to changing contexts and new methods to deliver patient care in already challenging healthcare environments is not an easy feat. This project responds to a call from medical experts in Precision Medicine in Switzerland, to design a national training programme that will equip PCPs with the competencies to deliver a precision approach to their patients. It is intended that this training programme will be a blended learning progamme (online and on-site learning) to allow flexible learning environments for busy healthcare professionals.

Online training offers an approach well-fitting with the rapid developments in PM as well as the need for timely updates and the transfer of new knowledge (Ruiz et al 2006). This expanding digital learning era does come with caution and a number of studies have reported the lack of guiding effective instructional design theories in the development of digital learning for health professions education (Dunleavy et al. 2019). The importance of applying a conceptual framework for project development, documented within the literature, is therefore a worthy consideration (Bordage 2009).

As an initial step in designing and implementing an online training platform, the project team introduces the use of existing educational frameworks that will guide development. To effectively deliver learning objectives, flexible instructional methods will support learner competency and a blended learning approach (Liu et al, 2016). The design and planning of this project will consider the need for a mix of online and on-site training to support the transfer of knowledge to applied practice (Dunleavy et al 2019). Table 1 shows the adapted model of Kern's 6 step approach to curriculum design and planned steps for project development (Thomas et al, 2016). It underlines the importance of using a general and targeted needs assessment. The paper reports on the first steps of a needs assessment for the target PCP population as well as the first four steps of *Table 1*.

Table 1. Application of Kern's Six Step Approach to design of a training programme for PCPs

Kerns 6 Step Approach	Planned Study Phases
1. Problem Identification and General Needs Assessment	Literature Review and Expert Opinion
2. Targeted Needs Assessment	Focus Group Study, Survey to experts
3. Goals and Objectives	Defining learning objectives with experts Content development with experts Content validation in peer review
4. Educational Strategies	Literature Review, Expert validation
5. Implementation	Delivering an online learning platform Supporting networking Developing on-site training
6. Evaluation and feedback	Participant Evaluation and Field Study

The skills required to deliver this project were recognised as an essential first step in building a diverse research team. These skills include experts in the following fields: Precision Medicine, family medicine, pharmacy, nursing, web-design, communication, e-learning and medical education. Regular project meetings have served as an essential point-of-contact to discuss key findings offering diverse perspectives not only from researchers but also *through the lens of topic experts and target study participants* (Creswell 2009). The research questions for this project are: Q1: What would motivate PCPs to attend online training for PM? Q2: What must be offered in online training programme, to enable PCPs to deliver PM to their patients? Q3: How can we ensure a best practice approach to design an online training programme?

2. METHODS

The systematic process of assessing needs is a means to determine the 'gap' between current practices and future expectations, as well as assessing what might be acceptable to a specific target group (Lockyer et al 1998). Figure 1 illustrates a mixed-method approach to needs assessment. Previously published articles advocating the use of multiple methods within Needs Assessment design and delivery (Fraenkel, Wallen & Hyun 2015) guide this approach. An essential strength is that information is gathered, validated, and refined from different sources offering new perspectives at each stage in the process (Creswell 2009; Keister & Grames 2012), striking a delicate balance between limitations of qualitative and quantitative research.

As part of the ***review of the literature***, a member of the research team searched through databases including PubMed, Medline, Google (also -Scholar and -books) with the following key terms: Precision Medicine in Primary Care/ Personalised Medicine in Primary Care/ Genomics in Primary Care/ Pharmacogenomics/ Shared decision-making in PM. The researcher gathered and logged publications based on (1) Opinion of relevance, (2) Formal and informal qualitative and quantitative studies, (3) Literature reviews and (4) Year of publication (2014 to date), to gather information on the 'new' field of PM across different sources and evidence (Druery et al 2013). The process documented a list of publications validated by members of the project team.

Expert validation or expert collaboration in qualitative research supports best practices purported within the literature that 'adds validity' and credibility to qualitative inquiry (Creswell & Miller 2000). With the view of building a working definition of PM for our project, key findings from the literature were discussed with interprofessional experts in order to validate extracted conceptual definitions. The targeted discussion groups included 2 PM experts, a pharmacist and an internist.

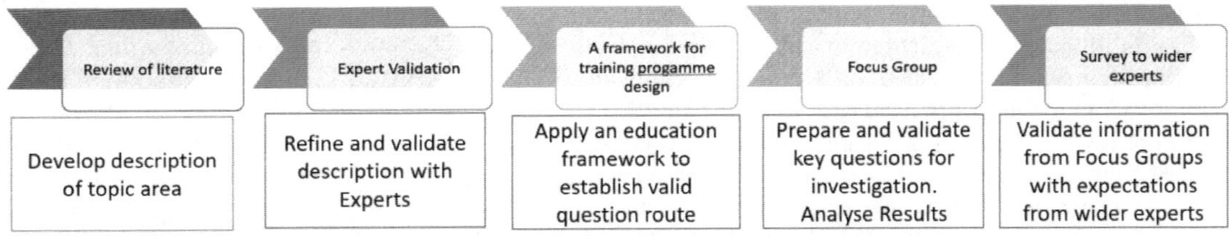

Figure 1. A multi-method approach to Needs Assessment

A framework for the training programme design for the research team shall ensure consideration of essential areas of development within this planning stage. Building upon the review of the literature and expert validation, the research team began the process of assembling key themes requiring further investigation during the qualitative study. In order to extract possible key terms (i.e. learners' motivation) addressing all relevant aspects of the intended training, a suitable educational framework was needed and sought for in the literature.

Focus groups are qualitative methods that have been widely used for the purpose of education needs assessments (Tipping 1998). For the purpose of refining scope within this study, we report on the design and **pilot** of a question route including main questions and sub-questions, to deliver 2 future inter-professional focus groups. The preparation for the focus groups has followed a design structure as shown in Figure 2 and following best practice approaches in the literature (Stalmeijer 2014).

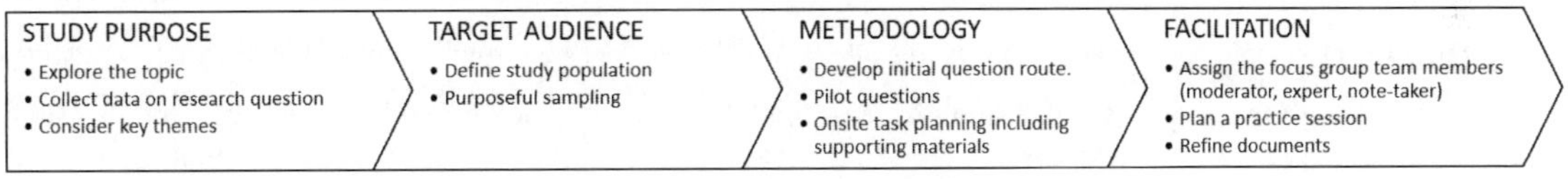

Figure 2. Focus group design adapted from Nagle & Williams 2013

The *question route* was developed aligned to the key themes from an educational framework guiding development. 4 members of the research team interviewed target group participants including 2 family doctors, a pharmacist and an applied practice nurse. This method follows a best practice approach to assess how questions are understood as part of the process to refine and improve research design (Adams & Cox 2008).

A follow up ***survey*** to a wider target audience will aim at: validate gathered perspectives of individual experts, test whether gathered perceptions of each target group profession is representative of that profession as a whole and validate to which degree our assumptions for methods of delivery reflect perceived needs. Relevance of content and levels of motivation represent the target audience in general.

3. RESULTS

The results of each step from Figure 1 show that within a short time frame an interprofessional project team agreed on clearly aligned stages, each bringing small but relevant insights for the project as a whole.

Table 2. Collation of key terms with perceived importance in Precision Medicine & expert validation result

Key terms linked to Precision Medicine Result of Literature Scope	Rejection or support Result of Expert Validation
Genomics	Yes, should be included
Clinical phenotypes	Not needed
Biological sampling	Not needed
Variability in genes, lifestyle and environment	Yes, should be included
Health records and big data	Yes, should be included
Customized prevention and treatment strategies	Yes, should be included

The ***review of the literature*** led to important findings in the scope and breath of the topic of PM as a newly evolving field, and the resulting learning objectives. In establishing the support of an online training programme in PM, the dominant perspective from the medical experts was to focus on the development of genomics, a topic synonymous with PM. A review of the literature on PM found additional key terms not isolated to genomics presented in Table 2. In the second step the key terms were ***validated with PM experts*** and consensus was reached on terms to include or dismiss as part of a definition of PM for project implementation in a long-term perspective (Table 2).

Selecting a framework for the design of an online training programme was an effort saluted to the well-known phrase *begin with the end in mind*, also recognised in curriculum design (Morrison 2003). We found that Kirkpatrick's 4 levels of evaluation, adapted from Barr et al 2006 offered a structured guide to determine overall themes and more specific objectives, see Figure 3.

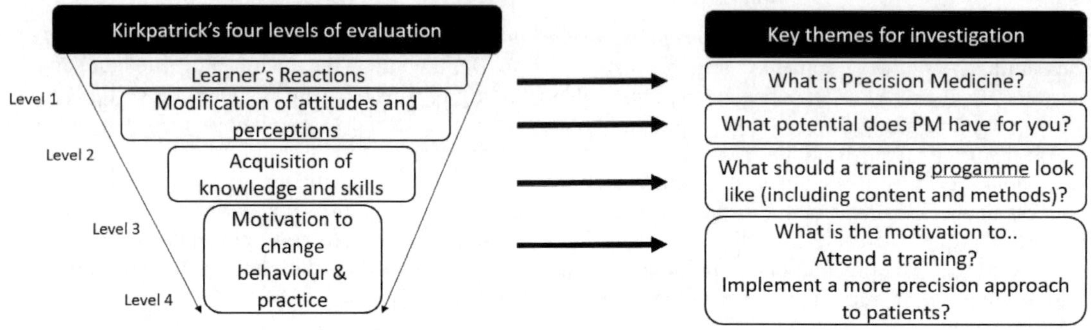

Figure 3. Developing essential objectives to explore 'key themes' derived from Kirkpatrick's levels of evaluation

The focus group design and planning phase followed the insights documented in Figures 2 and 3. Building upon the key themes from Kirkpatrick's model, the research team developed a specific question route covering the four theme questions from the model in Figure 3. Besides validating aspects related to the content***, the pilot study*** showed the importance of assessing the motivation to use an online training for PCPs. PCPs typically spend most of their time in clinics or their doctor's office and the topic of PM is also competing with many new areas and fields of study. Therefore, it does not help to build a quality online training programme, if the target group have no time or motivation to use it. The pilot offered valuable feedback that PCPs are not well informed about PM as this is a novel topic. Hence, the intention to optimise delivery and training of this new knowledge and possible skills to frontline professionals, using the opportunities of online training is assured at this stage of the development. Next steps of the Needs Assessment phase will deliver two focus group studies and a survey. Data of the focus group study will be ready for the conference in November.

4. DISCUSSION

This paper reports on the first steps in the design and implementation of an online training programme for PM. We have documented a process, confirming the need for further validation of the research questions through a systematic process for needs assessment (Figure 1). This process offers preliminary answers to the overall research questions.

Q1 addresses ***motivation*** to attend an online training programme in PM. Although results are preliminary, we can deduce that PM is a new field understood very differently across healthcare professionals. While participants responded that this may not be a topic relevant for today, the overall trend of responses from our initial pilot support the need for this training. The aspect of motivation and willingness to attend must continue to be monitored, also in terms of the means of knowledge delivery (on-line, mobile or more traditional) that can lead to implications in daily practice. Online delivery is only one part of the answer. *Q2* explicitly focuses on ***content***, the driver for success, and the particular granularity and the orientation of the needs of the different professions. The offered content must fit with the needs of the target groups, the clarification of which is the foundation of any curriculum development. Further, the content for development and means of delivery are intrinsically linked. It would be wrong to assume that all content is suitable for online delivery only, or that online training alone will meet the expectations of learners. The success of this training programme will be to strike a balance between the means of delivery, the content for training and the ultimate goal of meeting the expected needs of busy healthcare professionals. *Q3* has been a constant thread throughout the research to date and our experience shows that the use of existing ***frameworks*** has been of immense support in developing a complex online training programme, designed for continuing professional development for different target groups across PCPs.

The ***review of the literature*** led to important findings in the scope and breath of the topic of PM as a newly evolving field. While traditionally synonymous in the study of genomics, this is a field that is rapidly emerging into other areas including precision public health, environment and lifestyle, ethics, use of big data and health records, areas that are particularly fitting to frontline healthcare professionals. In establishing the support of an online training programme in PM, the dominant perspective from collaborating medical experts was to focus on the development of genomics. The most notable result has ensured that not only does the agreed definition (and future content of the planned training programme) include genomics but will also address other topics important for the future of PM and the role that PCPs will have in this approach to patient care. While the *literature review* was of a scoping nature, ***the expert validation*** of the finding supports the relevance.

The inclusion of ***theoretical frameworks***, including Kern's Model for curriculum development and Kirkpatrick's 4 levels of evaluation have helped the research team to prescribe specific milestones, align research themes, and support decision making in the project team. Kirkpatrick's model emphasises the importance of the learner at each level taking into account how the learner has reacted, acquired knowledge and skills, and changed behaviour to make a markable difference in the delivery practice performance. The project team will continue to keep the interests of the end users placed at the very centre of the development. Furthermore, the design and planning of 2 ***focus groups***, addressing the French and the German speaking Swiss target groups, has followed a documented process for development, for which the literature provides ample support and evidence. For the purpose of scope within this paper, we are assured of the importance of the essential role of ***piloting of questions*** prior to delivery of the focus group. The preliminary results led to extensive discussion, reorganisation and modification of central issues based on the collated responses during this pilot.

The immediate **limitations** of this paper is that it presents initial findings. Still, we regard the careful consideration of each step in the process to be important and in the end economical, supporting sustainable outcomes. It may be argued that the project is driven from frontline experts of PM with personal interests in dissemination. Yet, the interdisciplinary and multi-professional composition of the project team, as well as the documented development process serve the purpose of avoiding bias. This paper focuses on the online part of the learning programme. Also, the development of the full blended learning programme, integrating online and on-site training shall be given attention as the project develops. Some of the content needs hands on training (e.g. communicating with patients) and exchange of experience between PCPs (e.g. about patients reported needs), which best can be provided with on-site meetings. Further research shall help us find a balance between online and on-site training. It also may be argued that a theoretical framework for developing an online training programme is not an isolated method, however, further findings within this needs assessment fully support this process as a means to provide an intellectual structure that guides the development of the project as a whole.

5. CONCLUSION

This paper introduces the first steps taken in the design, planning and implementation of an online learning programme in PM for frontline healthcare professionals. We have reported on our initial findings that support the need to continue our investigations on (1) motivation of our target group (2) relevant content and means of delivery and (3) evidence-based frameworks to ensure acceptability of a high-quality training programme across the target population.

Our initial findings support that both the attractiveness and relevance of the content but also motivation of our target audience to attend a training programme are key elements to successful implementation. Further research aims at documenting these findings as well as implementation steps. The overall success of this programme will be measured by (1) the response and uptake of modules among Swiss frontline professionals, (2) the level of feedback received to disclose relevant information for improvements and (3) monitoring and evaluation of how this training infiltrates into a more precision approach to healthcare delivery. Additional modes of evaluation including the assessment of perceived relevance to daily practice and through subsequent and frequent participation to online modules will offer tangible insight into the 'success' of this training.

The emphasis on research within the domains of instructional effectiveness and satisfaction of online learning is well reported within the literature. The processes described within this paper respond to the call from systematic findings that more quality data is needed on the implementation and use of education frameworks in designing learning needs assessment, curriculum development and implementation for the purpose of online training. We have documented a multistep approach and use of an evidence-based framework for development to take decisions for implementation. Our first experiences have assured us that this approach is worth the effort. The development of an online interprofessional training programme for (inter-) national use is an expensive mission. The degree of success cannot be a surprise following the final dissemination. We must take every effort to ensure that the steps needed to build a quality, acceptable online training programme worthy of our target audience be built into the process from its inception.

ACNOWLEDGEMENT

The project team would like to thank Health2030 for their financial support.

REFERENCES

Adams A & Cox AL. 2008. *Questionnaires, in-depth interviews and focus groups*. In: Cairns, P & Cox, AL. eds. Research Methods for Human Computer Interaction. Cambridge, UK: Cambridge University Press, pp. 17–34

Barr H, Freeth D, Hammick M, Koppel I, Reeves S. 2006. The evidence base and recommendations for interprofessional education in health and social care. *Journal of Interprofessional Care.* Jan 1;20 (1):75-8.

Bordage G. Conceptual frameworks to illuminate and magnify. *Med Educ.* 2009;43 (4):312-319. doi:10.1111/j.1365-2923.2009.03295.x

Creswell JW. 2009. *Research Design Qualitative, Quantitative, and Mixed Methods Approaches*. Thousand Oaks, CA. SAGE Publications Ltd.

Creswell JW & Miller DL. 2000. Determining validity in qualitative inquiry. *Theory into practice.* Aug 1;39 (3):124-30.

Druery J, McCormack N, Murphy S. 2013. Are best practices really best? A review of the best practices literature in library and information studies. *Evidence Based Library and Information Practice.* Dec 8;8 (4):110-28.

Dunleavy G, Nikolaou CK, Nifakos S, Atun R, Law GC, Car LT. Mobile digital education for health professions: systematic review and meta-analysis by the Digital Health Education Collaboration. *Journal of medical Internet research.* 2019;21(2).

Feero WG. 2017. Is" Precision Medicine" Ready to Use in Primary Care Practice? Yes: It Offers Patients More Individualized Ways of Managing Their Health. *American family physician.* Dec 15;96 (12):767-8.

Fraenkel JR., Wallen, NE, & Hyun HH. 2015. *How to Design and Evaluate Research in Education*. McGraw-Hill International Edition ed. Vol. Ninth Edition. New York: Mc Graw Hill.

Keister D, Grames H. 2012. Multi-method needs assessment optimises learning. *The clinical teacher.* Oct; 9(5):295-8.

Liu Q, Peng W, Zhang, F., Hu R, Li Y. and Yan W., 2016. The effectiveness of blended learning in health professions: systematic review and meta-analysis. Journal of medical Internet research, 18(1), p.e2.

Lockyer J, Hanley D, Fidler H, Toews J, Lysholm-Andrews E. 1998. Physician educational needs in osteoporosis: An approach to needs assessment. *Journal of Continuing Education in the Health Professions.* Jun; 18(3):185-9.

Morrison J. 2003. *Ch 4. Evaluation.* In Cantillon & Wood. ABC of Teaching and Learning 2nd Edition. Wiley-Blackwell. Oxford.

National Library of Medicine. 2018. What is precision medicine? Online 24 August 2020 https://ghr.nlm.nih.gov/primer/precisionmedicine/definition

Nagle B. and Williams, N, 2013. Methodology brief: Introduction to focus groups. *Center for Assessment, Planning and Accountability,* (1-12). Online 24 April 2020 http://www.mmgconnect.com/projects/userfiles/file/focusgroupbrief.pdf

Ruiz JG, Mintzer MJ, Issenberg SB. 2006. Learning objects in medical education. *Medical teacher.* Jan 1;28 (7):599-605.

Stalmeijer RE, McNaughton N. and Van Mook WN, 2014. *Using focus groups in medical education research: AMEE Guide No. 91*. Medical teacher, 36(11), pp.923-939.

Thomas PA, Kern DE, Hughes MT, Chen BY. 2016. *Curriculum development for medical education.* JHU Press: Baltimore, MD, USA.

Tipping, J., 1998. Focus groups: a method of needs assessment. Journal of Continuing Education in the Health Professions, 18(3), pp.150-154.

APPLYING LAYERED GRAPHS TO EVIDENCE CENTERED DESIGN BASED SERIOUS GAMES ASSESSMENT

Jan K. Argasiński and Iwona Grabska-Gradzińska
Department of Games Technology, Faculty of Physics, Astronomy and Applied Computer Science, Jagiellonian University in Krakow, Poland

ABSTRACT

In this paper authors propose idea for inclusion of the Evidence Centered-Design (ECD) driven assessments into graph- based scenarios/levels generating system. The concept is to position ECD's *evidences* as elements of layered graphs representing game state and possible player's/student's actions. Graph's series of *productions* can be then compared to task assigned to player/student and evaluated. This mechanism combines one of the most popular methods of designing educational assessments with procedural generation of scenarios/levels and with core ideas derived from game design – such as concept of *mechanics*, represented here as the game design patterns.

KEYWORDS

Educational Assessment, Serious Games, Mechanics, Layered Graphs, Game Design Patterns, Evidence Centered Design

1. INTRODUCTION – KEY CONCEPTS

1.1 The Problem of Knowledge Representation and Open Assessment

Today serious games are becoming one of the most promising areas in computer-mediated education (Zhonggen, 2019). There are two main reasons behind that fact. First – the generation for whom playing games is one of the most important ways of consuming culture has long since entered schools (what is more – teachers are also increasingly people "brought up on games"). Second – games are more immersive, interactive, social objects than textbooks – which significantly influences the involvement of students in the teaching material (Almeida & Simoes, 2019).

Two main problems when it comes to serious games design are 1) methods of representation and transfer of knowledge appropriate for the medium and 2) ways to evaluate the educational progress of students in dynamic and open virtual environment. The goal of this paper is to outline possible solution to both these problems by applying the game design patterns and layered graphs for serious gameplay generation and assessment's *evidences* creation.

1.2 Key Concept: Educational Assessment and Evidence-Centered Design

Educational assessment is the process of systematic review of learning outcomes and progress using empirical data. Frequently, evaluation is framed into the canvas of *knowledge, skill, abilities* (KSA), and sometimes also *beliefs*. To achieve proper assessment there is a need for structured data on learning process and its outcomes. The simplest method in educational appraisal is testing. Nowadays, however, the methodology of *stealth assessment* is increasingly valued. The idea is that evaluation should be "seamlessly woven directly into the fabric of the instructional environment to support learning of important content and key competences. This represents quiet, yet powerful process by which learner performance data are continuously gathered during playing/learning (…)" (Shute, 2011, p. 504).

Evidence-Centered Design (ECD) is the framework for the design and implementation of assessments that provides systematic overview of evidences of educational progress (Arieli-Attali et al., 2019). It was introduced by Mislevy et al. (1994) and developed by many other scholars (Phelps et al., 2020; Johnson et al., 2018; Hao & Mislevy, 2018). The core idea is to provide system of models that describe various parts of educational endeavor. The ECD contains of the Students Model, the Evidence Model, the Task Model, the Assembly Model, and the Presentation Model (Mislevy et al., 2003). For us the most important is the Student Model which defines variables in relation to measured KSAs, and the Evidence Model which provide instructions on how to update the Student Model's variables in the light of work products from assigned tasks. Main mechanism of evaluation is hidden in the "identification and summary of evidence within tasks, in terms of observable variables" (Mislevy et al., 2003, p. 9). Variables are used for storing and updating the information about the student's proficiency in particular domains.

1.3 Key Concept: Patterns in (Serious) Games Design

Assessment in the ECD is performed based on *evidences* gathered from tasks assigned to student. In the realm of serious games tasks translate to game mechanics defined after Miguel Sicart (2008) as "methods invoked by agents to interact with the game state". Mechanics are means in which player (student) interacts with objects in environment to perform tasks. Outcomes from this interaction can be interpreted as evidences of knowledge, skill, ability of belief.

There are various definitions of mechanics, and there are various ways to systematize them (see: Sicart, 2008). Because all of them are essentially repetitive – they can be catalogued into patterns. The advantage of such approach is the ability to arrange mechanics into sequences and the possibility of automatic evaluation (*balancing*). Among the most interesting ways to systematize mechanics are propositions by Björk & Holopainen (2005) and Adams & Dormans (2012).

1.4 Key Concept: Layered Graphs in Serious Games Content Representation

Layered graphs are widely used in the fields, where data structures represent complex dependencies of real world, and where data manipulation and problem solving can be translated into well-defined graph algorithms (e.g. shortest path finding, BFS, DFS, etc.). It can be useful in serious games for e.g., user's behavior or multioptional choices analysis (Grabska-Gradzińska et al., 2012). Graph systems are also used in the design of support systems. (Vermeulen et al., 2016)

By graph model it is understood the system of nodes as information containers and edges as the representation of dependencies among the nodes. The layers help with assigning specific values or features to specific groups of nodes, which supports the flexibility of representation, and universality of structure. (Haahtela et al., 2015).

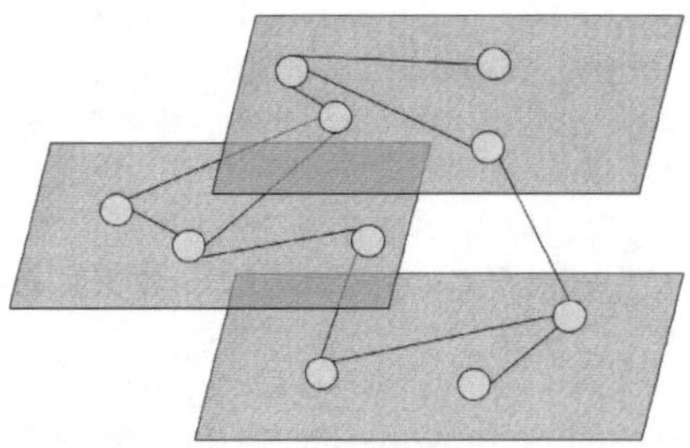

Figure 1. The idea of the layered graph: nodes (blue dots) gathered into three groups (red shapes) connected within one layer and between the layers (black lines)

The graph model, which represents the game state changes after every players' action. For the sake of formalization all these actions are mapped by the graph operations called "productions". It is the formal mechanism to connect player's behavior with its impact on the state of the game world.

2. PROPOSED SOLUTION – GRAPH GENERATED CONTENT

In this proposal the ECD's Task Model, generalized game mechanics (patterns) and in game world objects are mapped into graph model elements. Every node stands for the possible player's action. The graph's edges starting from first node represent the available choices of operations. Every node directly connected means the next possible operation. Some of nodes are collected in the Evidence Layer, which means, that they are crucial for player's evaluation. The path in the gameplay's graph represents the sequence of player's behaviors. The edges between nodes ensure that the cause and the effect relationship between succeeding actions is preserved. The assigned task is represented as subgraph with one initial node from any layer and group of nodes from the Evidence Layer, which collects player's responses to initial stimuli.

3. SIMPLE CASE STUDY: OSH SERIOUS GAME

3.1 The OSH Game Design Requirements

The Occupational Safety and Health (OSH) games are the specific category of serious games, because the procedures collected in the safety instruction manuals give small chance for spontaneity, but, depending on the circumstances, every single schema can be mixed with others or performed in different order. The evaluation of the course of the OSH games is not a trivial problem also because of the gravity of the matter. That being said - there are many ways to formalize player's behavior e.g., locating direct testing questions in the game narrative (Grabska-Gradzińska, 2016), using gameplay patterns (Argasiński & Grabska-Gradzińska, 2017), hazard control matrix (Greuter et al., 2013), etc. Another aspect of evaluation of the player knowledge is the idea of collecting additional information of player's physical reactions during the gameplay, e.g. time gap between question and replay, eye-tracking analysis, affective indicators of engagement etc. In every case the goal is to systematically assess changes in player's and game's states as evidences of some particular knowledge, skill or ability.

3.2 Patterns in OSH Game Design

For every serious game deigned in this framework there is a need for creation of an extensive, closed list of meaningful interaction that can occur during the gameplay. There is of course very large body of possible actions performed by player in the gaming environment but for purposes of educational assessment we need only catalogue of that which are in the first order 1) predictable (probable), and in the second 2) related to evaluation (linked to the tasks) or not.

For the purpose of this paper closed list of patterns with detailed description was not created due to lack of space – instead *ad hoc* and quite obvious mechanics (such as "reaching the doors" and "closing the windows") were used.

3.3 Graph Generated Content in OSH Serious Game

Let's take into consideration player's/student's task/goal based on fire safety instructions of one of the public institutions:

Task: Evacuation.

Initial production: Fire alarm (1).

Productions: Collecting personal belongings (2); Turning off electric devices (3); Closing the windows (4); Face covering (5); Location changing (6-11,13,14); Reaching the doors (7); Using the elevator (12); Reaching the meeting point (15).

Evidences: Finding the shortest path to the meeting point (subgraph: 6-13-14-15); Closing the doors while leaving the room (subgraph: 6); Turning off electric devices (subgraph 3); Closing the windows (subgraph: 4); Face covering [in case of fumes] (subgraph: 5); Using the elevator [negative evidence] (subgraph 12).

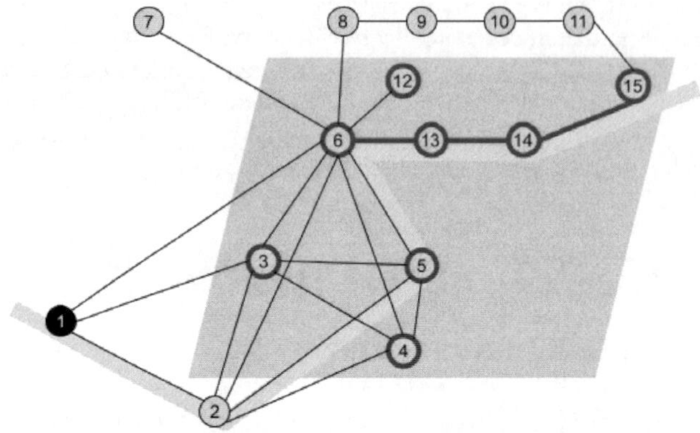

Figure 2. The game graph of the task "Escape": evidences (red subgraphs), other productions (blue dots), initial production (black dot), player's path (yellow line)

3.4 The Assessment

In the provided simple example there is the graph that describes possible player's actions that map to the ECD's *evidences* of the OSH knowledge, skills and abilities. Note that given proper boundary conditions and extensive catalogue of patterns various graphs can be generated for the purpose of similar assessments. The graphs can than serve as input to procedural content generating systems (such as level builders) to ensure that student's KSAs are assessed in multiple similar but different gameplays. This is the main feature of proposed solution.

4. CONCLUSION

In the above paper the outline of method of generating assessments for the serious games was provided. In the future follow up of the concept various detailed formalizations for generating graphs could be provided. There is also potentially interesting topic of using sophisticated statistical models (such as Bayesian networks) in order to generate the series of gameplay-based assessment. These topics, however interesting, are beyond the scope of the above paper - nonetheless they show the possibilities contained in the simple idea of combining the ECD, game design patterns and layered graphs.

REFERENCES

Adams, E. & Dormans, J., 2012. Game Mechanics. Advanced Game Design. New Riders, San Francisco, USA.

Almeida, F. et al., 2019. The Role of Serious Games, Gamification and Industry 4.0 Tools in the Education 4.0 Paradigm. Contemporary Educational Technology, 10, 120-136, 10.30935/cet.554469.

Argasiński, J. K., Grabska-Gradzińska, I., 2017. Patterns in serious game design and evaluation application of eye-tracker and biosensors. ICAISC 2017. LNCS (LNAI), vol. 10246, pp. 367–377. Springer, Cham

Arieli-Attali, M. et al., 2019. The Expanded Evidence-Centered Design (e-ECD) for Learning and Assessment Systems: A Framework for Incorporating Learning Goals and Processes Within Assessment Design. Frontiers in Psychology, 10, 10.3389/fpsyg.2019.00853.

Björk, S. & Holopainen, J., 2005. Patterns in Game Design. Charles River Media, Newton, USA.

Grabska-Gradzińska, I. et al., 2012. Towards a graph-based model of computer games. Advances in Information Technologies and Communication 2012: proceedings of Joint International Conferences on ICT, Computer Science Series, ISSN 2213-2805, 3.

Grabska-Gradzińska, I., 2015. How to predict behavior at risk: educational game story analysis using layered graphs and eyetracking system. Proceedings of the 23rd International Workshop on Intelligent Computing in Engineering: EG-ICE 2016, Kraków, Poland.

Greuter, S. et al., 2013. Designing a game for occupational health and safety in the construction industry. 10.1145/2336727.2336740.

Haahtela P. et al., 2015. Gamification of Education: Cities Skylines as an Educational Tool for Real Estate and Land Use Planning Studies

Hao, J. & Mislevy, R., 2018. The Evidence Trace File: A Data Structure for Virtual Performance Assessments Informed by Data Analytics and Evidence-Centered Design: The Evidence Trace File. ETS Research Report Series,10.1002/ets2.12215.

Johnson, E. et al., 2018. Using evidence centered design to create a special education teacher observation system. Educational Measurement Issues and Practice, 37, 10.1111/emip.12182.

Mislevy, R. et al., 2003. A Brief Introduction to Evidence-Centered Design. CSE Report 632. US Department of Education, 10.1002/j.2333-8504.2003.tb01908.x.

Mislevy, R. J., 1994. Evidence and inference in educational assessment. Psychometrika, 59, 439–483.

Phelps, G., 2020. Developing Assessments of Content Knowledge for Teaching Using Evidence-centered Design. Educational Assessment, 10.1080/10627197.2020.1756256.

Shute, V., 2011. Stealth Assessment in computer-based games to support learning. Computer Games and Instruction, 55.

Sicart, M., 2008. Defining Game Mechanics. Game Studies. The International Journal of Computer Game Research, 8.

Vermeulen M. et al., 2016. DISCO, a Formal Model of Serious Games to Help Teachers at the Design Stage. Doctoral Consortium CSEDU 2016 (DCCSEDU 2016), Apr 2016, Rome, Italy.

Yu, Z., 2019. A Meta-Analysis of Use of Serious Games in Education over a Decade. International Journal of Computer Games Technology, 1-8, 10.1155/2019/4797032.

IMPLEMENTING INTERDISCIPLINARY CONTENT AND NOVEL TEACHING METHODS AT AN EGYPTIAN UNIVERSITY: A CASE REPORT

Ly Lutter[1], Johannes Schrumpf[1], Felix Weber[1], Ahmed M. H. Abdelfattah[2] and Stefan Schneider[1]
[1]*Institute of Cognitive Science, Osnabrück University, Germany*
[2]*Faculty of Science, Ain Shams University, Egypt*

ABSTRACT

Shifting educational paradigms to facilitate knowledge transfer online is now more than ever needed, given the massive impact of a worldwide pandemic which impedes traditional face to face teaching techniques at universities. In this work, we present recent developments in an international cooperation project between a university in Egypt and a university in Germany, aiming at facilitating knowledge transfer between universities and introducing educational paradigms for interdisciplinary academic collaboration. When conducting such an educational venture boundary conditions such as cultural or infrastructural differences between partner universities need to be considered. In this article, we present the concrete measures we implemented that aim at bridging the educational, infrastructural and cultural gaps and reflect the implementation thereof given the contextual boundary conditions in Germany and Egypt. We conclude by identifying success factors that led to the efficacious implementation of an interdisciplinary pilot course for an Egyptian higher-education institution.

KEYWORDS

International Collaboration, E-Learning, Curriculum Development, Democratic Leadership, Moodle

1. INTRODUCTION

The report "Science and Innovation in Egypt" analyses the innovation and economic potential of Egypt, which it rates as promising, but also strongly recommends to "[u]pgrade school and university curricula and teaching methodology to ensure they reflect the needs of the marketplace, with greater emphasis on problem solving, critical thinking and communications skills. [Further, to r]evise science curricula to make them more interdisciplinary and to incorporate knowledge about new technologies" (Bond et al., 2012, p. 122). The higher education systems of Germany and Egypt differ significantly in structural aspects such as technical and study facilities or teaching approaches. Yet, the national research and innovation strategies of both countries agree that international research cooperations are suitable to tap into the knowledge of others, to foster excellence, innovation, economic development, and are vital to jointly tackle the immense recent global challenges (ASRT n.d., BMBF n.d.). The presented international cooperation project between a German and an Egyptian state university aims at building sustainable resources of novel educational and interdisciplinary content at the Mathematics department of the Egyptian partner university, following the example of an established study program in Cognitive Science at the German partner university. To this end, the on-going project has achieved to build a Cognitive Science laboratory at the Egyptian partner university, conducted annual summer trainings in Germany, supervised several research projects, and hosted two spring schools on Cognitive Science in Egypt.

However, during the course of the collaboration, three related but distinguishable gaps between the partner sites were identified: the *infrastructural gap*, including technical as well as educational aspects such as hardware, WiFi and approachability/ accessibility of lecturers; the *educational gap*, including didactical paradigms and content of teaching; and the *cultural gap* as visible in cultural codes, habits and norms taken for granted, the individual touch in the way of interacting and language differences.

Having identified these gaps, the current project phase (2019-2020) introduced new measures: A closer collaboration on the student level across universities, expanding available lecture content, on-site training for Egyptian students, and most crucially, digitalization of existing teaching resources from the German partner. The latter – digitalization – was intended to address availability of teaching content for Egyptian students, but also to allow a close collaboration with limited resources. This strategy inadvertently proved to be advantageous in facing the world-wide COVID-19 pandemic which we will expand on below.

In the following, we describe and evaluate the measures to address these gaps which evolved out of practical considerations and an in-depth look at the context of the project. We identify success factors for the effectuation of an interdisciplinary and intercultural cooperation project aiming at establishing sustainable educational resources and introducing new educational paradigms.

2. MEASURES

To address the infrastructural, educational, and cultural gaps we implemented the following measures. For each measure, we provide a design rationale.

DEVELOP AN E-LEARNING CURRICULUM: The project's long-range goal is to develop a full-fledged e-learning programme under the name "Interdisciplinary Computing Studies" (ICS). The envisaged ICS e-learning curriculum unites the strengths of both project partners: the technical skills and know-how of Computer Science (Egyptian partner), with inspirational fields of application from Cognitive Science (German partner) ranging from Artificial Intelligence to Neuroscience and Linguistics. Beyond that, ICS facilitates a stronger network among departments within the Egyptian university. The e-learning curriculum aims at implementing novel learning paradigms such as constructivist learning and learner-centered teaching approaches, which can be integrated into an existing learning context, bridging educational gaps between the partner universities.

LMS & ICS E-LEARNING ACADEMY: For facilitating knowledge transfer across continents, the project chose to implement an electronic learning management system (LMS) and instantiated an ICS e-learning academy. This platform allows to create and host teaching resources, and functions as a hub for future curriculum advances and various types of interaction among teachers and students. Furthermore, facilitating online education with its countless opportunities could potentially raise awareness and inspire stakeholders at the Egyptian institution to support the implementation of a full ICS curriculum.

JOINT STUDY PROJECT: For investigating how the educational gap between the partner universities could be bridged, a bilateral joint study project between Egyptian Computer Science students and German Cognitive Science students was formed which was dedicated to design, construct, and evaluate a pilot e-learning course for the ICS e-learning academy, following the ADDIE model (McKenny and Reeves, 2018). To facilitate mutual understanding across continents, intercultural workshops and exchange visits were organized. Disciplines of Cognitive Science were condensed for ICS. A complete tailor-made online course was implemented on Moodle based on multimedia learning principles (Mayer, 2014), minimalism of instructional design (Van der Meji and Caroll, 2018), gamification elements and learning theories.

ICS SPRING SCHOOL IN EGYPT: To raise awareness among students at the Egyptian partner and provide a basic level of training in ICS, a spring school was organized. The five-day conference with international experts aimed to cover a diversity of research areas that inspire the ICS program. Workshops and Q & A sessions enable close interaction between students and speakers in order to inspire new learning formats and low-threshold educational infrastructure with a learner-centered approach. Moreover, the high-stake conference aims to increase the visibility and prestige of the Computer Science members within the Egyptian partner university and whole Egypt.

3. OUTCOMES

We subsequently evaluate these measures in the context of the three gaps.

DEVELOPMENT OF AN E-LEARNING CURRICULUM: To develop an e-learning curriculum including innovative content while having to deliver a suitable infrastructure was challenging, given that the Egyptian context differs from the German context regarding technical resources, educational approaches, communication habits, language and culture. Apart from a lack of training in Cognitive Science, also the idea to develop an e-learning curriculum was initially not met with enthusiasm by representatives of the Egyptian partner institution. Nevertheless, with the help of the substantial network of the project managers at both sites and their persistent promotion among different political figures within and outside their universities resulted in support by content matter experts, educational- and technical advisors to the program. A fundamental milestone was accomplished as the project could attract high interest by the dean of the Egyptian institution to support the development of the ICS program and in offering to visit the German partner to tie a stronger cooperation and for an exploratory negotiation on how a full curriculum could be jointly instantiated.

LMS & ICS E-LEARNING ACADEMY: Moodle offers the required flexibility and variety regarding the design of learning tasks and assessments and is an easy access tool to administrate and expand. Two main considerations resulted in choosing Moodle as the free and open source LMS to host the ICS e-learning academy: Firstly, we could not yet foresee the detailed picture of the ICS e-learning academy's design and which options of the LMS we would want to make use of. Secondly, in the long run the ICS e-learning academy will be administered by local Egyptian project partners which puts their needs for usability as prior requirement.

JOINT STUDY PROJECT: In a joint effort, the study project developed the highly professional, tailor-made e-learning introductory course "Foundations of Cognitive Science". This was mainly a result of an open and trusting communication among all team members including the managerial team based on democratic collaboration so that new ideas could be brought up and solutions to problems were developed in a joint effort. Kick-off intercultural workshops and careful selection of students further strengthened communication, and short communication channels were established (e.g. Slack). Because of the diversity of skills among the student team and the support from the project's network of advisors, the whole team strongly believed in the project's potential, bolstering dedication and the utilization of skills, active boundary crossing by the students who reached out to external experts to seek feedback, and self-organization with regular realignments within the broader project team and context. Having several members of the German Cognitive Science program being well-disposed to the project helped to design solid teaching material, and creating micro lectures was a smooth and rewarding experience for the student speakers.

ICS SPRING SCHOOL IN EGYT: The ICS spring school promised to become a great success. First, raising awareness led to the official acknowledgement and support by the Egyptian institution, which gave high prestige to the event. Secondly, the school program with lectures by renowned speakers (international and Egyptian researchers), practical tutorials, lab visits and student presentations of outstanding projects attracted more than one-hundred students to register, so that the school was fully booked. Topics that attracted most interest were from Cognitive Science disciplines such as Artificial Intelligence, Cognitive Modeling, Computer Vision, Human-Computer Interaction, Computational Approaches to Cognitive Science and Educational Technologies.

However, due to the global COVID-19 pandemic, the Spring School 2020 was canceled as the Egyptian government closed universities, the German team being already in Egypt. Having the ICS e-learning platform at its disposal, the team quickly adapted to the situation and could record content in their hotel rooms and host it on the e-learning platform. Thus, the team was able to launch several already prepared workshops; other recordings were made in the professional recording studio at the German partner university, ultimately making the Spring School a success.

To this end, we had to engage in formal and informal interaction within the international cooperation project. Regular boundary crossing to content matter experts, educationalists and keeping in touch with externals to establish a supportive network were essential activities to this end. The enthusiasm for the project goals among team members produced a variety of well-suited ideas and so, flexibility and creativity in adopting and including different ideas in a way that fuels the project was fundamental for its current success.

4. CONCLUSION

The presented case report serves as example for international teaching collaborations. To conclude, we identify advantages of our approach and limitations we faced, and identify key success factors that may inspire similar projects that strive for a viable and sustainable international collaboration.

Employing a Systems Thinking approach (Dochy et al., 2012a), we connected and built synergies between the different project partners in order to actualize the measures for bridging the infrastructural, educational and cultural gaps. Embarking in such a cycle of expansive learning where we transferred existing knowledge to solve a new problem and to simultaneously construct new understanding resulted in a viable and sustainable cooperation project (Dochy et al., 2012b). This process was largely enabled by (1) open and trusting communication, (2) having a shared vision of the project goal established through regular realignments and discussion meetings and (3) mutual understanding of the Egyptian and German project sites with all their cultural implications.

Nevertheless, correctly identifying gaps to be bridged is only the first step. Our attempt to establish a more reliable technical infrastructure resulted in a well-equipped ICS lab. The intended purpose of illustrating possibilities that Cognitive Science offers to Computer Science students was turned down by existing dynamics of hierarchy and politics within the Egyptian context. However, with the installation of the lab, we could raise awareness and interest in ICS as a collaboration project between the German and Egyptian partners at these institutional figures on a fundamental level.

Utilizing democratic leadership within the team and especially in teaching the study project, might appear time consuming at first but bears the advantage of playing out expertise that might otherwise would have gotten lost. More so, implementing independent and sustainable measures highlights the importance of our bottom-up approach involving the Egyptian team members because it ensures support of locals and the target group. This groundwork thus must be increasingly solidified through raising awareness at the university administration, starting bilateral negotiations on teaching collaborations, and working towards institutionalization as accredited curriculum. For starting this process, integrating teaching in the form of a bilateral joint study project of graduate students, complemented by on-site trainings, proved to be a key component to foster a practice of a bilateral collaboration that introduces novel teaching content and new learning approaches to the Egyptian partner university.

ACKNOWLEDGEMENT

Our special thanks go to the participants of the incredibly engaged and lively joint study project between Egyptian and German students. We are grateful for advice and support from many content and educational advisors and technical personal who so selflessly supported the project, and without whom it would not have been possible. We are thankful that the project was generously funded by the German Academic Exchange Service (DAAD) with means from the German Federal Foreign Office (AA). Authors 4 and 5 are the principal investigators of the project.

REFERENCES

ASRT "International Cooperation" [WWW Document], n.d. URL http://www.asrt.sci.eg/index.php/international-cooperation (accessed 6.26.20).

Bond et al., 2012. *Science and innovation in Egypt*, London, England: The Royal Society.

BMBF "Internationalization Strategy" [WWW Document], n.d. URL https://www.bmbf.de/en/internationalization-strategy-2209.html (accessed 6.26.20).

Dochy et al., 2012a. Inter-organisational expansive learning at work, in: *Theories of Learning for the Workplace: Building Blocks for Training and Professional Development Programmes.*

Dochy et al., 2012b. Systems thinking and building learning organisations: P. Senge, in: *Theories of Learning for the Workplace: Building Blocks for Training and Professional Development Programmes.*

Mayer, 2014. *The Cambridge handbook of multimedia learning*, second edition. Cambridge University Press.

McKenney and Reeves, 2018. *Conducting educational design research,* second edition. London: Routledge.

Van der Meij and Carroll, 2018. Principles and Heuristics for Designing Minimalist Instruction, in: Carroll (Ed.), *Minimalism Beyond the Nurnberg Funnel*. MIT Press, Cambridge, MA, p. 19 -53.

WORK ON EXPRESSION-COMMUNICATION SKILLS AT THE UNIVERSITY BY PLAYING LORD OF THE RINGS ONLINE

Christine Bolou-Chiaravalli
University of Franche-Comté, France, PhD Student

ABSTRACT

The objective of this experiment, with an audience of Network and Telecommunications apprenticeship students entering their first year at university, was to have them work on their expression-communication skills through an online video game. The study is part of an action-research project and in the context of the reform of the University Institutes of Technology, the technical component of universities. This experimentation is discussed with regard to the skills-based approach it mobilizes.

KEYWORDS

Expression-Communication, Video Game, Skill-Based Approach, IUT, DGLB

1. CONTEXT AND OBJECTIVE

The French university has reached an important milestone with the decree of 6 December 2019 on the reform of the professional license carried by one of its components: the University Institutes of Technology (IUT). Its objective of professional integration is reinforced and completed. It must give "its holders the means to adapt to future changes in employment" (Article 4), accommodate various student profiles (Article 5) and offer training aimed at acquiring cross-disciplinary skills (Article 9). This development is in line with research recommendations (Chauvigné and Coulet, 2010; Tardif, 2006) which emphasize that future employees should not only be able to master the technical skills of their field, but also be capable of creating human value in their company, particularly through cross-cutting skills. These reforms are also linked to the Bologna process, within the European Qualifications Framework, and reflect the alignment of universities with the educational, economic and political issues associated with the competency-based approach (Chauvigné and Coulet, 2010).

Universities are moving from a disciplinary approach to a competency-based approach. Competency is understood as "complex know-how to act based on the effective mobilization and combination of a variety of internal and external resources within a family of situations" (Tardif, 2006, p. 22). The competency-based approach (APC) will be applied for students entering the IUT in 2021. It is considered to be more suited to their professionalization, since it must implement skills that can be mobilized in professional situations of a different nature, according to several levels of development for each skill at the end of the training. The APC requires situations and problem-solving activities that are learning triggers (Perrenoud, 2011). It diversifies the reflexive evaluation process: portfolio, self-evaluation, peer evaluation (Poumay et al., 2017). The APC will be organized into blocks of competencies around essential learning that define what is expected at the end of the training. Finally, it is based on resources that use groupings of courses and innovative pedagogical devices.

This context has allowed us to set up an APC experimentation whose objective is to propose a complex learning situation, adapted to the profiles of students in IUT, more specifically for student apprentices in Networks and Telecommunications. An experimental protocol was set up as part of an action-research project to make them play a massively multiplayer online video game to improve their expression-communication skills. Expression-communication is a disciplinary field common to the twenty-four departments found in an IUT and covers many crosscutting skills: teamwork, effective communication, critical thinking or judgement, project management and leadership. It was therefore a good candidate for the APC experiments. Our research question is to find out whether E-C skills can be improved by playing a MMORPG.

2. THEORETICAL ANCHORING

To create this complex situation, we used the theoretical framework of digital game-based learning (DGBL). It refers to the development and use of computer games for educational purposes (Prensky, 2001). It is a learning approach that focuses on student engagement through stimulating challenges in a collaborative and social environment (Cheng et al., 2013). Video games are increasingly used in higher education (Subhash and Cudney, 2018) because they are a powerful pedagogical tool that multiplies the possibilities for learning and information retention (Girard et al., 2013), allows the right to make mistakes and encourages trial and error (Chaudy and Connolly, 2018). Massively multiplayer online games (MMORPGs) are recognized for their ability to bring to bear the skills of collaboration and distributed thinking (Taylor, 2006). They allow people to build concepts by participating (Yang, 2012) and to experience communication relationships in authentic situations (Gee, 2008). They are recommended in subjects where students report greater anxiety (Crocco et al., 2016). However, little attention has been paid to the aspects related to communication (Sourmelis et al., 2017).

Their success has generated many models among learning theorists (Murphy, 2007) around motivation (Keller, 2008) and deep learning (Gee, 2008). There have also been attempts to create models combining learning theory, game design and flow theory (Kiili, 2005) and meta-models (Gentile et al., 2014). However, there is still conflict about how to effectively merge instructional design and. Therefore, we have generated a model that includes the three essential components of the DGBL: 1) **The characteristics of the game**: a stimulating universe, clear rules, a dynamic interface, the possibility of feedback, the increase in skills and levels, simulations of situations 2) **The related characteristics of the player**: a taste for challenge, fantasy, commitment to the task of achieving a goal and a reward, feedback linked to actions to progress, enjoyment of the game 3**) The characteristics of the targeted area of competence**: multimodal communicative interactions, team spirit, cooperation, development of the spirit of the player.

3. METHODOLOGY

The experiment was carried out in two distinct phases. The first was to establish a grid of expected skills in expression-communication (E-C) for students entering the IUT. The APC recommends reflexive evaluation methods based on a reference frame of competences, but no common evaluation grid for E-C competences at the IUT existed. In order to establish it, work was carried out at the local and national level involving twenty-three IUT E-C professors and two experienced researchers. The creation of this grid led to a submission and acceptance to Ludovia CH3 2020, and we summarize our work below. The final version of the grid is composed of three blocks of competences: Expression-Written Communication (**ECE**), Expression-Oral Communication (**ECO**) and Expression-Interpersonal Communication (**ECI**). The set brings together thirteen transversal skills that can be used in various professional activities. Seven for ECE: 1) mastering documentary research, 2) knowing the Net deontology, 3) using word processing tools, 4) analyzing documents, 5) synthesizing, 6) structuring, 7) writing professional documents. Three for ECI: 8) mastering oral presentation techniques, 9) professionally using digital tools, 10) knowing non-verbal communication. And three for ECI: 11) working in a team, 12) inserting oneself into the professional environment through life skills, 13) enriching one's personal culture. Each skill is associated with several tasks, for example, for skill n°11 we find the task "I think about staying in regular communication with the other members of the group". The degree of mastery of which is assessed according to five levels ranging from non-acquisition to complete acquisition of the skill. The ninety-three tasks are classified by increasing difficulty to acquire during the first or second semester. This reference grid was used for the pre- and post-tests of our experiment.

The second step was to build a scientific protocol. Within the framework of action research, an experimental protocol was built between the author, two researchers, and a pedagogical engineer. The experiment took place in 2019. The choice of the game was the Lord of the Rings Online (LotRO) software that met the DGBL's criteria. The target student audience is the first year students of Networks and Telecommunications at the IUT (N=14). The students' diverse backgrounds (3 vocational baccalaureate students, 4 technological baccalaureate students, 7 scientific baccalaureate students), their heterogeneous levels of competence in relation to academic disciplines and the professional world, their small number and their primarily masculine gender (M=13, F=1) made them good candidates. A questionnaire based on that of the fundamental research project *Ludespace* of the University of Tours determined that they were mostly experienced digital game players (1 moderate, 7 casual and 6 enthusiasts) and served as a basis for the constitution of five game teams. These teams were developed according to the "cross-functional teams" principle advocated by Gee (2008, p. 37). This team profile makes it possible to call upon the internal resources of each team member.

The first session, at the beginning of the school year, consisted in having a pre-test self-evaluation of skills completed in relation to the E-C reference grid. In addition, two argumentative writings in the first and last session were marked by an external expert on the basis of the ECE competence block. The second session was an opportunity to explain the whole sequence and the use of a wiki site on the digital workspace of the IUT. This wiki was used as a portfolio; the works and reflections selected and organized by the students were deposited there during the experimentation period and reported on the learning and development of the students' skills. The wiki was evaluated using the ECI competence block by the experimenters. Two sessions were devoted to creating the avatar and exiting the tutorial area. The next four sessions were dedicated to playing the game in the classroom: after a time of discovering the possibilities of adventures in LotRO, teams were asked to imagine an original adventure, outside of the quests of the game itself, and to make another team in the class experience it. The last session was a group oral presentation, where students were asked to discuss, in front of the class, the contributions of such a sequence in relation to their professional experience as an apprentice. An external expert using the ECO skills block evaluated the oral presentation. Afterwards, the students filled in the E-C reference grid as a post-test. The data concerning ECO, ECI and ECE have been entered in .xslx and .docx files. The total duration of the sequence was twenty-five hours spread over the first semester until December 2019.

4. RESULTS AND DISCUSSION

Compared to LotRO's gaming environment, the game's "old school" graphics did not prevent students from immersing themselves in this universe which presents families of situations that correspond to their taste for video games, but also to the professional world in the rationalization of tasks and professional postures to adopt in order to achieve a common goal. As for the students, it was difficult for them to use a video game as a serious game and to get out of the patterns imposed by the game's quests to imagine their own adventures. The variables of the levels of play and the origin of the baccalaureate that served as a basis for the team's compositions worked with four teams out of five. These four teams carried out all the stages of the protocol up to the final oral defense by helping each other. Although there was a general enthusiasm for these sessions, it was not the passionate players who made the most progress, but the teams that showed the most solidarity.

Student's tests revealed a significant p-value according to R. Fisher (1959) for the class on all blocks ($p=0.0371$) concerning their self-assessment. Six students made strong progress ($p<0.05$). Concerning the external examiner, only one statistical significance was found for the ECE skill block, the external examiner corrected the argumentative texts at the beginning and at the end of the sequence ($p=0.03$).

5. CONCLUSION

The purpose of our research was to verify if students with a specific profile can work on academic E-C skills by playing a MMOPG and improve them. A precise inventory of these skills was first necessary, and then academic activities related to LotRO were set up for experimentation. The advantages of such an experiment are threefold: 1) the game allows for the building of authentic communication situations related to the ninety-three tasks of the three blocks identified ECE, ECO and ECI. It confirms a similar result obtained with another MMORPG, World of Warcraft (Rausch, Faßhauer, Martens, 2012). 2) Digital game-based learning can be a powerful motivational engine for working on skills deemed difficult such as writing (ECE) with an audience of apprentice technicians. 3) Finally, student assessment to measure their trajectory meets the recommendations of the APC, putting into action skills that rely on the mobilization of a variety of LotRO resources works.

However, the experiment showed the limitations of a protocol that did not sufficiently distinguish between the tasks performed by each student, the acculturation necessary for the process of self-evaluation by the students, and the reference grid of skills that must be adjusted at each game session. These results have led us to carry out a new experiment in September 2020 that will be even more anchored in the logic of the APC.

These results could help to better integrate MMORPG-type games into targeted university curricula in France, which is lagging behind on this issue (Subhash and Cudney, 2018).

In January 2020, this project received a certificate of excellence from the French Ministry of Higher Education, Research and Innovation.

REFERENCES

Chaudy Y. and Connolly TM., 2018. Integrating assessment, feedback, and learning analytics in educational games: literature review and design of an assessment engine. *In* Azevedo A. and Azevedo J. (eds), Handbook of Research on E-Assessment *in Higher Education*. Idea Group Inc., pp. 127-169.

Chauvigné C. and Coulet J.-C., 2010. L'approche par compétences : un nouveau paradigme pour la pédagogie universitaire ? *In Revue française de pédagogie*, 172, pp. 15-28.

Cheng Y. et al., 2013. Investigating elementary school students' technology acceptance by applying digital game-based learning to environmental education. *Australasian Journal of Educational Technology*, Vol. 29, No.1, pp. 96-110.

Crocco F. et al., 2016. A Proof-of-Concept Study of Game-Based Learning in Higher Education. Simulation & Gaming, Vol. 47, N°4, pp. 403-422.

Fisher RA., 1959. *Statistical Methods and Scientific Inference*. (Ed 2). Oliver and Boyd, Edinburgh.

Gee J.P., 2008. Learning and Games. *The Ecology of Games: Connecting Youth, Games, and Learning*. Edited by K. Salen. MA: The MIT Press, Cambridge.

Gentile D. A. and al., 2014. The general learning model: Unveiling the teaching potential of video games. *In Learning by playing: Video gaming in education*, Blumberg, Oxford, UK, pp. 121–144.

Girard C. et al., 2013. Serious games as new educational tools: how effective are they? A meta-analysis of recent studies. *Journal of Computer Assisted Learning*, Vol. 29, No. 3, pp. 207-219.

Keller J. M., 2008. An integrative theory of motivation, volition and performance. *Technology, Instruction, Cognition, and Learning*, Vol. 6, No. 2, pp. 79-104.

Kiili K., 2005. Digital game-based learning: Towards an experiential gaming model. *The Internet and Higher Education*, Vol. 8, No.1, pp.13-24.

Murphy S., 2007. A Social Meaning Framework for Research on Participation in Social Online Games, *Journal of Media Psychology,* Vol. 12, No. 3, pp. 13-23.

Perrenoud P., 2011. *Quand l'école prétend préparer à la vie... Développer des compétences ou enseigner d'autres savoirs?* ESF Editeur, Paris.

Poumay M. et al., 2017. *Organiser la formation à partir des compétences : un pari gagnant pour l'apprentissage dans le supérieur*. De Boeck Supérieur, Louvain.

Prensky M., 2001. *Digital game-based learning*. McGraw Hill, New York.

Sourmelis, T. et al., 2017. Massively multiplayer online role-playing games (MMORPGs) and the 21st century skills: a comprehensive research review from 2010 to 2016. *Computers in Human Behavior*, Vol. 67, pp. 41-48.

Subhash S. and Cudney E., 2018. Gamified learning in higher education: A systematic review of the literature. *Computers in Human Behavior*, Vol. 87, pp.192-206.

Tardif J., 2006. *L'évaluation des compétences : document le parcours de développement*. Chenelière Education, Montréal.

Taylor T.L., 2006. *Play Between Worlds: exploring Online Game Culture*. MIT Press, Cambridge.

Yang Y., 2012. Building virtual cities, inspiring intelligent citizens: Digital games for developing students' problem solving and learning motivation. *Computers & Education*, Vol. 59, No. 2, pp. 365-377.

IMMERSIVE LEARNING FOR TEACHER EDUCATION

Eric Tarantini
University of St.Gallen, St. Jakobstrasse 21, 9000 St.Gallen, Switzerland

ABSTRACT

Virtual Reality technology (VR) offers new potentials for immersive learning and teaching. Nevertheless, its concrete use in education still lacks of a theoretical foundation and use cases. The present contribution describes the creation of a framework based on the concepts of Storytelling and immersive Learning to set a base for the beneficial use of VR in education. Furthermore, those results are transferred to the field of teacher education. Key findings are that (I): Educational Storyliving represents a promising method to be used for a didactically beneficial use of VR in education, (II): VR inherits the characteristic to foster the teaching of emotional and classroom management skills for novice teachers.

KEYWORDS

Immersive Learning, Digital Storytelling, Storyliving, Virtual Reality, Teacher Education

1. INTRODUCTION

Virtual Reality (VR) provides new perspectives in teaching and learning. It offers the opportunity to depict immersive worlds of experience and to immerse oneself in them (Hodgson et al., 2019; Parker et al., 2016; Google News Lab, 2017). Recent research efforts show, that immersive technologies are likely to produce positive emotions when used properly, which potentially lead to a relatively higher user performance (Hwang et al., 2016; Nissim & Weissblueth, 2017; Suh & Prophet, 2018). Moreover, it indicates that immersive pedagogy can be effectively strengthened and enabled by using VR (Schmoelz, 2018; Parker et al., 2016). Nevertheless, the didactically beneficial use of VR in education still represents an important question to be answered. Nissim and Weissblueth (2017) underline that "VR in education requires a detailed pedagogical examination of situations where students can be involved with educational creations". This paper focuses on the development of a theoretical framework to foster the pedagogically beneficial use of VR in education at high school and upper secondary level. In addition, the findings will be transferred to teacher education. However, a detailed statistical analysis is not subject of this paper and will be carried out will be carried out in future research projects on the topic. In light of this, the research question being discussed in this paper is the following one: *How can a theoretical framework for immersive learning be successfully integrated into teacher education?*. The paper is structured as follows: the first section focuses on the modelling process: 1) What concepts can be taken into account to create a solid base for VR use in education? 2) How can a framework be developed from those concepts for the beneficial use of VR in education as a core result and contribution of this research?; the second section transfers the result to the field of teacher education and shows perspectives for future research efforts.

2. CURRENT STATE OF RESEARCH

Raising the status of the current state of research sets the base for the modelling of a theoretical framework supporting the didactically meaningful use of VR in education.

Virtual Reality in Education. Virtual Reality can be defined as "experience in which agents interact within a three-dimensional (3D) world with movement of their body, experiencing images and sounds" (Sherman & Craig, 2002). Billingsley et al. (2019) defined "immersive VR" as "an advanced form of human-computer interface that allows the user to interact with and become immersed in a computer-generated environment in a naturalistic fashion". Summing up, Beck (2019) from the ILMxLAB (Lucasfilm's immersive entertainment studio) explained that "AR (Augmented Reality) lets you see the world differently, VR lets you see a different world". Consequently, it is important to underline, that the level of immersion and the resulting experience differs depending on the used technology. Concerning education, VR inherits the potential to "teach experientially about the real world whether in the past, present or future" (Nissim & Weissblueth, 2017). An interesting finding is that VR environments have a notable impact on feelings and emotions due to the immersive character of the technology (Beck, 2019; Nissim & Weissblueth, 2017). Especially when students face a complex challenge and manage to deal with it, positive emotions are unleashed. The fact that VR creates strong emotions is an important finding, which makes it very interesting for education and learning (Nissim & Weissblueth, 2017).

Digital storytelling. Classical sotrytelling can be enriched by modern, digital media (Donert, 2017). Consequently, digital storytelling represents a combination of multimediatic elements (such as video, text, music, etc.) used to energize a clear message and classical storytelling (Robin & McNeil, 2012). Stories naturally involve and emotionalize the participant, as they are usually written in the first person in order to hold his or her interest (Donert, 2017). A major benefit for educational purposes is the characteristic of digital stories to increase visual memory capacity (Robin & McNeil, 2012; Wu & Chen, 2020). Parker et al. (2016) found that VR acts very well as an enabler of digital storytelling as the participant can take action.

Immersive Learning Environments. Immersive learning represents a media-rich experience, which supports the creation of realistic real-life context simulations. It is important to mention that the level of immersion can vary from low to high density (Schmoelz, 2018). A highly immersive experience implies that the user is intensively involved with all his or her senses: Bodily, orally and visually (Schmoelz, 2018; Cooper et al., 2019). Studies revealed that first the level of immersion determinates resulting learning outcomes (Schmoelz, 2018). Secondly, also conceptual learning gains positively correlate with the level of immersion of a learning experience (Georgiou & Kyza, 2018; Hwang et al., 2016). Thirdly, with VR and IVR (Immersive VR) embedded in the classroom, the learning satisfaction and interest in the topic was remarkably higher (Hodgson et al., 2019; Parker et al., 2016). VR platforms can have a transformative effect on education (Cooper et al., 2019). This effect has been demonstrated in a fully immersive setting but also by using 360-degree video technology displayed with VR technology support (Rupp et al., 2019).

3. RESULTS

3.1 Educational Storyliving Framework

Arising from the world of gaming, the term "Storyliving" describes an immersive experience, where there is no "one-way communication" like in classical storytelling but a real interaction instead. The user can act in and influence a virtual environment (Beck, 2019). Consequently, Storyliving can result as a suitable concept to implement immersive VR meaningfully in education. In particular because it inherits the ability to shape and create emotions (Beck, 2019). To sum up, a theoretical framework for Storyliving can be established from the findings in chapter 2 of this paper. Accordingly, "Educational Storyliving" can be defined as a combination of two concepts: *(Educational) Digital Storytelling* (1), describing a facilitated production of a short digital story in an educational community setting (Wu & Chen, 2020) and *highly immersive learning through high immersive density* (2) (Schmoelz, 2018). This combination creates a pedagogically meaning- and useful base for the use of VR technology in education (Andone & Frydenberg, 2019). The following illustration shows the theoretical framework:

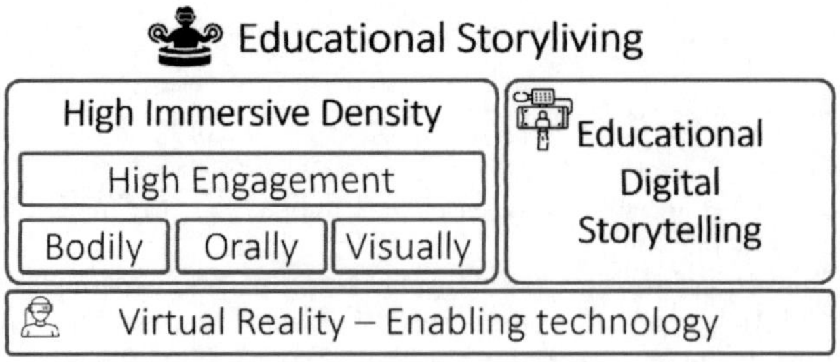

Figure 1. Framework for Educational Storyliving. Own illustration

"Educational Storyliving" can be implemented through the design of digital stories with an immersive character. The technical realization will be discussed in the following chapter. In consequence, this leads and enables a learning process driven by experience-making (experiential learning). To sum up, this framework can be used for upper-secondary but also for high school education.

3.2 Storyliving in Teacher Education

According to research from Nissim and Weissblueth (2017) and Theelen et al. (2019), VR offers potential for two specific areas in teacher education: 1) *Classroom management* represents an important skill to learn for every single novice teacher. In contrast to novice teachers, experienced teachers are constantly scanning the classroom. This allows them to notice events within the classroom at an early stage. 2) The further development of *emotional intelligence* and *teaching empathy* allows novice teachers to be more sensible regarding what is happening to themselves and their students in different situations (Snelson & Hsu, 2020). VR allows the display of real-life classroom events. The feeling of presence and emotional involvement it produces could result as highly beneficial for the development of these competencies (Billingsley et al., 2019; Cooper et al., 2019). Especially when the teaching sequences are realized by using Educational Storyliving to create an active experience, learning outcomes for the students could be enhanced (Nissim & Weissblueth, 2017). The arising question is, how to develop and technically enable digital stories in order to create Educational Storyliving. From personal experiences, a practical and cost-saving approach is to use 360-degree video technology (Theelen et al., 2019). A first example is described below:

Figure 2. Example for Educational Storyliving in Teacher Education with hotspots. Own illustration

As shown in figure 2, Educational Storyliving can be used to visualize decision situations. Being bodily, orally and visually immersed in a classroom with VR, the student can actively influence the teaching scenario with his or her decisions. The scenario of the teaching sequence can thereby be supported by telling the story of a teaching unit, where you as the responsible teacher have to prepare a group task. As illustrated in the picture, your next move could be to decide whether to "explain the taks in detail" or to "wait for the students to be silent". Technically, this can be realized by using 360-degree video technology and the implementation of "hotspots" (Fig. 2) via a software solution like Omnivirt (www.omnivirt.com). Creating and programming virtual environments is much more cost intensive and would require a partnership with a specialized firm. Theelen et al. (2019) argue, that 360-degree videos are highly useful in teacher education because they allow to individually choose a specific perspective when observing classroom interactions dynamically. Furthermore, online platforms like YouTube allow to easily share 360-degree videos (Aguayo et al., 2017). Generally spoken, it is important to consider, that "well working VR environments are required for an immersive learner experience" (Theelen et al., 2019). Therefore, it is indispensable to deliberately implement the technology.

4. CONCLUSION

To conclude, VR may be a promising digital tool for teacher education and education in general. Based on experiences from the gaming industry and educational experts, Educational Storyliving could result as a suitable approach to involve students in immersive teaching experiences. This method can transform VR in a didactically powerful medium. However, there are some limitations to this research. First of all, it would be interesting and insightful if this research would be challenged from experts in other fields. My perspective on VR mainly arises from the educational sector. Secondly, the pure conceptualization and modelling of framework is only the first step. A thourough investigation of the learning outcomes represents the next, crucial footmark. Future research should consequently explore how to realise effective Educational Storyliving by creating use cases (Snelson & Hsu, 2020). For example, STEM education may benefit from experiential learning processes supported by VR technology (Wang & Degol, 2017). To sum up, VR differentiates itself from other teaching mediums because of its characteristic to create emotionally involving immersive experiences. Through its proper implementation into education by using a concept like Storyliving, VR unfolds its potential and allows to experientially learn in another world.

REFERENCES

Aguayo, C. et al. (2017). Key themes in mobile learning: Prospects for learner-generated learning through AR and VR. *Australasian Journal of Educational Technology,* Vol. 33, No. 6, pp. 27-40. DOI: https://doi.org/10.14742/ajet.3671

Andone, D. & Frydenberg, M. (2019). Creating Virtual Reality in a Business and Technology Education Context. *In Tom Dieck, C. & Jung, T. (Eds.). Augmented Reality and Virtual Reality. The Power of AR and VR for Business*, pp. 147-160. Cham: Springer Verlag.

Beck, V. D. (2019). *ILMxLAB: From Storytelling to Storyliving.* Retrieved from https://www.youtube.com/watch?v=Or_U3K7TmtY

Billingsley, G. et al. (2019). A Systematic Literature Review of Using Immersive Virtual Reality Technology in Teacher Education. *Journal of Interactive Learning Research (JILR)*, Vol. 30, No. 1, pp. 65-90.

Cooper, G. et al. (2019). Using virtual reality in the classroom: preservice teachers' perceptions of its use as a teaching and learning tool. *Educational Media International*, Vol. 56, No. 1, pp. 1-13.

Donert, K. (2017). *Literature Review on Telling Digital Stories*. Salzburg: University of Salzburg.

Google News Lab. (2017). *Storyliving. An ethnographical study of how audiences experience VR and what that means for journalists*. Retrieved from newslab.withgoogle.com

Hodgson, P., Lee, V. Chan, J., Fong, A., Tang, C. & Wong, C. (2019). Immersive Virtual Reality (IVR)in Higher Education. Development and Implementation. *In Tom Dieck, C. & Jung, T. (Eds.). Augmented Reality and Virtual Reality. The Power of AR and VR for Business*, pp. 161-174.

Parker, M., Patton, K. & O'Sullivan, M. (2016). Signature pedagogies in support of teachers' professional learning. *Irish Educational Studies*, Vol. 35, No. 2, pp. 137-153.

Nissim, Y. & Weissblueth, E. (2017). Virtual Reality (VR) as a Source for Self-Efficacy in Teacher Training. *International Education Studies,* Vol. 10, No. 8, pp. 52-59.

Robin, B. & McNeil, S. (2012). *What educators should know about digital storytelling.* Texas: University of Houston.

Schmoelz, A. (2018). Enabling co-creativity through digital storytelling in education. *Thinking skills and creativity,* Vol. 28, pp. 1-13.

Sherman, W. R., & Craig, A. B. (2002). *Understanding virtual reality: Interface, application, and design*. Burlington, MA: Morgan Kaufmann.

Snelson, C. & Hsu, Y. (2020). Educational 360-Degree Videos in Virtual Reality: A Scoping Review of the Emerging Research. *TechTrends*, Vol. 64, pp. 404–412.

Theelen, H. et al. (2019). Using 360-degree videos in teacher education to improve preservice teachers' professional interpersonal vision. *Journal of Compuer Assisted Learning*, Vol. 35, pp. 582-594.

Wang, M.-T. & Degol, J. L. (2017). Gender Gap in Science, Technology, Engineering, and Mathematics (STEM): Current Knowledge, Implications for Practice, Policy, and Future Directions. *Educational Psychological Review,* Vol. 29, pp. 119-140.

Wu, J. & Chen, D. (2020). A systematic review of educational digital storytelling. *Computers & Education*, Vol. 147.

MAKE USE OF SELFIE DATA TO GENERATE TARGETED RECOMMENDATIONS FOR SCHOOL TEAMS: TWO INSTRUMENTS

Irina Dvoretskaya[1,2] and Alexander Uvarov[1,2]
[1]*FRC «Computer Science and Control», Russian Academy of Science, Russia*
[2]*Institute of Education, Higher School of Economics, Russia*

ABSTRACT

As SELFIE (Self-reflection tool for digitally capable schools) piloting has shown, self-assessment of the use of digital technologies (DT) in schools provides school teams with a lot of useful information. Nevertheless, as the feedback highlights, school team members are very interested in also getting the specific targeted recommendations for improving work planning in this area. Here we suggest two practical data-driven approaches for preparing such scale-based recommendations.
The first tool is based on Kruskal-Wallis non-parametric test of responses and helps to evaluate if the school develops and supports the shared vision on the integration of DT in the school. It allows us to correspond to the dichotomous scale of a shared vision. It was found out that on the sample level the influence of the shared vision formation is not tangible.
The second tool helps to classify across the sample schools, the progress in the use of innovative teaching and learning with DT. Each school was attributed based on the variability of teachers' and school leaders' responses. A cluster analysis was implemented to classify results. Ten clusters obtained were assigned to three out of five levels of the RISC (Reinventing School Coalition) metric/scale.

KEYWORDS

Self-Assessment Data, Cluster Analysis, Digital Capacity of Schools, Shared Vision, Digital Transformation of Education

1. INTRODUCTION

SELFIE (Self-reflection tool for digitally capable schools) is an online platform that provides assessment and insights of how digital technologies are used in the educational process through the eyes of its participants (Munoz Castano et al., 2018). Survey respondents of SELFIE are school leaders, teachers and students, to whom a special questionnaire is assigned, based on DigCompOrg model (Kampylis, Punie and Devine, 2015). As a result of processing the anonymous survey, each school gets an automatically generated report that indicates the average response rates. It is accepted that the teaching staff will use the report to analyze and discuss evidence-based strategies for improvement of their schools.

Schools for the study were chosen from IITE and UNESCO Associated Schools Project Network (UNESCO ASP), within the scope of the SELFIE pilot project in which Russia took part in October 2017. The pilot in Russia was conducted by UNESCO IITE. Three samples were surveyed: school principals (N = 206), school teachers (N = 685), and students (N = 3055).

During the SELFIE workshop, participants from 16 countries agreed that SELFIE reports help the teaching staff to evaluate the progress and results of their work on the DT integration in teaching and learning (Commission, 2019). At the same time, school staff expressed interest in receiving relevant and detailed recommendations to enhance digital transformation of their schools. The paper contributed to the specific recommendations development approach, and assumed an integrative assessment of the specific characteristics with their meaningful interpretation based on quantitative data. Analysis of the SELFIE pilot results has shown that, based on proposed data-driven scales, it is possible to develop the specific recommendations on the formation of a shared vision on the integration of DT in educational process, and the use of innovative teaching and learning with DT.

2. INSTRUMENTS DESIGN

2.1 A Dichotomous Categorization

The idea of dichotomous categorization is based on a theoretical grounded scale (Kools & Stoll, 2016) and on premise, that discussions in the school community serve as a tool to shape a shared vision. The assessment of the nature of such discussions can be treated as an indicator of the extent to which, the formation of a shared vision on the use of digital technologies in teaching and learning is endorsed in a particular school. It can serve as a basis for the development of certain recommendations that are provided as feedback to SELFIE school participants. The dichotomous categorization includes three steps:

1. To build a dichotomous scale, where 0 – shared vision is not shaped, 1 – shared vision is shaped.
2. To conduct a survey. This methodology can use Likert scale data collected from school leaders, teachers and students, with questions on the advantages and limitations of digital technologies (DT) in the classroom, and on the use of DT to enhance the effectiveness of teaching and learning.
3. To determine characteristics. A set of variables is defined as $\{V_d, V_e\}$ (table 1):

Table 1. Variables and statistical procedures

Variable	Type	Statistical procedures
V_d	Binary variable, characterized the discussion of the advantages and limitations of DT in the classroom	1. Levene's test 2. Kruskal-Wallis H-test 3. Post-hoc Dunn's test
V_e	Binary variable, characterized the use of DT to enhance the effectiveness of teaching and learning	1. Levene's test 2. Kruskal-Wallis H-test

4. To categorize variable states. When both V_d and V_e showed that there is no consistent difference in responses, it is treated as "Shared vision on DT in teaching and learning is shaped", otherwise it is treated as "Shared vision on DT in teaching and learning is not shaped".

2.2 A K-Mode Clustering Algorithm with Qualitative Validation

The idea of a combined procedure is based on the interpretation of quantitative data obtained after cluster analysis of a survey of teachers and school leaders (Vodopian and Uvarov, 2005), and the concept of the stages of development (maturity) of the school informatization (Lee and Broadie, 2016). It allows the matching of data on the use of innovative teaching and learning with DT, and judgments based on maturity models of the innovative processes in the school. The combined procedure includes four steps.

1. To conduct a survey in order to collect the data for further analysis. This methodology can use survey five-point Likert data collected, from at least two cohorts of actors of educational process, wherein a survey contains an item on innovative DT-supported teaching and learning.
2. To determine characteristics. For each school, a group of characteristics is calculated that reflects whether a school is working, both consistently and constantly on the use of innovative DT-supported teaching and learning. A set of variables defined at school level:

$$\{SL_{consensus}, SL_{coherence}, T_{consensus}, T_{coherence}\}$$

$SL_{consensus}$ – how coordinated are the efforts of school leaders to use innovative DT-supported teaching and learning;

$SL_{coherence}$ – how consistent are the efforts of school leaders to use innovative DT-supported teaching and learning;

$T_{consensus}$ – how coordinated are the efforts of teachers to use innovative DT-supported teaching and learning at school level;

$T_{coherence}$ – how consistent are the efforts of teachers to use innovative DT-supported teaching and learning at school level.

To determine the value of consistency variables, the proportions of positive answers ("agree" and "absolutely agree") are calculated for each group of respondents. If at least 60% of positive answers, the value of both variables is fixed as "high". Otherwise, it is fixed as "low". When determining the value of coordination variables, a standardized characteristic is calculated - a measure of variability (Allaj, 2018). The meaning of the coordination of efforts is evaluated as "low" if the variability measure of answers is far from 0.553 or 1, and "high" when the measure of the variability of answers is close to 0.553 or 1.

3. To cluster schools. The k-mode clustering algorithm is applied. When choosing the number of clusters, one uses qualitative descriptions of the resulting clusters after calculating the optimal number of clusters (using the elbow method). Here, one evaluates clusters in terms of significant differences in the use of innovative DT-supported teaching and learning at school level.

4. To correspond the cluster structure against maturity levels. At this step the resulting cluster structure is corresponded to the maturity scale of the innovation process by expert evaluation. We use the five-level scale of the innovation process maturity model of RISC model (DeLorenzo and Battino, 2008).

3. RESEARCH RESULTS

3.1 A Shared Vision on the Integration of DT in Educational Process

To assess a shared vision on the integration of DT based on the technique proposed, we used two triads of items of "Leadership and Management" component of the DigCompOrg framework (Dvoretskaya, 2018):

- Items on the discussion of the advantages and limitations of DT in the classroom, were coded as L1, T1, and S1 for school leaders, teachers, and students, respectively.
- Items on the use of digital technology to enhance the effectiveness of teaching and learning, were coded as L2, T2, and S2 for school administrators, teachers, and students, respectively.

Statistical results evidenced that respondents differ in how they view the advantages and disadvantages of digital technologies in teaching and learning ($p = 0.000$), and at the same time, they agree that it is desirable to use digital technologies in schools to improve the effectiveness of teaching and learning (table 2).

Table 2. Statistical results

	Levene's test		Kruskal–Wallis H test	
	F	p	H	p
School leaders, teachers, and students	7,38	0,000 ***	20,58	0,000 ***
L1, T1, S1 L2, T2, S2	5,91	0,003 **	0,003	0,998
Significance levels: ** p < 0.01. *** p < 0.001.				

As the Dunn's test shows, there is a statistically significant difference in the positions of the three groups of respondents regarding the discussion of the advantages and disadvantages of using digital technology in school. Categorizing results, we can conclude, that the shared vision needs to be developed.

3.2 The Use of Innovative Teaching and Learning with DT

To assess the use of innovative teaching and learning with DT, we used the combined technique in the processing of school principals ($N = 206$) and school teachers ($N = 685$) in SELFIE. The distribution of schools, according to clustering, showed that all schools already realized the need to use innovative DT-supported ways of teaching and learning. However, schools organize this work in different ways (table 3).

Table 3. School cluster structure against RISC maturity levels

Level of RISC scale	Clusters	Number of schools
Awareness	2, 3, 6, 7,8, 9	16
Understanding	1,5	5
First implementation	4	2
Usage	-	-
Elaboration	-	-

All schools are at least introducing innovative DT-supported teaching and learning. In most schools (the level of "Awareness"), the corresponding processes are ad-hoc. Individual teachers and / or school leaders initiate the use of innovative DT-supported teaching and learning here. One can distinguish a group of schools in which the use of innovative teaching and learning, using DT, has become manageable (the level of “Understanding”). In two schools (the level of “First implementation” on the scale), a manageable process has already been established for the implementation and use of innovative DT-supported ways of teaching and learning with a solid and systematic support of it.

4. CONCLUSION

The results of the assessment of two parameters, obtained using the procedures described, were discussed with SELFIE school coordinators, involved in piloting, during aftermath interviews and feedback collection. As these discussions have shown, additional feedback prepared in this way, enriches the computer generated basic SELFIE reports significantly. School coordinators and school teams found out that detailed and targeted recommendations on the formation of a shared vision and DT supported innovative teaching, can endorse digital transformation processes in their schools. Computations based on the procedures given above can be fully automated with the recommendations obtained that will be reverted to schools.

In future work, it will be required to check the validity of the developed procedures on sufficient sample size, reflecting the diversity of schools that participate in SELFIE. At the same time, it is necessary to prepare detailed guidelines for school teams that will help them, in cooperation with local communities, to interpret the results of SELFIE obtained together with targeted recommendations.

ACKNOWLEDGEMENT

The reported study was funded by RFBR, project number №19-29-14167. The authors would like to thank Prof. Alexander Khoroshilov, who initiated the piloting SELFIE in Russia, Marina Korobeinikova from UNESCO IITE, who led the piloting and Dr. Panagiotis Kampylis from EC JRC for the collaboration.

REFERENCES

Allaj, E. (2018) ‘*Two simple measures of variability for categorical data*’, Journal of Applied Statistics, 45(8).

Commission, E. (2019) *SELFIE Forum - teaching and learning in the digital age*, 4-5 April 2019, Madrid.

DeLorenzo, R. A. and Battino, W. (2008) *Delivering on the Promise: The Education Revolution*. Solution Tree.

Dvoretskaya, I. V. (2018) ‘*O sformirovannosti obshchego videniya na ispol'zovanie IKT v uchebnoj rabote v shkole*’, Nauka i shkola, 5

Kampylis, P., Punie, Y. and Devine, J. (2015) *Promoting Effective Digital-Age Learning - A European Framework for Digitally-Competent Educational Organisations*. Luxembourg: Publications Office of the European Union.

Kools, M. and Stoll, L. (2016) ‘*What Makes a School a Learning Organisation ?*’ (137).

Lee, M. and Broadie, R. (2016) ‘*A Taxonomy of School Evolutionary Changes: Evolution within the Threads*’, Igarss

Munoz Castano, J. et al. (2018) ‘*Within-School Differences In The Views On The Use Of Digital Technologies In Europe: Evidence From The Selfie Tool*’, in EDULEARN18

Vodopian G., Uvarov, A. (2005) *Ob odnom instrumente dlya ocenki i upravlenyia razvitiem processa informatizacii shkoly*’ // Voprosy obrazovanyia, №3, 2005. Available at: https://vo.hse.ru/2005--3/27044397.html

FAKE NEWS RESILIENCE THROUGH ONLINE GAMES? TENTATIVE FINDINGS FROM A RANDOMIZED CONTROLLED TRIAL IN HIGHER EDUCATION

Christoph Pimmer, Christoph Eisemann and Mateescu Magdalena
FHNW University of Applied Sciences and Arts Northwestern Switzerland
Peter Merian-Strasse 86, 4002 Basel - Switzerland

ABSTRACT

Learners' cognitive abilities to assess the credibility of information in digital spaces are part of 21st century skills. Emerging evidence suggests that gamification could be a suitable approach for learners to develop these skills independently of their educational level. This study examined two popular online fake news games in a higher education setting using a randomized controlled trial. 72 students were randomly assigned to one of two games. Their ability to classify news, i.e. to distinguish fake news from correct news, was tested before and after playing the game. The results from multiple regression analysis suggest that there was only a very modest increase in participants' news classification abilities in one game and no improvement in the other game. Contrary to some prior literature, these preliminary findings provide no evidence for the use of gamification in developing students' fake news resilience in higher education contexts and they call for more nuanced education and gamification approaches.

KEYWORDS

Fake News, Disinformation, Gamification, Serious Games, Fake News Resilience

1. INTRODUCTION AND BACKGROUND

False and fake news are a phenomenon which is deeply entrenched in today's information society. Fake news is connected to online media and social networks in particular, because on these platforms misinformation spreads remarkably farther, faster, deeper and more broadly than the truth (Vosoughi et al., 2018). The social and political consequences are potentially devastating. It has been suggested, for example, that false online stories can negatively impact political decision making in elections (Persily, 2017). In this light it is worrying that young people have little confidence in their ability to recognize fake news online (Notley & Dezuanni, 2019). The most promising strategy in fighting fake news is conceived to be the education of users (Waldrop, 2017). However, in many cases the attempt to correct false beliefs had limited effects or was even counterproductive, particularly regarding polarizing topics, such as vaccination (e.g. Pluviano, Watt, Ragazzini, & Della Sala, 2019).

A more pro-active way is thus to equip users with the methodological repertoire that permits them to detect fake news before misconceptions strike roots. A promising approach to achieving this is gamification. Games and gamified approaches are, according to a recent meta-reviews, more effective than many other forms of learning (e.g. Bai, Hew, & Huang, 2020). In the field of fake news and media literacy education there is an increasing number of online games and gamified approaches available. However, the evidence for their effectiveness is thin. There are many games which have not been researched and the few published studies often concentrate on design and usability (e.g. Urban, Hewitt, & Moore, 2018) or rely on self-reported measures. One of the few exceptions is the Bad News Game. A large-scale, pretest-post test study with 15'000 participants provides initial evidence for the effectiveness of this game (Roozenbeek & van der Linden, 2019) and a randomized controlled trial further affirmed these positive results (Basol, Roozenbeek, & van der Linden, 2020). The main finding was that playing the online game "bad news" increased people's ability to detect disinformation mostly independently of their socio-demographic and political backgrounds – for example, regardless of their education (Roozenbeek & van der Linden, 2019).

The Bad News game is also interesting because it presents one of two predominant gamification approaches in fake news games: Users assume the role of ***fake news spreaders*** (Roozenbeek & van der Linden, 2019). They learn about the mechanisms of deception by seeking to deceive others. The second main gamification approach is the classic, quiz-based concept of ***fake news detection***, where users need to evaluate the credibility of news items, receiving instructions and feedback in this process.

Against this background, the present study explores the effects of two fake news online games on learners' news classification skills in a higher education context. The specific question is whether the games would improve learners' news classification abilities and if so, to what extent?

2. MATERIALS AND METHODS

We examined two games which were representative of the two main game fake news gaming approaches. For the ***fake news spreader*** approach, the above-described Bad News Game (the German version) was chosen. For the ***fake news detection*** approach, the online game Fakefinder from the German public broadcasting corporation Südwestrundfunk was selected. Fakefinder requires users to evaluate a series of news and provides instructions, feedback and background information in this process. The two online games cover similar content and they have also crucial gamification concepts in common, such as progress bars and badges (Bai et al., 2020). Their most notable difference is, as indicated, that players immerse themselves in different, antagonistic roles: either as fake news detectors or as fake news spreaders.

The research questions were addressed by carrying out a two-arm (1:1) repeated measurement randomized controlled trial (n=72). Students from a bachelor degree program from a business school in Switzerland were randomized into two conditions (the two games). The randomization resulted in 19 male students and 17 female students in each of the two conditions. Before and after playing the game, a test was carried out which measured the participants' ability to correctly classify nine news items as fake news or correct news. The news presentation contained a screenshot and the link to the original news artifact that students could access in case they needed further background information. A score was calculated by crediting one point for each correctly classified news item.

3. FINDINGS

The descriptive statistics show a very small overall increase between the pre-test and the post-test across the two conditions. On average, participants increased their ability to detect fake news (i.e. their news classification score) from 6.29 points out of 9 (70%) in the pre-test to 6.58 (73%) in the post test. Table 2 shows the descriptive statistics per condition/game. It can be seen that the increase of the news classification score in the Fakefinder game condition was considerably more pronounced. (Table 1).

Table 1. Descriptive statistics in total and for each condition

News classification score	n	mean	sd	median	min	max	range
Pre-test total	72	6.29	1.76	6	2	9	7
Post-test total	72	6.58	1.57	7	2	9	7
Fake News spreader game: pre-test	36	6.5	1.63	6.5	3	9	6
Fake News spreader game: post-test	36	6.56	1.59	6.5	2	9	7
Fake news detection game: pre-test	36	6.08	1.89	6	2	9	7
Fake news detection game: post-test	36	6.61	1.57	7	3	9	6

In the next step, the connections in the data were analysed through a mixed model regression analysis. To account for the repeated measures, the participants' ID was included as a random factor. We followed a model-contrasting approach using likelihood tests to compare the models (Pinheiro & Bates, 2000). That is, various models were built in which the response variable *news classification score* was predicted by the group (the game), the interaction between time and group, and gender (see Table 2). The statistical analyses were performed in the computing environment R. The mixed models were fitted with the nlme package (Pinheiro & Bates, 2000), r-squared calculations drew on the MuMIn package (Nakagawa & Schielzeth, 2013). Table 2 shows that Model 3 is superior to a random model and to all other models ($LRatio_{Model3}$=9.91, p<.05). It has the highest predictive value, accounting for 28% of the variation.

Table 2. News classification score model and predictor variables

	Model 1	Model 2	Model 3
Condition	-0.18 (0.36)	-0.42 (0.40)	-0.42 (0.39)
Condition* Time (Fake News spreader game)		0.06 (0.23)	0.06 (0.24)
Condition*Time (Fake news detection game)		0.53^{*} (0.23)	0.53^{*} (0.24)
Gender (female)			-0.75^{*} (0.35)
AIC	527.35	526.28	523.70
BIC	539.23	544.10	544.49
Log Likelihood	-259.68	-257.14	-254.85
Adj. R2	.23	.25	.28
Num. obs.	144	144	144
Num. groups: Number	72	72	72

$^{***}p < 0.001$; $^{**}p < 0.01$; $^{*}p < 0.05$

The results show that there was a small but significant positive interaction effect between time and condition for the fake news detection game, but not for the fake news spreading game. In essence, the fake news detection game Fakefinder increased participants' news classification score very modestly whereas the fake news spreader game Bad News did not improve the score at all. Gender (i.e. being female) had a slightly negative effect on the news classification score.

4. DISCUSSION

The findings suggest that playing the fake news detection game amounted to a significant but very small increase in learners' fake news detection skills, whereas playing the fake news spreader game had no significant effects. These findings add to the current literature in that they relativize the impact of fake news games in higher education settings in general. They contrast with findings from Roozenbeek and van der Linden (2019) in particular, who reported that the fake news spreading game Bad News would increase people's ability to spot misinformation irrespective of their education level. The reasons for the limited impact in both games cannot be attributed to a ceiling effect in the response variable, as the learners' average pre-test score of 70% would have permitted room for improvement. These findings would not support the use of gamified interventions that draw on the design principles applied in the two games over other forms of learning and teaching. One way to achieve higher knowledge gains in a higher education context might be the integration of more advanced technical fake news detection strategies, such as image verification techniques (Katsaounidou, Vrysis, Kotsakis, Dimoulas, & Veglis, 2019). Another option could be the integration of further gamification elements that increase the level of engagement and learning, such as competition. Or the use of constructionist learning where users truly create (and not just select) fake news. One example for this is the game studied by Clever et al. (2020), who, however, restricted this idea to the creation of headlines.

Naturally, the study's findings are tentative in nature and need to be interpreted with respect to the methodological limitations. Firstly, the research involved a single site design and it is not clear to what extent the findings can be generalized across other, higher education contexts. Secondly, although we used a randomized between- group and within-group comparison design, the study involved a relatively small numbers of participants. And thirdly, the measurement approach of making users evaluate news, though quite common in the extant literature (e.g. Basol et al., 2020; Roozenbeek & van der Linden, 2019), does not reflect the full concept of digital literacy which might have been gained through playing the games. For example, knowledge about the underlying dynamics of the media system was not covered. Finally, it needs to be acknowledged that the experiment did not reflect real world conditions. The students were primed by the instruction of detecting fake news, which is atypical of their informal, day-to-day news consumption. Future work might thus consider more subtle measurements of learners' "fake news" and media literacy skills.

5. CONCLUSION

Although preliminary in nature, the study suggests that the two games did not impact learners' news classification abilities in meaningful ways, which is in contrast to results from some previous studies. From a practical perspective, these findings call for more nuanced gaming approaches in a higher education context, as outlined.

ACKNOWLEDGEMENT

We would like to thank Christian Tanner, Programme Head Bachelor of Science in Betriebsökonomie Basel and Markus Freiburghaus, the Head of Education, both from the FHNW University of Applied Sciences and Arts Northwestern Switzerland School of Business, for their support of this study. We are also very grateful for the students who agreed to participate in this research.

REFERENCES

Bai, S., Hew, K. F., & Huang, B. (2020). Is gamification "bullshit"? Evidence from a meta-analysis and synthesis of qualitative data in educational contexts. *Educational Research Review*, 100322.

Basol, M., Roozenbeek, J., & van der Linden, S. (2020). Good News about Bad News: Gamified Inoculation Boosts Confidence and Cognitive Immunity Against Fake News. *Journal of Cognition, 3*(1).

Clever, L., Assenmacher, D., Müller, K., Seiler, M. V., Riehle, D. M., Preuss, M., & Grimme, C. (2020). FakeYou! --A Gamified Approach for Building and Evaluating Resilience Against Fake News. *arXiv preprint arXiv:2003.07595.*

Katsaounidou, A., Vrysis, L., Kotsakis, R., Dimoulas, C., & Veglis, A. (2019). MAthE the Game: A Serious Game for Education and Training in News Verification. *Education Sciences, 9*(2). doi:10.3390/educsci9020155

Nakagawa, S., & Schielzeth, H. (2013). A general and simple method for obtaining R2 from generalized linear mixed-effects models. *Methods in ecology and evolution, 4*(2), 133-142.

Persily, N. (2017). The 2016 US Election: Can democracy survive the internet? *Journal of democracy, 28*(2), 63-76.

Pinheiro, J. C., & Bates, D. M. (2000). Mixed-effects models in S and S-PLUS New York. *NY: Springer-Verlag.*

Pluviano, S., Watt, C., Ragazzini, G., & Della Sala, S. (2019). Parents' beliefs in misinformation about vaccines are strengthened by pro-vaccine campaigns. *Cognitive Processing, 20*(3), 325-331. doi:10.1007/s10339-019-00919-w

Roozenbeek, J., & van der Linden, S. (2019). Fake news game confers psychological resistance against online misinformation. *Nature (Palgrave Communications), 5*(1), 12.

Urban, A., Hewitt, C., & Moore, J. (2018). Fake it to make it, media literacy, and persuasive design: Using the functional triad as a tool for investigating persuasive elements in a fake news simulator. *Proceedings of the Association for Information Science and Technology, 55*(1), 915-916.

Waldrop, M. M. (2017). News Feature: The genuine problem of fake news. *Proceedings of the National Academy of Sciences, 114*(48), 12631-12634.

PERSONALITY TRAITS AND PERCEIVED USABILITY EVALUATION OF E-LEARNING PLATFORMS: A CASE STUDY

Prokopia Vlachogianni[1], Nikolaos Tselios[1] and Michalis Xenos[2]
[1]*Department of Educational Sciences and Early Childhood Education, University of Patras*
[2]*Computer Engineering and Informatics Department, University of Patras*
26500 Patras, Rio, Greece

ABSTRACT

The impact of individuals' characteristics on the perceived usability of e-learning systems is a significant, but rather overlooked topic. The goal of this research is to investigate the relation between teachers' personality traits and their perceived usability of the e-class platform using the System Usability Scale (SUS) and the Big 5 Personality test. 1324 teachers of primary and secondary education in Greece participated in the study. Results indicated satisfactory usability levels for the e-class (M=69.68, SD=15.24). Moreover, SUS scores found to be correlated with teachers' ICT in education competency and educational stage. Furthermore, secondary school teachers and teachers holding a PhD or a master's degree rated significantly higher than the primary school teachers and teachers holding only BSc or high school diploma, respectively. However, SUS score was not correlated with age, gender, work experience, private/public school, work relationship (tenured or not) and general ICT competency. Finally, all five personality traits (Extraversion, Conscientiousness, Openness to new experience, Emotional stability, Agreeableness) found to be significantly positive correlated with perceived usability of the e-class platform.

KEYWORDS

Usability, Personality, User Experience, System Usability Scale (SUS), Big 5, E-Class, E-Learning, Learning Management Systems (LMS), Primary Education, Secondary Education, Teachers

1. INTRODUCTION

E-learning platforms are widely used in all educational stages. The successful adoption and use of a platform depends to a large extent on the satisfactory interaction with the user and consequently on its perceived usability (Ardito et al., 2006; Altanopoulou & Tselios, 2017; Tselios et al., 2008). However, even on the same platform the usability ratings may differ depending on the user. It is argued that participants' inherent personality characteristics as well as demographics influence their perceived usability ratings. Thus, the main goal of this study is to examine whether the teachers' personality traits are related with their perceived usability ratings of a widely adopted e-learning platform.

Perceived usability was evaluated by using System Usability Scale (Brooke, 1996) which is the most widely adopted questionnaire for perceived usability evaluation of software and products (Tullis & Albert, 2008). Personality traits were measured with the Big 5 Personality test developed by Goldberg (1992). The Big 5 model gives emphasis on five major personality dimensions: Extraversion, Conscientiousness, Openness to new experience, Emotional stability, and Agreeableness.

Previous research findings concerning the influence of personality to the perceived usability are quite inadequate. Kortum and Oswald (2018) in a dataset of 268 participants rated the perceived usability of 20 everyday products considering the personality traits. Openness to new experience and Agreeableness had the strongest positive correlations with SUS score. Furthermore, in a usability testing of a website conducted by Burnett & Ditsikas (2006) five participants with high scores at extraversion found 40% more usability problems comparing five participants with high scores at introversion. Using a sample of 603 participants, Oliveira et al. (2013) found that Extraversion and Conscientiousness had significant positive correlation with perceived usability of mobile services.

The study presented in this paper has been guided by the following research questions:

RQ1: What are the usability levels of the e-class platform used in primary and secondary education?

RQ2: Which factors seem to be related with SUS score (e.g. age, gender, stage of education, highest level of education, work experience, private/public school, work relationship, school district, and ICT competency)?

RQ3: Is there any relationship between the personality traits and the perceived usability evaluation of the e-class platform used in primary and secondary education in Greece?

2. METHODOLOGY

The participants were 1324 teachers of primary and secondary education in Greece who used e-class platform for distance learning purposes. E-class platform is a Learning Management System provided by the Ministry of Education in Greece. 72.7% of the participants were female, aged 24-67 with a mean age of 45.92 (SD=9.66) years. A questionnaire has been used which comprised a demographics section, and the Greek versions of the System Usability Scale (Brooke, 1996) and the Big Five personality test (Goldberg, 1992) The online questionnaire was distributed through e-mail and social networks from May 18, 2020 to June 20, 2020. SPSS v25 was used for the data analysis.

3. RESULTS

RQ1: Perceived usability levels of the e-class platform

Mean SUS score of e-class platform is 69.68 (SD=15.24). In specific, for primary education participants (N=545) mean SUS rating is 68.18 (SD=15.45) and for secondary education participants (N=779) mean SUS rating is 70.73 (SD=15). Considering the criteria set from Bangor et al. (2009) the e-class platform seems to have satisfactory usability levels but with some issues.

RQ2: Factors related with SUS score

Normal distribution is violated for SUS scores as it is demonstrated by using Kolmogorov-Smirnov and Shapiro-Wilk tests. Possible correlations between the age of participants, gender, stage of education, highest level of education, work experience, private/public school, work relationship, school district, ICT competency and the mean SUS score for the e-class platform were investigated.

No significant correlation was found between SUS score and a) age (rs=-0.017, p=0.545, ns), b) gender (U=169088, Z=-0.765, p=0.444, ns), c) work experience (rs=-0.013, p=0.635, ns), d) private/public school (U=4894, Z=-0.344, p=0.731, ns), e) work relationship (p=0.411, ns) and f) basic level ICT competency (U=109712, Z=-1.601, p=0.109, ns). Mann-Whitney U test examined the relationship between SUS score and educational stage. Teachers' ratings at secondary schools are statistically significantly higher than those of primary education (U=190537, Z=-3.179, p=0.001, s). In addition, teachers' SUS ratings holding a master's and/or a PhD degree were statistically significantly higher than those holding a bachelor's (p < .001, s, p=0.012, s) a degree of technological educational institution (p=0.029, s, p=0.023, s) or a high school diploma (p=0.021, s, p=0.013, s), respectively. A significant correlation was also found between SUS score and ICT competency specialized in educational purposes (U=1080063, Z=-5.621, p < .001, s). Teachers serving in urban districts gave statistically significantly higher SUS ratings than those located in semi-urban areas (p=0.018, s) and teachers in rural districts gave higher SUS ratings than those at semi-urban areas as well (p=0.045, s).

RQ3: Personality traits and perceived usability

Possible relationship was examined between perceived usability and the personality traits, as they were derived from the SUS scores at System Usability Scale and Big 5 personality test, respectively (see Table 1). All five major personality traits were significantly correlated with SUS score; Extraversion (rs=0.094, p=0.001, s), Agreeableness (rs=0.125, p < .001, s), Conscientiousness (rs=0.202, p < .001, s), Emotional Stability (rs=0.174, p < .001, s), Openness to new experience (rs=0.166, p < .001, s) and Total Big 5 score (rs=0.247, p < .001, s).

Table 1. Participants' personality traits and correlation with their SUS ratings
(* and ** indicate significance at the p=0.05 and 0.01 level respectively)

	Mean	SD	SUS-trait correlation (r)
Extraversion	*32.21*	*6.59*	0.094**
Agreeableness	*42.33*	*5.14*	0.125**
Conscientiousness	*40.23*	*6.1*	0.202**
Emotional Stability	*31.17*	*7.54*	0.174**
Openness to new experience	*37.88*	*5.70*	0.166**
Total Big 5 score	183.82	*19.01*	0.247**

4. CONCLUSIONS AND DISCUSSION

This paper sheds light in a significant research issue concerning the impact of personality traits on the perceived usability of the e-class platform. Individual-related factors which affect the perceived usability of a platform are often overlooked. Usability benchmarks are provided for the e-class platform and possible correlations between SUS score and a) gender, b) age, c) stage of education, d) teachers' highest level of education, e) work experience, f) private/public school, g) work relationship (tenured or not), h) school district and i) ICT competency were examined. The findings of this paper can be used as a useful benchmarking guide for improving the usability of e-class platform.

Regarding the research questions, e-class (M=69.68, SD=15.24) seems to have good usability levels but not without flaws, according to the criteria set by Bangor et al. (2009). This result comes in line with Vlachogianni et al. (2020) who analyzed usability benchmarks for 40 Learning Managements Systems and found their mean SUS score 66.88 (SD = 10.88). Furthermore, no significant correlation was found between SUS score and age (rs=-0.017, p=0.545, ns). Previous research results are quite contradictory regarding the relation of these two variables (Binyamin et al., 2016; Orfanou et al. 2015; Granić and Ćukušić, 2011; Bangor et al., 2008; Mujinga et al., 2018). No correlation was also found between gender and SUS score that is validated by previous research findings (Harrati et al., 2016; Kortum, & Sorber, 2015; Bangor et al., 2008; Ituma 2011; Orfanou et al., 2015; Ng et al., 2011; Berkman & Karahoca, 2016; Tossell et al., 2012).

Teachers of secondary education found e-class significantly more usable than those of primary education. This may be related to the general experience they gain interacting with their students using the platform. Students at secondary education usually have more advanced ICT skills compared to primary school children. Therefore, they might experience fewer issues when interacting with the platform. Teachers holding a PhD or a master's degree have statistically significant higher rates at SUS score than the rest. This could be explained by an underlying persistency which high achievers might possess. Thus, such persistency might have been expressed in the context of the study as an intrinsic motivation to learn how to effectively interact with the platform. Teachers at semi-urban school districts gave lower SUS scores in comparison to those at urban (p=0.018, s) and rural (p=0.045, s) districts, respectively. Moreover, teachers with ICT competency specialized in educational purposes rated statistically significantly higher at SUS.

Furthermore, all five personality traits found to be correlated with the perceived usability of e-class platform. That result is partially in line with the results reported by Kortum and Oswald (2018) who found Agreeableness and Openness to new experience have a significant correlation with SUS score.

The current study is not without limitations. First, teachers with lower internet competency skills may have been excluded since the questionnaire was distributed online. Second, generalization of the results obtained is questionable since they concern a partial and perhaps not representative sample of teachers in Greece. Thus, further research analysis using complementary approaches to refine the sampling procedure used might have a significant contribution in terms of validation of the current results.

As far as future work is concerned, it would be interesting to further investigate the impact personality traits have on the perceived usability of the e-class platform. In addition, the expected learning gain should be examined in relation to the perceived usability and the personality traits. Finally, the presented study can be expanded to consider more e-learning platforms used in primary and secondary education to reach more robust conclusions related to the influence of personality on the perceived usability evaluation.

ACKNOWLEDGEMENT

Part of the work presented in this paper has been completed in the context of the project: "ERMIS-F: Web services for environmental risk–Floods". Funding: Interreg V-A Greece – Cyprus.

REFERENCES

Altanopoulou, P., & Tselios, N. (2017). Assessing acceptance toward wiki technology in the context of Higher Education. *The International Review of Research in Open and Distributed Learning (IRRODL)*, *18*(6), 127-149.

Ardito, C., Costabile, M. F., De Marsico, M., Lanzilotti, R., Levialdi, S., Roselli, T., & Rossano, V. (2006). An approach to usability evaluation of e-learning applications. *Universal access in the information society, 4*(3), 270-283.

Bangor, A., Kortum, P. T., & Miller, J. T. (2008). An empirical evaluation of the system usability scale. *Intl. Journal of Human–Computer Interaction, 24*(6), 574-594.

Bangor, A., Kortum, P., & Miller, J. (2009). Determining what individual SUS scores mean: Adding an adjective rating scale. *Journal of usability studies, 4*(3), 114-123.

Berkman, M. I., & Karahoca, D. (2016). Re-assessing the usability metric for user experience (UMUX) scale. *Journal of Usability Studies, 11*(3), 89-109.

Binyamin, S., Rutter, M., & Smith, S. (2016, November). The utilization of system usability scale in learning management systems: A case study of Jeddah Community College. *In the 9th International Conference of Education, Research and Innovation (ICERI2016), International Academy of Technology, Education and Development*, Seville, Spain.

Brooke, J. (1996). SUS-A quick and dirty usability scale. *Usability evaluation in industry, 189*(194), 4-7.

Burnett, G. E., & Ditsikas, D. (2006, December). Personality as a criterion for selecting usability testing participants. *In Proceedings of the International Conference on Information and Communications Technologies*, 599-604.

Goldberg, L. R. (1992). The development of markers for the Big-Five factor structure. *Psychological assessment, 4*(1), 26-42.

Granić, A., & Ćukušić, M. (2011). Usability testing and expert inspections complemented by educational evaluation: A case study of an e-learning platform. *Journal of Educational Technology & Society, 14*(2), 107-123.

Harrati, N., Bouchrika, I., Tari, A., & Ladjailia, A. (2016). Exploring user satisfaction for e-learning systems via usage-based metrics and system usability scale analysis. *Computers in Human Behavior, 61*, 463-471.

Ituma, A. (2011). An evaluation of students' perceptions and engagement with e-learning components in a campus-based university. *Active Learning in Higher Education, 12*(1), 57-68.

Kortum, P., & Oswald, F. L. (2018). The impact of personality on the subjective assessment of usability. *International Journal of Human–Computer Interaction, 34*(2), 177-186.

Kortum, P., & Sorber, M. (2015). Measuring the usability of mobile applications for phones and tablets. *International Journal of Human-Computer Interaction, 31*(8), 518-529.

Mujinga, M., Eloff, M. M., & Kroeze, J. H. (2018). System usability scale evaluation of online banking services: A South African study. *South African Journal of Science, 114*(3-4), 1-8.

Ng, A. W., Lo, H. W., & Chan, A. H. (2011). Measuring the Usability of Safety Signs: A use of system usability scale (SUS). *In proceedings of the International MultiConference of Engineers and Computer Scientist*s, 16-18 March 2011, Hong Kong, China.

Oliveira, R. D., Cherubini, M., & Oliver, N. (2013). Influence of personality on satisfaction with mobile phone services. *ACM Transactions on Computer-Human Interaction (TOCHI), 20*(2), 1-23.

Orfanou, K., Tselios, N., & Katsanos, C. (2015). Perceived usability evaluation of learning management systems: Empirical evaluation of the System Usability Scale. *International Review of Research in Open and Distributed Learning, 16*(2), 227-246.

Tossell, C. C., Kortum, P., Shepard, C., Rahmati, A., & Zhong, L. (2012). An empirical analysis of smartphone personalisation: measurement and user variability. *Behaviour & Information Technology, 31*(10), 995-1010.

Tselios, N., Avouris, N., & Komis, V. (2008). The effective combination of hybrid usability methods in evaluating educational applications of ICT: Issues and challenges. *Education and Information Technologies, 13*(1), 55-76.

Tullis, T., & Albert, B. (2008). *Measuring the user experience: Collecting. Analyzing, and Presenting Usability Metrics.* Elsevier.

Vlachogianni, P., Tselios, N., & Xenos, M. (2020). Perceived usability of Learning Management Systems and University Websites: A systematic review. *In Proceedings of the 14th International Conference on Interfaces and Human Computer Interaction,* 23 – 25 July 2020, Zagreb, Croatia.

CONSIDERATIONS AND REFLECTIONS ON GLOBALIZATION OF RESEARCH-SUPPORTED BEST PRACTICES AND QUALITY STANDARDS FOR ONLINE EDUCATION AND DIGITAL LEARNING

Yaping Gao
Ed.D
Quality Matters, USA
1997 Annapolis Exchange Parkway, Suite 300, Annapolis, Maryland, USA 21401

ABSTRACT

As much of the world is still facing and coping with the COVID-19 pandemic, what can we do, as a connected global educational community, to share research-supported best practices and quality standards for teaching and learning to support each other and help institutions and students achieve their educational goals? Can a US-based, research-supported approach to quality assurance and continuous improvement in online and digital learning, developed for and adopted by over 1200+ higher educational institutions, K-12 schools, and other educational organizations mainly in English-speaking communities for over 15 years, be adapted to educational systems and environments outside of USA? What strategies work best and what considerations need to be employed in initiating and sustaining collaborations and globalizations of best practices in culturally and pedagogically different educational communities?
The presenter from a leading US-based quality assurance organization will share their experience working with various institutions and organizations in non-English speaking regions and their strategies and considerations applied to initiate and develop collaborations and partnerships with the goal to contribute to the establishment of quality assurance processes for online, blended and digital learning for international communities.

KEYWORDS

International Collaboration, Globalization, Online Education, Digital Learning, Quality Assurance, Best Practices

1. INTRODUCTION

Can a US-based, research-supported approach to quality assurance and continuous improvement in online and digital learning, developed for and adopted by over 1200+ higher educational institutions, K-12 schools, and other educational organizations mainly in English-speaking communities for over 15 years, be adapted to educational systems and environments outside of USA? What strategies work best and what considerations need to be employed in initiating and sustaining collaborations and globalizations of best practices in culturally and pedagogically different educational communities?

2. BODY OF PAPER

2.1 US-Based Research-Supported Quality Assurance Process:

The primary components of the US-based quality assurance process includes: 1) five sets of research-supported standards (or rubrics) to guide the design, development and review of online courses and the online components of blended courses; 2) variety of customizable professional development offerings and tracks for administrators, faculty and instructional design support staff to apply the standards for course design, development, and review; 3) a peer-review process for online and blended course reviews resulting in constructive recommendations for continuous improvement, certification of quality and national recognition, and 4) implementation of the quality assurance process as pathway on a continuum to program excellence and student success, achievement of institutional goals, and facilitation of accreditation process.

2.2 Reflections on Globalization of Best Practices and Quality Standards

Several years' efforts in international outreach initiatives in the identified priority communities by the US-based leading quality assurance organization have resulted in many reflections and takeaways on the globalization of research-supported best practices and quality standards, including but not limited to:

1) Just because the research-supported quality standards and related services and processes work well with the majority of US-based institutions and organizations does not mean they will work as well for the international community.
2) Translation is the easiest part of it, but truly accurate translation needs not only high language proficiency, but also acute cultural awareness and complete immersion into the local culture, in addition to deep understanding of and experience in implementing the US-based standards and tools.
3) Adaption is more than translation. When it comes to adaption and localization of standards and services, one size does not fit all. Considerations or adaptations that are important or even essential in one culture or educational environment may not be considered as important or essential.
4) Educational systems and environments vary vastly from country to country, from region to region, and even from local bureau to local bureau depending on the hierarchical governance and regional and national accreditation structure.
5) Although online and blended learning has become mainstream in US and other English-speaking countries, for the rest of the world, it is just starting but with great potentials as the COVID-19 pandemic has pushed quality online and digital learning to the top of priority lists. There are much to be learned from each other and many opportunities to explore collaborations.

3. CONCLUSION

Despite the vast difference among the diverse international education communities in terms of language, culture, pedagogy, technology infrastructure, governance, and more, core elements of teaching and learning remain the same for all. Based on years of working with numerous international communities with very culturally and pedagogically different educational environments, feedback has been collected to formulate a set of international standards, which can be adopted and adapted by any educational institution or organization to help achieve their goals in student-centered learning in their locally prevailing delivery formats, be it online, blended, or technology-enhanced teaching and learning during, after and beyond the COVID-19 pandemic.

REFERENCES

Ding, Y., Gao, Y., & Lu, F. (2017). *The Development of QM-Fudan Higher Education Online Course Quality Standards*, American Journal of Distance Education

Gao, Y.， Legon, R. (2015) *Internationalizing Quality Matters: The China Case*, American Journal of Distance Education, 29:3, 210-219

Quality Matters (2014), *Quality Matters Higher Education Rubric Workbook, Fifth Edition* Quality Matters website (www.qualitymatters.org). Quality Matters research and related documents may be found at *https://www.qualitymatters.org/research*.

Quality Matters (2016), *Quality Matters International Collaboration Principles and Guidelines*

United States Distance Learning Association 2017 International Awards: https://www.usdla.org/awards/2017-awards-winners/

TECHNOLOGIES FOR TRAINING AND INTENTIONAL STANCE

Oronzo Parlangeli[1] and Paul M. Liston[2]
[1]Dipartimento di Scienze Sociali, Politiche e Cognitive, Università di Siena, Siena, Italy
[2]Centre for Innovative Human Systems, Trinity College Dublin, The University of Dublin, Dublin, Ireland

ABSTRACT

Interactions with digital technologies can be based on the adoption of relational strategies which assume that these technologies have mental states. There are at least two reasons to support the hypothesis that intentional stance is the priority relational strategy. First, the evolutionary path that, at an individual level, leads us to take on a design stance towards artifacts and which appears slower, and later, than that relating to the intentional stance. Second, the fact that the recognition of interactive digital technologies as simple artifacts is something that requires commitment and is not immediate: when overloaded we can slide from design stance towards intentional stance.

KEYWORDS

Mental States, Theory of Mind, Relational Strategies, Digital Technologies

1. REFLECTION PAPER

Several studies highlight the ways in which interactions with digital technologies can be based on the adoption of mental models and relational strategies which assume that these technologies have mental states, or intentions. It seems that, at least in some circumstances, when we are dealing with digital technologies we sometimes implement interactive behaviors similar to those that occur between human beings (Parlangeli, Guidi & Fiore Farina, 2012; Thellman, Silvervarg, & Ziemke, 2017; Marchesi et al., 2019; Perez-Osorio & Wykowska, 2020).

Daniel Dennett (1971; 1987) advanced a theoretical framework which can be considered a point of reference, and which proposes three interpretative strategies of the world – the physical stance, the design stance and the intentional stance. The behavioral predictions of entities such as stones or stars are essentially based on the adoption of a physical stance. When, on the other hand, we enter into a relationship with artificial systems, the functional aspects become dominant and therefore relational strategies should be based on the use of the design stance. Finally, with regards to humans the predictions of behavior are based on the thoughts of others, their intentions, beliefs, and mental states, and in these cases we adopt an intentional stance. Dennett proposed that the assumption of one or other stance is due to the suggestions that the systems provide us directly and to the evolution of the interaction with them. However, the consideration that the intentional stance must refer to the capability to elaborate a Theory of Mind -ToM - (Baron Cohen, 1995) seems to suggest that intentional stance is the most complex and advanced form of interaction, and therefore the last to come into play both in the course of individual psychological development and in the evolution of interactions with the world

Nonetheless, various studies indicate the intentional stance as the basis of the possibility of establishing social and cognitive development, and it is thanks to this that various forms of cultural learning can be achieved (Tomasello et al., 2005; Perez-Osorio & Wykowska, 2020). And the elaboration of a thought which reduces artificial interactive systems to the rank of mere artifacts is probably the result of a path that develops more slowly, the result of our cultural evolution that allows us to slowly discriminate that which is natural from that which is not in a given context. In short, we can advance that the basic strategy in establishing a relationship with the world is that which foresees the supposition of a causative mechanism of behavior which is comparable to a mind. There are at least two reasons to support the hypothesis that intentional stance is the priority relational strategy with the world.

The first has to do with the evolutionary path that, at an individual level, leads us to take on a design stance towards artifacts and which appears slower, and later, than that relating to the intentional stance. Babies as young as 5 months-old already adopt initial forms of intentional stance since they are shown to be able to follow the gaze of adult agents on a screen (Senju, Csibra, & Johnson, 2008). When they are nine months old they understand that actions have goals and that if these goals are achieved then emotional states will emerge, such as happiness for example, that are different from those related to failure to achieve the goals (Tomasello et al., 2005). If we talk about design stance, however, the developmental path is probably different and slower. Indeed, children are shown to be sensitive to certain types of functional affordances of objects only after they are 12 months-old. And it's only after they are 24 months-old that they are able to attribute a sole function to an object, usually that demonstrated by an adult (Kelemen & Carey, 2007). From 4-6 years of age children start to have an ability to determine the category of an object according to the designer's intentions and the evolution of its use.

The second reason, refers to the fact that strategies of interaction with artificial systems can change according to the cognitive commitment in the execution of some tasks. In fact, some research has shown that participants who are induced to operate in a multitasking mode during the execution of a task, and consequently can devote less cognitive resources to the interpretation of the system with which they interact, are more likely to use intentional stance, and therefore to attribute mental states to this system (Parlangeli, Guidi, & Fiore Farina, 2012; Parlangeli, Caratozzolo & Guidi, 2014). It's as if the correct recognition of interactive digital technologies as simple artifacts is something that requires commitment, procedural resources on a cognitive level that, if removed, make the relationship slide towards less burdensome, more immediate modes, those that are based on the adoption of intentional stance. Relations with technology seem to be prioritising, you might say privileging, the adoption of intentional stance.

In the case of educational technologies this could have considerable relevance, it could completely change the underlying ideas about their design as well as the training aimed at their use. Maybe, for example, it is time to consider that a child who, for educational purposes, cooperates with a social robot will be led to think that it is equipped with a mind and, as such, capable of forming a relationship that provides mental states able to elaborate recursive and reflexive cognitive processes - even if robots were perhaps not designed precisely with these capabilities. Consequently, this would bring about implications for the training of designers and developers of education systems – competence development would need to include skills and techniques on the development and fostering of relationships among peers.

REFERENCES

Baron Cohen, S., 1995. *Mindblindness*. Learning, development, and conceptual change. MIT Press: Cambridge, MA.

Dennett, D.C., 1971. Intentional systems. *Journal of Philosophy*, 68 (February), 87– 106.

Dennett, D.C., 1987. *The intentional stance*. MIT Press: Cambridge, MA.

Kelemen, D. and Carey, S., 2007. The essence of artifacts: Developing the design stance. In S. Laurence and E. Margolis (eds) *Creations of the mind: Artifacts and their representation*. Oxford University Press, Oxford.

Marchesi, S., Ghiglino, D., Ciardo, F., Perez-Osorio, J., Baykara, E., and Wykowska, A., 2019. Do We Adopt the Intentional Stance Toward Humanoid Robots?. *Frontiers in psychology*, 10, 450.

Parlangeli, O., Chiantini, T. and Guidi, S., 2012. A Mind in a disk: The attribution of mental state to technological systems. *Work*, 41, 1118-1123.

Parlangeli, O., Guidi, S. and Fiore Farina, R., 2012. Overloading Disks onto a Mind: Quantity Effects in the Attribution of Mental States to Technological Systems. *Proceedings of the 18th international Congress, IEA - International Ergonomics Association*, Recife, 12-16 February, 2012.

Parlangeli, O., Caratozzolo, M.C., and Guidi, S., 2014. Multitasking and Mentalizing Machines: How the Workload Can Have Influence on the System Comprehension *11th International Conference, EPCE 2014*, Held as Part of HCI International 2014, Heraklion, Crete, Greece, June 22-27, 2014, 50-58.

Perez-Osorio, J. and Wykowska, A., 2020. Adopting the intentional stance toward natural and artificial agents, *Philosophical Psychology,* 33: 3, 369-395.

Senju, A., Csibra, G., and Johnson, M.H., 2008. Understanding the referential nature of looking: Infants' preference for object-directed gaze. *Cognition*, 108, 2, 303– 319.

Thellman, S., Silvervarg, A., and Ziemke, T., 2017. Folk-psychological interpretation of human vs. humanoid robot behavior: Exploring the intentional stance toward robots. *Frontiers in Psychology*, 8 (NOV), 1- 14.

Tomasello, M., Carpenter, M., Call, J., Behne, T., and Moll, H., 2005. Understanding and sharing intentions: The origins of cultural cognition. *Behavioral and Brain Sciences*, 28, 675– 691.

AUTHOR INDEX

International Association for Development of the Information Society (IADIS)
Rua Sao Sebastiao Da Pedreira
No. 100, 30, 1050-209
Lisbon, Portugal

ISBN 978-1-7138-2226-4
9 781713 822264

CURRAN ASSOCIATES INC.
proceedings.com